SENTIMENTAL

MATERIALISM

Gender, Commodity Culture,

and Nineteenth-Century American Literature

Lori Merish

DUKE UNIVERSITY PRESS *Durham and London 2000*

Printed in the United States of America on acid-free paper ∞
Typeset in Baskerville by Keystone Typesetting, Inc.
Library of Congress Cataloging-in-Publication Data
appear on the last printed page of this book.
Portions of chapters 2 and 3 are revised versions of previously published articles:
" 'The Hand of Revised Taste' in the Frontier Landscape: Caroline Kirkland's *A New Home, Who'll Follow?* and the Feminization of American Consumerism," *American Quarterly* 45, no. 4 (Dec. 1993): 485–523 (reprinted with permission), and "Sentimental Consumption: Harriet Beecher Stowe and the Aesthetics of Middle-Class Ownership," *American Literary History* 8 (Spring 1996): 1–33 (reprinted with permission).

SENTIMENTAL MATERIALISM

NEW AMERICANISTS

A series edited by Donald E. Pease

CONTENTS

ACKNOWLEDGMENTS

This book owes much to the assistance and generosity of countless colleagues, friends, and teachers, and I wish to thank some of them here.

This project began as a dissertation, and the guidance and support I received at Berkeley while writing it, as well as the intellectual community there, nourished my thinking from the outset. My intellectual and personal debts at Berkeley are numerous; the greatest is to my dissertation director, Carolyn Porter, whose scholarly example, intellectual passions, and abiding and generous belief in the project have been a fundamental source of sustenance. Carolyn has inspired and encouraged me over the years in more ways than she can know. Dell Upton's challenging criticisms and extensive knowledge of material culture studies and American studies scholarship contributed much to this project; his humor and steady encouragement smoothed its course. The late Jenny Franchot was an exceptionally generous and gifted second reader; her capacious and vibrant intellect, careful readings, and advice benefited this project in countless ways. Jenny's intellectual generosity and engagement and her unflagging commitment to this project immeasurably enriched it, as her friendship enriched my life. Completing the book without her has been a bittersweet accomplishment.

Other teachers at Berkeley provided invaluable support and encouragement. I especially wish to thank Alex Zwerdling, Don Friedman, Sam Otter, Janet Adelman, Sue Schweik, and Elizabeth Abel. Still others generously read and commented on the project in those early stages: I am grateful to Cathy Gallagher, Tom Laqueur, and especially Mitch Breitwieser, who read the manuscript in its entirety and whose thoughtful criticisms and ongoing belief in the project have at crucial points invigorated me.

The English Department at Miami University has been a vital, sustaining, supportive intellectual environment in which to revise and complete the manuscript. I am grateful to former chair C. Barry Chabot and our current chair, Dianne Sadoff, for their efforts toward creating and fostering such an environment. The intellectual wealth of a lively community of friends and colleagues at Miami has enriched my work: thanks to Alice Adams, Susan Jarratt, Tim Melley, Carolyn Haynes, Fran Dolan, Edgar Tidwell, Frank Jordan, Sheila Croucher, Mary Frederickson, Kim Dillon, Susan Morgan, Kate Rousmaniere, Mary Cayton, Keith Tuma, Laura Mandell, Kerry Powell, Scott Shershow, Cheryl Johnson, Vicki Smith, Jim Creech, and, most especially, Mary Jean Corbett and Kate McCullough for comraderie, inspiring conversation, and friendship. Former and current graduate students at Miami—especially Jill Swiencicki, Jennifer Thorington-Springer, Cara Ungar, and Malea Powell—have challenged me to refine and clarify my arguments. For their comments on portions or all of the manuscript I wish to thank Mary Jean Corbett, Scott Dykstra, Bruce Burgett, Glenn Hendler, Ann Cvetkovich, Jay Fliegelman, Kate McCullough, Anne Goldman, Barry Chabot, Karen Jacobs, Laura Mandell, Elizabeth Young, Gordon Hutner, Annmarie Adams, Richard Hardack, Liza Kramer, Judith Rosen, Cynthia Schrager, Mary Caraway, Jacqueline Shea Murphy, Margit Stange, and Cindy Weinstein, and my Miami reading group, Susan Jarratt, Vicki Smith, and Alice Adams. Dana Nelson and Lynn Wardley, my readers at Duke University Press, balanced astute criticisms and suggestions with warm support for the project and to both of them I am deeply grateful. My appreciation extends as well to my wonderful editors at Duke, Ken Wissoker and Katie Courtland, for their abiding support, professionalism, and good humor in coaxing the manuscript into printed shape.

During those seemingly endless final stretches in that process, conversations with Mary Jean Corbett, Ann Cvetkovich, Lori Varlotta, Glenn Hendler, Lynn Wardley, and Bruce Burgett encouraged and challenged me and ultimately helped me see my way. Family and friends, especially my mother, Elsie Riccardi Merish, my sister, Nancy Merish, Phil Soules, Julie Buckner, Mike Morris, Bob Gomez, Cay Lang, Yvonne Vowels, Debby Heim, Gloria Esenwein, and Beth Franks resourcefully supplied much-needed distractions and helped me keep the work in perspective. Lastly, I wish to thank Charles Rose, whose companionship and daily inspirations translate endings into beginnings.

For material support at various stages of the writing and revision process, I am grateful to the following: the Woodrow Wilson Foundation for a Charlotte W. Newcombe Fellowship; the Doreen B. Townsend Center for the Humanities at Berkeley for a Dissertation Fellowship; the Josephine de Karman Fellowship Trust; Miami University, for a semester research leave; and the Andrew W. Mellon Foundation for a postdoctoral fellowship in the English Department at Stanford.

INTRODUCTION:

THE FORMS OF CULTURED FEELING

A far-off friend familiar with my research project recently sent me a token of encouragement. A postcard, it pictures a gray, grainy photo of a woman's hand, fingers curved around a placard. Emblazoned in white on the red placard is the sentence, "I shop therefore I am." As though ironically endorsing the postcard's suggestion of an essential, metaphysical link between consumption and femininity, my friend added no words of her own, only signing its reverse side with an uncharacteristic flourish.

I begin with this reference to contemporary artist Barbara Kruger's well-known piece, parodying the Cartesian *cogito*, because it wittily invokes the gendered economy of subjectivity central to this book. Until recently, capitalism has usually been studied as a system of production: reflecting a bias in political economy and classical Marxism, economic historians have focused on the development and impact of capitalist production and the history of labor while ignoring "the demand side" of the "supply-demand equation."[1] Max Weber's Protestant ethic thesis, which has powerfully shaped subsequent studies of bourgeois ideology (and which Weber understood as especially relevant to American capitalism), defines the "spirit of capitalism" from the point of view of capitalist producer, bound by the pathology of capitalism to the severe requirements of reinvestment and accumulation. But such studies of economic processes and the subjects they constitute and engender are, as Kruger hints, invariably incomplete.

Scholarly attention has turned to the demand side in recent decades, following the groundbreaking theoretical work of the Frankfurt School. Cultural and social historians have provided comprehensive accounts of the birth and historical development of an American consumer culture, while materialist and postmodern critics have provided compelling theoretical analyses of its contemporary social forms. *Sentimental Materialism* builds on as well as revises this body of scholarship. Contemporary cultural historians locate the emergence of mass consumption in late-nineteenth-century America, while social historians point to the "feminization" of middle-class consumerism by the mid-nineteenth century. Investigating cultural representations of an "ethic" of feminine consumption by the late eighteenth century, *Sentimental Materialism* identifies the discourses that promoted these historical developments and their inseparability from emerging, historically specific forms of gender.[2] Materialist and postmodern theorists examine the complexities of consumer subjectivities and practices: identifying diverse consumer styles and subcultures in contemporary consumer culture, they describe modes of resistance (as well as complicity) available to the postmodern consumer. Providing a prehistory of consumer subjectivity and agency, this book maps the discursive processes through which commodities first became identified as privileged vehicles of subjective expression and civic identification.[3]

Sentimental Materialism demonstrates that the feminization of consumption in the late eighteenth century partook of new ideas, derived from eighteenth-century pietistic Protestantism and the emerging political discourse of liberalism, about gender, women's role in the public sphere, and the "civilizing" power of an array of mediating material forms—including luxury commodities and the bodies of "refined" and gracious women.[4] My thesis, concisely put, is that the sentimental discourses of consumption studied here instated a particular form of liberal "political subjectivity" and an identificatory logic interior to that subjectivity that is played out, rather than analyzed, in contemporary criticism about sentimental literature.[5] To unpack that logic of sentimental identification, I trace discursive processes through which middle-class consumption was *produced* in tandem with a new ideal of domestic womanhood. My analysis focuses on the affiliated emergence of an ethic of feminine consumption and the literary genre of domestic fiction, in which domestic material culture is often depicted in great detail, and in which personal possessions are endowed with characterological import. Part of the cultural work of domestic fiction, I demonstrate, was to construct equivalences between material and subjective "refinement"—between commodity and psychological forms—while suppressing the marketplace orientation of "private" life, often by advertising a distinction between home and market. Reinventing capitalist economic and commodity structures as the forms of interiority proper to "private," domestic life, these novels helped write into existence a modern consumer psychology in which individuals "express themselves" through consumption and "identify" with personal possessions.

Recovering these affinities between market laws and middle-class personal life and tracing their political effects, *Sentimental Materialism* addresses persistent critical questions about the politics of nineteenth-century women's fiction. To anticipate a complicated argument developed throughout this book, sentimental narratives engender feelings of power as well as submission endemic to liberal political culture; they thus instantiate a particular form of liberal political *subjection*, in which agency and subordination are intertwined.[6] Specifically, as codified within eighteenth-century sentimental historical narratives and nineteenth-century domestic fictions, sentimental sympathy prescribed forms of paternalism—specifically, of "benevolent" caretaking and "willing" dependency—suited to a liberal-capitalist social order that privileged individual autonomy and, especially, private property ownership. A particular reformulation of traditional models of political organicism within an individualist social framework, one that recast interdependency in psychological, affective terms, sentimental sympathy encompassed both a recognition of social hierarchy and a sense of spontaneous, heartfelt assent to power, thus reinventing political hierarchy as psychological norms reproduced within the intimate recesses of the desiring subject.[7] Critics of sentimental literature have often pointed out that sympathy conventionally operates across a status divide: typical objects of sympathy in these narratives are children, slaves, the poor, the disabled; and in sentimental narratives, it is the sympathy of the empowered for the disempowered, the "strong" for the "weak," the fully human for the dehumanized, that is enlisted as socially and ethically salient. (The "weak" in sentimental texts have ethical primacy through their intimate knowledge of suffering, a sign of Christ-like authenticity, but they have nothing politically useful to learn from the "strong"; becoming "civilized" in these texts entails a willing renunciation of power over others, cast in bodily terms, and marks the sublimation of aggression into sympathetic desire.) Sentimental narratives present a deeply conservative, paranoid view of power: power is figured as dangerous and intrusive, its effects uncertain and perhaps uncontrollable (power can hurt); satisfaction and ethical value lie in the voluntary, unregulated, deeply felt exchanges of interpersonal life. As a particular code of identification, sentimental sympathy can seem to neutralize the relations of political inequality it upholds; indeed, inequities structured into sympathetic identification are rendered invisible in theological and philosophical texts where sympathy is elevated into an inherent moral good. Similarly, the social, structural determinants of the bonds of sympathy and sentimental caretaking — the social, civil production of the "strong," the designation of some individuals as politically and economically empowered and capable of remedying the pain of others — are rendered invisible by the construction of sympathy as a spontaneously experienced emotion.[8] I argue below that sentimental sympathy promotes a deeply felt psychic investment in proprietary power over, and control of, objects of love, that I call "sentimental ownership." Constructed as an autonomous emotional response, sentimental ownership is a fantasy of intimate possession that is in fact — like the "free market" itself — produced and sustained by laws and economic policies. In a sense, sentimental ownership fosters those unspoken but deeply felt feelings of entitlement within liberal society — of male privilege, white privilege, middle-class privilege — that are both naturalized and envisioned as in the best interests of all. It represents both an enactment and a disavowal of proprietary desire in the social realm.

Sentimental sympathy, in this reading, is not a moral value; it is a significant element in those "affect reforms" through which the requirements of a capitalist market society were reproduced within individuals as the very stuff of subjectivity, and a means through which middle-class political hegemony was secured. I argue below that sentimental narratives themselves helped promote the emotional norms, and helped constitute the forms of subjectivity that they envision as the psychological basis of civil society. Extending Michel Foucault's analysis of how discourses of sexuality at once produce and regulate sexual desires and identifications, I envision sentimental ownership as a particular inscription of emotion, an eroticized formation of proprietary and political desire that sentimental narratives both describe and constitute.[9] Supplying the passional, erotic basis for both market society and what historians call the "companionate family," sentimental historical and literary fictions construct market capitalism and middle-class personal life as mutually determining spheres, each dependent on the other, and they inscribe sympathy as the spontaneous emotional faculty that enables the flourishing of both. Delineating a psychology of caretaking and sentimental cherishing, narrative inscriptions of sentimental ownership promote a passional investment in property, ascribing the accumulation of goods ethical value and marking as socially "progressive" a transition from a subsistence to a capitalist market economy. Specifically, sentimental ownership subtends a psychology of the "family wage," in which power is exclusively defined as the power of ownership (of labor and property), and in which female economic "agency" as market subjects (as consumers) is tied to the agency of the male "breadwinner" and located within the constraints of the what one legal scholar terms "possessive domesticity"; while sympathy diffuses the inequities of economic dependency through norms of emotional interdependency.[10] Signifying "care" of an object in both the ethical and aesthetic senses of the term, "taste" thus constitutes in these texts a sign of civility and socialized desire. In my reading, these narratives define a psychology of ownership that is both conservative and defensive: the desire for control over, and psychic investment in, domestic possessions is an index of a psychic sense of futility in the larger social realm, and the intensified affective investment in "possessive domesticity" marks a corresponding reduction in the sphere of effective social power and agency. Sentimental caretaking can thus be seen as a civil(izing) ritual in which feelings of political powerlessness are both enacted and held at bay; it thus both performs, and aims to redress, what Wendy Brown has termed the "woundedness" of the liberal subject.[11] Exhibiting while managing the dynamic of liberal political subjection, sentimental ownership can contain feelings of dependency, and promote feelings of agency, in liberal political subjects, modulating the emotions of interpersonal life in a social realm where sites of power are diffused and multiple.

Gender is a crucial political category in sentimental texts and in the production of sentimental ownership as the felt content of liberal agency: the political inscription of sentimental ownership depends on, and is inseparable from, a specific, and racialized, ideology of gender. Although it upholds male power and authority, sentimental ownership, or "taste," is envisioned in these texts as the natural property of women, spontaneously originating in the natural love and caretaking of the mother-child bond—a construction with complex political and social effects. The tie between sentimental ownership and reproduction is crucial, and clarifies the inextricability of the sentimental history of taste from the history of sexuality: the proprietary, domestic construction of sympathy discussed above regulates "taste" in accord with the demands of domesticity and middle-class intimacy, social forms (like the family wage) under contest in the revolutionary era and consolidated by the 1830s. What constituted in Hannah Foster's late-eighteenth-century novel, *The Coquette*, discussed in chapter 1, a didactic warning against its protagonist's "promiscuous" investment in (multiple and varied) objects of desire, a warning cast partly in political and social terms, would become, in the sentimental writings from the 1830s discussed in chapter 2, an investment in sentimental cherishing of domestic "objects" cast in a wholly different, moral and psychological, register.[12] In eighteenth-century Scottish writings, sentimental, domestic ownership regulates the male homoerotics of the market and the proliferation of market tastes, while by the 1830s, sentimental ownership helped regulate the erotics of the wage labor market, sanitizing labor of the obligations of interpersonal intimacy and differentiating the contracts and bodily claims of wage work from the eroticized contractual bonds of domestic life.[13] The erotics and bonds of wage labor were also managed by the emerging, ideologically freighted distinction between "public" and "private," which served as a prophylactic between forms of intimate bondage and the purported, public rationality of liberal political and economic subjects. (It is precisely this [ideological] distinction between erotic bondage and "free labor" that Marx challenged in his well-known assertion that "prostitution is only a *specific* expression of the *general* prostitution of the *laborer.*")[14] Finally, as I emphasize below and throughout this project, the intimate bonds produced by sentimental ownership were also naturalized and managed through a symbolics of racial difference, which helped distinguish the bonds of free labor from enslavement and feminine domestic dependency from female sexual slavery. As a code signifying both identification and desire, sentimental ownership helped constitute and circulate particular forms of desire within liberal society: specifically, it regulates the historically shifting distinction between being and wanting, the desire to be and the desire to possess, by at once facilitating social identifications and producing social differences—all the while obscuring its own role in the production of erotic norms by appealing to sympathy as a form of spontaneous recognition.

In the chapters that follow, I chart out the contested domestication of feminine taste and the corollary construction of the feminine consumer as a new civic identity for women and site of sentimental identification, a discursive process with important consequences for the emergence and ideological justification of commercial society, and for the expansion and feminization of consumption. Inscribing these new constructions of feminine consumption and taste and at times revealing their ideological contradictions, domestic fictions played a key role in the formation and dissemination of capitalist norms of personal life, facilitating those processes through which, in Judith Williamson's words, people's "wants and needs" were "translated into the form[s] of consumption."[15] But first, I will situate my argument in contemporary theoretical debates about the politics of feminine consuming, in order to draw out some additional implications of my analysis.

The Politics of Feminine Consumption

For the past three decades, Marxist and materialist feminists have reevaluated the political and economic stakes of feminine consumer desires and practices. In an important early example of this reassessment, Ellen Willis took issue with what was, by 1970, a familiar analysis of consumers as unwitting victims prone to the psychological manipulations of advertisers. Willis identifies what would become the most significant areas of contemporary theoretical debate. Questioning the "popular theory of consumerism"—namely, the leftist theory of commodity consumption as mass manipulation—Willis challenges the class elitism and sexism it implies, charging that "its basic function is to defend . . . the class, sexual and racial privileges" of its white middle-class male adherents. Noting that a primary assumption of this theory is that "the society defines women as consumers, and the purpose of the prevailing media image of women as passive sexual objects is to sell products," Willis makes three important counterclaims. First, she reminds her readers that the locus of oppression resides in the production process, emphasizing that "people have no control over which commodities are produced (or services performed), under what conditions, or how these commodities are distributed." Anticipating a line of analysis pursued by critics such as Janice Radway, she contends that the denigration of consumption as brainwashing denies the real (psychic) needs consumption fulfills, claiming that while the "profusion of commodities" is indeed a "bribe," it constitutes "a genuine and powerful compensation for oppression." Finally, identifying a central concern of Marxist feminists, Willis asserts that the theory of commodity capitalism as the root of women's oppression elides the role of patriarchy—and elite white men's stake in that system. According to Willis, "Consumerism as applied to women is blatantly sexist. The pervasive image of the empty-headed female consumer constantly trying her husband's patience with her extravagant purchases contributes to the myth of male superiority: we are incapable of spending money rationally; all we need to make us happy is a new hat now and then." She shrewdly notes that "there is an analogous racial stereotype—the black with his Cadillac and his magenta shirts."[16]

As Willis indicates, much anticonsumption discourse—from the left *and* the right—has been sexist and moralistic, informed as often by residual theological values as by a progressive political agenda. The extent to which critiques of consumerism have constituted a gendered discourse is itself telling, suggesting the inextricability of the discursive production of gender from discourses of consumption. A central claim of this study is that discourses about consumer culture are *always* discourses about female desire: since at least the late eighteenth century, consumerism has constituted a principal arena in which forms of female subjectivity and desire have been mapped out, articulated, and contested. As feminist critics of contemporary consumer culture insist, consumerism is a primary site in which femininity is imposed and enforced, and forms of femininity produced; this was no less true for the nineteenth century. In *Sentimental Materialism*, I demonstrate that the new consumer subject was inseparable from an emerging ideal of ("unproductive") domestic womanhood, and helped uphold the Victorian sex-gender system and its binary classification of sexed beings. Indeed, the production/consumption dichotomy has historically corresponded with male and female "separate spheres" and has helped constitute those historically specific forms of gender. Since the late eighteenth century, I will show, discourses about the social and political value of consumption have focused on gender as a primary analytic: consumer goods were widely depicted as "feminizing" material forms, instrumental in the production and representation of gendered forms of subjectivity and especially in what one critic calls the "feminization of women."[17] One consequence of this binaristic construction of consumption (consuming woman/productive man) is the tendency of contemporary theoretical and critical analyses to replicate it, focusing on sexual and gender difference as definitive categories of analysis while failing to historicize those very categories. Universalizing historically specific desires, material practices, and privileges (those of "first world," middle-class voluntaristic consumers), studies of consumerism that uncritically recycle this gender binary erase a range of race, class, sexual, and national differences among women, while rendering invisible those women who are *not* consumers.

Informed by the work of feminist theorists, *Sentimental Materialism* problematizes "woman" as an obvious and homogeneous empirical category to explore how "woman" as discursive category is historically constructed and traversed by more than one axis of difference.[18] At the same time, this book insists on interconnections between the discursively constituted forms of gender and their material loci in the densely mediated material practices of industrial and consumer capitalism. It thus calls attention to the systems of value, divisions of labor, and allocations of resources that the social construction of difference helps determine.

As Willis indicates, critics of consumer culture of varied political stripes have denounced consumption in part because of its association with the feminine and the private life of the family. As defined within the bourgeois gender hierarchy of public and private, consumption has been dismissed as apolitical and a form of disparaged women's work—a view that Marxism has done little to dislodge. Emphasizing "productive labor," narrowly defined, as the locus of collective struggle, Marxists often view commodity consumption as outside history, a form of mass distraction that blocks the development of historical consciousness.[19] Marxist feminists have critiqued both the failure of Marxism to deal adequately with questions of gender and the family, and the bourgeois dismissal of private life as outside politics altogether. In particular, Marxist feminists have contested the privileging of the "narrow, capitalist concept of 'productive labor' "—that is, the wage labor production of surplus for capital—in Marxist analyses of relations of production and exploitation under capitalism, arguing that such a concept ignores women's domestic work and forms of gender inequality (including relations of domestic labor, sexuality, and fertility) essential to the system's operation.[20] As Eli Zaretsky has demonstrated, the construction of the home as a private space segregated from the public, and the confinement of middle-class women to it, was an arrangement *produced* by capitalism and its social relations of production—as was middle-class subjectivity itself.

For Marxist feminists, women's (unpaid) domestic labor, including women's sexual labors (the reproduction of life) and the labor of consumption, are part of the reproduction of labor-power and the creation of surplus value within capitalism. Consumption, therefore, cannot be severed from production: home consumption is part of the production process—part of the reproduction of labor and the class relations that structure capital. Domestic labor (including the labors of consumption) is thus *necessary* labor; it secures the conditions of existence of capitalism. The (middle-class) feminine consumer charted out in the following chapters marks her distance from material "need" through the display of "taste," signified by fashionable clothing and consumer durables: taste constitutes both an expression of her "subjectivity" and symbolizes her class position and that of her family. From a Marxist feminist perspective, it is clear that part of what domestic consumption *reproduces* is not merely labor power, but class *relations* themselves—the social relations of labor, and the unequal allocation of resources, under capitalism.[21]

The reevaluations of consumerism by postmodern theorists have several points in common with Marxist feminists' revisionist analyses of women's consumer practices. But the postmodern critique takes the theorization of consumption further, asserting not only the centrality of women's consumption to political and economic life, but the *oppositional* potential of these practices. This emphasis was implicit in the Frankfurt School's critique: identifying a utopian, liberatory dimension of mass culture, Frankfurt School theorists saw in the commodity form a "utopian wish-image," a clue to the dream-form in which the genuine aspirations of the social collectivity are stored. For example, Theodor Adorno identified the "dual character" of luxury as its ability to figure social inequities as well as mask class differences. Challenging Thorstein Veblen's dismissal of conspicuous consumption as an expression of ruling-class competition and female domestic enslavement, Adorno contends that "those features of luxury which Veblen designates as 'invidious,' revealing a bad will, do not only reproduce injustice; they also contain, in distorted form, the appeal to justice." This "dialectic of luxury" allows consumer culture to be read as its opposite: personal ostentation, seemingly indifferent to the whole of society, can imply a vision of plenitude for everyone, the knowledge that "no individual happiness is possible which does not virtually imply that of society as a whole."[22] Similarly, Fredric Jameson emphasizes the utopian longings in mass cultural forms: "even the most degraded type of mass culture has a [utopian dimension] which remains implicitly, and no matter how faintly, critical of the social order from which (as a commodity) it springs." For Jameson, mass culture cannot hope to manipulate the public unless it holds out "some genuine shred of content as a fantasy bribe."[23]

The Frankfurt School's theoretical insights have been taken up by some U.S. critics. Analyzing the appeal of commodity culture for African Americans, Susan Willis argues that Michael Jackson's constant makeovers figure a utopian desire for social transformation, narcissistically displaced onto the desire for endless self-transformation. But for the most part, American critics have ignored the social, collective emphasis of the Frankfurt School's critique, embracing the potential of consumerism for individual fantasy-making and self-fashioning—a tendency that is, I would argue, symptomatic of the sentimental psychologizing of taste, discussed above.[24] Postmodern discourse about consumption as a site of desire and oppositionality often formalizes a notion of voluntaristic consumption that depends on possibilities of consumer "choice" unavailable to most consumers, in the United States and globally, while legitimating the erasure of the production process and the social relations of production from theoretical analysis. As Neil Lazarus argues in his critique of Jean Baudrillard, "Once society is defined exclusively in terms of consumption, those who are not consumers become invisible."[25] Whatever the political intentions of their authors, studies that construct consumption as an expression of individual subjectivity and desire formalize the individualist logic of the "free" market, and preclude more comprehensive analyses of the social value, production, and consequences of consumption—be they economic (involving class inequalities or relations of production in global capitalism), political (involving welfare-state policies), or environmental (involving the waste and destructiveness of the "cult of consumption" and its role in such trends as global warming).

Sentimental Materialism tracks the emergence of this individualist conception of consumption, as an expression of "subjectivity" (or what the mid-nineteenth-century author A. J. Downing would term "character"), and the social and material forms such a notion had to displace. In general terms, the discourse of "sentimental consumption" decontexualized commodities from politically and economically contested relations of labor and ownership, and rearticulated them as expressions of the formalized *desires* of individual consumer "subjects." Defining "taste" in a moral and psychological register and lodging these desires within the individual subject, this discourse obscured the complex social relations in which "tastes" emerge and to which they refer. As Antonio Gramsci writes, "food, dress, housing, and reproducing are elements of social life in which . . . the whole complex of social relations are most obviously and widely manifested."[26] These social dimensions are effaced in the texts I analyze, which write consumption as and into a specific liberal "identity politics"—an inscription that assigned consumption civic value while assimilating it to the identificatory processes of liberal subjectivity. In particular, this inscription removed consumption from public negotiation of questions of distributive justice and what Nancy Fraser calls "the politics of needs interpretation."[27] Sentimental consumption's ideology of subjective bonding with possessions reinforced the nuclear family as middle-class culture's privileged social form, even while it helped justify an unequal distribution of resources by appealing to the moral claims of ownership by the privileged few. In other words, the sentimental construction of feminine "taste" has operated to articulate the distribution of economic resources in *personal* and *moral*, rather than *collective* and *political*, terms.

The representation of consumer goods as a means of individual expression and "freedom (of choice)" obscures the social, collective processes through which commodities are invested with value, as well as the concrete material positioning of individuals with differing access to such "freedom." Indeed, I will argue that the critical valorization of consumer "choice" replicates a logic of consumer "subjectivity" and "agency" that the sentimental discourses analyzed here helped *produce*. Recent scholars have examined the fundamental conflict between republican and democratic ideals and the reality of chattel slavery in the

United States, arguing that the constitutional legitimation of slavery warped the republic from its birth, and produced a contradiction in American national identity and collective consciousness—a contradiction registered in literary discourse.[28] In ways entangled with race, class inequity was another such contradiction, one partially evaded through the utopian logic of the American dream and the myth of American "classlessness" first articulated by J. Hector St. John de Crèvecoeur. Intensified and insistently racialized with the Jacksonian establishment of "universal" white male suffrage, this contradiction was masked, in part, by the abstractions of liberalism itself: as feminist political theorists have argued, the subject of liberalism was usually defined as rational and disembodied, a construction that enabled the endorsement of formal "equality" at a remove from material conditions and contributed to an erasure of the historical and material specificity of subject-positions and needs.[29] Consumerism was a realm of public representation through which the racial and economic contradictions of American class society were both figured and (partially) resolved.

Inscribing a realm of "civilized" materiality, consumption has provided a body for the American liberal subject, at once a realm of desire and a site of state representation and regulation. Indeed, while American democracy and capitalism have been reciprocally defined—sutured under the sign of liberalism—commodity capitalism has been identified as a (if not *the*) principal material expression of American civic culture and "freedom," and has promoted the state's appeal in sensational, bodily terms. The strength of that appeal was fully understood by Franklin D. Roosevelt, who reportedly asserted that if he could place a single American book in the hands of every Russian, his choice would be the Sears, Roebuck catalogue.[30] Numerous immigrant narratives from the early twentieth century register this conflation of consumption and citizenship, figuring the purchase and ownership of goods as a definitive means of Americanization. For Roosevelt as for many others, commodity consumption has served as a primary means through which individuals come to identify as national subjects and learn to "love" America.[31] If consumption is a public erotics, it simultaneously incites disciplinary power—a fact particularly evident in Caroline Kirkland's *A New Home, Who'll Follow?* in which commodities are instruments through which subjects are disciplined and conscripted into the body politic. Kirkland's text shows that consumer goods were positioned within the realm of the "social," a realm of reform that, in the nineteenth century, was thoroughly entangled with the category "women."[32] As the culture's primary language for representing feminine sentiment and locating the female body *within* the social, sentimentalism helped inscribe—and was inscribed within—nineteenth-century constructions of gender, subjectivity, and civil society. Discourses of sentimental consumption encode the complexities of consumer culture's configurations of sex, gender, race, nationality, and power, and produced the female body as a central site of political struggle and contestation. In particular, sentimental consumption contributed to what Foucault calls the "hysterization of the female body": it produced an increasingly sexualized female body—one riddled with desires—while simultaneously promoting norms of taste, "proper" affect, and political and economic discipline.[33] In the nineteenth century, consumerism and its discourses established forms of political mediation through which feminine political subjectivities were defined, constituted, and contested.

Consumption and the Politics of Domesticity

Sentimental Materialism can be situated within the body of historical and literary scholarship, begun in the 1960s with the *Annales* school, that examines the ideological significance of "personal life." Drawing on the work of social historians, especially Lawrence Stone, Leonore Davidoff, and Catherine Hall, critics such as Nancy Armstrong and Mary Poovey have studied the cultural and political importance of representations of domesticity and the "domestic woman" in establishing and legitimizing bourgeois power and, indeed, in defining the cultural authority of imperial England. These critics show that several discursive traditions in the late eighteenth and nineteenth centuries represented gender difference as the dominant form of social difference, and constructed gender in such a way as to manage, symbolically, other, more overtly political, forms of social identity (such as class and race). As Poovey summarizes one version of this argument, representational "deployments" of the domestic ideal in mid-Victorian England "depoliticize[d] class relations" by "translating class differences into psychological or moral difference," by setting limits to competition, and by "helping subsume individuals of different classes into a representative Englishman, with whom everyone could identify, even if one's interests were thereby obliterated and not served."[34]

Similarly, Mary Ryan and Stuart Blumin have argued that the emergence of a distinct middle class in nineteenth-century America was largely dependent on the development of the domestic ideal. Ryan's studies of the mid-nineteenth-century "woman's sphere" explore how the middle-class family established boundaries between itself and other classes through gender construction as well as through the cultural production of specific kinds of psychological bonds and norms.[35] In his work on the emergence of an American middle class, Blumin addresses the changing significance of personal life during the late eighteenth and nineteenth centuries. In the mid–nineteenth century, Blumin argues, "white collar" families began to perceive "their homes and their domestic strategies to be distinct from those of manual workers, as well as from those fashionables who did not . . . aspire to the domestic ideal."[36] The pervasive ideology of the middle-class woman's sphere, articulated in an array of discourses, conveyed a newly psychologized understanding of the value of personal life as well as forms of cultural knowledge about what it meant to be fully "human." Building on the work of these scholars, *Sentimental Materialism* considers the role of domestic consumption in the construction of American personal life and a historically specific politics of gender. In doing so, I attempt to reassert "the specificity of the political content of everyday life and of the individual fantasy-experience and to reclaim it from [the] reduction to the merely subjective."[37]

What Blumin describes above as a model of middle-class self-definition via discursive differentiation is, according to Gramsci, paradigmatic of the hegemonic task in a class society. In Gramsci's account, a class becomes hegemonic by achieving self-conscious awareness of itself as a class — a process that entails distinguishing that class from competing social groups — as well as by representing its specific interests as "natural" and necessary. My understanding of middle-class self-definition is indebted to Ernesto Laclau and Chantal Mouffe's conception of hegemony as an "articulatory practice" in which contesting forces attempt to appropriate and reconfigure the signs and symbols of a culture.[38] In many of the texts I consider, "virtuous" middle-class women are identified through a class-inflected symbolics of differentiation, and are constructed in opposition to female characters notably lacking in the interior, emotional endowments of domestic womanhood.[39] But if the hegemonic task of the middle class entailed differentiating itself from alternate social groups, it also entailed incorporating idealized attributes of the previously dominant group — the aristocracy — as a means of ideological legitimacy.[40] Chapter 1 examines how late-eighteenth-century middle-class conduct books incorporated aristocratic attributes — such as gentility and politesse — into their version of domestic femininity. In these texts, aristocratic attributes were psychologized, privatized, and identified as the bodily signs of sensibility and psychological refinement. Politeness, for example, was often described as a "natural" capacity for spontaneous emotional response rather than a cultivated social code.

Class-specific forms of bodily life were endowed with emotional and moral import, and reconfigured as a semiotics of "civilized" subjectivity.

As Armstrong argues, following Foucault, the "political history" of the middle-class subject is organized around just such a semiotics of bodily life, and is inseparable from symbolic practices that affirmed the importance of sexuality and the care of the body—that created, in other words, a " 'class' body with its health, hygiene, descent, and race."[41] That " 'class' body" was also endowed with "taste": the political history of the middle class entailed a particular semiotics of private ownership—one articulated through novel constructions of gender and sex. For instance, numerous texts from the period represented mobile property, rather than land, as the basis of civil society, facilitating new forms of civic identification for both men and women. Discourses of luxury played a crucial role in this restructuring of political subjectivities: conventionally described as forms of personal property exceeding "mere" bodily needs for food, clothing, and shelter and thus satisfying aesthetic and ethical ("subjective") rather than physical wants, luxury goods were endowed with *emotional* import, and were being (re)constructed as signs of a specifically *feminine* civil subjectivity. Numerous antebellum domestic manuals and novels promoted an ideal of "pious consumption": tasteful domestic objects were frequently described as "spiritualizing," "civilizing," and "humanizing" the self, engaging an individual's sensibilities and "refining" her emotional repertory.[42] Overturning traditional Calvinist and civic humanist sanctions against luxury, tastemakers such as A. J. Downing contended that an aesthetically pleasing domestic environment presents an "unfailing barrier against vice, immorality, and bad habits." For Downing, "a good house (and by this I mean a fitting, tasteful, and significant dwelling) is a powerful means of civilization"; it exerts a "moral influence" and "elevates" character, resulting in the "refinement" of sensibility and manners which "distinguishes a civilized from a coarse and brutal people."[43] Pious consumption figured prominently in American nationalist rhetoric as well as discourses of internal and external imperialism. Rhetorics of pious consumption could serve to distinguish the "human" and "civilized" from the "nonhuman" and "savage" (to demarcate the "civilized" American) or justify imperial expansion in the name of maintaining a "humanizing" standard of living for the "civilized" few.

In nineteenth-century America, this ideological emphasis on the civilizing efficacy of mobile property promoted a general expansion in domestic consumption. Historians have observed that the "cult of domesticity" emerged simultaneously with an evident shift in the economic function of the family, from a unit of economic production (as in the colonial "family economy") to a unit increasingly dependent on consumption. Social historians of the standard of living have documented substantial increases in consumption levels during the three decades before the Civil War.[44] As Daniel Horowitz summarizes these findings, "members of the American middle class became more serious consumers" at this time, and he notes that a range of Americans during this period faced "a greatly expanded choice of consumer goods, many of them produced commercially for a mass market." According to Blumin, middle-class patterns of consumption operated as a principal tool or strategy through which that class defined itself in the mid-nineteenth century.[45]

Middle-class domesticity thus psychologized while transforming aristocratic material and social forms: the aristocratic ideal of inalienable (landed) property was rearticulated through mobile property, inflected with interiority, and transformed into a psychological necessity.[46] This psychologizing is still apparent in the work of contemporary sociologists and psychologists, who describe the importance of bonding with one's house, and institutions such as pet ownership and "plant companionship," in fully "humanizing" persons and training individuals in the experience of emotional intimacy.[47] This reconstruction of aristocratic material forms as signs of middle-class psychological complexity and moral superiority have often been obscured in accounts of the middle-class family and private sphere, which frequently rehearse bourgeois conceptions of the anti-aristocratic character of domesticity and a middle-class ideal of familial love divorced from property concerns. Most accounts of domesticity depict middle-class family relations as not about "property," but about "love." However, in middle-class texts, I argue below, *property* is represented as not about "property," but about "love." What constituted in aristocratic culture the openly political relations of kin and property were thus invested with moral and psychological import, and held apart from the public, manipulable realm of politics. Presenting a " 'class' body" inscribed with sentiment, these texts legitimated specific forms of material life as essential to "full" (middle-class) subjectivity.[48]

Rethinking the Feminization of American (Consumer) Culture

As I have suggested, the emergence of middle-class domesticity was inseparable from the "feminization of women": the (re)construction of "woman" from the embodiment of demonic, irrational forces, as she figured in Puritanism, into a paradigm of virtue, embodiment of moral sensibility, and shaper of "civilized" society.[49] As Armstrong, Blumin, and Ryan argue, middle-class construction was, in an important sense, "woman's work": the construction of the "feminine" woman and womanly domesticity fostered the symbolic constitution of the middle class. Essential to this womanly cultural work was creating and maintaining a tasteful domestic environment. As I demonstrate in chapter 2, the ideal of tasteful domesticity expressly authorized Caroline Kirkland's attempts to clean up the domestic "mess" of her frontier neighbors as part of her project to make them (civilized) "persons," even while it justified the "corrective domesticity" of antebellum middle-class reformers.[50] Members of Other races and classes—such as poor workers, widely depicted as spending wastefully to indulge their appetites rather than cultivate their emotions, and "savage" or "wandering" Indians, seen to lack a proper conception of private ownership—appear in Kirkland's writings as psychologically "unrefined" or inadequately "feminized," a psychological shortcoming that could be remedied by the proper practices of domestic consumption and good housekeeping.

The interrelations between consumption and feminine domesticity have been acknowledged by several scholars, most notably Ann Douglas. In her controversial study of the "feminization" of American literary and religious culture in Victorian America, Douglas sees in nineteenth-century sentimental "women's culture" the nascent origins of mass culture and women's "self-rationalization" for their new consumer role. Douglas situates these developments in the context of changes in the economic function of the family, correlating women's economic "disestablishment" and decline in household production with a general decline in women's social status and legal privileges. Focusing on what she perceives to be the devastating consequences of women's "influence" as consumers—specifically, the "debase[ment]" of American religious and literary culture—Douglas fails to provide a convincing theoretical account of feminine consumption and women's construction as (sentimental) consumers. Douglas deterministically construes the emergence of female consuming as an inevitable response to female boredom, an insignificant activity women engaged in to fill the domestic vacuum created by industrialism. Reductively presenting women's consumption (and sentimentalism itself) as a reflex of changes in economic production, Douglas fails to historicize the economic and gender relations she describes, and radically simplifies the ideological complexity of mass culture.[51]

While it may be true, as Douglas suggests, that sentimentalism served as an "introduction to consumerism," her work lacks an analysis of the political import of the symbolic practices and representations of domesticity that one finds in Armstrong, Poovey, or Ryan. Thus, she misses the constitutive ambivalence of consumption in political terms. Recent debates about female consumption — like debates about sentimentalism — have tended to focus on two questions: does consumption incite or express independent female subjectivity and desire, or does it negate or constrain, even "enslave" female subjectivity, subjecting it to the desires of men or advertisers? Replicating an ambivalence within liberal feminist subjectivity itself, such analyses miss the fact that what Foucault termed "subjection" is inseparable from the *constitution* of female consumer desire and the forms of subjectivity and agency ("freedom of choice") ratified by that desire. In the following chapters, especially chapter 1, I unpack the terms and gendered coordinates of that political subjection, and its specifically literary effects. For now, let me state that while feminine consumption was central to emerging forms of class, race, and national power, it also provided a new civic role and responsibility for (some) women, and consolidated while circumscribing their position within civil society. Viewed in its historical context, domestic consumption constituted a language of subjective expression and identification that facilitated middle-class women's civic agency, even while it enforced domestic conceptions of womanhood. Chapter 1 demonstrates that the "republican consumer" — along with the "republican mother" and the "republican wife" familiar from contemporary feminist historiography — constituted a new cultural type of feminine civil subjectivity in social discourse during the period. Endowing feminine taste and emotional preference with "civilizing" efficacy, early republican texts legitimized women's participation in the market as consumers and thus defined a new civic identification for women as liberal subjects. These texts ascribed to women a (mediated) form of political participation, while inscribing consumption with explicit civic value.[52] Elizabeth Cady Stanton affirmed the politicizing aspect of female consumption in her advice to the wife of a congressman — repeated before many of her audiences — to " 'Go out and buy!' " domestic conveniences and comforts without a husband's (or father's) approval or company.[53]

In late-eighteenth- and nineteenth-century American literary and political discourse, consumption is thus a practice that both facilitates and domesticates women's political agency. This cultural valuation of female consumption appears to be related to changes in property law that culminated in the mid-nineteenth-century Married Women's Property Acts, expanding the rights of married women to hold personal property.[54] The new authority accorded female consumption represented a new concern with the social significance of women's "taste" exercised in a number of different arenas — especially love relations and marketplace purchases. In other words, the construction of women as "civilized" and "civilizing" consumers, and the new social value accorded feminine emotional preference, contributed to a larger reconstruction of women as "consenting" political subjects. Consumption constituted a sociopolitical structure through which women were gendered "feminine" and were defined as "free" civil subjects. Historians have observed, although not theorized, this conjunction between consumption and feminine civic identity in the nineteenth century: "Within recent history decent clothing has been a necessity for any woman or girl child who wants to enter the social world. It's her means of entry, and there are rules that say so."[55]

As I demonstrate below, several narrative traditions from the period, such as white slave narratives, seduction narratives, and sentimental fiction, are preoccupied with the problematics of what I call "feminine consent" — a new category of feminine agency, derived from pietistic Protestantism, defined as voluntary emotional orientation or affiliation. Indeed, such texts define taste as constitutive of feminine civic identity — with taste constituting a gendered counterpart to masculine political rationality.[56] Feminine consent figured prominently in the rhetoric of American exceptionalism: early republican essayists, for instance, typically argued that the elevated social position of women and the increased social recognition of their sentimental choices and preferences exemplified the superior enlightenment of American men and the superiority of American social forms. This valorization of feminine taste as crucial to the development of civil society is apparent in much late-eighteenth- and nineteenth-century social discourse, and was a central element in nationalist narratives of social progress. This model of feminine consent simultaneously brings the previously socially dead to life and delimits the forms of feminine political agency.

These forms of feminine "subjectivity" and civic agency were articulated through race as well as class and nationality. Throughout this project, I analyze the racial parameters of feminine consent and forms of consumer refinement and commodity reembodiment. Following recent historians, I argue that the emergence and growth of capitalism, as well as its ideological justification in the United States, cannot be understood apart from the growing institution of chattel slavery: the American market system constituted, from the start, a racialized structure, one thoroughly implicated in the institutions and material practices of race. David Roediger demonstrates that the growth of the market system in the early nineteenth century, and capitalism's system of wage labor (on which the growth of consumption depended), were imagined as compatible with republican and democratic ideals of "freedom" because of the negative example of chattel slavery: the economic and political "freedom" of whites was symbolically articulated with reference to their perceived distance from black enslavement. In the words of Joel Kovel, who theorizes a racialized psychology of capitalist acquisition, "just as the creation of white wealth pushed Blacks down, so must the presence of degraded black bodies have exerted a continual stimulation to the continued pursuit of abstracted money."[57] The identification of capitalism as a realm of white entitlement is, I argue, central to the structure of liberal subjectivity and the political unconscious of white racism.

What Roediger views as the interdeterminations of "free labor" and chattel slavery, and Kovel views as the interdeterminations of the abstractions of market exchange and the emphatic (racialized) embodiment of "degraded" labor, are relevant to my analysis of the formation of the feminine consumer subject as an articulation of "racialized gender."[58] As I argue throughout this book, consumerism has been imagined as a site of feminine civic identification and "freedom" ("freedom of choice")—indeed, justified as a liberatory feminine role—only in opposition to the imagined position of women of color, and especially the negative example of black women's sexual slavery: women of color occupied the fantasmatic limits of feminine consumer subjectivity, marking and defining the constitutive boundary of that self. Extending Kovel's and Roediger's analyses, I would argue that the pursuit of the "civilized" (or cultured) body of consumption is similarly "stimulated" by the presence of culturally "degraded" racial bodies; similarly, I would contend that the construction of feminine consent (or taste) as the property of the "free" (feminine civil) subject is discursively and ideologically inseparable from, even dependent on, the construction of the nonconsent (what Patricia Williams terms the "antiwill") of the black female sexual slave.[59] These oppositions were highly unstable: as I demonstrate in my analysis of the consumer subject's formation in chapter 1, the abjected materiality of the Other's body (and the recognition of unfreedom) continued to haunt the edges of the subject's identity, threatening its fantasies of political liberty.[60] In the following chapters, I analyze the contradictions in the consumerist construction of feminine freedom and, especially, the limited power of feminine consent in a social field structured by male domination. In addition, I trace the entanglements of race and racial identification with the imaginary, discursive forms of feminine consumer subjectivity.

The construction of white women's subjectivity (specifically, their taste) as both index and agent of "civilization" is evident in an 1846 text by the antebellum feminist Eliza Farnham. *Life in Prairie Land* constructs feminine subjectivity as a site of racial and national contestation; in particular, it explicitly defines an ideal of (white, civilized) femininity against the deficiently developed (and inadequately protected) subjectivity of women on the racial "frontier." In the middle of her text, Farnham recalls a conversation with a newlywed "Westerner" which took place on the Illinois riverboat on which he is traveling with his new bride. Like many antebellum women's frontier narratives, Farnham's underscores the *national* resonances of sentimental ownership as a configuration that designates "civilized" Americans, and that is a central element in narratives of social and national "progress"; indeed, Farnham explicitly represents this proprietary model in opposition to "savage" cannibalism and other frontier consumption models.[61] As she recounts their conversation, Farnham's sentimental expectations clash vividly with the frontiersman's utilitarian concerns and evident insensibility. The unnamed Westerner had apparently married his bride out of economic rather than emotional motives, opting for a woman who will be a "useful" laborer rather than what Farnham terms "a pleasant face to meet you when you go home from the field, or a soft voice to speak kind words when you are sick, or a gentle friend to converse with you in your leisure hours."[62] For the frontiersman, "women are some like horses and oxen, the biggest can do the most work, and that's what I want one for"; thus, he has selected "a good, stout woman I should calculate was worth somethin. She can pay her way, and do a handsome thing besides, helpin me on the farm" (38, 36). Farnham is especially "disgusted" by the frontiersman's insensitivity to his wife's interior, emotional life and sentimental preferences (her "tastes"), his dismissiveness when she questions whether his wife won't be lonely on the frontier and miss her parents and friends (38). Farnham expresses her "indignation" in a lengthy exposition of the moral obligations of the marriage contract, highlighting a categorical distinction between sentimental property (which should be loved) and instrumental property (which can be used and consumed), between animate subject and inanimate tool or machine:

> [You] brought her away from her home to be treated as a human being, not as an animal or machine. Marriage is a moral contract, not a mere bargain of business. The parties promise to study each other's happiness, and endeavor to promote it. You could not marry a woman as you could buy a washing machine, though you might want her for the same purpose. If you take the machine there is

> no moral obligation incurred, except to pay for it. If you take the woman, there is. Before you entered into this contract I could have shown you a machine that would have answered your purpose admirably. It would have washed and ironed all your clothes, and when done, stood in some out-of-the-way corner till it was wanted again. You would have been under no obligation, not even to feed and clothe it, as you now are. It would have been the better bargain, would it not? (39)

In response to Farnham's complaint, the Westerner replies, in unabashed commercial terms, "Why that would be according to what it cost in the fust place" (39). In Farnham's account, the frontiersman clearly considers his wife an instrument of use rather than an object of love, a "machine" to be physically consumed through the performance of physical tasks; thus, he has chosen a woman with a strong physical constitution, one who is "stout and able to work" (37). Farnham's anecdote identifies the "moral contract" of middle-class marriage as a sign of civilized subjectivity, one imaged against the degenerate, destructive proprietary practices of savage Westerners. On the racial frontier, Farnham suggests, feminine subjectivity and desire (women's "happiness") is given neither full social recognition nor adequate legal protection, even while she images taste as constitutive of feminine civil subjectivity (that which distinguishes "woman" from "machine"). But the text also suggests the complexities of feminine consent in a political context where women were socially defined as dependents and objects of male property, a status promoted by law and economic policy. As Norma Basch has argued in her study of the nineteenth-century married women's property acts, "If one defines patriarchy in its purest form as the reduction of women to the status of property owned and controlled by men, then one can find many of its components in Anglo-American domestic relations law."[63] Sentimental texts such as Farnham's illuminate the gendered forms of liberal political subjection as well as the patriarchal parameters within which feminine consent and civil subjectivity are constituted.

The Politics of Sentiment

Farnham's text stages a dynamic of gendered identification central to sentimental cultural forms. Responding to the Westerner's brief narrative, the narrator "identifies" with his unnamed wife's imagined sentiments—the desires and longings the narrator would feel as a wife "brought away from home" by a new husband—a subjectivity notably invisible to the lower-class, masculine, and racialized frontiersman, and she incites the reader to "recognize" that subjectivity as well. Such forms of feminine identification have figured prominently in critical debates about the politics of nineteenth-century sentimentalism, especially since the feminist critical reevaluation of this literature began in the 1970s. Whereas early critics tended to read these novels' representations of feminine "sensibility" in positive terms, as an expression of a feminine counterculture (e.g., privileging domesticity over masculine adventure), recent critics have seen feminine sympathy as a form of race and class colonization. For example, Richard Brodhead sees feminine sentiment as a structure of Foucauldian discipline into middle-class affectional norms, while Laura Wexler sees the culture of sentiment as an instrument of racial domination. Both, however, neglect to theorize the production of (white, middle-class, feminine) sentiment on which this colonization depends: indeed, they seem to envision those emotional norms as anterior to the disciplinary, identificatory structure enacted by sentimental texts. In other words, both fail to analyze the form of feminine subjection these texts instantiate, and its consequences for a theory of sentimental readership.[64]

Farnham's text, in which the female narrator "recognizes" (the pain of) an abused wife, reveals much about these processes. In particular, it reveals how feminine "subjectivity" and sensibility are recognized—indeed, constituted—in scenes of subordination. It has often been noted that the conventional objects of sympathy in sentimental texts are socially marginalized and disempowered figures: criminals, the insane, children, slaves, and of course (abused) women. This has been read as enabling a sentimental "extension of sympathy" to previously "dehumanized," denigrated objects, and as instating sentimental condescension.[65] Both readings posit a fully "human," sentimental (reading) subject who preexists these exchanges, and whose subjectivity might be thus extended or withheld. Neither addresses or attempts to detail the psychological peculiarity of the identificatory dynamic these texts instantiate.

The absence of an analysis of that dynamic or any account of the production of feminine sentiment and subjectivity in criticism about sentimentalism should by no means be read as a willful mystification. Rather, it is symptomatic of the persistent effectiveness of sentimental texts in enacting forms of subjection and identification within liberal political culture. Drawing on the claims of theorists such as Catherine Belsey, I argue that the "subject of sentiment" does not preexist but is constituted through the identificatory exchanges of sentimental narrative. Indeed, the oft-noted conventionality of these texts should be understood as a kind of repetition-compulsion—one that might be interpreted, in psychological terms, as exemplifying that subject's need to revisit the scene of subjection through which it is formed, or in political terms, as an index of the social compulsion to repeatedly "perform" that subjectivity.[66] Indeed, I would argue that the binary structure of recent debates about the politics of sentimental sympathy (emphasizing, respectively, its politically transformative and its regressive or reifying dimensions) replays two different identificatory moments interior to the structure of sentimental subjectivity these texts enact: an identification with the progressive possibilities of liberal political agency and an identification with submission. Utilizing particular discursive and narrative cues (such as techniques of an "engaging narrator"),[67] these texts both thematize and instantiate the production of feminine subjection, in the Foucauldian sense of the term: these texts' constitution of feminine subjectivity and agency are inseparable from an identification with subordination and dependency; indeed, the production of feminine (sentimental) subjectivity depends upon that latter identification. The most detailed contemporary description of feminine subject-formation, Scottish Enlightenment moral philosophy (discussed in chapter 1), is quite explicit about this requirement; indeed, in the Scottish account, female subjection is foundational to modernity (and women occupy a "civilizing" and "socializing" role) precisely because the constitutive condition of female subjectivity, gaining agency in a state of subordination, is a model for the formation of *all* liberal political subjects.

This analysis of the psychic processes of sentimental subjection can illuminate the politics of sympathy and the particular narrative structure and effects of sentimental literary and philosophical texts. The Scottish inscription of sympathy, widely influential in America and often replicated in sentimental fiction, *narrativized* a developmental progression of sympathetic identification—from "enslavement" (savagery) to "agency" (civility)—and thus described and promoted particular normative identifications (especially gender, sexual, race, and class identifications) and forms of civil subjectivity. These forms of subjectivity are articulated through a traditional, philosophical opposition between "reason" and "passion": indeed, the very structure of psychological "development," agency, and self-management these texts inscribe (of control over, versus "enslavement" by, one's passions or bodily "appetites") promotes forms of (capitalist, middle-class) discipline by making self-control *feel like* "freedom." Sentimental literary and philosophical texts produce a narrative of "civilized" subject-formation through which certain "regressive" identifications are both registered and managed, sublimated in/by the diachronic progression of the narrative. Sentimental narrative's synchronic and diachronic temporal modes reinforce one another: indeed, the oft-noted scenes of recognition and emotional "conversion" common in sentimental texts (such as Farnham's), scenes frequently described as theatrical and pictorial, enact in miniature the trajectory of sentimental subjectification and consent to civil(ized) subjectivity described within the diachronic unfolding of the narrative. Throughout the book, then, I trace how liberal consumer subjectivity, and the dialectic of agency and subordination characteristic of feminine consent, is *constituted by* as well as *described within* sentimental narrative.

Sentimental Materialism thus focuses on the affiliated emergence of feminine consumer "subjectivity" and the literary culture of sentiment. In readings of fiction and domestic advice literature by a variety of American authors, I examine the ways in which these texts depict the materials of tasteful domesticity as markers of full subjectivity, and represent consumer artifacts as essential to "civilized" subjects' sentimental and moral education. Chapter 1 analyzes the reconstruction of "luxury" and "femininity" in the early republic, focusing on influential writings of Scottish Enlightenment moral philosophers and the reformulation of Scottish ideas in American conduct fiction and literature. Chapter 2, on the consolidation of sentimental ownership in the 1830s, traces ideologies of feminine domestic consumption in the fiction and advice literature of two of domesticity's most popular advocates, Caroline M. Kirkland and Catharine Maria Sedgwick. The third chapter, on Harriet Beecher Stowe's writing and the sentimental dimensions of Nathaniel Hawthorne's *The Blithedale Romance*, examines the import of sentimental constructions of property for the national debate over slavery and for the contested articulation of sentimental ownership as an expressly "American" proprietary configuration, discursively constituted in opposition to the "cannibalistic" practices of a range of ethnic, class, and national Others. Chapters 4 and 5 examine nineteenth-century African American women writers' creative engagement with domestic and sentimental literary conventions in their autobiographical and fictional inscriptions of black women as free subjects. Focusing on texts by Harriet Jacobs, Elizabeth Keckley, and Frances Harper, as well as Sojourner Truth's speeches and *Narrative*, the chapter explores how these writers manipulate the ties of sentiment in ways that both discursively produce black women as free civil subjects and expose the problematic nature of liberal models of freedom. The final chapter reads visual images of the cigar in advertising and popular culture as an index of public reformulations of consumer desire in the 1890s, an era of expressly gendered, "masculine" reaction to the increasingly visible cultural and economic authority of feminine consumers and feminine consumption. Last, my conclusion situates "sentimental materialism," as a particular aesthetics of ownership, within the history of aesthetics, as well as the history of American nationalism. Through short readings of texts by J. Hector St. John de Crèvecoeur and Lydia Maria Child, the conclusion suggests that sentimental ownership helped shape the passional, erotic attachment to nation that Benedict Anderson refers to in his description of nations as "imagined communities."

As an interdisciplinary project in cultural studies, *Sentimental Materialism* will, I hope, contribute to ongoing critical conversations in several areas: the politics of sentimental cultural forms, and their intersecting racial, class, gender, and national investments; the history and ideologies of domesticity, and the interrelationships between familial and economic structures in capitalism; the relationship between consumerism and feminism, and the place of consumption in the history of gender and historically specific forms of gendered subjectivity; the historical emergence and ideological and discursive articulations of capitalism and consumer culture in America; the place of affect in popular, commodity, and public cultures; the history and politics of "taste"; and the history of nationalism as sentimental affiliation. As an account of the emergence of sentimental subjectivity as a particular, conflictual form of liberal political subjectivity, the project contributes most forcefully, I hope, to our understanding of the discursive representation and constitution of political subjectivities; with Eric Lott, I see an understanding of "historical forms of consciousness and subjectivity" as the special ability of cultural studies work.[68] As my notes make clear, this project is indebted to the work of scholars in several disciplines; in my "home" discipline of American literary studies, I am especially indebted to the abundance of fine scholarship on domesticity and sentimentalism (some of which I have already noted) and a generation of feminist scholarship on late-eighteenth- and nineteenth-century women's literature, without which this book would have been unthinkable. To Gillian Brown's new historicist work on Stowe I am indebted for one of my central terms ("sentimental possession"); and indeed, Brown's very important account of "domestic individualism," and the ways in which possessive individualism "came to be associated with the female sphere of domesticity" in nineteenth-century America, has informed my own understanding of sentimental texts' instantiation of what I describe, in chapter 1, as the affectional dimensions of possessive individualism.[69] Brown's book brilliantly analyzes the ideologically occluded and mystified relays between market and home in antebellum literature, but—like much New Historicist scholarship in American studies—it seems to envision these relays as a closed system and to posit forms of economic determinism that marginalize the realm of politics, that realm in which domestic individualism and the institutions that subtend it are negotiated and, potentially, remade. *Sentimental Materialism* aims to articulate the unspoken investments and stakes of the bonds of sympathy and register their political effects, especially their gendered contradictions and the forms of political deference and political entitlement they enable. By mapping the emergence of sentimental ownership, starting in the eighteenth century, as a particular, liberal, erotics of property, I attempt here to historicize it, and to establish its contested place within the unwritten history of political subjectivities.

1

EMBODYING GENDER: SENTIMENTAL MATERIALISM IN THE NEW REPUBLIC

❀

In Charles Brockden Brown's *Alcuin; A Dialogue*, Alcuin, an "unpolished wight" and schoolteacher of "slender" stock, attends the coterie of Mrs. Carter, a decidedly middle-class *salonnière* whose "unbribed inclination" to superintend and serve constituted "the whole difference between her and a waiter at an inn, or the porter of a theatre."[1] When Alcuin awkwardly addresses the "mistress of the ceremonies" (4), "Pray, Madam, are you a federalist?" she responds with the following disclaimer:

> What! ask a woman, shallow and inexperienced as all women are known to be, especially with regard to these topics, her opinion on any political question! What in the name of decency have we to do with politics? If you enquire the price of this ribbon, or at what shop I purchased that set of China, I may answer you, though I am not sure that you would be the wiser for my answer. These things, you know, belong to the women's province. . . . The daringness of female curiosity is well known; yet it is seldom so adventurous as to attempt to penetrate into the mysteries of government. (7)

Of course, once she recovers from the "novelty" (7) of Alcuin's question, Mrs. Carter discourses quite eloquently on the subject of women's rights. Employing a rhetorical strategy widely used by republican women writers, Mrs. Carter mocks by hyperbolically articulating the sexist convictions of her age, her rhetorical performance dramatizing the distinction between the conventions of gender and the "natural" abilities of women. But what I wish to point to here is Mrs. Carter's demarcation of distinct, and distinctly *gendered*, "provinces" of male and female experience: the former encompassing the "mysteries of government" and public life; the latter, the seemingly less compelling (but, for Alcuin at least, equally daunting) "mysteries of tea-table decorum" (5) and the purchases that make these polite performances possible. The opposition was a convention of eighteenth-century Anglo-American social criticism and was used to mark the particularity of women's concerns, which purportedly rendered them incapable of disinterested rationality and, therefore, political virtue.[2] In line with a lengthy philosophical tradition that infused popular wisdom, these writers presumed that women, naturally deficient in reason and incapable of abstract thought, were inescapably buffeted about by the immediate and the contingent, the sensory and the sensual, excluded from the poise of reflection and the transcendental constancy of rationality. In the binary logic of eighteenth-century Anglo-American gender formulations, women were private and consuming, not public and political, creatures.[3]

But if shopping, to borrow Mrs. Carter's phrase, "belong[ed] to the women's province," exemplifying in its particularity something essentially *feminine*, it was also being rewritten by a variety of social discourses and legitimated as essential to an ethic of domestic sociability and social responsiveness.[4] The complex interconnections between the emerging familial form known as domesticity and what Neil McKendrick has called "the birth of a consumer society" have not been carefully explored—largely because historians of domesticity have tended to emphasize its spiritual and affectional, rather than its material bases. Cultural forms of domesticity adopted earlier, aristocratic ideals of courtesy, hospitality, and politesse to a more modest and—to borrow from the contemporary lexicon, less "promiscuous"—model of sociality, a model materially shaped by the democratization of consumption; in the words of one writer, "if a taste of any kind happen once to prevail among men of figure, it soon turns general." And what was "general" in eighteenth-century America, according to social historians, was a new taste for domestic commodities such as decorative furnishings, tableware, musical instruments, and the equipment of tea service, which helped form and express ideals of domestic sociability, comfort, and care.[5]

In this chapter, I discuss the genesis of a consumer ethic of feminine domestic sociality and aestheticism in eighteenth-century Anglo-American discourse, focusing on its contested articulation in a variety of texts published in the new republic, when an expressly "American" political economy and social ethic were first being formulated. This consumer ethic emerged out of a synthesis of Protestant and liberal discourses about the social significance of the family, the status of women, and the importance of mediating structures—economic, social, and aesthetic—in "civilizing" subjects and in promoting what eighteenth-century theorists termed "civil society." I will argue that the new feminine consumer ethic exhibited the constitutive ambivalence of liberal feminine subjectivity as an instance of what Hortense Spillers terms a "*patriarchilized* female gender."[6] In particular, it constructed women as *social* beings while falling short of positioning them as full participant citizens in American civic culture.

In a discussion of the moral philosophy of Scottish Enlightenment writers, especially Adam Smith, David Hume, John Millar, William Robertson, and Lord Kames, whose works were well known in America, I address representations of gender, property, and the emerging category of the "social" in Scottish liberalism. Although there are important differences among these writers, they share certain assumptions about the relationship among capitalism, sexual relations, and civil society, and it is their shared assumptions and rhetorical investments that interest me here. Consequently, I discuss these Scottish writings as a discourse, a representational matrix that (re)defined the ways in which commerce in general, and consumption in particular, could be "thought" in the new republic, and that set in place a network of discursive associations (e.g., among capitalist expansion, standard of living, and "civilization") that became unexamined conventions of U.S. writings about capitalism throughout the nineteenth century. In identifying luxury goods, which express "imaginary wants" and are thus explicitly invested with symbolic value, as vehicles of "civility" and "femininity," the Scots defined commodities as signifiers of subjectivity—specifically, of gender, sexual, and racial subjectivity—while they reified certain gender constructions as culturally normative.[7] Scottish discourse operated to define consumption and "taste" (that faculty that performs the selection of commodities) as constitutive of femininity and the realm in which feminine subjectivity is articulated and performed within culture, even while it worked to bifurcate capitalism according to a gendered division between production and consumption. Scottish Enlightenment discourse, I argue, enabled a profound reimagining of capitalism, in which constructions of gender played a key role. Crucially, this discourse created new ideals of refined, tasteful womanhood while valorizing capitalist exchange and consumption: indeed, the rhetorical rehabilitation of "luxury" was inseparable from, and effected through, the rehabilitation of the "feminine."

Eighteenth-century Scottish discourse (re)defined capitalism as a system propelled by desire, sympathy, and subjective identification rather than the often-violent expropriations of labor, land, and resources. Whereas earlier religious and political discourses (including civic humanism) had figured luxury as a means of political and ethical "enslavement" — a term with complex political and racial meanings in American republicanism — Scottish theory rearticulated luxury goods as expressions of subjective, imaginative "freedom" and, through what these writers described as the expansion of human sympathies in market society, the formation of ethical subjectivity per se. These formulations performed a series of displacements in American political discourse; in particular, they helped rearticulate capitalism — a highly contested system during this period — and distance it from slavery. By (re)defining capitalism's exchanges as mediated by sympathy, its privileged trope for reciprocity of both emotional and commercial exchange, Scottish discourse obscured the entanglements of capitalism with colonialism and slavery, entanglements that would resurface in the working-class republican rhetorics of "wage slavery" and "white slavery" in the 1830s and 1840s. Indeed, as the introduction to this book suggests, the dichotomy of enslavement and freedom was by no means stable in liberal constructions of subjectivity: "enslavement" was interiorized and often racialized as that subjectivity's constitutive limit, producing the interdeterminations of agency and constraint characteristic of liberal subjection.

Like other species of sentimental narration, Scottish narratives of the mutual evolution of civil society and civil subjectivity both describe and enact the psychodynamics of subjection in liberal political culture, with its intertwining of subordination and agency. This fundamentally ambivalent structure of political desire, alternating between moments of strenuous assertion of autonomy and submission to a "higher authority," has been described by Christopher Newfield as a fundamental "habit" of feeling of liberal "political subjectivity" in America: for Newfield, the "Emerson effect" has had a formative and devastating impact on American political life.[8] I have been suggesting that this dynamic assumes particularly gendered forms and habits of feeling in American public culture, and that the culture of sentiment is a primary place where the gendered processes of subjection are produced and instantiated. As I will show, in Scottish discourse, the formation of political subjectivity and desire through an identification with submission takes place in the realms of the family and the market, as well as through the "gentle suasion" of sentimental literary identification.

I argue below that the dynamic of sentimental subjection is distinctly proprietary: it generates what Scottish authors term the "sense of property," described as a spontaneous "affection" for private property implanted in man by the Creator to secure objects of labor "for himself and his family" — an erotics of ownership inextricable from relations of gender and the family.[9] Interweaving familial and property relations, sentimental subjection thus defines the affectional dimensions, indeed the attraction and erotic appeal, of possessive individualism. Further, I emphasize the performative dimensions of subjectivity this model enlists: rather than understanding sentiment as part of an individual's "private" life and interior endowments (that which defines identity per se), I argue that the "subject of sentiment," as a liberal, proprietary model of subjectivity, is produced in and staged by the repeated performance of emotion sentimental texts enlist. Staging and temporalizing an identificatory dynamic of agency and subordination, sentimental narratives enlist a subject's "consent" to capitalism at the most intimate level, grafting liberal-capitalist social forms onto that subject's most seemingly private, inalienable desires.

Turning from the Scots to late-eighteenth-century American conduct manuals such as Enos Hitchcock's *Memoirs of the Bloomsgrove Family* and Amos Chase's *On Female Excellence*, I examine how middle-class domestic advice literature synthesized Scottish conceptions of "civilizing" consumption and an aristocratic ethic of politesse, fashioning a new middle-class domestic model. Inscribing feminine taste and emotional preference with civilizing efficacy and political power, these texts construct the "republican consumer" as a new type of feminine civic identity. Finally, after examining configurations of domestic consumption and aestheticism in conduct literature, I turn to a discussion of Hannah Foster's *The Coquette*, in which the new domestic aesthetic is given complex articulation. Specifically, I examine the configurations of social difference through which Foster's text delineates the "proper" domestic practices of American women and envisions feminine taste as a site of political contestation and regulation. In the story of Eliza Wharton, Foster charts the contours of republican consumption by documenting the dangers of undisciplined consuming and an appetite for "fashion" that fragments, rather than bodies forth, the regenerate domestic community of the new nation.

"Luxury" in the New Republic

Few things seem as universally reviled in Revolutionary-era America as "luxury." Etymologically derived from the Latin noun *luxus*, meaning "excess," "luxury" possessed, as contemporaries never tired of noting, no fixed or absolute representational significance; however, this definitional obscurity only augmented the imaginative potency of the term as a source of imminent danger. Broadly stated, luxury connoted a realm of sumptuous superfluity and sensual gratification that lured men beyond a natural economy of needs.[10] According to most scholars, the predominant intellectual traditions in early republican America—religious, political, and economic—converged in an ideal of simple living and self-denial that rendered luxury anathema and a synonym for corruption. For orthodox Protestants, luxury connoted sensual indulgence and misplaced attachment to worldly ephemera, distracting individuals from divine truths. For civic humanists, luxury, signifying private acquisitive behavior and dependence on the market, corrupted republican virtue: undermining self-sufficiency and promoting insensibility to the common good, luxury was figured as a form of "enslavement" that rendered the citizen prey to despotism (as in the oft-invoked example of the Roman Empire's collapse). Finally, according to the colonial economic theory of mercantilism, liberal consumption practices—which during the eighteenth century chiefly meant buying foreign, mostly British commodities—created an unfavorable balance of trade, diminishing national wealth and draining the treasury: for mercantilists, luxury consumption wasted economic resources and weakened the body politic.[11] The traditional distrust of luxury was heightened during the Revolutionary era by a nascent nationalism and was given distinctly American form by the "myth of America"—a myth that coupled a redemptive pastoralism with a strong belief that Americans were, in Jefferson's words, "the chosen people of God," destined to transcend the corruptions of Europe and the contaminations of history.[12] Synthesizing Calvinist and civic humanist ideals and giving Puritan conceptions of communal exceptionalism a republican cast, Samuel Adams envisioned the new nation as a "Christian Sparta," an austere but virtuous society of independent citizens unselfishly devoted to the common good, and shielded from the corruptions of commercial advance that plagued Old World, European societies.[13]

However, one influential Anglo-American intellectual tradition rhetorically rehabilitated luxury by redefining its social and cultural effect as beneficial, supplying what John Pocock has called "an element of progress to pit against" the conventional "element[s] of conservation" and historical declension. For Scottish Enlightenment moral philosophers, whose arguments were frequently reiterated by American authors in the last decades of the eighteenth century, luxury was the favorable culmination of "civilization," human morality, and social advance.[14] According to Nicholas Phillipson, the tradition, which included the work of Adam Smith, David Hume, Henry Home (Lord Kames), William Robertson, and John Millar, first emerged during the late seventeenth and early eighteenth centuries in reaction to the backwardness of the Scottish economy. Intellectuals and politicians pressured Parliament to lift the restrictions on Scottish trade and open up Scotland's ports to ships of all countries. In 1707, the Scots received a compromise in the form of the Act of Union, which essentially exchanged Scotland's free political institutions for the right of free access to English markets at home and abroad. According to the Act of Union, Scotland would be allowed to trade freely, but at the cost of its political autonomy: henceforth, Scots would send members of Parliament to London, not to their own assembly. Grappling with this new situation, Scottish thinkers began to analyze the value of nonpolitical forms of association and to examine in new detail the relationship between commerce and society. Using civil law to organize their thinking, they emphasized the importance of the legal protections of the individual and his property *from* the state, as opposed to the participation of the individual *in* the state.[15]

As Pocock and others have demonstrated, Scottish Enlightenment moral philosophy emerged out of the tensions and conflicts within eighteenth century political discourse, especially those between court (or commercial) and country (or classical) republicanism. Organizing their polemics around the key terms of civic humanism — "luxury," "imagination," "passion," "credit," "property," and, most importantly, "virtue" — the Scots gave these terms new meanings, endowing their conceptual innovations with legitimacy by creating, rhetorically, the sense of historical continuity. While civic humanists insisted on a strict distinction between public and private spheres, the Scots qualified that distinction by delineating a group of mediating institutions — most prominently, commerce, property, and the family — through which individuals are "civilized," "socialized," and otherwise prepared for civil society.[16]

Like many of their contemporaries, Scottish Enlightenment writers were centrally concerned with the relationship between "virtue" and "commerce" in civil society. However, unlike most civic humanists, the Scots emphasized the beneficial consequences of trade, especially its "civilizing" effects on morals and manners. Although a few earlier writers such as Davenant had presented unelaborated rationales for economic "modernization" and the expansion of trade within a civic humanist frame, the Scots were the first to provide a theory of civic personality applicable to a commercial society. Rejecting as archaic, even "barbaric," civic humanist paradigms of Spartan, Roman, and Gothic virtue based on the possession of land, the Scots formulated a new social ethic suited to a "world of moving objects": they argued that it was only with the spread of commerce and the arts that men became socialized into the capacity for trust, friendship, and Christian love. In Pocock's words, they devised a "civic morality of investment and exchange" which equated "the commercial ethic with the Christian," recasting the Machiavellian antithesis between civic and Christian virtue in the form of a historical progression.[17] In America, this discourse performed several crucial ideological displacements: in particular, by construing mobile property as the basis of civil society, Scottish discourse shifted attention away from a Jeffersonian concern with economic self-sufficiency and ownership of *productive* property, even while it obscured the centrality of land as material basis (and site of violent struggle) of U.S. internal colonization and continental expansion.[18]

Indeed, Scottish discourse contributed to what would have seemed in the new republic an overwhelming ideological task: how to justify the growth of capitalism and a market system of commodity exchange that was, for many, antithetical to hard-won ideals of political independence. In part, as I will show, the rearticulation of capitalism as a "civilizing" social system was performed through its alignment with the "natural" discourse of gender, especially an explicitly gendered language of enslavement and race. Scottish discourse inscribes market capitalism as the system in which modern "subjects" are defined and interpellated into clearly gendered (and racialized) positions. As several historians have argued, the growth of market and industrial capitalism in the early nineteenth century was justified as compatible with republican and democratic ideals of "freedom" due to the negative example of chattel slavery: the economic and political freedom of whites was measured and symbolically articulated with reference to their perceived distance from black enslavement.[19] Scottish discourse itself was expressly racialized: the market was identified as a realm of freedom and full subjectivity through a symbolics of racial difference. For instance, William Robertson described Native Americans as "savage" precisely because of their alleged failure to assimilate into market culture, expressed in terms of absence of work discipline as well as an insufficient sense of private property, figured as an inadequate psychological and affectional "attachment" to things. Early-nineteenth-century writings on the market recycled this notion, often extending its logic to African Americans: for example, William Gilmore Simms argued that African Americans were constitutionally disqualified from participating in American civic culture because of their so-called insensibility to the attractions of consumer goods and material refinement—which is a way of saying that African Americans are both positioned outside civil society and insufficiently or deficiently gendered, positioned outside normative systems of gender difference through which full subjectivity is defined.[20] More specifically, such writings define liberal "consent" and its gendered models of consenting subjectivity, expressed in labor and commodity markets, as a *white* racial formation: identfying Native and African Americans with nonconsent, objecthood, and enslavement, these texts mark the racial limits of sentimental identification.

Capitalism's justification in this discourse pivots on the status of women, which the Scots conventionally termed the "treatment of women"—a rhetorical index of the condition of patriarchal subordination within which sentimental subjectivity takes shape. That status is measured in racial terms that were acutely resonant in America: implicit in Scottish discourse is the notion that while women in premodern or nonmarket societies are objectified, treated as drudges and slaves, white women are viewed as "subjects," as fully human persons with specific identities, desires, and emotions. Just as the position of white male "wage slave" was ideologically differentiated from that of chattel slave so that capitalism was defined as a realm of white privilege and "freedom," the position of white women in capitalism's private sphere—and the exploitation of white women's domestic and sexual labors within that sphere—was being articulated in Scottish discourse as distinct from the position and exploitation of women of color, especially Native American and African American women. This difference, it turns out, is wholly a matter of subjectivity: while women in premodern societies, especially women of color, are treated as drudges or (to borrow Farnham's metaphor) "machines," white women are socially acknowledged as consenting subjects and fully human persons.[21] In other words, Scottish discourse established a discursive structure through which white women were able to imagine themselves as free commercial subjects, and to imagine commerce itself as a realm of freedom, *in distinction from* the position of women of color, especially Native American and black women—a distinction challenged, in part, by the rhetorical identification of women and slaves in some feminist discourse.[22] Describing the socially progressive nature of commerce and modern heterosexuality, then, Scottish discourse represents market capitalism as supplying a new civic identification for women and depicts taste as constitutive of feminine political subjectivity—politically ambiguous constructions, I have suggested, that can help illuminate the complex interdependence of feminism and consumerism, and the fact that feminist longings have often been imagined in consumerist form. But by the late eighteenth century, the emerging market system and its gendered forms of civil subjectivity were subtly interwoven with discursive constructions of whiteness, and constituted a matrix of identifications within which white subjectivity and agency could be affirmed.

As we shall see, a fundamental psychic ambivalence, identifying with and disidentifying from "enslavement," was staged and engendered in Scottish philosophical as in American literary sentimental narratives. Scottish texts provide a narrative of liberal subject-formation that is both mythic-historical—an account of the "origin" of society—and developmental—a narrative of socialization. Because of these relays between the subjective and the social, Scottish sentimentalism enabled the "recognition" of a range of identifications (in terms of race, gender, age, etc.) and simultaneously mandated the regulation or repression of these ("regressive") identifications in the narrative teleology of "civilized" subject-formation. Temporalizing what I have described as the constitutive ambivalence of liberal subjection, they narrate the origin of liberal subjectivity as a transition from what Foucault terms punishment to discipline: from a state in which bodies are objects of force to one where power is internalized and consciousness is (self-) regulated in accord with the intersubjective, "consensual" relations of market exchange. In the Scottish model, the family plays a crucial role as the site where subjection, the interdetermination of agency and constraint, is originally as well as persuasively and habitually felt. Sentimental narrative both keeps alive those originary identifications while distancing or abjecting them through a symbolics of race, class, and gender difference, encoding differences of social status that both elicit and regulate the flow of sympathy.

I have suggested that these interdeterminations of gender, race, and economics in liberal economic discourse enabled Americans to negotiate various ideological contradictions in the new republic. On the one hand, with the emerging market structure in the United States being pressured by republican antimarket discourse and a critique of chattel slavery, Scottish discourse fostered the reconstruction of the market as a site of freedom; on the other hand, with patriarchal authority being pressured by revolutionary egalitarianism and the emerging discourse of feminism, Scottish inscriptions of the market offered a narrative of the voluntary and peaceful melioration of male domination in which white men (and, differently, women) could recognize themselves, and be assured of the superiority of their cultural forms, without sacrificing white male privilege and political power. Indeed, as we shall see, Scottish discourse did not negate but reconfigured male domination in accord with new social imperatives: it represented a (re)constructed, sympathetic masculine power, defined paternalistically as protective care and what I call in the introduction "sentimental ownership," as the enabling condition of feminine subjectivity, explicitly framing feminine subjectivity within the context of male authority and heterosexual desire. Although men and women are each dependent on the other in the Scottish model, it provides for a fantasy of male mastery, wholeness, and autonomy (identified with men's superior physical power and willfulness in the "state of nature"), while denying any such fantasy to women, who are envisioned as always subjected to male (physical or psychological) law.[23]

In Scottish discourse and in American texts, sympathy performed a crucial ideological function, encoding the emotional dialectic of identification and distinction. As a rhetoric of identification, sympathy could, of course, take a variety of social forms: for example, it could evoke male homosocial public desire and identification (as in Smith's *Theory*). In fact, in Scottish discourse, different formations of sympathetic identification correlate to different social spheres: for example, in the realm of the market, sympathy facilitates the sublimation of violence (in which others appear as mere objects or instruments of will) into the socially sanctioned aggressions of market competition and an identification with others as consenting subjects.[24] However, in Scottish discourse, heterosociality is envisioned as the origin of civilized life: thus, a particular formation of sympathy (one that operates across a status differential) is envisioned as *constitutive* of civil subjectivity, a formation that must be habitually returned to in order to enact socially that subjectivity.[25] As described in the introduction, sympathy was the eighteenth century's privileged trope to mediate relations between those unequally positioned within the social field (e.g., parents and children, husbands and wives, the wealthy and the poor, even people and animals), and constitute them as relations of intersubjectivity. Within the realm of the family, where legal relations were traditionally defined in terms of status, not contract, and where dependents were traditionally defined as male property, that recognition of intersubjectivity did not negate, but recast, patriarchal property relations, redefining them as relations of paternalism and protective care. The structure of liberal masculinity the Scots describe is characterized by its own constitutive ambivalence, facilitating an identification with dependency and a proprietary power over the dependent Other; indeed, liberal masculine political agency was enacted through this dynamic, in which powerlessness is both felt and disavowed. Although I focus on male subject-formation only briefly in this chapter, it seems clear that, in the Scottish narrative, a masculine proprietary relation is mobilized or recuperated defensively: the objectification of women as male property is internalized as a psychic mechanism through which men manage their feelings of powerlessness and their developmental dependence on women. Entangling constructions of gender and property, their narrative constitutes the property relation as at once a gender relation and a relation to gender: revealing the affectional dimension of possessive individualism, Scottish discourse construes property as a primary relation in which the dynamic of subjection (of agency inseparable from dependency) is instantiated and managed. I will argue below that a particular proprietary relation is central both to the structure of sympathy through which political subjectivities are constituted in Scottish discourse, and to the psychic effects of sentimental narrative.

Sympathy, Sex, and Commerce

Central to the Scots' commercial revisionism was a complex metaphorics of animation and social exchange: the Scots identified the market—the "sphere of moving objects"—as a domain of *animated* persons and objects, defined in opposition to the noncirculating property and immobile (non)persons of feudalism. Directly responding to Rousseau's narrative of cultural decline and challenging civic humanists' ritual invocation of the lost virtues of Spartan simplicity—which the Scots typically depicted as a state of barbarism and incivility—Scottish Enlightenment writers defended luxury as enabling the refinement, harmony, and polite sociability of civilized living. In the writings of the Scots, the twin significances of "decency"—connoting a material and an ethical standard—were indissolubly linked; in the words of David Hume, "the ages of refinement are both the happiest and the most virtuous." Like commerce, which facilitated its growth, luxury, by enlarging and varying the sphere of things and persons to which one's interests and affections are joined, would enable an expansion of social personality: it simultaneously promoted liberality of sentiment and the capacity for discriminating among objects of affection, stimulating what one writer termed an "enlarged" benevolence and the first stirrings of heterosexual love.[26] According to Lord Kames, a popularizer of Scottish ideas whose *Sketches of the History of Man* was widely read in America, the growth of luxury "multipl[ies]" individuals' enjoyments and "improve[s] their benevolence," and "soften[s] and humanize[s] our manners." Unlike "savage" society, "a society based on violence and brute force," a commercial society, and the desire for luxury which commerce awakens, sublimates divisive passions into the social sentiments of benevolence and encourages a well-mannered display of gentility. The "softening" and "domesticating" effects of luxury—bemoaned by civic humanists and Rousseauian primitivists alike — would improve, by rendering pacific and sociable, bellicose rulers and barbarous men.[27]

The Scots' commercial revisionism entailed a revisionism of gender and the family. Against the republican, neo-Machiavellian construction of political virtue, characterized by Spartan simplicity, disinterested rationality, and the manliness of military performance, the Scots assimilated Christian ethical ideals to reconstruct virtue as specifically feminine, emotional rather than rational, characterized by a disinterested benevolence infused through the refining comforts of domestic life. Modern or commercial societies, according to the Scots, were distinguished from premodern societies not only by the mobility of property but by the mobility of women and a new respect for feminine sensibility and refinement. Whereas in barbaric, premodern societies, women are physically enslaved or held captive, brutally used, and exploited, commercial societies are characterized by the "free" social circulation of women and a new respect for women's affectional choices within the heterosexual marriage and commodity markets.[28] In premodern societies, as in the hypothetical "state of nature," heterosexual relations are merely physical relations of what Immanuel Kant termed "sexual use": the use of another as sexual property, "in which one is really made a *res fungibilis* to the other," which is for Kant "on the level of cannibalism."[29] Countering Rousseau's contention that in the state of nature the sexes were physically equal, and that women's physical inferiority was both product and sign of cultural degeneracy, the Scots simultaneously represented feminine weakness as natural and reconstituted that weakness as embodying women's superior "sensibility."

Crucially, in the writings of the Scots, women's "natural" physical dependency and "natural" aesthetic and moral superiority are mutually constitutive. Because of the unremediable difference in physical strength between the sexes, heterosexual relations in the state of nature would inevitably be one-sided and lead to women's physical victimization. In contradistinction, "civilized" social relations were chiefly characterized by men's gentleness toward women and increased appreciation of women's interior, not just physical, endowments. Animating women's bodies by endowing them with sensibility, the Scots emphasized the socially regenerative nature of feminine refinement. According to John Millar, women in "refined and polished nations" were entitled to "the same freedom [as men], upon account of those agreeable qualities which they possess, and the rank and dignity which they hold as members of society." Similarly, Kames insisted that human history should be seen in terms of the "gradual advance of the female sex to an equality with the male sex," while Hume spoke of "that nearness of rank, not to say equality" which civilized life "establishe[s] between the sexes."[30]

Hume's subtle distinction between "nearness of rank" and "equality" exemplifies the complexities in Scottish constructions of woman's place in civil society. Indeed, the Scots did not so much negate women's status as male property as reconstitute it, simultaneously "animating" women and situating them within novel proprietary structures. I argue below that the Scots reconstructed women as sentimental property: a form of property that civilizes men, engaging their affections and inspiring their higher (aesthetic and social) sentiments, a form of property that men "love," cherish, and "care for." As I have suggested, "property" is a crucial term in the Scottish narrative and fundamentally informs the civilizing intersubjectivity of heterosexuality: because in the "state of nature" women are defined as male property objects, proprietary authority structures the forms of civil subjectivity this narrative outlines and the forms of political identification it engenders. Heterosexuality, structured across a formative difference in status and "originally" defined as a property relation, here *enables* liberal political subjection and its dual identifications with power and submission; and the form of (political) power it imagines is primarily the power of ownership. However, in the Scottish narrative, men and women have differing access to this power and it assumes particularly gendered forms, because of the narrative's inscription of women's "natural," essential status as male property. In particular, heterosexuality's civilizing exchanges here mandate men's and women's (prior) "recognition" of male power, so that women's consent to femininity requires, in a fundamental way, female self-abnegation. In this account, the "development" of capitalism and modernity is predicated on the existence of patriarchy, as well as white racial privilege: in fact, capitalism, patriarchy, and whiteness are affectively sutured together in the formation feminists term "white capitalist patriarchy."[31] As expressed by the oft-repeated phrase "treatment of women," Scottish discourse thus positions women ambivalently, as subjects with whom men "identify" and as objects over whom men have power—an ambivalence central, I have suggested, to processes and proprietary forms of masculine liberal subjection.

The view of women as male property objects is insistently figured in the Scottish equivalence of women and luxury. For the Scots, luxury goods perform the same function as virtuous women: "civilizing" men by meliorating their passions, polishing their manners, refining their ethical and aesthetic sensibility, tempering men's "ferocity with gentleness."[32] Hume applauds the aesthetic effects of feminine company: "What better school for manners, than the company of virtuous women; where the . . . endeavor to please must insensibly polish the mind, where the example of female softness and modesty must communicate itself to their admirers, and where the delicacy of that sex puts every one on his guard, lest he give offense by any breach of decency"; he speculates that the writings of ancient authors lacked polish and pleasantry, the graces of a refined style, because their women were excluded from the world of polite intercourse.[33] The civilizing power of luxury, like the civilizing influence of virtuous women, was seen to proceed from their status as objects of desire: for both, the capacity to stimulate male virtue depended on remoteness and exclusiveness, a *distance* that motivated the improving exertions necessary to attain them; both encouraged the virtue of deferral and self-restraint, the willingness to forgo immediate gratifications for the prospect of more refined pleasures later on.[34] Constituted as objects of erotic desire and enticements to market discipline, both embody what Georg Simmel terms the "essence of 'price' ": the simultaneity of availability and distance, invitation and aloofness, representative of the concurrent "ability and inability to acquire something" that produces commodity desire in market culture.[35]

Alternately, however, women are recognized in Scottish discourse as consenting *subjects* with whom men identify, and who are endowed with the civilizing faculty of feminine "taste." As Hume's statements indicate, a general desire for refinement was often attributed to the increased social influence of women and the hegemony of feminine taste, a historical sequence bemoaned by Rousseau and taken up more recently by historians.[36] For these writers, the "civilizing process" is a process of "feminization" whereby the elegancies women tastefully promote manage, in the words of an eighteenth-century American, to "tame what is wild, and conquer what is fierce, in man."[37] "Taste" here connotes a particular, expressly feminine, political faculty, associated for the Scots with female bodily weakness (and, indirectly, with the "natural" emotions of motherhood): not an expression of direct force or enactment of political will ("power over" an object), it connotes an act of will that turns against itself, sublimating "power over" or direct use of an object into the imperative to "care for" or preserve it. Encoding the identificatory dialectic of agency and subordination, taste constitutes a specific, gendered form of "possessive individualism": in the Scottish model, it is a relation to property and structure of political desire that men learn from women. Framing feminine subjectivity and "taste" within masculine proprietary power, these writers promote both the recognition and containment of masculine identification with women.

Before examining further the instability and psychic effects of the Scottish construction of feminine political subjectivity, it seems useful to pause to unpack the complex of meanings within Scottish discourse. In their rationale for capitalism and its sex-gender system, several aspects should be underscored: its rationalization of market discipline, especially its structure of delayed gratification, via a discourse of (hetero)sexuality; its scapegoating of women as enforcers of market discipline; its mapping of a binary pair of sexed, gendered (and racialized) subject-positions within civil society. Most importantly, these writers construct luxury and femininity as at once consequence and origin of progress and civilization, while defining each as constitutive of the other. The circularity of their logic, however, merely intensifies this discourse's rhetorical and ideological effectiveness, its ability to prescribe while describing certain subject-positions for those it addresses. "Sympathy" connotes the processes of identification that Scottish discourse both epistemologically requires and rhetorically performs: just as these texts describe forms of sympathetic exchange through which modern subjects are constituted, they promote forms of identification—of "recognizing" oneself in/as the "civilized" subject they represent—through which readers passionally engage with these writings. These texts are thus implicated in the processes they describe: the formation of specifically gendered forms of subjection within capitalism.

The Scottish reconstruction of female subjectivity and desire is fundamentally heterosexist: feminine taste is legitimated in terms of its salutary, civilizing effect on the masculine subject, a construction that both presents heterosexuality as the normative context for feminine consumption and relegates the politics of feminine desire to the prehistory of the masculine subject. Indeed, while Scottish theorists construct masculine taste as a consequence of male heterosexual desire, they don't theoretically account for the development of feminine taste: drawing on the lengthy, misogynist tradition dating back to classical Rome depicting women as possessed of a "natural" desire for luxury, Scottish writers naturalize feminine taste and a feminine consumer role; indeed, they present taste as constitutive of feminine subjectivity. Importantly, in the Scottish model, only certain forms of female desire are sanctioned: specifically, it valorizes as culturally progressive and civilizing only the forms of refinement that men themselves recognize and value. Thus, this discourse legitimates female consumption while framing or containing feminine taste within the rubric of male desire. The formulation of "sentimental property" encapsulates this tension and registers the instability of the feminine consumer subject-position within Scottish discourse: the feminine consumer subject is also imagined as a masculine property object, an object of male physical and social power. Recognized by men as constituting feminine civil subjectivity, taste also serves to differentiate "civilized" women from race and class Others: while the aestheticization ("refinement") of some women's bodies recasts, rather than negates, their status as male property, the aesthetic also serves as a vehicle to differentiate among different kinds of male property—to distinguish refined from unrefined bodies, feminine subjects from objects of physical and sexual utility.

Both the feminization and the social efficacy of taste, and its ambivalent effects on masculine subjectivity, are amply registered in the Scottish writings. No figure was as universally employed in discussions of luxury during the Enlightenment than the representation of luxury as "effeminizing." If luxury effeminized, it was marked as feminine property: as I argue more substantially below, luxury goods for personal and household consumption were conceived as material objectifications of feminine psychological and bodily attributes that extended—when enjoyed within certain bounds—the blessings of feminine civility, benevolence, and comfort. The new conception of luxury goods as embodying feminine "gifts" and "refinements" was given material form in the increased lightness of form and the fluid curvature of eighteenth-century furniture styles, from Queen Anne to Federal.[38]

This construction of luxury as "feminine" property was, however, double-edged. Like "woman," "luxury" remained a self-contradictory signifier, bearing persistent connotations of seductive physical pleasures which could undermine rather than promote sensibility and the bodily health and comfort on which sensibility depended.[39] If luxury was seen to impart the virtues and graces of femininity as conceived during the period—benevolence, gentility, and politeness—it could also transmit feminine pathology. The discourse of feminization as "degeneration," especially prominent in the late nineteenth century, was the dystopian version of the discourse of feminization as "progress," and is, I would argue, symptomatic of the liberal masculine need to manage its identification with "feminine" dependency. As my analysis of cigar imagery in chapter 6 suggests, the dynamic interrelations of gender, historical temporality, and power in Scottish constructions of the market indicate how a certain fantasy of aggression and unmediated physical power ("brute force"), associated with male mastery and wholeness and often located on the imperial "frontier," could be mobilized as a check on excessive "feminization" at home. As Amy Kaplan describes the intersecting and gendered rhetorics of domesticity and imperialism in U.S. discourse in the 1890s, "the empire figures as the site where you can be all that you can no longer be at home—a 'real live man'—where you can recover the autonomy denied by social forces of modernization, often aligned in this way of thinking with feminization."[40]

The ambivalent social effects of feminine subjectivity are abundantly evident in Scottish representations of luxury. Implicit in many of their writings is what Arthur Lovejoy calls the "ethics of the middle link," temporalized as a historical dialectic: the certainty that the benefits of civilization will, if immoderately indulged, foster cultural decay, transforming progress into decline. In the words of Lord Kames, great wealth produces a "lamentable effect: it enervates the possessor, and degrades him into a coward. He who commands the labour of others, who eats without hunger, and rests without fatigue, becomes feeble in mind as well as in body, has no confidence in his own abilities, and is reduced to flatter his enemies, because he hath not courage to brave them. . . . In the savage state, man is almost all body, with a very small proportion of mind. In the maturity of civil society, he is complete both in mind and body. In a state of degeneracy by luxury and voluptuousness, he has neither mind nor body." The excessive indulgence of luxury renders one weak, cowardly, "feeble in mind as well as in body"—in short, it makes one a(n embodied) woman, and imparts the constitutional dis-ease of femininity.[41]

Elaine Scarry has written beautifully of the "compassion-bearing" nature of material objects, the power of things to extend the body and relieve it of its problems and pains. But there is widespread suspicion during the eighteenth century that the expanding array of conveniences don't supplement bodily capacities but rather, through the dependency of habitual use, supplant and enervate them, a line of argument advanced by Rousseau and echoed frequently by Scottish and American authors. (In fact, several of these authors, including the American physician Benjamin Rush—who studied with William Cullen in Edinburgh—recommend as an antidote to the degenerative effects of material comfort the bracing tonic of physical pain: in a telling inversion of Scarry's central claim, Rush contends that bodily pain "gives a tone to the nervous system," "elevat[es]" the intellectual faculties, and even "rous[es] and direct[s]" the moral sense.)[42] According to these writers, material objects don't extend and enhance bodily powers but rather, by a process of substitution that encourages their relaxation and disuse, attenuate these powers and foster bodily "softness" and "weakness," the pathological debility of femininity. The Scottish historian William Robertson writes of the many "distempers which afflict polished nations" that are the "immediate offspring of luxury," maladies that "assault" and "enervate" the constitution, and consequently enfeeble and "abridge human life." And once again to quote Lord Kames: "The indulging in down-beds, soft pillows, and easy seats, is a species of luxury; because it tends to enervate the body, and to render it unfit for fatigue"; he goes on to describe "two young women of high quality, who were sisters, [who] employed a servant with soft hands to raise them gently out of bed in the morning."[43] The corruptive, contaminating power of luxury is discursively figured in this passage metonymically. Specific objects of luxury ("down-beds, soft pillows, and easy seats"), principally characterized by their "softness," are figured as the signs of feminine bodily attributes, an identity here highlighted by the adjectival link between the "soft pillows" and the female servant's "soft hands"; and these luxury objects produce bodies that are themselves "softer," themselves (more) "feminine." Indulgence in the luxuries and conveniences of life, "giving in" to the bodily support and pleasure they afford, implies a form of relaxation of both vigilance and exertion that compromises "manly" strength and enterprise. Mobilizing, figuratively, the ambiguities of gendered identification, Scottish writings on luxury mandate both the political deployment and the masculine regulation of feminine consumer desire.

The regulation of feminine taste was effected, in part, by the domestication of female desire, its confinement to the domestic realm of patriarchal property relations. The demarcation of taste and luxury as the special province of the feminine, and civilization itself as nourished by feminine advance, established "culture" as female property.[44] If culture was being feminized, it was also being domesticated: while Rousseau and the Scots were, no doubt, thinking especially of the salonnière in their discussions of the civilizing ministry of feminine taste, they were simultaneously constructing a new ideal of domestic intimacy that was absorbed into middle-class practice. Identifying the domestic sphere as a socially regenerative, humanizing realm, their texts gave the "ethics of the middle link" spatial dimensions, presenting the "natural society" of the family—a liminal construct positioned between the solipsistic privacy of "natural" man and the disinterested rationality of *zoon politikon*—as a space where the materials of culture could be safely enjoyed because thoroughly socialized, embedded within a nexus of intimate familial relations.[45] As I will show in my discussion of American conduct materials and in subsequent chapters, the Scots' commercial construction of liberal political subjectivities, and their emphasis on the companionate family as an originary realm in which these subjectivities are formed and habitually performed, enabled a particular middle-class construction of political subjectivity: establishing the middle-class subject as the legimate ("civilized") political subject, it reinforced the political and national hegemony of the middle class; at the same time, it inscribed class as a voluntary (and *malleable*) identification, one expressed and shaped by taste and domestic consumption—a configuration of class(lessness) central to the logic of the "American Dream," and one that could be mobilized at different political moments to diffuse and contain class antagonisms. But first, in order to elucidate the complex interrelationship between modernity and femininity in the sentimental model, I turn to the moral philosophy of Adam Smith, perhaps the best-known Scottish author in America, whose inscriptions of the regenerative, animating potency of intimate social exchanges were influential in the new republic.

Adam Smith and the Culture of Sentiment

The Theory of Moral Sentiments, first published in 1759, was well known among educated Americans in the early republic: common in American libraries, the text constituted a staple of the college curriculum by the Revolution.[46] Countering Thomas Hobbes's emphasis on the innate self-interestedness of persons, Smith depicted individuals as endowed with compassionate instincts and, especially, the capacity for sympathy, which he defined as "our fellow-feeling with any passion whatever" (49). "How selfish soever man may be supposed," the opening paragraph reads, "there are evidently some principles in his nature, which interest him in the fortune of others, and render their happiness necessary to him, though he derives nothing from it except the pleasure of seeing it" (47). Equally compelling, for Smith, was man's need to win the sympathy of others for himself, for man was naturally endowed with an "original desire to please, and an original aversion to offend his brethren" (212). Smith's *Theory* attempted nothing less than to show how the need for sympathy that the "Author of nature" had implanted within man could generate the entire structure of his moral and aesthetic judgment.[47]

As the primary medium of social animation, sympathy is, for Smith, a form of imaginative *exchange* that is simultaneously a form of imaginative *possession*: it entails imagining oneself in another's "place," placing oneself, but for an instant, in the visible context of another's life. "It is by the imagination only," Smith states early in the essay, "that we can form any conception" of the emotional experience or condition of another person (49). Sympathetic imagination operates by inference: the sympathizing individual perceives the material referents of feeling—contextual signs such as features of the environment, actions, manners, as well as the bodily "language" of emotional expression—and imagines, through the projections of imaginative identification, what it would be like to experience that emotion. Of particular importance for this empirical structure of social inference—this way of "knowing" persons—are the empirical "objects" with which individuals are most characteristically and habitually associated: thus, for Smith, the importance of property, long-standing social relations such as the family and, especially, bodies as indexes of an individual's subjectivity. Sympathy requires imaginatively projecting oneself into, or inhabiting, another's perceptible context or situation, imagining, that is, what it would be like to have his/her body (or his/her property or family). In Smith's account, sympathetic exchange entails both projection and introjection: it requires, in a double move, imaginatively projecting oneself into or inhabiting another's outward situation in order to promote a subjective, interior conception of the experience of the other. As Smith describes this structure of imaginative exchange: "By the imagination we place ourselves in [another person's] situation, we conceive ourselves enduring all the same torments, we enter as it were into his body, and become in some measure the same person with him, and thence form some idea of his sensations, and even feel something which, though weaker in degree, is not altogether unlike them. His agonies, *when they are thus brought home to ourselves, when we have thus adopted and made them our own*, begin at last to affect us" (48; emphasis added). The circuitry of sympathetic exchanges depends chiefly on the mediations of vision: according to Smith, it is precisely because "the eye is larger than the belly" that man leaves the insensibility of the state of nature and enters the "civilized" relations of society (304).

This process of imaginative projection and introjection animates both parties in the exchange: in Smith's account, being fully psychologically developed and socialized—situated, that is, within the social network of sympathetic exchanges—requires being imaginatively possessed, and *imagining oneself* imaginatively possessed, by others. Because of man's "natural" desire for sympathy, each person wishes to see him/herself imaginatively encompassed by the heart(s) of the other(s): "To see the emotions of [the viewers'] hearts in every respect beat time to his own . . . constitutes his sole consolation" and desire (67). The sympathy of others "enlivens" one's pleasures and moderates, by providing consolation for, one's pains: an individual who makes a joke, for example, experiences increased pleasure when others enjoy the joke, chiefly because of the "additional vivacity which his mirth may receive from sympathy with theirs"

(54); while a friend's pleasure in a book increases our own, since "we are amused by sympathy with his amusement, which thus enlivens our own" (55). Including oneself within the nexus of available sympathy requires a certain self-consciousness in one's emotional self-presentation, a certain theatricalization of one's inner life: it requires presenting one's emotional experience in a sympathetically recognizable fashion. (Like other eighteenth-century writers, Smith calls the requisite social structures of emotional performance "manners.") Indeed, self-consciousness for Smith entails the internalization of the other's perspective: incorporating the other as "the man within the breast" (352) and moderating emotional expression in accord with the other's internalized perspective. In a real sense, then, sympathy *animates* bodies, attaching empirical objects to normative conceptions of subjective, emotional experience by situating those objects within the circuitry of emotional identification and exchange, while multiplying the social emotions and, thus, "refining," the subjective interiority of social participants.

In *The Theory of Moral Sentiments*, the development of "sensibility" — the Scots' term for this quality of "animation" and emotional sensitivity — depends on the complex interplay of self-reflection and emotional experience. According to Smith, an unsocialized individual who had "grow[n] up to manhood in some solitary place," would be concerned wholly with objects of passion — sensory objects — rather than objects of reflective consciousness — the passions — themselves: "To a man who from his birth was a stranger to society, the objects of his passions, the external bodies which either pleased or hurt him, would occupy his whole attention. The passions themselves, the desires or aversions, the joys or sorrows, which those objects excited, though of all things the most immediately present to him, could scarce ever be the objects of his thoughts" (204). However, "bring [such an individual] into society, and all his own passions will immediately become the causes of new passions. He will observe that mankind approve of some of them, and are disgusted by others. He will be elated in the one case, and cast down in the other; his desires and aversions, his joys and sorrows, will now often become the causes of new desires and new aversions, new joys and new sorrows; they will now, therefore, interest him deeply, and often call upon his most attentive consideration" (205). Thus, self-reflection and socialization of the passions — multiplying and "refining" the social emotions by adjusting their expression to the norms of polite behavior — go hand in hand. In society, an individual, motivated by man's "natural" desire for approbation, learns to moderate his or her passions by experiencing them alongside what is imagined to be the view of the spectator(s): by "dividing [him or herself], as it were, into two persons," the socialized subject learns to "examine [his or her] own passions and conduct, and to consider how these must appear to [others], by considering how they would appear to [him or her . . .] when seen from that particular point of view" (206), and thus to adjust his or her affectional expressions in order to please and not offend. The individual in society must "flatten . . . the sharpness of [the feeling's] natural tone, in order to reduce it to harmony and concord with the emotions of those who are about him [or her]" (67). As Smith elaborates this process,

> In order to produce [the] concord [required for the harmony of society], as nature teaches the spectators to assume the circumstances of the person principally concerned, so she teaches this last in some measure to assume those of the spectators. As they are continually placing themselves in his situation, and thence conceiving emotions similar to what he feels; so he is as constantly placing himself in theirs, and thence conceiving some degree of that coolness about his own fortune, with which he is sensible that they will view it. As they are constantly considering what they themselves would feel, if they actually were the sufferers, so he is constantly led to imagine in what manner he would be affected if he was only one of the spectators of his own situation. (67–68)

Smith's intersubjective ethical model is succinctly articulated in his revision of the Golden Rule into the imperative "to love ourselves only as we love our neighbour, or . . . as our neighbour is capable of loving us" (72). Through such marginal adjustments in the general economy of social sentiment, the passions of "civilized" subjects, Smith suggests, achieve a kind of social equilibrium.

I use these economic metaphors intentionally: constituted through and enabling exchange and possession, sympathy is configured as a commodity; specifically, it is the affectional equivalent of the money form. Jean-Christophe Agnew has noted the commodity structure of sympathy in the *Theory*, observing that Smith's "social man," competing for the sympathetic attention of others, operates in an affectional economy of scarcity. As Agnew notes, Smith's representation of wealth and sympathy as mutually constitutive allows him to present exchange-value as the arbiter of all social relations and, ultimately, to represent "culture" as coextensive with the market and as contingent on a society's level of economic "development."[48] If sympathy is commodified in Smith's account, commodities are metaphorically constructed as bearers of sympathy. Because, Smith contends, we necessarily sympathize more fully with wealthy men than poor, sympathy is a form of (cultural) capital that inheres in and follows other forms. Indeed, wealth both enables and attracts sympathy. According to Smith, "before we can feel much for others . . . we must be in some measure at ease ourselves": in other words, those persons with "ease and prosperity" are better able to sympathize with others (79, 116). Further, "Our imagination, which in pain and sorrow seems to be confined and cooped up within our own persons, in times of ease and prosperity expands itself to every thing around us" (303). The wealthy are also more readily regarded sympathetically by others, chiefly because men are disposed to sympathize more fully with joy than with sorrow: "The rich man glories in his riches, because he feels that they naturally draw upon him the attention of the world, and that mankind are disposed to go along with him in all those agreeable emotions with which the advantages of his situation so readily inspire him. . . . Every body is eager to look at him, and to conceive, at least by sympathy, that joy and exultation with which his circumstances naturally inspire him" (113–14). For Smith, the wealthy man's "actions are the objects of the public care," and his words and gestures are "observed by all the world" (113–14). Conversely, the poor man "is ashamed of his poverty. He feels that it either places him out of the sight of mankind, or that if they take notice of him, they have, however, scarce any fellow-feeling with the misery and distress which he suffers. He is mortified upon both accounts" (113).

In his attempt to naturalize a "universal" desire for wealth — of crucial import for the author of *The Wealth of Nations* — Smith presents the markers of class as socially definitive delimiters of sympathy, a view which leads him to claim, tautologically, that a "natural" desire to admire the rich constitutes the origins of class society, and to suggest that the norms determining the evaluation of social distinctions both follow from and preexist those distinctions — to argue, in other words, that we admire the rich because the rich are most admirable. In Smith's words, "Upon [the] disposition of mankind to go along with all the passions of the rich and the powerful" — the "disposition to admire, and almost to worship, the rich and the powerful, and to despise, or, at least, to neglect, persons of poor and mean condition" — is "founded the distinction of ranks and the order of society" (115, 126). In fact, Smith naturalizes the attractions of wealth by constructing class power in terms of a social aesthetic. Presenting what Pierre Bourdieu has called an "ideology of charisma," Smith depicts upper-class social and material practices — the tasteful presentation of the refinements of bodily manner and luxury commodities — as inherently gratifying and appealing, "naturally" generating, in even the casual viewer, a response akin to "love at first sight."[49] For the upper-class individual, the object of what Smith calls "public admiration," continual self-consciousness of the public gaze promotes supreme self-possession:

> As all his words, as all his motions are attended to, he learns an habitual regard to every circumstance of ordinary behaviour, and studies to perform all those small duties with the most exact propriety. As he is conscious how much he is observed, and how much mankind are disposed to favor all his inclinations, he acts, upon the most indifferent occasions, with that freedom and elevation which the thought of this naturally inspires. His air, his manner, his deportment, all mark that elegant and graceful sense of his own superiority, which those who are born to inferior stations can hardly ever arrive at. (117)

Smith conceptualizes manners—the aesthetics of self-presentation—and the habitual, easy elegance of the upper class as instruments of power that, inspiring the "favor" of others, pleases those it subjects: elegant manners are the "arts" the well-bred employ "to make mankind more easily submit to [their] authority" (117). Aestheticizing the charms of wealth, Smith presents social power as a quasi-natural authority, a form of authority, habitually exercised, that elicits a seemingly immediate, unmediated emotional response.

It is crucial to note that Smith's account of the genesis of social sentiments and desires reifies the "social" ("the order of society") as a structure of social norms, presenting it not as a field in which subjectivities and actions are negotiated but, rather, freezing it in time as a static context—both origin and consequence of certain acceptable social sentiments—which preexists the individual and in which his or her actions and sentiments are produced. Society is not a complex entity individuals create, but rather an organized "system" (Smith also terms it a "machine") within which subjects assume fixed and necessary positions. Chillingly aestheticizing political power, Smith represents the citizen as characterized by a detachment that is not the rational disinterestedness of the republican citizen but rather the disinterestedness of an aesthete contemplating a perfectly ordered social sphere: Smith's model citizen would seem to be a perfect fascist. For Smith, social institutions (such as the market, the "political machine," the public police, the law) "are noble and magnificent objects. The contemplation of them pleases us, and we are interested in whatever can tend to advance them. . . . We take pleasure in beholding the perfection of so beautiful and so grand a system, and we are uneasy till we remove any obstruction that can in the least disturb or encumber the regularity of its motions" (305).

Smith and the Sentimental "Sexual Contract"

Smith also aestheticizes the power of gender and the "fair sex." Anchoring "taste" within the "civilizing" exchanges of heterosexual intimacy and personal life, Smith regulates the masculine homoerotics of public sympathy (envisioned largely as a vehicle of economic competition and class emulation, as discussed in the previous section), and binds taste to the requirements of biological and social reproduction. Smith thus fashions sentiment, in part, as a desire for social stability, a desire located in the female body.[50] Woman's privileged place within the sentimental cultural imaginary—her power to embody the attractions of culture and the graces of civilization—derives from her association with what Teresa de Lauretis calls her "consent to femininity—the impossible place of a purely passive desire": in other words, woman's *passivity* enables, by masking, her *activity* as positive site of collective identification.[51] Smith devotes less attention in his writings to the domestic "affections" (359) and the relationship between the sexes than Millar, Hume, Kames, or even Robertson. Still, Smith images the domestic sphere as the primary, indeed originary social institution, the social unit in which fellow feeling or "habitual sympathy" is most fully concentrated (362). Reinscribing a Puritan emphasis on the family as a principal site of spiritual regeneration, Smith, like all the Scots, emphasizes the *social* import of the modern family as an intersubjective realm in which individuals are "civilized," socialized, and endowed with psychological complexity. In a chapter entitled "Of the Order in which Individuals are recommended by Nature to our care and attention," Smith notes that a man's sympathies diminish as he moves outside the circle of his immediate associates: "After himself, the members of his own family, those who usually live in the same house with him, his parents, his children, his brothers and sisters, are naturally the objects of his warmest affections. . . . He is more habituated to sympathize with them: he knows better how every thing is likely to affect them, and his sympathy with them is more precise and determinate than it can be with the greater part of other people" (359). Within the "natural" institution of the family, animated by "natural affection" (366), nature and culture are interfused, and the acquisition of culture (socialization) occurs through insensible familiarization naturalized by habit.[52] Domestic education is, according to Smith, an "institution of nature," a pedagogy through which social norms are transmitted unconsciously and imperceptibly by emotional "contagio[n]" (367). In Smith's account, familial socialization lays the groundwork for the generation of all future relationships and forms of imaginative identification (such as institutional affiliations).

Mutual sympathy enlivens heterosexual relations. Endowed with a "natural" sensibility at once biological (a product of their "weak nerves" [91]), moral, and aesthetic, women animate men: "It is expected that [the] company [of women] should inspire [men] with more gaiety, more pleasantry, and more attention" (77). This process of heterosexual sympathetic exchange situates men within the human community of approbation and sentiment: "An entire insensibility to the fair sex renders a man contemptible in some measure even to the men" (77). Men's attentiveness to women—and thus women's capacity to "inspire" and "animate" men—ushers chiefly from men's sexual desire for women: according to Smith, the "passion by which nature unites the two sexes" is "naturally the most furious of all the passions" (76–77). However, the process whereby, in this model, heterosexual passion is socialized or sublimated into social sentiment is a circuitous one, and one for which Smith provides no convincing account. Why, one cannot help wondering, do men—since Smith is principally concerned with *men* here, whose "natural" physical superiority makes theirs the controlling desire—succumb to the social charms of women rather than enforce women's submission to their desires? Why does the mutual esteem of romantic love supplant the enforced subjection of women—for all the Scots, the characteristic heterosexual relation in "barbaric," premodern societies?

These questions are, on one level, misleading: it is wrong to ascribe an intentionality to this sequence, since, as I have suggested, the Scots' patriarchal "state of nature" is a fantasy of (imaginary) wholeness only narrated retrospectively from the perspective of the subject. Yet the narrative's gaps and discontinuities, even more than its explanatory logic, illuminate the formation of political desire and identification through which that subject is constituted. Many of Smith's contemporaries, following Shaftesbury and latitudinarians, rationalized the aforementioned transition in terms of a standard hierarchy of pleasures: because of desires implanted in man by the "Author of nature," these writers claimed, social and aesthetic pleasures are simply more pleasing than transient, "merely" physical pleasures. Hume and Kames, for instance, extolled the "refined" and varied pleasures of flirtation and animated heterosocial intercourse—pleasures derived from women's aesthetic charms of dress and bodily manner, as well as the graces of feminine conversation. Kames vividly embodied the distinction between the inexhaustible attractions of "culture" and the transient gratifications of "nature" in his description of the art of feminine dress: "Dress gives play to the imagination, which pictures to itself many secret beauties, that vanish when rendered familiar by sight: if a lady accidentally discover half a leg, imagination is instantly inflamed; tho an actress appearing in breeches is beheld with indifference; a naked Venus makes not such an impression, as when a garter only is discovered."[53] For Kames, the arts of feminine concealment, and the "accidental" discovery of women's charms, provokes male desire far more powerfully than the full, intentional revelation of the female body.

One could interpret this passage as expressing a traditional, Christian structure of delayed gratification: the view that the satisfactions of the material world, experienced now, are inherently less pleasing than the promised fulfillments of tomorrow. However, it becomes clear from Kames's account that what motivates male self-control — men's gentleness and social responsiveness to women — is, in part, *the promise of more complete possession of women*: a desire for possession of woman's hidden and interior, as well as exterior, charms. The art of feminine self-presentation — incorporating the material refinement of clothes and bodily manner — registers what would seem, for men, a gratifying self-consciousness of masculine spectatorship, an intentional concealment that signifies an awareness of, and responsiveness to, the masculine viewer. This, in fact, is the understanding of the art of feminine adornment advanced by Georg Simmel, a major early theorist of consumer culture. Writing more than a century after Kames, Simmel describes the flirtatious woman as enacting the variable interplay between "consent and refusal," "having and not having" (which constitutes for Simmel "the essence of price"):

> The distinctiveness of the flirt lies in the fact that she awakens delight and desire by means of a unique antithesis and synthesis: through the alternation or simultaneity of accommodation and denial; by a symbolic, allusive assent and dissent, acting "as if from a remote distance": or, platonically expressed, through placing having and not-having in a state of polar tension even as she seems to make them felt concurrently. In the behavior of the flirt, the man [for whom the behavior is intended] feels the proximity and interpenetration of the ability and the inability to acquire something.

In Simmel's account, this tension between consent and refusal, giving and withholding, identified as the defining characteristic of femininity, is emblematized by the clothed body: "It is remarkable how the historical development of the concealment of the body [or the history of clothing] demonstrates this motive of simultaneous presentation and refusal." Simmel observed that veiling the body with clothes such as "the girdles and petticoats that fulfill the function of a fig leaf" renders concealment itself ornamental, marking the body as "eminently worthy of attention" while concealing what is revealed. For Simmel, the "formula of all flirtation"—the concomitance of consent and refusal—is incorporated within the very structure of the development of "civilized" attire. The clothed female body emblematizes what Simmel calls the "unredeemed promise" of femininity—the "semi-concealment" and flirtatious foregrounding of the private, "not yet . . . apprehensible" female self—which magnetizes the male gaze and produces male erotic interest.[54]

For the Scots, as for Simmel, men's "recognition" of female civil subjectivity (women's "consent"), expressed through the seduction of flirting and the refinements of civilized heterosociality, can intensify male desire for erotic control, and indeed can reconfigure, rather than negate, the male fantasy of objectification and (collective) ownership of women ascribed to the "state of nature." This is the interpretation of the bourgeois ideology of romantic love offered by John Stuart Mill. Mill viewed modern love as an instrument of male domination that extends patriarchal authority from the physical to the psychological domain. "Consensual" marriage, according to Mill, is not distinct from "white slavery" but its modern incarnation, in which women's "masters require something more from them than actual service. Men do not want solely the obedience of women, they want their sentiments. All men, except the most brutish, desire to have, . . . not a forced slave but a willing one, not a slave merely, but a favourite."[55] Smith acknowledges this dynamic in his account of male desire within the (modern) family: "A husband is dissatisfied with the most obedient wife, when he imagines her conduct is animated by no other principle besides her regard to what the relation she stands in requires" (284). Domestic sympathy, in Smith's account, entails an erotics of female subordination.

It is crucial here to note that neither Smith nor any of the other Scots (not to mention Simmel) *theorize women's desire for men*. And, indeed, it is not clear from the Scottish model why *naturally* "refined" women—who are, by definition, more sensitive, beautiful, and well mannered than their male partners, more aesthetically and ethically pleasing—would desire men at all. Indeed, that the Scots take for granted women's desire for men (along with their corresponding omission of any account of female homosociality) is one of the most telling features of their speculative psychohistory. It seems clear that women's desire can thus be taken for granted because *women*, though positioned as "social" beings in Scottish discourse, *are defined as the objects of men's "natural" authority*—that is, *as the natural property of men*. While seemingly theorizing women's increased status in civilized society, and indeed while presenting women's position as a crucial evaluative index of social "development," Scottish authors present a sentimental version of what Carole Pateman has termed the "sexual contract": the "repressed" underside of the "social contract," according to which women are defined as the sexual property of men, and which forms the foundation of modern patriarchy.[56] The sentimental "sexual contract" reconfigured male authority, producing new categories of emotional domination and new species of feminine suffering along with new forms of what has been termed women's "emotional labor" to be exploited.[57] As the legal historian Michael Grossberg notes, in the late eighteenth and early nineteenth centuries women for the first time were able to sue in "breach of promise" and seduction suits for emotional "pain and suffering"—a novel form of (emotional) "damages" which suggested that a woman with a broken heart was indeed "damaged goods," unable to muster the emotional responsiveness and perform the emotional services that her position demanded. Antebellum judges, treating the suit like a tort, adopted an elastic measurement of damages to include such phenomena as "wounded feelings" and "mental pain," and decreed the need to protect what was termed "female delicacy": a deserted woman with a "wounded spirit," one jurist observed, "may mourn for years," and indeed, might never "fully recover."[58]

According to Pateman, the sexual contract, operative in a number of social arenas and practices (e.g., the workplace, prostitution, pornography, and surrogate motherhood), is largely "displaced" in the classic social contract texts "onto the marriage contract"—a contract that was being (re)conceptualized in sentimental terms, as a contract animated by mutual "love." As Grossberg has argued, in late-eighteenth- and early-nineteenth-century American family law, "affection began to replace status as the cement of domestic bonds."[59] This emphasis on familial love, as I have suggested, was central to the republican conception of the family: theoretically, love would equilibrate domestic inequities and revolutionize the American family, bringing it into accord with democratic political ideals. The tensions apparent in this new, middle-class ideology of marriage and consensual union are registered in Kant's contradictory concept of "personal right." Kant represents the marriage contract as the only context in which use of sexual property is converted into use of a person, or "personal right," defined as "the Right to the possession of an external object as a Thing and the use of it as a Person."[60] The Kantian opposition of the cannibalizing activity of sexual use versus the animating potency of love structured a range of texts from the period: *Clarissa*'s Robert Lovelace, for example, describes himself as a "notorious woman eater," while Clarissa's aristocratic brother tellingly states that, according to his class' practice of arranged marriages, "daughters are chickens brought up for the tables of other men."[61] Crucially, Kant's construction of mutual regeneration in marriage masks the disequilibrium between husbands and wives, the fact that—as Kant points out elsewhere—the husband is the wife's master, and thus that "personal right" is the right of a husband as a civil master. In "consensual" marriage animated by love, according to writers as diverse as Kant and Richardson, women's natural subjection would be magically transmuted into marital "equality."

It is important to remember that the structure of desire, described above, in which romantic love recasts male proprietary authority over women, is a specific, (liberal) male fantasy of political desire and agency: in the Scottish model, it both promotes a felt sense of proprietary power and manages a formative male identification with women and with "feminine" dependency. The proprietary structure of romantic love is made explicit in the pervasive trope of sentimental romance in the literature of colonization: as Peter Hulme and Mary Louise Pratt have pointed out, colonial narratives of interracial love form a crucial part of imperial mythology, reconfiguring relations of colonial domination as reciprocal relations of willing "consent." Importantly, the indigenous figure in these colonial romances is almost always a *woman*, a convention that illuminates the dynamic of seduction—the interrelation of dependency and equality, domination and respect—characteristic of feminine consent within "civilized" heterosexual relations.

Sentimental Republicanism

As several historians have argued, the sentimental ideal of consensual marital and familial relations was a prominent ideological configuration in early republican America and a favored figure for the regenerate social forms of American "union."[62] By the late eighteenth century, a range of American writers designated the prototypical "American" domestic model as consensual union mediated by love—a specific middle-class "code of consent" that equilibrated domestic disharmonies and inequities; this consensual domestic model was often defined against a

European, aristocratic model of coerced marriage for property or social position or to gratify other species of male lust. Early republican writers regularly employed the trope of consensual, voluntary domestic union to figure a regenerate American collectivity: Royall Tyler's *The Contrast*, for example, melodramatically configures Van Rough's patriarchal interference in his daughter Maria's romantic affairs, and his choice of the Chesterfieldian Van Dimple as her future spouse, against Maria's pure love for the republican hero, Manly, who ultimately exposes Van Dimple's rakish designs and wins Maria as his bride. Invoking this opposition between (Old World) enslavement and (New World) freedom, American essayists typically argued that the elevated social position of women in America was a sign of the enlightenment of American men and the superiority of American institutions. An anonymous author in *The Universal Asylum* writes, "How are those nations to be pitied and despised who consider the female part of the species as far inferior to the male, and in consequence, entirely disregard, and totally neglect to instruct, their daughters, considering them only as future slaves of some rightful lords and masters, who shall bid highest for them in their purchase." For Samuel L. Mitchell, "the condition of women is undoubtedly preferable to that of their sex in any part of the globe. They ought to know that Fredonia [the United States] is a woman's terrestrial Paradise. Here they are the rational companions of men, not their playthings or slaves."[63] This idea of the increased social mobility and respect for American women, especially for their sentimental preferences, was reiterated by Alexis de Tocqueville, and constituted part of the national mythology throughout the nineteenth century.

Scottish ideas about the refinements of culture and women's role in fostering them were reproduced in a variety of texts written for a broad audience during the late eighteenth century. Scottish ideas are apparent, for example, in the influential conception of "republican motherhood"; they also informed what Jan Lewis has termed the era's novel construction of the "republican wife." According to Lewis, Revolutionary-era writers popularized a new ideal of women's meliorating influence on the taste and manners of men, an influence attributed to female chastity (the withholding of sexual gratification) and primarily dispensed in the domestic sphere.[64] While Lewis focuses her analysis on magazine literature, other newly popular genres, such as conduct books and tracts on female education, similarly depicted a realm of improving domestic intercourse and harmonious sociability among intimates through which the passions were "civilized" and the social affections deepened and refined. In these texts, women, endowed with innate delicacy of moral and aesthetic sensibility, were constructed as the "natural" managers of the "culture of the heart" and the material culture of the home.[65] It is to these advice manuals, and the ethic of domestic aestheticism and sociability they promote, that I now turn.

Fashioning Femininity in the Early Republic

Joyce Hemlow describes the years from 1760 to 1820 as the "the age of courtesy books for women"; as Nancy Armstrong writes, "so popular did these books become that by the second half of the eighteenth century virtually everyone knew the ideal of womanhood they proposed."[66] Replacing the ideal of the aristocratic noblewoman, traditionally associated with lavish displays of status and leisure and the expression of hospitality, civility, and politeness, this new bourgeois ideal stressed woman's moral value, her spiritual depth rather than polite surface, and typically extolled the "passive virtues" of modesty, humility, and discretion coupled with the more practical skills of frugality and industriousness. According to Armstrong, middle-class conduct books "hollow[ed] out the material body of the woman in order to fill it" with the invented depths of "female psychology," thus establishing "the practice of secular morality as . . . woman's natural duty."[67]

Yet conduct books published during the period illuminate a complex interaction between surface and depth, and evince the persistent attractions of the body under the purportedly new ideology of femininity. Indeed, these texts did not so much reject what Armstrong describes as the aristocratic, ornamental body as reinscribe that body in accord with new moral imperatives. For Lawrence Klein, establishing "politeness" as a norm of social behavior by "absorbing it into a moral framework" was a major task of eighteenth-century social discourse, and is especially prominent in the writings of Shaftesbury, Joseph Addison, and Richard Steele.[68] In fact, middle-class conduct literature exemplifies the concern with manners and bodily comportment found generally in Protestant discourse, and illuminates the elevation of manners into a regenerative social aesthetic. In late-eighteenth-century America, this discourse of civility and refinement synthesized a Puritan ideal of "visible saints," emphasizing the representation and social performance of virtue, with the Enlightenment ideal of moral aestheticism that Klein examines. Conduct literature endorsed this new, synthetic ideal of regenerative aesthetic experience and incorporated it into a middle-class domestic model.

"Aristocratic" values of gentility and politeness were plainly endorsed in late-eighteenth-century American conduct literature, reconfigured as the basis of an expressly *feminine* social aesthetic. Indeed, early republican texts on feminine conduct disseminated a conception of women as instructors and civilizers of men, capable of polishing men's manners while cultivating benevolence and charity.[69] Enos Hitchcock, in his collection of didactic letters, *Memoirs of the Bloomsgrove Family* (1790), applauds the extensive "influence" that women have "over the manners of civilized society," owing to their "extensive sway over gallants and husbands," as well as their primary role in the socialization of children (I: IV, 2: 23). For the anonymous author of *Advice to the Fair Sex* (1803),

> When women, who are the ornament of society, unite a solid understanding and an honest heart to a graceful person, the natural inclination we have toward them, excites a mutual display of our most excellent qualities, then open in man a suitable desire to improve in every virtue. The pains we take to engage their affection, polishes and softens that asperity of temper, which is natural to us; their gaiety serves as a kind of counterpoise to our gravity and severity; in a word, men would be less perfect without female society. The man who is insensible to the attractions of their company is seldom a generous friend to human nature; he preserves an inflexibility which renders his very virtues ferocious.[70]

This passage is a good example of how eighteenth-century American social discourse presented, in secularized form, religious and Puritan concepts of grace, harmony, and spiritual conversion (reconfigured here as a process of emotional awakening). In particular, the passage exemplifies the simultaneous secularization and feminization of spiritual "grace," its incorporation within an aesthetics of feminine presence. Here, the "gracious," spiritually animated female body "engage[s]" men's emotions, transforming unregenerate "nature"—men's "natural" asperity of temperament—by converting male insensibility into a "suitable desire" for the good. Reformulating the contemporary theological language of spiritual perfectionism, the author images the "perfection" of men as effected not directly through divine grace but through the improving ministrations of heterosocial intercourse. In a process that engages while sublimating sexual desire (identified here as men's "natural inclination" toward women), women are seen to "polish" men's manners and meliorate male passions, transforming bestial "ferocity" into politeness and the civilized sentiments of benevolence. Similarly, Amos Chase argues in *On Female Excellence* (1792):

> As man is by constitution and employment, more robust, so by indulgence his manners usually favor more of a rugged fierceness than those of females. Hence, in an imperfect state, it might be expected—and hence, alas, it is found that his manners are too often uncomfortably rough. Now, to apply that happy influence which is most likely to moderate and cure such over-grown grossness in men, let an help-meet be found in the woman; For to her it belongs, not by a brazen brow but by a *soothing hand, to tame what is wild, and conquer what is fierce, in man.* (13; emphasis added)

Women, in these texts' standard language, would "humanize," "civilize" and "soften" men's manners by subduing the "savage rigour" and "violence" of their passions (*Advice*, 96). Like the fine art of poetry, which, in Hannah Foster's account, "soften[s] the passions, excite[s] sympathy, . . . meliorate[s] the affections . . . soothes the jarring cares of life, and, pervading the secret recesses of the soul, serves to rouse and animate its dormant powers," women, and the art of civilized living they embody, "soothe," "humanize," and "moderate the roughness of rash man."[71] The dangers inherent in this process—that love of a woman, and desire for her esteem, may excessively feminize the gallant and transmit the pathology, and not the virtue, of female nature—occasionally surface in these texts; one writer details the potentially dire consequences of unrestrained "female influence" when he notes that love "unmans the soul of the hero . . . and sinks him in all the downy softness of effeminacy, at the same time that he is frantic with all the rage of madness" (*Advice*, 39). Reasonably exercised, female influence would not compromise manly virtue but simply temper the "rugged fierceness" and "over-grown grossness" of men's manners (Chase, *Female Excellence*, 13). Their conduct typifying "the mild and gentle opposite of all that which is bold and ferocious, rough and daring" and exemplifying benevolence (for Enos Hitchcock, the "basis of true politeness" *Memoirs*, [24]), the "softer sex" would inculcate these civilized virtues—through an "artful train of management and unseen persuasions"—in men (Chase, *Female Excellence*, 12, *Advice*, 93).

Female influence depends above all on the display of good manners; for the anonymous author of *Advice*, "if a woman wishes to preserve the affections of her husband, she must be assiduous to persevere in the exertion of every talent that contributes to delight, as she was careful to display every charm, and anxious to exercise every pleasing faculty, to catch the attention of the lover, and win him to her breast" (78). The writer continues:

> The sex, therefore, should be extremely tenacious of those distant decorums and pleasing punctillos, which command respect to their persons, at the same time that they supply the place of familiarized beauties, with a kind of mysterious novelty; and fill the mind with that species of unsatisfied delight, which lies in its disappointments, and dies in its success. This is a pleasure, not unlike that of viewing a good piece of scene painting at a proper distance; we are delighted with the lively representation of nature, and our pleasure continues so long as we are kept at that distance; but if not satisfied we are suffered to take a nearer view; the pleasing effect is lost, as we approach; our satisfaction is diminished at every step; and whilst we indulge our curiosity at the expense of our pleasure, cannot help being disgusted at the coarse though just strokes of the ingenious artist; not avoid condemning him for discovering to us, the disagreeable mysteries of his art. (81)

Recommending the careful management of feminine bodily display that incorporates the material props of clothing as well as the refinements of good manners, the author converts the traditional feminine vices of duplicity, concealment, and changeability into social virtues, rearticulating Christian sanctions against spiritual complacency within a dynamic of socially regenerative heterosexual desire. Inscribing the surface of the female body as a site of "novelty" and endless aesthetic transformation, the passage assimilates that body into a cult of fashion and sartorial innovation, while simultaneously incorporating the ornamental (female) body within a middle-class social ethic. Proper feminine self-presentation here entails what Erving Goffman calls "impression management," the ability to maintain a formality of conduct that preserves the space of desire and with it, improving efforts to secure the beloved's esteem; as the writer reminds us, "where there is no mutual desire to please and be pleased, disgust and indifference must take the place of social intercourse, harmony, and cheerfulness" (*Advice*, 168).[72]

Underscoring the construction of this regenerative, expressly feminine aesthetic of social performance, the author of *Advice to the Female Sex* suggests that watching a virtuous and graceful woman is, ideally, like looking at a good painting: both depend on a "proper distance" to sustain their "pleasing effects"; and both meliorate the passions, fostering the sublimation of appetite (the "coarseness" of proximity) into the refined pleasures of aesthetic delight. Importantly, what "disgusts" is a collapse of respectful distance which exposes the corporeality of the object, the "coarse though just strokes" that assert the material basis of the illusion. Later, the writer suggests that a woman who shuns ill-mannered familiarity must take sufficient pains to hide her body; in a passage telling in its very profusion of detail (it is perhaps the most richly descriptive passage in the text), the author presents the negative example of the immodest Maria, who

> has been now a wife some time, and if you go into the house at ten in the morning, you will very likely find her at breakfast with her spouse tete a tete in her night cap, with her hair flowing in loose ringlets over her neck and shoulders; which are barely covered with a soiled gauze handkerchief, fastened behind with a single pin to a dirty short night gown, and tucked in her stays before, without an apron; and perhaps one of her black locks playing over her forehead, as she sips her tea; she is not at all discontented at your entrance now, for she is married. If you pop in at once it is not impossible but she is putting on her cap at the glass in the parlour, which is now decorated with the sweetly smelling spoile of her morning's dishabille. Her dear, is perhaps, reading a book; and as you enter, tells his wife in a churlish manner, that sure she might find some other place to dress in. Thus the poor man has lost all his affection and good humour to no purpose, for Maria will have her way. (*Advice*, 82–83)

This passage oscillates between voyeuristic fascination and repulsion, the apparent attractions of Maria's body (the "loose ringlets" falling on her bare "neck and shoulders") metonymically marked as "dirty" by the soiled garments that inadequately conceal them. Significantly, Maria's informality of conduct and careless display of her body result in the degeneration of domestic manners: her parlor (the room reserved for entertaining guests) has been transformed into a bedchamber, at the expense of hospitable civility; and Maria's inattentiveness is repaid by the "churlish manner" of her husband.[73]

According to the author of *Advice*, women inspire male desire not so much by maintaining a private self as by cultivating the *illusion* of a private self, a self which—like Maria's naked body—must always be withheld from view because it signifies the end of women's transforming potential. Because "men are civilized by the gentle intercourse of the fair sex" (*Advice*, 17), women's vigilance in self-presentation is crucial to the cultivation of virtuous subjects. Ideally, the virtuous woman should be so perfectly self-disciplined that she always displays her graces, even when alone: the author of *Advice* tells us of one Mrs. Medicus, whose husband ("a good natured but hasty man" [81]) would occasionally test her by visiting her chamber early in the morning to see "whether she was not affected neatly; but he had always the satisfaction to find her prepared to receive a visitor, though she did not expect one. . . . She would not more suffer her husband to be at her toilet, than a stranger; neither would she in a dishabille appear before him or any of the family, any more than she would in a front box of a theatre" (81–82). The exemplary Mrs. Medicus inhabits a private space that is oddly emptied of real privacy; she is always "prepared to receive a visitor" and, although she does not court an audience, she always acts with one in mind. While the negligent Maria treats her parlor like a bedroom, Mrs. Medicus exhibits such scrupulous social consideration that her bedroom easily becomes the setting for polite intercourse, her own unremitting vigilance making her husband's occasional inspections unnecessary. Because a woman's "conduct is generally . . . the criterion of the good or evil which runs through the whole house" (*Advice*, 77), self-restraint and the display of what another writer terms an "obliging deportment" are essential to the cultivation of social sentiments and good conduct throughout the household (Chase, *Female Excellence*, 9).

The account of Mrs. Medicus exhibits the principal tension that organizes these texts: a tension between the naturalization and cultivation of female refinement.[74] Indeed, these texts provide a pervasive language of social performance and theatricality, and exhibit the theatrical conception of virtue that the critics David Marshall and Jean-Christophe Agnew have seen in much eighteenth-century social discourse.[75] By focusing on the artfulness of female self-presentation, and indeed by instructing women in the proper performance of femininity, these texts raise the specter of female duplicity. These writers characteristically skirt this possibility, not by appealing to a model of manners as authentic expression of female interiority, but by anchoring female subjectivity within patriarchal heterosociality: by assuming that women exist *for others* and, especially, that their actions and exertions are performed for *men*. Women's artfulness of performance is legitimated, in pragmatic and political rather than ontological terms, in the service of male desire: as in Smith's moral philosophy, moral consciousness (or "conscience") is reconfigured and secularized as the internalized gaze of the (male) social collective. This construction detaches the female body from female interiority and desire, and reattaches it to male desire, so that men manipulate and control women's bodies—not directly and intermittently, as in expressions of violence and force, but indirectly, as an omnipresent disciplinary force. Just as female subjectivity is inseparable from patriarchal authority, female desire is constructed as the desire for what men (should) want in women: like Mrs. Medicus, women in these texts are magically constructed as always already socialized, always already dressed for (male) company. These texts, in other words, destabilize female subjectivity by opening up a potential distinction between feminine "surface" and feminine "depths," and attempt to restabilize that subjectivity by subordinating it to a governing male authority. However, the possibility of independent female interiority and desire is not so easily dismissed. Some of the tensions that these texts generate—in particular, the simultaneous invocation and circumscription or negation of female hypocrisy and agency—derive from the paradoxical construction of women as "sentimental property": as belonging (collectively and individually) to men, and yet as having subjective "feelings" of their own and, thus, at least potentially, exceeding male control.

Domesticity and the Performance of Feminine Virtue

If, according to American conduct books, women must display the graces of politeness, they must also be adept in domestic economy. Frugality is frequently invoked as an indispensable domestic virtue; women should observe what the anonymous author of "Reflections on Courtship and Marriage" called a "prudent frugality."[76] Indeed, these texts both aestheticize the female body and domesticate female desire. According to Enos Hitchcock, extravagant wives are a bad investment, because they subvert male domestic authority: "What kind of wives these have made, you may read in the shattered fortunes of many industrious husbands, who have been caught by the waving plumage." Training in the "useful branches of domestic economy" should complement the "arts of dress, music, dancing, paying and receiving visits, and the graces of an assembly room." Such training puts the finishing touches on the making of a good woman: just as "the portrait painter should never suffer an unfinished piece to go out of his hands, so a mother should never give her daughter in marriage, till she is qualified to fulfill the vow, of being 'a true and faithful wife.'" Training in domestic economy is especially important in America:

> If estates were as sure and durable as the everlasting mountains, [these precautions wouldn't be necessary]. But . . . in a free country, under a republican form of government, industry is the only sure road to wealth; and economy the only sure means of preserving it. . . . It is an old adage, "A man must ask his wife, whether he may be rich." He gets the estate by his industry; she preserves it by her economy. If she has no economy, he labors in vain. (*Memoirs*, 30–33)

Hitchcock takes pains to emphasize that such training need not detract from the virtues of a polished education but, instead, furnishes opportunities for "practicing many civilities which become easy and graceful by use only" (*Memoirs*, 38). The author of *The Female Guide* similarly defends daughters' instruction in the useful branches of domestic economy, insisting that an education that includes the virtues of "diligence, ingenuity, and industry . . . enlivens" the social arts, especially conversation, and "enhances sociability" in general.[77] Domestic economy thus does not threaten social culture and refinement but, rather, limits its expression and display to a finite terrain demarcated spatially (by the walls of the home) or psychically (by the ever reimaginable sphere of the "social circle"). The domestication of display ensures that feminine refinements are embedded within a nexus of intimate social relations: as Hitchcock states, "Her own house is the place for a lady to shine in" (*Memoirs*, 32).

As I have suggested, the domestication of display and politeness, and the consumption of goods that give shape to these practices, incorporates aristocratic categories of civility and politeness into a distinctly middle-class domestic ethic. This process of domestication, with its twin meanings of passional transformation and confinement to a limited social realm, circumscribes a sphere of investment (of affections and money) in which constricted spatial mobility figures female self-restraint. Conduct books' construction of the domestic reconfigures the Aristotelian golden mean as the "natural" sociability of the (middle-class) family, mapping ethical categories onto spatial ones in a novel social geography. According to Hannah Foster's *The Boarding School*, the "unbounded extravagance" of "fashionable dissipation" and a "fondness for company and public resorts . . . [are] incompatible with those domestic duties" which should be "the prevailing object of the sex" (59, 69–70). "Extravagance"—literally, "to wander beyond"—entails the simultaneous transgression of spatial and ethical boundaries: public space is inversely figured as a constriction of ethical subjectivity, a realm of "promiscuous" investment in persons and things. In place of the indiscriminate amusements of the profligate, Foster recommends the "local" pleasures of the "domestic circle," a social space of "comfortable subsistence" positioned midway "between sordidness and extravagance" (153, 150, 92). This social space, equally distinct from the "promiscuous" sociability of the "dissipated" and the miserly isolation of the "recluse" (153, 178), embodies feminine discrimination and self-restraint.

Industry and frugality were upheld by Poor Richard as the gospel of male economic success. And indeed, the synthesis of labor and virtue was a central preoccupation of early republican authors: attempting to reconcile an Aristotelian, classical republican ideal of leisure with a newer, Lockean (and Calvinist) ideal of work, late-eighteenth-century authors forged a construction of what might be called the "citizen-worker." Crèvecoeur's American Farmer, for example, whose "labor flows from instinct," composes "many a good sermon" as he "follow[s] his plough," and finds that labor inspires rather than impedes rational thought: as he puts it, "because a man works, is he not to think?"[78] While domestic manuals endorse the Franklinian virtues of diligence and frugality, they qualify their endorsement: according to these texts, women can easily be too industrious and too frugal. In this literature, the older, Puritan model of domestic frugality and diligence was partially displaced by a sentimental ideal of domestic comfort and refinement.

A stock figure in these texts is a woman who suffers from what Benjamin Rush calls "dirt phobia": she so zealously performs her housework that she destroys her home, its affectional and social value.[79] The anonymous author of "Reflections" is incensed by "that bigotry and passion for neatness, which makes a woman fretful and uneasy at every accidental or unavoidable speck of dirt, or the least disordering of her furniture" (43). Quite as unnatural as the "slattern"—such as the unruly Maria, discussed above—with whom she is frequently paired in domestic typologies, the zealous housewife performs her labors with an industriousness that undermines the virtues of domestic commerce:

> How necessary [cleanliness] is to the comfort and enjoyment of life, and how detestable a sluttish, nasty management must be, are things so very obvious that little need be said to enforce it [*sic*]. But . . . one [fault] in the execution of this part of housewifery . . . is the ill-timing of cleanliness, and the carrying it to such extremes, that a man's house is made an uneasy, and almost useless habitation to him. Some women have such amphibious dispositions, that one would think they chose to be half their lives in water; There is such a clutter of pails and brushes, such inundations in every room, that a man cannot find a dry place for the sole of his foot; so that what should tend to make a man's house an agreeable and wholesome dwelling, becomes so dangerous and unpleasant, that the desire of health and peace drives him out of it. (43)

In an elaborate conflation of domestic insubordination, female passion, and an atavistic identification with the "lower orders," this passage humorously fashions the "neat demon" as a liminal figure who undermines the harmonious "natural sociability" of domesticity, transforming (human) culture into (animal) nature. This conflation pivots on the imagery of flooding, imagery that operates on literal and figurative levels to signify specific excesses in housekeeping practices while figuring, with a traditional metaphor for unleashed passions, unsocialized feeling. Undue personal investment in one's work—a sign of impoliteness and ill-breeding—connotes an identification with the insufficiently refined lower orders, referring here to both amphibious beasts and the animalistic lower classes: "A prudent housewife should so time her neatness and cleanliness, that it may be as little inconvenient and troublesome to a man as possible, and support it with a graceful ease, and a good-natured sort of indifference. The contrary has more of the servant maid than the well-bred woman in it, and generally accompanies a low and mean education" (49). Immoderate ambition in domestic tasks (what this writer calls "overflowings of neatness" [43]) is designated a dangerous obsession, a constriction of subjectivity and vision whereby the material props of domesticity eclipse the affections of home life they are meant to support. Such practices undermine the attractions of home: as Amos Chase puts it, a man "might better enjoy himself on a housetop, exposed to the tempest and thunder in the heavens" than reside in a "wide house" with an intolerant female scold (*Female Excellence*, 13). In contradistinction, the good housewife exhibits an exemplary flexibility, a "graceful ease" in performing her tasks and an emotional openness to the needs of domestic inhabitants.

"Reflections" presents what seems to be a feminine, domestic (and Christian) version of the republican synthesis of virtue and work. In recommending that the domestic woman perform her household labors with grace, such texts also suggest that an aristocratic ideal of ease and effortlessness was being feminized during the period and absorbed into middle-class practice. The domestic woman embodies a complex synthesis of "nature" and "culture": because she is "well-bred"—her passions properly socialized—she can behave "naturally" and with a "graceful ease," her actions a spontaneous expression of gracious emotion. In texts such as "Reflections," we approach an ideology of "invisible labor," here presented as ethical prescription: insisting that domestic work be performed "naturally" and inconspicuously, these texts effectively erase domestic labor, subsuming women's work under the mantle of feminine modesty and grace. Just as her frugality must be tempered by sensitivity to domestic needs, the virtuous housewife "naturally" performs household tasks in accord with the demands of domestic sociability; her work is, first and foremost, a labor of love ("Reflections," 42).

The domestic woman should exhibit "mildness, moderation, and kindness towards all"; because she must be responsive to domestic exigencies, her personality is conceived as both flexible and constant. Possessed of an exquisite moral sense and "quick, instinctive sense of exact rectitude within," her conduct is regulated by divine precept even as it is alive to the particular needs of the household; if she is "pious," she is also "affable."[80] Unlike *homo economicus*, whose rational calculus of experience is regulated by the "theory of interchangeable participants" ("if one person doesn't pursue his self-interest to drive down a price or drive up a rate, someone else will"),[81] *feminina economica* operates in something like a gift economy, a network of social exchanges in which economic relations are rendered both personal and concrete. While her partner controls the accumulation of money, she manages the dispersal of economic fruits, binding individuals together through spiritual and material care. In Lewis Hyde's account, the gift economy is a network of "contracts of the heart" through which individuals are incorporated into a larger social whole. Gifts are embodiments of sentimental value, "enriched with social feeling, with generosity, liberality, goodwill," and their exchange shapes a realm distinct from legal contract and market exchange. Significantly, Hyde observes that, in twentieth-century America, "gift exchange is a 'female' commerce and gifts a 'female' property."[82]

In conduct manuals, the feminine virtue of benevolence—what Chase calls "the disposition of the heart that is practically distended with benevolent regard for mankind" and "a soul-full of friendship towards all around her"—is figured as a distension and fullness charitably expended, what Chase calls elsewhere a "bounteous diffusion" (*Female Excellence*, 8–9). Much like the construction in "Reflections" of woman's "natural" cultivation, Chase's imagery of distension and fullness metaphorically identifies benevolence with pregnancy, thus configuring social practices as a "natural" feminine response and grounding these (culturally specific) practices and emotions in the female body.[83] A similar conflation of female (bodily) "nature" and domestic "culture" is achieved through the metaphorical identification of hearts and homes: the good woman's heart is a "mansion of happiness" always open to those in need, while her hand "is ever ready to administer the needful assistance."[84] In these texts, the ideal domestic woman does not forgo the consumption of luxuries and conveniences—as one popular writer states, "there is no piety in bad taste"—but benevolently distributes the refinements of culture. The domestic woman, "so free, both from prodigality and meanness," generously distributes affection and the objects that bear it, her home the habitation of "comfort, neatness, . . . elegance . . . [and] plenty."[85]

Purchased artifacts, once "domesticated" as female property, support the forms of hospitality and domestic ritual. But if the circulation of domestic goods was essential to an ethic of domestic sociability and care, the act of purchasing was often depicted as fraught with potential danger. The tensions these texts exhibit between the valuation of domestic "refinement" and the suspicion of consumption replicate conduct books' construction of "home" as an extension of female bodily nature: the refinements of feminine "taste" and domestic culture are always already around, always already incorporated within the body of the home. It also illuminates these texts' emphasis on the domestic as the primary locus of socially regenerative sensibility, the setting in which the domestic woman's subjective endowments are freely expressed and equilibrated to her material and social surroundings. Constructing equivalences between domestic interior and subjective interiority, domestic manuals often represent persons outside the home as psychologically impoverished and "superficial." In Foster's *The Boarding School*, shopping is the paramount expression of female frivolity and caprice, expressing the unrestrained inclination of a "rambling disposition" (188). The occasion for impulse buying or the "insignificant amusement" of "tumbl[ing] over" goods, the "shopping tour" (185–86) affords unrestrained sensuous enjoyment in which pleasure is "the supreme object" (187). The *publicness* of the activity is one source of its potential danger: shopping provides an opportunity for public display in which women and goods compete for attention. Describing a visit by three fashionable ladies who invite her on a shopping spree, the virtuous Maria relates their description of its anticipated adventures:

> "Buying," said their principal speaker, "is no considerable part of our plan. . . . Amusement is what we are after. We frankly acknowledge it a delightful gratification of our vanity, to traverse Cornhill, to receive the obsequious congees, and to call forth the gallantry and activity of the beaux, behind the counter; who, you must know, are exceedingly alert when we belles appear. The waving of our feathers, and the attractive airs we assume, command the profoundest attention, both of master and apprentices; who, duped by our appearance, suffer less brilliant customers to wait, or even to depart without notice, till we have tumbled over and refused half the goods in the shop. We then . . . express our regret at having given so much trouble; are assured in return that it has been rather a pleasure; and leave them their trouble for their pains." (185–86)

Describing the public display of femininity by fashionable or upper-class women, the passage antithetically defines the feminine performance of virtue within the home. Specifically, it depicts an upper-class parody of women's domestic "improvement" of men: the women display their graces to "call forth the gallantry and activity of the beaux"; but rather than inspiring the sublimation of male desire through the effortless presentation of "natural" feminine virtue and refinement, the women perform their part with an eye to self-interested manipulation. The removal of feminine display from the domestic sphere and its economy of sympathy unleashes feminine self-interest, and is identified with a violation of the conventions of exchange: the men's "pains" reap no profit, but are repaid only by their "trouble." What Foster presents (admittedly, with apparent pleasure) as an inversion of sex roles—in the public space of the store, men serve women—is moralistically glossed as an exhibition of the monstrous, *unfeminine* nature of upper-class women, who reveal a shameful lack of female sympathy. Exhibiting the splitting of female characters into the "sexually predatory" and irrational "coquette" and the "idealized . . . true woman" that Ellen Rothman observes in the first century after independence,[86] the passage defines the properly domesticated Maria against the upper-class "public" women whose extradomestic involvement seems inversely related to a constriction of ethical subjectivity. The virtuous Maria has no taste for such diversions: insisting that she has "no occasion to purchase any thing," she recommends the "sweets" of one's "home" over the depraved pleasures of public exposure (185, 188). Shopping, with its meandering perusal of goods, especially endangers because, in its aimlessness, it exposes the self to the powerfully immediate attractions of objects, attractions that, in the words of one writer, "block up the avenues" of charity, and are unrestrained by an economy of domestic needs.[87]

The ethic of feminine domestic sociability and comfort analyzed in this chapter operated, I have argued, alongside the Weberian Protestant ethic and provided an ideological framework for American consumerism throughout the nineteenth century. Articulated through the gender binary masculine/feminine, this ideology of feminized domestic aestheticism was defined in opposition to masculine "worldly asceticism." In order to clarify the contours of this ethic of feminine consumption, I turn to a popular contemporary novel, Hannah Foster's *The Coquette*, which registers the social contradictions of women's place in the new republic and the gendered forms of republican power. Foster's novel illuminates the construction of feminine taste as a disciplinary tool and site of political contestation: the history of heroine Eliza Wharton reads like a cautionary tale, showing how an unrestrained female investment in objects of desire threatens the "refinements" of republican domestic culture. Indeed, *The Coquette*'s depiction of Eliza's consumer and erotic "extravagance" antithetically highlights the contours of republican domesticity and consumption. Like her *Boarding School,* Foster's *Coquette* stages widespread concerns about women's proper sphere: Eliza is a "first rate" coquette whose love of luxury, as much as her sexual indiscretions, betrays her affinities with the salonnière, the highly visible woman of the aristocratic public sphere; indeed, many of the arguments for and against domesticity voiced by various characters in the text echo quite explicitly those presented by seventeenth-century French writers in response to the salonnière's cultural authority and extradomestic roles.[88] *The Coquette* suggests the essential ambivalence of domesticity as a realm of community and reciprocal human relationships, as well as the seat of a disciplinary authority naturalized as emotionally authentic, animated by love and affection. In Foster's novel, the ideal of domestic sociability is both affirmed and challenged by pointing to just what it leaves out—specifically, independent female desire and pleasure.

The Coquette

Conduct books testify to what has been called the "privatization of virtue" in the eighteenth century, a process through which the collectivist values of civic humanism were subsumed into a secular Christian ethics and ideal of domestic intimacy. The "privatization of virtue," I have suggested, simultaneously entailed a reconfiguration of gender: the "feminine" functioned as a category through which virtue was detached from its political referents of active, independent citizenship and martial valor and made available to competing—especially middle-class—definitions.[89] While in civic humanism the "feminine" figured principally as the disruptive forces of Fortuna, the Enlightenment oversaw the "transformation of traditionally acknowledged feminine attributes" such as emotionalism and weakness "from liabilities into assets," a transformation legible in religious, philosophical, and literary discourses.[90] Hume, whose work illuminates this shift, believed that the "social virtues," compassion, benevolence, and humanity, are "very limited" in extension, principally "confined" to "that narrow circle" of those "who have any immediate connexion or intercourse with the person"; consequently, it is among intimates that virtue is nurtured and an individual's true "value" disclosed. For Hume, "proof of the highest merit" consists in an "extraordinary delicacy in love or friendship, where a person is attentive to the smallest concerns of his friend, and is willing to sacrifice to them the most considerable interest of his own," refinements of sentiment that inhere in nonpolitical forms of "voluntary" association such as friendship and family.[91]

For Hannah Arendt, these cultural processes—the privatization and "feminization" of virtue, and a new concern with the family as a socializing institution—mark the ascendancy of liberalism over republicanism and signal the erosion of public life: for Arendt, liberalism displaced the traditional republican distinction between "public" and "private" by a modern distinction between the "social" and the "intimate."[92] However, as Jürgen Habermas and others argue, the emergence of the "social" and, especially, the new emphasis on the social import of the family could have politicizing as well as privatizing valences—especially for those whom classical republicanism relegated to political invisibility. The "republican mother" and "republican wife"—concepts which ascribed to women clear civic functions, even as they enforced domestic conceptions of womanhood—were born out of these historical developments. The newly politicized position of domesticity and domestic womanhood is clearly registered in *The Coquette*. The novel's depiction of Eliza Wharton exemplifies sentimental gender revisionism: Foster's representation of Eliza emphasizes the (domestic) construction of *female* virtue and the effects of unregulated involvement in public life on female subjectivity and a specifically feminine republican community. Structured around the romantic history and downfall of Eliza Wharton, *The Coquette* takes as its subject the proper constitution of female personhood in republican America. The contradictory sentimental configuration of feminine subjectivity is legible both in Foster's frustration with the domestication of feminine affect, and in the novel's investment in a domestic economy of "cultured" feeling.

Like other seduction novels, *The Coquette* is concerned with the relationship between virtue and power, and has often been read as an allegory of republican political struggles and fears of the corruptibility of virtue. But the novel is equally concerned with the politics of gender: indeed, the text allegorizes the formation of republican womanhood, specifically the formation of "taste" as constitutive of feminine civil subjectivity. If *The Coquette* figures national politics through the trope of gender, it similarly figures gender *as* a politics, as a politically salient structure of social difference. I will argue that the novel's primary narrative problematic is the "nature" and political agency of feminine desire: the text represents female (consumer and sexual) desire as a locus of social struggle as well as an object of patriarchal regulation. Dialogizing the Declaration of Independence as a cultural text through which American identities are defined, Foster emphasizes Eliza's desire for independence and the opportunity to express and explore her "individual" subjectivity. Eliza's status as individual is underscored at the novel's outset: both her father and prospective husband, the Reverend Haly (a suitor selected by her parents), are dead when the narrative begins. For Eliza, the "pursuit of happiness" inheres in her agency as desiring subject and, in particular, in the free choice of objects of her desire: Eliza longs to choose her own companions and objects of romantic attachment, and to "indulge" her "taste for gaity (*sic*) of life" (100). While her friends wish to see her "suitably and agreeably connected" through marriage, Eliza wishes "for no other connection than that of friendship," and characterizes the "freedom" she prizes as the "opportunity, unbiassed by opinion, to gratify my natural disposition in a participation of those pleasures which youth and innocence afford," especially in the "festive haunts of fashionable life" (13, 6, 53). While her friends dismiss her views as merely a "play about words," contending that feminine "freedom" is realized rather than compromised in marriage (31), Eliza critiques feminine consent and the domestication of female subjectivity throughout the narrative, and views marriage and motherhood as vehicles of feminine regulation and discipline (e.g., 24–25, 44). For example, in an early conversation with her minister suitor, the Reverend Boyer, Eliza states, "From a scene of constraint and confinement . . . I have just launched into society. . . . I recoil at the thought of immediately forming a connection, which must confine me to the duties of domestic life, and make me dependent for happiness, perhaps too, for subsistence, upon a class of people, who will claim the right of scrutinising every part of my conduct; and by censuring those foibles . . . may render me completely miserable" (29). As Eva Cherniavsky argues, Eliza aims to disconnect sentiment from the constraints of the privatized domestic sphere; indeed, Eliza (re)articulates female emotion not as a medium of domestic interpellation, but as an expression of independent identity and agency.[93]

Foster's narrativization of Eliza's desire is ambiguous. On the one hand, the novel positions Eliza Wharton as an "excessive" woman, an embodiment of socially disruptive desires who must be contained and, indeed, punished within the narrative. But while moral didacticism is a significant language within the text, it is by no means the whole story. The novel also exposes the mechanics of the "feminization of woman" and the construction of "civilized" feminine subjectivity in the early republic, dramatizing its costs through the violence performed on the body/subject of the heroine. By framing Eliza's love of dress and fashionable living with the rhetoric of masculine seduction, the narrative explicitly situates feminine taste within a field of male power. In particular, Foster emphasizes the patriarchal political, economic, and legal parameters within which Eliza's subjectivity and desire are articulated and given social form. Eliza is a single woman "hitherto confined to the rigid rules of prudence and economy, not to say, necessity in my finances" (60–61); therefore, while she desires the pleasures of fashionable living—pleasures which, she repeatedly claims, are themselves wholly "innocent"—she can only gratify these desires by cultivating relationships with men who possess property and economic power. Although the "solution" the narrative ostensibly proposes to the reality of male power is a moral and "individual" one (i.e., by documenting "abuses" of male power, it encourages women to make better "choices" and thus to regulate their own desires), the novel simultaneously illuminates the larger structures that limit or determine those "choices" and promote Eliza Wharton's destruction, and calls into question the legitimacy of patriarchal authority in the new republic. Quite explicitly, in Foster's text, women's "choices" are either to be used or cared for by men: to be treated as sexual objects (as "slaves" to male passions) or to be treated as feminine "subjects," and thus subjected to the regime of patriarchal domesticity and its norms of affectional discipline. Framing Eliza's desire within the politically charged rhetoric of seduction, *The Coquette* illuminates relations of (male) power that constrain Eliza's "freedom," and shows how feminine consumption could extend rather than challenge male control.

Like other seduction narratives, Foster's novel about the seduction of the amiable but imprudent Eliza Wharton by an aristocratic libertine, Peter Sanford, is patterned on Samuel Richardson's *Clarissa*: Sanford is a "second Lovelace" (38), while Eliza is explicitly identified on several occasions with Richardson's heroine. A calculating and seemingly heartless rake, Sanford, like Lovelace, is a "woman-eater" whose physical passion for Eliza is depicted as degenerative rather than vivifying, its effects figured in the literal consumption or wasting of Eliza's body: as the dying Eliza asks Sanford at the end of the novel, "How . . . can that be love which destroys its object?" (158–59). Sanford crassly equates women with property and imagines them as solely available to gratify his economic and sexual demands. Writing to his friend Charles Deighton early in the text, he describes his "plan" to marry Miss Lawrence, whose "great fortune" will "mend [his] circumstances," while "enjoy[ing] [Eliza Wharton's] company as long as possible"; as Sanford puts it, "though I cannot possess her wholly myself, I will not tamely see her the property of another" (34–35). The text registers the violence of gothic ownership and the "lust and brutality" of relations of sexual use (163), and explicitly marks such relations as antirepublican: by the end of the novel, Sanford, having exhausted his "credit" and lost all his property, becomes a "vagabond," an invisible figure exiled from the domestic community of the nation (164–66). But if Sanford's violations of the norms of "civilized" masculinity are depicted as inexcusable and punishable, the text is more directly concerned with Eliza's "extravagance," her transgressions of the forms of domestic womanhood. Such transgressions are constructed as politically and ethically salient: taking as its principal subject matter the representation of feminine morals and manners, *The Coquette* endows feminine virtue with clear civic value. Performing true womanhood will, Foster insists, rehabilitate men as well as enact female power: it is only at the end of the text, when Eliza recalls the "counsels . . . and admonitions" of her "best friends" and treats Sanford as a "friend" rather than lover, that his "conscience" is awakened and he is—at least partially—reformed (160, 166).

I suggest above that Eliza's "choices" are either to be treated as a male property object or to be treated as a feminine "subject." It is crucial to point out that these "choices" are interior to the perspective and structure of feminine political subjectivity and "feminine consent." Indeed, as I argued in my analysis of Scottish discourse, that discourse constructed feminine "choices" in just those binary terms, providing an identificatory structure that mobilized women's consent to femininity. However, as I argue below, *The Coquette* registers possibilities of erotic and identificatory investment that escape this logic of liberal political subjection: the passional "excesses" of "Eliza Wharton," particularly her investments in public life and in a sphere of female homosocial desire (inscribed in the novel's feminine epistolarity), mark possibilities of political and erotic desire latent, if not institutionally recognized, in the founding moment of American republicanism.

Feminine Consent and Sentimental Literary Culture

The sentimental economy of intimacy that Hume defines as the site of moral value is legible in *The Coquette*'s epistolary form. The narrative features a selection of correspondence that embodies a social circle, shaping a sphere of sympathetic exchanges (principally among Eliza, Mrs. Wharton, Lucy Freeman, Ann Richman, and Julia Granby) that both mark and negate spatial distances. Letters shape a sort of informal coterie, a "respectable circle" (10) of intimates, engaging and refining social affections; writing to her clerical suitor, the Reverend John Boyer, Eliza notes that "an epistolary communication between the sexes . . . may be a source of entertainment and utility" through which social sentiments are "drawn forth and exercised by each other" (47). Inscribing a sphere of intimate sentiment, letters embed the self within a nexus of emotional exchange.[94]

The sentimental import of letters is clearly registered in the text's lapses in epistolary form. Sanford's status as a misanthrope who is ultimately banished from society, "debarred from every kind of happiness" (166), is marked by his exclusion from polite correspondence: although he writes to his friend Charles Deighton, he does not figure as the recipient of any letters in the text and, more significantly, he exchanges no letters with women. Tellingly, Sanford and Eliza do not correspond with one another: their relationship, Foster implies, is never given proper social form. Sanford's one note to Eliza (90), reminding her of her promise to inform him personally of a decision to marry Boyer, is written without any regard to polite convention: devoid of the refinements of style and punctuated with threats of revenge, it expresses the violence of unsocialized passion. Suggestively, it is also the letter that moves the plot forward most significantly; like Sanford himself, it disrupts the social world sympathetic exchange is meant to confirm. For all his gallantry, Sanford is betrayed as psychologically flawed by his ignorance of polite letters: in a tea-time conversation on "literary subjects," Sanford holds no "distinguished part" (38); and the one time we see him with a book, he feigns readerly interest while surreptitiously looking at Eliza, suggesting that his interest in women partakes of "mere sensual gratification" instead of the "nobler" refinements of polite intercourse (103).

The novel's intimate society of letters is, pointedly, a feminine one: although Eliza corresponds briefly with Boyer, the "bulk of the novel," according to Cathy Davidson, is " 'woman-talk': women confiding, advising, chiding, warning, disagreeing, misleading, confronting, consoling each other." Davidson suggests that the novel's emphasis on "female discourse" allows Foster to voice women's specific grievances against men's sexual and economic privileges, while offering practical advice on the "necessity of informed choice" in romantic matters, thus helping to shape women's collective consciousness.[95] As will become clear, I read the text's feminine pedagogy and its formulations of feminine "choice" more ambivalently: whereas Davidson views them in unproblematically positive, and familiarly feminist terms, I see the text's feminine pedagogy as constituting forms of liberal feminine subjectivity, agency, and taste that are inherently contradictory, and no less subject to male authority than the "seduced" Eliza. The problem with Davidson's reading, as I see it, is that it normalizes forms of feminine subjectivity which the text itself is engaged in constituting. Indeed, *The Coquette* allegorizes the formation of feminine subjectivity as well as the forms of literary identification through which readers such as Davidson "recognize" Eliza as a feminine (liberal) subject.

However, the novel's feminine culture of letters is, as Davidson argues, a primary locus of social value and narrative interest. Whereas the Scots had anchored female subjectivity within heterosocial relations and forms of identification, *The Coquette* organizes female sympathy around forms of female homosociality and homosocial desire. In particular, the text explores what remains a crucial issue in psychoanalytic theories of feminine gender development: what does it mean to "consent to (heterosexual) femininity" out of same-sex identification and, especially, a primary love for women? The novel's feminine epistolarity both facilitates forms of female identification and desire that unsettle what Eliza repeatedly terms women's domestic "confinement" through heterosexuality and motherhood, and works to inscribe Eliza into the affectional norms of a "*patriarchilized* female gender."[96] Indeed, the novel's sentimental register is not divorced from its didacticism but ambiguously interpolated within it. While letters in *The Coquette* embody a sphere of desire, they simultaneously enact an ethical standard; if they are gifts, they are also guides. As Eliza's closest friend, Lucy, writes, "It is the task of friendship, sometimes to tell disagreeable truths" (27). As material objects inscribed with sentiment, letters, which "alone can atone" for the "absence" of one's friends (33), both evoke bodily presence and enact social claims, reminding one to act with one's friends in mind.

Acting with one's friends in mind consists in seeking to please them even when they are not around; it means aspiring to live up to what they believe one to be, and entails the internalization of the conditions of esteem as a standard of ethical behavior, as conscience. In this ethical model, socialization is a voluntary not coercive process, and authority is exercised not by force, but through the psychological bonds of mutual respect; Eliza's mother's faith in her daughter's judgment renders her authority all the more potent, so that Eliza comes to fear her mother's censure more than that of God himself (154). Narrativizing the feminization of this ethical model, *The Coquette* depicts the dangers of forgetting one's friends: Eliza is punished for refusing the domestication of desire her friends want for her, instead engaging in a promiscuous investment in things and persons unconstrained by the demands of domestic benevolence. Sympathy is here a medium of social interpellation: Eliza's friends believe that Eliza, with her "correct taste" and "delicate sensibility," must want the refinements of domestic life, and their prescriptions follow from that certainty (58). Acting against her friends' wishes, Eliza pursues public pleasures which are marked, paradoxically, as private and unsharable, and invested in the novel with all the horror of gothic secrecy. Eliza's appetite for fashion is presented as feminine caprice: it contributes to her sexual fall—Foster pairs economic and erotic danger in the novel—and its wasting of affectional and economic resources is marked on Eliza's body by the novel's end (she dies, of course, of consumption). The principal threat of "luxury," in this account, is that it can make one antisocial; while itself the sign of the social, it easily converts into its own opposite. Luxury thus alienates the self, not from a natural economy of needs, as in Rousseau, but from a domestic economy of feminine affection.

The novel suggests, however, an alternative reading to that of feminine cautionary narrative. The problem with the above reading is that it is, in an important sense, ahistorical: it depends on forms of female subjectivity that the text itself participates in producing. Suggesting the tenuous organization of the domestic woman's self-restraint that the Scots had mystified as "natural" and conduct books strenuously enforced, the novel maps the social formation, as well as the costs, of republican forms of feminine civil subjectivity. *The Coquette* exposes the violence of republican gender structures, suggesting through Eliza Wharton's dramatic decline and death that a woman's very subjectivity in the new republic depends on the domestication of desire, the domestic, patriarchal regulation of feminine emotion.

Narrativizing Republican Womanhood

The novel opens with the expanding outward of Eliza's affections, as she surveys the prospect of release from her "paternal roof" and the constraints of an arranged marriage in which her "heart" was never "much engaged" (5). She had planned to marry Mr. Haly out of deference to her parents' desires: "like a dutiful child, [Eliza would have] sacrificed her own inclination to their pleasure" (11). Indeed, their relationship is marked as a vehicle for the family's social reproduction: thus, soon after Haly is chosen as Eliza's "future guardian" (5), Eliza's father conveniently dies. Haly's death, occurring directly before the novel begins, frees Eliza from what she calls the "shackles" of "parental authority" (13). The novel begins with a topos of republican literary discourse: the displacement of coercive patriarchal authority—embodied in the arranged marriage—by the binding love of an "unchanging friend" (39) and a form of consensual, voluntary, sentimentally engaging republican authority, embodied by Eliza's "indulgent and dearly beloved" mother (5). Producing a vacuum of patriarchal authority at the outset, the novel localizes "legitimate" republican government within a sentimental domestic economy, and constructs the (feminine) domestic as the proper context for republican virtue.[97]

If republican authority is an important problematic on which the narrative opens, so, too, is female desire. Invoking a foundational republican document, Eliza imagines the "pursuit of happiness" as the unconstrained, "free" choice of objects of her desire. Haly's death inspires in Eliza a desire for "mixing in the busy scenes and active pleasures of life" (7): as she confides to Lucy, "An unusual sensation possesses my breast; a sensation which I once thought could never pervade it on any occasion whatever. It is *pleasure*; pleasure, my dear Lucy, on leaving my paternal roof!" (5) This pleasure is not the mediated pleasure of aesthetic sensibility or benevolence, but a fully embodied *sensation*, its physical referent emphasized by the sensual language in which she expresses it: the sensation "possesses [her] breast," and enkindles in her a "gleam of joy" (5). Spatial and emotional release converge in Eliza's anticipations of independence: her emotions previously constrained by parental will and the "pleasing pensiveness" of bereavement, Eliza anticipates a descent into the world, "mixing" in its "busy scenes," that is simultaneously a movement outward, a diffusion of feeling beyond the circumscribed enjoyments of domestic society (7). As she playfully tells Lucy, "The mind, after being confined at home for a while, sends the imagination abroad in quest of new treasures, and the body may as well accompany it, for ought I can see" (15).

Going "abroad" in *The Coquette* is dangerous, since the pleasures it affords can contrive to unmake subjectivity itself. It is also, the novel suggests, powerfully attractive to women: reiterating the misogynist clichés of his age, one of the text's male correspondents, Selby, states that women are "naturally prone to gaiety, to pleasure, and, I had almost said, to dissipation" (53). While exposing the smugness of patriarchal judgment by "vicious character[s]" like Sanford as well as "virtuous" men like Selby and Boyer (31), the novel both invokes and reformulates this traditional view of women—a staple of Christian and civic humanist misogyny—as inherently seducible and passionally unstable. Eliza is, in her own words, "naturally cheerful, volatile, and unreflecting" (7), and her penchant for indulging her "natural disposition for gaiety" (16) lead to her "seduction" by the charms of "show and equipage" (35) and the "magic arts" (57) of her seducer (he captivates her through the senses of eye and ear). Such language, like the text's thematics of seduction, identifies Eliza's passions as a primary object of social, and discursive, struggle. As I have shown, sentimentalism reconfigured feminine sensibility as a virtue while simultaneously domesticating it, containing it within the socializing structure of domestic intimacy—and *The Coquette* bears traces of this restructuring. What the immediate attractions of extra-domestic pleasures threaten in Foster's novel is, quite simply, Eliza's self-consciousness—her self-recognition as a feminine subject—a sense of self anchored, in part, through epistolary writing and its forms of literary identification. When Eliza writes to her mother midway through the novel that "no other avocation could arrest my time, which is now completely occupied in scenes of amusement" (73), her use of a theatrical metaphor highlights the restoration of reflective detachment managed by composing with one's readers in mind.

For her part, Eliza finds the self-restraint necessary to "compose [one]self" (106) stifling just as she finds the marriage-plot constricting, and vows to remain single until she has "sowed all [her] wild oats" (68). While the novel didactically interprets Eliza's desire as a species of romantic folly, it offers clear insight into the unremitting self-discipline mandated by Eliza's social world: feminine subjection is doubly endorsed as a woman's most effective defense against male predations and the source of true feminine fulfillment. The preferred biography of middle-class womanhood is a narrative of progressive refinement and spatial constriction that recapitulates the historical succession of classes and serves as a paradigm of bourgeois social evolution. In the words of Eliza's friend Ann Richman,

> How natural, and how easy the transition from one stage of life to another! Not long since I was a gay, volatile girl; seeking satisfaction in fashionable circles and amusements; but now I am thoroughly domesticated. All my happiness is centered within the limits of my own walls; and I grudge every moment that calls me from the pleasing scenes of domestic life. (97)

As in the popular contemporary theory of the four stages of man, the "stages" of feminine development proceed from "promiscuity" to "intimacy," from the undifferentiated experience of "undistinguishing" social commerce to the more nuanced (and less restless) pleasures in one's "tender connections."[98] Ann Richman's voluntary confinement—her avowed preference for the "pleasing scenes" of domesticity at the expense of what Eliza terms "all the pleasing varieties of social life" (52)—evokes a social landscape in which middle-class limitations are redesignated the virtue of self-restraint: a frugal domesticity, the circumscribed social experience and limited range of "amusements" it affords, becomes a species of psychological enrichment. For Ann Richman, less is more. Exhibiting the refined taste characteristic of "civilized" femininity, she assures Eliza that "it is the glory of the marriage state . . . to refine, by circumscribing our enjoyments" (24).

While Ann Richman finds the transition from fashionable girlhood to tasteful domestic womanhood "natural" and "easy," Eliza Wharton does not. She continually calls domesticity a form of "confinement," boldly declaring that "I despise those contracted ideas which confine virtue to a cell" (13). Eliza's critique of domesticity in ethical terms as a "selfish state" in which one "neglect[s]" one's former acquaintances and "benevolence itself moves in a very limited sphere" (24) engages while inverting middle-class rhetoric, which figures domesticity as the realm of (feminine) fulfillment and full subjectivity. It also underscores the costs of feminine domestic subjection and its delimitation of feminine desire in accord with patriarchal scripts of heterosexuality and motherhood. Tellingly, the narrative is preoccupied with feminine loss and is marked by numerous sites of feminine mourning: Ann Richman's loss of her infant daughter Harriot, Eliza's loss of her friends to marriage and motherhood, her friends' (and her mother's) loss of Eliza. Eliza is particularly bereft following the loss of her best friend, Lucy Freeman, to marriage. In a letter to Ann Richman, Eliza writes:

> Yesterday . . . Lucy Freeman gave her hand to the amiable and accomplished Mr. George Sumner. . . . Every eye beamed with pleasure on the occasion, and every tongue echoed the wishes of benevolence. Mine only was silent. Though not less interested in the felicity of my friend than the rest, yet the idea of a separation; perhaps, of an alienation of affection, by means of her entire devotion to another, cast an involuntary gloom over my mind. Mr. Boyer took my hand, after the ceremony was past. Permit me, Miss Wharton, said he, to lead you to your lovely friend; her happiness must be heightened by your participation of it. Oh no; said I, I am too selfish for that. She has conferred upon another that affection which I wished to engross. My love was too fervent to admit a rival. Retaliate then, said he, this fancied wrong, by doing likewise. (70)

Employing the language of courtship and romantic passion, Eliza figures her desire for Lucy and registers her grief at the prospect of separation and possible "alienation of [Lucy's] affection." Although Boyer attempts to reclaim Eliza's desire within the forms of heterosexuality, seizing the occasion to renew his proposal of marriage, Eliza resists his efforts, firmly stating that "this was not a proper time to discuss that subject" (70). Embodying forms of feminine loss that occasionally disrupt the plot of heterosexual courtship and seduction, this passage bears traces of feminine "tastes" that exceed, and defy containment within, the affectional structures of patriarchal domesticity and feminine subjectivity.[99] Those possibilities are registered in the sympathetic exchanges of feminine homosociality: masking these feelings in public, Eliza preserves them for later disclosure and sympathetic transmission to Ann Richman. Eliza's critique of domesticity is quite powerfully presented in the text, so that her friends can do little more than protest, unconvincingly, that her "ideas of freedom, and matrimony" are all "wrong" (30).[100]

Of Eliza's suitors, it is Boyer who most closely embodies the domestic ideal of temperance and a "decent competency" (41): according to Eliza's mother, herself the widow of a clergyman, "No class of society has domestic enjoyment more at command, than clergymen. . . . They are removed alike from the perplexing cares of want, and from the distracting parade of wealth" (41). Boyer's ideal of an "elegant sufficiency" (42) entails a discriminating investment in and appreciation of objects that promotes feminine taste and self-restraint. After determining to renounce Eliza because of her apparent involvement with Sanford, Boyer, sounding pompous and self-satisfied, proceeds to enumerate a few of Eliza's "many faults":

> There is . . . an unwarrantable extravagance betrayed in your dress. Prudence and economy are such necessary, at least, such decent virtues, that they claim the attention of every female, whatever be her station or her property. To these virtues you are apparently inattentive. Too large a portion of your time is devoted to the adorning of your person. (84)

Dispensing both religious advice and fashion tips, Boyer invokes the entanglements of feminine virtue and domestic economy in ways that expose the patriarchal parameters of the emerging discourse of feminine taste as socially efficacious. "Prudence and economy" are depicted as virtues merited by *decency*: independent of one's "station" or "property," their practice is enshrined as a measure of psychological discrimination rather than material constraint. It is a want of discretion that Eliza's conduct betrays, an "unwarrantable extravagance" in her taste in both men and amusements. As Boyer sees it, Eliza acts like a "loose woman," exhibiting a volatility and intensity of response (what he calls a "levity" in her manner [84]) and a pleasure in her body which counter the virtues of domestic economy—itself identified, here, as the material expression of feminine ethical subjectivity. If Eliza roams too far in search of pleasure, Boyer suggests, it is because she is insufficiently appreciative of the refined enjoyments of domestic commerce.

In *The Coquette*, femininity is a matter of taste; or rather taste is depicted as constitutive of feminine subjectivity. Eliza's indiscriminate enjoyments result in the negation of her very subjectivity — a representation that figures both the violence of domestic norms and the dangers of feminine transgression. Eliza's preference for the "fashionable amusements" of public life — especially "brilliant assemblies, and crowded theaters" (76) — over the "calm delights" of domesticity (78), her inability to "consolidate [her] affections, and fix them" on specific objects (33), constitute an instability and multiplicity of erotic investments — specifically, investments in public life — that are rewritten as psychological deficiencies. Eliza's promiscuous tastes promote a kind of self- and world-unmaking, and entail an indulgence in unsocialized pleasures so threatening to the novel's domestic society that when the "secret" of Eliza's physical involvement with Sanford is finally revealed to her loved ones, it is invested with all the intensity of gothic sensationalism: Julia's "blood thrill[s] with horror" on discovering the "dreadful mystery"; Eliza's mother shrieks and faints (142, 151). Eliza's seduction by the "public" is inversely figured in the constriction of her social world: alienated from her circle of feminine confidantes and meeting secretly with Sanford, the "once happy and social" (137) Eliza becomes "what she once dreaded above all things, a recluse" (110). Importantly, as the novel progresses, she writes to her friends less and less: letter-writing, Eliza's "once favorite amusement" becomes "an employment, which suits me not" (134). Eliza's elopement to die among strangers, "where none knows, or is interested in my . . . story" (156), externalizes the psychic effect of her independent pleasures, "cut[ting her] off" from life, friends, and family (159).

Observing that after the affair with Sanford begins, Eliza "becomes less and less present in the text," Davidson sees a "negation of the female self" in *The Coquette*, which registers Eliza's "psychologically fallen status" after Boyer's rejection as well as women's legal (non)existence under coverture.[101] I am suggesting instead that Eliza's "absence" registers the failure of the text's forms of sentimental literary identification and feminine subjection to produce "Eliza" as a socially recognized civil subject. Registering instabilities within republican definitions of feminine civil subjectivity, the text appears to conclude that there is literally no space for feminine desire apart from its domestic interpellation. In the final pages, Foster maps the social negation of Eliza's self in a way that reveals the violence of its gendered operations. Publicly offering her story as a "beacon to warn the American fair" of the dangers of libertinism (159) and reducing her experience to a familiar moral allegory, Foster's heroine writes herself back into the social collective. An extraordinary reduction of the narrative complexity of Foster's novel and the erotic complexity of its heroine, the move chiefly serves to advertise the erasure of Eliza from the realm of social intelligibility, while underscoring the violence of feminine subjection itself. However, the fact that Foster's heroine remained a "cult heroine" through the nineteenth century suggests that "EW" remained alive to her readers—some of whom, one might imagine, recognized erotic and political possibilities in the text that exceed domestication and patriarchal control.[102]

2

GENDER, DOMESTICITY, AND CONSUMPTION IN THE 1830S: CAROLINE KIRKLAND, CATHARINE SEDGWICK, AND THE FEMINIZATION OF AMERICAN CONSUMERISM

Peter Cartwright, a popular Methodist preacher, rode the Sangamon Circuit on the Illinois frontier in the winter of 1824. Recalling his monthly appointment in a "certain brother's cabin" during his first year on the circuit, Cartwright, in his *Autobiography*, offers a telling description of his host's domestic environment, and his own response to it:

> There was but one chair in the house, and that was called the preacher's chair. The bottom was weak and worn out, and one of the upright back pieces was broken off. We had a hewed puncheon for a table, with four holes in it, and four straight sticks put in for legs. The hearth was made of earth, and in the center of it was a deep hole, worn by sweeping. Around this hole, the women had to cook. . . . When we came to the table there were wooden trenchers for plates, sharp-pointed pieces of cane for forks, and tin cups for cups and saucers. There was but one knife besides a butcher's knife, and that had the handle off. Four forks were driven down between the puncheons into the ground; for bedsteads, cross poles or side poles put in those forks, and clapboards laid crosswise for cords. The old sister kept up a constant apology, and made many excuses.[1]

Now, if "the brother had been really poor," Cartwright notes, "I could have excused everything." But knowing that "he had some three hundred dollars hoarded up to enter land" (251), Cartwright offers an impromptu sermon on the benefits of "cleanliness and decency," values dictated by the "Discipline of our Church" as well as a proper concern for "the great comfort of your family" (252): " 'Now, brother,' said I, 'do fill up this hole in the hearth, and go to town and get you a set of chairs, knives and forks, cups and saucers, and get you a couple of plain bedsteads and bed-cords. Give your wife and daughters a chance.' *I saw in a moment the women were on my side, and I felt safe*" (252; emphasis added). Cartwright surmises that "the females had taken my lecture to the old brother for a text, and they had preached successfully to him," because one month later, "the hole in the hearth was filled up, two new bedsteads were on hand, six new split-bottomed chairs were procured, a new set of knives and forks, cups and saucers, and plates, were all on hand. The women met me very pleasantly . . . and besides all this, the women all had new calico dresses, and looked very neat" (253). He concludes, "nearly all the children obtained religion and joined the Church, and those of them who still live, I number among my dearest friends" (254).

Cartwright's pious endorsement of the virtues of domestic "decency" and "comfort," values embodied in purchased rather than makeshift bedsteads and in matched sets of furniture and tableware, may surprise many of us. We have learned to see an apparent *contradiction* between revivalism and materialism in antebellum America, and we have come to characterize the Protestant work ethic—defined by Max Weber as a "duty of the individual toward the increase of his capital" and requiring the suppression of immediate consumer enjoyment—as the period's predominant social ethic.[2] It is precisely the brother's enterprising zeal in capital accumulation (he has saved three hundred dollars to purchase land) that so distresses the minister and, coupled with the women's encouragement, convinces him to speak out on behalf of household comfort and plenitude, and the legitimacy of expenditures that give form and substance to these values. Cartwright and the women's united sponsorship of an ethic of "comfort" and "decency" is imaged as sanctifying and salvific: the children who inhabit this more pleasing domestic environment, Cartwright observes, have since become church members and are among those for whom he feels a deep personal regard and attachment. Cartwright underscores the spiritual import of the brother's actions by identifying consumer purchases as visible signs of spiritual conversion. The acquisition of material objects is here construed as a kind of baptismal rite: the minister's words, repeated by "the females," apparently reach the brother's heart, and this spiritual transformation is marked by icons of regenerate materiality—sanctified actions and newly made artifacts.

Twentieth-century historians have located the "rise" of an American consumer culture, and a "shift" from an ascetic Protestant work ethic to a hedonistic consumption ethic, in the 1880s and 1890s, shaped by postbellum overproduction and the rise of a national market and promoted by therapeutic ideologues' endorsements of earthly self-fulfillment. In an influential analysis, T. J. Jackson Lears finds a transformation from Protestant producer culture to secular consumer culture in the late nineteenth century, arguing that "the crucial moral change was the beginning of a shift from a Protestant ethos of salvation through self-denial toward a therapeutic ethos stressing self-realization in this world—an ethos characterized by an almost obsessive concern with psychic and physical health defined in sweeping terms."[3] Cartwright's anecdote, however, suggests a far more complicated story. Indeed, by the time Cartwright was writing, a new ideal of "pious consumption," promoted by an array of theological, philosophical, and literary discourses, had gained widespread currency, and had legitimized an increased cultural and economic investment in domestic material and consumer "refinement." According to this ideal, a synthesis of pietistic Protestant and neoclassical aesthetic categories, "refined" domestic artifacts would "civilize" and "socialize" persons and awaken "higher" sentiments; such objects would seduce wayward individuals into the regenerative sociability of domesticity, and, by inspiring purified sentiments, could draw individuals to God.[4] Moreover, in a period when the domestic sphere was being redefined as a realm of redemptive, specifically *feminine* emotional expressivity and "taste," selecting and arranging the material "attractions of home" increasingly became women's work. Enabling what I theorize in chapter 1 as a specifically "feminine" property relation, "pious consumption" encouraged an emotional rather than a narrowly utilitarian relation to objects, and marked the very form of domestic artifacts: it shaped, for example, the nineteenth century's "ruling style," in which everyday objects were profusely ornamented and thus conspicuously marked as aesthetic artifacts by manufacturers.[5] This secularized Protestant ideal achieved its apotheosis in postbellum texts such as Elizabeth Stuart Phelps's bestselling *The Gates Ajar*, in which heaven is depicted as a consumer dream-world where individuals live in private homes with flower boxes, drink iced tea, play the piano, and possess "nicer objects" than are found in "the shops in Boston."[6]

The emergence of this new consumer ethic coincided with an expansion in what economists term "home demand": social historians of the standard of living have identified distinct patterns of mass commodity consumption—especially in household furniture and tableware—by the late eighteenth century, followed by a great expansion of commercial consumption after 1830 with the rise of industrialism.[7] To date, however, no one has developed a conceptual frame to account for this social transformation. In her controversial study of the "feminization" of American literary and religious culture, Ann Douglas has seen in sentimental "women's culture" the nascent origins of mass culture and women's "self-rationalization" for their new consumer role. Although Douglas rightly suggests that sentimentalism served as an "introduction to consumerism," the intellectual foundations of the antebellum consumer ethic were far more substantial than her analysis indicates.[8] Eighteenth-century American theologians, especially Jonathan Edwards and Samuel Hopkins, stressed the importance of beauty in the emotional experience of piety and endeavored to assimilate neoclassical aesthetic categories into the matrix of Protestant theology, thus tempering traditional Calvinist sanctions against luxury and art and reshaping the course of American Protestantism.[9] By the 1830s, a wide range of Protestant authors acknowledged the "civilizing" influence of luxury and tasteful surroundings, especially domestic surroundings, the material environment over which an individual exercised the most control and which would be most habitually experienced. Refined objects were, by many, deemed essential to the emotional culture of "civilized" persons.[10] Meanwhile, as discussed in chapter 1, emerging liberal-capitalist values were eroding the traditional republican hostility toward luxury and commerce. By the early decades of the nineteenth century, many political writers and orators, especially liberal and moderate Whigs, were arguing that the increased availability and circulation of luxury goods, along with education and the dissemination of cultural information, would increase workers' incentives by developing their tastes for the "artificial wants" of civilized society. Indeed, as Caroline Kirkland's narrative, discussed below, suggests, "pious consumption" was written into a Whig historical narrative of moral and economic "progress": constructing class as a malleable domestic identification, this narrative was invoked in the 1830s, a period of economic crisis and working-class radicalism, to diffuse public discourses of class conflict and political antagonism. In an 1836 address, Daniel Webster argued that increased consumption levels, paired with the expansion of industry and commerce, would increase and equalize national wealth, fueling economic progress while spreading "cheerfulness and animation to all classes of the social system."[11]

During the early nineteenth century, Protestant and liberal-capitalist traditions were forged into a novel synthesis of "pious materialism," in which luxury goods were seen as a primary means to civilize and spiritualize the self while animating economic and moral progress, and which legitimized a rise in living standards, especially among the middle classes. As I suggest in chapter 1, the domestication of feminine taste — a domestication Eliza Wharton resists — was being envisioned as a form of emotional as well as civic pedagogy: the "tasteful home" was specified as the site in which a feminine political subjectivity and proprietary relation are performed and transmitted. The significance of "pious consumption" as political pedagogy is evident in the depiction, widespread by the late nineteenth century, of consumption as an instrument of acculturation or Americanization, a trope especially prominent in immigrant fiction. America's "civilizing mission"—a complex ideological configuration which legitimated U.S. imperial expansion across the continent and overseas—would entail exporting a political ideology as well as shaving soap and white bread, ideals of democracy alongside seemingly more mundane and ephemeral cultural commodities.

Cartwright's *Autobiography* attests to the widespread legitimacy of "pious consumption" and suggests the importance of gender in the diffusion of consumer refinement. Evincing what Douglas depicts as an unholy "association" of ministers and women in antebellum America,[12] the anecdote strikingly casts the preacher as interior decorator. And Cartwright's household hints are timely: chairs, from ancient times associated with leadership and traditionally used for the purpose of enthroning authority and marking distinctions (hence, the solitary "preacher's chair") were during the eighteenth and nineteenth centuries increasingly produced and purchased in sets, embodying sociability rather than status; and trenchers and multipurpose eating implements (the brother's "tin cups" for cups and saucers, a "butcher's knife" for diningware) were gradually giving way to an array of specialized utensils, organizing the differentiation of impulses and material "needs," and a corresponding complexity of manners, that have been identified as central elements in the civilizing process.[13] More generally, Cartwright's concern with "comfort" and "decency" in the domestic environment, a concern motivated by both theological precept (the "Discipline") and secular moralism ("my good feelings toward you and your family"), exemplifies the alignment of piety and taste that was becoming conventional among evangelicals like Cartwright as well as more cosmopolitan, liberal Protestants such as Unitarians. In fact, the conception of a tasteful domesticity supplied a unifying symbol for American Protestantism amid interdenominational disputes and sectarian splintering, even as it eased Protestantism's accommodation to liberal ideals of material progress and plenty.[14] A range of antebellum texts about home life, including home decorating texts, conduct books, and domestic fiction, promoted an expanded consumerism and shaped an ideal of consumption in which material goods lift one beyond the body and are integrated with one's "higher" faculties and sentiments. In the words of the architectural pattern book author Gervase Wheeler, tastefully decorated homes are "sermons in stones" which cultivate religious and social sentiments and which constitute, in both theological and secular senses of the phrase, a means of grace.[15] Like Cartwright's, these texts marked out consumer refinement and gracious materiality as a specifically *feminine* province, the sign of feminine "influence" and presence and an index of male "respect" for feminine sensibility.

As I suggest in chapter 1, "taste" in sentimental discourse is a form of class authority as well as a vehicle of civic identification. Domestic texts such as Wheeler's construct class as a sentiment or psychological identification, fashioned in the home through domestic consumption—a construction with complex political effects in Jacksonian America.[16] In particular, as I demonstrate in chapter 1, the Scottish narrative creates a commercial structure of cross-class, *white* racial identification: mapping class differences onto a developmental narrative of "individual" and collective "progress," it facilitates fantasies of working-class mobility and middle-class identification (articulated through domestic taste) central to the logic of the American dream. In Jacksonian America, this Whig, liberal-capitalist narrative of middle-class, white identification was deployed against the ambivalent forms of workingmen's identification with African American slaves staged in minstrelsy and at times registered in political discourse.[17]

The consumerist ideal of feminine domestic aestheticism is vividly articulated in the writings of one of the most popular women writers of the 1830s—Caroline M. Kirkland. Kirkland was an essayist and literary journalist best known for her book-length, semi-autobiographical narratives and sketches of frontier life: *A New Home, Who'll Follow?* (1839), *Forest Life* (1842), and *Western Clearings* (1845). Ten years after Cartwright's arrival in Illinois, Caroline Kirkland moved to nearby Michigan, where her husband had purchased thirteen hundred acres of land and planned to supervise the development of a fledgling village. Her first frontier narrative, *A New Home*, was critically acclaimed and phenomenally popular, going into thirteen editions in eleven years; the narrative chronicles Kirkland's first three years at "Montacute," "beyond the confines of civilization," focusing on her efforts to set up housekeeping on the frontier with four children, a husband, and a wagonload of the "most needful articles" of domestic comfort and convenience.[18] In *A New Home*, the frontier constitutes a unique geopolitical and discursive space in which to explore the values of American "civilization" and its social and material relations. As a self-consciously feminine alternative to previous traditions of frontier literature and their masculine political fantasies, Kirkland's text registers in detailed form the role of feminine taste and domestic material refinement in the civilizing process and the formation of "civilized" subjectivities.[19] Rewriting the frontier as a *domestic* space (a "new home") and site of gendered struggle, Kirkland's text illuminates the expansionist, colonizing aspects of pious consumption, effected by its translation of political relations of race and class into relations of gender. By evoking and foreclosing on certain race and class identifications, the trope of gender and its symbolics of "civilizing" heterosociality becomes, in Kirkland's text, a vehicle for meliorating political conflicts and social differences, assimilating Others into a (white) national "family."

"The Hand of Refined Taste" in the Frontier Landscape: Caroline Kirkland's A New Home

Although she would doubtless agree with Cartwright about little else, Caroline Kirkland shared the minister's sense of the role of tasteful surroundings in promoting Christian nurture. Kirkland had little use for evangelical fervor: in *A New Home* she complains of an itinerant or "voluntary" preacher "with the dress and air of a horse-jockey who . . . rant[s] and scream[s]" until he can barely contain "the excitement into which he has lashed himself." But she fully appreciates the "gentle persuasiveness" of material "appliances" (comfortable seats, beautiful rooms) in "attract[ing] . . . the indolent, the careless, the indifferent, the self-indulgent" to Christian fellowship and virtue (128). The "meliorating influence" of religion, Kirkland notes, is "felt here [on the frontier] as everywhere else, and perhaps here more evidently than in places where society is farther advanced" (131). A primary "deficiency" of frontier living, however, is the absence of resident ministers, and thus the "lack of the ordinary means of public religious instruction" (127). This absence is replicated in Kirkland's text: the narrator discusses religion at length in just one chapter, focusing chiefly on the need for the meetinghouse to be made more comfortable (127–31). The "deficiency" of the minister's physical presence on the frontier is largely filled in Kirkland's text by the bodily surrogates of women and material refinement. If *A New Home* has seemingly little to say about the "state of religion" (130) on the frontier and avoids explicit theological discussion, it is nonetheless fundamentally shaped by Protestant ideals, especially Protestant concepts of redemptive materiality. Kirkland's narrative details the role of purchased objects—what the narrator calls "feminilities" (135)—as vessels of cultivation and refinement.

A New Home's opening pages identify the text as a feminine reworking of the nation's "myth of the frontier"—a myth chiefly forged from the materials of Puritan captivity and hunter narratives and secular frontier legends such as John Filson's biography of Daniel Boone.[20] Kirkland's text is especially indebted to the tradition of women's captivity narratives and to the synthetic frontier symbolism of James Fenimore Cooper's Leatherstocking novels. Nonetheless, Kirkland expressly identifies her text as a realistic alternative to the insubstantial fictions of frontier romance and adventure. In the opening chapter, Kirkland describes her text as a "veracious history of actual occurrences, an unvarnished transcript of real characters, and an impartial record of everyday forms of speech (taken down in many cases from the lips of the speaker)" (3). Such verisimilitude, she notes, departs from current literary tastes for romance and adventure stories: her text, she predicts, "will be pronounced 'graphic' by at least a fair proportion of the journalists of the day" (3). Further distinguishing her text from earlier models, she states that "I have never seen a cougar—nor been bitten by a rattlesnake" (3). In her feminine, realistic frontier narrative, Kirkland reconstitutes the primary metaphorical opposition of these earlier texts—the opposition between "savagery" and "civilization"—and details the explicitly social resonances of this pairing. The idea of the frontier—as metaphor and as geographical terrain—allows her to spatialize in her narrative the temporal dimensions of historical progress and to explore the ways in which the transformation of savagery into civility is mapped onto race, class, and especially gender relations.

Writing under the pseudonym Mary Clavers, Kirkland patterns her text on a collection of letters, a form of writing which, in the words of Kirkland's friend, the poet and conduct book author Lydia Sigourney, is a "natural vocation" of women because closely modulated by the pulses of the heart and because it "is but to talk upon paper."[21] The conversational ideal *A New Home* embodies is that of a "rambling gossiping style" and a "wandering wordiness" (82), "mere gossip about every-day people" (3), a rhetorical style which characterized much of antebellum women's writing and which mobilizes the emotional immediacy of "feminine" private language and romanticism's valuation of impulse and discursive fluidity. The text's informal, conversational style allows Kirkland a substantial flexibility of voice: the narrator alternates between sharp-edged, even satirical commentary, sentimental warmth, and poetic reverie, and combines sentences graced with French phrases and quotations from Romantic poetry with passages that are, in the narrator's phrase, "decidedly low" (4). In its replication of casual conversation and its apparent dismissal of a formal organizing principle or plot, the text simultaneously signals Kirkland's immersion in and emotional responsiveness to her "materials" (4) and serves as a rhetorical device to establish intimate, emotional engagement between reader and writer.[22] Kirkland's intended audience, as David Leverenz has suggested, is principally "fashionable," genteel Easterners whose values she both playfully mocks and shares.[23] In an important sense, this audience serves to stabilize her narrative, sustaining a community of shared values against the shocks of travel and an awareness of cultural differences, the destabilizing recognition that, in the narrator's words, "everything is relative" (15). The frontier is a crucial setting for Kirkland's rhetorical performances: locating herself within a community of "civilized" readers shaped by sympathetic identification, the narrator repeatedly performs her civil subjectivity, and invites her readers to do the same, by invoking and disavowing an identification with "uncivilized" frontier inhabitants. While Kirkland writes *for* an audience of genteel Easterners, she writes *to* her frontier neighbors, conceptualizing her narrative as an "opportunity" to "inspire" them with a love of refinement, a form of discursive "schooling" in politeness and "levelling upwards" (185). Like many of her contemporaries, Kirkland viewed literary texts as a means of gently disseminating values and securing "cheerful subordination" to authority; for example, in her "Essay on Fiction," she stresses the pedagogical significance of readerly identification, and describes narrative as a means through which the author "insinuate[s]" values and guides readerly emotions.[24] In her *A New Home*, Kirkland tactfully mobilizes the arts of culture—of voice and bodily manner, as well as material accoutrements—in order to transform a "rough" frontier population into a union of civility and social harmony. It is through the "irresistible power of... example" (78) that Kirkland hopes to refine and refashion them.

The commercial model of subjectivity Kirkland constructs is an expressly *white* racial formation: as for the Scots, racial Others, defined as nonconsenting objects rather than civil subjects, occupy that subjectivity's constitutive limits. Significantly, Kirkland does not write to or for Native Americans on the frontier, nor does she direct her rhetorical arts toward efforts to "civilize" and "improve" them. And indeed, this most familiar incarnation of "savagery" in the antebellum cultural imagination maintains, in the symbolic terrain of *A New Home*, only a shadowy, marginalized presence: while the proximity of the Indians on the frontier is signaled by white settlers' use of Indian terms (e.g., 16), Native Americans make their appearance in the narrative on just three brief occasions, in scenes that take place at the borders of the frontier towns, in the woods, or in the "unpeopled" wilderness (6–7, 28–30, 85). In fact, in *A New Home*, the structuring opposition of savagery and civilization is largely displaced from its racial referents and mapped onto class and gender relations. This displacement, and the narrative's (partial) erasure of Indians on the frontier, metaphorically registers the violence of Jacksonian policies of Indian "removal" while repressing the source of interracial struggle, translating, in Peter Hulme's words, the "topic of land" into the "topic of savagery."[25] Kirkland clarified the ideological complexities of *A New Home*'s representation of Native Americans in a preface she wrote for a collection of Dakotah legends transcribed and collected by the Southern author Mary Eastman, published in 1849. There, Kirkland called for humane "treatment" of Native Americans: defining native people as objects of white interest and proprietary care, she characterizes them as a doomed race for whom "annihilation" is "inevitable." Incapable of being integrated into civilized society, Indians nonetheless provide in their "history and character," Kirkland contended, the raw materials of a national literature, "all the distinct, poetic material to which we, as Americans, have an unquestioned right."[26] This double logic of appropriation and erasure is alluded to in *A New Home*'s opening chapters, where Mary Clavers describes the efforts to name the town that her husband has founded with an "aboriginal designation," efforts that concisely reveal that the Indians' symbolic value is contingent on their literal absence. In Kirkland's text, then, Indians are simultaneously memorialized and pushed to the boundaries of the social world the text constructs.[27] In a textual and social space effectively cleared of Native Americans' bodily presence, Kirkland directs her civilizing efforts toward those deemed more tractable and salvageable—explicitly, members of the lower classes, and men. Mapping the "frontier" as a white cultural space, the narrative constructs a sentimental structure of white racial identification that enables class mobility (the reproduction of "civility") and assimilation into a (white) national family.

The opposition between lower-class vulgarity and upper-class civility appears in *A New Home*'s opening pages, and is one of its structuring oppositions. Kirkland deploys the discourse of feminine taste and domestic civility to contain class confict, offering a Whiggish alternative to democratic rhetorics of class antagonism. Halfway through the narrative, Kirkland refers to a "class" of poor white settlers who are so "vicious and degraded" that they are insensible to civilization's charms—a class exemplified in the text by the Newlands. Unlike the Indians, the narrator observes, the Newlands work hard, but they dress "wretchedly" and "live in the most uncomfortable style in all respects," apparently wasting their economic resources in ephemeral commodities, such as alcohol and insubstantial finery, rather than investing their funds in more durable material improvements (101–10). To the problem of this undisciplined and intractable "class of settlers," Kirkland suggests a "solution" similar to that of Indian removal: the unregenerate Newlands, as their name indicates, are pushed west, beyond the bounds of American civilization. At the end of her account of the Newlands, Kirkland states that they "have since left this part of the country," and she asserts that "Texas and the Canada war have done much for us in this way; and the wide west is rapidly drafting off those whom we shall regret as little as the Newlands" (111). But in the main, the narrator incorporates her less "civilized" frontier neighbors into the text's social world: Mary Clavers "mingles" freely with them, and represents her neighbors as capable of material and psychological refinement. In a sense, the text allegorizes the expansion of American citizenship, enacted by law, performing the assimilation of newly enfranchised working-class and poor whites into the national culture. Taste and domestic consumption operated centrally in Whig narratives of domestic reform such as Kirkland's, and comprised a site of middle-class reform and working-class resistance.

Just how much work Kirkland's domestic reformer has cut out for herself is legible in the narrative's early pages. What Mary Clavers must do to "improve" her neighbors is cultivate their aesthetic and ethical sensibilities; it is to re-form, in other words, their most intimate sentiments and "wants." While civic humanism had equated unrestrained economic desire with anarchy and civic disorder, liberalism was establishing the proliferation of "wants" (and corresponding utilities) as the engine of economic and social progress. According to Adam Smith, for instance, although bodily needs are finite, "imaginary wants" are "infinite," and, thus, it is on imaginary wants, the aesthetic and ethical tastes, that civilization and collective improvement depend.[28] In *A New Home*, the frontier economy Mary Clavers enters resembles the undifferentiated, "primitive" economy of the Indians. On the frontier, Kirkland informs us, "the division of labor is almost unknown. If in absolutely savage life, each man is of necessity 'his own tailor, tent-maker, carpenter, cook, huntsman, and fisherman,' " on the frontier not even the gender division of labor is fully observed:

> Each woman is, at times at least, her own cook, chamber-maid and waiter; nurse, seamstress and school-ma'am; not to mention various occasional callings. . . . And every man, whatever his circumstances

> or resources, must be qualified to play groom, teamster, or boot-black, as the case may be; besides "tending the baby" at odd times, and cutting wood to cook his dinner with. (72–73)

This lack of economic complexity is reflected as well in frontier consumption patterns and in depressed levels of consumer demand. Indeed, the primary index of civility as Kirkland depicts it is the segregation and increased complexity of psychological desires and impulses, a psychological complexity that corresponded to an increasingly varied world of goods. "Modernization" has been characterized by social theorists from Adam Smith forward as entailing the increased specialization and rationalization of economic function in the sphere of production.[29] *A New Home*'s representations of economic progress suggest that the same specialization and differentiation of need and utility have organized the sphere of consumption as well.

The "primitive" nature of the frontier economy is immediately registered in *A New Home*. Upon her arrival at Mrs. Danforth's cabin, the "hotel" where she initially takes lodging in Montacute, Mrs. Clavers is at once offended by what she views as a "promiscuous" mixing of spaces, objects and uses. She must sleep in the same room with "all the men and boys" in the family, separated only by a "partial screen" constructed of "sundry old quilts . . . fastened by forks to the rafters" (9); she must perform her morning ablutions with the help of a "little iron skillet" that serves as a "wash-dish" (10); and she watches with some distaste while cooking utensils are hung on a "strip of dingy listing" with "a small comb" and other instruments of personal grooming (13). Dishes, rinsed in "equivocal looking suds," are set to drain on chairs (14); and the family's single wardrobe reveals "the go-to-meeting *hats and bonnets, frocks and pantaloons* of a *goodly number of all sizes*" (13; emphasis added). She is especially provoked by the habit of washing with one's handkerchief performing "the part of towels" (14), as she is by the individual who "pick[s] his teeth with his fork" and "us[es] the fire-place for a pocket handkerchief" (53). Mrs. Clavers's ideal of domestic propriety quite clearly entails a material environment differentiated in terms of gender, "size" (or age), and the discrete bodily and psychological needs of its inhabitants. Men and women should sleep separately and their personal belongings should be stored in individualized compartments (as Mrs. Clavers despairingly notes, the Danforths know nothing of privacy); children's belongings should be distinguished from adults', an extension of their specialized needs (one recalls that furniture designed specifically for children came into its own during this period);[30] distinct needs, especially grooming and eating, must be segregated and organized around distinct objects. Above all, things have proper uses: chairs are for sitting, forks are for eating, towels for washing one's face, pocket handkerchiefs for blowing one's nose. In Kirkland's text, "refinement" entails the multiplication of aesthetic and social wants; it simultaneously, through the differentiation of needs and utilities, incorporates into the structure of bodily experience social expectations and uses. The process of differentiation Mrs. Clavers promotes establishes distinct correspondences between subjective impulses and desires and the world of goods, thus establishing "impersonal" objects as mediating between the realm of private experience and the publicly sharable. Mrs. Clavers's sensibilities are "wounded" (183) by the Danforths' living habits because these habits seem nakedly to express unsocialized desires.

Kirkland's depiction of the Danforths' cabin reveals how broad cultural developments—such as the "invention of childhood" and its increased valuation as a unique stage of existence, and the accentuation of gender differences during the late eighteenth century[31]—have contributed to consumerism. It also illuminates how closely interwoven are middle-class psychological and emotional "needs"—such as the desires for privacy and intimate rather than "promiscuous" sociability—and the middle-class material landscape. Consumer goods, Kirkland's narrative suggests, are powerful means of *socialization*. They can shape the nuances of bodily experience and organize an individual's most intimate exertions and pleasures: as "object lessons" that embody culturally specific beliefs and usages, they give them a lasting physical presence, and can embed particular ideologies of subjectivity in the very structure of self and need. The metonymic slippage between the social and the material is vividly apparent in Kirkland's text: the narrator objects as much to the "promiscuous" domestic sociability of the frontier inhabitants as to their undifferentiated material environment. Kirkland's critique of the Danforths' domestic "mess," and her envisioned reorganization of their domestic environment through the compartmentalization of spaces, objects, and persons, were gestures mirrored in antebellum sociological texts on the urban poor, in which the material reform of the domestic environment was clearly linked with the disruption of preindustrial—and potentially "dangerous"—patterns of working-class sociability and collective activity.[32] On the frontier, Kirkland suggests, domestic reform through the dissemination of feminine "taste" takes place in several ways: through the power of "refined" example; through the circulation of texts, including her own, which inscribed domestic commodities with cultural value; and through what she depicts as the powerful attractions of objects themselves.

Mary Clavers's visit with the Danforths acquaints her with the unrefined nature of frontier living. But it is when she settles into her new home—a one-room log cabin with an "uneven floor"—that her reformist energies are first unleashed. The problem with her frontier neighbors, Mary Clavers soon notes, is that they *want* too little, and she hopes to develop and "refine" her neighbors' desires. When she unpacks her family's "movables," an "anomalous . . . congregation of household goods" recently arrived from the East, her neighbors respond amusedly "as each new wonder made its appearance" (32, 42):

> "What on airth's them gimcracks for?" said my lady [Mrs. Ketchum], as a nest of delicate japanned tables were set out upon the uneven floor.
>
> I tried to explain to her the various convenient uses to which they were applicable; but she looked very scornfully after all and said "I guess they'll do better for kindlin's than any thing else, here." (43)

The narrator's description of these tables and Mrs. Ketchum's response to them are revealing, and delineate the considerable social distance that Mary Clavers's efforts must bridge. The narrator's use of the adjective "delicate" evokes the aesthetic pleasure the tables are meant to afford as well as the care required in their use: they require a corresponding "delicacy" or self-restraint in their handling, and they call for an owner who will treat them with the "respect" a cultivated appreciation entails. Their fragility and their ornament suggest, above all, that they have been procured with an eye to something other than physical utility and bodily need: both mark the tables as satisfying *refined* uses and desires.[33] But the aesthetic value of the "delicate japanned tables," and the "various convenient uses" that Mrs. Clavers anticipates for them—a phrase which evokes a complexity of social rituals and needs—are quite lost on her neighbor Mrs. Ketchum. The latter can imagine only a single use for the tables—as a source of firewood, to provide heat for the household—suggesting in Kirkland's text a constricted psychological horizon, circumscribed by what was commonly called "mere animal enjoyments." Like others in the community who speak of carpets as "one way to hide dirt" and mahogany tables as "dreadful plaguy to scour" (184)—and not unlike the poor schoolteacher Mr. Whicher, who displays his insensitivity to the "magic" of musical performance by instead attending to its technology, "the construction of the instrument, which he thought must have taken 'a good bit o' cypherin' " (180)—Mrs. Ketchum, Kirkland implies, lacks the "refinement" of ethical and aesthetic sensibility necessary to "appreciate" the value of the objects Mrs. Clavers displays for her. In an important sense, the narrator ritualistically performs her "taste" in this scene, for her neighbors' but more importantly for her readers' consumption: she thus both marks her difference from her insensible neighbors, and her dependence on them for the performance of her refined sensibility and civilized subjectivity.

In her short story "Comfort," Kirkland depicts a concern with "present gratification at all hazards" ("as if a man whose fingers were cold, should make a fire of his chairs, or split up his piano, for comfort") as a principal sign of "savagery": signifying an inadequate *sense* of private property, it entails a failure of foresight as well as a lack of taste.[34] In her representation of Mrs. Ketchum's response, as elsewhere in *A New Home*, Mary Clavers's frontier neighbors exhibit an economic orientation toward subsistence rather than improvement, and push toward forms of consumption that are fully integrated with the body, and cyclical; in other words, they treat everything like food.[35] Refinement, on the other hand, is defined as the proliferation of social and aesthetic desires, and an appreciation of material objects that correspond with, or gratify, these desires. Like many of her Protestant contemporaries, Kirkland identifies the home as the primary site of emotional regeneration, and invests both the affectional and material culture of domesticity with spiritual efficacy. The liberal theologian Horace Bushnell, for example, in his influential treatise on the role of "Christian nurture" in childrearing, describes the domestic environment as a means of grace (Bushnell calls it the "church of childhood") which could "silent[ly]" and "imperceptibl[y]" impart a love of the good from an early age, thus rendering proper feeling a "habit of life" rather than the product of a "technical" conversion experience.[36] It is Mrs. Ketchum's indifference that Mary Clavers must work on and "convert"—the structure is essentially theological—through subtle "schooling" and the silent force of example and emulation.

In light of her neighbors' distaste, Mrs. Clavers begins to "cast a disrespectful glance upon [the tables] myself" (43) and promptly stows them away in the attic, to be taken down when her housing arrangements warrant them. Anything less than graceful adaptiveness would be seen as an assertion of social superiority, an attitude which, Mary Clavers repeatedly reminds us, is antithetical to the frontier "republican spirit" (184) and is "invariably met by a fierce and indignant resistance" (184). Such conciliatory behavior toward members of the lower classes constitutes an approach that, Kirkland suggests, does not come naturally to fashionable emigrants like herself. Significantly, English settlers "show little inclination to mingle with their rustic neighbors"—an oblique reference to the more rigid and permanent class distinctions in British society (139). Even recent transplants from Eastern cities, such as Mrs. Clavers's fashionable friend, Mrs. Rivers, who loves poetry and is "easily shocked by . . . sins against Chesterfield," must be continually persuaded to socialize freely with her neighbors and to "conceal her fatigue" at their frequent violations of genteel propriety (65). Mrs. Clavers's responsiveness to "common opinion" is largely pragmatic: as the narrator explains, "What can be more absurd than a feeling of proud distinction, where a stray spark of fire, a sudden illness, or a day's contre-temps, may throw you entirely upon the kindness of your humblest neighbour?" (65). But it is also an index of the class paternalism of her civilizing efforts. Placing the vessels of distinction "under wraps," Mary Clavers can, through a process of gentle habituation rather than affrontery, gradually insinuate her goods (and herself) into her neighbors' affections, so that, she believes, they will gradually grow to love rather than resent them. Like a good Whig orator, Mary Clavers comes "down to the people": she studies local customs and habits, and borrows her neighbors' colloquialisms in order more effectively to appeal to them and win their support.[37] Mrs. Clavers's conciliatory demeanor allows for the diffusion of refined tastes and facilitates the subsumption of class divisions, without physical violence and apparent coercion, within a harmonious union of interests. Kirkland thus inscribes taste and domestic consumption into the reproduction of civil subjectivity and the forms of class mobility.

In *A New Home*, suppressed ostentation inversely permits an expansion of what Kirkland terms "influence." According to the popular antebellum doctrine, influence was a form of authority, exercised on the passions rather than reason, which operated through persuasion instead of force: by appealing to an individual's love of virtue, influence engaged and subtly directed his or her affections. Influence was seen to be both so subtly and habitually exercised as to be imperceptible and irresistible: in the words of the conduct book author Rufus Bailey, influence "persuade[s], and compel[s] . . . so gently that there . . . seem[s] to be the absence of all authority or irksome constraint."[38] Influence, numerous antebellum authors claimed, was exercised by pleasing and refined material forms—such as gracious, cultivated women and elegant artifacts. Like the renowned influence of virtuous women, the influence of pleasing domestic possessions was seen to civilize and socialize the self: according to the prominent tastemaker A. J. Downing, the influence of a refined, comfortable domestic environment constitutes "an unfailing barrier against vice, immorality, and bad habits."[39] Refinement of sensibility, and an increased appreciation of objects and persons in one's daily surroundings, would be materially manifested in improved manners: gentleness toward others would indicate the incorporation of the Christian precept of benevolence, and as one's taste develops, one would gradually learn to keep one's feet off the mahogany coffee table and forgo spitting on the Brussels rug (common domestic insensitivities recorded during the period). The narrator of *A New Home*, for one, is confident that to *see* refinement is to *love* it:

> The silent influence of example is daily effecting much towards reformation [of my neighbors' habits] in many particulars. Neatness, propriety, and that delicate forebearance of the least encroachment upon the rights or enjoyments of others, which is the essence of true elegance of manner, have only to be seen and understood to be admired and imitated. . . . [Others in similar circumstances] will find ere long that their neighbours have taste enough to love what is so charming, even though they see it exemplified by one who sits all day in a carpeted parlor, teaches her own children instead of sending them to the district school, hates "the breath of garlic eaters," and—oh fell climax!—knows nothing at all of soap-making. (53)

Like the Scots' equivalence of women and luxury goods, the narrator's identification of feminine infuence with the influence of domestic objects entails a supression of female agency: Mary Clavers, who "sits all day" and meticulously avoids "encroach[ing] upon the rights and enjoyments of others," is absorbed into her parlor's domestic decor, and appears like one of its refined domestic objects. Feminine passivity and (self-)objectification enables the logic of sentimental identification: subjection to feminine domestic authority, and the form of feminine civil subjectivity (and class discipline) Clavers embodies, at once entails an identification with the passivity of domestic objects and a power over them. What Mary Clavers is doing here is inducting her neighbors into a feminine proprietary relation, and its complex pleasures of ownership. Refinement appears as that *je ne sais quoi*—it is not reducible to rules, unknown to the pedant—which charms against one's principles and subdues one's willful resistances. Domestic objects, on which "so much of the comfort of life depends," perform their "humanizing effect" by training domestic inhabitants' desires and sentiments (26); effective vessels of authority, they are experienced as pleasing, not coercive. In the words of one well-known proponent of domestic aestheticism, "in the place of prisons, laws, and preaching, [let us] substitute the statue, the picture, and the song. Let us look for a civilization which shall not be the result of Force, but of Pleasure; which, instead of compelling, shall attract men."[40]

An expanding array of consumer goods and aesthetically pleasing domestic artifacts performed a crucial function in the realization of the "civilization" pictured here, one characterized by a managed hedonism and the productive engagement rather than the repression of desire.[41] Mary Clavers's efforts to "civilize" her frontier neighbors and direct their desires is at least partly successful: at the end of three years, the narrator notes, "some few [of her neighbors have] carpets and shanty-kitchens; and one or two, piano-fortes and silver tea-sets" (187). But Kirkland delineates two persistent obstacles to progressive refinement on the frontier: Jacksonian republicanism and men. Although the historical accuracy of the link has been questioned by twentieth-century historians, *A New Home* employed the political designation "Jacksonian democrat" as a virtual synonym for "lower-class." As a result, class relations in Kirkland's text are largely constituted as relations of political allegiance: the social distinction between the refined and the uncultured classes is roughly translated in *A New Home* into an ideological opposition between Whiggism and Jacksonianism, a conflict between liberal-capitalist and republican attitudes toward luxury. Kirkland's Whiggish elitism is perhaps most clearly revealed in her disparaging account of her frontier neighbors' sense of civic duty and their determination to attend all local elections and town meetings at the expense of their business interests. When Mary Clavers questions one citizen, Mr. Fenwick, whose family is "suffering for want of the ordinary comforts," on the "sacrifice" he is making in spending two days at a political meeting, he responds with "virtuous indignation" and proudly states, "ought not a man to do his duty to his country?" (48). In a statement that juxtaposes "masculine" republicanism against "feminine" capitalist refinement, the narrator ironically notes, "This was unanswerable, of course. I hope it consoled poor Mrs. Fenwick, whose tattered gown would have been handsomely renewed by those two days wages" (48). Throughout the text, Kirkland represents Jacksonianism in negative terms, as a form of false consciousness that buttresses her neighbors' resistance to economic progress and material refinement.

Jackson himself was frequently represented in contemporary accounts as "rude" and "uncivilized": he reportedly ate with a "primitive" two-tined iron fork, for instance; and his inaugural reception in 1829 was described with horror as an event stormed by an undisciplined "mob," leaving in its wake fainting ladies, carpets and chairs smeared with muddy footprints, and several thousand dollars' worth of broken glassware and china.[42] Jackson's followers are depicted by Kirkland as equally tasteless. What particularly appalls the narrator is her neighbors' disrespect for refinement and cultivation, a disrespect bolstered by a spirit of democratic egalitarianism and republican pride. When, for instance, Mrs. Clavers's neighbor Mrs. Jennings comes to dinner—and she makes herself at home "with small urgency on [Mrs. Clavers's] part" (51)—she drinks from the spout of the teapot and cuts mouthfuls of meat directly from the roast, declining offers of help from the carver with defiant independence, "I'll help myself, I thank ye. I never want no waitin' on" (51). Jacksonian republicanism, Mary Clavers suggests, underwrites her neighbors ill-mannered usage of things, as well as their "reluctance to admire, or even to approve, any thing like luxury or convenience which is not in common use among the settlers" (184), the liberties taken in "slight[ing]" a French mirror of "unusual dimensions" with the flippant remark, "that would be quite a nice glass, if the frame was done over" (184). In Kirkland's depiction, Jacksonian republicanism also entails a commitment to communal consumption—Mrs. Jennings eats and drinks, the narrator pointedly notes, from the common vessels, ignoring the individualized plates and cups—which threatens to undermine social distinctions and the institution of private property on which they depend.

This Jacksonian emphasis on the *public* value of property ownership is clearly apparent in Kirkland's depiction of the frontier institution of "involuntary loans" (68). According to the narrator, "Your wheelbarrows, your shovels, your utensils of all sorts, belong, not to yourself, but to the public, who do not think it necessary even to *ask* a loan, but take it for granted" (67). Such collective claims are leveled not just at the implements of work, but extend "within doors" (67) to one's most familiar domestic and personal possessions: "For my own part, I have lent my broom, my thread, my tape, my spoons, my cat, my thimble, my scissors, my shawl, my shoes; and have been asked for my combs and brushes: and my husband, for his shaving apparatus and his pantaloons" (68); a neighbor has even been asked for the loan of her infant, to relieve a new mother whose baby is sick and cannot nurse (71–72). But "the cream of the joke lies in the manner of the thing": in the absence of "servile gratitude" (68) and the "fierce and indignant resistance" (184) to any suggestion of condescension and charity; in the presumption of entitlement; in the breezy complaints about the things sent; in the restoration of one's durable goods in worn or broken condition and the replacement of consumables with others of inferior quality (68). Kirkland's point is, in part, to show that unless positive rights to private property are absolutely secured, material improvement will be neglected. But she also suggests that the collectivist frontier economy violates not so much one's legal right to objects as one's emotional claims on them, entailing a recognition that one's most "intimate" possessions (one's clothing, one's implements of grooming, one's children) can never be satisfactorily valued by another because they are laden with personal emotions, rendered irreplaceable through familiarity and love.[43] Emphasizing the psychological rather than the political value of property, Kirkland here represents her Jacksonian neighbors' carelessness and resistance to private ownership as an index of their uncultured psychological state and, contrarily, represents exclusive, private attachments to particular objects as a measure of civilized, refined subjectivity. It is only through the security of continued possession, *A New Home* suggests, that objects are fully appreciated and "cared for."

But one's "roughest" neighbors can be discouraged and, even, avoided; men, on the other hand, are the enemy within (doors), representatives of "savagery" with whom one is intimately bound and against whom, in a seemingly ceaseless dynamic, one relentlessly struggles. In Kirkland's text, the most prominent manifestation of the structuring opposition between civility and savagery is a gender opposition, a conflict between women and men. By foregrounding gender in her text, Kirkland absorbs the divisive language of race and class divisions, and the historical specificities of these conflicts, within a transhistorical battle of the sexes—a rhetorical move that both buries the violence of these former struggles and neutralizes the potential force and divisiveness of social conflict, tempering perceptible tensions with the language of familial love.[44] This most prominent metaphorical translation also highlights the cultural import of the family during the antebellum period as a socializing institution, as a principal site of moral reform and the dissemination of values, and as a crucial source of both social stability and moral progress.

In *A New Home*, it is *women* who, by surrounding their loved ones with tasteful goods, direct "the refining process, the introduction of those important nothings on which so much depends" (147). In Kirkland's narrative, women and luxury goods are functional equivalents: both civilize and socialize subjectivity and engender refined sensibilities. Luxury goods constitute material markers and extensions of feminine presence.[45] Women's role in supervising the refining process is at least partly attributable to what Kirkland, like many of her contemporaries, paradoxically presents as (middle-class) women's "natural" cultivation and sensibility. Women, in Kirkland's account, "naturally" *want* more than men:

woman perceives "a thousand deficiencies which her rougher mate can scarce be taught to feel as evils. What cares he if the time-honoured cupboard is meagerly represented by a few oak-boards lying on pegs and called shelves? . . . Will he find fault with the clay-built oven, or even the tin 'reflector?' His bread never was better baked. What does he want with the great old cushioned rocking-chair? When he is tired he goes to bed" (146). The "rougher" sex, Kirkland suggests, is often mindless of aesthetic refinement and domestic comfort: primitive furnishings, unattractive and uncomfortable, are deemed sufficient by male inhabitants preoccupied with the satisfaction of bodily needs, such as eating and sleeping, at the expense of domestic sociability and harmony. Women, to be sure, must restrain their investment in material objects: in particular, that investment must be modulated with a concern for the social happiness of domestic inhabitants. Indeed, Kirkland suggests that women can "care" for things excessively, so that material objects engross their attention and affection at the expense of those they're meant to serve: the severe Polly Doubleday, for instance, possessed with a "neat devil," makes her husband and servant miserable with her relentless scouring and undue attention to the material appliances of living (69–71). But, Kirkland insists, it is chiefly the feminine touch that accounts for domestic refinement and supplies the "cherished features" of home, the "convenient furniture" of living:

> Small additions to the more delicate or showy part of the household gear are accomplished by the aid of some little extra personal exertion. "Spinning-money" buys a looking-glass perhaps, or "butter-money" a nice cherry table. Eglantines and wood-vine, or wild cucumber, are sought and transplanted to shade the windows. Narrow beds round the house are bright with Balsams and Sweet Williams, Four o'clocks, Poppies and Marigolds; and if "th' old man" is good natured, a little gate takes the place of the great awkward bars before the door. By and by a few apple-trees are set out; sweet briars grace the door yard, and lilacs and currant-bushes; all by female effort — at least I have never yet happened to see it otherwise where these improvements have been made at all. They are not all accomplished by her own hand indeed, but hers is the moving spirit, and if she do her "spiriting gently," and has anything but a Caliban for a minister, she can scarcely fail to throw over the real homeliness of her lot something of the magic of [the] Ideal. (147)

The problem is, one very well may have "a Caliban for a minister"; in fact, as Kirkland portrays things, one almost assuredly will. Examples of male "savagery" are everywhere present in *A New Home.* One example appears in the narrative's opening pages, in which Mary Clavers's refined sensibility, her susceptibility to nature's beauty and the attractions of Michigan wildflowers, is juxtaposed to the insensibility of her husband, who is so intent on his destination that he is abstracted from nature's aesthetic charms and devoid of even "one spark" of his wife's "floral enthusiasms" (5). Later in the narrative, women's civilizing influence on men is vividly registered in Kirkland's sketch of Mrs. Clavers's and Mrs. Rivers's encounter with a mob of Montacute citizens, a motley collection of men emitting shouts and "Indian yells" and bent on violence: the women's mere presence pacifies the crowd and diffuses its violent energies so that the "spirit of the thing was at an end" (118–19). But the opposition between male savagery and female civility is perhaps most distinctly evident in the narrator's account of the domestic situation of the "B——s," a neighboring family, recent Eastern emigrants of distinguished background, whose current fortunes are plagued by the dissipation and indolence of the "master of the house" (75). During a midsummer drive through the countryside, the Claverses come upon a house with a "smooth-shaven lawn," "beds of flowers of every hue," windows curtained with "French muslin," and a Spanish guitar with a "broad scarf of blue silk" arranged picturesquely near the door; as Mrs. Clavers puts it, "one glance told us that the hand of refined taste had been there" (74). Inquiring for directions, the Claverses are invited inside. Here, Mary Clavers sees a domestic setting lucidly divided into male and female spaces. Noting that "the interior of the house corresponded in part with the impressions I had received from my first glance at the exterior," she describes

> a harp in a recess, and the white-washed log walls were hung with a variety of cabinet pictures. A tasteful drapery of French chintz partly concealed another recess, closely filled with books; . . . before a large old-fashioned looking-glass stood a French pier-table, on which were piled fossil specimens, mosses, vases of flowers, books, pictures, and music. So far all was well; and two young ladies seated on a small sofa near the table, with netting and needle-work were in keeping with the romantic side of the picture. (74)

All the signs of culture and aesthetic refinement—books, pictures, a harp and sheet music—are clearly present in this scene. As in her treatment of the Danforths' cabin, Kirkland here depicts the domestic environment of her characters in fine detail, and represents the inhabitants' domestic setting and material possessions as telling indexes of their psychological condition. Kirkland's depiction of this feminine territory suggests psychological depth (the harp sits "in a recess"; the drapes partly conceal a nook filled with books), social consciousness (a looking glass is hung for checking one's appearance and seeing what others see; a "pier-table" displays for others one's personal possessions and mementos), and a taste for intimate sociability (extended by the "small sofa"). Nature is present indoors, but it is a nature whose value is chiefly aesthetic, one "improved" (the log walls are "white-washed"), cultivated (there are flowers that, notably, "Mrs. B——" tends), and discriminately selected and procured (e.g., bits of nature, such as mosses and "fossil specimens"). "So far," the narrator states, "all was well." But, she continues rather ominously, "there was more than all this":

> The bare floor was marked in every direction with that detestable yellow dye which mars every thing in this country, although a great box filled with sand stood near the hearth, melancholy and fruitless provision against this filthy visitation. Two great dirty dogs lay near a large rocking-chair, and this rocking-chair sustained the tall person of the master of the house, a man of perhaps forty years or thereabouts, the lines of whose face were such, as he who runs may read. Pride and passion, and reckless self-indulgence were there, and fierce discontent and determined indolence. An enormous pair of whiskers, which surrounded the whole lower part of the countenance, afforded incessant employment for the long slender fingers, which showed no marks of labour, except very dirty nails. This gentleman had, after all, something of a high-bred air, if one did not look at the floor, and could forget a certain indication of excessive carelessness discernible in his dress and person. (74–75)

Kirkland's depiction of the "B——s" presents the opposition between female refinement and male savagery as a vertical relation between high and low, a relation registered in various ways in this passage. After representing the "young ladies" seated on a "small sofa" and thus suspended within a cultivated interior, the narrator descends in perspective to the floor—a realm associated both metaphorically and metonymically with "coarse" physicality and animal life—before depicting the unkempt, "careless" "Mr. B——." The passage thus quite expertly marks the latter as an agent of domestic corruption, a defiling presence with whose "filthy visitation" the women vainly contend. The literal and figurative opposition between high and low frames the narrator's representation of "Mr. B——'s" resistance to feminine refinement and economic progress.

While the women's hands are busied with the feminine arts of needlework and netting, the "master's" hands, which "showed no marks of labour, except very dirty nails," are occupied with touching his own body and providing private physical pleasures. Instead of procuring economic resources for his family, "Mr. B——'s" hands are engaged in gestures that, in nineteenth-century codes, suggest masturbatory self-engrossment.[46] His ceaselessly moving hands caressing his "enormous . . . whiskers," like the cyclical motion of his rocking, constitute a repetitive rather than a productive or goal-oriented physical movement, and signify his withdrawal from a progressive economy grounded in refined domesticity. "Mr. B——'s" autoerotic caresses, like the alcoholism to which Mary Clavers indirectly alludes, betray the self-absorption of excessive embodiment, and are clearly paired with his unconcern with personal appearance, with the social attributes of self (his hands are dirty, his dress disordered). Significantly, while the "young ladies" sit together, "Mr. B——" sits alone—further signaling his alienation from feminine domestic refinement. If the feminine spaces are inviting and suggest a wealth of as yet undisclosed pleasures, masculine spaces repel and "embarrass," such as the small bedroom whose door Mrs. Clavers opens but sees "in a moment that I ought not to have gone there, and [I] shut it again instantly" (75). The "hand of refined taste" in this household is decidedly feminine.

Like Cartwright's anecdote with which I began this chapter, Kirkland's depiction of the living situation of the "B——s" represents the struggle between women and men as a struggle to define and control the domestic landscape. Male authority within the home, obstinately maintained in the presence of the manifestly superior refinement of women, is imaged in both these sketches of domestic life as the principal obstacle to social harmony and collective improvement. But in much of *A New Home*, Kirkland borrows from the developing ideology of separate spheres to map the conflict between men and women across a broader social terrain. In *A New Home*'s configuration of separate spheres, the opposition between female civility and male savagery is grafted onto a spatial distinction between domesticity and marketplace.[47] Charting civilization and savagery along a shifting class as well as gender continuum, Kirkland presents civility as a political identification that must be renewed through regenerative contact with feminine, middle-class domesticity. It thus identifies the home as primary site for the production and performance of civil subjectivity and middle-class identity.

The excesses of the male marketplace ethos, defined as a concern with immediate monetary gain at the expense of all social and aesthetic values, are attacked throughout *A New Home*. In the third chapter, for instance, Mary Clavers consults with the man her husband has hired to oversee Montacute's construction about the location of the town's "grand esplanade": desiring that the native beauty of the place be preserved, she recommends that the "fine oaks" that "graced" the area be spared during clearing. Mr. Mazard heartily agrees, but his economic interests evidently get the better of him and, in the narrator's words, "these very trees were the first 'Banquos' at Montacute" (11). A woman's influence, Kirkland here suggests, is powerless to direct the economic desires of any but her own husband and is insufficiently efficacious to transform extradomestic, "male" social spaces.[48] Men's market appetites, the narrator indicates, undermine benevolence and sociability as well as material refinement: while women exhibit a "feeling of hostess-ship" toward new settlers, men "look upon each one, newly arrived, merely as an additional business-automaton—a somebody more with whom to try the race of enterprize, i.e. money-making" (64). These male excesses are crystallized in Kirkland's discussion of *speculation*, described as an "unvarying theme" in the settlements that "fill[ed] the whole soul of the community" (26).

In her representation of the "B——s," Kirkland demonstrated that men succumb all too readily to the dangers of bodily engrossment and coarseness. In her account of speculation, she shows that they are alienated in yet another way from collective "improvement." Bodily indulgence alienates through an immersion in private experience; excessive imagination alienates through its displacement of common experience with fantasies that bear no relation to the probable, or even the possible. Speculation in *A New Home* is depicted as a species of "madness" (4) to which men are especially susceptible, an imaginary, empty enterprise that creates the illusion of value through the trafficking in profitable fictions. Like earlier moralists, Kirkland represents imaginative excess as a feminine danger: her Miss Eloise Fidler, for instance, is an avid novel reader who mistakes a clerk with a French-sounding name for a "young duke" (106), and a second "Female Quixote," Cora Marsden, is dangerously addicted to romance until the responsibilities of marriage and, especially, motherhood bind her securely to her social world. But if seduction by the "dream[s] of . . . fancy" (98) is endemic to a stage of feminine development (both Eloise and Cora "vanquish" their "follies" [106] through marriage and motherhood), in *A New Home* it is *men*, not women, who dwell dangerously and persistently in the realm of unfettered imagination.

As Kirkland represents it, speculation is a realm of "bubble-bubble," entailing a "necromantic power" that makes "poverty seem riches, and idleness industry, and fraud enterprise" (121), a "tricksy spirit" that prompts men to see in marshland the prospect of a thriving city and to reproduce these images in "choicely worded and carefully vague" advertisements (31). Kirkland's attack on speculation borrows from the traditional language of eighteenth-century civic humanism: republican authors frequently denounced stock jobbers and "paper men" for inhabiting a capricious world of fantasy and credit incompatible with civic virtue, which by contrast was sustained by the landed independence of free citizens. For civic humanists, speculation exemplified the insubstantial, politically vitiating character of commerce and undermined the stability of civic personality.[49] But, crucially, Kirkland reconstitutes the language of civic humanism, and redefines speculation's dangers in expressly economic rather than political terms. In Kirkland's text, speculation is opposed not to civic virtue but to gradual, economic "improvement," an improvement principally marked by durable goods.

Facilitated by inflationary, "Wild Cat" (121) banking and credit expansion, speculation seems to generate value that leaves no trace in the world and is not folded back into material reality. In *A New Home*, speculation entails fetishizing money, detaching it from the realm of tangible benefit. In fact, money itself seems to Mary Clavers exceedingly abstract and "valueless" once severed from the possibility of present enjoyment: "Money has never seemed so valueless to me as since I have experienced how little it will buy in the woods" (120). If, in the "magic cauldron" of feverish masculine imagination "burr-oaks were turned into marble tables, tall tamaracks into draperied bedsteads, lakes into looking-glasses, and huge expanses of wet marsh into velvet couches" (121), in reality these visions never materialize. As the narrator notes, "Comforts do not seem to abound in proportion to landed increase, but often on the contrary, are really diminished for the sake of it: and the habit of selling out so frequently makes that *home*-feeling, which is so large an ingredient in happiness elsewhere, almost a nonentity in Michigan" (22). Since a man considers his farm "merely an article of trade" and "holds himself ready to accept the first advantageous offer" for its purchase, he is less likely to "provide those minor accommodations, which, though essential to domestic comfort, will not add to the moneyed value of his farm" (22). As opposed to the chimera of the "speculation mania" (121) and the insubstantial promises of distant pleasures, Kirkland promotes a "feminine" orientation toward immediate particularity and a sense of rootedness in palpable experience—as the narrator states, "the conviction of good accruing on a large scale does not prevent the wearing sense of minor deprivations" (147).[50] The problem with men, Kirkland suggests, is that in their commitment to capital accumulation they are alienated from present enjoyments; they "always looked hungry, but never took time to eat" (25). In particular, they are insensible to *refinement*, to the social and aesthetic pleasures durable goods extend and afford.

The duplicitous fictions of male speculation recall another species of imaginative excess which Kirkland repeatedly invokes: the fictions of frontier romance. This fledgling genre—which included such works as James Hall's *Legends of the West* (1832) and Charles Fenno Hoffman's *A Winter in the West* (1835)—offered what Kirkland calls "pictures, touched by the glowing pencil of fancy," romantic legends of frontier inhabitants and blissful depictions of pastoral fulfillment. As she notes in her opening chapter, "When I first 'penetrated the interior' (to use an indigenous phrase), all I knew of the wilds was from Hoffman's tour or Captain Hall's 'graphic' delineations: I had some floating idea of 'driving a barouche-and-four anywhere through the oak-openings'—and seeing 'the murdered Banquos of the forest' haunting the scenes of their departed strength and beauty. But I confess, these pictures . . . gave me but incorrect notions of a real journey through Michigan" (6). Kirkland represents these disembodied representations as a masculine currency, employed by popular authors such as Hall and Hoffman as well as more elite writers such as Emerson, whose 1836 essay, "Nature," similarly vitiated and etherialized nature's body. As I have suggested, Kirkland critiques and satirizes in her text a range of male frontier narrative topoi and forms. Along with the insubstantial fictions of male romance, she debunks, for instance, the frontier adventure narrative of the Daniel Boone variety, parodying it in her depiction of her husband's camping party, comprised of mainly city gentlemen, who venture out in search of wilderness exploits and good hunting but instead get lost, fail to track down dinner, and must take refuge in a Frenchman's dwelling (25–32). Like speculators' "golden dreams" which are drawn on barroom tables and "splendidly emblazoned" on sheets of paper, these masculine fictions and "sketches of western life," Kirkland suggests, are detached from material referents and bear no relation to material reality (5, 30, 49).

In the place of these "floating visions" (49), Kirkland attempts to " 'body forth' an unvarnished picture of the times" (120), a "sort of 'Emigrant's Guide' " (1) which, though its depictions have been "softened" and delicately colored in order to gratify and not offend, is firmly rooted in the real. *A New Home*'s realism was noted by her contemporaries, including Edgar Allan Poe—who applauded Kirkland's "fidelity," "vigor," and fresh treatment of Western materials—and the text was subsequently acknowledged by modern critics as pioneering in its verisimilitude.[51] Recently, Kirkland's text has been situated by feminist scholars within an entire tradition of antebellum women's realist narrative, a tradition long overlooked and, indeed, obscured by the conventions of literary analysis and periodization.[52] Kirkland's narrative can be located more precisely within the newly emerging genre of the village sketch or "local color," a genre which focuses on the details of daily living and on residents' personal histories to present the dynamics of a village as community and culture, and which has been primarily developed by women.[53] In the symbolic economy of the village sketch, imagination is employed to "improve" and refine without supplanting reality, adding to the world without displacing it. In its alignments of form and content, *A New Home* suggestively correlates the division of the literary landscape into the separate discursive spheres of "male" romance and "female" realism with a sexual division of characteristic economic practices.

Later in her career, Kirkland identified the hallmark of "the novel feminine" as its unromanticized, meticulous representation of everyday domestic life.[54] *A New Home* indicates that the realist texture of antebellum women's local color and realist writings was rooted at least in part in an expanding, partially secular belief in the psychological and social significance of common household objects and the import of these objects in the symbolic ecology of the self—an imaginative investment which decisively shaped the domestic realism of nineteenth-century women's fiction, and which would be most fully realized in the detailed depictions of domestic material culture in postbellum realist novels and the late-nineteenth-century regionalism of Sarah Orne Jewett and Mary Wilkins Freeman. In such texts, as in Kirkland's narrative, the home is sacralized as a sphere of regenerate sentiment, and domestic artifacts are endowed with characterological import and serve metonymically to designate "civilized," or fully "human," emotional states. Put slightly differently, the principal sign of civility in Kirkland's narrative—a "feminine" attentiveness to refined material shapes—is registered not only thematically, in the text's representations of the forms of civilized housekeeping, but also formally, in Kirkland's literary technique. *A New Home* suggests that, in antebellum America, domestic realism and consumer "refinement" were twinned material expressions of a woman's touch and feminine presence.

Dispensing Comforts and Arranging the "Attractions of Home": Caring for Things in Catharine Sedgwick's Fiction

Thus far, I have been concerned with how property objects became entangled, by the late eighteenth century, with the emotional culture of persons. In particular, I have charted out the material dimensions of liberal sentimentalism, and a model of middle-class subjectivity constituted by an intimate emotional engagement with domestic possessions. Alongside the prototypical liberal subject, rational and calculating economic man, I have placed *feminina economica,* not a producer but a consumer, whose emotional complexity and refinement—her "inner wealth"—are secured and elaborated through "object relations," through caring involvement with a select group of objects. This model of subjectivity is empiricist, insisting that an individual's personal endowments—intellectual and emotional—are established through *experience* and rooted in the sensuous immediacies of empirical life. Hannah Arendt observes that the individual "retrieves" his or her subjectivity through continuous relations with durable goods: in a discussion that replicates the sentimental assumptions this book analyzes, Arendt describes the nineteenth-century tendency to invest one's intimate surroundings with "a care and tenderness . . . in a world where rapid industrialization constantly kills off the things of yesterday to produce today's objects," stating that this "may even appear to be the world's last, purely humane corner."[55] Like the woman in the Pledge commercial who announces proudly, "I can see myself," in her freshly polished table (this, it seems, is the psychological payoff of housecleaning, of preserving the identity of things and *making them last*), the sentimental subject is produced and sustained by attachment to and caring for a limited, domestic world of goods. Indeed, as I demonstrate in chapter 1, the sentimental subject, constituted in the domestic performance of taste, is *dependent on* those sentimental performances for its very existence. Hers is the emotional payoff of liberal economics, her subjectivity its very mark and seal: following Scottish Enlightenment writers, antebellum advocates of free-market capitalism regularly insisted that in increasing one's commerce with persons and things, capitalism challenges one's solipsism and expands one's sympathies, improving and refining emotional subjectivity. By diversifying an individual's "object relations" and refining the objects of her or his care, free-market capitalism, they suggest, has transformed violent, war-making societies into peaceful ones, and economic progress is reflected in civility and new ideals of intersubjective propriety and gentleness.

This, of course, is the received view among modern historians: that, in Edward Shorter's words, capitalism is "at the root of [a] revolution in sentiment," which included the invention of domestic intimacy and the "romantic love complex."[56] The civilized subject, for these writers, is endowed with a wealth of feelings, an enlarged and refined emotional repertory, liberality of sentiment as well as the corresponding capacity to discriminate, to cherish chosen objects of affection and establish long-standing relations that are continually deepened and nuanced.[57] What I've been suggesting is that liberalism has supplied an emotional and sentimental, as well as a rational and utilitarian, justification for private property, in which the protection of one's economic assets is underwritten not so much by a right to self-interested and rational profit-making as by an imperative to enjoy one's intimate belongings at length with the confidence of secure proprietorship, and thus to increase one's attachments and expand one's emotional endowments. By conditioning the subjective, emotional involvement of persons in the world of goods, sentimentalism has, I believe, made capitalism "habitable" and, indeed, seem necessary for the constitution and preservation of subjectivity per se.

In this model of sentimental possession, the experience of objects *constitutes* the individual's subjective endowments, so that these things are interwoven with the emotions that they shape. It is thus that things are imagined as "part of oneself," and that such occurrences as personal theft—and even voluntary rituals of divestment like garage sales—can be experienced as a "violation." Objects and an individual's treatment of them—her commitment to keeping them clean and neat, her attentive grooming of them, her careful arrangement and placement of them "just so"—ratifies her subjectivity as indexes of her emotional endowments, and produces and performs her capacity to "care." I use the word "care" here in both its senses, in terms of valuing something (caring about) and acting to preserve its well-being (caring for): at stake is a model of sentimental cherishing, a species of what Sara Ruddick has called "preservative love," in which the continued existence of beloved objects is essential to the subject's personal growth and emotional development. The sentimental subject can make a "commitment," and works to maintain and foster the relationships in which it is woven.[58] This emotional dynamic has often been viewed as part of a normative narrative of psychological "development": for psychologists, beloved objects guide the self beyond solipsism, and, in inspiring new feelings and desires and supplying new things to care for, they become themselves invested with these emotions.[59] They thus act as what psychoanalysts call "transitional objects," lifting the affections beyond the enclosure of self and ultimately transferring them to an intimate world of others. But rather than psychologize these property relations as inevitable expressions of "normal" self-formation, I wish here to emphasize their *performative* function: in particular I wish to stress how the "treatment" of domestic possessions occasions and renders habitual the (repeated) performance of the proprietary emotions that define subjectivity itself. Indeed, the attachment to things seen in sentimental cherishing is not an expression of an inherent emotional capacity or need; rather, it is partly *produced* by subjects' constitutive, formative dependency on the objects/materials of this performance.[60] The sentimental subject is "conservative" in the root sense of the term, hating to throw anything away (she is a sentimental version of the frugal housewife, husbanding her family's emotional resources), an avid saver of "baby's firsts" and a collector of mementos; and if there is a tension between conservation and improvement, preservation and growth in her household, it is partly resolved by the use of attics and trunks, not to mention lots of closet space.

One consumer artifact was considered especially effective in what was termed the "culture of the heart"—and that was the novel. As Steven Mintz observes, novels in antebellum America were being invested with a "new psychological and ideological significance," that of shaping moral standards and cultivating emotional sensibility. Antebellum moralists and pedagogues, increasingly less sanguine about the power of reason to guide the self in its choices and actions, typically stressed the importance of cultivating the emotions and directing them toward rational and moral ends, and looked to literature as a psychological device for fostering cultured feelings. Even the conservative Congregationalist minister Lyman Beecher advocated reading fiction on the grounds that it refines the emotions, elevates the sensibilities, and improves the tastes.[61] Narrative was widely viewed as a more effective instrument of moral and aesthetic instruction than the pronouncement of legalistic prescriptions, because it could engage and transform readerly emotions, cultivating a love of the good and the beautiful rather than a rational understanding of the identity of virtue and beauty; consequently, advice literature frequently featured case histories of virtuous and vicious characters, not so much to illustrate moral precepts as to encourage readers' proper feeling toward them.[62] The conventional distinction between intellectual and emotional cultivation, between fostering the rational apprehension of truth and encouraging what one author famously called "feeling right," was often conceptualized in terms of a gender division of labor: antislavery writer Hinton Rowan Helper, for instance, comparing his book of slavery statistics to Stowe's *Uncle Tom's Cabin*, wrote that "it is all well enough for women to give the fictions of slavery; men should give the facts."[63] If, as Nancy Armstrong has suggested, "the reading of fiction came to play an indispensable role in directing desire at certain objects in the world," the project of thus directing desire was being construed as the special province of women.[64]

The perceived pedagogical value of narrative is perhaps best illustrated by the numerous antebellum texts that it is difficult to classify as either advice manuals or fiction: apparently marketed as novels, these narratives of domestic living read as guides to domestic economy and home management, offering attenuated, barely visible plots and little sense of dramatic heightening and resolution. One such narrative was Catharine Maria Sedgwick's short novel *Home*. Described by contemporary literary critics as "America's most influential female novelist before Harriet Beecher Stowe" and "the pioneer" of antebellum women novelists, Catharine Sedgwick was one of the nation's first professional women of letters, and, according to most assessments, its most popular female novelist in the 1820s and 1830s.[65] The daugher of prominent Federalist politician and attorney Theodore Sedgwick, and related through her mother to the Dwight and Stoddard families of the Connecticut River valley, Catharine Sedgwick was a prison reformer who turned to writing in 1821; *A New-England Tale*, the first of seven novels, appeared the following year. Sedgwick's fifth novel, *Home*, first published in 1835, was phenomenally popular, appearing in twelve editions in two years, and by 1846 was in its twentieth. As I suggest below, Sedgwick was in temperament a very different writer from Kirkland: while Kirkland, a genteel Unitarian, writes with confidence in the Whig narrative of social "progress" and its forms of civilized agency, Sedgwick, influenced by her father's Federalism and the evangelical emotionalism of the Second Great Awakening, exhibited less faith in the power of liberal agency and its forms of emotional discipline. Indeed, *Home* registers "regressive" identifications and emotions (such as a nostalgia for lost wholeness that threatens to overwhelm the self, and irrepressible eruptions of male aggression and sadistic desire that threaten "civilized" social relations) that are foreclosed or managed in Kirkland's narrative. Inscribing these desires, Sedgwick also makes legible the psychic forms of gender and power (of masculine dominance and feminine submission) central to sentimental ownership and its institutional location in domesticity.

Helena Michie has observed that Sedgwick's use of domestic and maternal metaphors to describe her literary enterprise "collaps[es] the literary into the domestic" and constitutes a means of legitimizing the labor of writing.[66] These metaphors also mark the literary endeavor as extending the invisible labor of domestic influence — and the socializing force of feminine sympathy — beyond the circle of a writer's immediate associates. According to the narrator of *Home*, books effect an intimate, engaging communication, transforming "the spirits of the departed" and physically distant into "our familiar companions and instructors"; in the words of one sentimental review, books are "members of the family" — an anthropomorphizing metaphor that suggests how the moral justification of fiction-reading was often performed by assimilating it into the affectional structures of domesticity and its norms of proprietary authority. In sentimental literary culture, fictional characters, objects of identification and affection, would appear to instate the identificatory dynamic of sentimental subjection: a sympathetic identification with textual objects of affection that is at once an expression of proprietary desire.[67] In *Home*, Sedgwick documents complex emotional endowments of the sentimental subject that her text, in effect, works to constitute. The novel thematizes the power of sentimental ownership and the inscription of objects with affectional and psychological significance.

The narrative is in many ways a phenomenology of sentimental possession. It is structured by a thematics of nostalgia and loss: in *Home*'s opening pages, we learn that the central character, William Barclay, has lost his rural childhood home; now, as a young man, his vivid memory of that early object of affection fuels his lifelong desire to recover it. William Barclay is Sedgwick's response to European critics who had contended that Americans lack the delicacies of "home feeling" because they are consumed with the "fire of enterprise" (116). As a child, William had "knit his heart" to the "old fashioned parsonage" (3, 2), but on his grandfather's death, Greenbrook is sold, and William and his mother, the penniless "widow" of a once-prospering merchant, "shifted about . . . from pillar to post" to live with various friends, and were successively uprooted "according to the liberality or convenience of their patrons" (2, 5, 3). The novel highlights the psychological necessity and fragility of an individual's attachments to things and represents property objects as thoroughly interwoven with sentimental subjectivity; it simultaneously illuminates the sentimental impulse to secure species of property (such as the souvenir, the token, the photograph, the letter) whose value seems strictly personal, and which thus approaches the inalienability of memory, magically designating particular objects that cannot be stolen or "re-possessed." Unlike Kirkland's Whiggish narrative of progress on the frontier through the reproduction and advance of feminine taste, Sedgwick's narrative is infused with nostalgia, with a compulsive return to the subject's sentimental "origins" and a defensive fantasy of the restoration of lost wholeness. The market in *Home* appears as a mechanism governed by impersonal laws that radically restrict one's emotional experience of things, reducing their worth to the single index of cash value; the market is a realm from which one "rescues" things. The narrative is motivated by William's efforts to rescue the lost object of his affections, and delineates the obstacles—in particular, his business partner's unscrupulous practices that lead to his near-bankruptcy—placed in his way. The narrative justice of William Barclay's return to his long-lost home at the end of the text is defined less by the conventions of exchange (he has earned enough to buy it back) than by the sentimental imperative to retrieve what has been loved and lost. No one but William, Sedgwick implies, can sufficiently care for, and thus deserve, his ancestral home.

The house in sentimentalism is sanctified as a privileged object of attachment: as shelter for the individual's most intimate objects of affection as well as a monument to familial love, often remaining in the family's possession for generations, it is laden with a wealth of associations and emotions; as a result it is often accorded a "personality." William's love of his childhood home is not a fixation—it is not, in the language of the 1830s, "monomaniacal": since, according to Sedgwick, "the affections are given to us for activity and diffusion" (138), such brooding would entail a selfish hoarding of feeling. Instead, William's love for Greenbrook is the patient but committed desire of a "yearning heart" (76), one which accommodates, and leaves him emotionally available to, present objects of concern and care. That William's yearning doesn't monopolize his attention and occlude "all the charities of social life" (119) is evident in his readiness to make "sacrifices": the family takes in two orphans, for instance, though this delays their return to Greenbrook. Importantly, when finally reunited, both have changed: William is the father of a large family, and Greenbrook has been remodeled, looking to William like "an old friend in new apparel" (115). The forms of proprietary intimacy are deepened, rather than compromised, by William's earlier loss. Indeed, the enforced separation of William from Greenbrook—like the enforced separation of families conspicuous in so many nineteenth-century novels—occasions the dramatic performance of that original proprietary bond, and highlights its magical reconstruction or return as at once "voluntary" and inevitable.

Circumscribing the space closest to the self and constituting the realm in which the affections are concentrated, the house, I have suggested, played a crucial role in the emotional culture of persons. As a result, antebellum moralists frequently asserted the need to make the home "attractive" in order to appeal to and engage the subject's feelings;

the result was a consumer movement legitimating domestic aestheticism, which Neil Harris has called the antebellum home "beautification movement." By enlisting and developing the emotions, beautiful domestic surroundings were seen to promote aesthetic as well as social sensibility; according to Gervase Wheeler, making one's home "pleasant and beautiful" supplies a "wholesome influence," "attach[ing] the heart[s]" of family members so that "the inducement to wander from it would have but little power." He recommends the transformation of utilitiarian structures into "cheerful, smiling homes of the heart."[68] Sedgwick's William Barclay, for instance, favors the domestic incorporation of "whatever will increase the attractions of . . . home, and tend to raise [the family] above coarse pleasures" (35). By developing rather than deadening the self's emotional sensibilities and thus endearing home to self, pleasing domestic objects would extend and refine the subject's emotional repertory.

If antebellum moralists were concerned with making the home attractive, they were equally concerned with making the home comfortable. The nineteenth century witnessed what has been called the "democratization of comfort" in the middle-class home: in the 1830s, for instance, one species of goods still deemed essential to domestic comfort—upholstered furniture—was quickly becoming a "middle-class decency."[69] As Max Weber suggested, comfort was a privileged term in Puritanism, signifiying a middle ground between monastic asceticism and material indulgence, both of which were seen to entail an excessive preoccupation with the body. Comfort was associated with a "neutral" physiological state in which consciousness was freed to attend to divine truths. In the antebellum period, when Protestant theology was increasingly concerned with social obligation and secular human fulfillment, comfort was reconceived as the material basis of social consciousness.[70] By relieving the body of its privatizing pains and discomforts, sensations which, in the words of Lydia Maria Child, "block up the avenues of charity," comfort was seen to free the self to emotionally engage with, and care for, other people. According to one nineteenth-century commentator, "The popularity of comfortable furniture . . . goes a great deal toward civilizing the people generally. It seems to us impossible for the human race to be good-natured and good tempered if forced to sit in a 'bolt upright' position in the extreme corner of a horse-hair covered sofa, with arms and back built on the very straightest and most perpendicular principle. . . . It is not surprising that our forefathers were given to atrocities and cruelties when they were brought up to endure such tortures as could be inflicted by the furniture of even twenty years ago; it served to deaden the sensibilities."[71] Uncomfortable seating, like corporal punishment, was deemed unacceptable during the period because fraught with moral danger: domestic discomfort "hardens" the self, restricting one's sympathies so that one easily inflicts pain on others because one is insensible to their feelings.[72] Comforts are essential to the emotional culture of sentimentalism: expressions of care, they are distributed to ensure that the comforted self can care in return.

William Barclay's "strong love of birthplace" (116) derives in part from the rural location of the "old parsonage" (76). Urban living posed a grave danger for antebellum moralists: due to the abundance of things competing for one's attention, none are fully experienced; emotional involvement gives way to the detachment of spectacle. According to William Barclay, overstimulated city dwellers, their sensibilities deadened, no longer found "excitement" in a berrying frolic or a neighbor's twin lambs, and must instead seek pleasure in the exotic and the sensational, such as the attractions of "Scudder's Museum" or the otherworldly performance of "a mysterious or invisible lady" (118). In the country, "the social electric chain is bound so closely that the vibration of every touch is felt" and the "intrinsic [value] of each individual . . . known" and appreciated (120, 117); and the simple pleasures of nature "minister to" by engaging the affections (117). Nature in sentimental texts is a pastoral nature, a nature rendered intimate and familiar through metaphor; it is, in the language of aesthetic theory, a beautiful and not a sublime nature, reaffirming and not challenging socialized subjectivity. When the sentimental subject enters the natural world, her experience is neither romantic confrontation nor Adamic flight: she finds not a howling wilderness but a "smiling field" decorated, perhaps, by delicate flowers, and populated by a duck with her brood, the industrious spider, the busy bee, an ant colony. Sentimentalism entails a structure of psychic identification through which potentially alien natural objects are "recognized" and "identified with"; and sentimental nature would often be incorporated into the domestic environment in the form of houseplants, flowers, or curious bits of nature displayed in a Wardian case or on an etagère or pier table. The sentimental anthropomorphizing of nature—a characteristic of nineteenth-century nature-loving more generally, and a principal feature of the antebellum taste for natural history—is quite explicit in William Barclay's description of a brook that "winds through a lovely meadow, and then stretches round a rocky peninsula,—curving in and out, and lingering as if it had a human heart and loved that which it enriched" (2); nature is endowed with human feeling and care. Several historians have suggested that the sentimental familiarizing of the natural world—which diminished nature's otherness, and constituted a way of psychologically annexing natural objects to self—did much to underwrite the industrial appropriation of nature; Siegfried Giedion, for instance, writes of the willingness of anthropocentric nature before the machine.[73] However, as in Kirkland's text, the sentimental anthropomorphizing of nature could underwrite a preservative or conservationist impulse, entailing the insistence that natural objects should be preserved in their integrity so that we can continue to care for them, an impulse clearly legible in the antebellum beautification movements—such as the park and rural cemetery movements—which protected nature from the ravages of industry and the spirit of "grasping accumulation."[74] Importantly, technology's handmaid, science, is associated in Sedgwick's text with an impoverished sensibility, with distanciation rather than involvement, a coldness that entails not caring enough about what one sees and that reduces the wealth of psychic associations to the narrow dimension of cause and effect; as William Barclay advises his son Willie, for example, it is good to seek "the reason of the thing" unless "you are so brimful of satisfaction that nothing can add to it" (117). Sentimentalism's psychic structures of sympathetic identification could thus confer value on the integrity of natural forms and ensure that they would not be subordinated to "mere" physical uses; nature will not be treated as a "thing." In *Home*, the stable, sustained existence of natural objects prompts and develops William's capacity to care, and natural objects serve as vessels through which he learns to love God (he loved "to commune with God in his works" [3]) and other people (his love of nature "knit his heart to [the] home of his childhood" [3]). And in this process of emotional expansion and growth, his mother's place is central: it is through her "leading" that William is made receptive to the charms of "natural beauty," and through them, "the social spirit of the Christian religion" (119).

The mother plays a crucial role in sentimentalism: as the original object of affections—the "object" *that one can't remember not being there*—she is literally the sentimental subject's opening on the world. By the 1830s, as numerous historians have documented, the mother was widely assigned the crucial task of overseeing and guiding the emotional culture of young children in the years before reason reached its maturity, a task for which she was deemed especially equipped not only because of her physical availability while father was off at work, but also because of her emotional availability and sensitivity—what Sedgwick describes as her "inspiration" in performing the "delicate office" of "find[ing] the clue that leads through the labyrinth of another's heart" (132)—and the natural strength of the mother-child attachment. Because of the very intensity of that bond, the mother could lead children to internalize more completely any standards given them and to love, in effect, what she loves.[75] The mother's capacity to engage and direct the child's desires and values was widely known during the period as "influence," a form of authority so subtly and habitually exercised as to be both imperceptible and irresistible.[76] As I suggest above, "influence" is an antebellum rhetoric of feminine proprietorship, engendering the liberal identificatory dynamic of subordination and agency. Maternal influence should manage what Sedgwick called the "humble, womanly task of directing [the children's] domestic affections" (64) by supplying objects of affection that could not fail to please. In the domestic environment, influence was exercised through the "silent and gentle force of example" (122) as well as the careful selection of pleasing domestic objects: endowed with civilizing agency, domestic objects embody the ambiguities of femininity, extending maternal influence beyond the realm of bodily presence. According to Sedgwick, the mother oversees the sentimental economy, the cultivation of the emotional resources, of the family: "How she sees and foresees, provides against all wants, avoids irritations and jealousies, economizes happiness, saving those little odds and ends that others waste. How she employs the faculties of all, brings the virtue of each into operation, and if she cannot cure, shelters faults. She shows each in the best light, and is herself the light that shines on all,—the sun of her *home*" (123).

In *Home*, William's devoted mother plays a crucial part in her son's sentimental education, and love opens outward from the early attachments through which she guides him. When Greenbrook is sold, and William and his mother were compelled to leave it, they felt much as "might our first parents, when from Paradise they 'took their solitary way' " (3); stripped of his original objects of care, William's sense of loss is tempered by his friendship with, and eventual marriage to, his Greenbrook neighbor Anne Hyde. "Very early (so early that it seemed to him as a morning dream) the tenant and joint proprietor of all William Barclay's castles in the air" (12), Anne Hyde, as the novel opens, becomes the joint tenant of his home. For her part, William "seemed to her, in the memory of her childhood, to run, like a golden thread, through all its web" (12) so that "she could not remember . . . the time when she did not love him" (13). The two are knit together by early experiences and memories of incidental kindnesses, like the cold day he left a skating party to "drag her home on his sled," and the "unlucky day" when, after spilling a basket of strawberries, he "refilled her basket from his" (12). Like the nineteenth-century "ruling style," sentimentalism locates the attractive and the desirable in the most ordinary and familiar objects and inscribes them with "depth"; thus, the quasi-incestuous nature of sentimental love relations: the beloved object of affections is often a member of one's own household, or, as in this case, the girl next door, a liminal figure that both is and is not a family member. In the case of Anne Hyde, "affection had grown with their growth" (13), and their sympathetic union is so perfectly fulfilled that their legal union seems inevitable and natural.

William and Anne's intimacy is perfected because they care for the same things: William's mother's happiness is wife Anne's "first care" (7); and William Barclay can independently select and furnish the house the couple will move into because he is intimately acquainted with his wife's taste. But it is Anne's approval and woman's touch that establishes the value of this structure as home. In fact, the novel's opening scene, in which William and Anne visit together for the first time the "small, newly-built, two-story house in Greenwich Street" (4), reads like a test of the sentimental woman's inner resources. William worries out loud that the house is too small and that his wife will inevitably "contrast this little dwelling with [her] father's spacious house" (5) and compare its small New York yard with the "golden harvests" and "beautiful view . . . of mountain and meadow" offered by her paternal homestead. But to William's observation that the "parlor is scarcely big enough to turn in," Anne responds that "it struck me as just of the right size. I always had a fancy for a snug parlor. Nothing looks so forlorn as a large, desolate, cold, half-furnished, shabby parlor," and she assures William that "I will try my best to make the small one agreeable" (6). Anne's response illuminates the necessary resourcefulness of the sentimental subject: because of the complexity of her emotional endowments, she can find something to care about in everything and make emotional capital out of apparent waste; a measure of this faculty is Anne's desire to savor by retelling again and again the story of the "long and checkered track by which Providence had led" the couple to marriage, as well as her capacity to appreciate, "after an instant's survey," the "neat" bureau, the "nice little closet," and "what a blessing!—a grate too!" in a bedroom that William has complained contains an "ugly jut" (6). Performing her superior taste and delicacy of sentiment, Anne, in a ritual of sentimental heterosexuality, successfully "converts" William to her views. The chapter concludes with William's apparent satisfaction in Anne's response and his renewed pleasures in his domestic surroundings. The virtuous woman views nothing with indifference and makes the best of what she has, ensuring that no detail, no matter how small, goes overlooked and unappreciated.

William and Anne's intimate dwelling is furnished with an eye to "substantial comforts": "ample stores of household linen, fine mattrasses [*sic*], as nice an apparatus for ablutions as a disciple of Combe could wish, jugs, basins, and tubs large enough, if not to silence, to drown a travelling Englishman," as well as "a book-case filled with well selected and well bound volumes" (8). Books, according to William, are "productive capital, from which we may derive exhaustless pleasure which hundreds may share, and which those who come after us may enjoy" (10); "instructive and entertaining" (11), they are objects that, through attentive familiarity, continue to sustain an individual's interest and gratify her taste for novelty. As the "best productions of the best minds" and endowed with "living and immortal souls" (10), they afford, in their complexity, a wealth of private experience; in the words of the twentieth-century sentimentalist and greeting card designer Mary Engelbreit, "A book is a present you can open again and again."[77] Some books are reserved for Martha, the domestic, with an eye to "improv[ing]" her mind and heart (11): such gifts integrate her fully into the family through the cultivation of shared sentiments and tastes. Like Kirkland, Sedgwick envisions the performance of domestic taste as a vehicle for socializing lower-class individuals (here, a domestic servant), enlisting their "consent" to the civilizing sentiments of ownership. William Barclay concisely articulates the text's synthesis of sympathetic identification and authoritarian control: "Every wise provision for [servants'] happiness multiplies the chances of their attachment and fidelity" (11). Anne Barclay, too, is concerned with Martha's pleasure, noting with satisfaction that the kitchen is not a dark and dismal "New York cellar kitchen" but a room on the main floor, and claiming that "home should be the sweetest of all words even to the humblest member of a family" (8).

In *Live and Let Live*, Sedgwick expressly defines proper management of servants as a species of "home missionary work," an opportunity to apply improving benevolence to the domestic and, through her, to all the poor. The narrative's exemplary domestic supervisor, revealingly named Mrs. Hyde, aims through her efforts "to qualify those she employed for the happier condition that probably awaited them—to be the masters and mistresses of independent homes." *Live and Let Live* envisions the deployment of cross-class, gender identification, cast in a developmental narrative at once psychological, moral, and historical, in order to mobilize workers' "consent" to submission and forms of labor discipline.[78] In *Home*, Anne and William both intend that the household should "present as perfect an image of heaven, as the infirmity of human nature, and the imperfections in the constitution of human affairs, would admit" (14). The remainder of the narrative is meant to disclose how fully their efforts succeed.

The text depicts a series of crises threatening the "bonds of natural affection and Christian love" (102), crises surmounted by a resurgence of "humane" feeling; indeed, such crises occasion the performance of sentimental sympathy and promote forms of readerly identification, through which "civilized" subjects are constituted. The first of such crises comes when Wallace Barclay, in a fit of youthful rage, responds to his baby sister's destruction of his beloved kite, which she has transformed into a ruff for her pet Maltese kitten, by placing the animal in a pot of scalding water. What Mr. Barclay calls his son's "violence towards such a dear good little girl as [Haddy], and murderous cruelty to an innocent animal" (18) is answered by a "few weeks' confinement" (20) in his room and the following stern words: "Go to your own room, Wallace. . . . You have forfeited your right to a place among us. Creatures who are the slaves of passions, are, like beasts of prey, fit only for solitude" (17). Aligning "slaves of passion" with "beasts of prey" (characteristic of the state of savagery), the scene makes explicit the forms of psychological self-control that, for the liberal civil(ized) subject, constitute (indeed, *feel like*) "freedom"; it also suggests that those subjective forms are exemplified in a relatively recent practice that has generated a multi-billion-dollar consumer industry: the keeping of pets. Gilles Aillaud describes pet-keeping as "part of that universal but personal withdrawal into the private small family unit, decorated or furnished with mementoes from the outside world, which is such a distinguishing feature of consumer societies"; as a form of property that its owner "identifies" with and that calls forth her capacity to love and cherish, the pet is an exemplary object of sentimental proprietorship.[79] Significantly, many contemporary Anglo-American psychologists continue to invest in the emotional value of pet-keeping: pets, widely seen to help children learn gentleness and responsibility and to help young couples prepare for parenthood, are used in many kinds of psychotherapy and family therapy. Wallace's act violates a number of sentimental taboos: he doesn't appreciate his family's feelings (the "one lesson" his siblings learn is "if you commit sin . . . all that love you must suffer with you" [18]), and he doesn't appreciate his sister's feelings and the things she cares about (his action expresses "violence towards such a dear good little girl" [18]). Finally, he doesn't appreciate the kitten's feelings and pains: he treats the pet like something Other — like an *animal*, and, more specifically, in a way *pets* are never to be treated, like food.[80] Elder brother Charles, "at the risk of his own hand, rescued the kitten," his own pain easily exchanged to amend the kitten's insensitive treatment; "but seeing its agony" he sympathetically and "with most characteristic consideration . . . gently dropped it in again, and thus put the speediest termination to its sufferings" (17). Even little Haddy, whose "tender heart" is "touched" by her brother's apparent misery, says appealingly, "I guess you did not mean to, did you, Wally?" (17), indicating a desire to sympathize with even a bestial (domestic) Other that suggests the kitten has served its function well. A rhetorical performance that fuses the descriptive and the prescriptive, Haddy's plea facilitates a sibling version of the ritual of heterosexual seduction the Scots narrate: "little Haddy's" performance derives its sentimental and erotic appeal—its "cuteness"—from her sex as well as her dependency, explicitly framed as it is by the threat of her brother's physical power and violence.[81] Wallace, whose passionate rashness has constituted a drastic act of selfishness that has alienated him from sentimental involvement, is sent to his room, a physical replication of his psychological state and a form of domestic captivity that will, his parents hope, mobilize his "consent" to familial forms of affectional discipline. His punishment is also a form of moral quarantining, for, as Mrs. Barclay states, "How much worse" than physical illness is "a moral disease!" (20).

The emotional culture of sentimental subjectivity entails the expansion of sympathy, the capacity to care for an increasing array of persons and things so that all are bound together by the "vivifying spirit of love" (110). Sedgwick envisions a millennial future of universal sympathy and harmony, when "the terrestrial shall put on the celestial" (111) and the "tie of human brotherhood [will be] felt [all] through the social circle" (117). But that emotional culture also entailed the development of taste and the refinement of feeling, which during the antebellum period chiefly signified "uplift," the orientation of one's desires toward objects that gratify "refined" (e.g., social, aesthetic, religious) wants.[82] The indulgence of bodily appetite was aligned with an unfeeling solipsism, constituting an immersion in private experience that entailed a radical constriction of sympathy. This is the significance of the sentimentalist cult of mourning: the death of a loved one supplied a crucial occasion for emotional pedagogy: purifying an individual's attachments of sensual desire, the disappearance of the flesh could refine and elevate emotions and purge them of what was commonly termed "mere animal attachment."[83] For Sedgwick, dining in particular constitutes "an important item in *home* education" (27), an occasion for taming the animal within, called in *Home* the "monster appetite" (33).[84] After Wallace is sent to his room, the family convenes in the dining room; but they eat that night with limited enjoyment. The parents' sadness is conveyed like an "infection," and "scarcely a word was said above a whisper. There was a favorite dish on the table, followed by a nice pudding. They were eaten, not enjoyed. The children realized that it was not the good things they had to eat, but the kind looks, the innocent laugh, and cheerful voice, that made the pleasure of the social meal" (18). Wallace, eating in his room, finds " 'how different [his dinner] tastes from what it does at table!' and though he did not put it precisely in that form, he felt what it was that 'sanctified the food' " (19). The sacramental nature of the middle-class family meal derives from the love and social regard the food is meant to embody. Since the gratifications of "appetite . . . were felt to be inferior pleasures,—to be enjoyed socially and gratefully, but forbearingly" (33), the Barclays regard meals as "something more than means of sustaining physical wants,—as opportunities of improvement and social happiness" (28), a chance to "develope [*sic*] the mind by conversation, and cultivate refined manners" (28). In an important sense, the meal ritually enacts this distinction: food is inscribed as the medium of social affection. After two weeks of solitary confinement, during which his "affectionate heart" gains ascendancy over his "passionate temper" (18), Wallace is restored to the family, his reintegration completed by being welcomed to a table set with "scrupulous" care (28), served by an attentive sister who selects for her brother his favorite foods and brushes his place with "double pains," and offered his siblings' portions of the strawberries they've been given for dessert (31).

The second crisis facing the Barclays is a business crisis: Mr. Barclay's elder partner in his printing firm, Mr. Norton, had independently endorsed the business ventures of his son John, who had invested in mercantile concerns and, in the narrator's words, "had plunged deeply into that species of gaming called *speculation*" (81) to support an extravagant lifestyle. John loses everything in the fluctuating market, and tragically commits suicide; his father's death closely follows. Norton and Co. is liable for John Norton's debts, and Barclay loses all his capital but the printing presses. As a result, the move back to Greenbrook—which had recently been placed on the market and purchased by Barclay—is delayed indefinitely. Old Norton's younger son, Harry, a frequent visitor to the Barclays, delivers the news of John's death on Christmas morning; and while "it certainly was a severe disappointment to have the accumulations of years of vigorous labor swept away from him by the profligacy of others,—to have his dearest plans thwarted at the moment of their accomplishment," Barclay bears the disappointment bravely and visits Old Norton on his deathbed in the Christian spirit of "forgiveness and infinite compassion" (85).

Speculation was amost universally denounced in antebellum America; the antispeculation rhetoric of civic humanism was employed by both Whigs and Jacksonians during the period. In sentimental texts, however, speculation appears not so much as a threat to political virtue, as in civic humanism, but as an unsurpassed form of selfishness that puts one's family's treasured possessions at risk and endangers the security of sustained proprietorship; its horrifying outcome is conventionally the furniture sale, in which beloved objects are exposed before the unfeeling gaze of strangers, and sentimental value reduced to cash value.[85] Like the restless vagabond with whom he was frequently compared, the itinerant speculator represents a danger to society because of his refusal to care for things. The Nortons' extravagance similarly marks them as superficial and emotionally impoverished. Certainly, the shame of monetary waste is legible in Sedgwick's account of their lavish lifestyle, particularly in her description of the aftermath of their Christmas Eve party, a veritable orgy of conspicuous consumption: "Some of the lamps were still burning, or smoking in their sockets. . . . There still stood the relics of the feast—fragments of perigord pies, drooping flowers, broken pyramids, and piles—literally piles—of empty champagne bottles; an enormous whisky-punch bowl, drained to the last drop, stood in a niche in the entry" (82). But in Sedgwick's account, an additional, psychological connotation is legible: the slave of fashion, due to the promiscuous nature of her attachments, doesn't have time to bond. John Norton's wife, "a poor stylish girl, who immediately [upon marriage] introduced her notions of high life into her father-in-law's house" (79), is represented as cold and insensible; having taken up Old Norton's youngest child, Emily, as a favorite, removing her from all her old associates and "inducting [her] into a genteel circle" (80), she betrays how little she really feels for Emily by abandoning her after the family crisis. Mrs. John Norton, Sedgwick implies, has used Emily: instead of sympathizing with her, she has treated her as a doll, as a thing. But for Emily the family's financial crisis is a fortunate fall, and provides a conversion experience: stripped of objects—she sells even "her little trinkets . . . her watch, her gold chain, and her real enamel buckle" (93) to pay her chambermaid—her "heart is melted" (93) and rendered susceptible to the Barclays' loving care. The Barclays determine to take Emily in, offering in the place of insignificant baubles objects worthy of her esteem.

Emily's entry into the family precipitates its most difficult crisis, one surmounted and resolved by a final surge of sympathy. In a chapter entitled "Cross-Purposes," Sedgwick reveals that some ten years after Emily's arrival, both Charles and Wallace Barclay have fallen in love with her. According to the narrator, "Nothing was more natural, than that an intimate intercourse with a girl very lovely in person and character, and attractive in manners, should excite their affections, and that affection in the boy should ripen into love in the man" (129). The young men's "jarring hopes" (129) are reconciled and their love "unimpaired" (129, 133), but the resolution of the narrative's attenuated love-plot foregrounds the political complexity of sentimental gender constructions. William Barclay and his son Charles, with whom he closely identifies and feels bound in "perfect sympathy" (153), are represented by Sedgwick as true gentlemen, part of an American "natural aristocracy"; they are also depicted in *Home* as feminine. Charles's patience and gentle service to his family—we first see him, for instance, holding a skein of yarn for his grandmother to wind—are represented by Sedgwick as "most *unboyish*" (16); and sensitivity and tenderness are coded throughout the text as "feminine" gifts (e.g., 126). The fiery and passionate Wallace is the text's single "boyish" male, and Sedgwick features him in just two scenes: one is the kitten episode, and the other follows the revelation of Charles's love for Emily, and depicts Wallace as he wanders in impassioned self-absorption through the garden and unwittingly snaps the heads off the carnations that Charles has planted and tended for Emily's pleasure. And importantly, Wallace, who is attracted to Emily in part because of her passivity and because her heart "takes any impression you please to put upon it" (93), gets the girl. By presenting male brutality and insensibility as the incitement to feminine affection, Sedgwick's text here (as throughout Wallace's characterization) replicates the Scottish narrative of civilized heterosociality, a heterosocial dynamic produced within the sympathetic bonds of domestic intimacy; it also foregrounds the omnipresent threat of male violence that is both necessitated by and managed within the sympathetic performance of that relation. Indeed, as in Susan Warner's *The Wide, Wide World* (which includes a memorable incident in which the heroine, Ellen Montgomery, observes her future husband, John, beat someone up for her as a prelude to their courtship), Sedgwick's text registers a violent subtext often present in sentimental novels, which threatens to disrupt the text's representation of heterosocial domestic harmony.[86] In pairing Wallace and Emily, Sedgwick is clearly implying that the temperamental Wallace needs a good woman's influence more than Charles does; and certainly that even a kitten-cooker like Wallace is not insensible to what Effie Barclay calls the lesson Emily "teach[es] best,—and without seeming to try": the lesson of loving her (125). Sedgwick is also testifying to Emily's wealth of being, that she can see the good in the Barclays' temperamental son. But although Sedgwick wishes to present feminine sympathy as an inescapable social(izing) force, the threat of male imperviousness to a good woman's care haunts the novel. Numerous texts by antebellum women (including many temperance narratives) documented the abuses suffered by women at the hands of unfeeling and unregenerate husbands. Lurking near the surface of sentimental texts such as Sedgwick's is the threat of male physical and institutional power. Although *Home* seemingly invests in the sentimental utopia of universal care and harmony, the millennial incarnation of heaven on earth, when the "social spirit of the Christian religion" will prevail and "society will only be an extension of the intercourse of home" (119), the text also suggests the inadequacy of "influence" and emotional cultivation as a form of female power. Since a woman cannot force a man to care, "normal" heterosexuality can easily degenerate into abuse. Although Sedgwick insists on the social sufficiency of the private sphere and the power of "*home* influences" to "reform the world" (63, 60), the text at moments pointedly exposes the relations of power that undergird sentimental paternalism, and arguably points toward the need for legal and political reform as a means to compensate for a potential scarcity of sympathy. Thus, while Kirkland envisions a social world where progress and the civilizing ministrations of feminine taste are inevitably victorious, Sedgwick's less sanguine vision of the power of liberal agency and self-control is registered both in the pull of the past (nostalgia) and its power to overwhelm the present, and in the recurring threat of "enslavement" to (male) passion that repeatedly surfaces in the novel.

The brothers' rivalry tests their love, but does not threaten it: sympathy overcomes discord, proving that the market ethos of competition is no match for the "*home* cultivation of the affections" (134). The event and its aftermath convince Charles to move west: the desire for "possession of [Emily's] pure and tender heart" had "shaped the plan of his life" (134) so that "there was not a walk, a view, a tree, or a plant at Greenbrook, that did not tend by its associations to keep alive feelings" of love (136); as a result, a change of scenery is called for. But even spatial distance is surmounted by the power of sympathy; familial bonds are marked and sustained through the exchange of letters and, especially, gifts. Gifts are a critical category of antebellum material life, exemplifying the Protestant emphasis on the role of possessions in imparting and conveying personal feelings and sentimental commitments. Most contemporary conduct books included a section on the etiquette of gift selection and exchange, and literary annuals known as gift books—collections of sentimental essays, sketches, and poems, published with such titles as *Affection's Gift* and *The Token*—were a phenomenally popular form of literary culture between 1825 and 1865, a period during which, according to one assessment, over a thousand different volumes were issued.[87] While usually bought and sold in the market (though home-made gifts were highly valued during the period), gifts were represented as freed from the cold rationality of marketplace calculation because invested with, and inspiring, a wealth of feeling. In *Home*, Charles's family's gifts serve a substitutive function: they mark the subject's emotional attachments in the face of absence, reminding Charles of those he has left behind. They also work to stabilize subjectivity: such tokens of affection provide a continuity of environment that makes selfhood retrievable; they ensure, in other words, that Charles will continue feeling the same. And by distributing his family's gifts among his new neighbors—especially the books they send him, and "package[s] of flower seeds" and "slips of fruit-trees" they provide (objects that, in circulation, continue to produce pleasure for an expanding array of persons)—Charles generates a new sphere of sympathy: "We are but an extended family circle, perfectly acquainted with each other's condition, and feeling one another's wants" (140).

I have attempted to show how sentimentalism has conditioned middle-class culture's investment in the world of goods and legitimized an expanding consumerism, and to challenge the view, widespread among American historians, that a Weberian work ethic, emphasizing economic rationality and the accumulation of capital, constituted the dominant economic ethos in antebellum America. Women's historians have done little to disrupt this view: in analyzing domestic ideology, they often read what has been termed its "anti-pecuniary bias" as evincing an opposition between home and market, and they typically characterize antebellum domesticity as a sanctuary outside market exchange.[88] But domesticity is not threatened by the market per se; in fact, domestic refinement and comfort depend on it. Rather, what threatens is the impoverishment of feeling that habitual attention to business and cash value entails. The threat, then, is not "contamination" by the market, but the inability to extricate oneself from it and cultivate a wealth of sentiments, attending to aesthetic and ethical as well as market value. Domesticity—described by Sedgwick as a "safe and convenient shelter for private feelings" (129)—is conceptualized as a realm where emotions are concentrated and refined. In other words, domestic writers like Sedgwick seem to counsel that it's fine to shop and buy things; but once at home, be sure to take the price-tag off.

3

SENTIMENTAL CONSUMPTION: HARRIET BEECHER STOWE, NATHANIEL HAWTHORNE, AND THE AESTHETICS OF MIDDLE-CLASS OWNERSHIP

In her third novel, *The Minister's Wooing*, Harriet Beecher Stowe—member of one of the most influential Protestant families in America, daughter of prominent Congregational minister Lyman Beecher, and wife and sister of two other ministers—presents what surprisingly seems like an extended tribute to Roman Catholicism. A work of "local color" realism set in late-eighteenth-century Newport and loosely structured around the fictionalized romantic history of New Divinity pastor Samuel Hopkins, the novel is punctuated with references to the aestheticism of Roman Catholic religious culture and, especially, its redemptive, expressly *feminine* religious iconography. The novel's heroine, Mary Scudder, compared on several occasions to St. Catherine of Siena, is identified throughout the text with the Virgin, an identification established less by scriptural reference and interpretation than by appeals to the sensuous immediacy of Italian art. In a radical revision of Puritan typology, Stowe presents Mary Scudder, "transfigured by a celestial radiance," as the antitype of Christ's mother as portrayed by modern painters, a living incarnation of pictorial representations such as the Sistine Madonna and other "pictures of the girlhood" of Mary.[1] Recasting the Neoplatonic doctrine of a "ladder" of earthly material forms—what Stowe calls "sacraments of love" (166)—through which "the soul rises higher and higher, refining as she goes, till she outgrows the human, and changes, as she rises, into the image of the divine" (66), Stowe's narrative animates a religious pictorial tradition, conflating the iconography of Catholicism with a semisecular aesthetics of feminine presence. Indeed, Stowe presents the "face of woman" as a kind of democratized, everyday version of the "gorgeous paintings" and "lofty statuary" of Rome, "that work of the Mighty Master which is to be found in all lands and ages" (69). As feminine embodiments of God's handiwork, women, Stowe suggests, themselves labor to beautify the landscape of daily life, inspiriting the unregenerate and calling forth the perfected or "resurrection form[s]" of those they encounter (96). Women, Stowe writes, are "God's real priests" on earth, "soul-artists, who go through this world looking among their fellows with reverence, as one looks amid the dust and rubbish of old shops for hidden works of Titian and Leonardo, and, finding them, however cracked or torn or painted over with tawdry daubs of pretenders, immediately recognize the divine original, and set themselves to cleanse and restore" (97).

Stowe's interest in Roman Catholicism was prompted by a series of European excursions in the 1850s, and was registered in many of her writings from the period: for example, in *Agnes of Sorrento*, a historical novel set in fifteenth-century Italy, Stowe identifies "the rosary, the crucifix, the shrine, the banner, the procession" as spiritual object lessons, "homely rounds of the ladder" through which divinity "gave itself to the eye and touch."[2] Indeed, Stowe's eventual shift from the Congregational to the Episcopal church marked the culmination of her frustration with Calvinism's theological asceticism and her growing reverence for Catholicism's humanizing, mediating forms.[3] However, Stowe's midcentury fascination with Roman Catholic aestheticism has more than simply biographical relevance; rather, it signals a broader historical development in American Protestant culture. While the 1850s saw the emergence of Know-Nothing nativism and the publication of many anti-Catholic texts (including *The Papal Conspiracy Exposed*, by Stowe's brother, Edward Beecher), an increasing number of Protestant commentators—many influenced by John Ruskin—wrote appreciatively of the aesthetic richness of Roman Catholic culture. During this period, as Neil Harris has shown, Protestant Americans began visiting Catholic Europe in increasing numbers and frequently expressed in their public and private writings a new faith in the spiritual efficacy of the aesthetic: as Harris demonstrates, it became something of a commonplace in midcentury America that "art objects were powerful means of bringing men to God."[4] Not surprisingly, Catholic—and *European*—aesthetic forms were not absorbed intact into American culture but, rather, were transformed and reconstructed in accord with "native" institutions and ideals. As Stowe's novel suggests, the gracious "material shapes" of Roman Catholicism were, in American Protestant culture, simultaneously "domesticated" and (theoretically) "democratized": regenerative aesthetic artifacts were removed from the public space of the church and dispersed—in vernacular forms—among private households, where their inspiriting influence would be continually felt. At the end of *The Minister's Wooing*, Mary Scudder passes into what Stowe calls "that appointed shrine for woman, more holy than cloister, more saintly and pure than church or altar, a Christian home," in which are installed emotionally engaging artifacts, "memorials" and "relics" of intimate affectional experience and private attachments (410, 149–50). Stowe's domestic aesthetic simultaneously sacralizes everyday life and divests aesthetic objects of the significances and temporal rhythms of collective ritual, reconstituting them as the stuff of personal possessions. In Stowe's version of "home religion," artifactual incarnations of God's grace are to be consumed—along with His Word—at home.

As *The Minister's Wooing* indicates, midcentury Protestant discourses both approached and diverged from traditional, Catholic views of the regenerative power of mediating forms—a fact with significant implications, not only for American religious history, but for economic and literary history as well. Twentieth-century historians have located the rise of an American consumer culture, and a shift from an ascetic Protestant work ethic to a hedonistic consumption ethic, in the 1880s and 1890s, shaped by postbellum overproduction and the rise of a national market and promoted by therapeutic ideologues' endorsements of earthly self-fulfillment.[5] However, the antebellum work ethic coexisted with an emerging consumer ethic, which both challenged and helped define it: worldly asceticism and domestic aestheticism were distinct, and distinctly *gendered*, cultural ideals. As I demonstrate in chapter 2, by the time Stowe was writing, a new, semisecular Protestant ethic of "pious materialism," promoted by an array of theological, philosophical, and literary discourses, had gained widespread currency, and had legitimized an increased cultural and economic investment in domestic material and consumer "refinement."

In this chapter, I examine ideologies of domestic materialism in midcentury fiction, focusing on the work of Stowe and Hawthorne.[6] Specifically, I argue that these writers' reformulations of sentimental ownership were responding to the crisis in liberal social forms generated by the national debate over slavery. Stowe's homemaking writings and novels construct the "inside" realm of domesticity as the sphere of fulfillment and plenitude, and indicate the new, quasi-spiritual significance of consumer goods in establishing what one writer called the "attractions of home."[7] I trace the structure of sentimental proprietorship in Stowe's texts, a structure which undergirds her ideal of domestic consumption, and which defines a (paradoxical) model of "consensual," spiritually redemptive property relations seemingly compatible with America's democratic ideals. Instantiating what I have described as the proprietary forms of liberal subjection, sentimental ownership expressed a complex array of class, ethnic, gender, and national identifications, and was constituted in opposition to a range of proprietary models, differentiated spatially as well as temporally—specifically, "savage" cannibalism and the degenerative patriarchal proprietary relations of gothic or feudal ownership. My discussion of Stowe's household writings focuses especially on *House and Home Papers*, a collection of essays published in the *Atlantic Monthly* under the pseudonym Christopher Crowfield, and issued in book form in 1865. Stowe's homemaking writings exemplify what was becoming an influential bourgeois discourse of sentimental proprietorship, a discourse which highlights the significance of objects in the emotional culture of persons, and which extends from Scottish Enlightenment moral philosophers' rhetorical rehabilitation of luxury consumption to twentieth-century Anglo-American psychologists' and sociologists' accounts of the emotional value of "object relations" and a sense of "relatedness" to the nonhuman environment.[8] Depoliticizing relations of family and property by depicting them as expressions of essentially "human," emotional *needs*, *House and Home Papers* naturalized middle-class patterns of private ownership and helped establish consumerist domesticity as an instrument of cultural hegemony.

My discussion of Stowe's work concludes with an analysis of *Uncle Tom's Cabin*, which demonstrates how Stowe's ideal of sentimental ownership authorized her imaginative reconstruction of the relationship between owner and owned under slavery—a reconstruction that simultaneously "humanized" and "feminized" African Americans while falling notoriously short of representing them as full participant citizens in American civic culture. Indeed, I argue that, during the national crisis of the 1850s, the threat of political and economic "enslavement" was registered and managed principally through a racialized discourse of gender. While proslavery writers had called attention to the similarities between the bonds of slavery and the bonds of liberal market culture and its norms of personal life, Stowe boldly reasserted sentimental ownership as the antidote to black enslavement.[9] In examining the political effects of sentimental abolitionist texts such as Stowe's, I argue that these texts make explicit the racial parameters within which sentimental subjectivity takes shape: the interracial "extension" of sympathy described in and facilitated by this literature generated forms of (white) liberal political "agency" as well as outrage at African American enslavement. The final pages of this section examine the larger implications of sentimental possession for sentimental aesthetics, and for the proprietary forms and "structures of feeling" of antebellum readership.

As I demonstrate in chapter 2, the new emphasis on the emotional value of consumer goods in antebellum America was registered in the very *form* of domestic realist fiction, a literary genre in which domestic material culture is represented in great detail, and in which personal possessions are endowed with psychological or characterological import. Stowe, for instance, typically introduces her fictional characters by first presenting the particulars of their domestic environment, to show her readers whether or not the signs of civility and refinement are present there, and to indicate whether an individual "cares for" his or her possessions—a sentimental reformulation of a traditional Christian ethic of stewardship and care that is, for Stowe, an essential sign of "civilized" personhood. One of the chief representational strategies through which Stowe represents the full "humanity" of members of Other races—for example, African Americans in *Uncle Tom's Cabin*, and Native Americans in *Oldtown Folks*—is showing that these individuals do indeed "keep house," and either reside in, or aspire to, something like middle-class domesticity. Constructing formal and thematic equivalences between material and subjective "refinement"—between commodity and psychological forms—sentimental texts such as Stowe's helped write into existence a modern consumer psychology in which individuals "express themselves" through consumption and "identify" with personal possessions.

In my discussion of "white slave" narratives and Hawthorne's *The Blithedale Romance*, I continue to analyze sentimental texts' negotiation of the racialized problematic of enslavement. Narratives such as Maria Ward's *The Mormon Wife*, like Hawthorne's *Blithedale*, record the racialized ambivalence of liberal subjectivity discussed in my introduction: they exhibit an eroticized fascination with "enslavement" and a containment of its threat. Feminizing and sexualizing the condition of enslavement, these narratives both inscribe the forms of erotic bondage legitimated within domesticity, and contain the threat of that recognition by symbolically divorcing sentimental ownership from enslavement and reclaiming the former as the safeguard of feminine freedom. White slave narratives such as Ward's generate forms of white subjectivity that depend on an ambivalent identification with racialized bodies in pain, and promote gendered fantasies of proprietary power that give liberal selves a stake in capitalism. Similarly, Hawthorne's *Blithedale* foregrounds conflicting desires within liberal subjects by presenting competing types of male characters—incarnations of phallic power and corporeal agency, and "civilized" feminine men. Thus bifurcating constructions of masculinity, the text mobilizes masculine fantasies of autonomy and wholeness, while envisioning the "voluntary" renunciation of patriarchal power through the civilizing identificatory exchanges of heterosexuality. Representing the eroticized dynamic of "consent" first described by the Scottish writers discussed in chapter 1, *Blithedale* records Hawthorne's fascination with the bonds of sympathy, and with the forms of emotional and erotic bondage legitimated within liberal "public" and "private" cultures.

Love's Body: Building the Domestic Interior

The dynamic interplay between affectional and material forms—between, in other words, middle-class interiority and the middle-class interior—central to sentimental discourse is foregrounded in a standard topos of sentimental fiction: the window scene. Window scenes explore the powerful meaning of the *boundary*, the charged threshold between inner and outer, in the period's material and psychological landscape. One such scene appears in the opening chapter of Susan Warner's 1850 bestseller, *The Wide, Wide World*. In that scene, the heroine, Ellen Montgomery, sits in the parlor where her invalid mother rests and gazes out the window into the street:

> There was no one else [besides her mother] in the room. Driven thus to her own resources, Ellen betook herself to the window and sought amusement there. The prospect without gave little promise of it. Rain was falling, and made the street and everything in it look dull and gloomy. The foot-passengers plashed through the water, and the horses and carriages plashed through the mud; gayety had forsaken the sidewalks, and equipages were few, and the people that were out were plainly there only because they could not help it.[10]

A second, especially telling example of the sentimental window scene, from Maria Cummins's *The Lamplighter* (1852), is in important ways a structural inversion of the first. In Cummins's text, the heroine, Gerty, and her young friend Willie accompany Truman Flint, the lamplighter, while he performs his evening labors. The children stop, enchanted, before the window of a "great stone house," a home less "screen[ed]" from the "public gaze" than many of those surrounding it:

> It was now quite dark, so that persons in a light room could not see anyone out of doors; but Willie and Gerty had so much the better chance to look in. It was indeed a fine mansion, evidently the home

of wealth. A clear coal-fire, and a bright lamp in the centre of the room, shed abroad their cheerful blaze. Rich carpets, deeply-tinted curtains, pictures in gilded frames, and huge mirrors, reflecting the whole on every side, gave Gerty her first impressions of luxurious life. There was an air of comfort combined with all this elegance, which made it still more fascinating to the child of poverty and want. A table was bountifully spread for tea; the cloth of snow-white damask, the shining plate, above all, the home-like hissing tea-kettle, had a most inviting look. A gentleman in gay slippers was in an easy-chair by the fire; a lady in a gay cap was superintending a servant-girl's arrangements at the tea-table, and the children of the household [were all] smiling and happy. . . .

Gerty's admiration and rapture were such that she could find no expression for them, except in jumping up and down, shouting, laughing and directing Willie's notice first to one thing and then another.

"O, Willie! isn't she a darling? and see what a brilliant fire, — what a splendid lady! And look! look at the father's shoes! What is that on the table? I guess it's good! There's a big looking-glass; and O, Willie! an't they dear little handsome children!"[11]

In sentimental novels, as well as in texts such as architectural pattern books and home decorating manuals, which codified domestic ideology, "inside" was being established as the realm of fulfillment and emotional satisfaction: the Jeffersonian political ideal of the economic self-sufficiency of the individual homestead was being reconfigured as the domestic ideal of affectional self-sufficiency.[12] Countering the structures of desire identified by Leslie Fiedler and others as paradigmatic, these novels do not depict the open space of "outside" as aspiration's aim or the object of obsessive fantasy; when "outside" *is* longed for and presented as the object of desire, it offers only temporary exhilaration or, more typically, a refuge from an unhappy, unappealing home life. In fact, *The Lamplighter* opens with a description of the orphan Gerty sitting on the wooden doorstep of "a low-roofed, dark, and unwholesome-looking house," gazing up "with much earnestness" at the street, which offers temporary respite from her working-class stepmother's abuse. But the street is represented as cold and impersonal, a space in which "no one noticed the girl" (1), so that Gerty's longing to move *out* of one household space is immediately redirected into the longing to move *in* (somewhere else). Being "outside" in these texts signifies, like Gerty on the doorstep, the absence of domestic warmth, both emotional and physical; it signifies exclusion from care and interest; it signifies "neglect." In sentimental narratives, liberal and Protestant discourses intersected to define the private sphere of the family as the sphere of fulfillment and shelter—the space of an attenuated Christian community of care—in which needs are satisfied and attended to, and human relations mediated by love. While liberalism carved out the private sphere as a realm of individual autonomy and freedom, sentimentalism filled this same sphere with *psychological* content, depicting it as site and constitutive sign of emotional "refinement."

Antebellum novels' window scenes encode, in condensed form, nineteenth-century women's fiction's "overplot" or standard trajectory of desire, a trajectory whose arc carries the heroine out of the home and into the workplace, and whose culmination or telos is a chastened domestic intimacy.[13] The movement of psychic and physical energy in these passages is unidirectional: persons always want to cross the threshold from outside to inside, from street to household; everybody wants a "good home." This trajectory of desire is a decidedly middle-class formula, as Christine Stansell has shown; indeed, the sentimental configuration of domesticity as regenerate and regenerative emerged in distinct opposition to a diverse array of cultural practices—especially the social and material practices of the working class, immigrants, Native Americans, and African Americans. Stansell's work suggests the significance of extradomestic forms of collectivity for working-class men, women, and children during the period, and demonstrates that street culture was essential to working-class identity and consciousness. Stansell finds that urban laboring women "observed no sharp distinction between public and private," and their lives "spread out to the hallways of their tenements, to adjoining apartments and to the streets below. . . . It was in the urban neighborhoods, not the home, that the identity of working-class wives and mothers was rooted." Middle-class reformers registered an awareness of these differences in their attempts to reshape working-class home life in accord with middle-class domestic imperatives: labeling working-class forms of socializing "promiscuous," they legitimized their interventions in lower-class families by appealing to an ideal of domestic intimacy, and they consistently envisioned "scattering" working-class children among middle-class households as the most effective means of promoting moral and social reform.[14]

An expanding consumerism, and the new world of goods being brought into the home, played a central role in the sentimental recoding of the domestic sphere as the site of fulfilled desire. A multiplying array of consumer goods and embellishments helped substantiate and define the "attractions of home." In the passage from *The Lamplighter*, Gerty's "admiration and rapture" are inspired as much by the array of material objects—the "rich carpets, deeply-tinted curtains, pictures in gilded frames, and huge mirrors," the "easy-chair" and "gay slippers," as well as the "snow-white damask, the shining plate, [and] the home-like hissing tea-kettle"—as by the "splendid" lady and "handsome" children who enjoy these objects. Wanting a happy home, for Gerty, is thoroughly interwoven with wanting domestic "elegance" and "comfort," so that after just a glance inside the Clintons' house she determines that "she meant to work, and grow rich" (47). Gerty's gaze into the interior of the Clintons' home replicates a familiar consumerist formula, a formula which organizes her experience in the novel and which entails, in often-rapid succession, looking (through a window), wanting, and (finally) owning. This consumerist structure of desire can in fact be traced back to the eighteenth and early-nineteenth centuries, when shopping was pushed indoors from open-air marketplaces and new technologies made expanses of plate glass readily and cheaply available.

In Cummins's novel, "home" is both instrument and end of redemption: both persons and objects *belong* "inside," and those with value ultimately make their way there. Antebellum sentimental novels typically map conventional liberal and Protestant oppositions—such as civility/savagery, salvation/corruption, heaven/fallen world—onto a gendered division between private and public, thus spatializing a Protestant structure of temporality and spiritual "progress," and reconfiguring spiritual conversion in terms of the sentimental motif of "coming home." This delineation of domesticity as a regenerative, spiritually *animating* space is especially apparent in these novels' characteristic and often-noted depictions of domestic animism: it is precisely when objects cross the threshold from outside to inside, and enter the humanizing realm of the home, that they are represented as having *feelings* rather than as inanimate "things."[15] Assimilating Puritan metaphors of emotional regeneration and an Enlightenment rhetoric of sensibility, these texts characteristically present an individual's subjective condition—more or less "hardened" and insensible, more or less "human"—as contingent on his or her location in cultural space. In a real sense, then, these texts problematize any stable, ontological distinction between subjects and objects, simultaneously providing an opening for social transformation—the social regeneration and elevation of those previously "dehumanized" by dominant classifications—while engendering forms of identification between persons and things essential to a consumer sensibility. However, the socially transformative, liberatory potential of sentimental animism is strictly, indeed materially, delimited. As the structure of the window scenes clearly indicates, these texts bifurcate cultural space according to a rigid binarism, so that the domestic is inscribed as a fully human and humanizing domain *only in opposition to* an extradomestic space whose inhabitants are necessarily characterized as less than human. In other words, the "inside" realm of spiritually regenerate, animated objects is structurally opposed to an "outside" world of unregenerate and inanimate objects. Not coincidentally, sentimental novels' representations of emotionally engaged, loving ownership within the home emerged during an era of tremendous industrial expansion in the fallen world "outside," where persons and natural objects were often brutally exploited. Indeed, cultural configurations of sentimental ownership, and the spatializing strategies that organize them, rationalized the exploitation and instrumentalization of persons and objects in the world "outside."

Like *The Lamplighter*, Stowe's homemaking writings and fiction testify to the centrality of consumer goods in establishing the "inside" space of domesticity as the site of fulfillment and plenitude, and they illuminate the relations of emotionally engaged, sentimental ownership which characterize this interior domain. The sentimental reconfiguration of ownership and ideal of caring proprietorship had significant legal consequences in nineteenth-century America, particularly in adoption and custody issues: as the historian Michael Grossberg has noted, maternal custody rights were increasingly recognized during the antebellum period, a recognition based on an emerging "best interests of the child" doctrine in American family law and a new concern with the feelings of (domestic) property.[16] But this configuration of sentimental ownership—which promoted forms of feminine taste and civil subjectivity, and which conflated property rights and certain (class- and culture-bound) structures of feeling—could easily be used to discount the proprietary claims of those individuals whose material and affectional practices didn't quite square with sentimental norms. In mid-nineteenth-century America, then, the discursive configuration of sentimental ownership both legitimized the proprietary authority of previously disenfranchised social groups *and* identified specific, class-based social and material forms as constitutive signs of "civilized" personhood.

Eros and Ownership

In the summer of 1874, in the midst of an adultery scandal involving Stowe's brother Henry Ward Beecher, Stowe's half-sister, the feminist activist Isabella Beecher Hooker, fled to Europe, hoping to avoid the controversy generated by her brother's trial and the family resentment produced by her refusal publicly to proclaim his innocence. In her Paris hotel room, Isabella began to experience visions of her mother, Harriet Porter Beecher, who had died nearly forty years earlier. Harriet Porter Beecher offered her daughter love and unconditional acceptance, as well as comforting assurances of Isabella's moral rectitude: she predicted, for instance, that a contrite Henry Ward Beecher would one day kneel before Isabella in an agony of remorse for the way he had treated her. In the years that followed, the spectral Harriet Porter Beecher reappeared on several occasions to offer maternal support and to assist her daughter in meeting her earthly responsibilities, announcing that Isabella would be called to lead a worldwide matriarchal government that would be merged with the kingdom of Christ in a feminine, and feminist, millennium. As Isabella reports them in her diary, Harriet Porter Beecher's messages about her daughter's spiritual and political destiny were punctuated by equally earnest recommendations on home management and what was termed at the time "household taste." Isabella's descriptions of these visions include detailed accounts of her mother's advice on such matters as proper clothing, household budgeting, and the selection and care of the material "appointments" of home.[17]

Isabella's spiritualist exercises suggest the importance of domestic consumption and domestic economy in shaping the bounds of female community, a community that could extend beyond the domestic circle into the political and, apparently, even the celestial spheres. They also suggest the moral and spiritual *seriousness* with which home decoration was invested in the mid–nineteenth century. Antebellum tastemakers such as A. J. Downing stressed the pedagogical import of domestic aesthetics, and represented tastefully decorated homes as instruments of "civilization" and emotional refinement. Their writings arguably helped shape what has been identified as the nineteenth century's "ruling style," in which "objects of everyday use" were "adorned with a profusion of ornament" and conspicuously marked as aesthetic artifacts by manufacturers.[18] Similarly, sentimental authors underscored the psychological and moral significance of material comfort, and featured in their novels and advice manuals sentimental culture's familiar interweaving of bodily comfort and emotional well-being. Since sensibility was a bodily as well as a psychological capacity, preserving the body's aliveness to sensation, its capacity to feel pleasure and pain, was endowed with moral urgency, and was seen to have profound ethical and social consequences. Most antebellum reformers assumed that those who were insensitive to their own pains couldn't be sensitive to others'; and it was in the nineteenth century that "mean"—which originally meant "common," and usually referred to lower-class living conditions—began to take on the moral connotations of "vicious," "brutal," and "cruel."[19] Genteel authors as well as sentimentalists legitimized an increased investment in domestic comfort and refinement in specifically psychological and emotional terms, and discursively identified middle-class forms of private ownership with norms of subjective emotional experience. This identification—as diverse writings by contemporary analytic philosophers, psychologists, and sociologists testify—remains a cultural commonplace today.[20]

Stowe's writings on domestic economy strengthened this association, affirming and extending what Ann Douglas has called sentimentalism's "commercialization of the inner life."[21] Stowe represents the home as a sphere of love, intimacy, and solace, and thoroughly implicates domestic objects in the formation of that sphere. Her writings delineate an aesthetic and sentimental, rather than an instrumental and utilitarian, approach to domestic possessions, endorsing a disposition that allows for a full emotional engagement with things. These delineations place Stowe's ideal of sentimental domesticity in explicit tension with both a Calvinist ideal of strenuous labor, and a Puritan ideal of frugal housekeeping. Historians have long argued that a Weberian work ethic, emphasizing economic rationality and the accumulation of capital and mandating the suppression of immediate consumer enjoyment, was hegemonic in antebellum America. However, Stowe's constructions of sentimental, consumerist domesticity suggest that the home was organized by a distinct economic ethos, by an explicitly feminine and domestic ideology of both consumption and work.[22]

A Home Is Not a Factory: Stowe's House and Home Papers

The project of carving out the home as a sphere of love and emotional involvement requires Stowe to reimagine radically the practice of work. Because of the predominance of the utilitarian, Franklinian model of labor as rational calculation and methodicalness, as well as labor's biblical associations with pain, work would have to be reconstituted in order to be fully synthesized and modulated with an economy of domestic happiness and emotional fulfillment. Dolores Hayden and Gillian Brown have examined parallels between home and workplace in Stowe's household writings, especially in *The American Woman's Home*, a text she coauthored with her sister, Catharine Beecher; Hayden argues that the text inaugurates the home efficiency movement with its emphasis on domestic efficiency and professionalism. But Beecher and Stowe insist that standard economic virtues must be tempered by domestic sentiments and constrained by the collective aims—the promotion of "comfort" and emotional "well-being"—to which these virtues are meant to contribute.[23] As Stowe writes in "What Is a Home?" included in *House and Home Papers*, "Order was made for the family, and not the family for order": systematic efforts should be fully integrated with a sentimental ideal of harmony, emotional intimacy, and care.[24] If the home in Stowe's writings is demarcated as distinct from the street, a space of neglect and cruelty, it is also distinguished from the factory, a space in which objects and bodies are used orderly and methodically for economic gain rather than nurtured and cared for. Stowe counters utilitarian and Calvinist models of work with an essentially romantic model of labor as inspired spontaneity, encoding a resistance to order that signifies sympathetic responsiveness. In Stowe's sentimental economy, the domestic woman's muscular exertions are tempered by the delicate perceptions of sensibility; and the hand as instrument of labor is partially reconstructed into a vessel of aesthetic genius and emotional nurture, complementing manual exertion with a gentle caress and a "light touch." Stowe's imaginative reconstructions thus contributed to the process through which the body of the industrious frugal housewife was assimilated into that of the tasteful female shopper.[25]

The potential conflict between, and necessary merger of, labor and sentimental subjectivity is explicitly invoked throughout the *House and Home Papers*. Stowe's chief aim in "The Lady Who Does Her Own Work," for instance, is to coordinate and carefully synthesize manual labor with feminine delicacy, beauty, and emotional refinement. While women sweep floors, make fires, and cook breakfast, Stowe assures us, they chat of books and their studies; occasionally they discuss embroidery, poetry, or perhaps a rural ball. Describing one such "famil[y] of daughters," Stowe writes approvingly that "they spun with the book tied to the distaff; they wove; they did all manner of fine needlework; they made lace, painted flowers," and did impressive and elegant fancywork (89). As Stowe insistently reminds us, the "same ladies who" do housework "find quite as much time for reading, letter-writing, drawing, embroidery, and fancy work as the women of families otherwise arranged" (89–90); sensibility need not be compromised or "deadened" by labor's muscular exertions (88). In addition, Stowe observes, such women also come up with labor-saving methods for performing needed tasks—as she asserts, "cultivated, intelligent women . . . are labor-saving institutions"—which both "save [the] body" and provide more time for emotional availability. The exertions of domestic labor should be "inconspicuous," all the better to produce a nonrational, emotional response (53). In Stowe's household, the woman's domestic tasks need not "harden" her sensitive touch nor compromise "the gift . . . in her finger-ends" (60): hers is the capacity to arrange domestic objects and direct familial sociability to produce an emotionally engaging home environment.

In *House and Home Papers,* Stowe rejects both a Puritan model of domestic frugality and a genteel model of domestic formality, offering in the place of these models an evangelical, sentimental ideal of domestic warmth and comfort. In "What Is a Home?" Stowe criticizes the "blessed followers of Saint Martha, . . . the dear, worthy creatures, up before daylight, causing the most scrupulous lustrations of every pane of glass and inch of paint in our parlors" because in their industriousness they make a house seem uninhabitable, "like a tomb" (45). Traces of labor in the home of the frugal housewife, Stowe here suggests, are altogether too conspicuous. Christopher Crowfield, Stowe's persona, recounts the fear and trembling he experienced as the youthful resident of such a place, and acknowledges that such a home feels like a prison: "My only idea of a house was a place full of traps and pitfalls for boys, a deadly temptation to sins which beset one every moment; and when I read about a sailor's free life on the ocean, I felt an untold longing to go forth and be free in like manner" (46). Stowe's sentimental domicile, a site of "inviting" relaxation and easy elegance (46), would make Fiedleresque, expansive longings for male flight unlikely and unnecessary.

Stowe's social and psychological ideal of domestic sensibility and harmony dovetails with, and indeed defines, her theological critique of orthodox Calvinism, identified in *House and Home Papers* with an uncharitably rigid preoccupation with domestic order and a frugality that tends toward discomfort. Framed by an opposition between Calvinist legalism and evangelical pietism, a little domestic mess signifies a lot of love. In the place of the frugal housewife, Stowe constructs a new middle-class domestic type, the charmingly scattered, forbearingly slack and flexible homemaker, whose housekeeping expresses the impulses of devotion and love, and is comprised of a collection of kindly actions from which feeling is never far. This romantic model of work, partaking of an exemplary flexibility and emotional openness—a form of work which doesn't disrupt, but is rather in tune with, the emotional nuances and intimate particulars of daily life—absorbs an ideal of aristocratic ease and effortlessness into sentimental, middle-class practice. This was the model of domestic labor Stowe seems to have practiced in her own housekeeping, to husband Calvin's vexation and dismay; it also inflected her literary labors and shaped her prose style, which has been described as "associative," "conversational," and "chatty."[26] A discursive enactment of her formulation of domestic labor, Stowe's writing practice mobilized the emotional immediacy of "feminine" private language and romanticism's valuation of impulse and discursive fluidity, buttressing a stereotypically feminine penchant for "pointless" gossip with evangelical sanction. Indeed, in the second chapter of *The Minister's Wooing*, Stowe explicitly identifies inspirational housekeeping and inspired authorship, and confesses with mock dismay her own taste for authorial meandering: "You see, instead of getting our tea ready, as we promised at the beginning of this chapter, we have filled it with description and meditations, and now we foresee that the next chapter will be equally far from the point. But have patience with us; for we can write only as we are driven, and never know exactly where we are going to land" (21). Stowe's reconstruction of the domestic woman's "hand," spiritually animated by "the gift . . . in [its] finger-ends," apparently entailed a reconfiguration of the domestic work of "feminine" writing.

The "feminine" model of uncalculating emotional responsiveness legible in Stowe's descriptions of affectionate housekeeping and inspired authorship informed as well the sentimental woman's extradomestic practices, undergirding, for instance, the antebellum construction of the "impulse buyer." Importantly, this model naturalizes female labor and incorporates it seamlessly into a sentimental emotional economy. Stowe's sentimental reformulation of domestic work as spontaneous labor of love performs an erasure of domestic effort, and sanctifies the institutionalization of what Marxist feminists term "invisible labor." Stowe's sentimental housekeeper would seem to be the antithesis of Stowe's contemporary Melusina Fay Peirce's politicized housewife, the woman who organizes and collectivizes domestic labor in order to charge her husband for her services.[27]

Creating the Lived-in Look: Objects in Stowe's Sentimental Economy

Inspirited by the sentimental woman's gentle touch, objects as signs of labor are remade in Stowe's writings into vessels and expressions of shared sentiments. Distinct from the well-scrubbed premises of the frugal housewife and the showy households of the rich (described in *House and Home Papers* as "mere sets of reception rooms" that showcase great politeness but express little love [41]), Stowe's ideal domicile is arranged in accord with the "close intimacies of Anglo-Saxon life" (41), offering "inviting" comforts and "a little appearance of wholesome neglect combined with real care" (48). A home, Stowe advises in "What Is a Home?" should offer "something that doesn't seem like a hotel,—some bit of real, genuine heart life . . . a little of your heart, a little home warmth and feeling" (51). Dining rooms and parlors should be "cosy and inviting" spaces in which "one feels like taking off one's things to stay" (80, 77); and objects within these rooms should be intimately embedded in the animation of social contact. While possessions in "best rooms"—an unfortunate remnant of aristocratic formality in middle-class households—are "mute and muffled," things in comfortable and cozy spaces come to life and "have a sort of human vitality in them," bodying forth social sentiments so that visitors feel they "are taken into the family, and are moving in its inner circles" (82–83). As Stowe puts it in "Raking Up the Fire," "How many people do we call in from year to year and know no more of their feelings, habits, tastes, family ideas and ways, than if they lived in Kamtschatka. . . . One hour in the back room, where the plants and canary-bird and children are, might have made you fast friends for life" (82–83). In place of the formality of fashionable "best rooms" and the frugal housewife's rigid orderliness, the sentimental woman establishes what we today call the "lived-in look," a domestic style in which objects express "*homeliness*" (82). Such objects are fully incorporated into a sentimental economy of feeling.[28]

Throughout *House and Home Papers*, objects are closely conjoined with the representation and production of intimate feelings. Guests in Stowe's universe visit one's home laden with their own sentimental longings and belongings: she describes one visitor who "would like better than anything to show you the last photograph of his wife, or to read to you the great, round-hand letter of his ten-year-old which he has got to-day. He is ready to cry when he thinks of it" (51). Such guests appreciate informality—"a bit of your average home life"—much more than "fuss." Indeed, in the sentimental home, the ritual of sharing one's often-used, familiar possessions signifies not disrespect but trust, and occasions not genteel resentment but a deepening of sympathy through the revelation of mutual vulnerability and imperfection. Domestic informality, sharing everyday and even broken objects that display one's lapses in vigilance, creates gaps in social performance that are coded in Stowe's domestic writings as "inviting," constituting openings for sympathy and domestic closeness. Such objects become material signs of relaxation, incorporating into social life the Christian virtues of forgiveness and love, and shaping a sentimental social contract that seems to say, "I see your flaws and imperfections, but I like you anyway."[29] Broken domestic objects signify tolerance as well as intimacy and coziness, and a prioritizing of what Stowe calls "comfort and liberty" (43). Such objects are to be cherished and carefully but "freely handled" (44).

Unmended domestic possessions are thus represented in *House and Home Papers* as tokens of sentimental involvement: bearing traces of a history of "free handl[ing]," they are markers of emotional engagement and intimacy. Objects thus interwoven with "heart-life" seem to come alive and "have a sort of human vitality in them" (82). Domestic objects, Stowe counsels, should not be (merely) "used" or displayed; they should be cared for, and loved. But the moral and emotional stakes involved in loving one's possessions—legible in what Baudrillard calls the "moral fanaticism" of middle-class housekeeping, and in what Arendt describes as a modern tendency to invest intimate surroundings with unmistakable "care and tenderness"—are most clearly manifest in Stowe's discussions of objects that are "really" alive, especially pets and plants.[30] According to the historian Keith Thomas, pet-keeping and the tending of household plants were practices that became popular in the eighteenth century, particularly among the middle class, and were centrally implicated in the emergence of a sentimental and "non-utilitarian attitude" toward the natural world. This inscription of animals and plants as means of emotional satisfaction rather than as instruments of utility or the gratification of "animal needs" is clearly legible in *House and Home Papers*.[31] Stowe's ideal housekeeper, tending her plants and pets, displays her sentimental endowments by demonstrating an emotional involvement in nature that is simultaneously a resistance to appetite, enacting a cherishing appreciation of natural objects rather than the destructive ritual incorporation of natural objects as food.[32] Stowe's text conspicuously brings plants and animals out of the fields—and out of the kitchen—and into the parlor.

In Stowe's household writings, plants and pets serve as exemplary objects of sentimental proprietorship, developing and extending an individual's capacity to "care." Promoting feminine taste and sympathetic identification with objects of property, these writings constitute what I have described as the proprietary forms of feminine civil subjectivity. According to Stowe, a dog is "nothing but organized love—love on four feet encased in fur and looking piteously out at the eyes—love that would die for you yet cannot speak"; such a creature, Stowe believes, cannot fail "to win out philanthropy in our boys and girls." Pet-keeping thus accomplishes—to borrow a phrase from the nineteenth-century antivivisectionist Ralph Waldo Trine—"heart-training through the animal world."[33]

Houseplants perform a similar function. In "Raking Up the Fire," Stowe contrasts the fashionable "Aunt Easygo," who regularly replaces her plants rather than tend them properly, with the fully sympathetic domestic woman. "I can tell you what [such a woman] puts into her plants," Stowe insists, "just what she [puts] into her children, and all her other home-things,—her heart. She loves them; she lives in them; she has in herself a plant-life and a plant-sympathy. She feels for them as if she herself were a plant; she anticipates their wants,—always remembers them without an effort, and so the care flows to them daily and hourly"; she endows them with "all the habitual care of love" (71). In Stowe's writings, beloved objects such as pets and plants figure centrally in the rites of intimate emotional experience in which the self's inner resources are constituted and preserved. *House and Home Papers*' depictions of pet-keeping and plant companionship crystallize her conceptualization of proprietary relations as bonds of love, and exemplify the possibilities, and the moral and psychological imperatives, of loving one's possessions.

Stowe's sentimental housekeeper is the prototype of the modern consumer, whose sympathetic extensions of self have been banked on and encouraged—often in quite explicit terms—by nineteenth- and twentieth-century advertisers.[34] In an important sense, Stowe's depictions of sympathetic ownership constitute a *reductio ad absurdum* of liberalism's ideal of consensual authority, articulating a fantasy of noncoercive ownership in which relations of power and force are imaginatively reconstituted, and masked. To the question, "What do objects want?" Stowe's sympathetic consumer would seem to answer, "They want *me*!" (This fantasy of consensual ownership is especially legible in Victorian narratives about pets, in which animals travel for miles in order to reclaim their "families" and reenter the humanizing, spiritually animating realm of the home.) But Stowe's animistic representations also helped shape a historical moment when the material loci of sentience—and the lines separating "human" from "nonhuman," "person" from "thing"—were being problematized and reformulated. These loci and boundaries were urgently and powerfully reimagined in Stowe's most sustained meditation on the feelings of property, *Uncle Tom's Cabin*.

Uncle Tom's Cabin

Philip Fisher has described the sentimental novel as "a romance of the object rather than a romance of the subject," because it "draws on novel *objects* of feeling rather than novel feelings." This expansion of sympathy to novel objects resulted in the extension of "full and complete humanity to classes of figures from whom it ha[d] been socially withheld" — especially, Fisher contends, prisoners, madmen, children, the aged, and slaves. Fisher's list of what Stowe calls "human things" could itself be expanded to include animals, plants, and even rocks, minerals, and manmade artifacts, as Keith Thomas has demonstrated in *Man and the Natural World*.[35] As Thomas's book shows, sentimentalism oversaw the restructuring of the Great Chain of Being through the inscription of objects previously considered subhuman with human feelings and sentiments. This sentimental reconstruction of the object world is clearly registered in *House and Home Papers*, which delineates a model of sentimental possession that both animates objects and constitutes sentimental subjects. Inscribing the "feelings of living property" (81) is a central concern in *Uncle Tom's Cabin*. There, Stowe's construction of loving proprietorship simultaneously animates the socially dead, and situates "living property" within the bounds of normative, middle-class structures.

My discussion of the racial reformulation of sentimental ownership in Stowe's work can shed light on the politics of sentimental abolitionism and its relation to the forms of liberal subjection. Critics have long assessed the racial politics of white women's abolitionist literature; recently, many have argued that, while texts such as Stowe's work to promote white readers' identification with African Americans in order to bring home to readers the dehumanized treatment of African Americans in slavery, this extension of sentimental sympathy is a form of emotional colonization that inscribes "black" subjectivity according to white, middle-class norms.[36] Certainly, texts such as Stowe's endeavor to promote such racial "extensions" of sympathy, in part by rendering black "subjectivity" and "feelings" using conventions intelligible to middle-class white readers. For Saidiya Hartman, the representation of black bodies in pain in cultural forms such as sentimental texts forges "ties of sentiment" that reinforce rather than contest black bondage, enabling white readers/spectators to "slip into" or "figuratively occupy" the black body and transmuting black pain into the pleasures of white mastery. Analyzing the "complex nexus of terror and enjoyment" facilitated by representations of black suffering, Hartman comes closest to what I am after here; although by focusing her polemic on exposing the "repressive effects of empathy" she does not consider the constitutive instability of white subjectivity in these texts and, indeed, the precarious dependency of white subjects on the scenes of racial subjection she describes.[37] Most accounts of the colonizing, racist effects of sentimental sympathy are not ideologically neutral: they seem to assume that the white, middle-class emotional norms that produce the "ties of sentiment" stand outside sentimental texts' identificatory exchanges. Instead, I have argued here that sentimental abolitionist literature, by staging the dialectic of sentimental subjection and enlisting "civilized" emotional performances by/of white readers, worked to *constitute* the forms of sentimental subjectivity described so persuasively by critics. Texts such as Stowe's are as invested in inscribing forms of feminine political agency ("influence") as in protesting the horrors of the peculiar institution; indeed, these investments are inseparably conjoined. In particular, by racializing (the threat of) "enslavement" and proprietary dependency, an identification both acknowledged and disavowed, these texts inscribe, and could help readers *feel*, the agency and proprietary power of liberal civil subjectivity. In a sense, Stowe's sympathetic inscription of white maternal care for and of black slaves both reasserted the moral authority of her class and recuperated the felt forms of liberal agency, both of which were undergoing a political challenge in the 1850s.

Like *House and Home Papers*, *Uncle Tom's Cabin* envisions taste, cast as maternal care, as a vehicle of social reform; and like Kirkland, Stowe relies on a sentimental ideology of gender to invest feminine emotional "influence" with the efficacy to curb the excesses of male economic and political power. However, Stowe's construction of maternal care as the basis of racial reform in *Uncle Tom's Cabin* is, as many have noted, extraordinarily problematic, principally because it unleashes the proprietary dynamic of sentimental ownership into the realm of racial politics. Stowe's sentimental inscriptions of slaves as objects of white maternal care (a care partly performed through writing) both invest black bodies with forms of "white" (feminine, middle-class) emotion, and define black subjects as objects of "legitimate" (white) proprietary authority. The novel thus inscribes a particular, racial formation of sentimental ownership, one that sustains white economic entitlement and asserts black dependency.

In Stowe's novel, the sentimental mitigation of hierarchy is represented as a form of democratic revisionism, connoting a "mingl[ing] of class[es]" distinct from the rigid status classifications of the English (340–44). But it is the "dividing line . . . of color" as a restrictor of sympathy that is especially interrogated (335). Stowe's sympathetic representations of black slaves constituted a powerful form of cultural and legal revisionism. Employing definitions of slavery derived from Roman and civil law traditions, antebellum jurists and lawmakers collectively defined slave chattel as instruments of *use*, as extensions of their owner's will and physical nature. According to the Southern novelist and essayist William Gilmore Simms, for instance, the African American, whom Simms described as morally primitive, would never "be other than a slave," and was "designed" to be "an implement in the hands of civilization."[38] In the words of Patricia Williams, slave law, which was "rooted in a concept of black 'antiwill' " ("the antithetical embodiment of pure will"), pursued "a vision of blacks as simple-minded, strong-bodied economic 'actants.' "[39] Against the instrumentalism of this concept of the slave as a tool, Stowe deployed another ethical and perceptual structure, Christian in origin and defined by philosophers and theologians from Augustine forward as the essential antithesis of proprietary instrumentalism. That structure was love. Stowe's synthetic construction of loving ownership was, as I have shown, part of an overall reconfiguration of domestic property relations during the late eighteenth and early nineteenth centuries. Not only slaves, but women, children, pets, and other traditional forms of patriarchal property were sentimentally redeemed, and reconstituted as "animated" proprietary objects whose "feelings" and "well-being" were increasingly attended to and socially and legally recognized.[40] For Stowe, the sentimental property relations of family and familiar possessions are assimilated into an ideal of intersubjective intimacy, and serve as the nexus in which sentimental personhood is constituted. In *Uncle Tom's Cabin,* I will show, Stowe strategically represents blacks as (already) "inside," within the home and the family: discursively substituting sentimental property relations for the property relations of slavery, she marks slaves as recognizably "human."[41]

The project of endowing black slaves with feelings, reconstructing them as objects of love rather than objects of use, was one that met with much cultural and discursive resistance. American theorists of racial difference from Samuel Stanhope Smith and Benjamin Rush to Silas Weir Mitchell contended that sensibility, the capacity to feel pleasure and pain as well as to experience attachments and love, varied among the races. Responding explicitly to *Uncle Tom's Cabin,* the Virginia essayist George Frederick Holmes declared that "what might be grievous misery to the white man . . . is none to the differently tempered black. Identity of sensibilities between the races of the free and the negroes is an entire fallacy."[42] In Stowe's sentimental reconstruction, the recently rehabilitated white female body was of much use. Since white women were supposedly endowed with the most refined and sensitive bodies, positing alignments between the bodies of white women and the bodies of slaves could endow black bodies with feeling. The often-discussed "feminization" of the black slave was a means of rhetorically recuperating the body of the slave and endowing that body with sensibility and life.[43]

Stowe's feminized blacks possess a "soft, impressible nature" (231), and their feelings are signified through the sentimental codes of weeping, fainting, and blushing. Such bodily signs comprise an irrepressible "natural language," "indubitable" evidence of black sensibility (56). Stowe represents blacks as individuals who "feel as keenly—even perhaps more so" than whites, and whose "local attachments are very abiding" (200, 164). Utilizing midcentury identifications of women with domesticity, she depicts slaves as "home-loving and affectionate," and identifies a "gentle, domestic heart" as the "peculiar character" of the African race (162–64). Stowe's domesticated and feminized black slaves are acutely "sensitive" to household beauty (275), and experience deeply their "local attachments," as is evidenced by their visibly painful partings from familiar objects of attachment (e.g., 104). Countering proslavery depictions of blacks as savage cannibals, creatures driven by voracious and destructive appetites, Stowe animates blacks with the preservative impulses of aesthetic sensibility and sympathy. She thus (re)constructs black slaves as gendered "subjects" by situating them within the sentimental bonds of domestic intimacy.

In Stowe's text, slaves' natural emotional responsiveness is manifested and materialized in their *responsibility*: as domesticated, "animated objects," African Americans—like women—are represented as "natural" proprietors, that is, as "naturally" endowed with sentimental proprietary emotions.[44] Stowe's depictions of African Americans' sensibility and "taste" are squared both with her identification of slaves as loving proprietors and caretakers and her figuring of Christian ownership as legalized cherishing. In her representations of African Americans' caretaking in *Uncle Tom's Cabin*, as in *House and Home Papers*, Stowe figures property relations as bonds of love, the product of natural sentiments and intimate attachments. But the tragedy she documents in the novel is that these bonds among the slaves are neither legally acknowledged nor socially respected. Southerners, denying the existence of the slaves' attachments, joke about black promiscuity and indiscriminate coupling, and assume the substitutability of the slaves' objects of affection: traders justify separating families with the claim that "thar's women enough everywhar" (170), and they imagine that the gift of "some ear-rings, or a new gown" can satisfy a slave mother whose child has been sold, contending that with them it is "out of sight, out of mind" (47–49). Stowe's representations of black slaves as loving owners and caretakers countered familiar representations of black insensibility and was an active rejection of paternalistic proslavery rhetoric portraying black slaves as requiring the care of whites and as incapable of taking care of themselves.

The feminization of the body of the black slave culminates in Stowe's depictions of black women, who, along with white women, perform most of the preservative caretaking the novel's world. Aunt Chloe exemplifies the ideal of the black woman as caretaker: indeed, she is the only black woman in the novel whom we see embody her sentimental impulses in the practices of independent homemaking. We first meet her at home in "her own snug territor[y]" (66) of Uncle Tom's cabin, a structure whose name serves less to connote patriarchal proprietorship than to highlight poignantly the unprotected status of the black slave's attachments, the disjuncture between law and feeling. The intimate relation, for Stowe, between having a home and being a person is measured by the fact that she typically frames her introduction of new characters with descriptions of their domestic surroundings; and her chief narrative strategy for representing the humanity of members of different races is showing that they do indeed keep house. Stowe, in fact, shares the contemporary tastemaker A. J. Downing's assumption that the home is an infallible expression of its residents' "character."[45] In *Uncle Tom's Cabin,* the domestic environment is figured as the female body turned inside out: it externalizes and represents its female inhabitant's interior, emotional endowments; and it constitutes a womb-like space for the extension of feminine psychic and bodily nurture. The psychological, affectional import of domestic material culture is registered in Stowe's literary technique. In *Uncle Tom's Cabin,* this pervasive cultural valuation of the *emotional* significance of familiar objects, the belief that domestic possessions both constitute and metaphorize their owners' internal, psychological condition, is formally registered in the novel's domestic realism.

This representational investment is legible in the narrative's detailed depictions of Aunt Chloe's domestic environment. We first see Chloe engaged in the domestic labor of cooking Tom's dinner, "presiding with anxious interests over certain frizzling items in a stew-pan, and anon with grave consideration lifting the cover of a bake-kettle" (66); and as she cooks, her "whole plump countenance beams with satisfaction and contentment from under her well-starched checked turban," a description that suggests that Chloe has achieved a pleasing synthesis of loving tolerance (coded by her plump body) and domestic orderliness (evidenced by the "well-starched" turban). Chloe's loving care of the home is legible in the "neat garden-patch" in which "strawberries, raspberries, and a variety of fruits and vegetables flourished under careful tending" and especially in the beautiful flowers, the begonia, rose, and diverse array of "brilliant annuals" that were "the delight and pride of Aunt Chloe's heart" (66). The neatness and rudimentary comforts of the one-room cabin register her domestic efforts and expertise (she is recognized, we learn, as the "first cook of the neighborhood" [66]), as do her manifest attempts at home decoration. In fact, Stowe's representation of Aunt Chloe's designation of one corner of the room, which contains a large bed "covered neatly with a snowy spread," as "the drawing-room of the establishment" (67–68) is intended less to provide an occasion for readerly condescension than to signal slavery's delimitation of slaves' aspirations. The "decency" (74) of the cabin as a space of love and care is indicated as well by its designation as the neighborhood's weekly meeting-place, the structure's ready transformation into the house of God (74–80).

Chloe's sensibility is clearly legible in the body of her home, and in her loving care of her children and husband. But it is the figure of the mulatta that best effects, for Stowe, the sentimental regeneration of blackness, the construction of a body that is both "black" and "white." The "tragic mulatta" was a common figure in antebellum antislavery stories, and she served a double function: to represent the history of sexual violence and coercion under slavery, and simultaneously to make that violence intolerable for white readers. The tragic mulatta, a woman "delicately bred" and pampered who is suddenly exposed to the full force of slavery's legalized injustices, makes several appearances in *Uncle Tom's Cabin*, and is most powerfully represented in the characterization of Eliza Harris. Eliza's sentimental pedigree is legible in her tidy, neat apartment in the Shelby household, and especially in her deep attachment to her son, an attachment which leads her to risk her own domestic protection and sever all her other ties, and which constitutes, on leaving the Shelbys' home, all she has (151). In the figure of Eliza, who flees and successfully evades the slavetraders, the strength of maternal love is tested, and responsiveness and responsibility are conjoined.

Our first meeting with Eliza serves to delineate the realm and conditions of caring proprietorship in Stowe's world and begins to identify two distinctly gendered models of ownership. In chapter 1, ironically entitled "A Man of Humanity," Stowe describes a meeting between a Kentucky slaveowner, Mr. Shelby, and the slavetrader Mr. Haley, in which Shelby arranges to sell some of his slaves to repay business debts. Eliza follows her son Harry into the room:

> The door was pushed gently open, and a young quadroon woman, apparently about twenty-five, entered the room.
>
> There needed only a glance from the child to her, to identify her as its mother. There was the same rich, full, dark eye, with its long lashes; the same ripples of silky black hair. The brown of her complexion gave way on the cheek to a perceptible flush, which deep-

> ened as she saw the gaze of the strange man fixed upon her in bold and undisguised admiration. Her dress was of the neatest possible fit, and set off to advantage her finely moulded shape;—a delicately formed hand and a trim foot and ankle were items of appearance that did not escape the quick eye of the trader, well used to run up at a glance the points of a fine female article. (45)

The passage moves from a suggestion of Eliza's feelings—marked by her blush of discomfort at the "strange man's" gaze of "bold and undisguised admiration" and, according to sentimental codes, her delicate body and refined dress—to the trader's utter disregard of these feelings as he assesses their material traces as the "[selling] points of a fine female article." Narrative perspective in the passage is complex, and works, rapidly, to evoke Eliza's subjective interiority and to situate that interiority in a nexus of intimate familial relations. First described as an anonymous "young quadroon woman, apparently about twenty-five," she is immediately identified not as "Eliza" (she is not named in the passage) but as *someone's mother*; and the physical description that follows ("there was the same rich, full, dark eye") refers us constantly back to that relation. The intensity of that attachment, and her urgent concern for her child's well-being, are conveyed by the fact that her attention is absorbed in looking for him to the extent that she does not at first notice the "strange man's" gaze "fixed" on her. We are again reminded of Eliza's feelings in the detailed description of her response—a blush—when she notices the stranger's disrespectful bold stare. The abrupt transition to the trader's perspective, from which Eliza's subjectivity is flattened out and viewed as a collection of "points" that make up a "fine female article," forcefully drives home the violence of that perspective. The trader assesses Eliza according to what Stowe calls elsewhere "present attractions" and their possible benefit to him: his perspective detaches Eliza's body from the feelings and personal history with which the narrator carefully invests it, thus freeing that body for his use as an instrument of anticipated profit-making. The reader is invited to interest her/himself in Eliza's subjectivity and feelings, and in the maternity to which her physical features refer; the slave trader views Eliza and sees nothing but valuable surfaces.

Stowe's introduction of Eliza in this passage begins to mark out distinct perspectives and structures of perception, which are identified in *Uncle Tom's Cabin* with different spheres and with the genders that inhabit them: a "male" look characterized by insensibility, and identified with using objects of perception and treating them as things, and which is aligned with the unrestrained imposition of (male) will; and a "female" look characterized by a layering of perceptions, a look of sympathy and responsiveness that sees in objects traces of sentiments and depth.[46] This insensitive male gaze, exemplified in the passage above by the "callous" (363) gaze of the trader, is an act of perception that does not provoke sympathetic identification but rather objectifies its object, and easily gives way to an impudent sordid touch (e.g., 477), and even whipping and abuse. These two perspectives—emphasizing, respectively, "inside" and "outside"—are, through a complex series of identifications, aligned with distinct spheres: the female look, which sympathizes with objects and endows them with depth, is affiliated with the "inside," domestic sphere, where the nuances of subjective interiority are assessed and appreciated; and the male look, of superficiality and rational conquest, is identified with the sphere of economic calculation and self-interest. These conventionally gendered perspectives correspond with and entail, I have been arguing, equally gendered structures of ownership, structures that are perhaps most explicitly defined in Hawthorne's work. Instrumental ownership—its framing type entails treating "persons" as "things"—is gendered male, and is frequently figured as mesmeric possession, while (regenerative, domestic) sympathetic ownership—its framing type entails treating "things" as "persons"—is gendered female, and is probably most clearly embodied in *The House of the Seven Gables*' Phoebe Pyncheon, who cares for household goods "as though they had a human heart in them."[47] Like Hawthorne—and like Warner and Cummins—Stowe designates the interior domestic space as the space of human fulfillment and the satisfactions of intimacy. The domestic sphere both spatially represents subjective interiority and materially protects that subjectivity—and the relations that define it—from the encroachments of male aggression.

The male realm of insensibility and coldness is identified in the text with the market, and with a politics subordinated to concern with economic profit. The *dehumanizing* effects of the market are, for Stowe, the consequence of two things: the superficiality of marketplace encounters with, and investments in, persons and things; and the *risk* that the pursuit of profit often entails. To the extent to which parties in economic exchanges view one another as "free" agents, a concern with them as individual subjects with specific feelings and specific, individual pasts is bracketed and delimited; and to the extent that capital investment in objects and persons is temporary and transient, emotional involvement with these objects is circumscribed by, and subordinated to, the desire for monetary profit. The risks inhering in self-interested profit-making are encapsulated for Stowe in one word, "speculation." Most of the tragedies Stowe documents—from Shelby's sale of Tom and Eliza, to Cassy's forced sale and sad plight—can be traced to a male act of speculating "largely and . . . loosely" (51). Speculation, which offers the "prospect of sudden and rapid gain," is described by Stowe as a "temptation to hard-heartedness," and exemplifies the imposition of "independent" male will without regard to the feelings and desires of others, an act in which these are not sufficiently "weighed in the balance" (50). The market, Stowe suggests, "hardens" men, socializing them into insensibility and unconcern with the social consequences of their actions. This insensibility increases under slavery, which effects the expansion of the market and its dangerous intrusion into the protective, humanizing domestic sphere. The psychological "hardening" produced by viewing persons as things is clearly illustrated in Stowe's characterization of the plantation owner Simon Legree. Legree's plantation emblematizes the unrestrained intrusion of the market into the home, an intrusion that is identified with white women's absence (Legree is unmarried) and is signified by his once-beautiful house and garden's neglected, unkempt appearance; in Stowe's words, Legree "used [his home], as he did everything else, merely as an implement for money-making" (491). Slavery—associated above with a "coldness" of the eye and an insensitive, bold gaze—completes, in the figure of Legree, the transformation of the body from an instrument of feeling into an insensible weapon: his head resembles a "bullet" (477), and his fist a "blacksmith's hammer" (483). Slavery especially effects the transformation of touch: the hand is transformed from instrument of sympathy and care, whose touch promotes and symbolizes interracial connection and sympathy (as in Eva's touching and embracing the slaves) into an instrument of violence and force.

Materially demarcated from the realm of male aggression and exploitation, the female, domestic realm in Stowe's novel is characterized as a sphere of care and physical and emotional protection. *Bringing things home* in this novel is an act of love, an act invested with emotional and moral urgency. The construction of the home as the realm of sentiment and loving proprietorship aligns the act of purchase with a thematics of rescue; it also assimilates proprietorship into adoption and "the labor of . . . conversion" (353). Within the bounds of domestic safety, objects in Stowe's text literally come alive: importantly, it is within the secure, idealized Quaker household of the Hallidays—a household notably free of slaves—that we hear a "motherly and old" rocking chair with "wide arms" and feather cushions "breathe hospitable invitation" and speak appealingly to the family with a "kind of subdued 'creechy crawchy,' " the result of "having taken cold in early life, or from some asthmatic affection" (214–5). In such a home, Stowe suggests, the feelings of property can be fully nurtured and attended to. Once assimilated into the sphere of protection and taking their place within it, domestic objects are represented as extending that protection. This protection is a protection of the body as well as the protection of what Augustine St. Clare calls one's "moral nature" (363). The (limited) power of things to extend domestic protection is especially legible in the novel's numerous scenes of packing, scenes in which a select group of treasured possessions are lovingly assembled as a defense against a family member's leavetaking, his or her entry into the "cold world." Such scenes are poignant because they figure the anticipated removal of the leavetaker from the sphere of domestic protection while making the fragility of the body, and the person's need for ongoing care, vividly apparent. Stowe's identification of the horrors of slavery with its dehumanizing power to strip the slave of his objects of attachment is vividly registered in her description of Legree "ransacking" and auctioning off Tom's carefully tended trunk filled with the possessions Chloe had packed for him, and then rifling through the slave's pockets, appropriating for himself a silk handkerchief and laughingly tossing into the river unnamed "trifles, which Tom had treasured, chiefly because they had amused Eva" (482). Once removed from the bounds of the home, beloved possessions are easily lost, stolen, or—as in the case of Tom's trunk—violently expropriated and stripped away.

Stowe's sentimental "romance of the object," then, is a materially bounded romance, one localized in the practices of a sentimental domestic economy. It is within the realm of the home that "objects" are endowed with personal affectional significance and reconstituted as containers of "sensibility." Significantly, it is in this feminized domestic ethic that recent critics such as Jane Tompkins have seen sentimentalism's public power and political import. However, although Tompkins (like Stowe) invests in the redemptive social value of "sentimental power," I would argue that such power is constitutively ambivalent, with ambivalent political effects: enacting the gendered dynamic of sentimental subjection, texts such as Stowe's produce forms of feminine political "agency" that are inextricable from submission and dependency. Without question, Stowe's reconstruction of domestic proprietary relations, and her inscription of blacks within this sentimental proprietary structure, had significant legal and political implications in mid-nineteenth-century America. But while the "male" practices of economics and politics are shown to impact on the domestic world, there is a real sense, I think, that novels like Stowe's instruct us not to care (very much) about them. Presenting a thematics of redemption based on the gendered bifurcation of cultural space, sentimental texts such as Stowe's work to universalize domestic (and class-specific) forms of subjectivity and ownership by assimilating these with "natural" sentiments, thus simultaneously affirming the need for legal *protection* for these forms while removing them from the arena of public negotiation. Significantly, as numerous critics of *Uncle Tom's Cabin* from James Baldwin forward have pointed out, looking especially at the novel's final configuration, Stowe plainly fails to imagine African Americans as full participant citizens in an American democracy. Sentimental discourse such as Stowe's helped expand a *protective* rather than an *enabling* conception of rights and legal/political identity, and helped construct a semisecular model of caretaking and benevolent ownership that became codified in the liberal welfare state.[48]

Sentimental Consumption and Domestic Fiction

The domestic "romance of the object" figured in Stowe's writings—the sentimental construction of the home as an animating, humanizing domain that transforms insensible "objects" into sensible, hybridized "animated objects"—shaped, I have suggested, the consumption of diverse commodities during the antebellum period—including the consumption of novels. It also has clear implications for Stowe's sentimental realism. Like many antebellum women writers, Stowe employs an informal, conversational prose style that captures the cadences of oral language and serves as a rhetorical device to establish intimate, emotional engagement between narrator and reader; she also uses what narratologists call metalepsis (crossing diegetic levels to imply that figures inside and outside the fiction exist on the same plane) to suggest that her fictional characters are "real"—possibly as "real" as the narrator and reader. (Indeed, the main purpose of "Concluding Remarks," the final chapter of *Uncle Tom's Cabin*, is to reassure the reader that the text's principal incidents are "authentic" and "sketches drawn from life" [618], while Stowe's *Key to Uncle Tom's Cabin*, first published in 1853, provides further documentation of the novel's "realism.") Stowe suggests the proper orientation of sentimental readership in a short sketch, "Feeling," in which she delineates three distinct "ways of seeing"—what might be called the "instrumental" look, the "aesthetic" look, and the "sentimental" look—that have clear implications for readerly practice:

> There is one way of studying human nature, which surveys mankind only as a set of instruments for the accomplishment of personal plans. There is another, which regards them simply as a gallery of pictures, to be admired or laughed at as the caricature or the beau ideal predominates. A third way regards them as human beings, having hearts that can suffer and enjoy, that can be improved or be ruined; as those who are linked to us by mysterious reciprocal influences, by the common dangers of a present existence, and the uncertainties of a future one; as presenting, wherever we meet them, claims on our sympathy and assistance. Those who adopt the last method are interested in human beings, not so much by present attractions as by their capabilities as intelligent, immortal beings.[49]

Stowe's endorsement here of the sentimental, *humanizing* gaze—a look of sympathy and responsiveness, which sees in what she calls "human things" traces of sentiments and depths, as opposed to the mere "present attractions" of bodily surfaces—informs her novelistic practice, and, especially, her representation of fictional characters. Sentimental texts such as Stowe's typically represent "persons" through the depiction of material and bodily signs of certain conventional emotional states—signs that include weeping, blushing, and fainting, as well as the "refined" materials of an individual's domestic environment—and they often encode clear ethical resistances to a more nuanced, modulated psychological realism. As Jane Tompkins describes *Uncle Tom's Cabin*'s discursive practice, through which bodily signs constitute the privileged locus of emotional expression, "not words, but the emotions of the heart bespeak a state of grace, and these are known by the sound of a voice, the touch of a hand, but chiefly, in moments of greatest importance, by tears."[50] In a sense, sentimental texts construct persons as "animated (representational) objects," objects of readerly proprietary desire that are animated by the "mind's eye" and the mediations of readerly sympathy.

Emphasizing empirical objects (such as bodies, families, and property) with which characters are habitually associated, and employing rhetorical devices that foster narrative intimacy, Stowe encourages her readers to "sympathize" or sympathetically "identify" with her characters, to imagine these characters as "persons"—as complex, emotionally nuanced *subjectivities* that must be fully *experienced* to be appreciated and evaluated—rather than objects of allegorical abstraction. Such allegorical renderings, Stowe's novel suggests, are always insufficient, because devoid of the felt particularity of intimate involvement and the emotional experience of "knowing" a person, an experience that, in *Uncle*

Tom's Cabin, is localized in the "private" life of the domestic sphere. The reader of *Uncle Tom's Cabin*—consuming the text, one recalls, *at home*—can project herself within an idealized, intimate community of sympathizers—to modify Benedict Anderson's phrase, an imagined *domestic* community—which extends beyond the bounds of her individual household and which is mapped onto the domestic community of the nation.

Stowe's sentimental realism was reinforced by numerous additional commodities produced for domestic consumption: *Uncle Tom's Cabin* inspired dolls, songs, poems, plays, and toys—including a parlor game, "Uncle Tom and Little Eva," introduced in 1852, with pawns that represented, according to the manufacturer, "the continual separation and reunion of families."[51] (Perhaps thinking of the generativity of this consumer industry, national advertisers in the early twentieth century referred to the " 'Topsy' element in advertising," formulated by one writer as "Turn the advertising out, and let it grow up like Topsy.")[52] These "secondary" commodities would be textualized—invested with narrative content—even while they substantiated the novel's realism and the phenomenal reality of its events and characters, loaning their empirical weight to Stowe's fictional representations. These commodities also reinforced the proprietary forms of sentimental readership, bodying forth a personalized relationship between reader and text, and apparently establishing that the novel's characters and their stories can (indeed, perhaps should) "belong" in some personal way to each individual reader. It is precisely such humanizing exchanges between the material and the affectional that sentimental consumption both promises and promotes.

"A Woman's Heart Is Truly Worth Possessing": Nathaniel Hawthorne and the Aesthetics of American Romance

In her 1855 bestseller, *The Mormon Wife: A Life Story of the Sacrifices, Sorrows, and Sufferings of Woman*, Maria Ward describes her marriage to a Mormon man, their subsequent migration to Salt Lake City, and the frontier or "border life" carried on there.[53] A literary variant of the popular urban exposé narratives that appeared in the sensationalist press in the 1840s and 1850s, Ward's narrative employs the journalistic device of the skeptical and detached participant-observer to uncover the "mysteries" of Mormonism for an uninitiated readership. Ward focuses in her narrative on the dangerous "antirepublican" aspects of Mormon spiritual and social practice—including the despotism of charismatic church leaders, the virtual negation of "individual rights" among the Mormon population, and the church's illiberal economic policies, which impede the "free circulation" of both objects and persons (50, 83–84). But Ward particularly documents abuses of patriarchal power in the Mormon community, institutionalized in spiritual wifery and polygamy. As a Mormon woman, Mrs. Bradish, describes it, "The perfect development of Mormonism will restore women to their primitive condition," identified as "a state of utter and entire dependence on their male relatives," who will then "have the power of disposing of them in marriage as they see fit" (307). Such practices were "sanctioned," she continues, by "patriarchal usage" as recorded in Scripture—specifically, the examples of Jacob, David, and Hosea (307). For Maria Ward, however, such power entails the "enslavement" of Mormon "females" (321): removing to Utah "for the avowed purpose of being beyond the surveillance and influence" of civil law, rejecting republican principles in favor of a patriarchal theocracy, the Mormons reduce the status of women from subjects with "individual rights" to chattel without any legal existence or authority of their own (380). Expressly identifying the "primitive condition" of Mormon women with the status of Englishwomen under coverture (375), Ward makes it clear that Mormon women are defined wholly as patriarchal property: "One by one the rights to which [women] had been accustomed, as well as the courtesies generally conceded to them, were taken away"—including the right of a woman to choose her own husband, the privilege of hiring domestic service, and, especially, a woman's right to hold property of her own (321). Indeed, to establish women's status as patriarchal property, the Mormons deny women independent property rights—newly instituted by the legislatures of most federated states—and, even, their claim to dower. "It is the policy of these men," one woman informs Ward, "to keep everything like money out of the reach of the women" (90).

In Ward's narrative, Mormon men's virtually unlimited authority over women easily leads to male "licentiousness" and the abuses of male sexual predation (307). Indeed, the thrust of *The Mormon Wife* is to show that, trapped in a wilderness community where men exploit their sexual dominion through polygamy, women are nothing more than sexual slaves. Church founder Joseph Smith—a man who, according to Ward, "outraged and insulted all woman-kind" by his "maltreat[ment]" of women and absolute disregard for their feelings (118)—makes a point of seeking out and converting "young and beautiful girls" for the purpose of the "gratification of lawless passions" (60, 65). One young woman is seduced by Smith, who then informs her that she will be passed around to other men; unable to face a brutal fate and knowing there is no escape, she drowns herself (79). Smith's successor, Brigham Young, is even more lustful, promising to make a favored girl "something like chief sultana in the Turkish harems" (218) and shamelessly awarding male initiates "beautiful girls" in exchange for their contribution to the "coffers of the church" (101). The sexual commodification of women is melodramatically rendered in a chapter entitled "Church and State," in which Ward stages the sale of two sisters by a mercenary father who "looks on his daughters as legitimate subjects of speculation" and who "paid little attention to the inclinations of [his] children," conceiving "the marriage of his daughters [as] an occasion of enriching himself" (357, 321, 359). Mr. Melton selects for his daughters' husband Old Weldy, a leering, lascivious old man, "uncouth in form and feature" with the air of a "hungry lion" (322, 359), who already possesses a dozen wives. When the sisters and their mother tearfully remonstrate, Mr. Melton responds that his daughters "should be married to Weldy if [they] went to the altar in chains" (358). Old Weldy himself scoffs at the girls' passionate entreaties and their avowal that they do not love him, refuting their claim that "marriage without love must be unhappy" with the argument that "marrying for love [is] an antiquated notion . . . unsuitable for this utilitarian age" (361), and menacingly insisting that "you are mine—legally mine" (360). Weldy has his way: the girls are "purchase[d]" in exchange for a few "horses and cows" (358), and are forced to join his household. In a scene worthy of *Uncle Tom's Cabin*, Mrs. Melton turns to one daughter "with a mute glance of despairing agony," while "the girl sat with her hands clasped, her cheeks blanched, the picture of utter despair" (328).

Ward's portrait of the Melton women's victimization clarifies the terms of her denunciation of Mormonism as an "antirepublican" social and religious institution: specifically, it locates her critique within the far-reaching cultural context known as sentimentalism. Presenting Mormonism as a barbaric anachronism, *The Mormon Wife* contrasts the sentimentalism of "civilized" modernity—in which social relations are mediated by sympathy and love, and the subjectivity and feelings of society's "weaker" members (here, women and children) are "respected," socially acknowledged, and attended to—with the "antisentimentalism" or unrestrained patriarchalism of "primitive" societies (such as the Mormons'), in which social relations are mediated by "brute" physical force. Indeed, the great crime of Mormonism, in Ward's account, is its antisentimental "degradation" of the marriage tie, its transformation of the "domestic altar" into a "shrine of legal prostitution" (314). According to Ward, the "abomination of polygamy" is that marriage is emptied of the "finer and gentler feelings" of love and transformed into a business arrangement or "mere means of propagating the human species": specifically, in Mormon marriages, men are encouraged to view women as objects of transient physical passion instead of subjects with feelings and desires of their own. Ideally a loving union in persons who "through life, are bound to each other" so that "neither absence nor distance can break the tie" (42), marriage under Mormonism is reduced to a relationship of sexual utility, and wives become instruments of sexual use—mere "tools" of male sexual passion (101)—traded to gratify men's "passion for variety" (219): Mormon "wives may be multiplied like garments, and with every one that is worn, an old one must be thrown off" (312). Instead of being viewed as objects of love, whose "heart[s]" as well as their bodies are deemed "truly worth possessing" (220), Mormon women are viewed as "machines" (40, 205)—as *insensible* bodies—and are subsequently treated "with the most brutal indifference" to their feelings (80). In Ward's view, such marriages are not the sanctified, legally sanctioned unions of civilized society: expressing lust rather than love, they *dehumanize* husbands and, especially, wives. Mormon women, Ward writes, "were treated little better than slaves, were required to do all the drudgery, were frequently subjected to corporeal punishment, and painfully impressed with a sense of their inferiority in a thousand ways" (103).

Ward's sensationalistic narrative was one of the earliest examples of a popular American genre: more than fifty novels and adventure tales about Mormonism were produced between 1852—when the Mormon church publicly disclosed its endorsement of polygamy—and the turn of the twentieth century.[54] *The Mormon Wife* was itself reissued many times in the second half of the nineteenth century, the last edition appearing in 1913—some twenty years after the church hierarchy officially renounced the practice of plural marriage. The anti-Mormon narratives, featuring the twin ideas of captivity and sexual danger, exemplified a broad cultural fascination with what was commonly termed "white slavery." (In *Boadica, the Mormon Wife*, for example, Alfreda Bell depicts Mormonism as a degenerate social state in which women were nothing more than "white slaves.")[55] A range of popular antebellum narrative forms—including anti-Catholic narratives such as Maria Monk's *Awful Disclosures*, sensationalistic gothic novels such as George Lippard's *Quaker City*, "Oriental" tales and travel narratives such as Bayard Taylor's *The Lands of the Saracen*, and a host of Indian captivity narratives—presented sensationalistic, often lurid accounts of young, beautiful white women captured, brutally treated, and confined against their will, often for explicit sexual purposes.[56] Indeed, *The Mormon Wife* expressly identifies Mormons with Catholics (e.g., 99–100) and Indians (e.g., 132, 381–83), as well as "Orientals" such as Turks (e.g., 287, 300), and the text punctuates its dominant narrative theme—the seduction and captivity of Mormon women by Mormon men—with brief, contrapuntal narratives of Indian captivity. A descendant of the sensationalistic, melodramatic Indian captivity narrative popular in the late eighteenth century—itself a secularized variation on the seventeenth-century Puritan genre—the antebellum "white slave" narrative captured the imaginations of many Americans, and constituted a resonant cultural form.

Below, I examine the ideological import of that resonance: white slave narratives, I argue, were engaged in negotiating a pressing cultural problematic—that of the status of civil "subjects" in a democratic republic. Like the related term "wage slavery," the term "white slavery" had a complex political history. As David Roediger has demonstrated, the terms "white slavery" and "wage slavery," which underscored connections between wage labor and "unfreedom," circulated widely in political discourse during the 1830s and 1840s, in part because the rise of a highly visible movement to abolish slavery prompted a reexamination of the line between slavery and freedom. These terms were highly unstable, expressing both renewed republican fears about the loss of liberty under capitalism *and* assurances of white privilege and entitlement; in Roediger's words, "for all but a handful of committed abolitionists and labor reformers, use of [the term] white slavery was not an act of solidarity with the slave but rather a call to arms to end the inappropriate oppression of whites."[57] Solidarity with African Americans was perhaps especially charged for the white male artisans who led the first labor movement, who frequently applied the term "white slavery" to factory workers (often women and children) without necessarily applying it to themselves. For instance, Seth Luther's 1832 *Address to the Workingmen of New England* does not refer to American male journeymen as slaves, but it does describe factory women in bondage and quotes sentimental verse describing child laborers as "little sinless slaves." As Roediger points out, in the 1850s, slavery metaphors largely disappeared from labor's language, while the term "white slavery" came to be applied exclusively to the arena of sexual politics and the exploitation, especially sexual exploitation, of women (a meaning evident in earlier discourse as well). Indeed, while some factory women used the term "white slave" to identify with the abolitionist cause, others, such as Clementine Averill, rejected the term as "degrading," in part because of its association with sexual exploitation.[58] As with the "feminization" of black slaves in Stowe's novel, the gendering and racialization of "enslavement" in the evolving political discourse of white slavery could distance white men from the threatening loss of political agency, while facilitating complex forms of identification and disidentification between white women and African Americans. In an important sense, white slave narratives, like Stowe's novel, define slavery as the problem and offer gender as the solution. In other words, mapping forms of patriarchal "enslavement" of women onto a developmental (and racialized) narrative of individual and social "progress," these narratives reframed slavery from a political and economic condition that undermined the liberty of citizens into the effect of a particular, gendered dynamic within patriarchal heterosexuality. That rewriting could mobilize "regressive" fantasies of masculine power and ownership of women, while promoting "consent" to the civilizing, proprietary agency available to liberal subjects within capitalism.

The discourse of white slavery in the 1850s was thus, I would argue, a response to first-wave feminism and the national crisis over slavery, as well as the expansion of industrial and commercial capitalism. As Averill's example suggests, the term "white slave" was ambiguous and charged, registering both white women's identification with slave women and the assertion of their racially privileged status as civil subjects (and indeed, their collective authority over black women). Indeed, part of the rhetorical effectiveness of the term "white slave" in political discourse, as well as the horror white slave narratives evoke, derives from the (temporary) erosion of race distinctions. White slave narratives capitalize on this ambivalence, in particular by narrativizing white women's "captivity" as a temporary condition, and by associating forms of "enslavement" with the desires of racial and class Others. Documenting the (regressive) return of "savage" patriarchal power, here displaced onto religious and racial Others, narratives such as Maria Ward's work to normalize particular forms of liberal civil(ized) subjectivity and proprietorship. Employing as autobiographical narrator the properly distressed (and no longer physically captive) "*Mrs.* Maria Ward," the narrative enlists readerly identification with the sentimental performance of that free (white) civil subject by evoking and then containing (or abjecting) an identification with the "enslaved" racial body.

Narratives such as *The Mormon Wife* thus performed a crucial ideological function: depicting the property relations of racial and religious Others, they worked to define dominant, specifically "American" proprietary and affectional relations and subjectivities.[59] Indeed, by the late eighteenth century, as historians have pointed out, American writers regularly designated the prototypical American domestic model as a consensual union mediated by love — a specific middle-class code of consent that would, ideally, equilibrate domestic disharmonies and inequities. J. H. Beadle, author of the inflammatory anti-Mormon text *Life in Utah* (1870), makes this process of discursive Othering explicit: "polygamy," Beadle writes, "could not have been established in a purely American community"; the Mormon practice, which demonstrated features "probably worse than in any Mohammedan country," could flourish only among "alien" women and men, those of foreign birth and of the class "among whom men have never been accustomed to respect women very highly."[60] Appealing to a symbology of gender and proprietorship first articulated by Scottish Enlightenment moral philosophers, a wide range of midcentury texts defined respect for women — a new concern with the *feelings* of male property — as an index of American civilization.

As I have argued, the sentimental paradigm did not so much *negate* women's status as property as *reconstitute* it, simultaneously "animating" women and situating them within novel proprietary structures. As the hero in a Catharine Sedgwick novel remarks, after the woman he loves has professed her undying devotion, "I feel a sort of unratified property right in her."[61] Against what one might call the gothic or patriarchal ownership of white slavery — a configuration in which temporal primitiveness and ethnic Otherness are conflated — texts like *The Mormon Wife* construct an ideal of what I have been calling "sentimental ownership," a (paradoxical) model of "consensual," socially regenerative property relations seemingly compatible with America's democratic ideals. A prominent moral formulation presented in a wide range of antebellum texts, this model of loving ownership, I have demonstrated, connoted a synthesis of class, race, gender, and national identifications, and was a foundational construction of a specifically American "private life."

Below, I examine these "American" configurations of domestic proprietorship and affection in the work of Nathaniel Hawthorne, an author whose popular and sentimental dimensions, long obscured by his canonical status, are only recently being explored.[62] No nineteenth-century American author delved more deeply into the entanglements of sympathy and seduction, love and power, outlined in Scottish discourse and American sentimental fiction. Indeed, like the Scots, Hawthorne explores in his writings the emotional and ethical consequences of what Adam Smith terms "living inside another's heart"; like Smith in particular, he emphasizes in his work the perceptual structure of vision that mediates the imaginative exchanges that make sentimental possession possible. Hawthorne was apparently familiar with Smith's moral philosophy: according to Marion Kesserling, he borrowed a copy of *The Theory of Moral Sentiments* from the Salem Athenaeum when he was in his early twenties.[63] Hawthorne delineates in his writings, especially *The Blithedale*

Romance, the Smithian interrelations between loving and owning, animation and affectional involvement, localized in the "civilized," regenerate domestic sphere. In Hawthorne's *Blithedale Romance*, as in Smith's essay, the family is constituted as a socially redemptive sphere in which bodies are "animated" and endowed with emotional sensibility. However, Hawthorne's text, more clearly than Smith's, exposes the extent to which the bourgeois ideology of romantic love and consensual familial ties produces new species of patriarchal power, reconfiguring, rather than undermining, women's construction as property. Indeed, recounting the Blithedale experiment from the perspective of the male narrator, Coverdale, Hawthorne foregrounds the forms of masculine desire within which sentimental subjectivity takes shape.

Like Smith's *Theory*, Hawthorne's text underscores the importance of vision as arbiter of social animation and, thus, an instrument of social power. This concern with the politics of looking is thematized in much of Hawthorne's fiction: it is central, for example, to Hawthorne's narrative explorations of the romantic theme of the overreaching scientist, who irreverently aims to penetrate the secrets of nature and other people, and who looks at persons not with sympathy and respect but with calculating detachment. Hawthorne's Smithian understanding of the social power of the "look" also underlies his preoccupation with the moral dimensions of his own authorial practice and his concern that he was, in fact, a voyeur by profession: envisioning himself as a "spiritualized Paul Pry," Hawthorne apparently imagined himself as a detached observer situated outside the bounds of everyday social intercourse.[64] However, again more fully than Smith, Hawthorne registers the gendered disequilibrium in social power that structures relations of vision. Because of this disequilibrium, it is *men's* visual power, and the power of the *male* look to animate or destroy bodies—to constitute them, that is, as (animate) objects of love or (inanimate) instruments of use—that is socially determinative. In *The Blithedale Romance*, this male power is partially registered in the mesmeric potency of Hollingsworth's and Westervelt's gazes. However, the significance of vision as a medium of social interpellation is principally figured in the visual practices of Coverdale, whose penchant for voyeuristic speculation frames, indeed motivates, Hawthorne's narrative.

"White Slaves" and Feminine Subjects in The Blithedale Romance

What I've described as a nexus of Scottish, Smithian interrelations of emotional animation and emotional control appears in much of Hawthorne's fiction. Sympathy in Hawthorne's work is inseparable from domination: Hawthorne repeatedly explores the gothic underside of the bonds of sympathy, the ways they constrain and "enslave," as well as constitute and empower, gendered liberal subjects. These Smithian interrelations are evident in his first major work, *The Scarlet Letter*. *The Scarlet Letter* is the story of an arranged union between an aged scholar and a young, beautiful woman, a union forged not by mutual love (as Hester frankly tells Chillingworth, "I felt no love, nor feigned any") but by law and male ambition.[65] Early in the text, Chillingworth describes his love for Hester in metaphorical language that suggests both illicit, gothic possession—she is imprisoned within his heart's "innermost chamber," consumed by the fire her presence generates—and the alignment of "hearts" and "homes" essential to the sentimental ethos: "My heart was a habitation large enough for many guests, but lonely and chill, and without a household fire. I longed to kindle one! . . . And so, Hester, I drew thee into my heart, into its innermost chamber, and sought to warm thee by the warmth which thy presence made there!" (81). As in Smith's *Theory*, the text's public/homoerotic and domestic/heterosexual spheres of sympathetic exchange overlap, and indeed constitute one another: commercial and familial forms of liberal political subjection, their relations of dominance and submission, are mutually reinforcing. In *The Scarlet Letter*, Chillingworth's illicit possession of Hester is displaced onto his diabolical psychic pursuit and captivity of Dimmesdale: practiced by the text's "potent necromancer" (281) and unmoored from the "civilizing" practices of domestic exchange, sympathy is transformed from an instrument of love into a weapon, employed in the service of revenge (as Chillingworth melodramatically states of Dimmesdale, "Sooner or later, he must needs be mine!" [81]). Like many of his male contemporaries, particularly Whitman, Melville, and Emerson, Hawthorne explores in his imaginative writing the masculine homoerotics of public life; but unlike Whitman's political-erotic vision of egalitarian fraternity and radical democracy, Hawthorne's inscriptions of public sympathy between men are marked by inequality, and involve relations of dominance and submission characteristic of marketplace competition and especially the bodily bonds of wage labor. Indeed, in Hawthorne's work, public/commercial homoerotic desire entails forms of bondage and penetration that are powerfully desired and powerfully feared, and to which the "civilized," sympathetic relations of patriarchal domesticity appear as both escape and antidote.

In *The Scarlet Letter*, whereas Dimmesdale, as masculine public figure, is invested with a dangerous excess of sympathetic interest, Hester, as a woman who has transgressed patriarchal domesticity, is positioned outside the realm of sympathetic exchange. Publicly branded as an adulteress, Hester lives on the "outskirts" of the Puritan settlement, indeed on the "frontier" of civilization (87); thus liminally situated, Hester is represented as a spectral being, her insubstantial material presence figuring her exclusion from the "sphere of human charities" and the social network of sympathetic vision centered in domesticity (87):

> In all her intercourse with society . . . there was nothing that made [Hester] feel as if she belonged to it. Every gesture, every word, and even the silence of those with whom she came in contact, implied, and often expressed, that she was banished, and as much alone as if she inhabited another sphere, or communicated with the common nature by other organs and senses than the rest of human kind. She stood apart from moral interests, yet close beside them, like a ghost that revisits the familiar fireside, and can no longer make itself seen or felt; no more smile with the household joy, nor mourn with the kindred sorrow; or, should it succeed in manifesting its forbidden sympathy, awakening only terror and horrible repugnance. (90–91)

But the regenerating power of familial love is especially apparent in the depiction of Hester's illegitimate daughter, Pearl. Over the course of the narrative, Pearl is transformed from an inhuman "airy sprite" (99) and "imp of evil" (101), situated "entirely out of the sphere of sympathy or human contact" (145), into a recognizably "human" child who displays the conventional signs of sympathetic emotion. Described as a "born outcast of the infantile world" (101), having by her own account "no heavenly father" (106) as well as no earthly one, Pearl is persistently identified with liminal figures such as Indians (e.g., 266) and witches (e.g., 101, 267); Pearl seems strikingly oblivious to the feelings of others, violating norms of Puritan propriety by irreverently dancing on the tombstones of church elders and shrieking wildly when one of her "moods of perverse merriment" overtakes her (145). Tellingly, it is Dimmesdale's public acknowledgment of "my little Pearl" (274) and especially his kiss that animates Pearl, situating her within the bonds of love and the (reconstructed) patriarchal family: "Pearl kissed his lips. A spell was broken. The great scene of grief, in which the wild infant bore a part, had developed all her sympathies; and as her tears fell upon her father's cheek, they were the pledge that she would grow up amid human joy and sorrow, nor forever do battle with the world, but be a woman in it" (279). *The*

Scarlet Letter makes it clear that the metaphorics of sympathy and civil subjectivity constitute a patriarchal metaphorics: the animating, "civilizing" exchanges of sympathetic identification are localized within the patriarchal domestic economy of sex and gender.[66]

These metaphorics also inform *The Blithedale Romance.* A narrative commentary on the project of utopian socialism executed in George Ripley's Brook Farm experiment, an experiment in which Hawthorne briefly participated, *The Blithedale Romance* emphasizes the *national* significance of the Smithian, sentimental construction of domestic "animation." Situated by Hawthorne in a long tradition of American utopian experiments, Blithedale is expressly identified with the Puritans' foundational "errand." Like the Puritans, the narrator states, the Blithedale community aims to effect the "reformation of the world" by beginning their lives anew and thus "showing mankind the example of a life governed by other than the false and cruel principles" on which the rest of human society has been based.[67] Blithedale is depicted by its members as a new Eden, a society in which regenerate individuals can escape the "shackles" of worldly existence and lead the "life of Paradise" (16). And like the Puritan—and later on, the American republican—collective undertaking, Blithedale's utopian community is figured in familial terms, as a heartfelt and consensual union. Images of domestic warmth and animation versus extradomestic coldness and unregeneracy abound in Hawthorne's text: in the opening narrative sequence, for example, the new community members arrive in the midst of a snowstorm, and find a "cheery" and "abundant" fire burning in the kitchen-hearth (9, 23). In the narrator's description, the blaze "flickered powerfully" on the walls of the farmhouse, "comfort[ing]" and "cheer[ing]" its inhabitants, and contrasting powerfully with the "chill and dreary" situation "on the other side of [the] illuminated windows" (23, 25). Thus situated domestically, members of the community are described as joined together by "familiar love" (19), an egalitarian and voluntary union that prefigures the earthly "millennium of love" (24). Blithedale's reconstructed family, in Hawthorne's account, is a community of "regenerated men" (12), a redeemed, and consensual social body defined in contrast to the "fallen" world outside, which is peopled by what Coverdale calls "outside barbarians" (20). Coverdale makes explicit this dynamic of communal love and collective antagonism in Blithedale's collectivity: "I very soon became sensible that, as regarded society at large, we stood in a position of new hostility, rather than new brotherhood. Nor could this fail to be the case, in some degree, until the bigger and better half of society should range itself on our side. Constituting so pitiful a minority as now, we were inevitably estranged from the rest of mankind, in pretty fair proportion with the strictness of our mutual bond among ourselves" (20). This regenerate collectivity is mapped temporally as well as spatially: "estranged from the rest of mankind," the members of Blithedale are similarly estranged from their personal and collective past(s), their aspirations interpolated in a narrative of social "progress." As Coverdale astutely observes, "Our bond . . . was not affirmative, but negative. We had individually found one thing or another to quarrel with, in our past life, and were pretty well agreed as to the inexpediency of lumbering along with the old system any farther. As to what should be substituted, there was much less unanimity" (63). Thus distinguished from the fallenness of contemporary society in spatial and temporal terms, Blithedale is depicted as an incarnation of American utopianism: a familial union that regenerates bodies through sympathetic exchange, the segregated, domestic community at Blithedale is, like Hawthorne's romance itself, a "world elsewhere," a kind of political and erotic theater that stages the performance of "consent" and civil(ized) feeling. Framed by Coverdale's normalizing gaze, the production of such civil(ized) feeling in Blithedale entails managing forms of male homoeroticism and interpellating sexed and gendered subjects within the identificatory forms and emotional structures—specifically, forms of dominance and submission—of liberal political subjection.[68]

Imaged as an "earthly paradise," Blithedale is mapped as the site of perfected, spiritualized embodiment and reconstructed eroticism. Bodies are literally remade at Blithedale, a process especially evident in the text's depictions of Coverdale and Priscilla. When Coverdale arrives at Blithedale, he experiences an illness that is clearly configured as a death and rebirth, occasioning his reincarnation into a new, less material body. Invoking an antebellum cliché about the spiritualizing power of illness, Coverdale observes that "the soul gets the better of the body, after wasting illness" or during a "reduced state of the corporeal system" (46), and this process of re-embodiment resembles "the exultation with which the spirit will enter on the next stage of its eternal progress, after leaving the heavy burthen of its mortality in an earthly grave" (61). Treated with homeopathic medicine, Coverdale "speedily became a skeleton above ground" (41), and emerges from the sick chamber—appropriately, on May Day—in a new, regenerated form. Employing the threshold imagery so common in Hawthorne's work, Coverdale tellingly figures this transformation as a passage from one house—a dark, restrictive architectural structure—to a "freer" space beyond:

> My fit of illness had been an avenue between two existences; the low-arched and darksome doorway, through which I crept out of a life of old conventionalisms . . . and gained admittance into the freer region that lay beyond. . . . The very substance upon my bones had not been fit to live with, in any better, truer, or more energetic mode than that to which I was accustomed. So it was taken off me and flung aside, like any other worn out or unseasonable garment; and, after shivering a little while in my skeleton, I began to be clothed anew, and much more satisfactorily than in my previous suit. . . . I was quite another man. (61)

Zenobia later satirizes this vision of utopian bodily reconstruction. Coverdale, she states, will indeed be given a new body, but of a distinctly earthly kind. Instead of being purged of "masculine grossness" and endowed with sensibility, Coverdale's body will be more thoroughly materialized, converted from human flesh into food: his brain will be a "cauliflower," and his "physical man" will be "transmuted into salt-beef and fried pork, at the rate . . . of a pound and a half a day" (67).

Priscilla, too, is reborn at Blithedale, "budding and blossoming, and daily putting on some new charm" (72). When Priscilla arrives at Blithedale, she is wan and "unsubstantial" (26), and lacks the power to speak (28); indeed, she seems to Coverdale a liminal being, "some desolate kind of a creature, doomed to wander about in snow-storms," who had been momentarily "tempted" by the "ruddiness of our window-panes" to enter a "human dwelling" (27). Complying with Hollingsworth's request that they "warm her poor, shivering body with this good fire, and her poor shivering heart with our best kindness. Let us feed her, and make her one of us" (30), the community takes her in; soon, she begins "to look like a creature of this world" (31). At Blithedale, Priscilla is transformed from a spectral being—"unformed, vague, and without substance" (72)—into a flesh and blood person with a "woman's soul and frame" (73); her gestures and smile, "like a baby's first one," possess a "wondrous novelty" (73). Thus re-embodied, Priscilla gives herself over wholly to the utopian impulse, describing Blithedale as "a world where everybody is kind to me, and where I love everybody" (75), and insisting on the community's escape from history and its relations of social dominance, announcing to Coverdale that "the past never comes back again" (76).

Describing her body as a "delicate" instrument and her nerves as "fragile harp-strings" (75), the narrator emphasizes the fluidity of Priscilla's body, its unpredictable, "ever-shifting" (73) movements registering its sensitivity as an emotional receptor. Priscilla's body epitomizes for Hawthorne the "feminine" body, a body that is a medium of sensibility rather than an instrument of rational will (a "tool"). Priscilla's sensibility, her capacity to feel what others feel, is best exemplified in the text during a visit to Coverdale's sick chamber: delivering a letter from Margaret Fuller, she sympathetically assumes the writer's shape, resembling through her "air" and "the expression of her face" the letter's sender (51). As in Stowe's writings, the "regenerated" feminine body is here endowed with sensibility; and Priscilla's value as an empathic instrument is depicted as proportionate to her failings as a diligent, organized domestic laborer (74). Appealing to a model of action as inspired spontaneity rather than the product of rational will, Hawthorne thus images Priscilla's bodily actions as the unmediated impulses of regenerate feeling. This resuscitation of bodily action, of course, constitutes one of the community's principal aims: the community arrives at Blithedale motivated by "delectable visions of the spiritualization of labor," the sanctification of work as a "form of prayer, and ceremonial of worship" in which heart, mind, and body are conjoined (19, 65).

The locus of collective regeneration, the reformed social body at Blithedale would, its members believed, undo the social divisions and forms of "unfreedom" in the world "outside." Love relations at Blithedale are imaged as voluntary and consensual, exemplifying in particular the increased respect for women's choices often considered characteristic of American society. According to the narrator, "While inclining us to the soft affections of the Golden Age, [Blithedale's mode of association] seemed to authorize any individual, of either sex, to fall in love with any other, regardless of what would elsewhere be judged suitable and prudent. Accordingly, the tender passion was very rife among us, in various degrees of mildness or virulence, but mostly passing away with the state of things that had given it origin" (72). Amidst this free, "consensual" heterosocial intercourse, the "example" and influence of women, coupled with the "education of Christianity," would ideally "soften" male violence and will to power (41). However, in the narrator's account, the utopian collectivity does not undermine but merely recasts relations of dominance and "enslavement." Far from forming an idealized, utopian common body bound together by love and sympathy, bodies at Blithedale materialize persistent signs of social distinction and inequality. On his arrival at Blithedale, for example, Coverdale is distressed by the uncouth table manners and inferior "refinement" of the hired farm manager, Silas Foster, whose "terrible enormities" perpetrated with the "butter-plate" and diverse additional "amiable exploits" at supper mark him as less a "civilized Christian than the worst kind of an ogre" (30). Not only are class practices and distinctions indelibly marked on the body, but some (working-class) bodies are represented as incapable of regeneration: Silas's wife, Mrs. Foster, knits in her sleep, and her mechanical performance of labor radically enacts the segregation of mind and body while defining work as the province of inhuman machines rather than a virtuous, spiritualized enterprise (32).

Similarly, the domination of women is not undermined by the proposed equality of the sexes and the forms of "feminine consent" facilitated by/in Blithedale's "union." As I argue more extensively below, it is crucial to emphasize that the narrative's construction of "Blithedale" is an expression of *Coverdale's* desire: Coverdale takes on himself the project of investigating and "exposing" the utopian community's failures, and his investment in this project is erotically charged and deeply *interested*, as well as a measure of his political cynicism. Indeed, Coverdale's "recognition" of the persistence of gender inequality and feminine submission at Blithedale, like his efforts to debunk the community's political ideals as veiled expressions of self-interest (what Zenobia terms "playing at philanthropy and progress" [227]), suggests his eroticized, identificatory investment in the social forms that sustain liberal subjectivity. If Blithedale promotes the unsettling sense that "everything in nature and human existence was fluid, or fast becoming so," Coverdale takes refuge in his habitual inclination, "a decided tendency towards the actual" and a felt "sense of what kind of world it was" (140). Framed by Coverdale's desire, Hawthorne's text registers both the forms of gender inequality—specifically, women's construction as objects of masculine proprietary desire—within liberal political culture, and the dependency of masculine subjectivity on *reproducing* and *performing* those proprietary forms of gender. Indeed, politics are insistently eroticized in Hawthorne's text, and political desire circulates principally through the heterosexual couple: as I demonstrate below, Coverdale's profession of feminism and rhetorical and erotic investment in feminine moral "superiority" is as much an attempt to seduce Zenobia (and rhetorically outperform Hollingsworth) as an expression of his identification with feminine submission (121–24). As in the Scottish narratives discussed in chapter 1, the production of masculine "possessive individualism" *depends on* this proprietary construction of femininity—a construction Coverdale invests in and repeatedly enacts, although his efforts inevitably fall short. In narrativizing Coverdale's desire, Hawthorne documents in rich detail the psychic, identificatory structures of liberal masculinity: the ambivalent forms of masculine "identification with" feminine submission and proprietary "power over" women that *instantiates* masculine political subjectivity.

Coverdale's "work" at Blithedale is thus a narrative labor: it involves inscribing Zenobia and Priscilla—female objects of erotic interest in the text who, with Hollingsworth, comprise the members of Coverdale's "private theater" (153)—within the normative, proprietary forms of heterosexual desire through which civil(ized) subjects are constituted. For example, immediately on his arrival, Coverdale observes that women's work at Blithedale is neither socially nor spiritually redeemed. Learning from Zenobia that a nineteenth-century gender division of labor is upheld in the community "as a matter of course" (16), Coverdale pointedly notes that "the kind of labor which falls to the lot of women" (what Zenobia calls "the domestic . . . part of the business" [16]) is just that which chiefly distinguishes . . . the life of degenerated mortals" from the "life of Paradise" (16); he adds, "Eve had no dinner-pot, and no clothes to mend, and no washing-day" (16). Associated with tending and maintaining the unregenerate, material body, feminine labor is, in Coverdale's account, positioned outside the realm of animating and consensual social exchange. Men's possession of women's bodies, their (collective) sense of entitlement to female labor and to women as sexual property, is thus not negated at Blithedale but instituted in new forms.

Initially presented as a refuge from gothic proprietorship and the illicit power of Westervelt, who apparently has mysterious claims on both Zenobia and Priscilla, the experiment at Blithedale, in Coverdale's construction, reconstitutes rather than undoes the domination of women. Like *The Mormon Wife*, *The Blithedale Romance* employs pervasive "Orientalist" imagery (Blithedale is repeatedly figured as a seraglio), here referring not to the illicit ownership of women by religious Others but to relations of gender and property within the "regenerate" American collectivity: both principal female characters appear to be under the sway of Hollingsworth's "animal magnetism," and by the end of the text one of the women has died. Indeed, part of the utopian promise of the collectivity—the (unspoken) return for men's entry into the social contract—is what Pateman calls the "sexual contract," the construction of the collective's women as the (potential) property of each man, and of each male citizen as a (potential) proprietor/owner. Thus, the bachelor Coverdale imagines himself not as propertiless—bereft of particular attachments and objects of love—but, rather, as the *potential* owner of all women; this fact accounts for his emotional waverings at Blithedale as well as his disappointment when he "intuits" that Zenobia has been married, a disappointment that evinces lost possibilities as well as the proprietary construction of gender that underpins liberal subjectivity. As Coverdale tellingly states, "A bachelor always feels himself *defrauded*, when he knows, or suspects, that any woman of his acquaintance has given herself away" (48; emphasis added). In Coverdale's Blithedale, "white slavery" is not localized "outside" or a vestigial remnant of "primitive" social forms, but is situated at the very heart of utopian union: in Zenobia's words, women are marked as "hereditary bond slave[s]" both within and without the community (217). Narrowing his vision from the extended collective to the trio of characters he fixates on, Coverdale both aims to resolve the erotic ambiguities of the quartet by reframing them within the "civilized" desires of the heterosexual couple, and registers alternate erotic possibilities (especially his desire for Hollingsworth, a desire both clearly inscribed and disavowed). Indeed, Coverdale's oft-noted social liminality and detachment, as well as his ambiguous sexual impulses, registers his ambivalence about acceding to heterosexuality and the forms of liberal political subjectivity it subtends. Coverdale's compulsion to "know" the "truth" about the erotic lives of his "three friends" (153), and specifically his voyeuristic stake in "unveiling" hidden operations of "white slavery" within the collective, both fuels the narrative—constitutes its principal narrative desire—and reveals his erotic investment in the interrelations of gender and power (specifically forms of feminine submission and masculine force) he both "discovers" and fears.

The construction of women as the collective property of men and the importance of visual desire in sustaining that relation are evident in the narrative "treatment" of Zenobia. Again, this *narrative* "treatment" is, of course, the *narrator*'s "treatment": Hawthorne's utilization of a first-person (and *male*) narrator in *The Blithedale Romance*, and his foregrounding of Coverdale's voyeuristic desire, expressly aligns the text's erotic and proprietary impulses with *male* desire, and with the narrative enactment of masculine subjectivity. As Lauren Berlant has argued, Zenobia is the main recipient of the narrative gaze of heterosexual desire in the text, and the main object of the text's voyeuristic speculation.[69] In the narrative's treatment of Zenobia one can see the reduction of an intellectually complex, articulate woman into an effect of male sexual desire, a reduction epitomized in Coverdale's negation of the intellectual content of Zenobia's feminism and his persistent deflection from her "fine intellect" to the "admirable figure" in which it is "fitly cased" (15). Acknowledging that the "sphere of ordinary womanhood was narrower than her development required" (190), Coverdale nonetheless confidently states that "women, however intellectually superior . . . seldom disquiet themselves about the rights or wrongs of their sex, unless their own individual affections chance to lie in idleness, or to be ill at ease. . . . I could measure Zenobia's inward trouble by the animosity with which she now took up the general quarrel of woman against man" (120–21). Framing Zenobia's desire within his heterosexualizing, domesticating gaze, Coverdale attempts here to confine that desire to the reflection of (some) man's desire for her—in his Byronic formulation, that love for man is woman's whole "existence" (241). However, it is precisely what Coverdale calls Zenobia's "sex" (17)—her "uncomfortable surplus of vitality" (96)—that fuels his visual and erotic interest.

As Berlant notes, when Coverdale first sees Zenobia, he responds to her verbal invocation of Paradise by undressing her with his eyes, rationalizing his fantasy of sexual possession as an "irresistible" response to Zenobia's imagined sexual invitation: "Zenobia['s] . . . words, together with something in her manner, irresistibly brought up a picture of that fine, perfectly developed figure, in Eve's earliest garment. I almost fancied myself actually beholding it. Her free, careless, generous modes of expression often had this effect of creating images which, though pure, are hardly felt to be quite decorous, when born of a thought that passes between man and woman" (17). Aiming to "know" and "possess" Zenobia's body in any way possible, Coverdale's visual fascination with Zenobia's vital and attractive person is gradually translated into a fascination with her sexual history. Performing an act of "masculine grossness," Coverdale reads Zenobia's "womanly frankness" as the sign of sexual guilt. Zenobia, Coverdale intuits, is a sexually experienced woman: " 'Zenobia is a wife! Zenobia has lived, and loved! There is no folded petal, no latent dew-drop, in this perfectly developed rose!'—irresistibly that thought drove out all other conclusions, as often as my mind reverted to the subject" (47). In telling imagery, Coverdale fears that Zenobia will deceive Hollingsworth by pretending to be "a free woman, with no mortgage on her affections nor claimant to her hand, but fully at liberty to surrender both, in exchange for the heart and hand which she apparently expected to receive" (127). It is Zenobia's "freedom" and (questionable) status as consenting feminine "subject" that is at stake here; and the imagery of male property Coverdale employs *performs* the proprietary, domestic containment of Zenobia that his interpretation purports to "discover." Henceforth in the narrative Coverdale's "eyeshot" (47) and his efforts at what he terms "wicked interpretation" (47) will be directed less at the surfaces of Zenobia's body than at what Coverdale calls "the mystery of [her] life" (47): specifically, Zenobia's subjective interiority—in particular, her (sexual) experience—whose physical correlative, the hymen, is visually inaccessible and hidden from view.

This view of Zenobia as sexual property—indeed, in Coverdale's assessment, damaged goods—is reinforced by Coverdale's construction of events at Blithedale and his interpretation of Zenobia's desires and actions. While Zenobia rails against the patriarchal domestication of feminine desire—the fact that "fate has assigned [woman] but one single event [i.e., marriage], which she must contrive to make the substance of her whole life" while "a man has his choice of innumerable events" (60)—she herself, in Coverdale's view, is seduced by the domestic, heterosexual construction of feminine subjectivity. Zenobia, in Coverdale's account, craves Hollingsworth's loving, animating gaze (72) and seeks his "strong and noble" influence (68)—and he describes her acquiescing before Hollingsworth's conventionally sexist disquisition on woman's place and the "unmistakeable . . . sovereignty" of men, a bald expression of "masculine egotism" which, Coverdale states, "centred everything in itself" and represented woman as "a mere incident in the great sum of man" (123). Evidently bereft of Hollingsworth's desire at the end of the text and possibly stripped of her inheritance, Zenobia apparently commits suicide. After Hollingsworth departs during their final confrontation at Eliot's pulpit, Coverdale watches while Zenobia sinks to the ground, "as if a great . . . irresistible weight were pressing her to the earth" (221): her face and brow whiten to a "deathlike hue" (223), and her white hand feels cold and "deathlike" (227). Bitterly complaining that Hollingsworth "has flung away what would have served him better than the poor, pale flower he kept" (224), she tells Coverdale she plans to leave Blithedale in search of "new faces—unaccustomed looks," escaping the pain of familiar scenes and the mortifications of "eyes that knew her secret" (225). Ironically aware of Coverdale's desire to turn "this whole affair into a ballad," Zenobia appears to enact the part of mortified, "cast-off" woman with a "battered heart" who has "sacrificed the honor of her sex, at the foot of proud, contumacious man" (223–25), and she appeals to Coverdale to incorporate her story in his song and purvey it to Hollingsworth as something "tender and submissive" (226). What Zenobia appears to perform in this scene is the feminine desire to be the object of male property, the desire to be possessed by Hollingsworth—a desire that both titillates and distresses Coverdale. Zenobia speaks of becoming a nun, thus fully removing herself from social visibility and exchange: "When you next hear of Zenobia, her face will be behind the black-veil" (228). Zenobia's absorption into nature's inanimate substance literalizes her social death, her removal from the sphere of heterosexual commerce and social "animation."

But if Zenobia's fate is to be "reduced" through the operations of Coverdale's gaze from a vital, complex person to play the part of victim in a seduction narrative, Coverdale's fantasies of possession consistently come up short: indeed, like Foster's Eliza Wharton, the "queenly" Zenobia remains in excess of liberal patriarchal scripts of sex and gender. In his inscription of Priscilla, Coverdale similarly, and evidently with greater success, attempts to confine her within the proprietary, domestic forms of feminine liberal subjection. To some extent, Priscilla's trajectory is the inverse of Zenobia's: at the start of the narrative, she is situated outside the realm of sympathetic exchange. Priscilla's father, old Moodie, exemplifies Smith's claim that the poor man is invisible, placed "out of the sight of mankind" and removed from the animating power of others' "fellow-feeling." An "elderly-man of rather shabby appearance" (5), Moodie is figured as a spectral being, an "old grey shadow" (87) who slinks around like a "gray kennel-rat" (181) and who seems "ashamed of his poverty," shrinking from the "eye of the world" in order to escape the mortification of its judgment (82, 83). As Coverdale discovers during his meeting with the old man, Moodie is in fact a "decayed gentleman" (181), a profligate who long ago exhausted his wealth and abandoned his well-bred wife and daughter; with the waste of his estate, and because he had "laid no real touch on any mortal's heart," Moodie's "physical substance" was similarly wasted, "literally melt[ing] into vapor" (183). A ghostly, insubstantial being (83), Moodie fathers an equally spectral daughter. Born to Moodie and his second wife—a "meek-spirited, feeble" young seamstress who "faded . . . out of the world" shortly after giving birth—Priscilla is a "pale and nervous child" who "in her densest moments" could never "make herself quite visible," a mere "reflection" of her parents' condition (185, 187). The lower-class, not-fully-human status of this "ghost-child" (187) both frames and enables Priscilla's availability to her father's exploitation of her and Westervelt's nefarious designs. Moodie, impressed by his daughter's "gift of second-sight and prophecy," colludes with Westervelt's mesmeric captivation of Priscilla and his use of her as a medium of necromantic power (188). Priscilla becomes the Veiled Lady, a mysterious figure publicly displayed before the eyes of thousands and subjected to the "will and passions" of Westervelt (198), who is consistently imaged as an "Oriental" enchanter (e.g., 199). (The text's Orientalism is furthered by the imagery of Priscilla's veil, identifying her with the illicit sexual property of the harem.)[70] As the townspeople melodramatically construe these occurrences, "They averred that the strange gentleman was a wizard [who] . . . had taken advantage of Priscilla's lack of earthly substance to subject her to himself, as his familiar spirit, through whose medium he gained cognizance of whatever happened, in regions near or remote" (188).

In a well-known interpretation of the novel, Allan and Barbara Lefcowitz have argued that Priscilla is less a "personification of pure spirit" and Victorian "true womanhood" than a sexually ambivalent being whom Hawthorne identifies, albeit with characteristic indirection, as a prostitute.[71] Certainly, mesmerism and sexual exploitation were closely linked in the antebellum imagination; and, indeed, there are clear sexual overtones in Hawthorne's description of mesmerical phenomena (e.g., chapter 23). What the Lefcowitzes identify as the "ontological ambivalence" of Priscilla's characterization registers, I would argue, Hawthorne's shifting construction of Priscilla as object of illicit as well as "legitimate," *consensual* sentimental ownership. As in *The Mormon Wife*'s (re)constructions of femininity, Hawthorne maps Priscilla's "progressive" reconstitution from "white slave" to domesticated, consenting "sentimental property." Indeed, narrativizing this transformation, repeatedly invoked with the recurring threat of Priscilla's (re)enslavement, Hawthorne allegorizes in *The Blithedale Romance* the production of feminine (liberal) political subjectivity. Apparently betrayed by her own father and with no mother to protect her, situated outside the bounds of the animating community of love and sympathetic exchange, Priscilla is constructed as an object of male physical and economic exploitation: "enthralled in terrible bondage" (190) to Westervelt, she is, in John Stuart Mill's words quoted above, a "slave" rather than a "favourite." Zenobia's ghost story recounted at Blithedale, "The Silvery Veil," a "spectral legend" (107) based on the history of the Veiled Lady, expressly figures the constancy of sentimental love—specifically, the performance of sympathetic identification within the heterosexual relation—as an antidote to such bondage. The story's young hero, Theodore, desiring to uncover the "mystery" of the Veiled Lady, is told by that Lady that only a kiss—with which he must pledge his love for "all eternity"—would be sufficient to "lift th[e] mysterious veil, beneath which I am a sad and lonely prisoner, in a bondage which is worse to me than death" (112–13).

Emotionally regenerated at Blithedale and physically "rescued" from the threat of Westervelt's bondage, Priscilla appears to be transformed from instrumental into sentimental property. However, Coverdale makes it clear that Priscilla is not so much "protected" from male proprietary authority as the object of subtler forms of emotional subjection. According to Coverdale, her "pleasant weakness" (74) and helplessness endear her to the group (although Zenobia seems to resent it), and she is imaged on several occasions as a gentle animal or pet, a "bird," a "young colt," and a butterfly (73, 74). She idolizes Zenobia and apparently desires to be her "slave," a desire Coverdale characterizes as "feminine" as well as "beautiful" (33); Zenobia reciprocates by decking Priscilla out in ornate clothing and looking at her "as a child does its doll" (59). Priscilla is also drawn to Hollingsworth, who first brings her to Blithedale; apparently under his "sway," she is typically imaged as sitting at his feet (76) and waiting upon his words in "perfect content" (123). Ominously revising a standard image of antebellum courtship, Coverdale describes Priscilla's heart as "held in [Hollingsworth's] hand" rather than warmed within his own breast. Partially re-embodied at Blithedale, Priscilla apparently remains under Westervelt's demonic influence—a mesmeric force registered in Priscilla's "sudden transformations," her dramatic physical alternation between periods of intense liveliness and static immobility (e.g., 61). Most importantly, although Priscilla "deemed herself safest near Zenobia, into whose large heart she hoped to nestle" (190), in Coverdale's view, Priscilla does not find safety in Zenobia's "large heart" but rather gothic entrapment. Spying on the trio in their boardinghouse during his interlude in the city, Coverdale imagines that Zenobia and Hollingsworth have captured Priscilla and intend to purvey her to Westervelt in order to protect Zenobia's inheritance. Fascinated, indeed enthralled by Priscilla's synthesis of agency and submission, Coverdale is consistently drawn to the gothic underside of the "ties of sentiment," the relations of dominance and submission that persist within the modern family and subtend liberal political subjection.

Finally, the climactic performance at the Lyceum—which turns on what is essentially a confrontation between Westervelt and Hollingsworth and a test of each man's authority over Priscilla, and in which she is clearly positioned as a medium of male power—makes it starkly apparent that the relations of heterosexual love are continuous with the exploitative relations of "sexual use" and patriarchal possession (203). The Veiled Lady's performances, the narrator states, embody both availability and distance—concealment and the promise of revelation—and thus provoke (generalized) male proprietary desire; indeed, the "interest of the spectator" is chiefly "wrought up" by the "enigma of her identity" (6), which promotes a good deal of collective speculation among the audience and which is, of course, eventually "unveiled" in the narrative. Tellingly, Hollingsworth only grows conscious of his love for Priscilla—and his desire to "protect" her—during her performance, when she is being gazed at by a "thousand" other pairs of eyes (203). (Of course, in

Coverdale's view, news of Priscilla's possible inheritance contributes to the redirection of Hollingsworth's desire.) Joining Westervelt and the Veiled Lady on the platform, Hollingsworth gazes at Priscilla "with a sad intentness that brought the whole power of his great, stern, yet tender soul, into his glance" (202–3). Hollingsworth's powerful, intense look alone animates Priscilla, so that she responds to his command, "Come. You are safe," by standing up and "thr[owing] off the veil" (203): according to the narrator, "The true heart-throb of a woman's affection was too powerful for the jugglery that had hitherto environed her" (203). Like the ending of Henry James's *The Bostonians*, the scene concludes with a sentence imbued with resonant irony, destabilizing while invoking the myth of male protection: "[Priscilla] uttered a shriek and fled to Hollingsworth, like one escaping from her deadliest enemy, and was safe forever" (203).

The publicness of this scene is crucial: mapping relays between forms of masculine public competition and the production of sentimental subjectivity, the scene stages the performance of feminine consent within the exchanges of (companionate) heterosexual intimacy. In other words, the final scene dramatically produces Priscilla's status as a feminine civil "subject" by spectacularly inscribing her body within the animating, intimate exchanges of the (companionate) heterosexual couple. In an important sense, Coverdale's "Confession" at the end of the text merely renders explicit his ambivalent erotic investment in the normative forms of gender and affect that have been intermittently performed throughout the narrative.

Voyeurism, the "Male Gaze," and Patriarchal Property

As I have suggested, *The Blithedale Romance* is a narrative enactment of Coverdale's desire. The issue of Coverdale's voyeurism—his visual interest in the persons and events at Blithedale, and his corollary posture of emotional detachment and disengagement (in Coverdale's words, the tendency to "take an exterior view" of his personal relationships [140])—has received a good deal of critical attention. By his own account a "frosty bachelor" (9), Coverdale is apparently unfamiliar with the intimate social exchanges of domestic life; at Blithedale, he soon becomes alienated from the community and, even, his "three friends" Zenobia, Hollingsworth, and Priscilla. Coverdale's subjectivity and desires are not domestically located, nor are they confined or "socialized" within the "civilizing" affectional exchanges of the heterosexual couple. Indeed, his desire in the text is most consistently and powerfully directed toward Hollingsworth, alternately envisioned as a gentle nurse and a strong, "powerfully built" man who attempts to impose his will on Coverdale as well as the others (e.g., 49–57). Furthermore, it is arguable that Coverdale directs his attentions toward Zenobia and Priscilla as a way of managing his feelings of powerlessness before Hollingsworth's forceful, attractive presence. In fact, during the initial exchanges at Eliot's pulpit, Coverdale makes explicit the political sources and effects of his attraction to women and feminine "influence" while revealing the complex identificatory dynamic of liberal masculinity. In response to Zenobia's feminist declamation for women's "wider liberty" and inclusion in public life, Coverdale responds,

> I will give you leave, Zenobia . . . to fling your utmost scorn upon me, if you ever hear me utter a sentiment unfavorable to the widest liberty which woman has yet dreamed of. I would give her all she asks, and add a great deal more, which she will not be the party to demand, but which men, if they were generous and wise, would grant of their own free motion. For instance, I would love dearly—for the next thousand years, at least—to have all government devolve into the hands of women. I hate to be ruled by my own sex; it excites my jealousy and wounds my pride. It is the iron sway of bodily force, which abases us, in our compelled submission. But, how sweet the free, generous courtesy, with which I would kneel before a woman-ruler! (121)

Making explicit the interdependency of public and domestic psychic forms, Coverdale locates the attractions of heterosexuality and the "civilizing" influence of domestic(ated) women as a refuge from the "wound[ing]," compelling force of masculine power. Foregrounding the erotics of the Scottish opposition of force and consent, Coverdale despises the "iron sway" of masculine power "which abases us, in our compelled submission," preferring instead to willingly "kneel before a woman-ruler" with "free, generous courtesy," a courtesy that characterizes the "civilized" heterosexual relation. Naturalizing the patriarchal rule of women, Coverdale paternalistically envisions women's "widest liberty" as an expression of masculine generosity, something that men willingly and voluntarily grant. Coverdale's erotic and political fantasies here oscillate between a scenario of forceful masculine penetration (a male rape fantasy) to a scenario of voluntary subjection to the "gentleness" of feminine rule. Furthermore, in Coverdale's scenario, liberal political consent is structured by masculine homophobia and a proprietary authority over women, an authority that enables, indeed instantiates masculine political agency.

These twinned identifications through which liberal masculine subjectivity is constituted (an identification with masculine "brute force," and a "willing," consensual and feminine submission to that authority) are registered in the text's thematics of vision, a thematics construed in moral terms. Specifically, Coverdale mobilizes fantasies of violence and submission in a visual register. Considering Zenobia, Priscilla, and Hollingsworth his "private theater," Coverdale, throughout the narrative, views these objects of his gaze not with sympathetic involvement but with the detachment of a scientist or a detective: he attempts to "penetrate" their "secrets" by asking hypothetical questions to see how they'll respond, and he secretly watches them hoping they'll "give [themselves] away" (48). As Coverdale frankly states, Hollingsworth, Zenobia, and Priscilla "were separated from the rest of the Community, to my imagination, and stood forth as the indices of a problem which it was my business to solve" (69). Analyzing his own visual practices later in the narrative, Coverdale acknowledges that the "cold tendency, between instinct and intellect, which made me pry with a speculative interest into people's passions and impulses" could easily go far toward "unhumanizing my heart" (154). Such passages express Coverdale's—and Hawthorne's—ambivalent investment in a fantasy of masculine power through authorial practice.

As I have suggested, Hawthorne—like Smith—represents vision as the primary medium of social judgment and social animation. The social gaze, wielded or withheld, can animate or "dehumanize" its objects: it can constitute a life-giving instrument of love or a destructive weapon. Throughout *The Blithedale Romance*, Coverdale envisions his "look" as an instrument of power—and, especially, an instrument of male domination of women. The potential violence of the male gaze is evident in Coverdale's figurative language (e.g., he describes his look as "eyeshot" [47]) and self-critique of his visual practices. Describing the dangers of "making my prey of other people's individualities" (84), Coverdale admits that "it is not, I apprehend, a healthy kind of mental occupation, to devote ourselves too exclusively to the study of individual men and women. . . . If we take the freedom to put a friend under our microscope, we thereby insulate him from many of his true relations, magnify his peculiarities, *inevitably tear him into parts, and, of course, patch him very clumsily together again*" (69; emphasis added). Revealing the characterization of the male look as a vehicle of masculine penetration to be a product of (Coverdale's) male fantasy, Hawthorne foregrounds the instability of the male look as an instrument of power, as well as the precariousness and vulnerability of liberal masculinity. Indeed, Coverdale's fantasies of visually enacted violence are inseparable from his feelings of impotence and isolation. More importantly, Coverdale's self-critique manifests his ambivalent investment in these practices, his simultaneous assertion and renunciation of them. Hawthorne suggests that the fantasy of masculine force and power Coverdale invests in enables the performance of sentimental sympathy as a voluntary suspension of corporeal power, one that constitutes or instantiates liberal agency.

Hawthorne's novels are preoccupied with the ethical dangers, and the eroticized satisfactions, of voyeurism, and often construe voyeuristic interest as a gendered practice of sexual violence. As a young man Hawthorne fantasized about "hovering invisible round man and woman, witnessing their deeds, searching into their hearts, borrowing brightness from their felicity and shade from their sorrow,"[72] and he explored the nuances and moral implications of that fantasy in his stories (such as "Ethan Brand") and in his major novels. Such preoccupations reconfigured traditional, Christian strictures against irreverent looking/inquiry and pursuit of forbidden knowledge in human and psychological terms, so that the transgression of divine command becomes a transgression of the forms of psychological "respect" and the norms of polite intercourse.[73] For example, *The House of the Seven Gables'* Holgrave, a clear surrogate for the author, is a detective who is tempted by the opportunity to "fathom" his objects to "the full depth of [his] plummet-line" (178), thus attaining "empire over the human spirit" (212), and whose moral salvation is only secured by his possession of a characteristically "feminine" trait, "the rare and high quality of reverence for another's individuality" (212). Holgrave's "acute" (179) and penetrating gaze is expressly gendered, and contrasted with the gaze of his beloved Phoebe, who "venture[s] to peep in" to the private life of others "just as far as the light reaches, but no farther. It is holy ground where the shadow falls" (178).[74] In *The Blithedale Romance,* which narrativizes Coverdale's visual desire and proprietary "will to power," Hawthorne denaturalizes liberal proprietary and erotic configurations by identifying them as a masculine currency, as the effects of explicitly male desire. *The Blithedale Romance* reveals that the "sexual contract" structures the performance of liberal subjectivity and is located at the very heart of Hawthorne's American "romance."

4

DOMESTICATING "BLACKNESS": HARRIET JACOBS, SOJOURNER TRUTH, AND THE DECOMMODIFICATION OF THE BLACK FEMALE BODY

This chapter begins an analysis, concluded in chapter 5, of the entanglements of race, sex, and property in nineteenth-century African American women's literature. Specifically, these two chapters attempt to account for what Claudia Tate has described as nineteenth-century "black women writers' general preoccupation with fine clothing and expensive household articles" in their autobiographical and fictional prose—a "preoccupation" or representational investment which suggests the pervasive cultural identification of consumer refinement and sentimental subjectivity, and which suggests the oppositional uses of consumption as a code to designate a "feminine" civic identity.[1] I argue that African American women's texts expose the complexities of race in sentimental cultural forms; in particular, they foreground the racial exclusions in sentimental constructions of gender, "feminine consent," and civil(ized) subjectivity analyzed in earlier chapters. Focusing on Harriet Jacobs's *Incidents in the Life of a Slave Girl, Written by Herself* and the *Narrative of Sojourner Truth*, I demonstrate how Jacobs and Truth, in writing black female autobiographies, "tactically" inscribe liberal political fictions of gender and civil subjectivity that are founded on black women's absence.[2] Published under the pseudonym Linda Brent, Jacobs's *Incidents*, as several critics have noted, borrows conventions from sentimental fiction to narrate her passage from slave to "free" black female subject.[3] In analyzing Jacobs's narrative inscriptions of sentiment, I focus on their political effects; in particular, I chart Jacobs's disarticulation of sentiment from white masculine proprietary authority and the "civilizing" exchanges of heterosexuality central to liberal philosophical narratives and often foregrounded in white women's fiction. Foregrounding the political limits of sentimental sympathy discussed in chapter 3, Jacobs represents white women's sympathy as an ambivalent emotional performance, one delimited by white privilege and promoting forms of race and gender colonization. In my discussion of Truth, I am interested in her words as well as her image as a public figure; thus, in addition to her *Narrative*, a dictated autobiography inscribed by the white feminist Olive Gilbert, I consider extant transcripts of her speeches, as well as the *Book of Life*, a collection of letters and biographical sketches of Truth's life compiled by another white feminist, Frances Gage, and appended to the 1878 edition of the *Narrative*.[4] In the *Narrative*, and in speeches such as the well-known "Ain't I a Woman?" delivered at the 1851 Women's Rights Convention in Akron, Truth rejects sentimental, domestic models of femininity, and converts black women's exclusion from norms of antebellum "true womanhood" into an enabling political strategy.[5] Highlighting instead the muscularity and physical power of her body, Truth destabilizes liberal constructions of gender and civil subjectivity and accesses a republican political register identified in midcentury America with the performance of "manliness" and, especially, the right to *labor*. I argue that Truth's problematization of gender categories and her rhetorical appropriation of republican codes of "manliness" enable her to invent a new political subject—the black female citizen.

My decision to focus on slave narratives in this chapter derives from that genre's emphasis on the discursive scripting of the self.[6] Antebellum slave narratives document the transformation of a continuous, single self from slave to free subject, and thus chart the discursive making (and racial marking) of "free" subjectivity. Narratives by antebellum African American women highlight the contours—both the politically enabling and the disabling features—of the fictions of gender and civil subjectivity analyzed in previous chapters. But while I will be interpreting these texts with an eye to how they inscribe as well as interrogate prevailing fictions of feminine subjectivity, it is crucial that the specific conditions of ex-slave authorship during the period be fully attended to. As Albert E. Stone has written, autobiographies by ethnic minorities exhibit a "belief not only in individualism but also in *identity* as a vital personal achievement."[7] For example, as I argue in my discussion of *Incidents*, Jacobs's appropriation of sentimental tropes and topoi in her account of a slave woman's self-affirmation through maternal resolve serves to challenge the culture that denies black women the civil status and legal rights of white women—especially the right to participate in the institutions of parenthood and family—even while it affirms and symbolically instates Jacobs's claims to social equality. My examination of what Stone calls "strategies of self-construction" in African American women's texts aims to keep their fundamentally *oppositional* aspects in clear view; to do so, I read these narratives as compelling and coherent literary acts *and* as interventions in a larger field of social discourse. In addition, it seems crucial to remember that the self-representations of African Americans in these texts, for particular historical reasons, would have been formulated in dialogue with the conventions and expectations of antebellum white literary culture, and the terms in which subjectivities would be intelligible within that literary culture.[8]

Registering and discursively performing the decommodification of the black female body and black women's movement from "object" to "subject," both Jacobs and Truth engage with the codes of gendered identity that measure black women's exclusion from full (civil) subjectivity in nineteenth-century America, codes that were juridically and discursively established under slavery. They expose the ways in which sentimentalism both constitutes and delimits forms of female political agency, subjectivity, and desire in liberal political culture. As I demonstrate in chapter 1, sentimental narratives construct proprietary power and agency as the natural authority of white men, and encode forms of identification through which Others could be socially recognized as civil subjects. For example, in the sentimental texts discussed in chapters 2 and 3, white women are articulated as subjects through the "civilizing" exchanges of heterosexuality and its forms of racial identification; for instance, white slave narratives capitalize on race privilege to narrate the horrors of enslavement and the production of taste and feminine consent. In addition, for a mixed-race, fugitive-slave author and orator such as Frederick Douglass, sentiment could inscribe an identification with the white father and could facilitate, through that identification, forms of liberal masculine agency and gender privilege. With liberal political agency defined as white and masculine, slave women are positioned at the boundaries of civil subjectivity, doubly marginalized by race and gender. Representing particular experiences of black female bondage, Jacobs and Truth rearticulate and reject, respectively, the forms of sentimental subjectivity and consent mobilized in white women's fiction. Registering slave women's position as chattel with no civil status and the brutality of white patriarchal slave power, Jacobs's and Truth's narratives demystify sentimental fictions of white male protection, sentimental ownership, and "civilized" masculine authority. In particular, inscribing what Hortense Spillers terms the " 'mark' " of the black mother, established by the American slave code, in determining the social identity of black subjects, their texts detach sentiment from white male power, thus reshaping black women's political identifications.[9]

Several critics have examined black women writers' engagement with sentimental narrative forms. For example, Valerie Smith and Henry Louis Gates have argued that writers such as Harriet Jacobs and Harriet Wilson borrow from the languages of antebellum "women's fiction," in part to win the sympathies of white women readers. Claudia Tate makes a powerful argument for understanding these sentimental gestures as politically oppositional, expressing black women's entitlement to the gendered privileges of civil subjectivity.[10] However, antebellum black women writers' relationship to sentimentalism would inevitably be complex, given that sentimental narratives both describe and constitute forms of feminine subjectivity and consent predicated on black women's absence. As I argue in chapter 1, the construction of "feminine consent" (or taste) as the property of the "free" (feminine civil) subject depends on the construction of the nonconsent (what Patricia Williams terms the "antiwill") of the black female sexual slave. Indeed, in white women's fiction as well as white slave narratives, forms of consent articulated through both proximity to and distance from enslavement—a distance inscribed through a symbolics of racial difference—are repeatedly and insistently performed. The performance of cross-racial sympathy in the sentimental texts I discuss in chapter 3 both facilitates white women's recognition of their own gender oppression and construction as male property, and can foreclose that identification by instantiating a feminine property relation; in these sentimental texts, free white liberal subjectivity is constituted through an identification with, and proprietary power over, black women's bodies. This dynamic is registered in Jacobs's narrative.[11] Jacobs explores and exploits the limits of sentimentalism as abolitionist rhetoric, and construes feminine sentimental sympathy as politically problematic, because the forms of political agency it evokes are racialized and aligned with particular gender and (hetero)sexual investments. Specifically, Jacobs' narrator writes from the position of the black female sexual slave, a position that defines the racial limits of sentimental identification, a situation she exploits in complex and ingenious ways. For example, *Incidents* disrupts female pity, and the proprietary forms of sentimental sympathy, while calling attention to white women's racial privilege, which underwrites their dubious "freedom," even while its narrator invites readers (as well as women such as her white mistress, Mrs. Flint) to "identify" with her in awareness of shared oppression by patriarchal power. The ambivalence of sentimental sympathy is legible in the character of Mrs. Bruce, ambiguously positioned as Linda Brent's owner and domestic employer, whose identification with Brent's desire for freedom coexists with a sense of entitlement to Brent's affections and domestic labor. Registering these ambiguities in liberal codes of gender, Jacobs and Truth rewrite the slave woman's status as commodity through accession to forms of femininity and masculinity; at the same time, they rewrite the forms of gender from the vantage point of the decommodified female subject.

The dialogic structure of black women's narratives, their engagement with the forms of gender and civil(ized) subjectivity, cannot be understood apart from their political contexts of their discursive production and consumption. Engaging with the forms of gender, Jacobs and Truth are able to rewrite themselves as subjects and, in their rewriting, to undo the effects of the social death of individuals in slavery. Black women authors simultaneously appeal to and reformulate Anglo-American literary conventions and self-constructions by dramatizing their racial limits and interrogating their symbolic production of subjectivities. Their autobiographical narratives constitute texts in which, in the words of Gayatri Spivak, "so-called marginal groups, instead of claiming centrality, redefine the big word human in terms of the marginal."[12]

Gender, Race, and African American Subjectivities

African American women's slave narratives engage quite explicitly with forms of gender and gendered discourse. For slaves violently displaced from traditional structures of social practices and kinship relations—including gendered identities and roles—in West African societies, gender would have constituted an important problematic as they negotiated their lives in the United States. According to most historians, in the primarily agricultural, precolonial West African societies, gender was a primary form of social organization. Many of these societies, for instance, ascribed to women special economic functions (such as agricultural labor and marketing), while gender influenced the development of such political institutions as the position of Queen Mother among the Ashanti. In addition, while West African societies exploited women's labor, many also endowed femininity in general, and especially motherhood, with a sacred character.[13] Calling attention to West African survivals in slave society, Elizabeth Fox-Genovese suggests that African American gender identifications and relations would have borrowed both from "whites' notions of domesticity and African notions of tribe and lineage."[14] In other words, the black female slave would have negotiated her gendered position in a complex sociosymbolic field in which both dominant (U.S.) and residual (African) forms of gender are articulated—even if the latter are not given official (juridical) sanction.

Clearly, for slaves drawn from a variety of peoples and places, the period of the middle passage and relocation to the South was an event of unspeakable violence, one that disrupted the social structures within which the very forms of social identity were shaped. For Spillers, the middle passage commenced a process of commodification so radical that the slave would have been decisively "ungendered." According to Spillers, the commodification of the African slave and her/his reduction to an object of property would have dissolved forms of gendered identity, transforming embodied "subject" into undifferentiated "flesh": as defined by the slave codes, "every feature of social and human differentiation disappears . . . regarding the African American person," so that "the respective subject-positions of 'female' and 'male' adhere to no symbolic integrity." In severing "the captive body from its motive will . . . we lose at least *gender* difference *in the outcome*, and the female body and the male body become a territory of cultural and political maneuver, not at all gender-related, gender-specific." Under these circumstances, gender is reduced to its Euro-American articulation, so that the slave (captive body) exists between two positions: the dominant (domestic) construction of feminine gender, and an objectification so radical it ungenders. In Spillers's formulation the black female slave can only articulate her (un)gendered position as an absence in the cultural symbolic: the black female slave is not intelligible as a subject within the forms of civil identity that accrue juridical and political legitimacy. Indeed, under the slave codes, gender had no symbolic value: "In the absence of legally binding slave marriage, and because slaves' access to property was negligible and therefore devoid of political significance, the law of slavery had no cause to differentiate between women and men."[15] As defined within the official realm of patriarchal law, the black female slave is locked outside the legitimating structures of gender.

If slavery constituted a condition in which slave bodies/subjects are "ungendered," in the United States the political rhetoric of liberty and forms of liberal political subjectivity were explicitly articulated through categories of gender as well as race. Ownership of persons, within the contexts of political, economic, and familial relations, has had a relatively continuous existence in Western cultures. But, as David Brion Davis has argued, property claims on persons would necessarily be viewed as problematic in a democracy, a political system predicated on the freedom and natural liberty of all persons. Classical liberal and sentimental texts supply distinct, and distinctly gendered, "solutions" to what Davis has called the "problem of slavery" in Western thought. Liberalism's solution came in the form of an ideal of *self*-ownership, or what C. B. Macpherson has called "possessive individualism." In classical liberal thought, the self is conceptualized as essentially an owner, an owner of his own bodily capacities and labor; such ownership was for Locke a natural right. This (possessive) individual is defined as "free" because he can choose, rationally and independently, when and where to sell or alienate these bodily capacities and this labor.[16]

This contradictory model of liberal proprietary "agency" is constitutively racialized. As David Roediger and others have shown, constructions of wage laborers as "free" depended on the negative example of chattel slavery: in the rhetoric of Anglo-American freedom lovers, "the opposite of 'liberty' was 'slavery.' " For Eric Lott, the subjectivity of the "free laborer" is structured by a fundamental psychic ambivalence, an identification with enslaved blacks, and a disidentification from them and (re)assertion of white privilege and economic entitlement. White, working-class masculine subjectivity, in Lott's account, is not a stable, coherent identity but a field of multiple and contradictory identifications; in particular, it is constituted through an ambivalent dynamic of "love and theft," both identification with and desire for blackness (specifically the black male body), and an appropriative, proprietary authority over black culture and black labor—which, at particular historical moments, is effected through an identification with middle-class whites.[17] However, the racial parameters of possessive individualism (i.e., its formulation as a sign of white privilege) served to mystify its social contradictions and the constitutive ambivalence of liberal political subjectivity itself. The liberal ideal of "free labor" depends, as socialist critics of contractarianism have contended, on the *political fiction* of "labor power"—the fiction that an individual can alienate the labor of his body, even for an entire lifetime (in contemporary contractarianism, selling oneself into civil slavery is an extreme expression of such freedom), while not alienating him/herself and therefore remaining "free." According to this ideal, the capitalist can buy an individual's labor power, but that individual—the embodied person, the owner of labor power—remains somehow magically detached from these transactions.

In sentimental texts, which focus chiefly on the proprietary relations of the domestic sphere, the problem of slavery is negotiated by substituting for the absolute property claims of slavery a model in which traditional objects of male property are reconstituted as "social" beings whose feelings and interests were increasingly attended to and socially and legally recognized. Like the liberal construct of free labor, sentimental property relations pivot on consent, the sign of which in sentimental texts is love—a specific code of (feminine) consent which, as in the rhetoric of romantic love and sentimental accounts of a natural mother-child bond, can serve to naturalize volitional allegiance.[18] As John Stuart Mill noted in his analysis of marriage, which he depicted as a form of white slavery, married women's "masters require something more from them than actual service. Men do not want solely the obedience of women, they want their sentiments. All men, except the most brutish, desire to have . . . not a forced slave but a willing one, not a slave merely, but a favourite."[19] The sentimental restructuring of property relations simultaneously constitutes women as sentimental subjects with feelings and emotional interiority, and promotes what Mill describes as a masculine "will to power," a desire to possess women's interiority as well as their bodies. In sentimental culture, the body can be illegitimately possessed (as in captivity narratives) and even bought and sold (as in accounts of arranged marriages, or the traffic in white slavery), but there is something that can never be purchased or nonconsensually possessed—and that something is "love." The separability of the body from feelings is staged in narratives of patriarchal entrapment such as white slave narratives, in which possession of the body and possession of the heart are clearly distinguished. In sentimental texts, then, an individual's body can be sold, but his or her feelings—his or her (sentimental) person—can never be purchased or nonconsensually owned; it is in that sense that the sentimental subject is imagined and can imagine herself as existentially "free." Like the (masculine) "free laborer" vis-à-vis his labor power, the (feminine) sentimental subject is in a possessive relation to her emotional endowments (she "has" feelings), but she is "free" to choose who, and what, to emotionally "invest" in—figurative phrasings that suggest the very parallels I wish to call attention to—between masculine and feminine consent, between the "rational" consent of the masculine (free) laborer and the "emotional" preference of the feminine consumer. In sentimental texts, to borrow Mill's terminology, "slaves" are distinguished from "favourites" by the existence of socially recognized feminine tastes: property in persons is represented as consensual and emotionally fulfilling, and is assimilated with interpersonal ideals of "trust," "love," and "commitment." Like the fiction of consensual "free labor," this fiction of sentimental, loving ownership habituates subjects to forms of ownership, rendering tolerable the existence of property claims on persons in a democracy.

The distance as well as the constitutive relays between slaves and liberal and sentimental proprietary subjects are measured in antebellum slave narratives, whose inscriptions of freedom, as experiential condition and narrative *telos*, are visibly shaped by existing cultural paradigms.

Fictions of identity constructed in slave narratives—the movement from chattel to free subject—frequently borrow from prevailing, conventionally gendered liberal and sentimental vocabularies. As I demonstrated in chapter 1, the African slave is positioned at the fantasmatic limits of liberal and sentimental constructions of civil(ized) subjectivity: it was precisely in terms of their perceived difference from African American slaves that (white) masculine wage laborers and (white) feminine consumers were able to imagine themselves as "free" liberal subjects. Indeed, the performance of "feminine consent" described within and instantiated by sentimental texts requires both an identification with the slave and disavowal of that identification: liberal political agency is constituted through an identification with the (racialized) object of property and a felt proprietary power over the racial body. Douglass's and Jacobs's narratives relocate the figure of the African American slave from margin to center, from dehumanized object to speaking subject. That relocation fractures liberal and sentimental paradigms of white subjectivity and desire. Indeed, Douglass's and Jacobs's narratives both remap the racial coordinates of gendered subjectivity *and* problematize the imagined freedom of liberal subjects.[20]

Noting that market society defines the "display of unremittingly controlled wilfullness" as "the closest equivalent of nobility," Patricia Williams has argued that slave law embodied a "belief structure rooted in a concept of black . . . antiwill, the antithetical embodiment of pure will." This belief structure was expressed through slave law's representation of slaves as "embodied" beings while negating slaves' minds and hearts: "To define slave law as comprehending a total view of personality implicitly accepts that the provision of food, shelter, and clothing (again assuming the very best of circumstances) is the whole requirement of humanity. It assumes also either that psychic care was provided by slaveowners (as if an owned psyche could ever be reconciled with mental health) or that psyche is not a significant part of the whole human." Severing "psyches" from bodies, slave law "pursued a vision of blacks as simple-minded, strong-bodied economic 'actants' ": "while blacks had an indisputable generative force in the market place, they had no active *role* in the market."[21] Douglass and Jacobs challenge slave law's construction of slaves as the antithesis of market society's willful subjects by ascribing to blacks just such an active role: in particular, they inscribe gendered models of consent and liberal political agency. Frederick Douglass's 1845 *Narrative*, for instance, reconstructs the proprietary object of slavery as the (liberal masculine) subject of free labor and possessive individualism. In Harriet Jacobs's *Incidents*, a text plainly shaped by the conventions of sentimental fiction, the passage from slavery to freedom is symbolically marked by her representation of her "choice" of a sexual partner, her inscriptions of loving ownership of her children, and her habitation of the constricted "homeplace" of the attic space within her grandmother's house. The cultural force of Douglass's and Jacobs's destabilization of the commercial categories through which "free" subjects are engendered is evident in the violent response that destabilization provokes: in Douglass's narrative, white wage workers respond with racist violence to African American slaves who hire out their labor (and thus act the part of free laborers), while in Jacobs's narrative, the white mistress, Mrs. Flint, terrorizes the slave woman who insists on the prerogatives of feminine gender.

Douglass's and Jacobs's dramatic enactments of gendered forms of liberal civil subjectivity instantiate what Homi Bhabha terms the "ambivalence" of colonial "mimicry," which he describes as "one of the most elusive and effective strategies of colonial power and knowledge." Bhabha observes that the discourse of the "civilizing mission" often constructs the colony ambivalently, as the effect of a flawed colonial mimesis: "colonial mimicry is the desire for a reformed, recognizable Other, *as a subject of a difference that is almost the same, but not quite.*" The effect of a colonial desire for sameness, colonial "mimic-men" constitute "authorized versions of otherness" that reinforce colonial authority; at the same time, by disclosing the ambivalence of colonial discourse, they "menace the narcissistic demand of colonial authority" by inscribing the colonized as " 'inappropriate' colonial subjects," evoking the "partial presence" of an ineluctable Otherness. "The effect of mimicry on the authority of colonial discourse is profound and disturbing," Bhabha argues, because "in normalizing the colonial state or subject, the dream of post-Enlightenment civility alienates its own language of liberty and produces another knowledge of its norms." Strikingly, to illustrate the disruptive effects of the "recalcitrance" of mimicry, Bhabha turns to the ambivalence of enslavement in Locke's Second Treatise: in this foundational liberal text, slavery appears both as illegitimate power and antithesis of "free" civil subjectivity, and as a legitimate form of colonial authority. Locke's Second Treatise, Bhabha argues, "*splits* to reveal the limitations of liberty in his double use of the word 'slave': first simply, descriptively as the locus of a legitimate form of ownership, then as the trope for an intolerable, illegitimate exercise of power. What is articulated in that distance between the two uses is the absolute, imagined difference between the 'Colonial' state of Carolina and the Original State of Nature." The psychic and political disturbances produced by this "difference" make ambiguous the "post-Enlightenment . . . language of liberty" and destabilizes its cultural authority.[22] In particular, because Douglass and Jacobs are defined by the slave codes as commodities with no civil status or rights, their texts problematize liberal and sentimental fictions of "civilized" ownership. Describing conditions of enslavement within America's Christian democracy as well as their accession to the status of "free" subjects, Douglass and Jacobs unsettle dominant fictions of civil subjectivity even while inscribing them.

In most slave narratives, the alienation and alienability of the body is an acute and crucial concern. The dehumanizing spectacle of the slave auction, often represented in slave narratives, in which the bodies of slaves were disrobed, prodded, and inspected, made graphically clear that what was exchanged in the purchase of slaves was the embodied person of the slave. In his 1845 *Narrative*, Frederick Douglass characterizes this exchange as involving the unjust expropriation—what Douglass refers to as the "robbery"—of the fruits of slave labor; appealing implicitly to a labor theory of value, he presents in his narrative a shrewd economic analysis of the sources and injustices of the slave system.[23] Douglass's refiguring of enslavement (ownership of the body) as capitalist expropriation of labor power enables him to write himself into existence as a (possessive) individual, and amounts to a discursive investment in liberal political subjectivity—one that would have had particular resonance with middle-class white abolitionists. While his fight with the slavemaster Covey graphically exemplifies Douglass's efforts to take possession of his own body (just as learning to read enacts taking possession of his own mind), Douglass's movement out of slavery is in fact chiefly charted by transformations in his status as a worker: the narrative allegorizes the passage from chattel to free labor in Douglass's progression from house slave, to hired field hand and ship caulker, to ship hand who contracts independently to hire himself out, to free laborer in Massachusetts. For Douglass, slavery denies the slave's individuality, defined according to contemporary liberal ideals as the right to make contracts, a power he discursively recuperates in his *Narrative*.[24]

Douglass's inscription of the liberal ideal of self-possession through labor is an expressly masculine construction. As several critics have noted, Douglass's writings, especially his *Narrative* and his antislavery novella *The Heroic Slave*, script the slave's escape from bondage in gendered terms, as the heroic achievement of *free manhood*—a form of masculine self-invention that marginalizes, indeed effaces, the role of black women in the fugitive slave's accomplishment as well as in the slave community's collective resistance. Rhetorically invoking the (contradictory) revolutionary legacy of the founding fathers, Douglass calls attention to the construction of political freedom as a masculine identification: by claiming for the African American "son" the revolutionary legacy of the "fathers," Douglass repositions the black male slave within the body politic while countering the slave's exclusion from the politically salient privileges of gender.[25] In other words, Douglass's inscriptions of liberal civil subjectivity have a gendered, indeed patriarchal cast: as Jenny Franchot has argued, the mixed-race son's self-construction as free "subject," and inscribed identification with the political privileges of the white father, is achieved by objectifying, indeed abjecting the black female body, which appears in the *Narrative* as an object of illicit proprietary desire and patriarchal violence. It is important to point out that Douglass's opportunity to be hired out as a slave—a development that provided opportunities for unsupervised mobility and thus made possible his successful escape—is itself a political articulation of gender: according to Fox-Genovese, "whether as a result of white or black male bias—or more likely a combination of the two—female slaves were unlikely to be trained in carpentry, blacksmithing, masonry, coopering, or other specialized crafts that would lead them to be hired out"; consequently, "they were less likely than men to have an excuse to be abroad alone."[26] Inscribing the liberal construct of free masculine subjectivity while making spectacularly apparent that construct's constitutive exclusions, Douglass both invests in and problematizes gendered forms of civil subjectivity.

Jacobs's *Incidents* is similarly a double-voiced text, one that both invests in the conventions of sentimental womanhood and registers their discursive and political limits. Specifically, *Incidents* exposes contradictions within feminine consent and taste as forms of feminine political agency. Giving voice to the boundaries of gender, Jacobs, I will argue, addresses white "women of the North," her designated readers, by both invoking and unsettling dominant discourses of free subjectivity. As in Douglass's *Narrative*, in Jacobs's *Incidents*, inscribing the sanctity and independent integrity of her body is a crucial narrative purpose; however, Jacobs focuses less on the contracts of free labor than on what Carole Pateman has called the "sexual contract." Jacobs's determination to escape from slavery begins with her recognition that as a slave *woman*, a specific, and specifically sexual, form of possession of her body is at stake; as the narrator tells us, "[Slave] women are considered of no value, unless they continually increase their owner's stock" (380).[27] Rejecting the claim of her master, Dr. Flint, that "I was made for his use, made to obey his command in *every* thing" (352)—refusing, that is, to be sexually used by a man she hates—"Linda Brent" staves off his sexual advances and chooses to take as her sexual partner another white man, Dr. Sands. As the narrator explains her decision, "It seem[ed] less degrading to give one's self, than to submit to compulsion. There is *something akin to freedom* in having a lover who has no control over you, except that which he gains by kindness and attachment" (385; emphasis added). The act also constitutes something akin to revenge: "I knew nothing would enrage Dr. Flint so much as to know that I *favored* another; and it was something to triumph over my tyrant even in that small way" (385). The narrator's use of the verb "favor" here is both striking and ambiguous, possessing clear sexual overtones ("sexual favors") while connoting (feminine) condescension and sentimental preference. Appropriating the language of romantic courtship, the narrator figures her sexual experience as the voluntary granting of (sexual and emotional) privileges, equated here with resistance to tyrannical male power. Jacobs thus depicts her sexual experience as an act of sexual giving to the man who "pleases" her, and situates that act in the context of masculine deference and romantic involvement, as well as political resistance.

This rescripting is evident as well in the account of Linda Brent's extended harrassment by Flint. Critics have frequently commented on *Incidents*' representation of Brent's extended, dramatic resistances to Dr. Flint's sexual threat: Flint proclaims that Brent, as his daughter's (and therefore his) property, is "subject to his will in all things" (361) and that he "can kill [her] if [he] please[s]" (371), but while he beats her on several occasions, Brent manages to stave off the seemingly imminent sexual assault. The narrator attributes Flint's "restraint" to "the master's age, my extreme youth, and the fear that his conduct would be reported to my grandmother" (361), and thus that the rape's horror would publicize what Jacobs depicts as the South's repressed secret of black women's sexual exploitation. Clearly, the prolonged struggle with Flint measures Brent's ingenuity, improvisational facility, and desire, as well as the force of her resistances. I would suggest that this scripting of their struggle also defines something crucial about the narrative: Jacobs's rearticulation of the exercise of what Pateman terms "patriarchal sex right" as (foiled) seduction narrative, one that inscribes a distinction between body and feelings, between possessing the body and "winning" the heart. Contrary to Flint's statement that he owns her "body and soul" (370), the narrator emphasizes that there is something that he does not own, something that is truly "hers" (and which he desires)—that is, her "favor." This construction is legible in the language with which Flint's thoughts and feelings are rendered in the text. Describing Brent as a "poor child" who doesn't know her "own good," Flint assures her that "I would cherish you. I would make a lady of you" (368), and he labors to convince her, through "leniency" and attentiveness, that her "master" is her "best friend" (389). When Brent turns him away, he assumes "the air of a very injured individual" and is reduced to the pathetic entreaties of a repulsed lover (367). This sentimental reconstruction is similarly legible in Flint's repeated claim that he would not sell Brent for any amount of money, and his promise that she will be his "for life," a promise that is increasingly ironized as the narrative progresses until it becomes a parody of the marriage vow (e.g., 407–8).

As Lauren Berlant argues, Flint is trying here to conscript Linda Brent into his "parodic and perverse fantas[y] of masking domination as love and conjugal decorum," a fantasy that "disguised enslavement as a kind of courtship." This fantasy is not the individual project of Flint but a collective form of white male desire for mulatta women, who signified "white" but provided white men a different access to sexuality. As Berlant points out, mulatta women's European-style beauty justified a "specific kind of exploitation by whites" that mimicked white domesticity: white men set up "a parallel universe of sexual and racial domestic bliss and heterosexual entitlement: this involved dressing up the beautiful mulatta and playing white-lady-of-the-house with her, building her a little house that parodied the big one, giving her the kinds of things that white married ladies received, only in this instance without the protections of law." But while this fantasy, as Berlant observes, is "a production of the intentions and whims of the master," such a reading presents the danger of negating the agency Jacobs's narrator exercises, as well as the destabilizing force of domestic parody the fantasy engenders.[28] This parodic construction of Brent as gendered, feminine subject structures her narrative: indeed, unlike Douglass's, Brent's "choices" are primarily romantic and familial, and involve her performance of particular affectional attachments. Indeed, I would argue that *Incidents'* appropriation of the language of heterosexual courtship (of feminine consent and masculine recognition of feminine subjectivity) constitutes a form of what Bhabha terms "mimicry," ironizing and destabilizing the cultural authority of dominant constructions of gender and civil subjectivity. Representing her relationship with Flint through the codes of heterosexual courtship, the narrator denaturalizes feminine freedom while claiming for herself the emotional leverage of sentimental subjectivity.[29] Brent performs (the withholding of) her feminine consent here, and that performance instantiates what Bhabha terms the constitutive, destabilizing *ambivalence* of colonial subjectivity.

This destabilizing mimicry is similarly evident in the sentimental narratives of the colonial "contact zone" studied by Mary Louise Pratt, in which Eurocolonial constructions of indigenous and slave women's loving "consent" served to dramatize Other women's willing capitulation to the European master and to validate European authority: "From the viewpoint of European hegemony, romantic love was as good a device as any for 'embracing' such groups into the political and social imaginery—as subalterns."[30] However, Jacobs's narrative gives voice to the colonial woman officially excluded from the culture's legitimating structures of gender. When Brent falls in love with a freeborn black man, a carpenter, who proposes marriage (369), Flint behaves like a "jealous lover" (408) and resolutely refuses to allow the marriage to take place, insisting that "if you *must* have a husband, you may take up with one of my slaves." Brent replies, "Don't you suppose, sir, that a slave can have some preference about marrying? Do you suppose that all men are alike to her?" (371). Publicly professing these emotional "preferences" is, for Linda Brent, symbolically crucial: it establishes her entitlement to the prerogatives of feminine gender, and it constitutes an overt rejection of pervasive racist stereotypes of African Americans as naturally promiscuous, incapable of forming discriminating sentimental attachments—a racist characterization is implicit in Flint's assumption that he can dictate her marriage arrangements.[31] Positioned within a legal system organized around the nonrecognition of her desire, Brent construes feminine consent as what Michel de Certeau calls a "tactic," a "maneuver 'within the enemy's field of vision' . . . and within enemy territory" that opens up a provisional space from which to negotiate legal and cultural exclusions and dramatize her claims to personhood.[32] Jacobs thus claims, within the interstices of heterosexual ritual, a certain room to maneuver; there is a certain space for recognition of her desire even while white patriarchal power and the coercions of heterosexuality are on full display.

Jacobs's language in these passages suggests her astute *performance* of the codes of gender and heterosexual exchange, as well as her recognition of their white patriarchal parameters. For example, she suggests that the "freedom" a woman gains by choosing a lover is a mere approximation of the real article ("something akin to freedom"), while calling attention to the specific forms of "submission" to (white, patriarchal) power to which slave women are subject. Indeed, rather than construing her "choice" of Sands as embodying her feminine consent to his authority as lover, Jacobs depicts their relationship as necessarily triangulated: manipulating the bonds between men constitutive of patriarchy, Linda Brent takes pleasure in her choice as a challenge to Flint's patriarchal power: "I knew nothing would enrage Dr. Flint so much as to know that I favored another; and it was something to triumph over my tyrant even in that small way." Last, Jacobs describes her "choice" in language devoid of sentimental mystification: choosing Sands is simply the "less *degrading*" in what Brent envisions as her two choices.

Linda Brent's decision to sleep with Dr. Sands, while an index of her practicality and strength, dramatizes more than anything else her limited range of choices: for Brent, the "choice" is not *whether* one will give one's body, but rather *to whom* one will give one's body. Brent's action both ironizes and throws into relief the dominant culture's mystified relations of courtship and marriage. Feminists have long argued that the radical economic, political, and social inequities between men and women make the notion of marital union as a voluntary "contract" an audacious falsehood. The socialist feminist William Thompson made the point memorably when he blasted "that most unequal and debasing code, absurdly called the *contract* of marriage":

> Women may or may nor marry! they may refuse to "enter into this contract." So when, in happier times of East India monopoly, the food of provinces was bought up by individuals under the shield of mercantile political power, the poor people were kindly told, "they were at liberty to buy or not to buy." . . . So by male-created laws, depriving women of knowledge and skill, excluding them from the benefit of all judgment and mind-creating offices and trusts, cutting them off almost entirely from the participation, by succession or otherwise, of property, and from its uses and exchanges—are women kindly told, "they are free to marry or not."[33]

Legally and economically defined as male dependents, women, Thompson argued, are (collectively) coerced into marriage, although any individual woman is "free" to remain single. Carole Pateman has devised the phrase the "sexual contract" to refer to the mystified, pseudo-contractual status of heterosexual relations amidst devastating structural inequities. Pateman argues convincingly that these inequities guarantee that men *as men* have claims on women's bodies; women's "choice" within this structure is, at best, which man (or men) to whom that claim will be granted. Pateman sees this "patriarchal sex right" exercised in a number of cultural arenas, including home, street, and workplace, and in such practices as prostitution, pornography, and surrogate motherhood. As I have argued throughout, the liberal construction of feminine choice depends on, and is sustained by, women's belief in male proprietary power: that investment constitutes a form of domestic colonization (what Spillers terms "patriarchilization") of the "female gender."[34] As I demonstrate in chapter 1, the "dominant fiction" of masculine power thus structures the performance of feminine consent to heterosexuality and disables other political identifications—such as, for example, women's collective identification or organization around the domestic and sexual labors on which capitalism depends. What Jacobs's text effects in parodying feminine consent is to denaturalize these forms of gender while mapping clear differences between black and white women's position vis-à-vis patriarchal "sex right" and ownership. Indeed, Jacobs suggests it is white women's identification with male proprietary power that underlies their constitution as feminine "subjects," enabling them to sympathize with slave women but ultimately disabling a more radical political identification with black female slaves. In other words, *Incidents* both performs and denaturalizes liberalism's conflation of choice and consent, and demonstrates the inadequacy of feminine consent as a vehicle and sign of female subjectivity and freedom. *Incidents*' appeal to dominant fictions of selfhood authorizes Brent's self-construction as a "woman" rather than chattel while simultaneously underscoring the unfree status of free (white) women.

White women's less-than-free status—they paradoxically constitute, in the words of Spillers, "a privileged class of the tormented"[35]—is registered throughout Jacobs's narrative. It is especially legible in Jacobs's representation of her white mistress, Mrs. Flint, who appears as both oppressor and victim. Like Douglass's portrait of Sophia Auld, transformed from domestic angel to demon by the "fatal poison of irresponsible power" (*Narrative*, 274), Jacobs's characterization of Mrs. Flint exemplifies the abolitionist slogan that complete power corrupts, threatening even that culturally sanctified wellspring of virtue—white womanhood—and extending slavery's power to ungender to the bodies of white women. Jacobs documents several incidents of white women's betrayal of black women: Brent's first mistress, her mother's "whiter foster sister," who provides the black slave girl with a "happy" home," fails to free Brent as expected on behalf of her mother's "love and faithful service" and instead bequeaths her to her niece, Mrs. Flint's five-year-old daughter (343–44); this same "kind" mistress also reneges on a promise to Linda's grandmother that, when she died, the old slave woman would be freed. Jacobs also catalogs Mrs. Flint's cruelty toward Linda's Aunt Nancy (who is "slowly murdered" by her mistress's maltreatment) and her vindictive treatment of Linda Brent as well.

However, Jacobs also represents white women such as Mrs. Flint as themselves victimized by white men and by a sexual double standard. Jacobs presents a sympathetic psychological analysis of Mrs. Flint's behavior: powerless to control her husband's sexual appetites, her pride "wounded" by his desecration of their marriage vows, she redirects her anger at the object of his desire—the slave woman (365–66). According to the narrator, "I could not blame [Mrs. Flint for her vindictiveness]. Slaveholders' wives feel as other women would under similar circumstances" (366), and she states that "I, whom [Mrs. Flint] detested so bitterly, had far more pity for her than [her husband] had, whose duty it was to make her life happy. I never wronged her, or wished to wrong her; and one word of kindness from her would have brought me to her feet" (365). The passage subversively inscribes the black slave woman with the ability to sympathize more than the white mistress, while showing how the mistress's white privilege—and constitutive disidentification from black women—prevents her from gaining a clear understanding of the complexities of slavery's politics of sexuality and her own unfree position. While cataloging painful instances of white women's betrayal of black women, *Incidents* also includes several examples of white women's—even white slaveholders'—solidarity with female slaves. In addition, Jacobs directly appeals to white women readers' sympathy at several points in the narrative. In fact, Jacobs expressly identifies her narrative's audience as *female*—the only slave narrative by a black woman, according to at least one scholarly assessment, to so identify its readership. As Jean Fagan Yellin argues, "Jacobs' book . . . represents an attempt to establish an American sisterhood and to activate that sisterhood in the public arena."[36] While I would argue that *Incidents'* vision of the possibilities of cross-racial identification and gender solidarity is more vexed and complicated than Yellin suggests, Jacobs's text is clearly engaged with exploring possibilities of identification between black and white women.[37] Frances Smith Foster has argued that, by claiming for black women "the same roles and the same level of respect accorded free white women," *Incidents* held up a "new mirror which did not show white women as essentially different from black women."[38] Strategically appealing to the rhetorical codes of sentimental femininity, *Incidents* vividly represents the inequitable social relations that these codes often mystify.

In the oft-cited "confession" of her loss of virtue, in which she directly addresses her white women readers not to "judge the poor desolate slave girl too severely" for her sexual fall (384), the narrator both appeals to white women's sympathy and contests that identification, emphatically inscribing the distance that separates slave women from the free white woman in her ideal habitus. Characterizing her readers as "happy women" who "have been free to choose the objects of your affection" and "whose homes are protected by law," the narrator asserts that, "if slavery had been abolished, I, also, could have married the man of my choice; I could have had a home shielded by the laws" (384). Depicting free white femininity as characterized by the performance of feminine taste and patriarchal domestication, Jacobs both maps the racial parameters of civil subjectivity and undercuts the sentimental ideal she invokes: as I have suggested, white women are largely depicted in *Incidents* as "a privileged class of the tormented," victims of white male perfidy, debauchery, and violence (e.g., 381–82). At the same time, addressing her readers in a complex fashion, she disrupts the racialized performance of sympathy to which novels such as *Uncle Tom's Cabin* readily appeal.

Importantly, in the apologetic "confession" of sexual "shame" to her middle-class female readers, what is problematized (and requires extended explanation) is not Linda Brent's "fall" per se, but her *consent* to sex (her "choice" of Sands) — a fact that underscores the sentimental suturing of feminine consent with the patriarchal regulation of women's bodies. Characterizing Sands as "my friend" and "a man of . . . generosity and feeling" (385–86), Linda Brent "trust[s]" that he will buy her, out of his feelings for her and out of a wish to make her happy. She thus envisions the plot of her life as the upward arc of the familiar narrative of the "tragic mulatta," conventional in antebellum antislavery fiction, in which a young slave woman is purchased by her white male lover, but whose tragic outcome (eventually he abandons her or dies, and she is sold back into slavery) measures the distance between extralegal and legalized sentiment. Besides constructing Sands as someone on whom she bestows her "favors," Brent chooses Sands because she believes that he will be a good and loving father. In fact, Brent agrees to have sexual relations with Sands because she believes that he will behave more like a father to his children than a master. Apparently investing in Sands's paternal authority (i.e., believing that he views her as an object of sympathy rather than sexual use), Brent feels "confident" (386) that Sands will support her children, and that he will purchase and manumit them. Unfortunately, Sands (as his name suggests) fully betrays Brent's trust: he buys her children but does not emancipate them, and Brent is uncertain throughout most of the narrative as to whether he stands in relation to her children as father or as slaveowner, and whether he treats them as chattel or objects of real care (e.g., 462). Sands's actions make it painfully clear that Brent's formulations of their relationship, and her inscribed claims on him, are not recognized by law, and thus are subject to the whims of masculine fancy. Again, Brent's mimicry of feminine gender both serves to negotiate the sex/gender system and explodes the sentimental myth of male protection; crucially, Linda is conspicuously hindered by her false belief that she could depend on Sands, or any white man, to "care for" herself and her children. While proslavery writers such as George Fitzhugh were defending slavery by invoking a model of benevolent white paternal authority and a loving family of slaves and master, Jacobs's decolonization of the black female subject is performed through a demystification of white male authority and disinvestment in the white father—a disinvestment that calls into question slave power as well as patriarchal constructions of feminine sentiment.

Jacobs's inscriptions of freedom, and her constructions of "free" subjectivity, are thus inflected by gender, and engage substantially with the prevailing sentimental vocabulary.[39] The second ambiguous characteristic of white women's freedom that Jacobs identifies in her direct address to her readers—being "protected" in a home of one's own—is claimed in a complex fashion, discussed below. But Jacobs also invokes the sentimental investment in the "natural" affectional power and cultural authority of maternity, and inscribes the mother-child bond with a politically destabilizing force. Describing the conditions of "happiness" to her brother William, Linda states that "those who ha[ve] pleasant homes, and kind friends, and who [are] not afraid to love them," live happy lives; and these conditions engender Linda Brent's aspirations. If being unafraid to fight constitutes the essence of true manhood, as suggested in the chapter entitled "The Slave Who Dared to Feel Like a Man," being "[un]afraid to love" constitutes the essence of womanhood "dar[ing] to feel" like a woman. In *Incidents*, Linda dares to feel for her lover, her grandmother's family, and especially her children. Although she asks in the narrative's most sentimental passage, "Why does the slave ever love? Why allow the tendrils of the heart to twine around objects which may at any moment be wrenched away by the hand of violence?" (369), she describes her two children, Benjamin and Ellen, as her "link[s] to life," and she represents her love for them as a powerful counter to her growing conviction that "death is better than slavery" (404). Linda Brent's resolution to escape from slavery is explicitly motivated by her love for her children, and by her willingness to "sacrifice" herself to secure their freedom (433). As the narrator notes, "It was more for my helpless children than for myself that I longed for freedom"; and she states that "I had a woman's pride, and a mother's love for my children; and I resolved that out of the darkness . . . a brighter dawn should rise for them" (416, 412). Countering slaveholders' contention that a slave mother hasn't "so much feeling for her children as a cow has for its calf" (427), Brent asserts the force of maternal feeling, attributing her resolution to escape slavery to the desire to be "free to act a mother's part" (486).[40] In a complex move, Jacobs recuperates motherhood, defined under slave codes as the (re)production of nonpersonhood, as constitutive of black female subjectivity. Just as Douglass dialectically recuperates his body and his labor as the objectified (exploited) properties of his person, configuring them as the instruments of his liberation, Jacobs recuperates her sexual and reproductive labor as her "link to life," transforming herself from what Patricia Williams terms a will-less "economic 'actant' " and moving her from sexual slavery to free civil subjectivity.

Brent's achievement of freedom is sealed by her physical possession of her children in the North and, especially, by her identification as their sole parental authority. This inscription of black women's maternal authority unsettles the absolute property claims of slavemasters as well as the social death of slaves, the contention that "a slave, *being* property, can *hold* no property" (342, 345; emphasis in original). This displacement of the white father by the black mother is vividly performed in the chapter entitled "The Confession," in which Linda Brent reveals to Ellen the identity of Ellen's white father. Ellen responds, "I know all about it, mother. . . . I am nothing to my father, and he is nothing to me. All my love is for you. . . . I used to wish that he would take me in his arms and kiss me, as he did Fanny [his daughter by his white wife]. . . . I thought if he was my own father, he ought to love me. I was a little girl then, and didn't know any better. But now I never think any thing about my father. All my love is for you" (501). As Linda Brent does throughout the narrative, Ellen here performs her disidentification from the paternal authority and proprietary desire of the white father. Deterritorializing the black female body by registering what Spillers terms the "mark" of the black mother and recuperating black maternal desire, Jacobs remaps the gender and racial parameters through which black social subjects are constituted.

The discursive space Brent's maternal commitments generate in the narrative is marked by that powerful antebellum cultural icon—the home. Jacobs's understanding of the power of domestic material "refinement" to signify free civil subjectivity and the privileges of gender, and her political deployment of domestic symbols to contest white male power and economic entitlement, are both clearly legible in *Incidents*. For example, relating the aftermath of Nat Turner's insurrection, the narrator observes that whites are outraged when they "see colored people living in comfort and respectability" (393). In response, Brent prepares with "especial care" for the arrival of the poor white soldiers sent to search the houses of blacks: "I arranged everything in my grandmother's house as neatly as possible. I put white quilts on the beds, and decorated some of the rooms with flowers" (393). Whereas the narrator of Kirkland's *A New Home*, certain in the authority of her class and its domestic symbols, utilizes feminine domestic display to disseminate taste among her poor white neighbors, thus interpolating feminine taste within a narrative of class hegemony and race privilege, Jacobs challenges these forms of cross-class racial identification that, for Kirkland, diffuse class tensions, and constitute part of the matrix in which white class identities are constituted. In Jacobs's text, the performance of feminine taste is expressly politicized—indeed, cast in metaphors of racial warfare—as a vehicle to contest white economic entitlement. Just as "free" black economic successes in the urban North were often met with acts of retaliatory violence by economically disenfranchised whites, Linda Brent's resistance here is framed by the ominous threat of violent retribution. In its performance of class and gender identifications, Brent's action here is ambivalent, asserting her entitlement to domestic taste and the performance of (middle-class) femininity (she depicts her family as more "civilized" than the poor whites), while contesting hegemonic identifications that disable political resistance to white slave power.

Throughout the narrative, the house of Brent's maternal grandmother—a surrogate mother to her grandchildren when their mother dies (345)—is symbolically crucial. This house is the space that Linda feels is her *real* home: after she is bought by Flint, for example, Linda regularly stops during her frequent errands in order to get some breakfast, dinner, or dessert, as well as love, comfort, and care. The grandmother's house is a "snug little home" with a "grand big oven" that provided sweets and biscuits, and Linda receives there not only food, but other material provisions as well (351–52). According to the narrator, "I was indebted to *her* for all my comforts, spiritual or temporal. It was *her* labor that supplied my scanty wardrobe" (346; emphasis in original). The slave code claimed that slave labor was exchanged for "protection," defined as subsistence and physical care. In representing her grandmother's provisions for Linda's well-being, and in insisting that she is indebted to her grandmother, not Flint, for "all [her] comforts, spiritual or temporal," the narrator inscribes her grandmother as her *true* "protector" and thus her (symbolic) owner. Linda replaces the "linsey-woolsey dress" given her every year by Mrs. Flint (which she describes as "one of the badges of slavery" [346]) with her grandmother's lovingly offered garments; and she supplants the gruel and "scrapings" provided by the Flints with her grandmother's pleasing cookery. These exchanges are subtle forms of resistance, pitting black familial and proprietary relations against those of slavery, and consequently provoke the master's and mistress's outrage. Recalling the "first time I was punished," Linda Brent notes, "It was . . . February. My grandmother had taken my old shoes, and replaced them with a new pair. . . . When I walked through Mrs. Flint's room, their creaking grated harshly on her refined nerves. She called me to her, and asked what I had about me that made such a horrid noise. I told her it was my new shoes. 'Take them off,' said she; 'and if you put them on again, I'll throw them into the fire.' " Brent is then ordered to perform errands outside without shoes or stockings (353–54).

The geographical theorist Henri Lefebvre has characterized the appropriation of the social spaces of everyday life as a precondition for the political empowerment of subordinated social groups: "Groups, classes, and fragments of classes are only constituted and recognized as 'subjects' through generating (producing) a space." In Jacobs's text, the grandmother's house defines the space in which subjects are "constituted" and socially "recognized" as such.[41] Indeed, *Incidents* exemplifies what bell hooks has described as the importance of "homeplace" in African American culture. Recollecting her own visits to her grandmother's house, hooks suggests that such spaces "belonged to women, were their special domain, not as property, but as places where all that truly mattered in life took place — the warmth and comfort of shelter, the feeding of our bodies, the nurturing of our souls." According to hooks, homeplace is a site of intellectual and emotional "decolonization" that enables the movement from object to subject:

> Since sexism delegates to females the task of creating and sustaining a home environment, it has been primarily the responsibility of black women to construct domestic households as spaces of care and nurturance in the face of the brutal, harsh reality of racist oppression, of sexist domination. Historically, African-American people believed that the construction of a homeplace, however fragile and tenuous (the slave hut, the wooden shack), had a radical political dimension. Despite the brutal reality of racial apartheid, of domination, one's homeplace was the one site where one could freely confront the issue of humanization, where one could resist. Black women resisted by making homes where all black people could strive to be subjects, not objects, where we could be affirmed in our minds and hearts despite poverty, hardship, and deprivation, where we could restore to ourselves the dignity denied us on the outside in the public world.

Hooks develops this analysis through a discussion of the devaluation of the maternal in Douglass's *Narrative*, in which he writes that he never enjoyed a mother's "soothing presence, her tender and watchful care," although his own mother—who was hired out twelve miles from his place of residence—returned on foot to see him at night and hold him while he slept, thus, in hooks's words, "resist[ing] slave codes, risking her life, to care for her son." For hooks, recollections such as Douglass's which denigrate, by omission, the role of maternal care present the danger of "forgetting the powerful role black women have played in constructing for us homeplaces that are the site for resistance" and thus "undermine our efforts to resist racism and the colonizing mentality which promotes internalized self-hatred." "Failure to recognize . . . the remarkable re-visioning of both woman's role and the idea of 'home' that black women consciously exercised in practice," hooks continues, "obscures the political commitment to racial uplift, to eradicating racism, which was the philosophical core of dedication to community and home."[42]

Incidents makes visible black women's labor in resisting slavery and in promoting the process of decommodification, the movement from "object" to "subject." Explicitly locating freedom in her African American grandmother's "homeplace," Linda Brent thus invokes a conception of home and domestic personhood intelligible to white readers, while expressing a distinctly politicized sense of home that both exposes white privilege and unsettles white norms. Indeed, unlike Anglo-American domestic texts in which home is imaged as the "natural" province of women—its privileges and protections legitimated by patriarchal law—in *Incidents* home is a politically contested space, something black women must struggle to achieve and preserve. Brent's escape from slavery is scripted in expressly gendered terms: unlike the heroes of slave narratives, Brent escapes not by running but by active "retreat" into domestic space. Although Linda Brent is turned away from her grandmother's house when the older woman learns of her granddaughter's pregnancy—an event that is represented as a kind of death sentence (387–88)—she returns to that house to give birth to her baby boy and girl, and then, in secret, to hide from Flint for seven years in its tiny garret. Recalling while unsettling white women's protestations against domestic "confinement," Linda hides in a "little cell"—or "loophole of retreat"—that is slightly larger than her body (437–40); constituting a prison that is also a womb, the garret gives Linda her body back, and completes her transformation into a free black woman.[43] The symbolic import of that space is signaled by the language of Christian resurrection and rebirth with which she describes her experience (e.g., 440, 445). It is here, in the (constricted) space within her maternal homeplace, that Linda Brent's "decommodification" is completed.

Jacobs's narrator's final plea, after she escapes to the North and is joined by her children, is for a home large enough to contain herself and the objects of her love: "The dream of my life is not yet realized. I do not sit with my children in a home of my own. I still long for a hearthstone of my own, however humble. I wish it for my children's sake far more than for my own" (513). Significantly, she configures the conditions of her habitation with employer/owner Mrs. Bruce—the woman who, in the narrative, purchases her from the Flints but does not free her—by invoking while denaturalizing the proprietary relations of sentimental domesticity. While the narrator notes that "circumstances" are such as to "keep [her] with . . . Mrs. Bruce," she describes her employer/owner as "my friend" and claims that "love, duty, gratitude also bind me to her side. It is a privilege to serve her who pities my oppressed people, and who has bestowed the inestimable boon of freedom on me and my children" (513). That "freedom" is of course more than ambiguous: at the end of the narrative, Brent is owned by Mrs. Bruce, although *Incidents* represents this ownership as mediated by relations of sentimental sympathy and care. Notably, Linda Brent's official, juridical transformation from slave to free subject takes place within the bonds of sympathetic, domestic identification. Rewriting the bonds of slavery as the bonds of love and service as the moral "duty" of friendship, Brent instates her claims to feminine gender, and contests the forms of racial power on which her (non)recognition as feminine subject depends. This is the significance of the narrator's pointed representation of the events surrounding her sale to Mrs. Bruce as exemplifying trust, love, and mutual commitment: Mrs. Bruce entrusts Brent with her baby daughter so that the runaway slave can travel, disguised, as a nursemaid, an act that works to reconstruct Mrs. Bruce's purchase of Brent as an act of trust and sympathetic identification, through which the former voluntarily (if temporarily) relinquishes both her maid's labor and her own baby's presence in order to "protect" the slave. Crucially, this sequence, in which Brent pretends to be what she is (a servant) in order to protect herself from her enemies (i.e., owners who don't love her as well as Mrs. Bruce does), reimagines service as a charade whose "real" content is friendship and love. The transaction concludes with a sentimental reunion, and is sealed with a mingling of tears (512). If it is literally true, as the narrator contends in a statement that invokes sentimental convention to suggest a departure from it, that "my story ends with freedom; not in the usual way, with marriage" (513), this "freedom" is one that bears uncanny resemblance to "marriage," a freedom which entails a voluntary, heartfelt commitment to share a happy home with a "master" who is also a "friend," and which constitutes giving herself in service to someone she loves.

The final conscription of Brent's body in *something resembling* sentimental domesticity—an ambiguity legible in its gender/sexual coordinates—would appear to bear out the truth of Spillers's argument, that black female subjectivity both exceeds the patriarchal symbolic and is denied its juridical protections. The social liminality of her position is both recognized and voiced by Linda Brent. Recording her response to the news of Mrs. Bruce's purchase of her, the narrator states:

> My brain reeled as I read these lines [describing the sale]. A gentleman near me said, "It's true; I have seen the bill of sale." "The bill of sale!" Those words struck me like a blow. So I was *sold* at last! A human being sold in the free city of New York! The bill of sale is on record, and future generations will learn from it that women were articles of traffic in New York, late in the nineteenth century of the Christian religion. . . . I well know the value of that bit of paper; but much as I love freedom, I do not like to look upon it. I am deeply grateful to the generous friend who procured it, but I despise the miscreant who demanded payment for what never rightly belonged to him. (511–12)

In Harriet Beecher Stowe's fiction (e.g., *The Minister's Wooing*), black women who are liberated from slavery over the course of the narrative are usually reconfigured as household servants: "free" black women are reconstituted as "willing" and loving domestic workers. Jacobs represents this sentimental proprietary reinscription as plainly insufficient: in the end, Linda Brent still longs for "a home of my own"—a space where she can *claim possession* of the domestic rather than *be* the domestic. Emphasizing her ambiguous legal status, the narrator suggests that the performance of her "generous friend" Mrs. Bruce's sentimental sympathy is inseparable from sentimental ownership, and entails a felt sense of entitlement to Brent's labor and affections. Jacobs's tactical appropriations of the codes of gender and sentimental domesticity reveal the political limits of these codes and unsettle their racial investments, even while they open up a space for the decommodification of the black female body. The sentimental, proprietary construction of "freedom" with which *Incidents* ends is thus, in the narrator's evaluation, "not saying a great deal, [but] it is a vast improvement in *my* condition" (513).

Sojourner Truth's Incarnations of Black Womanhood

In her famous speech delivered before the Akron Women's Rights Convention in 1851, Isabella Bomefree, popularly known as Sojourner

Truth, articulated her pointed and provocative question, "Ain't I a Woman?"[44] Recently, critics have reopened that question. Examining the social construction of race and gender during the antebellum period, these critics have argued that African American women were not defined as "women" according to the dominant culture's conceptions of femininity inscribed in religious tracts, secular treatises, and novels, as well as legal statutes and judicial opinion. According to Evelyn Brooks Higginbotham, "Gender [in the antebellum period] was both constructed and fragmented by race. Gender, so colored by race, remained from birth until death inextricably linked to one's personal identity and social status. For black and white women, gendered identity was reconstructed and represented in very different, indeed antagonistic, racialized contexts."[45] Harriet Jacobs, I have suggested, invokes sentimental constructions of femininity in order to register her entitlement to these constructions and map their racial exclusions. (Re)inhabiting the liminal position of the black female sexual slave, Jacobs's narrator ambiguously inscribes the black female body with sentimental consent. Sojourner Truth, on the other hand, performs gender differently: powerfully challenging sentimentalism's domestic construction of femininity, Truth denies that this construction circumscribes possibilities of feminine fulfillment. Rather than appealing to sentimental codes of gendered identification and civil subjectivity, Truth represents the black female body as a site of gender contestation. As Hazel Carby argues, the domestic construction of antebellum femininity—that of the cult of domesticity's "true woman"—was symbolically coded "white": "The cult of true womanhood drew its ideological boundaries to exclude . . . black women from 'woman.'" Sojourner Truth converted this exclusion into an enabling discursive and political strategy, one which allowed her to invent new forms of black womanhood.[46]

Truth characteristically transformed the "liability" of black women's marginality into a vitalizing opportunity through the rhetorical strategy of *inversion*. For example, in a speech delivered at a northeastern religious convention in the early 1860s, Truth is reported to have stated, "We has heerd a great deal about love at home in de family. Now, children, I was a slave, and my husband and my children was sold from me. . . . Now, husband and children is *all* gone, and what has '*come* of de affection I had for dem? *Dat is de question before de house*!" (*Book of Life*, 150; emphasis in original). Elsewhere, Sojourner Truth converts this experience of personal loss—an experience that vividly registers the unequal political standing of black and white families—into a sign of political authority and and patriotic commitment: brilliantly troping on the traditional argument that motherhood undermines civic disinterestedness and thus unfits women for politics, Truth claims that having been "robbed of her own offspring," she "adopted her race," and considers the "whole United States . . . more her home than any single locality of town or State. She loves her country with truest love" (*Book of Life*, 194, 254). Employing such patterns of discursive reversal, Truth turns black women's exclusion from dominant definitions of femininity to her own account, and capitalizes on black women's gender ambiguity. Converting this exclusion into an enabling occasion, Truth shifts prevailing codes and attempts to invent herself as black female citizen.

Sojourner Truth's rejection of the signs of sentimental femininity, including the material refinement of bodily manner and fashionable dress, is registered throughout the *Narrative* and the *Book of Life*. In a famous passage from the *Narrative*, the narrator describes Truth's experiences as a guest at the home of benevolent and welcoming Quakers. Truth gazes with wonder at the " 'nice, high, clean, white, *beautiful* bed' " provided for her and determines to camp out underneath it, only deciding to sleep on *top* of the bed out of concern for her hostess's wishes (47). This passage cannily illuminates the cultural, class values embedded within domestic objects and the specific forms of bodily life they help shape; it simultaneously figures "refined" domesticity as a socializing ritual—one that Truth only reluctantly, and comically, complies with. (The comic overtones of this scene are exaggerated in the account presented by Harriet Beecher Stowe in her widely read essay "The Libyan Sibyl," a text which illuminates the racial stereotypes Truth both appealed to and contested in constructing a public self.)[47] In her speeches, Sojourner Truth railed against the frivolity of women's dress. Admonishing women at women's rights conventions during 1870–71, she complained, "You rig yourselves up in panniers and Grecian-bend backs and flummeries . . . and mothers and gray-haired grandmothers wear high-heeled shoes and humps on their heads, and put them on their babies. . . . What kind of reformers be you, with goose-wings on your heads, as if you were going to fly, and dressed in such ridiculous fashion . . . ? 'Pears to me you had better reform yourselves first" (*Book of Life*, 243).

Truth's rejection of conventional (white) femininity is registered—with significant impatience and discomfort—in two of the best-known contemporary descriptions of Sojourner Truth: those of Douglass and W. E. B. DuBois. Both represent Truth's unconventionality and willful rejection of refinement as an affront to the black race and especially black womanhood. Recalling his first meeting with Truth in the 1840s in Florence, Massachusetts, during a visit to the Northampton Association of Education and Industry, a socialist community where she was living at the time, Douglass describes Truth as a "strange compound of wit and wisdom, of wild enthusiasm and flint-like common sense, who seemed to feel it her duty to trip me up in my speeches and to ridicule my efforts to speak and act like a person of cultivation and refinement. . . . Sojourner Truth . . . was a genuine specimin [*sic*] of the uncultured Negro. She cared little for elegance or refinement of manners. She seemed to please herself and others best when she put her ideas in the oddest forms."[48] DuBois referred to Truth along with Harriet Tubman as "two striking figures of war-time," and lists Truth among seven people (the other six are men) who "made American slavery impossible." But he regrets that Truth and Tubman's "strong primitive types of Negro womanhood in America seem to some [white Americans] to exhaust its capabilities. They know less of a not more worthy, but a finer type of black woman wherein trembles all of that delicate sense of beauty and striving for self-realization, which is as characteristic of the Negro soul as is its quaint strength and sweet laughter."[49] Both Douglass and DuBois deploy dominant codes of "femininity," "civilization," and "progress" in order to contain the black female body within nineteenth-century parameters of gender and civil subjectivity. Douglass represents what he sees to be Truth's intentional repudiation (even critique) of "elegance" and "refinement," while DuBois contrasts Truth's "primitive" quaintness with the "delicacy" and aesthetic sensibility of "refined" black womanhood. Douglass in particular seems to view Truth's public persona as a personal affront—a representation perhaps partly attributable to Truth's rebuke to Douglass—"Frederick, *is God dead*?"—during an 1849 speech in which he recommended that slaves claim their own freedom, if necessary, by physical force, a rebuke made famous by Stowe's essay. But it is more likely that Truth's "uncultured" body evoked, for both Douglass and DuBois, the personal-historical memory of slavery itself: behind Truth's body is the "degraded" (abjected) body of the slave (m)other, whose negation and denigration founds the "free" black male subject. Douglass's and DuBois's constructions of political "freedom" are predicated on the transcendence of the maternal origin and the abjected materiality of the black female body, which signifies non-being in the symbolic economy of slavery. Thus, Douglass protests what he perceives to be Truth's attempts to "ridicule my efforts to speak and act like a person of cultivation and refinement," his very phrasing indicating both the ambivalence of his performance and Truth's assigned role as (frustratingly persistent) embodiment of Douglass's own (slave) past. The maternal identification evoked by Truth's persona, evident in her self-construction as foster mother of her "race," is legible in the popular legend that she nursed George Washington—a subversive construction of Truth as "national mammy." Truth's maternal self-representations foreground black women's sexual and reproductive labors, signify on racial stereotypes, and figure the racial ambiguities of American genealogies. Staging the "return of the repressed," these representations (re)locate the "degraded" black female body within American civic consciousness.

Truth's rejection of conventional codes of femininity, and her destabilization of the gender categories that structure nineteenth-century civil society, is especially evident in her own and others' descriptions of her body. As in Douglass's and DuBois's accounts, the black female body was a charged political symbol and site of political contestation. When a black female speaker mounted the platform in midcentury America, she presented a powerful civil drama, publicly representing persons deliberately excluded from the American political sphere. While black women writers' physical presence was mediated by the literary text, black women public speakers such as Truth staged—and negotiated in various ways—their bodily difference from cultural norms of white masculinity which obstructed their claims to full public personhood.[50] In speeches and in the *Narrative*, Sojourner Truth addressed the cultural problematics of black female embodiment, manipulating an array of corporeal codes in order to turn the bodily signs of racial and gender difference to her own account. Truth represented her body not as a fixed sign but as a fluid, protean vehicle of self- and social transformation. In a sense, Truth undoes the "theft of the body" under slavery, transforming the black female body from what Hortense Spillers has called a "territory of cultural and political maneuver" to an extension of active, subjective desire.

Truth vividly exemplifies contemporary feminist theorists' concept of gender identity not as natural fact but as embodied performance. In several of her speeches, as well as in the *Narrative* and the *Book of Life*, there are references to her impressive physical capacities, and especially to the immense strength of her body. While Jacobs focuses on the performance of sentiments and sentimental attachments in scripting her claim to civil subjectivity, Truth emphasizes the physical power of her body and her labor. In most transcripts of the Akron speech, Truth refers directly to her muscularity, and especially her capacity to perform strenuous physical labor, as evidence of the physical equality between men and women. In the version of the speech printed in the Garrisonian *Anti-Slavery Bugle*, for example, Truth states, "I am a woman's rights. I have as much muscle as any man, and can do as much work as any man. I have plowed and reaped and husked and chopped and mowed, and can any man do more than that? I have heard much about the sexes being equal; I can carry as much as any man, and can eat as much too, if I can get it. I am as strong as any man that is now."[51] Truth's self-representations seem to have powerfully shaped her auditors' conceptions of her as a public figure. In the *Book of Life*'s" description of the Akron speech, for instance, Frances Gage images Truth as an "Amazon" who stood "nearly six feet high, head erect, and eye piercing the upper air"; and she depicts Truth foregrounding her own body during the speech by baring "her right arm to the shoulder, showing her tremendous muscular power" (133–34). The power of her body is matched by the power of her voice, which is described as spellbinding, "magnetic," and capable of drowning out a "fearful thunder storm" (136).

In the *Narrative*, too, Truth emphasizes the power of her body. For instance, she notes the satisfaction she had experienced when her master, Dumont, claimed that she was worth more to him "than a *man*—for she will do a good family's washing in the night, and be ready in the morning to go into the field, where she will do as much at raking and binding as my best hands" (33). Although she ironizes her ambitions to please Dumont and speaks with contempt of her earlier complicity in his exploitation of her to increase his property, Truth describes in detail and with evident pride her ability to work for long hours without sleeping or with just sleeping standing up, and to labor effectively and proficiently even with a "badly diseased hand" (37, 33, 39). Direct references to the body in Truth's speeches and the *Narrative* suggest her rhetorical emphasis on enactment—a reflexive rhetorical form in which the speaker incarnates the argument and is the proof of what is said—which she shared with other African American speakers, an emphasis partly encouraged by white abolitionists' reliance on ex-slave orators to supply embodied evidence of black humanity and the injustices of slavery.[52] But Truth's representations of corporeality—and especially the particular emphasis of these representations on the body's muscularity and physical power—would seem to serve Truth's own purposes as well, and are central to her efforts to challenge rigid, binaristic constructions of gender and race. Highlighting the "manly" power of her body, Truth does not so much transcend the opposition between "male" and "female" as embody an amalgamation of these opposing identifications, a particular configuration and conflation of binary gender categories. Specifically, these representations allow Truth access to a working-class republican political register identified in mid-nineteenth-century America with the performance of "manliness" and, especially, the right to labor. Truth's inscriptions of "masculine" muscularity and physical strength are politically charged representational "tactics" which permit Truth to inscribe herself within the nineteenth-century public sphere as a republican citizen.[53]

Truth's reconfiguration of the codes of gender is complex. On the one hand, by foregrounding the power of the black female body to signify gender differently, she calls attention to the exclusions of nineteenth-century codes of gender and the political limitations of the proprietary construction of sentimental femininity. In other words, Truth attempts to open up the category "woman" to include possibilities of desire and identification disabled within the sentimental model. Conspicuously scripting and performing the black female body as a laboring body, she makes visible the political and economic centrality of the black female body while exposing the exploitative organization of labor that structures the capitalist and slave economies. As Richard Dyer argues, the body is a potentially subversive site in those economies, because it forces a recognition of human physical and reproductive labor (rather than the magically self-multiplying power of capital) as the source of economic value. Dyer observes that the black body in particular has served as the site of both "remembering and denying the inescapability of the body in the economy," a representational function that Truth's performances foreground.[54] Finally, in performing the codes of masculinity and masculine embodiment, Truth lays bare the political economy of racialized gender and the construction of citizenship as masculine entitlement. Indeed, she contests black male writers' and orators' purchase on codes of masculinity to signify the political privileges of gender and full access to the public sphere—a rhetoric of gender legible, for instance, in Douglass's *The Heroic Slave.* Underscoring her body's position as a site on which the political practice of "ungendering" is performed, Truth deploys gender codes as political "tactics"—a strategy that allows her to carve out a provisional social space for black female subjectivity.

Sojourner Truth's symbolic access to the "masculine" political register was so successful that she was accused of being "a man disguised in women's clothing" by proslavery Democrats at an Indiana abolitionist meeting, and was asked to "submit her breast to the inspection of some of the ladies present, that the doubt might be removed by their testimony" (*Book of Life,* 138). Publicizing this offense in an act that symbolically replicated the involuntary exposure of slave women on the auction block, Truth proceeded to expose her breast to the whole congregation, telling them "that it was not to her shame that she uncovered her breast before them, but to their shame" (*Book of Life,* 139). Sojourner's hybrid body encoded her reshuffling of gender categories and her symbolization of new possibilities of black female subjectivity. Truth reportedly described herself to Horace Greeley as a "self-made woman," a phrase that pithily exemplifies her strategy of appropriating codes of masculinity and incorporating them into novel fictions of feminine selfhood (*Narrative*, vi). Apparently, Truth's contemporaries saw her as someone who defied conventional classifications; Stowe's "The Libyan Sibyl," for example, describes Truth as an "original," a phrase that was picked up and reiterated in newspaper articles and in announcements of Truth's speaking engagements (e.g., *Book of Life*, 201).

Truth's body, in the *Narrative* and the *Book of Life*, is a resonant symbol, a means of literalizing some of her favorite metaphors of self and signaling her spiritual and political commitments. That body is conspicuously lifted out of the domestic seclusion to which white women were viewed as ideally confined, and its boundaries mapped onto the boundaries of the nation. Truth's manipulation of the political articulation of the African American (female) body is concisely and brilliantly expressed in her contention that the American flag's stars and stripes symbolized, under slavery, the " 'scars and stripes' upon the negro's back" (*Book of Life*, 254). In the *Narrative*, Truth's body is represented as a vessel of divine truth, and a register of the nation's moral condition. In Gage's preface, for instance, Truth's body registers her status as an African American citizen, and is described as miraculously bearing the signs of Africa as well as the marks of American redemption and regeneration. As Gage puts it, Truth's "blood is fed by those tropical fires which had slumberingly crept through many generations," and her tall body sways like her "lofty cousins, the Palms" (vi). But since the Civil War, Gage tells us, Truth has experienced "a new baptism . . . of physical and mental vigor": her "health is good; her eyesight for many years defective, has returned. Her gray locks are being succeeded by a luxuriant growth of black hair, without the use of any other renovator than that which kind Nature furnishes. She hopes that natural teeth will supersede the necessity of using false ones" (xii). Truth's body registers the moral health of the nation instead of domestic sensibility, and is incorporated into a spiritually sanctified polis. Synthesizing the blood of black, white, and Indian —her paternal grandmother was a Mohawk—Truth's body emblematizes the union of the nation's principal racial groups, and anchors her authority to speak as America's conscience. This synthesis feeds her immense physical and spiritual strength: as the *Narrative* inscribes her words, "I felt so *tall within*—I felt as if the *power of a nation* was with me!" (45; emphasis in original).

Truth's representation here of physical strength as *feeling tall* encodes in miniature one of the *Narrative*'s chief legitimizing strategies: specifically, that text casts the making of Truth's masculinized, politicized female body in the form of a narrative of origins. In the *Narrative,* Truth's tall, straight body is imaged as inherited from her black father, who was given the name "Bomefree," which was "low Dutch for tree," because of his slender and stately physique (15). Her father's legacy is in fact crucial for Sojourner, and inspires her transformation from chattel to person and from "Isabella Bomefree" to "Sojourner Truth." Her father's homelessness after his master, Charles Ardinburgh, "frees" him (rheumatic and crippled, he is no longer valuable chattel) and her mother, Mau-mau Bett, dies—his pathetic "migration" from the house of one surviving Ardinburgh to the house of another—prefigures Isabella's transformation into "Sojourner." Indeed, her pilgrimages to spread God's word and enlighten the nation redeem and sanctify his own. Her father's circumscribed travels, in fact, inspire Isabella's flight from slavery—a situation registered in the text in explicit and concrete terms. Noting that "the slaves often assist each other, by ascertaining who are kind to their slaves, comparatively; and then using their influence to get such an one to hire or buy their friends," Isabella asks her father when he visits to attempt to "get her a new and better place" than she has with the brutal Mr. Nealy; after this, she returns to the spot where they speak every day to walk "in the tracks her father had made in the snow" until her wish is granted and she is purchased by Scriver, where she remains for one and one-half years (*Narrative,* 28). The steps Isabella takes in her father's footprints constitute her first steps out of slavery.

The *Narrative* thus constructs the original motive for Isabella's conversion into the holy pilgrim Sojourner Truth as a cross-gender, paternal identification. Sold by Scriver, Isabella is bought by John Dumont, who seems to Isabella a kind, decent master: he praises her hard work, and intervenes to protect her from harrassment by his cruel and jealous wife. But she determines to escape from slavery when she sees all too clearly that masters cannot by any means be entrusted with their slaves' welfare. Dumont promises to free Isabella one year before she will be legally freed under New York state law. When the time arrives, Dumont reneges on his promise, ostensibly because Isabella has been ill during the previous year and was "less useful than formerly"; the narrator, however, surmises that "[Isabella's] very faithfulness probably operated against her now, and he found it less easy than he thought to give up the profits of his faithful Bell, who had so long done him efficient service" (39). After witnessing the "murderous neglect" of her father and the fate of local slave Ned

Brodhead, who is literally killed by his master's faithlessness, Isabella has seen and heard enough to explode the myth of the slavemaster's paternal protection. When she learns of Dumont's betrayal, Isabella "concluded to take her freedom into her own hands," and she sets off with "her infant on one arm and her wardrobe"—insubstantial enough to be packed in a cotton handkerchief—in the other (*Narrative*, 41). Trusting entirely to God's care and direction, she leaves just before dawn one morning with no thought as to intended destination; after she climbs a hill and prays to Him, she remembers that safe asylum could be obtained in the direction that she had been luckily but unconsciously pursuing. She continues in her inspired travels until she reaches the home of the Van Wagenens, who gladly take her in.

Isabella's conversion experience, when she takes on the divinely authorized identity Sojourner Truth and begins "*agitatin*" and preaching in a series of lecture tours that would extend for the rest of her lifetime, would not take place until sixteen years later, in 1843. But her escape from Dumont begins to mark out the contours of her later identity and adumbrates her transformation into politicized pilgrim. Sojourner's sojourns enact her "unwavering faith" in God's protection: heeding her mother's "treasured" religious instructions to look to Him for help in "every affliction," she represents her flight from slavery as a going to God, and her inspired steps testify to her absolute trust in His presence and aid (*Narrative*, 27, 17). Here, as elsewhere, Truth's evangelical faith, and sense of an unmediated relation to divine truth, authorizes her defiant rejection of established social and material forms.[55] Christianity for Truth is a democratizing force: her heartfelt religious experience and sense of God's "all-pervading presence" allow her to contemplate "the unapproachable barriers that existed between herself and the great of this world, as the world calls greatness, and [make] surprising comparisons between them" (*Narrative*, 68). Truth's antinomianism is legible in her emphasis on *oral* communication with God and her unmediated knowledge of His presence: following her mother's advice, she engages in frequent and familiar "talks with God" (*Narrative*, 60), and represents herself as an inspired receptacle of God's wisdom and words (e.g., *Narrative*, 101). (Crucially, Truth refers repeatedly in her speeches and *Narrative* to her illiteracy, although, as modern critics have noted, the evidence is not definitive that she could not read and write.)[56] Truth's emphasis on the tropes of orality and self-presence suggest her apparent awareness of print culture as a technology of white domination, and her resistance to the forms of white mediation of African American texts (such as authenticating documents) prevalent in nineteenth-century literary culture. It also suggests her rejection of the fixed materiality of the written word in favor of the living, transformative corporeality of embodied performance.

In the *Narrative*, Truth's inspirited, regenerative body is not a fixed, static entity; rather, it is constantly in motion. In particular, the act of walking — of embodied movement — is constructed as a willed transgression of both gender and race boundaries, and emblematizes Truth's self-scripted public identification. In an analysis of the importance of the body for Western ideas of political agency, Elaine Scarry has noted that "discussions of freedom are almost invariably couched in terms of physical movement," and that bodily mobility, especially walking, connotes the most basic, direct expression of political will.[57] Truth's walking emblematizes, at once, her ownership of her body — it enacts her own will and intentions (authorized by God), not her master's directives and commands — and her entitlement to a public, political identity. Some of her peripatetic travels are fueled by her familial relationships: she walks for miles and miles, for instance, to retrieve her son Peter who has been illegally sold by Dumont, and to establish her legal claim to him as the child's "sole master" (*Narrative*, 53). Much is made in these descriptions of the lightness of her body — which is typically "not encumbered with stockings, shoes, or any other heavy article of dress" — and the speed or "peculiar gait" with which she moves (*Narrative*, 51). But these travels also advertise Truth's rejection of domestically defined womanhood — she is clearly not homebound — and instate her claims to political citizenship. It is the "pure air" of "outside" that is Sojourner Truth's true element; and she explicitly identifies her journeying with freedom and independence (*Narrative*, 105). In an important sense, Truth, like Scarry's Socrates, patrols in her wanderings the boundaries of the polis: she travels all over the nation and — according to the catalog in the *Book of Life* of places she visits — unifies through her physical travels all the country's regions. During her lifetime, she visited and lectured in states as far north as Maine, as far south as Virginia, and as far west as Kansas (*Book of Life*, 308). The circulation of her body is reproduced and extended in the circulation of her photograph, sold at her speaking engagements in order to sustain that body physically and pay for her travels; as she puts it, "She sells the shadow to support the substance" (*Book of Life*, 203). As the *Narrative* contends, "every pedestrian . . . is not a vagabond" (105): if Truth's destinations are often unplanned, the act of walking — of moving and removing — emblematizes her self-scripted public agency, and entails a willed transgression of gender and race boundaries. Her belief in her right to traverse and occupy *all* the spaces of the republic, including those socially deemed off-limits to a black woman, is vividly enacted in her successful protests against Jim Crow policies and her efforts to desegregate the trolleys in Washington, D.C., described by Gage in the *Book of Life* (184–87). Sojourner's sojourns thus constitute an expression of freedom as well as a cogent political statement.

Sojourner Truth, at the age of fifty-nine, finally purchases a home; but as the *Book of Life* pointedly states, she rarely stays there. Frances Gage reports that "about the year 1856, [Truth] came to Battle Creek and bought a house and lot, since which time her home has been in Michigan. She still continues her itinerant life, spending much of her time in the neighboring States, especially in Indiana, which she felt needed her missionary efforts" (*Book of Life,* 136–37). Similarly, an article first published in the *Detroit Post* notes that "Sojourner calls Battle Creek her home, but as she is constantly on the move, she visits that place but seldom" (*Book of Life,* 234). The house at Battle Creek is imaged as a way station, a place for recovery and convalescing (e.g., *Book of Life,* 252) until the pilgrim is able to resume her work promoting social reform and laboring "for the good of humanity" (*Book of Life,* 253). In fact, when homeownership is invoked in the *Narrative* and the *Book of Life,* it is always in the context of political rights and a triple alignment of physical labor, self-support, and citizenship. In Elizabeth Cady Stanton and Susan B. Anthony's *History of Woman Suffrage,* Truth is quoted as saying, "I would like to go up to the polls myself. I own a house in Battle Creek, Michigan. . . . Well, there was women there that had a house as well as I. They taxed them to build a road, and they went on the road and worked. It took 'em a good while to get a stump up. Now, that shows that women can work. If they can dig up stumps they can vote."[58]

The association invoked here between property ownership, the power to labor, and the rights of political citizenship constituted, as I have noted, a central configuration of midcentury republicanism. Truth signifies on this tradition in her analyses of the exploitation of slave labor and of capitalism's "great system of robbery and wrong" (*Narrative,* 98) from which she attempts to extricate herself by living on voluntary donations and gifts; these republican associations also inform her postwar analysis of the economic *right* of free blacks to Western lands, which pivots on Truth's contention that "[African Americans] have been a source of wealth to this republic. . . . Some of its dividends must surely be ours" (*Book of Life,* 196–97).[59] She also strategically deploys these associations to lift women's bodies out of the private, domestic sphere and into the public, political sphere. Her rhetorical emphases on women's muscularity and physical strength, as well as their unconstrained mobility, structure her demand for women's political rights and authorize her inscriptions of female citizenship. Such depictions propel, as I have been arguing, the representation of female embodiment into the public register. The public orientation and character of Truth's embodied existence are everywhere manifest in the *Narrative* and the *Book of Life*. She "counts her years," for instance, not from the year of her "natural" birth within the slave family (1797) but from the year of her "social" birth, the "time she was emancipated" (1827), emphasizing the social and political parameters of her identity. And while it is difficult to extricate Gage's mythologizing in that text from Truth's own, the *Book of Life* images Truth—whose "natural" life began nearly simultaneously with the nation's own and spanned almost an entire century—as the nation's "twin sister," and her personal memory is depicted as a national archive, "the shelves of which contain a history of the revolutions, progressions, and culmination" of the nation's past (*Book of Life*, 224, 254). Indeed, the autographs of public figures, such as Abraham Lincoln, William Lloyd Garrison, and Lydia Maria Child, that Truth carried around in her "Book of Life"—names "indelibly stamped upon the pages of their country's history, and inseparably connected with it" (*Book of Life*, 316)—serve less as authenticating documents, in the standard understanding of that apparatus (though they certainly testify to Truth's "truth") than firmly to establish Sojourner Truth's inclusion in a community of public figures, and to emblematize her participation in the political life of the nation.

5

FASHIONING A FREE SELF: CONSUMPTION, POLITICS, AND POWER IN THE WRITINGS OF ELIZABETH KECKLEY AND FRANCES HARPER

This chapter continues my analysis of black women writers' reformulations of sentimental consumption, "taste," and "feminine" civil subjectivity. Particularly in post-Reconstruction America, an era when the voting and civil rights of African Americans, secured by the Fourteenth and Fifteenth Amendments, were largely undermined by reactionary state legislatures and local governments in both North and South, sentimentalism could provide African American writers with a significant vocabulary of political expression. The sentimental trope of affectional preference or taste constituted a specific code of consent within gendered categories of civic identification, one that could authorize African Americans as subjects within nineteenth-century civil society.

Focusing on Elizabeth Keckley's *Behind the Scenes, or, Thirty Years a Slave and Four Years in the White House* and Frances E. W. Harper's *Iola Leroy*, I examine the importance of tasteful domestic consumption and, especially, fashionable clothing in black women's writings published in the decades after the Civil War. Following the critic Claudia Tate, I read these texts' sentimental formulations of commodity consumption as fictive figures of "gendered racial desire" for racial justice and female autonomy.[1] Denied access to the political public sphere, nineteenth-century African Americans, I argue, appropriated the discourse of fashion as an alternative, competing register of publicity and social recognition. In particular, the representational emphasis on clothing in African American narratives could problematize binaristic constructions of racial embodiment, while registering the dependence of the "fashion system" on slave labor and the slave economy.[2]

As I demonstrate in chapter 1, Scottish sentimentalists had interpolated feminine taste within a narrative of heterosexuality and male visual desire, a dynamic often redescribed in feminist analyses of fashion. For example, Kames inscribes women's dress within the "civilizing" exchanges of heterosexual seduction, thus aligning sartorial expressions of feminine taste with forms of masculine authority and desire. In their foundational narrative of the social efficacy of feminine sentiment, Scottish writers establish taste as the property of what Spillers terms a "*patriarchilized* female gender." As Spillers asserts, " 'gendering' takes place within the confines of the domestic, an essential metaphor that then spreads its tentacles for male and female subjects over a wider ground of human and social organization. Domesticity appears to gain its power by way of a common origin of cultural fictions that are grounded in the specificity of proper names, more exactly, a patronymic."[3] Registering what Spillers, among others, has identified as the ambiguities of gender in slavery, especially slave law's negation of the white patronymic in mapping the symbolic location of black bodies/subjects, both Keckley and Harper disarticulate feminine sentiment and taste from patriarchal domesticity and its forms of white male power and desire. In *Behind the Scenes*, Keckley detaches the fashionable body from its masculine referent and resituates fashion commodities within a complex circuitry of black female erotic and political desire. In *Iola Leroy*, published during a decade of imperial expansion abroad and an intensification of racial violence at home, Harper adapts sentimental narration to address the historical legacy of slavery and contest the institutionalization of Jim Crow segregation. *Iola Leroy* appropriates the language of sentiment to signify race differently; in particular, the novel inscribes the social import of the black family—especially what Spillers terms the "mark" of the black mother[4]—while divorcing feminine sentiment from a legitimating narrative of white male power and "protection."

Fashion, Feminine Taste, and Cultural Forms of African American Womanhood

Keckley and Harper illuminate the racial politics of nineteenth-century consumption—the politically enabling as well as disabling aspects of pervasive sentimental codes of feminine taste and domestic civility. As I have argued throughout this book, forms of "civilizing consumption" were positioned within what Robyn Wiegman calls the "regimes of corporeal visibility" through which race was objectified, and racial identities defined, in nineteenth-century America. Wiegman has described the efforts of nineteenth-century "scientific" discourses about race (especially comparative biology and ethnology) to locate an ontological basis for racial identity by defining empirical, visible evidence of racial difference. Analyzing a variety of cultural contexts in which specific racial categories are rendered "real" through "the naturalizing discourses of the body," Wiegman documents the ways in which "race has been constituted as a visual phenomenon" and a racial "epistemology of vision" has been established. Increasingly, over the course of the century, what Foucault terms the human sciences, especially ethnology, included material culture within the rubric of the interpretable, reading artifacts as signs of cultural development which expressed the relative "savagery" or "civilization" of a given social group.[5] The popular conception, regularly repeated in architectural pattern books and home decorating texts, that domestic possessions constitute a "second body" illuminates the extent to which material culture signified within racialized discourses of the body and constructions of embodied racial identity. Signifying social subjectivity and desires, domestic objects were clearly positioned within the "regimes of corporeal visibility" Wiegman describes: just as tribal specimens were seen to objectify a "savage" condition, forms of "civilizing consumption" were part of the regime through which race was materialized in nineteenth-century America. Clearly, the language of consumer refinement—the widespread perception that commodities "spiritualize" and "refine" the body—carried explicit racial overtones: commodity re-embodiment was positioned against the excessive (uncivilized) embodiment of racial and cultural Others.

As I argue in chapter 1, commodity culture thus supplied a symbology of whiteness and white racial identification: consumption was defined as a means to perform one's taste and construct and display a "white" body. That commodity culture was both a politicized site for performing civil subjectivity, and a realm of racial contestation and struggle, is indicated by the public claims to fashionable dress made by African American freedmen and women in the years after slavery, actions often met by hostility and, at times violence on the part of whites. I will argue below that these economic sites of racial contestation multiplied, and took on new significance, in post–Civil War America, an era of economic and political restructuring, with African Americans' emergence from slavery to citizenship.

However, if norms of taste and consumer "civility" enact racial distinctions, they also foreground the body's construction as a malleable *cultural artifact*, produced within culture rather than defined within the realm of nature—an identification that problematizes essentializing models of racial difference. This denaturalizing of the body and its racial meanings was fueled by a broad trend in postbellum and late-nineteenth-century commodity culture, one especially evident in advertising. Increasingly, advertisements mapped out the body as the primary target of mass commodity culture: in the burgeoning industry of commercial advertising, the body was being constructed as a "problem" for which commodities would provide the "solution."[6] Advertisements regularly presented the body not as a static organic entity but as something manipulable and changeable: indeed, a central promise of commodity culture was then—as it is now—the power to transform and "perfect" the body. This trend was especially evident in soap advertisements, an innovative advertising market in the late nineteenth century.[7] Importantly, soap advertisements from the period (see figs. 1–3) frequently depict the body of the racial Other as the primary object of commodity concern, synthesizing images of imperial conquest and corporeal transformation and configuring that synthesis in both domestic and international terms. Employing the clichéd visual trope of "washing blacks white,"[8] an advertisement for Pears's soap (fig. 1) endows the commodity with the power to "whiten" African Americans, thus re-forming their very bodies. Employing racist identifications—most obviously, the association of blackness with dirt—that reinforce white supremacy, and visually encoding race hierarchies through the vertical ordering of "high" and "low," advertisements such as this one situate commodities within the imperial "civilizing mission" and emphasize their power to transform and "civilize" the (Other's) body.

While the Pears's soap advertisement clearly employs racial and imperial stereotypes, it is not solely a representation of what Anne McClintock calls "commodity racism."[9] Like other forms of mass-mediated culture, these advertisements connote a range of cultural meanings, some of which exceed and unsettle "dominant" racial categories; at times, they mobilize a playfulness of racial signification found in popular culture forms such as blackface minstrelsy. For example, the "whitened" black body featured in these advertisements recalls the figure of the mulatto, a figure that confounds racial classification at the level of the body and is often envisioned as a "black" subject who could "pass" as "white"—frequently, in African American narrative traditions, through self-conscious manipulations of commodity significances and styles. More importantly, as an embodiment of interracial sexual relations, the mulatto insistently evokes a register of U.S. historical countermemory: specifically, such advertisements represent, under the sign of commodity representation, what Jacobs described as the culturally repressed history of the sexual exploitation of black women in slavery. That history is explicitly referenced in an extraordinary advertisement for Bell's Soapona

1 Pears's Soap Advertisement (c. 1884).
Printed by permission of Joseph Boskin.

2 Bell's Soapona Poster (c. 1889).
Library of Congress.

3 Cuticura Medicated Soap Advertisement.
Harper's Weekly (9 April 1887).

soap powder, which expressly links the commodity's power to "whiten" the body with the racial ambiguities of paternity (fig. 2). Like the advertisement for Pears's soap, this advertisement problematizes ideals of consumer civility (and a "civilized" commercial nation) by alluding to the violence enacted in their service—here, the historical dependence of capitalism on slavery and its racialized sex-gender system. Identifying the "civilizing," racializing commodity with the patronymic or name-of-the-father, the Soapona advertisement foregrounds the power of commodities to legitimize the cultural body and position it within the realm of the social, with its culturally intelligible forms of gender and race.

A form of culture closely and habitually associated with the body, clothing was woven into the symbology of the racial body, and similarly enabled a reconfiguration of the material grounds of race. Writing of the enormous appeal of fashion in Western capitalist nations, Elizabeth Wilson observes that self-adornment "link[s] the biological body to aesthetics," and represents "enduring efforts to change the biological given of one's body."[10] Clearly, clothing was a medium of class and race, as well as gender struggle, for nineteenth-century women. As fashion historians have shown, by the mid–nineteenth century, fashionable dress was redefined as a marker of femininity: during the late eighteenth and early nineteenth centuries, ornate dress — comprised of vivid colors, luxurious fabrics, elaborate decoration, and defined by the rapidly changing codes of fashion — previously a prerogative of the aristocratic elite and a sign of social class, was increasingly associated with women, while most men adopted some version of the plain, dark, uniform three-piece suit. With gender replacing class as the primary category of sartorial distinction, fashionable appearance and sumptuary display became material markers of femininity.[11] As several historians have shown, antebellum sentimental womanhood was defined in part through particular class and racial codes of feminine dress, a complex of signifying practices defined in texts such as *Godey's Lady's Book.* By midcentury, fashion was (re)defined as a historically specific "technology of gender," a system of signs through which individuals were constituted as gendered subjects and conscripted into socially normative gendered positions.[12]

The social significance of fashion was not lost on those excluded by its codes. Working-class women, for example, saw in taste and the codes of fashionable dress an arena of social recognition and a locus of political contestation. Writing of the significance of clothing as a representational matrix for nineteenth-century British workingwomen, Carolyn Kay Steedman observes that "within recent history decent clothing has been a necessity for any woman or girl child who wants to enter the social world. It's her means of entry, and there are rules that say so." Similarly, in her study of New York workingwomen at the turn of the century, Kathy Peiss emphasizes the significance of dress in working-class women's public self-presentation, especially the representation of sexuality (the ability to project respectability and desirability).[13] Just as working-class women claimed access to dominant codes of fashion as a means to appropriate, and thus contest, the signs of middle-class women's privilege, newly freed

African American women (such as Keckley) attempted, through dress, to claim publicly their right to full social subjectivity, contesting black women's exclusion from full participation in civil society in expressly gendered terms. Observing that black women often scorned the old forms of dress — utilitarian work garments that were "plain, drab, and heavy" — in favor of "more colorful, elaborate garments," and that clothing served to announce freedwomen's awareness of their new status, the historian Jacqueline Jones relates an incident, reported by Henry W. Ravenel, that conveys both the widespread understanding of fashion as white privilege, and black women's contestation of that view. Depicting a Charleston street scene in the mid-1860s, Ravenel describes "Negroes shoving white persons off the walk — Negro women drest in the most outré style, all with veils and parasols for which they have an especial fancy — riding on horseback with negro soldiers and carriages."[14] Like contemporary accounts of workingwomen's usurpation of the sartorial markers of class privilege, Ravenel's description records whites' obsession with policing the forms of dress, as well as newly freed blacks' repudiation of that authority and their contestation of white economic entitlement. For Ravenel, modes of freedwomen's dress — specifically, their access to the material signs of gentility (veils, parasols) — signified a dangerous departure from codes of racial deference; such practices comprised endlessly proliferating evidence of black insubordination. Although the political significance of such gestures was routinely contained by white observers such as Ravenel by invoking a bourgeois rhetoric of authenticity, they clearly indicate black women's awareness of a postbellum "politics of dress" as a realm of racial, and class, struggle.

As a dominant nineteenth-century technology of gender, fashion could negate the process of "ungendering" which, according to Hortense Spillers, constituted black women's condition under slavery. In "Mama's Baby, Papa's Maybe," Spillers argues that the quantification of the African body under slavery — especially the transformation of the African into an economic abstraction during the middle passage — displaced gendered subjectivity: "the respective subject-positions of 'female' and 'male' adhere to no symbolic integrity" under slavery, for in severing "the captive body from its motive will . . . we lose at least gender difference in the outcome, and the female body and the male body become a territory of cultural and political maneuver, not at all gender-related, gender-specific."[15] Black women's appropriation of fashion commodities can be read as an effort to dislodge the black female body, symbolically, from slavery's processes of ungendering and inscribe that body as "feminine," thus claiming the privileges of gender in nineteenth-century civil society. At the same time, the appropriation of signs of taste, feminine consent, and civilizing consumption for those constitutively excluded from those codes entails a form of what Homi Bhabha terms "mimicry," a performance of the material markers of civil(ized) subjectivity that destabilizes liberal constructions of freedom (what Bhabha terms "the dream of post-Enlightenment civility" and liberty) by exposing incivilities and forms of constraint liberal discourses disavow.[16] Nineteenth-century representations of fashion as a site of class and racial struggle indicate the inadequacy of feminist critiques that read fashion practices solely in terms of sexual difference and the sexual objectification of women by men. The politics of fashion are more complex and multivalent than such analyses allow.

Clothing, Publicity, and Power in Elizabeth Keckley's Behind the Scenes

African American writers emphasized the display of the fashionable and commodified body as a form of political and racial contestation. In nineteenth-century America, I have suggested, "fashion" constituted a terrain on which the politics of class, gender, and race were played out. Women's rights advocates such as Elizabeth Cady Stanton and Amelia Bloomer established dress reform as a central concern of nineteenth-century feminism; middle-class writers protested what they saw to be the democratization of fashion among the working classes, especially working-class women; while proslavery writers such as William Gilmore Simms represented slaves' alleged insensibility to contemporary canons of taste as indicative of African Americans' inassimilability into American "civilization" and a market economy.[17] Clothes were important signifiers of status under slavery: indeed, plantation slaves' distance from the symbolic codes of "fashion" was conspicuously marked by the widespread use during the 1840s and 1850s of what was commonly termed "slop" or "Negro clothing"—cheap, plain, mass-produced clothes made of inexpensive cotton fabric. Some states had slave codes that strictly regulated dress: for example, South Carolina's slave code of 1740 dictated that, except for livery which was viewed as properly servile, slaves were to wear only coarse and plain clothing. Slaves apparently resisted these prescriptions by dressing in colorful and fancy clothing, decorated with buttons and other finery, for church on Sundays and on holidays. Several Works Progress Administration narratives refer to slaves' sensitivity to the social significance of clothing and the pleasure taken in dressing up on Saturday night and Sunday—rituals performed, significantly enough, not for white masters, but out of respect for the slave community. These "fancy clothes" were sometimes given to slaves on holidays or were hand-me-downs from masters and mistresses; but often they were purchased with the slaves' own earnings from gardening or baking, or were made by the slaves themselves. In response to slaves' efforts to manipulate the language of dress to express both individuality and community, the masters apparently attempted to maintain control over the circulation of clothing and to contain the meanings of clothes within the forms of racial hierarchy. The distribution of clothes on plantations was often treated by slavemasters as a paternalistic ritual: often a master would make a special trip to his plantations to hand out clothing personally, in a manner designed to underscore his own benevolence and to signify his proprietary authority.[18] For both slaves and masters, dress was a site of struggle: and what is at stake in conflicts over dress would seem to be—quite literally—control over, indeed ownership of, the slave's body. That slave practices of dress could threaten the master's control is made explicit in the 1822 "Memorial of the Citizens of Charleston," sent to the legislature in the wake of the Denmark Vesey plot, which recommended the adoption of stricter laws regulating slaves' clothing. According to the memorial, slaves' apparel has given them "ideas not consistent with their condition" and made them "insolent to whites"; most importantly, their clothing has rendered them "so fond of parade and show as to cause it extremely difficult to keep them at home." Clothing was a medium of gender as well as race discipline under slavery: for example, in one recorded incident, a slave woman, wrongfully accused of theft, was punished by being forced to wear trousers for a year.[19]

Nineteenth-century African American writers registered their awareness of the politics of fashion in diverse ways. In numerous midcentury slave narratives, clothes figure centrally at the level of plot: the dramatic progression from slavery to freedom recounted in these narratives often depends on the slave's ability to manipulate the signs of dress and to successfully perform cross-racial, and often cross-gender, masquerade. In narratives such as Jacobs's *Incidents* and William and Ellen Craft's *Running a Thousand Miles for Freedom*, as well as in novelistic representations of slavery such as *Clotel* and *Uncle Tom's Cabin*, fugitive slaves flee from slavery disguised as white as well as the opposite sex: racial and gender code-crossings are mutually articulated. Such texts emphasize the importance of dress in the reinscription of the slave as free subject. For example, *Running a Thousand Miles for Freedom*, which recounts William and Ellen Craft's dramatic escape from Macon, Georgia, in 1848 disguised as a white man and his slave attendant, depicts the symbolic uses of dress to problematize racial boundaries and hierarchies instutionalized under slavery. The Craft narrative figures the transgressive power of slaves to appropriate the signs of an authoritative whiteness and to confound a "white gaze" which would aim to enact clear racial distinctions. By identifying race with sartorial display and the manipulable signs of bodily appearance, narratives such as the Crafts' suggest the futility of stabilizing racial identity at the level of the body—whether in blood (the "one-drop law") or in the racialized physical features classified by the new ethnology.

The Craft narrative registers the political significance of clothing in slavery, as well as slaves' utilization of dress to both mark and transgress social boundaries. The narrative recounts how William and Ellen Craft design an ensemble to facilitate their escape from slavery: the fair-skinned Ellen poses as a white gentleman, with her husband as her slave attendant. William purchases clothing "piece by piece (except the trousers, which Ellen found necessary to make)" and his wife, a ladies' maid, hides them in a locked chest of drawers. Once Ellen is dressed in her disguise, William writes, "I found that she made a most respectable looking gentleman." The narrative uses the trope of disguise to foreground the instabilities of race and to figure the fact of miscegenation, a racial mixing replicated here on the body's surface. Undermining the security of racial distinctions, the narrative challenges the foundation of slavery; at the same time, it destabilizes whites' sense of a protective distance from the terrors of the institution by extending slavery's power to "disappear" persons and dissolve identities—to enact a person's social death—to "whites" as well as "blacks." The narrative presents several instances of white children who are, like Ellen, racially "misrecognized," including "the case of a white boy who, at the age of seven, was stolen from his home in Ohio, tanned and stained in such a way that he could not be distinguished from a person of color, and then sold as a slave in Virginia." Signifying on the darkening of white bodies in blackface, the tanning of the white boy in this incident entails not a subversive and pleasurable "trying on" of the black body but a terrifying captivity, loss of white privilege, and erasure of socially recognized civil subjectivity. The racial body in the Craft narrative is a manipulable entity, and such racial masquerades—and the misreadings they generate—threaten to undermine the race distinctions institutionalized in slavery. Clothes in narratives such as the Crafts' provide a means to control and manipulate the white gaze, problematizing, indeed deconstructing the binaries on which race hierarchy depends.[20]

In *Behind the Scenes*, fashion is again the symbolic matrix within which desire—especially the desire for "freedom"—is negotiated. In

Keckley's text, however, black women's *labor*, and productive control over the public "language" of dress, are foregrounded: specifically, fashion constitutes the discursive terrain on which Keckley establishes her political as well as her literary authority. While as a slave Keckley's access to the vocabulary of dress is radically constricted, as a free woman she turns the tables on the (ex-)masters, exercising the power to dictate the appearance of Anglo-Americans. Keckley is a seamstress who gains freedom for herself and her children by hiring out her labor; as a free woman she moves to the nation's capital, where she designs and makes clothes for Northern and Southern leaders, including Jefferson Davis and, during the Civil War, President and Mary Todd Lincoln. The public, political import of fashion for Keckley is apparent in the pride and pleasure she experiences when she discovers that a wax statue of Jefferson Davis on display in Chicago wears a gown made by her own hand. In addition, the final sections of the narrative are devoted to providing an authoritative, intimate account of the history of Mary Todd Lincoln's clothes, which Mrs. Lincoln, destitute after her husband's death, had been forced to sell at public auction—an event which produced quite a scandal. Throughout *Behind the Scenes*, fashion constitutes a medium through which Keckley establishes her political authority and inscribes herself within the body politic.

In her narrative, Keckley weaves fashion commodities into a complex signifying practice, laden with a range of historical and contemporary meanings. Weaving and sewing clothing were traditional female skills in certain West African cultures, and these skills were exploited under slavery: as Ann duCille observes, before their reproductive profitability was discovered, their skill at sewing and weaving helped make black women valuable slaves.[21] Slave women in plantation households were involved in all aspects of clothing production, from spinning and weaving to dyeing wool to sewing garments and fancywork. Although mistresses sometimes taught their slaves specific skills, slave women normally transmitted those skills from one generation to the next and made clothing for their own families as well as for the master and mistress. According to Elizabeth Fox-Genovese, "Slave women sewed in the big house under the direction of their mistresses or a slave seamstress. They sewed in their own cabins with the assistance of their daughters, and they sewed and quilted with the other women of the quarters."[22] In addition, many free black women relied on their skills in sewing and dressmaking as the basis for their income. According to the historian Dorothy Sterling, records suggest that a significant percentage of the free black female workforce in 1860 were dressmakers. Black newspapers and magazines often publicized black women's dressmaking businesses: one Brooklyn business advertised "Fashionable Dress Making, Shirt Making, Embroidering, and Quilting," promising "Ladies' and Children's dresses cut and made in the most fashionable style and warranted to fit."[23]

As Fox-Genovese observes, slave women were responsible for most of the textile production in the plantation household, including producing the "Negro clothes" that masters paternalistically distributed. But while in some households black and white women would sew together side by side, mistresses typically "did not 'see'—or at least did not bother to write down [in household record books]—most of their slaves' textile work."[24] Recording and publicizing that "invisible labor," Keckley's narrative reclaims slave women's appropriated labor, dialectically refiguring her skill as seamstress as the basis of her liberation from slavery; more generally, she foregrounds the productive centrality of black women's labor within the slave economy. Like Sojourner Truth, Keckley takes great pride in her ability to work, emphasizing her tremendous productivity even as a young child, when she "knit socks and attended to various kinds of work"; and she refers repeatedly and with resentment to a remark by her first master that "I would never be worth my salt" as a laborer, clearly taking pleasure in proving her doubters wrong.[25] While still a slave, Keckley is given leave to sell her sewing during a period when her master suffers economic hardships, and subsequently supports the entire family: as she states with pride, "with my needle I kept bread in the mouths of seventeen persons for two years and five months" (45). According to Keckley, "I was fortunate in obtaining work, and in a short time I had acquired something of a reputation as a seamstress and dressmaker. The best ladies in St. Louis were my patrons, and once my reputation was established I never lacked for orders" (45). Her labor enables Keckley to prevent her aging mother from being placed out at service in her old age, and facilitates Keckley's freedom in a direct and material sense. She persistently asks her master whether he would permit her to purchase herself and her son, and when Garland sets the price at twelve hundred dollars, Keckley's wealthy clients in St. Louis, whom she terms "friends" and whom she had impressed by her dressmaking, arrange to raise the money among themselves (51). Freed, she moves to Washington, where she again supports herself with her needle. She opens a dress shop, employs several other women, and secures numerous clients, including the families of the most prominent political figures in Washington. Whereas slave codes had institutionalized white men's effort to control the appearance of blacks and the meaning(s) of the racial body, Keckley's narrative appropriates that authority, emphasizing a black woman's power to fashion the public identities of whites while registering the centrality of black female labor to Anglo-American culture.

In Keckley's narrative, slavemasters' attempts to control the dress and appearance of their slaves appears as part of their broader project to control the labor (including sexual and reproductive labor) of black bodies and to dictate the public definition of black identities. Writing as a former slave, Keckley is acutely aware of the specificities of black women's oppression, and, in particular, the sexual vulnerability and exploitation of black women in slavery. As a slave, Keckley is raped by a white man, an incident she refers to only briefly, and consequently conceives a child. Giving birth to her mixed-race son, Keckley critiques the slave codes that legitimate white men's sexual predations: "Why should my son be held in slavery? . . . The Anglo-Saxon blood as well as the African flowed in his veins. . . . Must the life-current of one race bind the other race in chains as strong and enduring as if there had been no Anglo-Saxon taint? By the laws of God and nature, as interpreted by man, one-half of my boy was free, and why should not this fair birthright of freedom remove the curse from the other half—raise it into the bright joyous sunshine of liberty?" (47). Rhetorically counterposing redemptive nature with corrupt, Anglo-American culture and the "taint" of white blood, Keckley challenges the authority of white laws to designate and sort racial bodies. Foregrounding her agency as a seamstress and, through that agency, her ability to (re)inscribe racial bodies, Keckley intervenes in structures of Anglo-American authority—legal, political, and cultural—through which racial identities are publicly defined.

Charting her transformation from slave to free woman, Keckley's metaphorics of dress register the meanings of clothing as both a vehicle of racial contestation in slavery, and a signifier of freedom among freedmen and women. According to Jacqueline Jones, for newly freed women, fashionable dress constituted an assertion of control over one's physical appearance and a way to mark one's distance from slavery's vestimentary economy. Jones cites several sources, by both African Americans and Anglo-Americans, which suggest that freedwomen repudiated the old forms of slave dress—plain, utilitarian clothing rationed in the form of one or two shifts a year—in favor of more colorful, stylish garments. For example, Jones relates telling comments by Rosa Cooley, a New England white woman who taught on the Sea Islands in the early twentieth century, on the role of women's clothes during the transition from slavery to freedom:

> Slavery to our Islanders meant field work, with no opportunity for the women and girls to dress as they chose and when they chose. Field workers were given their clothes as they were given their rations, only the clothes were given usually as a part of the Christmas celebration, "two clothes a year," explained one of them as she remembered the old days. With the hunger for books very naturally came the hunger for clothes, pretty clothes, and more of them! And so with school and freedom best clothes came out and ragged clothes were kept for the fields. Work and old "raggedy" clothes were . . . closely associated in the minds of the large group of middle-aged Island folk.

According to Jones, colorful clothes served to announce a woman's awareness of her new status; they also expressed changes in male-female relationships from slave unions to legal marriages. As Jones puts it, "Black husbands took pride in buying fashionable dresses and many-colored ribbons, pretty hats and delicate parasols for their womenfolk. When a freedman walked alongside his well-dressed wife, both partners dramatized the legitimacy of their relationship and his role as family provider."[26]

Keckley's narrative testifies to this broader symbolic matrix in which fashionable clothes, denied to slaves, are taken on as emblems of freed status. Keckley seems to have enjoyed manipulating these signs in her own self-presentation. A fellow member of Washington's Fifteenth Street Presbyterian Church vividly describes Keckley's impressive appearance: "Mrs. Keckley was one of the most picturesque women that walked the streets of Washington, and wherever she went, people would turn to admire her carriage. . . . Members of the Presbyterian Church would often come on Sundays to see Mrs. Keckley walk down the aisle to her pew, and every eye would turn to see her because of her queenly walk, and to admire the beautiful and fitting way that she was gowned; refined and rich, but not gaudy."[27] But while Jones emphasizes a husband's patriarchal pride in orchestrating the public presentation of his fashionable wife, Keckley's striking appearance and "queenly walk" connote gestures of self-fashioning and self-possession. When Keckley enters the church, she enters alone: she designs and controls her self-presentation, and the freedom it signifies is decidedly her own. For Keckley, fashion signifies not only her escape from slavery, but also particular forms of "gendered racial desire" and the meaning of her freedom as a slave *woman*.

This rescripting of the body is inseparable from slavery's racialized sex-gender system and the black female body's position within that sexualized matrix. Thus, in Keckley's narrative, clothes take on a crucial, gendered significance: in particular, the clothed body is placed in opposition to exposed, and sexually vulnerable, female flesh. One episode in Keckley's narrative serves to contextualize the desire for dress within the sexual relations of slavery. In the second chapter, entitled "Girlhood and Its Sorrows," Keckley describes how as a young woman she was given to her master's eldest son, a minister named Burwell, and his wife. Although she "did the work of three servants," Keckley was "scolded and regarded with distrust" (32). Mrs. Burwell enlists a frequent visitor, the village schoolmaster, Mr. Bingham, a "hard, cruel man" and a "ready tool" in Mrs. Burwell's vindictive designs. One day, the schoolmaster asks Keckley into the study and then abruptly announces, "I am going to whip you, so take down your dress this instant" (33). She bravely resists this threat: "I drew myself up proudly, firmly, and said: 'No, Mr. Bingham, I shall not take down my dress before you. Moreover, you shall not whip me unless you prove the stronger. Nobody has a right to whip me but my own master, and nobody shall do so if I can prevent it' " (33). These words seem to "exasperate" Bingham, who seizes a rope and succeeds in binding Keckley's hands and "tearing my dress from my back" (34). When she appeals, bruised and bleeding, to her master and mistress, demanding an explanation for the flogging, he responds with yet another act of violence, striking her with a chair and felling her to the floor (35).

As critics have often noted, the whipping scenes of female slaves so frequently depicted in African American narratives (such as Douglass's representation of his aunt Esther's whipping in all three autobiographies) can be read as metaphorical representations of the rape of black women under slavery.[28] Like the exposure of slaves' bodies on the auction block, the stripping and flogging of the black female slave is meant to figure the absolute power of the slave master over the body of the slave, and the corollary negation of the black woman's desire and self-possession. This metaphorization is literalized in Keckley's narrative in a telling narrative sequence in chapter 2: immediately after Keckley describes the whipping incident, she recounts her "persecution" over four years' time by a white man with "base designs" on her, leading to the birth of a son (39). Although Keckley does not "dwell" on a subject that is "fraught with pain," she, like Jacobs, protests angrily against "the edicts of that society which deemed it no crime to undermine the virtue of girls in my then position" (39). In Keckley's account, the brutalized and suffering female body *is* endowed with a kind of charismatic authority, a Christ-like power to convert those who would oppress her. However, the whipping scenes acutely convey the vulnerability, especially sexual vulnerability, of the black female body under slavery: the denuded female body is positioned as both ground and reflection of the master's absolute power. In this symbolic matrix, reclothing the body serves as a way to recontextualize the slave woman's body in a different semiotic and erotic structure, reattaching that body to black female desire and inscribing it within a dense web of cultural meanings. Clothing constitutes a protection of the flesh and the subject's self-inscription, a way to "write over" the victimized body of the slave woman with a proliferation of meanings of the self's own devising. Clothing also serves as a way of controlling and deflecting the white gaze, enacted in the whipping scenes in all its sexualizing and punitive power. As though to signal the self-protective, indeed liberatory significance of fashion in the narrative, Keckley concludes chapter 2 with an abrupt segue to a transcription of a letter to her mother, the single one included in the text, which is replete with references to clothing. She mentions presents her mother had sent, as well as a gift from Aunt Bella which, Keckley owns, "I have been so particular with . . . that I have only worn it once" (41). She describes various "frocks" that she is making, concluding the letter with a request: "I wish you would send me a pretty frock this summer" (42). Easily viewed as concerned with matters trivial and incidental, passages such as this have often led critics to dismiss the narrative as an unrealistic and at times, nostalgic portrait of women's lives under slavery. But I would argue that this passage foregrounds Keckley's awareness of the political meaning of clothing in slavery, and reveals her strategic inscription of clothing as signifiers of female pride and self-possession. Importantly, the passage positions *black women* as the agents of slavery's vestimentary exchanges, and presents clothing as a basis of black women's community. Bearing garments produced by black women and given with love, the clothed female body is inscribed by the desires not of white men, but black women.

The representation of clothing in Keckley's narrative clearly expresses black women's control over their sexuality, the power to deflect as well as to court the gaze of others. Keckley rewrites the meaning of clothing in slavery in a number of additional ways: for example, where slavemasters had utilized the distribution of clothing to reinforce paternalistic forms of benevolence and deference, Keckley reverses these relations, even describing an incident in which a white mistress must appeal to the "generosity" of her slave to borrow a silk dress. Most importantly, she inverts the slavemasters' control over slaves' dress, claiming for herself not only the ability to provide satisfactory clothing for a large number of white clients (thus documenting white dependence on her labors), but the power to fashion public identities for national luminaries. As Mary Todd Lincoln's "regular modiste" (89) and chosen confidante, Keckley makes all Mrs. Lincoln's clothing, starting with Mrs. Lincoln's dress for the first inaugural ball (86–87), an occasion for which Keckley not only designs and sews the dress but arranges the First Lady's appearance (as she puts it, "I dressed her hair, and arranged the dress on her" [88]). For Jefferson Davis, Keckley designs a silk dressing gown as well as a chintz wrapper that she later views, displayed on a wax figure of the Confederate president, at a postwar benefit in Chicago. When Keckley makes the "pleasing discovery" and recognizes the gown, reportedly the garment Davis was wearing when captured, there was "great cheering and excitement, and I at once became an object of the deepest curiosity. Great crowds followed me, and in order to escape from the embarrassing situation I left the building" (74–75). Keckley's position as seamstress for the nation assigns her a publicity both desired and feared, and endows her acts with clear civic value.

Clothing and/as a Politics of Black Womanhood

The political inscription of clothing, registered in part through Keckley's visible presence in Washington and her role as fashioner of the "body politic," takes on, I have argued, expressly gendered meanings. In addition to registering black women's control over their sexuality and self-inscription as desiring subjects, discussed above, Keckley's emphasis on clothing figures her identification with other women; more particularly, it expresses her entitlement to and complicated identification with the privileged, protected femininity of white women. Unlike Harriet Wilson's *Our Nig*, which characterizes the (white) seamstress, Frado's mother "poor Mag," using a conventional melodramatic vocabulary of working-class exploitation and suffering, Keckley's narrative constructs its protagonist as a modiste with mastery of the "fashion system" and its forms of tasteful consumption; this position enables Keckley to recuperate black female labor and to reconstruct taste (with its particular gender and class investments) as a vehicle to map conflictual forms of cross-racial identification. Indeed, by manipulating the signs of dress, Keckley extricates her body from a network of white and male power and resituates that body in an interracial network of women. In other words, Keckley draws on the gendered symbology of dress to figure forms of identification and desire between white and black women.

Complicating earlier feminist critiques of the "fashion system" as wholly organized by heterosexuality and sexist imperatives of feminine objectification and display, contemporary feminist theorists have begun to analyze fashion as an expression of feminine community and homosocial, indeed homoerotic desires. In an essay entitled "Women Recovering Our Clothes," Iris Marion Young attempts to theorize the psychic and physical pleasures of dress apart from the "orbit of self-reference" that the "male gaze" establishes. Young identifies three possible sources of "women's pleasures in clothes": the autoerotic sensuality of touch, the pleasure of fantasy (especially the "fantasy of multiple and changing identities"), and the empowering possibilities of female bonding. For Young, "clothes often serve for women in this society as threads in the bonds of sisterhood. Women often establish rapport with one another by remarking on their clothes. . . . Often we share the clothes themselves."[29]

Keckley's narrative illuminates what Young describes as the power of clothes to function as vehicles of female homosocial desire and gender identification. As in Keckley's references to her aunt's and mother's gifts, clothes in *Behind the Scenes* instate forms of female bonding and familial identification. Specifically, they bear what Spillers terms the "mark" of the black mother with its subversive entailments of maternal identification and desire, and embody forms of maternal care recuperated in Jacobs's narrative. In addition, dress functions in Keckley's narrative as a means to contest white entitlement and envision shared "tastes" between black and white women, mapping complexities of homosocial and (homo)erotic desire that, historians have suggested, were part of the sexual matrix of the slave system. Observing that "the personal relations between house slaves and the white family could range from love to hatred, but whatever their emotional quality, they were more likely than not to include a high level of intimacy," Elizabeth Fox-Genovese writes that "mistresses whipped slave women with whom they might have shared beds, whose children they might have delivered or who might have delivered theirs, whose children they might have suckled and who frequently had suckled theirs." Similarly, Spillers suggestively points to homoerotic possibilities that the female slave's "ungendering" would have facilitated.[30] As the stereotypical figure of the "black mammy" suggests, the black female body was an object of intense affective and erotic investiture for whites, including white women.

Such erotic complexities are evident in an anecdote Keckley relates involving her aunt, a slave named Charlotte, and Charlotte's white mistress. This story, transcribed in the narrative, is recounted in the words of the mistress's daughter. Charlotte's mistress, after punishing Charlotte for some unnamed offense, attempts to apologize by making two "extravagant promises": "on condition that her maid would look cheerful, and be good and friendly with her, the mistress told her she might go to church the following Sunday, and that she would give her a silk dress to wear on the occasion." This present, it turns out, is the mistress's only silk dress; and two weeks later, when she is invited to a neighbor's house, the mistress realizes she has nothing suitable to wear. . . . "She had but one alternative, and that was to appeal to the generosity of Charlotte. . . . [The mistress] made her appearance at the social gathering, duly arrayed in the silk that her maid had worn to church on the preceding Sunday" (255–56). The passing of garments from master to house servant, a gesture familiar to readers of texts such as *Uncle Tom's Cabin*, could serve to reinforce the mythology of white paternalism and to figure the allegedly "imitative" nature of the slave.[31] What Keckley focuses on in this passage is not the desire for the slave to inhabit the body or position of the white master or mistress (notably, the narrative says nothing about Charlotte's feelings), but the mistress's desire for the slave. Indeed, in Keckley's account, the dress passes from white woman to black and back to the white woman, mapping forms of exchange that problematize white authority and racial power, as well as the stability of racial embodiment. In addition to recording what is clearly, for Keckley, a gratifying role reversal in slavery's relations of economic control—here, the mistress must appeal to the "generosity" of the slave to receive what she needs—the incident also evokes the submerged eroticism Fox-Genovese describes, an eroticism evident in many accounts of relations between house slaves and mistresses. It is hard not to see Keckley's inscriptions of shared clothing, as well as her representations of the fittings of garments with their ritualized intimacies of touch and visual pleasure, as erotically charged events, expressing white women's desire for the love, care, and proximity of black women.[32]

Intriguingly, Charlotte is positioned in this anecdote not as a slave whose labor and obedience are demanded but as an object of desire and sympathy whose favor is courted: in a familiar ritual of domestic seduction, the mistress gives Charlotte the dress in exchange for the slave's evident pleasure in serving her, so that Charlotte will "look cheerful, and be good and friendly with her" mistress. The passage demystifies sentimental sympathy as it emerges in, and is shaped by, the proprietary relations of slavery. The mistress's sympathy is here deployed in the service of domestic fantasy and "consensual" relations of domestic affection: while the mistress wishes to apologize to Charlotte for an unnamed slight as a purchase on Charlotte's affections, so that Charlotte's domestic service can be seen as willingly, indeed affectionately performed, Keckley makes it clear that such sympathetic performances are subject to slavery's economic coercions. Significantly, Charlotte's feelings are not recorded; we have no evidence that the mistress's request and tokens of affection are met with anything but suspicion and detachment. More importantly, the narrative's silence on that point underscores that the sympathetic exchanges envisioned here are dictated by the mistress's desire, and constitute a species of narcissism. This refusal of sympathetic exchange extends to the reader as well: by refusing to inscribe Charlotte's sentiments, Keckley, in a sense, withholds Charlotte's feminine consent, and disrupts the forms of readerly identification on which, I have argued throughout this book, sentimental subjectivity depends. But Keckley's account doesn't end here: instead, it ends with the humiliation of the mistress, who must appeal to the generosity of the slave so she herself can publicly perform her gender, race, and class privilege. The incident thus suggests both slaves' ability to manipulate sentimental sympathy and white women's dependency on a proprietary authority over black women. Detaching the performance of sympathy from white male desire and power, Keckley's narrative explores complexities of erotic desire and identification under slavery. At the same time, it exposes the entanglements of cross-racial sympathy with forms of power and aggression.

Behind the Scenes documents strong emotional ties between black and white women. Throughout the narrative, Keckley records what she terms the "heartfelt bonds" between white and black women in slavery, bonds signified most plainly in a letter to her mother, where she writes, "Give my love to all the family, both black and white" (41). Indeed, the most powerful bonds in the narrative are female bonds—between Keckley and the female friends and clients who purchase her from slavery; between Keckley and her Washington clients (especially Mrs. Lincoln); and between Keckley and the Garlands, the family from whom she had purchased her freedom, and who invite her for a visit after the war (she describes her visit to Virginia in a chapter entitled "Old Friends"). According to Keckley, "Ann Garland, the mistress from whom I purchased my freedom . . . had five daughters. . . . I used to take pride in dressing the two eldest, Miss Mary and Miss Carrie, for parties. Though the family labored under pecuniary embarrassment, I worked for these two young girls, and they were always able to present a good appearance in society. . . . I loved them both tenderly, and they were warmly attached to me. Both are now dead, and when the death-film was gathering in the eyes, each called for me and asked to die in my arms" (238–39). Keckley describes with evident satisfaction her warm "reunion" with the Garlands, and their solicitousness and attachment to her; she includes in the chapter extracts from a letter from Maggie Garland (who had subsequently visited her in Washington), which is signed "Your child, Mag,"—"an expression of love," Keckley writes, "warmly appreciated by me" (264). Passages such as this, one which testify to the "warm attachment between master and slave" (242), have led some critics to characterize the narrative as an apology for slavery. But while Keckley includes these passages to illustrate her claim that "love is too strong to be blown away like gossamer threads" (257), she plainly registers the complexities of "friendship" between white and black women. Inscribing similarities as well as differences between black and white women, such passages call attention to the ways in which white race privilege remains embedded within women's interracial relations. Indeed, Keckley plainly shows that the forms of cross-racial "intimacy" were structured by the proprietary relations of slavery, while white women's desire for slave women's affection was shaped by relations of paternalism and sentimental ownership—proprietary investments that Keckley acknowledges and contests.

For example, in narrating her visit to the Garlands, Keckley recounts not only the pleasure of reunion but the pain and indignity of discrimination: she describes, for instance, looking for her mother's grave in a public burial ground, where the "marks of her grave . . . were so obscure that the spot could not be readily designated" (240), noting that "somber threads" are woven into the "sunny picture" of the past. She is more explicit about the politics of interracial intimacy in a conversation with her former mistress, confronting Ann Garland with resentments that darken the other's nostalgic, "golden" picture of the past (241). When Ann Garland asks, "Do you always feel kindly towards me, Lizzie?" the latter responds, "To tell you candidly . . . I have but one unkind thought, and that is, that you did not give me the advantages of a good education." Ann Garland acknowledges that Elizabeth is right, owning that "I did not look at things then as I do now," but observing that "you have not suffered much on this score, since you get along in the world better than we who enjoyed every educational advantage in childhood" (257). What Ann Garland wants here is Keckley's sentimental consent, a performance of sympathy that would legitimate Garland's identity as a "good mistress," and she stages a ritual in which Keckley refuses to participate. Keckley does not "identify" with her mistress here; instead, she takes evident pleasure in bearing out the truth of Ann Garland's statement, and documenting reversals in status and power between (former) slave and mistress. Keckley suggests that slavery had ill-suited the Garlands to adapt to their lives as mature women: Ann, the wife of a former Confederate officer, complains that she has "had to be at times dining room servant, house-maid, and the last and most difficult, dairy-maid"; while Maggie is "buried in the wilds of Amherst" where she works as a governess and where her room is too cold to compose long letters (260, 265). Keckley's current position, comfort, and social prominence contrast plainly with the Garlands' situation. In passages such as this, Keckley constructs interracial female relationships to acknowledge both sameness and difference: in particular, she depicts relations of mutual attachment and identification in order to register black women's exclusion from the privileges of gender and to highlight her own independent achievements. Writing here in the guise of deferential former slave, Keckley exposes the complexities and veiled aggressions of interracial intimacy under slavery.

The Textual Metaphorics of Dress: Writing the "Lincoln Dress Scandal"

Behind the Scenes' inscriptions of the politics of cross-racial female "friendship" and feminine identification culminate in the representation of Keckley's relationship with Mrs. Lincoln. Keckley documents Mrs. Lincoln's affection for her throughout the narrative: Mary Todd Lincoln devises "pet names" ("Lizabeth" and "Lizzie") for Keckley, and refers to her at various points in the narrative as her "best friend" (e.g., 210). Indeed, on the night of President Lincoln's assassination, it is Elizabeth Keckley that Mary Lincoln sends for (as Keckley puts it, "She denied admittance to almost every one, and I was her only companion, except her children, in the days of her great sorrow" [193]); and when Mrs. Lincoln leaves the White House and returns home to Chicago, it is Elizabeth Keckley's company she seeks for her trip west. Keckley relates Mary Lincoln's words during that trip: " 'Lizabeth, you are my best and kindest friend, and I love you as my best friend' " (210). The tone of these passages is quite complex. Keckley is absolutely explicit about the relations of power that mediate interracial "intimacy" between women, and she repeatedly stresses Mary Todd Lincoln's presumptuousness and imperiousness in arranging "their" plans. For instance, recounting their exchange before the Chicago trip (a trip "devoid of interest" for her [210]), Keckley relates how, after she voices reservations because of work commitments, Mary Lincoln answers her objections as follows: "Now don't say another word about it, if you do not wish to distress me. I have determined that you shall go to Chicago with me, and you *must* go" (210; emphasis in original). As in her depiction of the Garlands, Keckley conveys her resentment at this treatment, and demonstrates how presumptions of "intimacy" can serve as a cover for white women's privilege, precluding consideration of black women's independent interests and needs. In particular, Mary Lincoln seems to feel herself entitled to the labor as well as affection of Elizabeth Keckley—suggesting that forms of cross-racial sympathy between white women and "free" black domestic workers are here, as in Jacobs's narrative, structured by sentimental proprietorship and continuous with the proprietary relations of slavery. Nonetheless, Keckley seems proud to have secured this woman's favor and trust (which, at least for a time, aided her in business and elevated her public reputation), and labors to preserve it. I would suggest that she employs this identification strategically: both as a source of pleasure and self-legitimation, and as a form of (inter)racial pedagogy. In other words, Keckley depicts her intimacy with Mary Lincoln as a means both to register the entitlement of black women to the privileges of "femininity," and to disrupt the privileged, domestic enclosure of white womanhood.

In *Behind the Scenes*, Keckley manipulates forms of cross-racial identification and disidentification to her own advantage. Mary Todd Lincoln serves as both intimate "friend" and foil for Elizabeth Keckley throughout the narrative. In various ways, Keckley contrasts Mary Lincoln's story of dependence and increasing victimization with her own story of independence, self-sufficiency, and ascendant heroism. Like many nineteenth-century African American narratives, *Behind the Scenes* undercuts stereotypes of blacks as childlike dependents by documenting the dependency of whites on African American's care, labor, and resourcefulness. While Mrs. Lincoln is emotionally and financially dependent, and especially dependent on a man (Lincoln calls her, to her evident gratification, "his child-wife" [236]), Keckley is self-supporting and self-sufficient; indeed, she resolves to separate from her husband when he "proved dissipated, and a burden instead of a helpmate" (50, 64). Whereas Mrs. Lincoln is financially imprudent and neglects to secure a pension for her support, Keckley is financially competent and secures her own widow's pension. Indeed, Keckley is positioned as an adviser to Mary Lincoln (in one instance, Mary writes letters with Elizabeth positioned "at [her] elbow" [294]), whose guidance is solicited on a range of subjects, from interior decoration to White House political matters to Mary Lincoln's financial affairs; on at least one occasion, Keckley suggests, her own sense of female respectability and decorum restrained the impulsive Mrs. Lincoln from irregularities of behavior that would have exposed her to public censure (283).

Such interracial relationships enable Keckley to draw contrasts as well as necessary parallels between whites and blacks. The occasion for one such comparison is a remarkable incident of textual "signifying": Keckley relates young Tad Lincoln's reading lesson, when he identifies the letters "A-p-e" as the word "monkey." According to Keckley, "Tad had always been much humored by his parents, especially by his father. He suffered from a slight impediment in his speech, and had never been made to go to school; consequently his book knowledge was very limited. I knew that his education had been neglected, but had no idea he was so deficient as the [incident] proved him to be" (216–17). Keckley offers the following explanation for Tad's mistake, "The word was illustrated by a small wood-cut of an ape, which looked to Tad's eyes very much like a monkey; and his pronunciation was guided by the picture, and not by the sounds of the different letters" (217). This incident clearly "represents," for Keckley, much more than its literal value as an episode in the Lincolns' private life: indeed, the passage stands out, in a largely episodic narrative, for its figural complexity. In particular, Keckley signifies on the racist identification of African Americans with apes—an identification drawn, at least partly, because of Africans' reputed "lack" of letters—in order to destabilize conventional racial hierarchies.[33] Keckley explicitly draws out such conclusions for her readers: "Whenever I think of this incident I am tempted to laugh; and then it occurs to me that had Tad been a negro boy, not the son of a President, and so difficult to instruct, he would have been called thick-skilled, and would have been held up as an example of the inferiority of race" (219). Keckley continues: "I know many full negro boys, able to read and write, who are not older than Tad Lincoln was when he persisted that A-p-e spelt monkey. . . . If a colored boy appears dull, so does a white boy sometimes; and if a whole race is judged by a single example of apparent dulness [*sic*], another race should be judged by a similar example" (220).[34]

Keckley's use of the rhetorical strategy of inversion to destabilize race relations is especially evident in *Behind the Scenes'* account of Mary Lincoln's trip to New York, where she arranges to sell her dresses, recounted in the long, concluding chapter of the narrative ("The Secret History of Mrs. Lincoln's Wardrobe in New York"). Keckley had already discussed Mary Lincoln's tremendous expenditures on clothing while in the White House, noting that "in endeavoring to make a display becoming her exalted position, she had to incur many expenses," so that at the time of the president's death she owed "different store bills amounting to seventy thousand dollars" (147, 204); afterward, when Congress neglects to provide Mrs. Lincoln a pension, the latter determines to divest herself of her wardrobe in order to generate funds to live on. Aware that the mission is a "delicate" one (269) and aiming to avoid public attention, Mrs. Lincoln travels incognito, calling herself "Mrs. Clarke" and disguising herself in public places by wearing a heavy black veil (288, 297). This sequence allows Keckley to reconfigure, in racial terms, tropes of disguise and "passing" central to slave narratives and later African American literature. In one instance, Mary Lincoln and Elizabeth Keckley, on a ride through Central Park, are nearly run into by a passing carriage, creating "a spasm of alarm, for an accident would have exposed us to the public gaze, and of course the masquerade would have been at an end" (289). In another, extraordinary passage, while traveling on a train between New York and Chicago, the veiled Mary Lincoln finds herself seated beside an old acquaintance, who recognizes her, to their mutual distress and embarrassment (299). Recalling similar incidents of threatening recognition in slave narratives, this episode is, in miniature, a narrative of "passing" and disguise in which the burden to "pass" (as well as the "veil" of color) are displaced onto Mary Todd Lincoln's body. In Keckley's narrative the representation of cross-racial intimacy engenders forms of displacement, enabling Keckley to re-present, and effectively invert, racialized relations of surveillance, power, and embodiment.

In particular, this section of the narrative depicts Mary Lincoln's painful "exposure" before the public gaze. Although Mary Lincoln initially attempts to conduct her business secretly, privately commissioning two male advisers to sell the garments for her, her plan is unsuccessful, and she at last resolves to "place her wardrobe on exhibition for sale, and . . . publish the letters [describing her plight] in the [New York] *World*" (296). Keckley includes excerpts from an article in the New York *Evening Express* reporting on the event:

> The attraction for ladies, and the curious and speculative of the other sex in this city . . . is the grand exposition of Lincoln dresses at the office of Mr. Brady, on Broadway, a few doors south of Houston Street. The publicity given to the articles on exhibition and for sale has excited the public curiosity, and hundreds of people, principally women with considerable leisure moments at disposal, daily throng the rooms of Mr. Brady. . . . Twenty-five dresses, folded or tossed about by frequent examinations, lie exposed upon a closed piano, and upon a lounge; shawls rich and rare are displayed upon the backs of chairs, but the more exacting obtain a better view and closer inspection by the lady attendant throwing them occasionally upon her shoulders, just to oblige, so that their appearance on promenade might be seen and admired. Furs, laces, and jewelry are in a glass case. (302–3)

The *Evening Express*'s description of this scene is erotically charged, suggestive of the intimacy of the boudoir, with garments "tossed about," fondled, and intimately "exposed." What might be called the passage's construction of a pornography of dress is particularly evident in the newspaper's discursive emphasis on, and evident fascination with, the worn spots and stains on the dresses, indicating garments clearly touched and "marked" by Mary Lincoln's body (304): the garments are explicit metonyms for Mary Lincoln's body, and their exposure is expressly eroticized. For placing her intimate possessions on public display, Mary Lincoln met with much public censure: the *Evening Express* reports that "the feeling of the majority of visitors is adverse to the course Mrs. Lincoln has thought proper to pursue, and the criticisms are . . . severe" (303). In part, the incident allows Keckley to challenge white privilege and disrupt barriers and institutionally enforced forms of disidentification between white and black women. Employing the language of "inspection," "expos[ure], and illicit public display," the passage depicts Mary Lincoln as publicly disrobed—thus recalling the stripping of the black female body described in the narrative's earlier sections. If clothes in *Behind the Scenes* enable Keckley to imagine and represent forms of interracial identification, they also provide materials for an inversion of power relations and racial hierarchies. Here, the "exposure" of Mrs. Lincoln's body is contrasted with the conspicuous and prudent covering of Keckley's own.

Though she clearly sympathizes, at least in part, with her former employer, in relating these incidents Keckley also gains a certain power over her, disrupting, indeed reversing paternalistic relations on which sentimental subjectivity depends. As I have argued, as dressmaker, Keckley controls the public "image" and appearance of political luminaries and inverts the vestimentary logic of slavery, asserting the power of dress while registering the dependence of whites on black female labor. As writer, Keckley furthers this logic: writing "The Secret History of Mrs. Lincoln's Wardrobe" places Keckley in a position to control Mary Todd Lincoln's public "appearance," to publicly "dress" and even "undress" her. The title of the chapter directly invokes the genre of midcentury sensation fiction, in relation to which Keckley's narrative is ambiguously positioned. Nineteenth-century sensationalism employed an eroticized vocabulary of nakedness, embellishment, dress, and undress which encoded the reader-text relation through a gendered metaphorics of eroticized voyeurism. Indeed, the rhetoric of sensation fiction was explicitly intertwined with the cultural logic of gender, with the (literal and metaphorical) "veiling" and "unveiling" of the female body.[35] Writing constituted an opportunity for Keckley to gain control over the materials of her life, to determine which incidents she would relate while organizing them in a certain pattern—to control, that is, what was publicly viewed and what would remain private and unseen. Writing thus enables Keckley to challenge the compulsory, disciplinary visibility and emphatic embodiment of the black body, and even to (re)direct the public gaze—here, to the body of a white woman. Writing about the dress scandal further encodes, and complicates, relations of power, visibility, and control. The text offers what is, at best, a mixed representation of the First Lady's "private" character: Keckley plainly registers Mrs. Lincoln's faults and idiosyncracies (at one point she calls her the "most peculiarly constituted woman" she has ever met), her jealous and suspicious nature, and her occasional cruelty, in addition to paying tribute to her warmth, affection, and loyalty. In *Behind the Scenes*, Keckley metaphorically "undresses" Mrs. Lincoln in public, thus inscribing—even while attempting to distance herself from—the narrative logic of sensational exposé.

Keckley was well aware of the dangers of sensationalism as a political language, dangers registered in slave narratives such as Jacobs's. For instance, Jacobs repeatedly invokes the language of sensationalism, its rhetoric of secrecy and exposure, to underscore the ethical and political necessity to expose the repressed truth of slavery—specifically, the institutionally sanctioned rape of black women by white men—even while she recognizes that such revelations violate the conventions of "polite" female speech. In Keckley's case, writing explicitly about Mary Lincoln would violate conventions of gender and female privacy, as well as expected forms of race and class deference. In her preface, Keckley acknowledges that "it may be charged that I have written too freely on some questions, especially in regard to Mrs. Lincoln" (xiii). In framing her defense, Keckley tellingly employs a metaphorics of unveiling and veiling, nakedness and masking, that figuratively connects her dual occupations as seamstress and writer, while implicating the cultural dynamics of writing and publishing in the text's politics of dress:

> Mrs. Lincoln, by her own acts, forced herself into notoriety. She stepped beyond the formal lines which hedge about a private life, and invited public criticism. The people have judged her harshly, and no woman was ever more traduced in the public prints of the country. The people knew nothing of the secret history of her transactions, therefore they judged her by what was thrown to the surface. . . . If the world are to judge her as I have judged her, they must be introduced to the secret history of her transactions. The veil of

mystery must be drawn aside; the origin of a fact must be brought to light with the naked fact itself. (xiii–xiv)

Further, she contends, "I do not forget . . . that ladies who moved in the Washington circle in which [Mary Lincoln] moved, freely canvassed her character among themselves. . . . If these ladies could say anything bad of the wife of the President, why should I not be permitted to lay her secret history bare, especially when that history plainly shows that her life, like all lives, has its good side as well as its bad side?" (xv) Although she uses the tropes of unveiling and nakedness associated with sensation fiction, Keckley defends her actions by contending that Mary Lincoln, as a public figure who had arranged a public sale of her clothing, has willingly removed herself from the protections of private life and "invited" public scrutiny. Furthermore, Keckley notes that Washington "ladies" had freely made Mary Lincoln a topic of unflattering gossip, to which she envisions her text as response and rebuttal. In addition, Keckley assures the reader that she has carefully screened and selected the materials for publication, including, for example, only those extracts from her personal letters that "refer to public men, and are such as to throw light upon her unfortunate adventure in New York" (xv). Keckley states that her efforts are unquestionably justified, since the close association between the two women necessarily raises questions about her own role in the scandal: "My own character, as well as the character of Mrs. Lincoln, is at stake, since I have been intimately associated with that lady in the most eventful periods of her life" (xiv). By presenting her own text as authoritative version of Mrs. Lincoln's life, Keckley positions herself as purveyor of the true portrait of Mary Lincoln, "as she is, free from the exaggerations of praise or scandal" (xv). Through writing and especially the medium of print, metaphorized as dress, Keckley controls the public image of the First Lady, while insisting on the honorable nature of her efforts.[36]

Keckley's efforts to control the text's metaphorics of unveiling and secrecy and manipulate the logic of sensational exposé ultimately failed. Against her wishes, Keckley's publisher, G. W. Carlton, and her literary adviser, James Redpath, published Mrs. Lincoln's letters almost verbatim (Keckley had loaned Redpath the letters so that he could help her choose appropriate excerpts) rather than the edited selections Keckley had determined to include. Although Keckley attempted carefully to control the public image of Mrs. Lincoln and herself, Carlton and Redpath appropriated that position, claiming for themselves the prerogative to frame the women's representation in a way that capitalized on the text's potential sensationalism. Advertisements for the book intensified the sensational dimension of the narrative (its "White House Revelations") and downplayed its value as autobiographical memoir: for instance, in the New York Library, Carlton advertised the book as "The Great Sensational Disclosure by Mrs. Keckley." Reviews recirculated this rhetoric of scandal and exposé, framing the narrative in moral terms: for example, the editor of the *New York Citizen* pronounced it "grossly and shamelessly indecent . . . an offence of the same grade as the opening of other people's letters, the listening at keyholes, or the mean system of espionage which unearths family secrets with a view to blackmailing the unfortunate victims." After the book's publication, Mary Todd Lincoln never spoke with Keckley again; because Mary Lincoln's son, Robert, demanded that the book be suppressed, it was withdrawn from the shelves.[37] The outcome was tragic for Keckley: not only did she receive no royalties from the book's publication, but her wealthy clientele disappeared, and newspapers criticized her for what was conventionally viewed as an act of disloyalty. Suppessing her story, the reviews thus publicly reframed Keckley within the paternalistic relations of servitude she had repeatedly challenged. Keckley attempted to defend herself, insisting in the *New York Citizen* that "all I have written of Mrs. Lincoln has had a tendency to place her in a better light before the world" and that "the impartial reader of the book" will "agree that it is not written in the spirit of 'an angry negro servant' "—but her efforts were in vain. After *Behind the Scenes,* Keckley's writing life ceased: she never attempted to publish anything again. Her book suppressed, Keckley appears to have consigned herself to private life: she lived the remainder of her life a recluse, residing in a boardinghouse and supporting herself on the twelve-dollars-a-month pension she received as a widow whose son was killed in combat.[38] The reversals that Keckley's narrative inscribe, and her efforts to control codes of public "appearance," were deemed unseemly, a threatening expression of black female independence that challenged racial hierarchies and conventional forms of deference, authority, and power.

Harper, Hopkins, and the Domestication of "Blackness"

As many critics have noted, late-nineteenth-century black women authors deployed images of sentimental, refined femininity in order to reconstruct the public face of the black race and help forge the era's politically potent trope of the "New Negro." The turn-of-the-century "trope of the New Negro," described by Henry Louis Gates, was a vehicle for "rewriting" blackness for both blacks and whites, and served to transform racist images of African Americans by signifying the culturally "progressive" features of the black race and by conferring on the black self the symbolic attributes of the "civilized" subject—especially education, refinement, and property.[39] In post-Reconstruction America, this trope would serve as a critical intervention into the racist discourse of black degeneracy and what Herbert Gutman has identified as the "retrogressionist" arguments of white radical conservatives, arguments which centered on the imputed sexual excesses of African Americans and their unrestrained regression into savagery.[40] In the writings of black women authors, such as Frances Harper, Pauline Hopkins, and Emma Dunham Kelley, this trope was textually embodied primarily in the character of the educated, cultured mulatta.[41] Signifying cross-racial, gender identification, this figure allowed black women writers to tap into the privileged position of white women, widely seen to exemplify the apex of civilization, as a means of "elevating" the black race from within and without. Specifically, the "cultured mulatta" conspicuously marked African American women as "women" (as defined by sentimental codes) and claimed for black women the politicizing potentiality of "feminine consent." The productive interplay of gender and race identifications are legible in Fannie Barrier Williams's essay on the "Club Movement among Colored Women," printed in the 1900 collection entitled *A New Negro for a New Century*, edited by Booker T. Washington. In that essay, Williams places black femininity at the center of the New Negro's philosophy of self-esteem: "To feel that you are something better than a slave, or a descendant of an ex-slave, to feel that you are a unit in the womanhood of a great nation and a great civilization, is the beginning of self-respect and the respect of your race."[42]

Black women authors self-consciously contributed to this project of race reconstruction and elevation, and attempted to further what Williams refers to as the "progress" of the "mind and spirit of the race."[43] Harper, for instance, expressly saw her fiction as participating in the contemporary movement of racial uplift, a movement led by a widespread network of black clubwomen whose motto was "lifting as we climb."[44] Her narrative representations of cultured mulattas, exhibiting cultivation and the material signs of refined sensibility, were situated within this broader narrative and political project. As critics have noted, these images served several different functions; in particular, they enabled sympathetic alignments with a white readership, mitigating Jim Crow segregation by symbolically mediating between proscribed white and black worlds; and they were used to refute racist, pseudoscientific theories of black degeneracy, and to counter images of the uncultured, quaint, and comic black of white plantation and Reconstruction humor, a stereotype that could all too easily be used—as Stowe's "Libyan Sibyl" attests, and as Douglass and DuBois apparently feared—to define and contain the cultural presence of an "original" like Sojourner Truth. During a period when charges of black male "savagery" prompted the horrors of retaliatory violence through the brutal white ritual of lynching, images of African American women as civilized and civilizing, incorporated within the gendered structures of civil society, would have constituted a powerful protest against whites' conspicuous lack of civility. Countering racist stereotypes by claiming for black women the familiar signs of idealized white femininity—sensibility, refinement, and *home*—authors such as Harper maintained in their fiction the domestic emphasis characteristic of nineteenth-century "woman's fiction." While late-nineteenth-century African American men's protest fiction emphasized male efforts to secure civil rights and suffrage, African American women's fiction from the period often highlighted the traditionally "feminine," domestic themes of marriage and motherhood as markers of black women's accession to full (civil) subjectivity.

Black women writers' investments in the figure of the cultured mulatta and middle-class domestic themes have generated much critical debate. Certainly, these images were not unproblematic, revealing a conservative stake in middle-class norms of subjectivity, sentiment, and gender; further, they mobilize a rhetoric of "civilized" subjectivity that, by the 1890s, had clear imperialist connotations. Indeed, as I will show in chapter 6, depictions of consumer "refinement," in the 1890s, were expressly entangled with a politics of empire, race, and gender: political writers and policymakers envisioned U.S. imperial exploits in Cuba, the Caribbean, and the Philippines as a response to what was widely termed "overcivilization" through excessive (feminine) consumption, an attempt to restore male authority at home by remasculinizing American manhood and securing new markets for the "surplus commodities" that were seducing the American consumer public.[45] I will argue here that the figure of the cultured mulatta, and the performance of taste, domestic display, and feminine consent these texts stage, not only worked to inscribe black women as civil(ized) subjects according to sentimental codes; these representations also constitute an instance of colonial "mimicry," a repetition with a *difference*, that had destabilizing discursive and political effects. These texts stage the performance of domestic civility, but with a difference: in particular, exposing the white male sexual predations at the heart of slavery's racialized sex-gender system, these texts disarticulate feminine sentiment from white patriarchal authority, encoding and inscribing other structures of racial feeling.[46]

The central place of black women and domesticity in the reconstruction of "race" is a recurring theme in the fiction, lectures, and essays of Frances Harper, described by one critic as "the most popular African-American writer of the nineteenth century."[47] In a lecture entitled "Enlightened Motherhood," delivered before the Brooklyn Literary Society in 1892, Harper characterizes the recently emancipated African Americans as a "homeless race" who need to be "gathered into homes of peaceful security and to be instructed how to plant around their firesides the strongest batteries against the sins that degrade and the race vices that demoralize." Appealing to the sentimental construction of the home as an earthly heaven and a Christian community of care overseen by women, Harper states that "while politicians may stumble on the barren mountain of fretful controversy, and men, lacking faith in God and the invisible forces which make for righteousness, may shrink from the unsolved problems of the hour, into the hands of Christian women comes the opportunity of . . . striving to make their homes the brightest spots on earth and the fairest types of heaven." Mothers, Harper contends, must endeavor to be "true artists" capable of inspiring their children with a love of virtue and shaping the emotional repertory of the "cultured heart." In instructing "mothers of our race" on the performance of their "grandly constructive" labors of racial uplift, Harper especially emphasizes what she terms the "influence" of "environment"—of domestic material and emotional forms—on the moral "condition" of the race. The identification between domestic environment and proper sentiments is tropologically conveyed in Harper's chiastic coupling of "homes" and "hearts": benign "home influences" metaphorically signify the refined emotions of "cultured heart[s]," and these hearts are themselves figured as the "*homes*" of "high and lofty enthusiasm" and "noble devotion."[48] Bringing a recently "homeless race" *inside*, within the home and the family, Harper (re)situates African Americans within a nexus of sentimental familial and proprietary relations. Like bell hooks's conception of "homeplace" discussed in chapter 4 above, "home" in Harper's text represents a site of decolonization, enabling African Americans' transformation from property object to civil subject, and configuring that process in expressly erotic terms. Specifically, home—as a space claimed for the African American family—constitutes a site where African Americans' affectional investments and erotic desires are publicly marked and given a symbolic location within the social realm.

Harper's best-known work, *Iola Leroy*, similarly emphasizes the feminine, domestic reinscription of racial identity. The novel revises the well-known antebellum antislavery story of the tragic mulatta in order to document black women's sensibility and refinement, and to refute the proslavery argument that—in the words of the novel's heroine—"slavery is not wrong if you treat [the slaves] well and don't sell them from their families."[49] The conventional tragic mulatta, a figure whose refinement and sensibility make the crime of slavery all the more palpable and render her utterly unable to bear the degradation of the slave's condition, makes several appearances in the text: in Camille Lecroix's story of the two "cultivated" Creole girls who, through a reversal of fortune, were brought to the auction block, and whose knowledge of their "tainted blood" is described as a "blow" which killed them "as if they had been shot" (99–100); and in the story of Iola's sister Gracie, whose acute sensitivity is clearly registered in her "perfectly dazed" condition when she learns of her race status, and in the literal wasting away and spiritualizing of her body (96, 108). Like these other figures, the novel's heroine, Iola Leroy, the daughter of a Southern plantation owner who married one of his slaves, is a well-educated, pampered, and sheltered young woman with great "refinement and magnificent beauty," a young woman who has been raised by her white father and mulatta mother without "the least idea of her negro blood" (100). But unlike Gracie and the unnamed Creole girls, Iola doesn't die as a consequence of her knowledge. After struggling with her own racism (the narrator tells us that, as a "southern girl and a slave-holder's daughter," Iola had "always defended slavery when it was under discussion" [97]), she fully embraces her identity as a black woman. Iola rejects the opportunity to marry a prestigious white man and pass in white society, proudly announcing that "the best blood in my veins is African blood, and I am not ashamed of it" (208). The novel ends with Iola's marriage to a black man and the couple's return to the South in order to work together to uplift and "elevate" the race.

Harper's uses of sentimentalism in *Iola Leroy* serve to address, as well as redefine, contemporary languages of race and civil subjectivity. Invoking sentimental tropes and narrative conventions to figure black women's sensibility, Harper demonstrates that black women's sentiments—especially maternal sentiments and erotic desires—are neither socially legitimated nor legally protected. The rapid, seemingly inevitable demise of Iola's sister Gracie and the two "cultivated" Creole girls serves to mark in dramatic fashion the social death of the black female "subject"—the negation of her sentiments—and the abjection of the black female body from the social. But, principally through Iola's own story, the novel also invokes the languages of sentiment to expose the racial exclusions of gender and civil society, and to contest black women's sexual commodification under slavery. Indeed, the text performs the processes of the decommodification in expressly sentimental terms. By registering within the narrative Iola's affectional preferences and family bonds, and especially by inscribing within the text feminine erotic and maternal sentiments, *Iola Leroy* redefines black women as sexual *subjects* and repositions the black female body within the social collective.

The symbolic import of the family and domesticity in the reconstruction of race is everywhere apparent in *Iola Leroy*. Indeed, in Harper's novel, racial identity (or race "loyalty") is conceptualized chiefly in sentimental, familial terms. The sentimentalization of race plainly reinscribes the family from the locus of biological determinism and the "one-drop law" to the site of "voluntary" sentimental identification and what Harper calls "race sympathies" (265)—a construction which serves to undo the "social death" of enslavement and the civil nonrecognition of African American subjectivity. The sentimental reconstruction of race is especially evident in narratives of passing, which serve to de-essentialize racial identification and reconfigure it through the feminine consent of sentimental allegiance and emotional preference. In particular, passing—what Robert calls "masquerading as a white man" (203)—is imaged by both Iola and her brother Harry as a betrayal of their (black) *mother* (e.g., 117, 203). As in Jacobs's narrative, this performance of maternal identification is symbolically crucial: specifically, it inscribes what Spillers terms the "maternal function"—derived from (but in excess of) the American slave code, and a redemptive antidote to the marks the patriarchal symbolic order inscribes on slave bodies—as the origin of the black social subject. Signifying non-being in the symbolic economy of slavery, the black maternal body is here repositioned *within* the social order and reinscribed, through the operations of sympathetic exchange, as a site of sentimental identification. The personal history of Iola's future husband, Dr. Frank Latimer, a light-skinned black man, contributes to this thematic: Latimer rejects the offer of his paternal grandmother—an aristocratic Southern lady in whose family his mother had been a slave—to adopt him as her heir if he promises to "ignore his identity with the colored race" (239), on the grounds that his love for his mother is too strong to forsake her race "for the richest advantages his grandmother could bestow" (240). This wedding of race loyalty and intimate sentiment is emblematized in the marriage of Iola and Frank, a union, as critics frequently note, based not on physical passion but on shared social commitments. As the narrator describes that union, "Her noblest sentiments found a response in his heart. In their desire to help the race their hearts beat in loving unison. One grand and noble purpose was giving tone to their lives and strengthening the bonds of affection between them" (266).

This sentimental reconfiguration of racial identification is apparent as well in Harper's narrative poem "Moses: A Story of the Nile," first published in 1869. In that poem, as in *Iola Leroy*, Harper conflates racial identification and particularized, sentimental commitment. Moses was a key figure in Harper's personal mythology. In an earlier essay, Harper had expressed her admiration for Moses as a "disunionist" who "would have no union with the slave power of Egypt": "The magnificence of Pharoah's throne loomed up before his vision, its oriental splendors glittered before his eyes; but he turned from them all and chose rather to suffer with the enslaved, than rejoice with the free." In Harper's poem, Moses is a foundling who escaped the enslavement of his group and is adopted into a family of leaders where he receives the advantages of education and material comfort. Rather than enjoy these class privileges, Moses chooses to identify with his oppressed race. As Moses states in the poem's opening stanza, in which he informs his adoptive mother, the Princess Charmian, of his decision:

> I go to join
> The fortunes of my race, and to put aside
> All other bright advantages, save
> The approval of my conscience and the meed
> Of rightly doing.

The Princess, stunned by his "strange election," asks in disbelief,

> Thou who
> Hast only trod the court of kings, why seek
> Instead the paths of labor? Thou, whose limbs
> Have known no other garb than that which well
> Befits our kingly state, why rather choose
> The badge of servitude and toil?
> . . . .
> I cannot comprehend thy choice.

To these questions, Moses responds,

> Within [bondage-]darkened huts my mother plies her tasks,
> My father bends to unrequited toil;
> And bitter tears moisten the bread my brethren eat
> . . . .
> I cannot live in pleasure while they faint
> In pain.

Renouncing all ties with his royal Egyptian family, Moses chooses to recognize as "mother" the Hebrew nurse who had suckled and cared for him, and from whose "lips" Moses had learned "the grand traditions of our race."[50]

Like Harper's poem "Moses," *Iola Leroy* emphasizes the power of the black family and homeplace to make and unmake the (racial) body, and to forge racial identifications and sentimental commitments. The novel, in fact, is visibly preoccupied with the fragmentation and reconstruction of the racial body, and with the establishment of loving environments in which that body can be nurtured and preserved. As in most sentimental novels, bodies in *Iola Leroy* are represented as acutely sensitive and painfully susceptible to injury, vulnerable to wounding not just by the physical contact of touch but by all forms of painful sensory experience, and especially painful words and images; bodies are also unmade by the emotional hurts of separation, hurts vividly rendered in standard sentimental metaphors of being "wrenched" and "torn away" from loved ones (e.g., 142–43). While the novel's tragic mulattas are fatally injured by the shock of painful words and stories and the violence of extradomestic exposure, such bodies in Harper's text can be recreated and protected within the domestic sphere, and remade with expressions of care and love. The importance of the loving care of the body in establishing sentimental bonds is registered in the fact that the love between Iola's father, Eugene, and mother, Marie, develops when Marie's careful nursing saves him from the grave and restores him to comfort and strength (68–70). It is similarly apparent in the fact that Dr. Gresham falls in love with Iola when, during their work in the hospital, he observes the "tenderness of her ministrations" as a nurse, "bestowed alike on black and white" (58–59).

Along with and inseparable from the (re-)making of the individual racial body in the novel is the reunification of a "social" body held together expressly by love—the family. Iola's most important task in the narrative is to reconstruct her black family, and to reassemble the objects of her care in a place or home of its own. The sacred, healing nature of the gathering together of "remnants of broken families" (179) is reflected in the fact that most of the reunions take place at church meetings (e.g., 178–83, 194–95) and at hospitals (e.g., 191, 139–43). But the *home* is represented as the most significant, emotionally laden setting for familial healing. While there are few detailed descriptions of domestic spaces in the text, the Northern home of Iola's grandmother, which serves as the setting of the family's reassembly and in which Iola, her uncle Robert, and grandmother await the arrival of Iola's mother, is described with special care, chiefly because of the care with which the family invests this space. As the narrator tells us, Iola personally oversaw getting things "in order for her mother's reception. Her room was furnished neatly, but with those touches of beauty that womanly hands are such adepts in giving. A few charming pictures adorned the walls, and an easy chair stood waiting to receive the travel-worn mother" (209). The room's neatness, adornments, and comfort serve both to materially signal and to make possible the cultivation of sentiment. The sacralized, sentimental import of objects in the novel is registered in the significance of tokens and gifts—such as the pocket handkerchief decorated with cats' heads (201), and Iola's locket, which contains her mother's picture (142)—in reconstructing the family and drawing together the dispersed family members. Such representations are means to remind us that, if slavery and racism are cruel and divisive, familial love can counter these forces and engender psychic and collective wholeness.

Several of Pauline Hopkins's novels and stories share the domestic focus of *Iola Leroy*. Hopkins's fiction would seem to bear out the truth of Anna Julia Cooper's claim that "a race is but a total of families. The nation is the aggregate of its homes."[51] Hopkins's work testifies to the significance of household space in the formation of personal and collective identity. In *Contending Forces*, a novel whose sentimental allegiances are signaled by its epigraphs from the Fireside poets, the cultural import of the "refined" domestic environment is both metaphorically registered and explicitly stated. According to the narrator, "Inborn love implanted in a woman's heart for a luxurious, esthetic home life, running on well-oiled wheels amid flowers, sunshine, books and priceless pamphlets, easy chairs and French gowns, may be the means of developing a Paderewski or freeing a race from servitude."[52] The novel's investment in the content of domestic surroundings is especially apparent in its depictions of the living arrangements of the heroine, Mabelle Beaubean. Mabelle is a young Southern mulatta who was raped by her white uncle and who has since moved north and changed her name to Sappho Clark. "Sappho's"

Boston home is represented as a carefully arranged domestic space filled with "the refinements of living," what the narrator calls "all those things which make a man, and sweeten toil" (86, 60). Sappho is staying in the boardinghouse of the Smith family, and while, as the narrator notes, the rooms are plain but "substantially and well" furnished, Sappho decorates hers with "beautifully embroidered" drapes and tablecloths and "two good steel engravings," thus transforming it into a "pretty" and "very inviting interior" (98). The novel's detailed depictions of Sappho's carefully ornamented and arranged domestic space vividly establish its heroine's refined tastes and sentimental pedigree. But this narrative interest in Sappho's domestic surroundings also serves as an index and expression of Sappho's will and self-possession, her power to shape a space and to determine, by selection and arrangement, what objects touch her body—an act especially crucial for Sappho, a victim of rape. This symbolic gesture of bodily (re)possession and sentimental self-inscription prefigures Sappho's reclamation of her personal history and prior identity as Mabelle, as well as her son, Alphonse, whom she had renounced out of shame (although she had secretly visited him and paid for his support). This maternal "pride of possession in her child" is sanctified in the novel by Mabelle's explicit association with the figure of the Virgin Mary (e.g., 386), an association underscored by her residence during Alphonse's birth at the Convent of the Holy Family: crucially, this association sacralizes maternity while negating the proprietary claim of Alphonse's white father. The redemption and sanctification of black women's maternity in the novel—an experience degraded and exploited under slavery—is here symbolically crucial to the re-possession of African American women's personal and collective integrity.

Contending Forces identifies domesticity as the creative core of the black world, "the place," in the words of the novel's representative clubwoman, Mrs. Willis, "which the virtuous woman occupies in upbuilding a race" (148). Like Harper's novel, Hopkins's narratives figure the home as the site of emotional "culture" and sentimental expression, the space in which identifications are re-formed as well as performed and socially acknowledged. In Hopkins's texts, as in Harper's, racial identifications are particularized and cast in terms of sentimental commitment. In particular, in Hopkins's stories and novels, especially "The Test of Manhood" and *Hagar's Daughter*, as in Harper's *Iola Leroy*, "masquerading" as white is imaged as censurable and immoral not because it alienates one from one's culture or "true self," but principally because it involves separation from and betrayal of one's *mother*. "The Test of Manhood," a story which explicitly thematizes the equation of passing and familial betrayal, recounts its central character's intentional renunciation and final, public acknowledgment of his black mother; while in *Hagar's Daughter*, Hopkins's second novel, the recovery of "blackness" is thematized as the reconstruction of the "sacred family relation," specifically of the mother-child relationship, through which internalized racism is mitigated by filial devotion.[53] This construction is rendered explicit, with some variation, in *Contending Forces*, in which the "passing" plot is reformulated to involve not *racial* but *sexual* status, and in which Mabelle's attempts to pass as a "respectable" middle-class woman directly pivot on her denial of the mother-child bond.

These narratives, in different ways, conspicuously deconstruct the black family in order to reconstruct that family through an act of social recognition and sentimental identification. In particular, by appealing to sentimental codes of "consensual" familial union, these texts problematize essentialist models of racial identities, and reconfigure race as a *political affect*, an emotionally inscribed political identification. Certainly, such narratives derive their literary and emotional force from the widespread cultural sentimentalization of maternity, as well as the historical fact that "blackness," as a legal and social construct under slavery, was a maternal heritage. Betraying the "mark" of the slave mother on the child's body and its sentiments, these texts envision the reconstruction of black social subjectivity and its political and erotic desires.

These texts are, however, double voiced: even while they appropriate conventions of Anglo-American women's fiction to inscribe a different racial politics of sentiment, they underscore the contradictions embedded within these conventions. In particular, they problematize, even while inscribing, sentimental consent as a code of civic agency: the public articulation of black female desire is limited by persistent cultural codes that consolidate race and gender hierarchies. Harper's and Hopkins's texts depict the forms of sentimental, bourgeois femininity (i.e., pleasing manners and forms of bodily propriety, material "refinement," and home) as not so much voluntary as compulsory, an (albeit tenuous) safeguard against male sexual rapaciousness. In *Iola Leroy* and *Contending Forces*, the distinction between "civilized" consumer (or "respectable" woman) and sexual commodity is insecure and highly unstable; indeed, these texts emphasize persistent structures of social surveillance and classification—the differentiation of "good" women from "bad," of "refined" and "cultured" from "sexualized" body—which undermine feminine civic and sexual agency. In other words, in Harper's and Hopkins's texts, the threat of racial exposure always coexists with, and in some instances clearly motivates, the "passing" self's ultimate gestures of racial reconciliation. Sentimental "voluntarism" and feminine consent are compromised and powerfully critiqued in these texts' representations of a legal institution bent on enforcing racial distinctions, and a social world intent on classifying bodies according to ethnic, class, and sexual status.

6

NOT "JUST A CIGAR":
COMMODITY CULTURE AND THE CONSTRUCTION
OF IMPERIAL MANHOOD

Out of the agricultural and industrial development of these amazing plants were to come those economic interests in which foreign traders would twist and weave for centuries to form the web of our country's history and the motives of its leaders and, one and the same time, the shackles and support of its people. Tobacco and sugar are the two most important figures in the history of Cuba.

—Fernando Ortiz, *Cuban Counterpoint*

Sometimes a cigar is just a cigar.—Sigmund Freud

This chapter continues my analysis of the gendered metaphorics of commerce in nineteenth-century America, and the ways commodity consumption constitutes gender, sexual, racial, and imperial subjectivities and practices. In particular, I address the entanglements of race, sex, and nation in cultural representations of commodity consumption in the 1890s. Focusing on popular visual representations of one highly visible and symbolically charged imperial commodity, this chapter examines the role of advertising in the construction of imperial subjectivities and of what Mary Louise Pratt calls the "domestic subject[s]" of empire.[1] Specifically, I chart the symbolic import of the cigar in the U.S. imperial imaginary during the late nineteenth and early twentieth centuries, a crucial era in the rise of the United States as an imperial nation-state and in the development of modern U.S.-Cuban relations. Popular representations of the cigar are a significant cultural form for imparting an imperial worldview in the United States and constituting emergent imperial identifications. As an expression of what Anne McClintock has recently termed "commodity racism," cigar advertisements articulate imperialism in a domestic context, and register the complex ways in which gender, race, sexuality, and nationality interact in the formation of imperial subjectivities and practices.[2] A multivalent and culturally resonant erotic signifier, the cigar, contextualized within popular representations, can help illuminate the racial and sexual unconscious of American imperial whiteness at the turn of this century.

As an examination of the (contested) interpellation of imperial masculinity in U.S. visual culture, this chapter both contributes to and intervenes in current debates in American cultural studies about cultural and representational forms of U.S. imperialism, and the interrelations between imperial and domestic race, gender, and sexual politics.[3] In a groundbreaking essay on the representation of American masculinity in popular historical novels of the 1890s, Amy Kaplan deftly exposes the imperial dimensions of "domestic" constructions of gender, and the interrelations between gender, sexuality, and nation.[4] Kaplan argues that, in response to a perceived threat of "overcivilization" and "feminization" on the homefront, white American men sought manly "re-embodiment" on the Cuban "frontier" through imperial violence. But Kaplan seems to assume that imperial masculinity is a much more stable construction than it could ever be. Contrary to Kaplan's account, imperial constructions of gender are highly conflictual and contradictory, fraught with a range of (often disavowed) identifications and erotic investments. In particular, late-nineteenth-century configurations of imperial masculinity were articulated within — and manifested the erotic instabilities of — what Eve Kosofsky Sedgwick has called the "male homosocial bonding" of capitalist economics.[5] The so-called crisis of masculinity registered by American men in the last decade of the nineteenth century (and oft-discussed by historians) was not so much a moment when "manliness" was threatened by a collection of new sociohistorical forces (e.g., the rise of feminine consumerism and the new woman, changes in the structure of capital and male labor, the much-heralded "closing of the frontier") as a moment when social changes forced the internal contradictions and fractures in white masculinity to the surface. At a time when the geopolitical dimensions of "America," as well as its domestic gender, race, and sexual relations, were everywhere contested, the racial/imperial coordinates of white masculinity were mapped out quite plainly in cultural representation.

In the United States, white male subjectivity has always been constituted in dynamic interrelations and identifications with a range of Other (racial, sexual, and gender) identifications. In the late nineteenth century, there were three prominent and overlapping sites of public contestation over the cultural definition of white masculinity: one was a site of sexual contestation, involving the cultural definition of homosexuality as an identity category; another was a site of gender struggle involving various challenges to the hegemonic middle-class model of gender relations, patriarchal domesticity; and the last was a site of racial contestation, involving the racial realignments of Reconstruction and its challenges to (and the ensuing, violent reassertion of) white supremacist masculinity. As Eric Lott, Kobena Mercer, and others (starting with Leslie Fiedler) have shown, white masculinity in America has historically been constituted through a complex interaction with black masculinity, a dynamic Lott calls "love and theft." This involves identification with/desire for black masculinity (signaled through erotic investments in the black male body, especially the black penis) as well as the appropriation of black culture and black labor (the "theft" of Lott's phrase)—a dynamic often disavowed through violent repudiation. As Lott describes this structure of identification, instantiated in blackface minstrelsy: "To assume the mantle of whiteness . . . is not only to 'befriend' a racial other but to introject or internalize its imagined special capacities and attributes. . . . The black male and fantasies about him supply the content of the white male Imaginary, they make up its repertoire. This (racial) splitting of the subject actually makes possible one whole area of white desire—but it also insures that the color line thus erected is constantly open to transgression or disruption."[6] This process—oscillating between the sexual idealization of the racial Other and anxiety in defense of the identity of the white male ego—is the mixed erotic economy, what Homi Bhabha terms the "ambivalence," of American whiteness.[7]

The psychodynamic of the erotic investment of white men in black masculinity (specifically the fascination with black male sexuality), a complex forged in the context of colonialism, was first described by Frantz Fanon. Analyzing the sexual stereotyping of Africans (including African Americans)—specifically, the view that the black man "is the incarnation of a genital potency beyond all moralities and prohibitions"—Fanon explains that black men symbolize a "sexual potency" that white men both desire and fear. In particular, the black penis, representing the "tremendous sexual prowess" of black men, is an object of white male (identificatory and erotic) desire, as well as anxiety (evoking the fear that the Other is more sexually potent than the white "master"). Defined through eroticized images and myths in the white racial imaginary (such as the stereotype of black penis size), the black man, according to Fanon, "is eclipsed. He is turned into a penis. He *is* a penis."[8] In the late nineteenth century, as the United States entered the stage of imperial nation-states in the Spanish American War, the preoccupation with the phallus of the Other was culturally pervasive on the imperial battlefield as well as the homefront, and could take particularly violent forms. As I will show, the crisis of white masculinity was registered in lynching, a horrific practice in which white male castration anxiety was both manifested and disavowed, displaced onto the black male body.

Below, I read how these interactions, forged in the racial and imperial imaginary of the late nineteenth century, are inscribed in popular representations of one specific and culturally contested imperial commodity—the cigar. The symbolics of the cigar are rich and complex: cigar advertisements register how distinct cultural binaries (masculine/feminine, white/black, heterosexual/homosexual) constitute one another as well as the civilized/savage binary central to the U.S. imperial project; they also foreground the instability of these binaries and the centrality of Other forms of identification and desire to normative constructions of white masculinity. For example, cigar advertisements activate a desublimated orality in excess of heterosexist, "civilized," erotic imperatives. Cultural representations of the cigar make legible the complexities of masculine subject formation—in particular, the inextricability of identification (with phallic masculinity) and erotic desire (for the body of the Other).

Modulating commodity and imperial desires, cigar advertisements articulate imperialism in a domestic context. In addition, the specifically *oral* desire associated with and engendered by the cigar manifests the cross-racial homoerotics of white male subject formation (cigar smoking as fellatio) as well as a historically resonant, cultural metaphorics of imperial cannibalism (cigar smoking as "eating the Other"). These metaphors of imperial cannibalism were reversible, figuring the white male subject's culturally engendered anxiety about engulfment by (racial, gender, and sexual) Others as well as a projection of white phallic domination. Cigar iconography, by staging phallic masculinity as *performance* (and by representing the phallus itself as a detachable floating signifier), figured the construction and deconstruction of phallic male subjectivity, and simultaneously acknowledged and disavowed the ways in which male subjectivity is always fractured by the threat of castration. If cigar consumption facilitated what Amy Kaplan describes as imperial masculine re-embodiment through imperial exploit, it also foregrounded the fragility and tenuousness of this phallic (commodity) re-embodiment. A culturally resonant erotic signifier, the cigar, contextualized in popular imagery, constitutes an index of the racial and sexual unconscious of American imperial masculinity in the late nineteenth century.

In unpacking the cultural meanings of the cigar, I will examine not only the construction of the new "imperial subject" (partly achieved through domestic consumption), but the interconnections between U.S. imperialism and domestic race, gender, and sexual politics. The prominence of the cigar in the late nineteenth century's cultural imaginary constitutes a highly unstable, contestatory dramatization of imperial/race politics *and* an effort to reinscribe capitalism as a masculine terrain and site of male bonding (i.e., a way to wrest authority from increasingly visible *consuming women*). Mapping the connections between internal and external colonization by focusing on a particular and resonant commodity-text, I attempt to show how international relations of race, gender, sexuality, and nation reciprocally shape a dominant imperial culture at home, in which imperial relations are re-presented and contested. In the words of Eric Lott, "representations of national racial difference often provide displaced maps for international ones. . . . The domination of international others has depended on mastering the other at home—and in oneself: an internal colonization whose achievement is fragile at best and which is often exceeded or threatened by the gender and racial arrangements on which it depends."[9]

Blake

Toward the beginning of *Blake* (1861–62), the only novel by the radical African American author Martin Delany, Judge Ballard, a Northern slaveholder and planter with holdings in Havana, and Major Armsted, a Southern slavetrader, hold the following conversation about Cuba:

> "I consider that colony . . . a moral pestilence," [Judge Ballard stated,] "a blighting curse, and it is useless to endeavor to disguise the fact; Cuba must cease to be a Spanish colony, and become American territory. Those mongrel Creoles are incapable of self-government, and should be compelled to submit to the United States."
>
> "Well, Judge," [Major Armsted replied,] "admit the latter part of that, as I rather guess we are all of the same way of thinking—how do you manage to get on with society when you are there?"
>
> "I cannot for a moment tolerate it! One of the hateful customs of the place is that you must exchange civilities with whomsoever solicits it, consequently, the most stupid and ugly Negro you meet in the street may ask for a 'light' from your cigar."
>
> "I know it, and I invariably comply with the request. How do you act in such cases?"

"I invariably comply, but as invariably throw away my cigar!"

" . . . Why throw away the cigar, Judge? What objection could there be to it because a Negro took a light from it?"

"Because they are certain to take hold of it with their black fingers!"

" . . . You Northerners are a great deal more fastidious about Negroes than we of the South, and you'll pardon me if I add, 'more nice than wise'. . . . Did it every occur to you that black fingers made that cigar, before it entered your white lips! — all tobacco preparations being worked by Negro hands in Cuba — and very frequently in closing up the wrapper, they draw it through their lips to give it tenacity."[10]

This passage, foregrounding the Pan-American nexus of colonialism, gender and race relations, and slavery, registers several of *Blake*'s key political themes: the economic and moral complicity of the U.S. North (represented by the Northern slaveowner, Judge Ballard) in the Pan-American institution of slavery; Anglo-American fears of black Cuban insurrection and the so-called Africanization of Cuba; and white Americans' imperialist ambitions in the Caribbean, first articulated by James Madison and intensified in the "Southern dream of a Caribbean empire" that emerged during the antebellum period as a way to preserve and extend the slave empire.[11] The exchange between the two men maps interconnections between national and imperial identifications, and demonstrates how domestic relations of race, gender, sexuality, and nation extend and, indeed, shape those relations in different national/imperial contexts. The "Spanish colony" of Cuba is here not only an object of U.S. imperial ambitions (registered most plainly in the judge's statement that Cuba must be "compelled to submit to the United States"), but also a site of national subject formation, a territory on which racial, gender, and sexual identifications are performed. Mapped out most explicitly in this passage are relations among men: even more strikingly than the domestic scene, imperialism establishes itself here as a homosocial space in which women have no real presence or currency.[12] Positioned in this passage as the imperial "frontier," Cuba is a site where boundaries are transgressed, a space where (racial, sexual) desires disallowed at "home" can be tested and explored. In particular, what gets explored (and, by the judge at least, repressed) are forms of interracial intimacy between white and black men.[13]

Prominent in this passage's configuration of race politics is a seemingly mundane, but nonetheless symbolically charged object — the cigar. The cigar mediates social relations in this passage, constituting its primary locus of economic and representational contestation. At stake in that contestation is the possession and symbolic expression of "manliness." For Judge Ballard, the cigar figures prominently in an allegory of social disorder, signifying the destruction of rituals of social deference and Afro-Cubans' transgression of their "place." The fact that "the most stupid and ugly Negro you meet in the street may ask for a 'light' from your cigar" epitomizes, for the judge, the class and racial confusions of Cuban society (they are a nation of "mongrel Creoles" incapable of self-government)[14] and is an invitation to U.S. military intervention; in the judge's words, Cuba must be "compelled to submit to the United States." Viewing the cigar as a high-status *Anglo* commodity, one significant chiefly as an object of consumption, the judge protests what he perceives to be an illicit appropriation of the cigar by Afro-Cubans.[15] The judge's proprietary chauvinism is challenged by his cultural displacement, which he depicts as intolerable and "hateful." Moving from America (a place where, he implies, Anglo property rights are respected) to the carnivalesque terrain of the Cuban street, the judge finds that his (Anglo) "ownership" of the cigar—his mastery of its political and symbolic economies—is called into question. Faced with what were powerful signs of Cuban national identity—the cigar, and the concept of *mestizaje*[16]—the judge sees only civil disorder, and responds to the perceived affront to Anglo-American proprietary authority by recuperating that authority in the imagined form of racial and imperial domination.

Imagining that he can enforce racial hierarchies (and contain same-sex, interracial desire) through the performance of ruling-class manners, the judge is a poor reader of the complexities of racial intimacy. The Southerner Armsted directly confronts the judge's views (and gives the lie to his racial fastidiousness) by recovering the cigar's history as an object of *production*. What Armsted recovers is the suppressed erotics of the commodity form—an erotics registered here through the vehicle of a resonantly phallic commodity. Armsted calls attention to an alternative history of the cigar, one both invoked and physically *represented* by the "Negro" on the street. In this history, the cigar constitutes a container of Afro-Cuban labor rather than a marker of status distinctions among (Anglo-American) consumers and a sign of white supremacy. The meaning of consumption in Armsted's account is anticipated and shaped by the process of production: the "Negro's" act of "borrowing" the cigar on the street is not illicit appropriation but, rather, a performance of the black worker's "original" relationship to the commodity and, for Delany, his right to ownership. When Judge Ballard complains that his cigar has been illicitly touched on the street by "black fingers," Armsted points out that "Negro hands" made the cigar: the ritual of white consumption is anticipated by techniques of black production, through which the cigar was rolled by such "black fingers" and, indeed, the wrapper "draw[n] ... through [black] lips to give it tenacity." A container of black labor, the cigar, in Armsted's account, constitutes a symbolic extension of the black body. Consequently, consuming the cigar is an act of interracial communion, against which the judge's gesture of repudiation (he inevitably "throw[s] away [his] cigar") is fundamentally useless as a defense.

Armsted's identification of the cigar as an embodiment of Afro-Cuban labor and, thus, as a prosthetic extension of the (Cuban) black male body places the cigar at the center of a highly charged, and contested, national erotics. For both Armsted and the judge, albeit in different ways, "Cuba" is a field traversed by structures of male homosocial and interracial desire, and the cigar constitutes a principal embodiment of that desire.[17] Leslie Fiedler has described Anglo-American male "flight" from feminine "civilization" and homoerotic union with the racial Other as the prototypical American fantasy; Delany removes this union from the national frontier of the "wilderness" to the imperial frontier of the Caribbean.[18] Described by the judge as a nation of "mongrel Creoles" (the judge's pejorative gloss on the Cuban national symbolics of mestizaje, and a phrase which appears frequently in nineteenth century U.S. texts), "Cuba" here constitutes a site in which the fantasized interracial male union is consummated and nationally embodied. In Delany's passage, the cigar at once constitutes a sign of male homosocial, cross-racial desire (marking the Anglo-American "consumption" of the Afro-Cuban body) and marks the repression of that desire.[19] The cigar figures prominently within competing economies of political desire, each inflected by race, gender, and nationality: for the black Cuban, the cigar signifies desire for social equality and economic and political rights, inscribing the black male body within the (homosocial) union of the Cuban nation; for the white American, the cigar embodies Anglo-American men's desire for Cuban "manliness" and, simultaneously, repudiation of that desire, a repudiation that takes the form of an insistence on white supremacy over blacks and U.S. imperial dominance over "unruly" and excessively independent "mongrel Creoles."

The complex erotics of this scene—the circuitry of (homo)sexual, interrracial, national, and imperial desires—can be mapped onto domestic as well as international imperial contexts. By the late nineteenth century, when U.S. imperialism became national policy, the fascination with the phallus of the racial Other registered ambivalently in the figure of Judge Ballard—a fascination both homoerotic and cannibalistic—was ritualized in diverse cultural practices. Indeed, this fascination figured not only in the "civilized" and seemingly trivial ritual of cigar smoking, but in the savage and altogether serious ritual of lynching. Partly in response to the vocal critique by many black Americans of U.S. imperial policy, the war in Cuba and the Philippines coincided with a wave of antiblack violence throughout the South, fueled by the racist rhetoric of imperialists and white supremacists in Congress.[20] The period of expansion, from 1889 to 1901, saw almost two thousand black men, women, and children lynched in the South. Many critics of U.S. expansionism saw connections between imperial and domestic racial violence: for instance, commenting on the Philippine independence movement in 1899, one black newspaper editor wrote that "maybe the Filipinos have caught wind of the way Indians and Negroes have been Christianized and civilized" in America; while Ida B. Wells, speaking in 1898 to a gathering on "Mob Violence and Anarchy, North and South," urged blacks to "oppose expansion until the government [is] able to protect the Negro at home."[21] As domestic expressions of white male supremacy, constituted in complex interaction with techniques of colonial subjection enacted abroad, lynching and rape were terrorist practices designed to perform, in Hazel Carby's words, the "internal colonization" of black men and women in the late nineteenth century.[22]

As Trudier Harris has shown, lynching emerged as a ritualized form of violence in the United States after the Civil War in order to keep blacks contained politically and socially during the years of Reconstruction. Part of a "counter-revolutionary carnival" of violence intended to beat back the temporary gains of Reconstruction, lynching continued to be used by whites as a form of racial terrorism and social control through the 1950s.[23] It is crucial to recognize that lynching in the United States was an intensely and blatantly sexualized form of ritual violence. Lynching expressed the intensity of white investment in the black male body, an investment (as *Blake* suggests) at once erotic and economic.[24] Both the motive for and the enactment of lynching were characteristically sexualized. White supremacist mob violence was largely a response to the perceived threat of black male sexuality: as Harris states, "the one 'crime' for which lynching became the only punishment for black men was sexual indiscretion with white women."[25] It was in the later nineteenth century that the myth of the "black male rapist" was forged, a crystallization of the sexual fears and anxieties (and the repressed desires) of whites.[26] The sexualized nature of the ritualized violence performed in lynching both indicated the imputed sexuality of the original "crime," and measured the intensity of white sexual obsession. As Harris explains,

> Castration quickly became a part of the summary hanging prescribed for black males accused of sexual offenses. In history as in literature [by black writers about lynching], the crowds would gather to punish the black offender in a mood which bordered upon hysteria. White men, women, and children would hang or burn (frequently both), shoot, and castrate the offender, then divide the body into trophies. The white participants in the mobs would frequently bring food and drink to the place of execution and would make a holiday of the occasion. To insure that an audience was available for really special lynchings, announcements of time and place were sometimes advertised in newspapers.[27]

Clearly, the American historical practice of lynching black men betrays complex anxieties about black male sexuality and interracial, homoerotic desire. Richard Wright, in his novel *The Long Dream*, captures the nature of white ambivalence — the dynamic of attraction / repulsion of white men toward the black male bodies they mutilate — that fuels mob hate and, indeed, constitutes the distinctive identity of white masculinity in the United States. Chris, a young black man, is lynched as a result of his apparently consensual involvement with a white woman. The novel describes the response of the local doctor, Tyree, the town's undertaker preparing the body for burial, and Tyree's son Fishbelly, to what has taken place:

> "The *genitalia* are gone," the doctor intoned.
>
> Fishbelly saw a dark coagulated blot in a gaping hole between the thighs and, with a defensive reflex, he lowered his hands nervously to his groin. . . .
>
> "Killing him wasn't enough. They had to *mutilate* 'im. You'd think that disgust would've made them leave *that* part of the black boy alone. . . . No! To get the chance to *mutilate* 'im was part of why they killed 'im. . . .
>
> "You have to be terribly attracted to a person, almost in love with 'im, to mangle 'im in this manner. They hate us, Tyree, but they love us too; in a perverted sort of way, they love us."[28]

What Wright's doctor terms the "perverted" love performed on and over the body of the "black boy" — a love that transgresses bisecting boundaries of race and sexuality — is both enacted and disavowed in lynching. The white man's "terrible attraction" to black men — specifically, the fixation on the black male penis — expressed in Wright's account suggests the complex forms of white male homoeroticism, identification, and envy at stake in the act of lynching. As Lillian Smith astutely points out, "The lynched Negro becomes not an object that must die but a receptacle for every man's dammed-up hate, and a receptacle for every man's forbidden sex feelings."[29] Trudier Harris, who emphasizes (hetero)sexual competition and downplays homoeroticism in her analysis of lynching, nonetheless indirectly suggests the inextricability of the two: "In simultaneously perpetuating and attempting to destroy the myth of black male sexuality, the white men involved in the lynchings and burnings spent an inordinate amount of time examining the genitals of the black men whom they were about to kill. Even as they castrated the black men, there was a suggestion of fondling, of envious caress. The many emotions involved at that moment led the white men to slash even more violently at what could not be theirs, but which, at some level, they very much desired."[30] Or, in Daryl Dance's formulation, "The very nature of the lynch mob's punishment of Blacks—the sexual mutilation of the victim—suggests the white man's efforts to wrest from the Black man that symbol of manhood . . . which he so fears."[31] The appropriative fixation on the black male penis is evident in some historical accounts, in which the lynchers were reputed to have divided pieces of the black man's genitals among themselves as trophies. An object of desire as well as retributive aggression, the black penis symbolizes a sexual potency that can be "detached" from the black male body and controlled and possessed by white men, affirming white masculinity and dominance.

Oral and written descriptions of lynchings suggest their connection to other acts of racial and sexual violence, and their position within a broader context of imperial domination and affect. In African American oral culture, descriptions of lynchings sometimes refer to a gruesome act in which the severed penis is placed in the mouth of the lynched man. The choreographer and dancer Bill T. Jones recalls a story he was told as a child about the South's history of racial violence:

> I was very fortunate to have the mother I did because she understood these events [of the Civil Rights Movement] in a context that was very personal and very historical. She tells us two stories, one was about a man who was the best worker on a farmer's farm and had sons. Something happened between he [*sic*] and the farmer and the farmer, who had known the black man his whole life, has him and his sons all hung up in bags and he burns them one by one. They ask him if he had a cigarette, I remember, and he cut off the guy's penis and shoved it in his mouth and said, "Smoke that, nigger." Now that was my mother telling us this story as children.[32]

Such accounts invoke what I am describing as the circulating forms of power and desire — of orality, interracial homoeroticism, and racial domination — between domestic and imperial racial contexts, and serve to map out resonant connections between U.S. internal and external imperialism. As a metonymic representation of the black penis, the cigar is at once racial fetish, object of homoerotic desire, and site of retributive violence.[33]

"Tobacco Is a Masculine Thing": The Cigar as Gendered Sign of Imperial Contest

The phallic symbology of the cigar has often been noted, most famously by Sigmund Freud. The cultural critic Fernando Ortiz extends the metaphor in his groundbreaking study of the Cuban colonial economy and its "social repercussions": "Tobacco is a masculine thing. . . . Twisted and enveloped in its wrapper as a cigar . . . it is always a boastful and swaggering thing, like an oath of defiance springing erect from the lips."[34] Delany's text suggests that the phallic connotations of the cigar are inseparable from their political context, and must be mapped along racial and national, as well as gender, axes. At stake in Delany's text is the performance of "manliness" — precisely who will be permitted to accede to the status of "manhood" and display its symbolic attributes. *Blake* makes it clear that manhood is a *political* construct, and is inseparable from international and racial, as well as domestic and gender, relations of domination. The cigar-wielding white American man displays not only the power and authority of his gender, but those of his race and nation as well.

In the United States, the imperial symbology of the cigar emerged dialogically, out of a struggle with the particular symbologies and representations of the (Cuban) Other. In a recent study, Vera M. Kutzinski has examined the significance of the exquisitely crafted Cuban cigarette and cigar labels known as *marquillas* in constructions of Cuban national identity. According to Kutzinski, these marquillas, through which numerous tobacco manufacturers advertised their products for the domestic and international market, constituted an important instance in the nineteenth-century gendered and racialized discourse of Cuban nationalism, exemplifying how one of Cuba's two major industries represented the fledgling nation at home and abroad.[35] Fernando Ortiz emphasizes the significance of the cigar in constructions of Cuban national identity; for Ortiz, while sugar equals slavery, tobacco (and especially the "manly" cigar) equals "Cubanness." (The symbolic resonance of the cigar in expressions of Cuban national identity was utilized by Fidel Castro and Che

Guevara, who would often, and theatrically, pose for photographs with cigars.) Like the marquillas in Cuba, cigar labels in the United States constituted an important locus of national identity and, in the late nineteenth and early twentieth centuries, served as a vehicle for the expression of U.S. political desires. Grappling with a central symbol of Cuban nationalism and independence, U.S. advertisers and cultural producers aimed to recontextualize the cigar within the U.S. national imaginary, a task especially charged (and particularly pressing) during the Spanish American War period. Because of the cigar's metonymic association with "Cuba," depictions of the cigar could synthesize proprietary and imperial fantasies, and served as a means for representing and negotiating who "owned" Cuba itself. Cigar advertisements and popular imagery both performed the cultural work of U.S. imperialism and made visible the violence and repression of imperial expansion.

The construction of the cigar as a site of contestation owes much to the complex history of tobacco as a colonial commodity. Tobacco had long served as a medium of racial and colonial exchange in the Americas. From Columbus's simultaneous "discovery" of Indians and cigars in Cuba and the subsequent prominence of tobacco in the Cuban colonial economy, to the central role of tobacco in the development of the U.S. slave trade, to the prominence of ethnic imagery (such as the dime-store Indian) in tobacco advertising in the United States and Europe, tobacco has been a contested commodity, the site of complex and conflictual racial, gender, sexual, and national investments. In the late nineteenth century, with changes in patterns of tobacco consumption and production and extended U.S. involvement in Caribbean tobacco culture, these investments were reconfigured. The cigar became the most popular tobacco product in the United States, overtaking the traditionally popular pipe: per capita consumption of the cigar was seventy by 1900.[36] Meanwhile, U.S. corporate involvement in the Cuban tobacco industry expanded rapidly, culminating during and after the Spanish American War.[37]

In the late nineteenth century, the cigar brought the empire home to Americans, inscribing commodity desire within what William Appelman Williams has termed "empire as a way of life." A traditionally masculine commodity, the cigar configured imperial desire in gendered as well as racialized terms—a fact with important domestic and international implications. By the late nineteenth century, commodity culture was widely viewed as a conspicuously feminine terrain: most statistics suggested that women controlled, on average, nine-tenths of a family's purchases. In addition, with the much-heralded closing of the frontier and the absence of new continental territories for incorporation within the national market, there was a widespread concern with what was often called "overcivilization"—a phenomenon identified with excessive domestic consumption and closely associated with women. When Henry James's Basil Ransome in *The Bostonians* speaks contemptibly of the "damnable feminization" of American society, he is voicing a general cultural conviction.[38] This perception of overcivilization had international dimensions: specifically, it fostered and legitimated U.S. expansionism and the search for new markets abroad for American "surplus." Political theorists and military strategists such as Alfred Thayer Mahan preached what was known in the 1890s as the "large policy," and argued that the United States must look outward to "new frontiers" beyond its national boundaries, especially to further commercial expansion. Mahan, for instance, recommended the acquisition of naval bases in Cuba, the Caribbean, and the Philippines, chiefly to protect national commercial interests.[39] The imperial outlet for American surplus constituted a violent reassertion of the social body, what the cultural historian Ronald Takaki calls a "masculine thrust" toward Asia and Latin America.[40]

In the late nineteenth century, the cigar engendered a conspicuously *masculine* preserve in an increasingly feminine consumer landscape: as a racialized signifier of phallic power, it signified a resurgence of manly frontier spirit in opposition to domestic feminization and overcivilization. Emblematizing the "masculine thrust" of the United States, especially its military and economic intervention into Cuba, the cigar connoted the assertion of male authority at home and abroad. A commodity that signified phallic imperial masculinity, the cigar intervened in the intersecting, hom(m)osocial realms of international and domestic capitalism: it served as a medium for the external colonization of the Cuban economy and the internal colonization (or "re-masculinization") of domestic capitalism. With the mass marketing of the five-cent cigar by 1900, the cigar, traditionally an expensive and high status good, was marked as a commodity every (American) man could enjoy and/or identify with: "every" American man was invited to participate symbolically in the imperial reconstruction of American masculinity. The marketing of the cigar to working-class men, a development closely tied to increased U.S. control over Cuban tobacco production, suggests the correlation between domestic capitalism and imperialism, a correlation figured in the entanglements of class, race, gender, and nation in cultural representations. The mass-marketed cigar configured imperial masculinity as a *national* construction, smoothing over class difference while heightening gender, racial, and national distinctions.[41]

The emblematic masculinity of the cigar was especially prominent during the Spanish American War. The war itself was conceived in therapeutic terms, as a crucible for a new American manhood. War correspondents and historians widely depicted the Spanish American War as a showcase for the conspicuous enactment and display of American virility and manly chivalry.[42] The wartime performance of masculinity was aided by programs on the homefront devised to effect the regeneration of American masculinity and corporeal power. Teddy Roosevelt's 1899 men's club speech "The Strenuous Life," in which he spoke urgently of restoring through sport "that vigorous manliness for the lack of which in a nation, as in an individual, the possession of no other qualities can possibly atone," epitomizes this generalized resurgence of masculinity, but the phenomenon was more generally expressed in the sport and physical culture movements, Boy Scouts, and other cultural phenomena.[43] As Ernest Thompson Seton, co-founder of the Boy Scout movement at the turn of the century, put it, physical culture was necessary "to combat the system that has turned such a large proportion of our robust, manly, self-reliant boyhood into a lot of flat-chested cigarette smokers, with shaky nerves and doubtful vitality." For Thompson Seton, the scouting movement would provide recreation as national "re-creation," "the physical regeneration so needful for continued national existence."[44] If national degeneration was exemplified by "a lot of flat-chested cigarette smokers," the imperial (re-)making of Americans during the Spanish American War period was often represented by the cigar. In popular imagery from the period, the cigar constituted a potent phallic symbol, synthesizing gender, race, and national significances. Cigar representations both alleviated and intensified late-nineteenth-century gender and sexual insecurities, and registered the complex erotics of white imperial manhood.

Traditionally associated with Cuba (an association as old as the earliest European narratives of exploration), the cigar was especially available to U.S. imperial fantasies. However, due to its powerful resonances in Cuban political culture, the cigar was enmeshed in an intercultural debate and nexus of intertextual revisionism.[45] In the Cuban political imaginary, the cigar has served as a prominent symbol of Cuban political radicalism, revolution, and manliness, associations which Fernando Ortiz forged into cultural theory in his influential treatise on the Cuban colonial economy. In *Cuban Counterpoint,* Ortiz contends that "tobacco has always been more Cuban than sugar," that it spelled liberty rather than slavery, and "that in the history of Cuba sugar represents Spanish absolutism; tobacco, the native liberators"—an analysis which, while it vividly registers nationalist sentiments, has been discounted as a nostalgic mystification of Cuban history.[46] To be sure, Cuban cigarmakers were a highly politicized group of workers: cigarmakers were at the vanguard of nineteenth-century Cuban independence movements and were an important source of support for José Marti's Cuban Revolutionary Party, while cigar shops were among the first structures to be taken over and collectivized in Castro's revolution.[47]

The cigar's significance as a symbol of Cuban independence is evident in the Cuban legend that Marti, exiled in Florida, sent home revolutionary messages rolled in cigars—an account that foregrounds the literal inscription of the cigar as a revolutionary artifact. This tradition of depicting the cigar as a symbol of Cuban revolutionary manhood was critical to the (re)articulation of the cigar, in the U.S. political imaginary, as a symbol of revitalized imperial masculinity. In other words, the Cuban tradition of representing the cigar as a symbol of national solidarity and manliness constitutes part of what was appropriated/cannibalized in the symbolic regeneration of American manhood.

In the late nineteenth century, the imperial articulation of the cigar as a political sign was inseparable from transformations in the structure of international capital: U.S. symbolic appropriation or recontextualization of the cigar within the national imaginary, and increased U.S. economic intervention into and control over the Cuban tobacco industry, were interrelated phenomena. Throughout the first half of the century, U.S. tobacco trade with Cuba was chiefly mercantile: U.S. wholesalers and retailers principally bought Havana cigars made in Havana. With the rapid rise in U.S. cigar consumption during the nineteenth century, the domestic cigar industry expanded, and mercantile trade with Cuba gave way to the large-scale purchase of Cuban tobacco leaf for U.S. home production. The consolidation of U.S. tobacco monopolies in the late nineteenth century brought further changes. In particular, the monopolies speculated on the crisis years of the war and bought up Cuban tobacco land and businesses, so that by 1902 the American Tobacco Company controlled 90 percent of all Cuban cigar exports.[48] These changes in the structure of U.S. capital, changes bound up with and furthered by the war, are registered in complex ways in popular imagery. Social representations of the cigar accompanied, adapted to, and even formulated the nature of changes and trends in the capitalist economy. Such representations, in the words of Paul Smith, legitimate contemporary social and economic structures "at the level of the *consumer*, who is never the consumer of just a commodity but equally of the commodity's *text* and ideology."[49]

Advertising the Nation

The cultural prominence of the cigar as an imperial "commodity-text" was facilitated by broad changes in U.S. commodity culture. By the late nineteenth century, the commodity was fully articulated within the U.S. national imaginary, and figured centrally in public discourse about international expansion as well as gender anxieties on the homefront.[50] The national articulation of the commodity in the late nineteenth century is especially evident in advertising, the principal form of cultural representation in which the social meanings of commodities are formed.[51] Frank Presbrey has identified the 1890s as the period that marked the birth of modern advertising, the period when manufacturers and advertising agencies began conducting carefully strategized national campaigns to increase consumer demand nationwide for particular products.[52] Making use of new printing technologies such as the half-tone, national advertisers increasingly incorporated political iconography into their advertisements, especially images of national public figures, such as Columbia and Uncle Sam, and national symbols like the eagle and the flag.[53] By the late nineteenth century, in a range of advertisements, the "nation" and the "commodity" were mutually articulated: during this period, commodities played an increasingly important role in mobilizing political identities and identifications. National advertising imagery synthesized commodity and political desire in a truly *national* consumer culture.

Part of what was promoted in turn-of-the-century advertising was the new identity of the United States as an imperial nation, an identity much contested in political discourse. Modern advertising in the United States literally came of age in an imperial era, and was from the start saturated with imperial import and imagery.[54] Advertisements and the commodities they represented brought the empire *home*, embedding it within the affective structures of daily life.

Cigars were spectacularly advertised imperial commodities. Cigar labels were particularly innovative in terms of chromolithography, requiring an elaborate printing process: up to twenty-two different colors could be used, along with bronzing powder and fancy silk- or satin-finished papers; many labels were also decorated with detailed embossing. What collectors have termed "cigar label art" was fully embedded within everyday life: people collected labels and bands, and forms of folk art were made out of them.[55] Cigar advertisements, valued as artifacts in their own right, would usually be consumed along with the cigars: cigars were sometimes smoked with the bands on, and a cigar box would typically be opened and its label displayed while the cigars were smoked. Cigar labels, bands, and boxes were deemed valuable and significant forms of culture, shaping the complex of the cigar's meanings as an imperial commodity-text.

The cigar was a particularly suitable commodity to figure in the imperial (re)construction of American manhood. Traditionally, cigar smoking in the United States had been marked out as male enterprise, and the cigar was saturated with gender significance. In the mid–nineteenth century, for instance, men dropping cigar ashes on the Brussels rug constituted a stereotypic image of male brutality and resistance to domestication, and smoking was widely imaged as a male rite of passage (and site of male bonding).[56] When Mark Twain's Huck Finn "lights out" in what has been called his paradigmatic flight from civilization, he also lights up, an act that at once signifies a rejection of feminine gentility and respectability and an expansive movement outward from "civilized" domestic space.

"Ubiquitous symbol[s]" of the gaudy, freewheeling Gilded Age, cigars were familiar props in late-nineteenth-century male culture, and served as a medium of male homosocial/homoerotic exchange. In homes of the well-off, men withdrew from the ladies after dinner to enjoy fine cigars and brandy while they discussed politics and other "male" matters. Similarly, workingmen gathered in popular saloons after work to talk and enjoy a smoke and stein of beer, while male politicians and businessmen crowded into proverbial smoke-filled rooms to cut deals. The cigar was a virtual appendage of turn-of-the-century financiers and industrialists like J. P. Morgan (who had eight-inch cigars specially rolled for him) and became an emblem of male corporate power. Passing around cigars was a male corporate ritual, and signified the consolidation of capitalism as a male homosocial preserve and a site of homosocial and homoerotic desire.[57]

The consumer industry of the cigar constituted a markedly masculine space in the increasingly feminized landscape of consumer culture. In the United States, the cigar embodied the antithesis of the model of feminine "pious consumption" predominant in Victorian domestic culture. Whereas "feminine" consumer practices such as sentimental cherishing staged the suppression of appetite and the cultivation of domestic sentiments, cigar smoking constituted a "masculine" paradigm of consumption, one along the lines of the frontier model described by Richard Slotkin, Anne Norton, and others. This masculine paradigm was a model of what Slotkin terms "regeneration through violence," entailing the cannibalistic, oral incorporation of the savage Other as a way of taking on its power.[58] According to this paradigm, the cigar connoted escape from pervasive feminization through regenerative contact with—and ritual incorporation of—the "savage" (Cuban) Other. As opposed to feminine sentimental consumption localized in heterosexual domesticity, the masculine practice of "regeneration through violence" occurs on the boundaries of civilization and is clearly identified with imperial expansion.[59] However, the specifically oral, homoerotic desires engendered by (and performed through) cigar consumption deconstruct these spatial boundaries and make explicit the "uncivilized" desires at the heart of "civilized" culture. Cigar consumption enacts forms of Other (homoerotic, interracial) desire which are both central to and regulated by imperial practices.

A series of political cartoons by the war journalist Red ("Bart") Bartholomew clarify the contours of this "masculine" consumer paradigm and illuminate the role of gender in writing the cigar as an imperial commodity-text. Bart's work was widely circulated: it appeared regularly in the *Minneapolis Journal*, a midwestern daily with an extensive readership, and was reprinted in various national collections of cartoons about the war.[60] Bart's cartoons exemplify the virtual identification of "Cuba" with "cigar" in the U.S. political imaginary, as well as the homoerotics of phallic imperial contest. In "Sampson Takes Havana" (fig. 4), "Havana," imaged as a cigar, is passed from General Blanco to General Sampson (significantly, no Cuban appears in the picture). Configuring Cuba as a

4 Red Bartholomew, "Sampson Takes Havana." *Minneapolis Journal* (19 August 1898).

phallic cigar, the cartoon registers a central strategy of colonial discourse more generally: the representation of cultural Others as objects, the "metonymic freezing" of whole cultures and populations in time.[61] The metonymic freezing of Cuba in this cartoon recalls Fanon: "One is no longer aware of the . . . [Cuban], but of a penis. . . . [The Cuban] is turned into a penis. He *is* a penis." Depicting the two generals in military attire, the cartoon foregrounds the shared masculinity of the two men (as successive "owners" of "Havana," the right hand of each grasps the cigar), a masculinity from which the Cubans are excluded by their conspicuous absence. But while in Fanon's account, the Other's penis is a phobic object which signifies a threat—namely, the fear that the Other is more sexually potent than the (white) Self—that object is here safely domesticated and contained, its powers harnessed by the white generals. The text, reiterating Blanco's reported statement that Havana is "better than the pipe of peace and answers the same purpose," explicitly connects histories of internal and external U.S. colonialism—here by recalling the imperial history of tobacco and by drawing parallels between Native Americans and Cubans as objects of U.S. imperial expansion and economic appropriation.

Another cartoon by Bart expressly invokes the masculine consumer paradigm of frontier cannibalism, registering how U.S. imperial desires are fused with fantasies of oral consumption and aggression (see fig. 5). In "Havana Filler" (the remainder of the caption reads "How Uncle Sam will Smoke the Spanish Out"), the image features Uncle Sam "smoking" a cigar that is also a cannon, through which he blows both smoke rings and bombs, aimed across the water at the city of Havana. Placed at the center of the cartoon, the cigar mediates between the United States (personified by Uncle Sam) and Havana while visually connecting the two. The cigar instantiates a relationship between the United States and Havana, defining that relationship as one of U.S. domination and ownership. In Bart's cartoon, Uncle Sam is both smoking or consuming a "Havana"—ritually incorporating Havana—while simultaneously killing off his rivals, the Spanish. Here, Havana—both cigar and place—are securely in possession: Uncle Sam's massive hands are raised to his shoulders (with phallic fingers extended), suggesting both his rather ominous proprietary power and the ease and effortlessness of U.S. possession. While hands are central to the homoerotics of "Sampson Takes Havana," here the cartoon emphasizes a dynamic of oral desire (cigar smoking as fellatio) and retaliatory aggression. The homoerotics of cigar smoking are both acknowledged and disavowed: the cigar is transformed into a weapon turned against Cuba and its Spanish inhabitants.

U.S. cigar manufacturers capitalized on this wartime symbolism of the cigar and its role as an imperial commodity-text. The "Victory" label (fig. 6), from the turn of the century, employs the medieval iconography common in cigar advertisements, and performs the work of situating the cigar within the Anglo-American imperial imaginary. The label sports martial imagery of jousting knights and coats of arms, presented in bright primary colors. The "Victory" label exemplifies the era's larger fascination with the Middle Ages, what one writer calls its "medieval mentality," and particularly its fascination with medieval martial valor.[62] This "medieval mentality" was clearly bound up with U.S. nativism: it worked to define a "pure" and valiant Anglo-American ethnicity against the immigrants who were entering the United States in great numbers as well as those racial and ethnic Others within and beyond its national borders. In "Victory," medieval iconography works to reconstruct the cigar as an Anglo-Saxon commodity, symbolically incorporating the cigar within a fundamentally *Anglo*-American past. Deploying what Eric Hobsbawm calls "tradition," the label configures the U.S. appropriation of the cigar—effected through the geographic expansion of the market and secured by overseas conquest—as a temporal return to ethnic origins.[63]

The national recontextualization of the cigar, enacted in the "Victory" advertisement, is expressly performed in the "American Presi-

5 Red Bartholomew, "Havana Filler." *Minneapolis Journal* (23 April 1898).

6 "Victory" Cigar Box Label.
Collection of thc author.

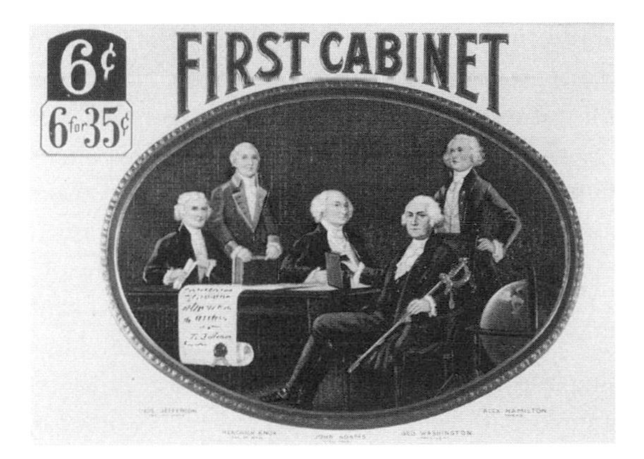

7 "First Cabinet" Cigar Box Label.
Collection of the author.

dents" series of cigar bands and labels from the early twentieth century. Exemplifying what Robert Heimann calls the "great man" theme that distinguishes cigar nomenclature, this series foregrounds the political significance of the cigar, articulating that commodity within the national imaginary by linking it with national heroes and leaders.[64] The "First Cabinet" cigar label similarly employs the presidential motif (fig. 7). Significantly, the tendency to name the cigar after political and military figures of national stature was not characteristic of other tobacco products—a fact that would seem to be bound up with the cigar's role in the international economy and its powerful and contested gender and ethnic significances. The "great man" theme prominent in cigar advertising both registered and aimed to allay pressing political anxieties about who "owned" the cigar itself. Advertisements such as the "American Presidents" series and "First Cabinet" contributed crucially to the cigar's (re)construction as an imperial commodity-text.

Consuming (a) Havana: The Cigar and the History of Western Cannibalism

Cigar imagery embodies, and elicits, fantasies of oral desire and consumption that historically have been fundamental to the U.S. imperial imaginary. Imperial fantasies of oral incorporation were essential to popular imagery of the cigar as well as its symbology in everyday life. The cigar is a commodity that is slowly and leisurely consumed in an act of uninterrupted oral pleasure. (Many cigar advertisements from the period emphasized this temporal dimension, distinguishing the confident masculinity of the cigar consumer from that of the less mature and less successful cigarette smoker.)[65] The orality of cigar consumption is bound up with its cultural location on the imperial "frontier." Historians typically discuss the frontier as a space of racial transgression and the formation of "masculinity." But it is also a space where social boundaries (of race, nation, sexuality, and gender) are tested and contested. As cigar iconography suggests, the imperial frontier—the field of imperial expansion—is a site of homoeroticism and desublimated orality, a terrain where gender and sexual identifications are challenged and affirmed.[66] In the late nineteenth century, U.S. male "incorporation" and "possession" of Cuban manhood were both enacted and *ritually performed* in the very consumption of cigars.

As the "Havana Filler" cartoon (fig. 5) suggests, explicit imagery of imperial cannibalism—of orality and violent oral incorporation—was a fixture of U.S. expansionist rhetoric. Indeed, this imagery was as old as the nation itself.[67] The antebellum journalist and reformer Parke Godwin, for example, expressly described U.S. continental expansion as a process of bodily growth, entailing "the incorporation of . . . foreign ingredients into our body." Such expansion, for Godwin, would not "swell us out to an unmanageable and plethoric size." Rather, "this tendency to the assimilation of foreign ingredients, or to the putting forth of new members, is an inevitable incident of our growth. . . . Cuba will be ours, and Canada and Mexico too—if we want them—in due season, and without the wicked impertinence of a war."[68]

Like many of his U.S. contemporaries, Godwin conceptualizes the rest of the Americas (especially bordering countries such as Cuba, Canada, and Mexico) as assimilable raw materials—specifically, as food which exists to expand the life and strength of the United States. Economically, this identification of peripheral societies (such as Cuba) with unprocessed foodstuffs ensured the extraction of economic rewards by the imperial center.[69] Noting the frequency with which these tropes appear in nineteenth-century U.S. political discourse about the continental frontier, Anne Norton observes that frontier life was widely represented as "one long meal." Frontier lore featured prodigious feats of consumption: Davy Crockett alone reportedly swallowed Indians whole, devoured thunder, rattlesnake eggs, and bears, and washed his breakfast down with spike nails. Norton argues that metaphors of eating encapsulate the twinned features of expansionism: violent conquest and self-aggrandizement, aggression and assimilation into the national body.[70] The insistent orality of these metaphors also suggests the complex (homo)erotics of frontier masculinity.

Cultural representations such as advertisements served to print these political practices within the fantasy lives of individual consumers, inscribing them on the body. The imperialist bodily economy of oral consumption is highlighted in an 1882 Burpee seed company advertisement for the "Cuban Queen" watermelon (fig. 8).[71] The name "Burpee's Cuban Queen," an obvious reference to the traditional colonial designation of Cuba as "Queen of the Antilles," is inscribed directly on the melon (foregrounding William Atlee Burpee's appropriative agency), while the remainder of the text lists other "specialties for 1882" (including "Burpee's netted gem muskmelon" and the "Giant Rocca Onion"). The advertisement obviously appeals to the traditional rhetoric of American abundance (it shows an "81-pound" watermelon), and the standard European depiction of New World as an idyllic garden overflowing with sustenance for European consumption. Invoking an imperial rhetoric of discovery and collection, the "Cuban Queen" advertisement foregrounds Burpee's ability to collect and rationally organize an ever-expanding array of "New Vegetables" for the American consumer.

This representation of Cuba as an object of oral consumption was featured in cartoons as well. Red Bartholomew's "A Valuable Addition to the Repast" (fig. 9), for instance, depicts Uncle Sam on an eating spree, and metonymically figures the islands as tropical fruits. The sign on the wall reads, "The expansion restaurant: tropical fruits a specialty"; in the restaurant, Jamaican ginger offers itself, spoon in hand, to ease Uncle Sam's indigestion after devouring the islands/fruits on the table (including the Philippines, Puerto Rico, Cuba, and the Hawaiian Islands). An-

81 LB. CUBAN QUEEN WATER-MELON.

This new Melon from the West Indies is certainly **The Largest and Finest Variety** in the world. Flesh, bright red, remarkably *solid, luscious, crisp* and *sugary*—far surpassing all others, and on a Melon of enormous size there is barely half an inch rind! The first-prize Melon the past dry season weighed **81 Pounds.** We offer **$50.00 IN CASH PRIZES for 1882** for the three largest Melons grown from our Seed. Do not fail to try and see how large the Cuban Queen can be grown.

☞ **OTHER SPECIALTIES FOR 1882.—Burpee's Netted Gem Musk-Melon** (see illustration), the earliest, most productive, *sweet as honey* and a gem indeed! **Burpee's Surehead Cabbage,** the very best, *all head* and always *sure to head.* **Lemon Pod Wax Beans,** marvellous for great beauty, fine quality and *immense productiveness.* **Livingston's Perfection Tomato,** bright red and smooth as an apple. **Giant Rocca Onion,** grown from our seed last year to weigh 1½ lbs. each. **Burpee's Improved Long Orange Carrot,** finest strain. **Peerless White Spine Cucumber,** best for table or pickling. **Giant White Stuttgart Radish,** early, large and fine **Red Top White Globe Turnip,** very handsome. **Philadelphia White Cabbage Lettuce,** and **Bassano Beet.** Illustration and full directions for culture printed on each packet.

A REMARKABLE OFFER! ☞ The above **12 Packets** of the choicest and **New Vegetables** at our catalogue prices are **worth $1.15,** but we will send the entire collection by mail, *post-paid,* to any address, for **ONLY 50 CENTS,** or 5 collections for $2.00. Our Seeds are all **Warranted First-Class,** *unrivalled in quality,* and this remarkable offer is made to induce thousands of new customers to give them **a fair trial**

FLOWER SEEDS! Another Great Offer! BURPEE'S GEM COLLECTION FOR 1882, embracing *Asters, Balsams, Pansy, Petunia, Phlox Drummondii, Verbena Hybrida, Double Zinnia,* &c.—in all **10 packets**—*most beautiful varieties,* with full directions for culture, for only **30 Cents,** or ten 3-cent stamps, sent *post-paid* to any address. ☞ **Both Collections,** of Flower and Vegetable Seeds—in all 22 packets—will be mailed for **75 Cents.** ☞ *Postage stamps accepted same as cash.* **Order now,** and ask for **BURPEE'S FARM ANNUAL for 1882,** beautifully illustrated, tells all about the best Garden, Field and Flower Seeds, Bulbs, Plants, &c., and is **Sent Free to any Address.**

W. ATLEE BURPEE & CO.
219 & 221 Church St. Philadelphia, Pa.

8 Burpee "Cuban Queen Water-Melon" Advertisement. (April 1882).

9 Red Bartholomew, "A Valuable Addition to the Repast." *Minneapolis Journal* (24 August 1898).

other cartoon, "Uncle Sam's territorial expansion dinner," similarly develops this expansionist vocabulary of food and oral consumption. On the table, draped with an American flag, Uncle Sam has served up his new "possessions," represented by "Hawaiian Poi," "Porto-Rico Coffee," and "Ladrone Melon"; off to the side appears a box of cigars designated "Smaller West Indies."[72] These associations between eating and territorial expansion illuminate the slogan featured in Beech-Nut Tomato Catsup advertisements in the early twentieth century, usually attributed to Charles Dudley Warner: "It takes more Brains to run a Grocery Store than to govern an Island." Running a grocery store and governing an island were being depicted as virtually identical.

Bringing "Havana" Home

Staking out, on a national level, ownership of the cigar—claiming the cigar as a national possession—is part of what is represented in U.S. cigar ads and imagery. Contributing to this translation was a marketing tactic that destabilized the very geographic identity of an "independent" Cuba. Cigar companies in the United States often used Spanish brand names and had labels designed in Spanish; indeed, cigars made in the United States were often designated authentic "Havana" cigars (e.g., fig. 10, "The Velocipede").[73] According to one 1875 commentator, "All the cigars made in the United States are invariably put up in imitation Havana boxes, with imitation Havana labels and brands. It is doubtful, how-

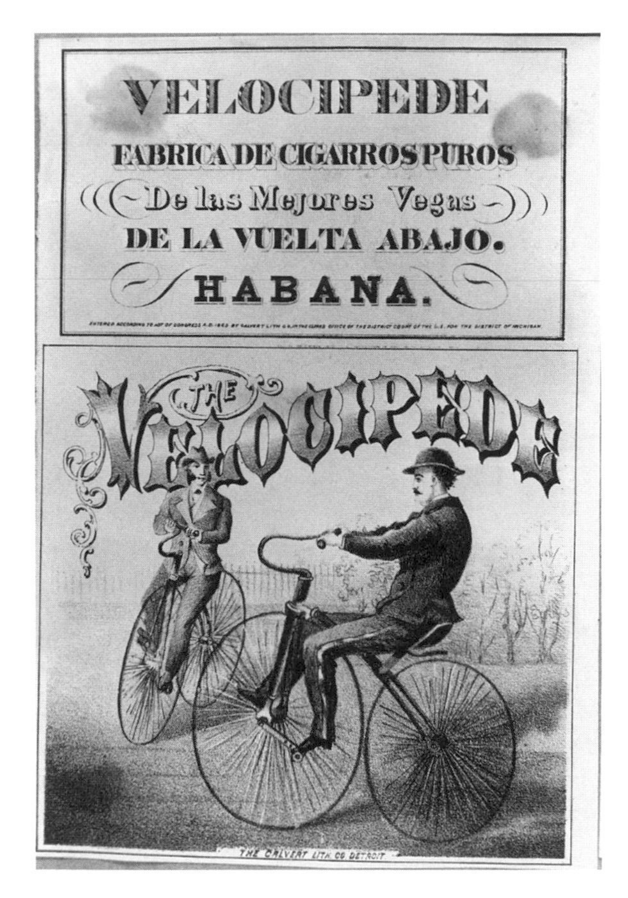

10 "The Velocipede" Cigar Box Label.
© Collection of the New York Historical Society.
Printed by permission.

ever, whether this transparent device deceives anybody."[74] However, given extended U.S. involvement in the Cuban tobacco industry in the last decades of the nineteenth century, the labels' "transparent device" seems more serious than this writer allows. What he represents as an innocuous Barnumesque ploy in fact registers confusion about who "possesses" Havana as well as where (indeed, what) "Havana" is. The deterritorialization of Havana, configured in these labels, both *represented* and *facilitated* Cuba's incorporation within a U.S. imperialist economy.

The translation of "Havana" or "Habana" (the Spanish form of the name) from geopolitical site to commodity signifier itself signaled the shifting importance of land in U.S. imperial policy. In the late nineteenth century, as Amy Kaplan notes, the nature of U.S. expansionism was undergoing a broad shift: continental land-grabbing gave way to the expansionism of investors and a more generalized economic imperialism. U.S. policymakers during the period envisioned what historians have called an "informal empire," expressing a fantasy of worldwide "Americanization" through shifting and intangible marketplace relations, a desire for total control disentangled from direct political annexation.[75] Many believed that with the end of continental expansion, national power would be measured by the extension of vaster yet less tangible networks of international markets and political influence. According to Emily Rosenberg, Cuba in particular "became a laboratory for methods of [commercial] influence that fell short of outright colonialism."[76] The dis-placement of Havana performed in cigar advertisements helped facilitate, symbolically, Cuba's incorporation within these shifting networks of international exchange.

Certainly, the use of the designation "Habana" and the Spanish names in labels such as "The Velocipede" inscribe U.S. imperialist designs. However, these representational practices also register the ethnic and linguistic complexities of domestic U.S. culture—especially the inclusion of some cities and regions within an "extended Caribbean."[77] Many Cuban radicals who emigrated to the United States worked in the cigar trade, and in centers of the cigar industry—such as New York, New Orleans, and especially Florida—there was a flourishing Cuban-American culture. Key West, for instance, the center of "Clear Habana" production in the United States, was widely known as "Little Havana." The city offered Spanish-language newspapers and Cuban restaurants, small Cuban-style groceries and taverns, and coffee vendors who walked the streets and the aisles of cigar factories. Ties with Havana remained strong and cigarmakers moved freely back and forth between the two cities throughout the late nineteenth and early twentieth centuries.[78] Cities such as Key West thus constitute what Antonio Benítez-Rojo has called "imperfectly integrated" areas of the United States, in which vestiges of Spanish colonization persist and where heavy island populations thrive; such areas, Benítez-Rojo contends, destabilize any narrow geographical understanding of the "Caribbean."[79] The pervasive designation "Habana" on cigar labels in the United States thus represented and made visible the "imperfectly integrated" areas of "Cuban-America." Embodying Cuban-American "borderlands," cigar labels register the ethnic and racial complexities of "American" culture and the instability of U.S. and Cuban national boundaries.

Rolling and Stripping: Engendering an Imperial Politics of Affect

It is always worth asking [when analyzing international politics], "Where are the women?" . . . Enjoying Cuban cigars together after dinner while wives and mistresses powder their noses has been the stuff of smug cartoons but not of political curiosity. — Cynthia Enloe, *Bananas, Beaches and Bases*

Sexual difference has always been essential to ideologies and practices of both internal and external imperialism. As Said and others have shown, in literature, popular iconography, and political discourse, racial Others were often marked as "feminine," a conflation that could justify, indeed mandate imperialist policies and practices.[80] Thus far in this chapter, I have addressed the imperial representations of gender largely in terms of a *homoerotics* of capitalist expansion, and its deployment of an implicit and, at times explicit, ideology of *masculinity*. To return to the passage from *Blake*, the Afro-Cuban man, laying claim to the Anglo-American man's cigar, conspicuously intervenes in imperialist ideologies that would negate Cuban and black manhood, performing in his gestures the symbolic recuperation of that manliness. *Blake* suggests that Anglo-American men both desire the masculinity of Afro-Cubans and aim to negate that masculinity (and that desire) under the sign of imperial domination. While the metaphorics of cigar consumption make visible the homoerotics of capitalism and imperialist expansion, representations of sexual difference in cigar advertisements work to domesticate these relations, resituating the cigar within a heterosexual domestic context.

Sexual difference was, from the outset, fundamental to the securing and maintenance of the imperial enterprise. Cynthia Enloe's "where are the women?" is thus a relevant, indeed critical question to pose in analyzing the imperial culture of the cigar.[81] Tobacco growing and manufacture in the nineteenth century, in both Cuba and the United States, followed a gender division of labor. As in many kinds of agricultural labor, field hands on large tobacco plantations were divided by age, sex, and strength, and a gendered work hierarchy was enforced. Skilled tasks such as plowing and mowing were assigned to men, while tasks designated as unskilled, such as weeding, harvesting, and cleaning, were assigned to women. Cigarmaking, in Cuba and the United States, was traditionally a masculine trade, one especially characterized by a working-class ethos of "manliness." Within the industry, there was a standard gender division of labor: women typically performed low-status tasks, such as stripping the leaves from the stems of the tobacco plant, while men usually performed the skilled craft of rolling the cigars. (This status-based division of labor, inflected by race and age as well as gender, was recorded in James Weldon Johnson's *Autobiography of an Ex-Colored Man,* in which young black men, including Johnson's protagonist, work in a cigar factory as strippers, while older Cuban creole craftsmen work as rollers.)

If women's physical labor in the trade was circumscribed, the cultural work of gender in the industry as a whole was diverse and varied. Women sold cigars in a variety of U.S. social spaces: women sold cigars in booths at the 1893 Columbia exposition; while "Cigarettes, Cigars!" immortalized in Ziegfeld Follies routines, would become a feminine refrain at the speakeasies. Selling femininity along with cigars was a common marketing strategy: many early advertisements used the new strategy, in the early 1900s, of what one advertising historian has called the "pretty girl picture" to "attract attention" to a product. Images of erotically appealing women were commonly found in in cigar labels and posters, as in the 1906 poster for the "Colonial Club" five-cent cigar (fig. 11). Posters such as this one would appear especially in male spaces such as taverns, tobacco stores, and barber shops. Featuring an attractive, and smiling, young woman in a low-cut dress, her hair, face, neck, and shoulders framed by her bonnet, the advertisement directs the (male) viewer/consumer's gaze toward these sexualized areas of her body. Advertisements such as this mask the homoeroticism of capitalism while simultaneously repositioning women from consumer subjects to commodity objects. Advertisements such as "Colonial Club," in other words, constituted early examples of selling femininity along with commodities; in doing so, they fueled and gratified male fantasies of (sexual) ownership.

This imperial (re)positioning of women as sexual objects is evident in much nineteenth-century political discourse about Cuba. The uses of gender in imperial discourse were related to, and generated out of, particular anxieties and desires on the homefront: indeed, "saving" Cuba could recuperate, on an international scale, patriarchal prerogatives challenged at home. In literature and popular culture, Cuba (the "Pearl" or "Queen" of the Antilles) was traditionally represented as feminine and in need of (U.S.) masculine protection. Narratives featuring Cuban women captured and preyed on by a degenerate Spain fused anti-Catholic and imperial sentiments, and were a standard feature of U.S. literary nationalism throughout the nineteenth century.[82] The construction of Cuba as feminine and dependent fanned annexationist desires, as an especially lurid example of antebellum political rhetoric suggests: "Cuba admires Uncle Sam, and he loves her. Who shall forbid the banns? Matches are made in heaven, and why not this? Who can object if he

11 "Colonial Club Cigar" Poster (c. 1906).
Collection of the author.

throws his arms around the Queen of the Antilles, as she sits, like Cleopatra's burning throne, upon the silver waves, breathing her spicy, tropic breath and pouting her rosy, sugared lips? Who can object? None. She is of age—take her, Uncle Sam!"[83] The passage configures political annexation in gendered, explicitly sexual terms, as at once rescue and rape. Specific adjectives—"silver waves," "sugared lips"—obliquely refer to colonial commodities drawn from Cuba and other Caribbean islands, commodities which served as a primary topic in annexationist debates. The passage modulates erotic and commodity desire in an imperial politics of affect.

Late-nineteenth-century cigar labels recycled these traditional representations. For example, in the "Cuban Winner" cigar label (fig. 12), a young Cuban girl's face and and shoulders are juxtaposed against a background image of a tobacco plantation. The plantation appears as a harmonious, picturesque setting viewed from a distance, its visual charms emphasized by the frame of flowers, palm trees, and a palm-like tobacco plant which appears in the foreground and which forms the lithograph's borders. Signs of labor have been strategically omitted and obscured; the only kind of human activity represented in the print is that of contemplation, of looking (a visual metaphor for the consumer's gaze). A caballero appears, elevated on horseback, in the left foreground, surveying the expanse of the plantation and the river, buildings (perhaps the owner's residence), and mountains in the distance. The scene is presented from an elevated perspective, so that the viewer is placed in the classic position of the imperial subject, what Mary Louise Pratt has termed the "master of all I survey."[84] The plantation is imaged as a space of consumption rather than production, available to the (male) consumer's visual and proprietary pleasure. The femininity of the figure in the foreground—the young girl—effectively synthesizes commodity fantasy and erotic seduction. The brand name, "Cuban Winner," is productively ambiguous. is the Cuban Winner the cigar (and by extension the young girl) who has been "chosen" by the American consumer? Or is the Cuban Winner the (American) consumer, the anticipated victor over Spain, and thus the "winner" (i.e., the "legitimate" owner) of both Cuba (here figured by the young girl) and the cigar? Crucially, the young Cuban girl looks away from the tobacco plantation and directly out at the viewer: her smile is an invitation to enter the scene in which she stands poised, and her role is to eroticize this visual exchange.

12 "Cuban Winner" Cigar Box Label. Collection of the author.

13 "Bloomer Club" Cigar Box Label.
Collection of the author.

The "Cuban Winner" label works to stabilize (hetero)sexual relations, and the sexual identity of the masculine consumer, by positioning women as "passive" commodity-objects. But labels such as one for the "Bloomer Club" cigar (fig. 13) reverse conventionally gendered relations of proprietorship, and foreground a more complex set of issues involving sexual, gender, and racial identification. This label can be considered one in a long tradition of female (often lesbian) appropriations of the cigar, appropriations that trope on the cigar as a cultural sign of phallic masculinity. In the late nineteenth century, sexologists such as Richard von Krafft-Ebing and Havelock Ellis were defining a cultural identification between lesbians and cigars: Ellis, for example, in his description of "sexual inverts" in *The Psychology of Sex*, writes that the "masculine" characteristics of some lesbians include "a decided taste and toleration for cigars."[85] The "Bloomer Club Cigar" advertisement clearly tropes on this identification and markets the cigar under the sign of the "New Woman," signified here by the bicycle, the cricket pin, and above all the bloomer, from which the cigar derives its brand name. In an important sense, this label (like the work of Ellis and others) displaces the male homoerotics of cigar consumption onto a specifically lesbian context.

Crucially, the New Woman in this advertisement is, conspicuously, the New *White* Woman: the consumer of the "Bloomer Club Cigar" is constructed in opposition to the black woman worker represented in the background, whose labors here *produce* the pleasures of the "Bloomer

Club." Indeed, the New (White) Woman's escape from confinement by Victorian domesticity and femininity is facilitated, materially and symbolically, by the presence of the black woman, who quite literally here becomes "*the* domestic." One particular feature of the label is that the white women are represented in pairs or female dyads, which convey a sense of homosocial or lesbian desire as well as racial "mirroring" as constitutive of identity and desire. The African American woman has no such mirroring counterpart: she stands alone, and her gaze is directed toward a white female couple, who sit absorbed in conversation and whose gazes are directed not at the black woman (they seem not to notice her) but at one another. Clearly, the consumer pleasures of the "Bloomer Club" are not available to black women: instead, those pleasures produce and enforce their (colonial) domination. Here, the circuitry of transracial desire evoked by the cigar is differently coded: the black woman's body does not signify "savage" sexuality but is domesticated and contained; her labor provides the grounds for the sexual "transgressions" of the white women. The destabilization of gender foregrounded in this label depends on the rigid stratification of race. For the female consumer of the "Bloomer Club Cigar," fantasies of gender/sexual transgression and racial/colonial dominance are mutually intertwined.

Late-nineteenth- and early-twentieth-century advertising conventionally employed such images of racial stratification and imperial appropriation, and continued to represent consumer subjectivities in the (white) racial terms discussed throughout this book. The gender significance of the cigar, apparent in "Cuban Winner," was heightened by its symbolic opposition to the increasingly popular (and equally gender-coded) cigarette. Feminists have long critiqued the aggressive advertising campaign in the 1920s, which inscribed the cigarette as an icon of women's liberation, as a cheap commercialization of feminist goals, an example of capitalism's appropriation of the languages and symbols of feminism to its own oppressive ends. However cheapened, the feminist resonance of the cigarette in the 1920s would seem to owe something to the imperial articulation of the cigar in advertising and popular culture three decades earlier. It is possible to see in the later commercial campaign a rearticulation of imperialist imagery in "feminine" terms, marking white women's inheritance of the "world" and expansive movement into public space.

Conclusion

Whenever I go abroad, it is always involuntary. I never return home without feeling some pleasing emotion, which I often suppress as useless and foolish. The instant I enter on my own land, the bright idea of property, of exclusive right, of independence, exalt my mind. Precious soil, I say to myself, by what singular custom of law is it that thou wast made to constitute the riches of the freeholder? What should we American farmers be without the distinct possession of that soil? It feeds, it clothes us; from it we draw even a great exuberancy, our best meat, our richest drink; the very honey of our bees comes from this privileged spot. No wonder we should thus cherish its possession; no wonder that so many Europeans who have never been able to say that such portion of land was theirs cross the Atlantic to realize that happiness. . . . These images, I must confess, I always behold with pleasure and extend them as far as my imagination can reach; for this is what may be called the true and the only philosophy of an American farmer. . . .

I endeavour to follow the thread of my feelings, but I cannot tell you all.—Hector St. John de Crèvecoeur, *Letters from an American Farmer*

Enjoy the land but own it not.—Henry David Thoreau, *Walden*

These two epigraphs suggest a genealogy of what I have been calling sentimental ownership as a form of national pedagogy. Not only does each writer aestheticize property, endow it with an aesthetic dimension and depict it as a site of aesthetic investment; each illuminates how the category of the aesthetic itself emerged to reconfigure ownership, to displace preexisting proprietary claims (based on positive law or natural rights) by positing a moral and spiritual claim, a morality of proprietary entitlement that, because spiritualized, is infinitely expandable and expansive—indeed, what constituted, for Crèvecoeur, the imagined expanse of the continent, and the infinite reproducibility of independent freeholding, would be matched by the imagined elasticity of consumer demand. Tracing out that genealogy, and its alignment with particular ideology of gender, has been the project of this book; and Crèvecoeur and Thoreau, in aestheticizing the land, fashion an agrarian aesthetics and proprietary logic that was reconstituted, in sentimental fiction, as "household taste," and configured around mobile property, domestic virtue, and femininity. In (re-)imagining the land, both writers counter a rational, utilitarian calculus of private property by illuminating the *feelings* of ownership, envisioning imaginative or aesthetic possession as an intuitive, spontaneous excess of emotion. In the epigraph from *Walden*, Thoreau draws on an emerging distinction in British aesthetic theory between owning and aesthetic contemplation, a distinction articulated by Shaftesbury and Addison. In Addison's Spectator essays, the "Man of Polite Imagination," like Thoreau, feels "a greater Satisfaction in the Prospect of Fields in Meadows, than another does in the Possession." But while the disinterested gaze augments the spectator's pleasure, the desire to possess does not wholly disappear from aesthetic contemplation as Addison describes it: "It [aesthetic contemplation] gives him, indeed, a kind of Property in every thing he sees, and makes the most rude uncultivated Parts of Nature administer to his Pleasures." As Mary Poovey argues in her reading of this passage, "Addison's elaboration of aesthetic contemplation [and virtue] functioned to admit into the behavior . . . associated specifically with leisured gentlemen men of a more middling rank—men for whom possession would have been linked to commerce, not inherited property"; it thus enabled men from the middle class, as well as the geographic "fringes," "to rival aristocratic prerogative by claming a superior social role as moral conscience for the nation."[1] Indeed, in America, envisioned by many as "nature's nation," aestheticizing the landscape would have not only class, but nationalist import: specifically, it generated national sentiment by promoting an aesthetic investment in the land, and a sense of imaginative possession of or entitlement to it; it inscribed a collective sense of the land as cherished cultural and national resource, as common "home." Devising an aesthetics of national possession, texts such as *Walden* helped create an emotional sense of belonging to/in the nation, and constituted the passional, erotic attachment to nation that Benedict Anderson refers to in his description of nations as "imagined communities." Aestheticizing the land and writing (our) collective title to it, *Walden* helped produce Walden Pond as national monument.

Thoreau suggests the role of the aesthetic in shaping a sense of imaginative possession central to the experience of nationalism. Crèvecoeur's text more thoroughly delineates an aesthetics of ownership, and illuminates the structure of feeling central to this book. In "following the thread of [his] feelings," which he invites the reader to complete and imagine for herself, Crèvecoeur evokes the feelings of home, and imbues property with an aesthetic, imaginative, indeed sentimental dimension—one central to the forms of "sentimental property" described throughout this book. In Crèvecoeur, the irrepressible "pleasing emotion" of attachment to home is by no means "useless and foolish": indeed, the defamiliarizing effect of travel and return imbues with Humean vivacity "the bright idea of property, of exclusive right, of independence"; the land, in Crèvecoeur's account, generates both imaginative and material "riches," inspiring sentiments through which "*we* . . . cherish its possession" (54; emphasis added). Crèvecoeur imagines these sentiments as primary, anterior to law rather than constituted by law; indeed, the "bright idea of property" as sentimentally experienced generates, in Crèvecoeur's account, "our" attachment to law and the nation's juridical structures. Using the metaphor of the plant, his favorite trope for figuring the "natural" expansion of human faculties, Crèvecoeur envisions the generation of sentiment, like the generation of wealth, as a process of organic unfolding and expansion, a natural process to which law is secondary: "The laws, the indulgent laws, protect [the immigrants] as they arrive, stamping on them the symbol of adoption" (69). Law here is envisioned, in antinomian fashion, as stamp and symbol, as physical sign and benign "protector" of a primary process of emotional realignment, here and elsewhere cast in domestic terms (i.e., as maternal "adoption"). In Crèvecoeur, conspicuously, national attachment follows from his attachment to both land and family, and his felt sense of patriarchal pride of possession in both; indeed, in the final letter, when Crèvecoeur's persona, James, anticipates abandoning his home to escape Revolutionary strife, he writes as a man in exile, one whose national allegiances are undone by the failure of "indulgent laws" to protect his ties to home; his retreat into domestic seclusion is a retreat into the security of these "natural" attachments.

Crèvecoeur's text illuminates the role of private property, of "exclusive right," in the making of Americans, and in delineating and expanding "our" personal, emotional investment in the nation. Designating a social and national realm of affect, it also illuminates a history of political subjectivity, a structure of feeling endemic to liberal political and social subjects. That history is evident in late-nineteenth-century immigrant stories, in which mass-produced commodities, rather than land, generate forms of emotional transformation ("refinement") in a process often called "Americanization." In such texts, as in Crèvecoeur, "taste" is a signifier of class, as well as national, affiliation, and enables forms of imaginative identification which constitute (middle-)class and national subjects. I have argued throughout this book that the aestheticization of property is linked to an aestheticization of femininity and the emergence of "modern" forms of gendered subjectivity; the aesthetics of ownership are also constitutively racialized. Indeed, in Crèvecoeur, the process of emotional regeneration that the laws "symbolize" and protect is also a process of ethnogenesis, the production of what Crèvecoeur terms a "new race": the making of Americans as "free" civil subjects and property owners through the "melting together" of diverse European races entails the making of whiteness as racial and economic prerogative. Crèvecoeur's text also illuminates the peculiar ambivalence of liberal forms of "free" civil subjectivity, in which agency and submission are inextricable: and here, what Wendy Brown terms the "woundedness" of the liberal political subject marks her dependence on property and the laws that sustain it.[2] In other words, just as rationalist liberal theorists naturalize industriousness and economic self-interest, sentimental texts envision social(ized) affect (including the emotions of private ownership) as prior to social law; at the same time, they betray, in the structure of subjectivity they generate, the subject's *interpellation* by and *dependence* on the law, and with it, recognition of the constructedness of political subjectivity. Sentimental texts thus engender attachments to particularized property objects, as well as an attachment to, and proprietary stake in, the nation whose laws enable and secure these attachments.

Both Thoreau and Crèvecoeur illuminate, in different ways, the aesthetics of American nationalism. Committed to regeneration in/as America(ns), both evision their imaginative apprehension of America as transformative, the occasion for singular and collective rebirth: as "western pilgrim" who exemplifies the doctrine of *imperio translatio*, the American, Crèvecoeur writes, "received in the broad lap of our great Alma Mater," "ought . . . to love this country much better than that wherein either he or his forefathers were born" (70). As both "man of feeling" and "family man," Crèvecoeur is invested in the reproduction and intergenerational transmission of what he terms "national pride" (66), although this remains hypothetical in *Letters*: the Revolution intercedes, and the threat of warfare, as well as the American farmer's now-divided loyalties, threaten the security of his attachments to "his" land and family. The final letters, in which utopia becomes dystopia, produce (inter)-

national crisis as emotional turmoil, and underscore, above all else, the primacy of his emotional attachments to family and property. The Revolution, which forces a realignment of national attachments, is primarily registered as an unwanted disruption of domestic harmony. Indeed, the increasing incoherence of the final letter, a discursive reflection of his passional instability, suggests how his very subjectivity is at stake, and depends on the security, and constancy, of his emotional attachments. The text ends with a fantasy of domestic retreat on the frontier, a "haven in a heartless world," indicating that the Revolution's realignment of sentiments has yet to take shape.

Writing on the brink of war, Crèvecoeur brings the Revolution home by casting it in emotional and domestic terms. By the 1820s, Lydia Maria Child can more effectively envision the reproduction of national attachment, and constructs a familial genealogy for the transmission of "civilized" national sentiments, one in which sexual difference plays a central role. In *Hobomok*, published in 1824, Child both registers and critiques the reconfiguration of sentiment and gender which was becoming institutionalized by the 1820s. A historical romance about seventeenth-century New England, *Hobomok* produces a genealogy of feminized sentiment as the ground for American political subjectivity. It does this by presenting a gendered history of Puritanism as national origin: like Perry Miller's foundational account of the "marrow of Puritan divinity," Child's novel operates by dissociating Puritan rationalism from its "marrow" or true essence in Puritan piety; Child then retroactively maps these onto the emerging, and gendered, separate spheres of the 1820s.[3] Midway through the text, the mother of the heroine, Mary Conant, gives authoritative voice to this view: "I have lately thought that a humble heart was more than a strong mind, in perceiving the things appertaining to divine truths. Matters of dispute appear more and more like a vapor which passeth away. I have seldom joined in them; for it appears to me there is little good in being convinced, if we are not humbled; to know every thing about religion, and yet to feel little of its power."[4] Thus figuring feminine sentiment as the regenerate "heart" of the American nation, envisioned as both prior to and outside of the law (defined here as the coercive, expressly masculine juridical apparatus of the state), Child's novel places the female body at the center of forms of imaginative identification through which social subjects—including national subjects—are constituted. Theorizing the principle of social reproduction as feminine "sympathy," a generative agent lodged in the female heart, Child sutures the female body to forms of intimacy through which national subjects are produced and reproduced. By virtue of her gender—

the collective construction of women as property objects—the feminine subject of sentiment/object of sentimental identification engenders a sense of imaginative possession and a proprietary stake in the nation ("my nation") associated with nationalism. As originary, indeed exemplary national subject, the feminine subject of sentiment also, like Crèvecoeur's James, registers forms of dependency on the state and what Brown terms the "woundedness" of liberal subjectivity.

Registering the domestication and feminization of sentiment, *Hobomok*, I have suggested, maps a discourse of feminine "heart" central to the reformation of American collectivity in the 1820s, locating its genealogic origins in Puritan piety. Writing seventeenth-century history as the plot of romance, *Hobomok*'s two aims are intertwined: it anchors the "true" history of Puritan religious practice not in the theology of the Puritan fathers but in the piety of Puritan mothers; and it fleshes out the "bold outlines of [the forefathers'] characters" and public actions by supplying "varying hints of domestic detail" (6). Interweaving theological and social aims, it identifies the feminine domestic as the repository of the "pure flame" (6) of Puritan piety and the site where that originary emotion is socialized and embodied. Theological disputes are personalized in the novel and emplotted in domestic terms: Mary Conant is in love with an Episcopalian, Charles Brown, and her father forbids their union; Mr. Conant's congenital severity—described as "feelings too rigid and exclusive" and attributed to the "narrow prejudices of the time" (114, 106)—and lack of sympathy for Brown's perspective and his daughter's preference breeds familial disharmony, and ultimately drives his daughter from his household and leads to the "scandal" invoked in the title—her marriage to the Native American man after whom the novel is named. The novel relates this plot in a revolutionary language of thwarted emotion, of natural and socially regenerative feminine desire repressed and constricted by an oppressive and unyielding patriarchal law. The novel ultimately reasserts the authority of feminine affect, in Mrs. Conant's deathbed request that her husband allow the union between Mary and Charles, a request to which Mr. Conant assents. However, Child's inscription of a sentimental version of the repressive hypothesis obscures the extent to which feminine sympathy is discursively and indeed juridically produced. This opposition of "natural" feminine emotion and restrictive patriarchal law, an opposition that enables the antinomian identification of female affect as a revolutionary sentiment and basis of social reform, masks the interpellation of sympathy by the law. Mary Conant's feminine "conscience" is an effect of patriarchal law: Mary had "no sympathy with her father's religious scruples," the narrator states, because "her heart very naturally bowed down before the same altar with the man she loved" (46). In *Hobomok*, feminine "conscience" and affect are envisioned as a "natural," willing submission to the law of (white) masculine desire.[5] As one undergraduate pointedly asked during our class discussion of the novel, "Why is Mary Conant's 'feminist' rebellion represented as her willing submission to another man?"

This structuring opposition of feminine affect and patriarchal law, as well as its collapse, are foregrounded in chapter 7 of *Hobomok*. Grafting the secular category of sentiment onto the theological category of piety, the chapter appears to map out an arena of "private" attachments and desires into which masculine law cannot encroach. In chapter 7, the church elders convene a public assembly to respond to the complaint of one member, Mr. Hopkins, that his friend Collins had betrayed his confidence and trust by determining to marry a woman Hopkins had considered plighted to himself. In having the tribunal dismiss the complaint as outside its proper jurisdiction, the novel conspicuously constructs love as outside the law, an affair of "conscience," prior to and unconstrained (indeed, uncontainable) by law. In the words of the assembly: "We do not see that we have a right to constrain the consciences of men in these particulars" (56). "Conscience" is inscribed in the text as a revolutionary impulse, a realm of feminine authority as well as liberty, associated with Anne Hutchinson's antinomianism and especially with Mrs. Conant: indeed, the novel insists that in affairs of "conscience," Mrs. Conant knows best. (For example, when Mary asks for maternal approbation of her desire to see Charles without her father's knowledge, she tells her mother, "In your conscience you can't think it's wrong," to which Mrs. Conant replies in sympathetic communion, "You well know my heart, my dear Mary," and instructs her daughter to "follow your own dictates" [46].) Conspicuously depicting the legal tribunal as the domain of Puritan fathers, chapter 7, and the text as a whole, envisions feminine "conscience" as outside and prior to legal interpellation; at the same time, however, it naturalizes and eroticizes female political subordination. The masculine heart's conversion is domestically effected: as I have suggested, Mr. Conant is finally converted to his wife's perspective through her deathbed request, and his conversion is a product of his identification with his wife and his love for her (which should, Child suggests, supersede any "mere" doctrinal commitment).[6] The scene suggests the significance of the feminine deathbed plea, conventionalized in women's fiction; specifically, it theatricalizes feminine abjection and physical powerlessness as the enabling condition of both feminine authority and masculine desire.

From its opening pages, the novel maps these gendered economies of emotion and enlists the reader's participation in their production and recognition. Explicitly aligning its narrator with the authority of feminine "heart," the novel images male theological debate as exceedingly rationalistic and, indeed, irrelevant to the true spirit of Puritanism and the national project that issues from it: the novel's women characters dismiss those debates and largely ignore them, offering instead a counterdiscourse of domestic suffering; and, from the "enlightened" contemporary perspective of Child's nineteenth-century narrator, "most of the points for which they so strenuously contended, must appear exceedingly absurd and trifling" (6). However, the narrator insists that, although the Puritan "forefathers" "exhibited a deep mixture of exclusive, bitter, and morose passions," they also sustained the "pure flame" of true divinity: "Without doubt, there were many broad, deep shadows in their characters, but there was likewise bold and powerful light" (6). In capturing that light, the feminine literary imagination provides "the varying tints of domestic detail" needed to soften the "bold outlines of their character," generating requisite forms of national appreciation and attachment (6). Inciting while directing her reader's emotions, Child encourages a more "sympathetic" view of Puritan history than is currently "fashionable": "in this enlightened and liberal age, it is perhaps too fashionable to look upon those early sufferers in the cause of the Reformation, as a band of dark, discontented bigots." In the place of unmitigated judgment, Child proposes a properly sympathetic, indeed filiopietistic approach, one that will renovate the nation's historical genealogy: "The peculiarities of their situation occasioned most of their faults, and atoned for them. . . . Whatever merit may be attached to the cause of our forefathers, the mighty effort which they made for its support is truly wonderful; and whatever may have been their defects, they certainly possessed excellencies, which peculiarly fitted them for a vanguard in the proud and rapid march of freedom" (6). Sympathetic emotion is depicted as the vehicle of both narratorial and readerly identification with the Puritan forefathers: the spontaneous emotion of feminine sympathy engenders the recognition of Puritan forefathers as prototypical revolutionaries; a principle of cultural reproduction, it enables an identification with, and as, national subjects. According to the narrator, "the heart pays involuntary tribute to conscientious, persevering fortitude, in what cause soever it may be displayed" (6).

In Child's text, then, the discourse of the feminine heart is assigned national import; it also promotes a national aesthetics of sympathetic ownership. The narrator's opening gesture is an invitation to the reader to apprehend imaginatively the setting of the novel's action, New England, as the scene of national origin, and to feel "a glow of national pride" and possession in surveying it: to say, along with the narrator, "this is my own, my native land" (5). The land is, of course, a crucial thematic in *Hobomok*: if the novel is plotted through romance, and routes feminine affect through the institutions of heterosexuality and marriage, it is also a novel about property, about the legitimacy of patriarchal ownership of the land and patriarchal authority within the family, one that adjudicates, and finally dismisses, Native Americans' claims to the land as well as white women. Like early imperial narratives of discovery and conquest, the novel entangles these two plots of romance and property: in these symbolic terms, the novel aligns Hobomok's entitlement to the land (against the "usurpers," as Hobomok's Indian enemy terms the English [30]) and his entitlement to Mary; and the novel concludes with the spectacle of Hobomok's dispossession, his "voluntary" renunciation of his native land as well as his wife and son—significantly, out of "respect" for Mary's emotions, his sympathetic recognition of her preference for Charles over himself. (Explicitly interpellating feminine conscience as an imperial emotion, Child tells us early in the text that, through his love for Mary, "Hobomok's loves and hates had become identified with the English" [31].) In the novel, the category of the aesthetic (sentimental ownership) is invoked to authorize English (and through the sympathetic extension promoted by the narrator, Anglo-American) title to the land, to anchor the American collective as "nature's nation." Throughout the novel, Child envisions the pure feminine affect of piety as in part an aesthetic emotion: while the Puritan forefathers, "little thought . . . amid the fierce contests of opinion" of the "rich sympathies of taste" (91), the religious affections of the Puritan mothers encompass an appreciation of the beauties of nature, called by Mrs. Conant "God's library—the first Bible he ever wrote" (76). Significantly, we see Mary Conant in private aesthetic contemplation of nature's beauty on several occasions, and her aesthetic responsiveness exhibits her "native elegance of mind" while designating a wealth of private feeling (the "recesses of . . . her heart") that differentiates her from less "refined" characters, such as Sally Oldham, who "saw nothing in the setting sun but a hint to do her out-door work" (36). Invoking a distinction, emphasized in Thoreau, between physical use and imaginative contemplation, while feminizing aesthetic contemplation by embodying it in the person of Mary Conant, the novel constructs feminine taste as a socializing force and, specifically, a form of national pedagogy. "Sympathizing" with Mary Conant and engaging in such acts of imaginative possession she exemplifies—in readerly terms, projecting oneself into the landscape and the domestic scenes that Child describes—engender, Child suggests, an imaginary relation to the land (and national past), that constitutes a kind of national identification, and a sense of proprietary stake in the nation.

The ambiguous position of the female body as both proprietary subject and property object enables its pedagogic function. The aestheticization of Mother Nature is matched by the aestheticization of the female body: indeed, Child writes that the superior beauty of the white woman established Hobomok's preference for Mary and ensured her "empire in his heart" (84). The aestheticized female body socializes individuals into forms of imaginative contemplation and imagined possession, distinct from lust or "mere" physical use. Women's role as agents of socialization, and the cultural production of the feminine body as a site of national identification, is signified by the fate of the child Hobomok. According to Indian custom, the child "took the name of his mother," and his assimilation to her Englishness is sealed by his Harvard and later English education and by the gradual erasure of his father from his genealogy. "his father was seldom spoken of; and by degrees his Indian appellation was silently omitted" (150). The novel's adherence to matriarchal "Indian custom" (149) is not gratuitous: that reference anchors the antebellum empire of the mother in an expressly Anglo-*American* past, while assigning the "omi[ssion]" of Native Americans from the national culture a kind of multicultural sanction. (Re)located within the white, English, patriarchal family, the virtuous, aestheticized female body exerts a socializing force, generating forms of national identification and possession, and a promise of imagined fulfillment, that could compensate for real disaffiliation and dispossession in the present; specifically, it generates fantasies of entitlement and power that we have come to call the "American Dream."

Crèvecoeur and Child illuminate a national romance of property embedded within the structure of sentiment. Indeed, they help us see "sentimental materialism" as a particular aesthetics of ownership, as well as a white racial fantasy of economic, political, and national entitlement—one that has shaped the forms of collective remembering, and forms of political desire, available to us. Addressing interrelations of capitalism, politics, and affect, this book has explored the place of sentiment in the history of liberal political and economic subjectivities and the constructions of racialized gender that have sustained them. Discussing an important chapter in the history of bourgeois taste, it has identified entangled fictions of property and sentiment in sentimental literature, and their role in forging private and public attachments. However, as eighteenth-century philosophers repeatedly emphasize, emotion is notoriously difficult to fix, to describe or to prescribe; and while the body and its passions have been a primary locus of social regulation in capitalism, they also continue to hold forth the promise of transformation. As Lawrence Grossberg notes, affect, which represents the "enabling distribution of energies" within social life, is "constantly being articulated to ideological, economic, and state politics, but it does not follow that it can be explained solely within [those] terms." For Grossberg, it is precisely "in an understanding of 'the popular' as an affective plane, that one can find any grounds for an 'optimism of the will' today, any space to negotiate between utopianism and nihilism."[7] This book has identified one scene of the ideological "articulation" Grossberg describes, in the suturing of nineteenth-century literary sympathies and liberal proprietary forms. Recording both the erotic appeal of liberal social forms and their inherent dissatisfactions, *Sentimental Materialism* aims to problematize and unsettle them, in the hopes that we might imagine other political intimacies, other narratives of nation.

NOTES

Introduction: The Forms of Cultured Feeling

1 Introduction to Neil McKendrick, John Brewer, and J. H. Plumb, eds., *The Birth of a Consumer Society: The Commercialization of Eighteenth-Century England* (Bloomington: Indiana University Press, 1982), 5.

2 On the late-nineteenth-century emergence of consumerism, see T. J. Jackson Lears, *No Place of Grace: Antimodernism and the Transformation of American Culture, 1880–1920* (New York: Pantheon, 1981), and "From Salvation to Self-Realization: Advertising and the Therapeutic Roots of the Consumer Culture, 1880–1930," in *The Culture of Consumption: Critical Essays in American History 1880–1980*, ed. Richard W. Fox and T. J. Jackson Lears (New York: Pantheon, 1983), 3–38. While the social history of female consuming remains to be written, several historians have suggested that during the late eighteenth and early nineteenth centuries the responsibility for purchasing domestic goods shifted from husband to wife in many households. According to Mary P. Ryan, for example, in the second half of the eighteenth century, "the activity of shopping played an increasingly prominent role in personal accounts of how American women spent their days"; Ryan, *Womanhood in America from Colonial Times to the Present*, 2d ed. (New York: New Viewpoints, 1979), 50. See also Ann Douglas, *The Feminization of American Culture* (New York: Anchor, 1988), and Carole Shammas's suggestive work on the "influence" of women consumers in colonial America: "How Self-Sufficient Was Early America?" *Journal of Interdisciplinary History* 13 (autumn 1982): 247–72, and "The Domestic Environment in Early Modern England and America," *Journal of Social History* 14, no. 1 (1980): 3–24.

3 On the semiotic function of commodities, see especially Jean Baudrillard, *For a Critique of the Political Economy of the Sign*, trans. Charles Levin (St. Louis: Telos Press, 1981), Michel de Certeau, *The Practice of Everyday Life* (Berkeley: University of California Press, 1984), Dick Hebdige, *Subculture: The Meaning of Style* (London: Methuen, 1979), Judith Williamson, *Consuming Passions: The Dynamics of Popular Culture* (London: Marion Boyers, 1979), and Anne Norton, *Republic of Signs: Liberal Theory and American Popular Culture* (Chicago: University of Chicago Press, 1993).

4 For a theoretical account of the emergence of modern consumerism, see Colin Campbell, *The Romantic Ethic and the Spirit of Modern Consumerism* (London: Basil Blackwell,

1987). I agree with Campbell that a "Romantic ethic," deriving out of pietistic Protestantism by way of sentimentalism, helped promote mass consumption; however, I believe this argument can more convincingly be made by identifying specific ways these discourses legitimized consumerism than by positing a vague association between Romantic expressivity and the "self-illusory hedonism" of modern consumerism.

5 For "political subjectivity," see Christopher Newfield, *The Emerson Effect: Individualism and Submission in America* (Chicago: University of Chicago Press, 1996), 10.

6 Foucault theorizes "subjection" or "subjectivation" as the effect of a power that at once produces and dominates or regulates subjectivity; in Foucault's account, the subject is founded through a primary submission to power. See Michel Foucault, *Discipline and Punish: The Birth of the Prison*, trans. Alan Sheridan (New York: Random House, 1979). In *The Psychic Life of Power: Theories of Subjection* (Stanford: Stanford University Press, 1997), Judith Butler elaborates the processes of subjection as envisioned in the work of several different theorists; her suggestive discussion of the role of "passional attachments" in securing the subject's subordination aided me in understanding the erotic forms of liberal consent, below.

7 Sympathy translated the traditional status of dependency in preindustrial societies into a moral and psychological register, and helped transform "dependency as political subjection into dependency as psychology," assigning it markers of class, race, and gender. Nancy Fraser and Linda Gordon, "A Genealogy of 'Dependency': Tracing a Keyword of the U.S. Welfare State," in Fraser, *Justice Interruptus: Critical Reflections on the "Postsocialist" Condition* (New York: Routledge, 1997), 129. Fraser and Gordon identify the emergence of certain figures (women, children, slaves, Native Americans) as personifications of dependency, a definition which they locate in the 1830s as a consequence of new rhetorics of white male economic and political independence, rhetorics that divested wage labor of its traditional and republican association with dependency and reinterpreted it as freedom.

8 As a code for authorizing certain emotions within the social realm, sympathy is indeed a form of emotional tutelage or what Richard Brodhead terms "disciplinary intimacy": it is a code of "identification" that is at once a code of socialization, reproducing norms of emotional experience and "taste" and consolidating socially recognizable identities. Brodhead, "Sparing the Rod: Discipline and Fiction in Antebellum America," *Representations* 21 (1988): 67–96. On "taste" as a vehicle of class differentiation and a form of middle-class discipline, see Pierre Bourdieu, *Distinction: A Social Critique of the Judgment of Taste*, trans. Richard Nice (Cambridge: Harvard University Press, 1984), and Laura Kipnis, *Bound and Gagged: Pornography and the Politics of Fantasy in America* (New York: Grove, 1996).

9 On the political history of bourgeois "affect reforms," see Kipnis, *Bound and Gagged.* Foucault, *The History of Sexuality*, vol. 1, trans. Robert Hurley (New York: Pantheon, 1978).

10 "Possessive domesticity" appears in Amy Dru Stanley, "Home Life and the Morality of the Market," in *The Market Revolution in America*, ed. Melvyn Stokes and Stephen Conway (Charlottesville: University of Virginia Press, 1996), 90. S/M scandalizes defenders of liberal erotic norms not only because it advertises these unspoken but deeply felt relations of power, but because it frees them from their institutionalization in forms of domestic dependency, redefining bondage as sex, not love.

11 Wendy Brown, "Wounded Attachments: Late Modern Oppositional Political Forma-

tions," in John Rajchman, ed., *The Identity in Question* (New York: Routledge, 1995), 199–227. For Brown, this woundedness is a consequence of a fundamental contradiction in liberal ideology, between formal and substantive equality, and is expressed as feelings of powerlessness to remedy existing social inequities in the face of market laws.

12 The anxiety about the alienability of property, expressed in the sentimental writings discussed in chapters 2 and 3, should be understood in terms of this history of erotic realignment.

13 Thus, the prostitute is a highly charged figure in sentimental discourse starting in the 1830s, and is often identified with independent workingwomen more generally, because she threatens these distinctions between male and female consent, between consenting to work and consenting to love, and because her affections and her body are envisioned as the site of competing male claims. For an important argument about the role of the capitalist wage economy in the emergence of modern homosexuality, see John D'Emilio, "Capitalism and Gay Identity," in *The Gay and Lesbian Studies Reader*, ed. Henry Abelove, Michèle Aina Barale, and David M. Halperin (New York: Routledge, 1993), 467–76.

14 Karl Marx, *The Economic and Philosophical Manuscripts of 1844*, in *The Mary-Engels Reader*, ed. Robert C. Tucker (New York: Norton, 1978), 68 n. 7.

15 Williamson, *Consuming Passions*, 230.

16 Willis, "Consumerism and Women," *Socialist Review* 3 (1970): 76–82, reprinted in *Popular Writing in America*, ed. Don McQuade (New York: Oxford University Press, 1974), 358–61.

17 Ruth Bloch, "The Gendered Meanings of Virtue in Revolutionary America," *Signs* 13, no. 1 (1987): 37–58.

18 Drucilla Cornell, *Beyond Accommodation: Ethical Feminism, Deconstruction, and the Law* (New York: Routledge, 1990); Norma Alarcon, "The Theoretical Subject(s) of This Bridge Called My Back and Anglo-American Feminism," *Making Face, Making Soul/Hacienda Caras*, ed. Gloria Anzaldúa (San Francisco: Aunt Lute, 1990), 356–69.

19 Max Horkheimer and Theodor Adorno, *Dialectic of Enlightenment*, trans. John Cumming (New York: Continuum, 1988), 120–67.

20 Maria Mies, *Patriarchy and Accumulation on a World Scale: Women in the International Division of Labour* (London: Zed, 1986), 48.

21 Pierre Bourdieu, *Distinction: A Social Critique of the Judgment of Taste*, trans. Richard Nice (Cambridge: Harvard University Press, 1984).

22 Adorno, *Prisms*, trans. Samuel and Shierry Weber (Cambridge: MIT Press, 1982), 87; Jane Gaines, "Introduction: Fabricating the Female Body," in *Fabrications: Costume and the Female Body*, ed. Jane Gaines and Charlotte Herzog (New York: Routledge, 1990), 11–15.

23 Jameson, "Reification and Utopia in Mass Culture," *Social Text* 1 (1979): 132.

24 Willis, *A Primer for Daily Life* (New York: Routledge, 1991), 108–32; Joel Pfister, "The Americanization of Cultural Studies," *Yale Journal of Criticism* 4, no. 2 (1991): 199–229.

25 Lazarus, "Doubting the New World Order: Marxism, Realism, and the Claims of Postmodern Social Theory," *differences* 3, no. 3 (1991): 94–138.

26 Antonio Gramsu, *The Modern Prince and Other Writings* (New York: International Publishers, 1959), 79.

27 Nancy Fraser, *Unruly Practices: Power, Discourse, and Gender in Contemporary Social Theory* (Minneapolis: University of Minnesota Press, 1989), 145.

28 Eric Sundquist, *To Wake the Nations: Race in the Making of American Literature* (Cambridge: Harvard University Press, 1993); Eric Lott, *Love and Theft: Blackface Minstrelsy and the American Working Class* (New York: Oxford University Press, 1993).
29 Zillah R. Eisenstein, *The Color of Gender: Reimaging Democracy* (Berkeley: University of California Press, 1994).
30 As reported in David M. Potter, *People of Plenty: Economic Abundance and the American Character* (Chicago: University of Chicago Press, 1954), 80.
31 For an analysis of the role of mediating cultural forms in configurations of the U.S. "national symbolic," see Lauren Berlant, *The Anatomy of National Fantasy: Hawthorne, Utopia, and Everyday Life* (Chicago: University of Chicago Press, 1991). For a general theoretical account of the ways in which nationalism mobilizes love in the service of the state and state-supported institutions, see Benedict Anderson, *Imagined Communities: Reflections on the Origin and Spread of Nationalism* (London: Verso, 1983).
32 Denise Riley, *"Am I That Name?" Feminism and the Category of "Women" in History* (Minneapolis: University of Minnesota Press, 1988).
33 Foucault, *History of Sexuality,* 104.
34 Poovey, *Uneven Developments: The Ideological Work of Gender in Mid-Victorian England* (Chicago: University of Chicago Press, 1988), 9.
35 Ryan, *Cradle of the Middle Class: The Family in Oneida County, New York, 1790–1830* (New York: Cambridge University Press, 1981).
36 Blumin, *The Emergence of the Middle Class: Social Experience in the American City, 1760–1900* (New York: Cambridge University Press, 1989), 190–91.
37 Fredric Jameson, *The Political Unconscious: Narrative as a Socially Symbolic Act.* (Ithaca: Cornell University Press, 1981), 22.
38 Gramsci, *The Modern Prince*; Laclau and Mouffe, *Hegemony and Socialist Strategy: Towards a Radical Democratic Politics,* trans. Winston Moore and Paul Commack (London: Verso, 1985).
39 According to Nina Baym, aristocratic "fashionable" women were frequently depicted as foils to the heroines of nineteenth-century woman's fiction; Baym, *Woman's Fiction: A Guide to Novels by and about Women in America* (Ithaca: Cornell University Press, 1978), 22.
40 Karl Marx, *The German Ideology,* in *The Marx-Engels Reader,* 110–64.
41 Foucault, *History of Sexuality,* 124.
42 The term "pious consumption" is borrowed from Thomas Richards, *The Commodity Culture of Victorian England: Advertising and Spectacle, 1851–1914* (Stanford: Stanford University Press, 1990), 104. Robert T. Handy analyzes the pervasive Protestant ideal of a "Christian civilization" in nineteenth-century America which synthesized Protestant millennialism and a secular, liberal conception of historical progress, and which correlated a liberal opposition between savagery and civility and a Christian distinction between salvation and corruption; *A Christian America: Protestant Hopes and Historical Realities* (New York: Oxford University Press, 1971). In an important sense the Puritan "myth of America"—the corporate ideal of a purified community of saints visibly identified with the national body politic—was mapped onto the consumer utopia of a "culture of abundance." For an analysis of the role of consumer goods as markers of inclusion within the national body politic, see Philip Fisher, "Democratic Social Space: Whitman, Melville, and the Promise of American Transparency," *Representations* 24 (fall 1988): 60–101.
43 Downing, *Cottage Residences* (New York, 1847).

44 Edgar S. Martin, *The Standard of Living in 1860: American Consumption Levels on the Eve of the Civil War* (Chicago: University of Chicago Press, 1942); Alice H. Jones, *American Colonial Wealth: Documents and Methods*, 3 vols. (New York: Arno, 1977), and Alice Jones, *Wealth of a Nation to Be: The American Colonies on the Eve of Revolution* (New York: Columbia University Press, 1980).

45 Horowitz, *The Morality of Spending: Attitudes toward the Consumer Society in America, 1875–1940* (Baltimore: Johns Hopkins University Press, 1985), xxv; Blumin, *Emergence*, 187–90.

46 These relays between the affectional and the material (re)appear in Elaine Scarry's important work. In *The Body in Pain: The Making and Unmaking of the World* (New York: Oxford University Press, 1985), Scarry powerfully recycles the identification, central to antebellum sentimental culture, between material and subjective refinement, between having a certain level of physical "comfort" and being a fully "human," affectionally and psychologically engaged social being (278–326). Scarry's work is itself deeply sentimental, and her interpretation of the psychological consequences of material life is not historicized. While there are, I believe, sound political reasons for forging the identifications she makes between "sentience" and material comfort (or standard of living), she casts her argument in ontological rather than political terms; thus, she misses the cultural and class specificity of the identifications she tracks.

47 Marc Fried, "Grieving for a Lost Home," in *The Urban Condition: People and Policy in the Metropolis*, ed. Leonard J. Duhl (New York: Basic, 1963), 151–71; Boris Levinson, *Pets and Human Development* (Springfield, Ill.: Charles C. Thomas, 1972); Olive Stevenson, "The First Treasured Possession: A Study of the Part Played by Specially Loved Objects and Toys in the Lives of Certain Children," *The Psychoanalytic Study of the Child* 9, no. 1 (January 1954): 199–217.

48 Especially in chapters 1–3, I attend to the religious underpinnings of "pious consumption"; I thus follow many previous scholars in asserting the formative impact of religion on American kinship relations, family life, and the development of capitalism. The middle-class domestic model I examine is a Protestant one, opposed to the claustrophobic, dangerous privacy depicted in gothic texts. That this Protestant domesticity entails a socially oriented privacy is suggested by the emphasis on the social performance of good manners and the pervasive language of theatricality in domestic fiction and advice literature. This *social* orientation is legible in the very *form* of domestic fiction, a genre devoted to publicizing the everyday practices of the private sphere. Protestant religious culture profoundly shaped the form and thematic content of domestic texts. The sacralization in New England Puritanism of the concrete behaviors and relationships of everyday domestic life, perhaps most apparent in the writings of Thomas Shepard and Anne Bradstreet, had important implications for the aesthetics of nineteenth-century domestic texts, which memorialize and sacralize domestic practices and affectional ties. The social and institutional emphases of American Puritanism—the Puritans' rhetorical and conceptual identification of the covenant of grace with the institutional forms of church and domestic covenant—long obscured by the influential work of Perry Miller, are currently undergoing critical reevaluation; e.g., Mitchell Robert Breitwieser, *American Puritanism and the Defense of Mourning: Religion, Grief, and Ethnology in Mary White Rowlandson's Captivity Narrative* (Madison: University of Wisconsin Press, 1990); Amanda Porterfield, *Female Piety in Puritan New England: The Emergence of Religious Humanism* (New York: Oxford University Press, 1992). Miller's "negative theology" essentially suppressed the Anglican aspects of American Puritan-

ism — such as the importance of what Ann Kibbey has termed "material shapes" in Puritan religious experience — as well as the social dimensions of Puritan theology, the "institutionalization of spirit" in an array of concrete social practices and institutions; Kibbey, *The Interpretation of Material Shapes in Puritanism: A Study of Rhetoric, Prejudice, and Violence* (New York: Cambridge University Press, 1986). Indeed, the Puritan conception of a community of "visible saints" — in which saving grace and inclusion within the covenant is manifested through bodily, material signs — informed the development of ideologies of American consumerism and the perceived social import of consumer "refinement."

The social ideals of American Puritanism, especially the ideal of a select and exclusive social body bound together by love, informed late-eighteenth- and nineteenth-century Anglo-American norms of domestic intimacy and familial affection. There is, indeed, an important connection between the early Protestant ideal of an exclusive body politic composed of regenerate Christians and the sentimental ideal of domestic intimacy and the selective sociability of the intimate social circle. The Puritans, as Edmund Morgan has noted, interpreted both figuratively and literally the biblical injunction to "do good to all, especially the household of faith"; *The Puritan Family: Religion and Domestic Relations in Seventeenth-Century New England* (New York; Harper, 1944), 16ff. The memorializing of domestic rituals in sentimental texts owes much to the Puritan emphasis on the home as a redeemed and redemptive social form. In these texts, the material boundaries of the home typically define and mark out the distinction between those within and without the covenant, between members of a regenerate, sanctified union and the unredeemed.

49 Bloch, "Gendered Meanings"; Jan Lewis, "The Republican Wife: Virtue and Seduction in the Early Republic," *William and Mary Quarterly* 44, no. 4 (1987): 688–721.

50 Christine Stansell, *City of Women: Sex and Class in New York, 1789–1860* (Urbana: University of Illinois Press, 1986), 193–216.

51 Douglas, *Feminization*.

52 On liberalism's identification of "choice" with "consent," see Norton, *Republic of Signs*, 4, 66–67. In a study of the rhetoric of advertising, William O. Beeman describes "freedom of choice" as the primary expression of "American symbolic culture." Beeman quotes the text of a 1948 Sun Oil Company advertisement, "There is only one freedom. Freedom of Choice"; Beeman, "Freedom to Choose: Symbols and Values in American Advertising," in *Symbolizing America*, ed. Hervé Varenne (Lincoln: University of Nebraska Press, 1986), 52–65.

53 Quoted in Lloyd Wendt and Herman Kogan, *Give the Lady What She Wants! The Story of Marshall Field and Company* (South Bend, In.: And Books, 1952), 28–29.

54 Ronald Hoffman and Peter J. Albert, eds., *Women in the Age of the Revolution* (Charlottesville: University of Virginia Press, 1989); Norma Basch, *In the Eyes of the Law: Women, Marriage, and Property in Nineteenth-Century New York* (Ithaca: Cornell University Press, 1982).

55 Carolyn Kay Steedman, *Landscape for a Good Woman: A Story of Two Lives* (New Brunswick: Rutgers University Press, 1988), 67.

56 Nancy Armstrong, *Desire and Domestic Fiction: A Political History of the Novel* (New York: Oxford University Press, 1987), 3–27.

57 Roediger, *The Wages of Whiteness: Race and the Making of the American Working Class* (New York: Verso, 1991); Kovel, *White Racism: A Psychohistory* (New York: Columbia University Press, 1970), 197.

58 Eisenstein, *Color of Gender*, 201.

59 Williams, "On Being the Object of Property," in *The Alchemy of Race and Rights* (Cambridge: Harvard University Press, 1991), 220–21. For feminist critiques of consent as liberal mystification of women's position in patriarchal societies, see Carole Pateman, *The Sexual Contract* (Stanford: Stanford University Press, 1988), Catharine A. MacKinnon, *Toward a Feminist Theory of the State* (Cambridge: Harvard University Press, 1989), and María Herrera-Sobek, "The Politics of Rape: Sexual Transgression in Chicana Fiction," in *Chicana Creativity and Criticism: Charting New Frontiers in American Literature*, ed. Herrera-Sobek and Helena María Viramontes (Houston: Arté Público, 1988).

60 Such psychological inextricability of "enslavement" from "freedom" in forms of liberal subjectivity suggests that what Lott terms "love and theft"—the dialectic of identification and disidentification from the black slave body characteristic of white male working-class subjectivity—is a form of ambivalence that inheres in middle-class subjectivity as well, although with its own specific class configuration. On the ambivalent psychology of liberal masculinity, see Newfield, *Emerson Effect*.

61 On the frontier consumption model of "regeneration through violence" and oral incorporation, see Richard Slotkin, *Regeneration through Violence: The Mythology of the American Frontier, 1600–1860* (Middletown: Wesleyan University Press, 1973). On the prevalence of images of eating in antebellum frontier political discourse and mythology, see Anne Norton, *Alternative Americas: A Reading of Antebellum Political Culture* (Chicago: University of Chicago Press, 1986).

62 Farnham, *Life in Prairie Land* (New York: Harper, 1846), 38. All further references are to this edition.

63 Basch, *In the Eyes*, 38.

64 Brodhead, "Sparing the Rod," 67–96; Wexler, "Tender Violence: Literary Eavesdropping, Domestic Fiction, and Educational Reform," in *The Culture of Sentiment: Race, Gender, and Sentimentality in Nineteenth-Century America*, ed. Shirley Samuels (New York: Oxford University Press, 1993), 12–32.

65 E.g., Philip Fisher, *Hard Facts: Setting and Form in the American Novel* (New York: Oxford University Press, 1985); Saidiya V. Hartman, *Scenes of Subjection: Terror, Slavery, and Self-Making in Nineteenth-Century America* (New York: Oxford University Press, 1997).

66 Belsey, *Critical Practice* (New York: Methuen, 1980), 56–84; Judith Butler, *Gender Trouble: Feminism and the Subversion of Identity* (New York: Routledge, 1990).

67 Robyn R. Warhol, "Toward a Theory of the Engaging Narrator: Earnest Intervention in Gaskell, Stowe, and Eliot," *PMLA* 101, no. 5 (1986): 811–18.

68 Lott, *Love and Theft*, 11.

69 Brown, *Domestic Individualism: Imagining Self in Nineteenth-Century America* (Berkeley: University of California Press, 1990), 2. "Possessive individualism" comes from C. B. Macpherson, *The Political Theory of Possessive Individualism: Hobbes to Locke* (New York: Oxford University Press, 1964). For a groundbreaking feminist account of the "politics of affect" in nineteenth-century fiction, see Ann Cvetkovich, *Mixed Feelings: Feminism, Mass Culture, and Victorian Sensationalism* (New Brunswick: Rutgers University Press, 1992).

1 Embodying Gender: Sentimental Materialism in the New Republic

1 Brown, *Alcuin; A Dialogue*, ed. Sydney J. Krause et al. (Kent, Oh.: Kent State University Press, 1987), 6, 4. All further references are to this edition.

2 As J. G. A. Pocock notes, "woman as capricious consumer is a recurrent feature of the rather prominent sexism" of Enlightenment social criticism; *The Machiavellian Moment: Florentine Political Thought and the Atlantic Republican Tradition* (Princeton: Princeton University Press, 1975), 465.

3 Thomas Laqueur, "Orgasm, Generation, and the Politics of Reproductive Biology," *Representations* 14 (1986): 1–41; Bloch, "Gendered Meanings."

4 According to Ruth Bloch, in late-eighteenth-century America, republican notions of political virtue as characterized by spartan simplicity, military prowess, and male disinterested rationality had been largely superseded—or at least contested—by a (secular Christian) notion of virtue as specifically feminine, emotional rather than rational, characterized by disinterested benevolence infused especially through the refining, domestic comforts of home life. In an important sense, the collectivist values of civic humanism were absorbed into the virtues of the domestic woman, whose graceful manners and tasteful surroundings, as much as her moral sensibility, were conceptualized as instruments of social influence and redemption ("Gendered Meanings," 42).

5 See Shammas, "How Self-Sufficient Was Early America?" and "The Domestic Environment"; and Alice Jones, *Wealth of a Nation to Be*.

6 Hortense Spillers, "Mama's Baby, Papa's Maybe: An American Grammar Book," *diacritics* 17, no. 2 (1987): 73; emphasis in original.

7 This definition, for most theorists, characterizes the commodity per se; Baudrillard, *For a Critique*. My characterization of Scottish writings on luxury as a "discourse" is indebted to Stuart Hall's Gramscian adaptation of Foucault's analyses of the material operations of the discursive: "Discursive formations (or ideological formations that operate through discursive regularities) 'formulate' their own objects of knowledge and their own subjects; they have their own repertoire of concepts, are driven by their own logics, operate their own enunciative modality, constitute their own way of acknowledging what is true and excluding what is false within their own regime of truth. They establish through their regularities a 'space of formation' in which certain statements can be enunciated"; Hall, "The Toad in the Garden: Thatcherism among the Theorists," in *Marxism and the Interpretation of Culture*, ed. Cary Nelson and Lawrence Grossberg (Urbana: University of Illinois Press, 1988), 51.

8 Newfield, *Emerson Effect*. Although Scottish writings, like virtually all eighteenth-century American political writings, employ a mixture of liberal and civic humanist vocabularies, for reasons that will become clear I view Scottish writings as an important contribution to American liberalism, principally because they promote a commercial model of subjectivity realized through the unregulated exchange of private property; furthermore, I argue that these writings have helped constitute the structure of liberal political feeling Newfield describes, which alternately asserts and undermines a robust, Lockean conception of political automony. (Because of its commercial coordinates, the Scottish, sentimental construction of civil subjectivity, as I suggest throughout this book, emerged as a fundamentally bourgeois social formation: indeed, the Scottish conflation of civil, "civilized," and commercial subjectivity promoted middle-class hegemony as well as white racial entitlement.) Although the Scots, like civic humanists, were concerned with the collective significance of property ownership and the link between property and virtue, they saw the value of both property and virtue in social, not political terms. Indeed, property was viewed by the Scots not as a means for maintaining independence and a publicly active, self-governing citizenry (as for most civic humanists), or as the means through which autonomous individuals shield themselves

from the potential of collective tyranny (as for Locke), but as a medium of socialization, enabling sympathetic, intersubjective exchanges among often unequally positioned individuals in the social realm. Crucially, as we shall see, in the Scottish narrative, sympathy originates in an essentially feudal relation of paternalism and ownership, and reconfigures that relation as the product of mutual desire and "consent" through sympathetic identification. In fact, the Scottish narrative of the "origin" of society relies on a certain (feudal) construction of sexual difference, of masculine mastery and feminine dependency, as necessary for the production of civil society and its subjects. By associating virtue with femininity, the Scots sever the republican connection between economic autonomy and virtue; indeed, effectively inverting that requirement, the Scots locate the "origin" of civil subjectivity in an identification with feminine dependency. Entrance into civil society for the Scots is thus not the product of rational political will (as in social contract theory) but rather of a formative sentimental identification with feminine dependency; hence, the peculiar construction of "consent" in Scottish writings (what I call "feminine consent"), which is more precisely a taste. Deploying a particular, feudal construction of sexual difference and sexual ownership, the Scottish narrative reinforces feminine subordination and what feminists term the "myth of male protection," while habituating subjects to the forms of submission Newfield describes and undermining the robust conception of autonomy central to the liberal tradition. Still, by construing women, specifically feminine "taste," as the medium of social interpellation, the Scottish narrative keeps alive imaginary fantasies of masculine autonomy and power. For further elaboration of the Scottish deployment of sexual difference, its promotion of interdependent fantasies of masculine autonomy and feminine socialization, see note 23 below. Elaborating the political effects of sentimental narration, this book thus extends, and is indebted to, Gillian Brown's important account of "domestic individualism," the ways in which possessive individualism "[came] to be associated with the feminine sphere of domesticity" in nineteenth-century America (*Domestic Individualism*, 2).

9 Henry Home, Lord Kames, *Sketches of the History of Man* (Edinburgh, 1778), 1: 117. Theorized as a "natural" affection like the moral sense, the sense of property (the "foundation of yours and mine") evidences, for Kames, that "things destined by Providence for our sustenance and accommodation, were not intended to be possessed in common" (1: 117).

10 See John Sekora, *Luxury: The Concept in Western Thought, Eden to Smollett* (Baltimore: Johns Hopkins University Press, 1977).

11 My outline of these traditions is based on Bernard Bailyn, *The Ideological Origins of the American Revolution* (Cambridge: Harvard University Press, 1967); Gordon S. Wood, *The Creation of the American Republic, 1776–1787* (Chapel Hill: University of North Carolina Press, 1969); Pocock, *Machiavellian Moment*; and Drew R. McCoy, *The Elusive Republic: Political Economy in Jeffersonian America* (New York: Norton, 1980). The most recent wave of republican revisionism has resuscitated the importance of Locke and the tradition of natural jurisprudence extending through Adam Smith, which emphasized the virtues of industriousness and frugality; Isaac Kramnick, *Republicanism and Bourgeois Radicalism: Political Ideology in Late Eighteenth-Century England and America* (Ithaca: Cornell University Press, 1990).

12 McCoy, *Elusive Republic*, 76–104, 166–84.

13 Wood, *Creation*, 118.

14 Pocock, *Machiavellian Moment*, 415. Assigning Locke's philosophy of mind a historical

dimension, Scottish Enlightenment writers were principally concerned with how unmediated bodily experience (the state of nature) gave way to the reflective, psychological relations of civilized society, a process they saw structured by the invention of private property. It is precisely because, as Adam Smith tells us, "the eye is larger than the belly" that man advanced from the hand-to-mouth existence of the state of nature (or a subsistence economy) to the civilized social organization of modernity; *The Theory of Moral Sentiments*, introduction by E. G. West (Indianapolis: Liberty Press, 1976), 304. All further references are to this edition. On the influence of Scottish thought in America, see D. H. Meyer, *The Instructed Conscience: The Shaping of the American National Ethic* (Philadelphia: University of Pennsylvania Press, 1972).

15 Phillipson, "Towards a Definition of the Scottish Enlightenment," in *City and Society in the Eighteenth Century*, ed. Paul Fritz and David Williams (Toronto: University of Toronto Press, 1973), 125–47, and Phillipson, "Adam Smith as Civic Moralist," in *Wealth and Virtue: The Shaping of Political Economy in the Scottish Enlightenment*, ed. Istvan Hont and Michael Ignatieff (Cambridge: Cambridge University Press, 1983), 179–202; J. G. A. Pocock, "Cambridge Paradigms and Scotch Philosophers," in *Wealth and Virtue*, ed. Istvan Hont and Michael Ignatieff (Cambridge: Cambridge University Press, 1983), 235–52.

16 On the emergence of the "social" as a category specific to modernity, see Riley, *"Am I That Name?"*

17 Pocock, *Machiavellian Moment*, 440, 441.

18 Peter Hulme, *Colonial Encounters* (New York: Methuen, 1986); William B. Scott, *In Pursuit of Happiness: Conceptions of Property from the Seventeenth to the Twentieth Century* (Bloomington: Indiana University Press, 1977).

19 Roediger, *Wages of Whiteness*; see my discussion of the racialized ideology of the "free market" in the introduction.

20 Robertson, *The History of America* (London, 1777), 1: 309–10; Simms, "Miss Martineau on Slavery," *Southern Literary Messenger* 3 (November 1837): 641–57.

21 Native American women were conventionally depicted as objects of routine abuse and sexual and economic exploitation. Jefferson figures gender relations as a template of cultural advancement: whereas white men's treatment of white women reveals their regard for women's "natural equality," Native American men assert the right of the "stronger sex" to simply "impose on the weaker"; *Notes on the State of Virginia*, ed. William Peden (New York: Norton, 1972), 60.

22 Jean Fagan Yellin, *Women and Sisters: The Antislavery Feminists in American Culture* (New Haven: Yale University Press, 1989). In the United States, I am suggesting, white women and white men's sense of "freedom" within capitalism depended from the outset on the exclusion of racial Others from the labor and consumer markets—indeed, the formation of liberal subjectivity depended on that exclusion. For examples of the pervasive whiteness of advertising imagery, see chapter 6.

23 This fantasy of masculine wholeness, power, and privilege comprises what Kaja Silverman terms the "dominant fiction," an ideologically sustained collective belief in the commensurability of penis and phallus—in other words, in an exemplary masculinity unimpaired by castration (in Lacanian psychoanalytic terms, the subject's subordination to a discursive and social order that preexists it). Deftly elaborating intersections between Marxist (especially Althusser's) theories of ideology and psychoanalytic theories of subject formation, Silverman argues that the dominant fiction or ideological be-

lief in the adequacy of the masculine subject operates "not at the level of consciousness, but rather at that of fantasy and the ego or *moi*, and that it consequently comes into play at the most profound sites of the subject's formation"; *Male Subjectivity at the Margins* (New York: Routledge, 1992), 16. Asserting that "even the earliest and most decisive of the subject's identifications may be ideologically determined," Silverman argues that the dominant fiction is a central part of the *méconnaissance* or self-recognition/misrecognition on which the ego is founded (primary identification in the Lacanian mirror stage) and is sustained by cultural images of unimpaired masculinity; while female subjectivity is the site at which the male subject "deposits" its lack. Further, Silverman observes that "capitalism would . . . seem to 'need' the dominant fiction, or [rather] . . . to constitute one of the important forces sustaining it" (49). I am arguing here that Scottish narratives of sexual difference instantiate the dominant fiction, and a masculine fantasy of unimpaired political will (and feminine castration) that can, as Silverman puts it, "cover over" male lack and political and economic subordination (46). Silverman's analysis suggests that what Newfield terms the "Emerson effect"—an alternation between autonomy and submission central to the affective structures of American liberal masculinity—is sustained by the dominant fiction and its organization of sexual difference, and is an effect of an ambivalent masculine identification with "feminine" castration.

24 In Scottish discourse, sympathy mediates and facilitates market exchanges, (re)configuring these exchanges as "consensual" relations between equals and thus translating relations of power into relations of consent and mutual desire. Positing a connection between capitalism and an expanded humanitarianism (a connection made more recently by the historians John Nef and Thomas Haskell), the Scots contended that capitalism, through its proliferation of market exchanges, is a *socializing* force, enabling the extension and expansion of the social sentiment of sympathetic identification—a formulation that, conversely, delimits the extension of sympathetic subjectivity to those made intelligible through commercial exchange. Sympathy was an especially resonant trope within Scottish constructions of the "free" market precisely because, to paraphrase Mary Louise Pratt, reciprocity has always been capitalism's ideology of itself: "As an ideology, romantic love, like capitalist commerce, understands itself as reciprocal. Reciprocity, love requited between individuals worthy of each other, is its ideal state." This ideal of sympathetic exchange is, as Pratt argues, a mystification: "Only under the fetishized social relations of capitalism does reciprocity disappear altogether, however loudly its presence is trumpeted"; *Imperial Eyes: Travel Writing and Transculturation* (New York: Routledge, 1992), 97, 84. The contradictions within the sentimental formulation of the market are perhaps best evident, as Pratt suggests, in eighteenth-century colonial literature, where the interdeterminations of sympathy and power are clearly displayed. In these texts, the social contract is clearly doubled by the "antisocial contract," in which the idea of "equality among equals" instead signifies an equal opportunity to disappropriate and exploit; Y. N. Kly, *The Anti-Social Contract* (Atlanta: Clarity Press, 1989). For a political critique of sympathy as a white racial response to economic inequality, see Pascal Bruckner, *Tears of the White Man: Compassion as Contempt*, trans. William R. Beer (New York: Free Press, 1986).

25 Butler, *Gender Trouble.*

26 Hume, "Of Refinement in the Arts," in *Essays*, 1: 300; John Millar, *The Origin of the Distinction of Ranks* (London, 1806), 3.

27 Home, Kames, *Sketches*, 1: 219, 2: 144; Millar, *Origin*, 14–46; Albert O. Hirschman, *The Passions and the Interests: Political Arguments for Capitalism before Its Triumph* (Princeton: Princeton University Press, 1977).

28 Contemporary women's historians have charted out historical links between the rise of personal property ("personalty"), women's property rights, and women's greater freedom and flexibility in marriage choices. See the essays by Gloria L. Main, Carole Shammas, and Marylynn Salmon in *Women in the Age of the American Revolution*, ed. Ronald Hoffman and Peter J. Albert (Charlottesville: University of Virginia Press, 1989).

29 Kant, *The Philosophy of Law*, trans. W. Hastie (Edinburgh, 1887), 239.

30 Millar, *Origin*, 101; Home (Kames), *Sketches*, 2: 64; Hume, "Of Polygamy and Divorces," *Essays*, 1: 234.

31 Donna J. Haraway, *Simians, Cyborgs, and Women* (New York: Routledge, 1991), 145–46. The Scots thus describe how, in MacKinnon's words, patriarchy gives men "a stake" in capitalism (*Toward a Feminist Theory*, 67).

32 Adam Ferguson, *An Essay on the History of Civil Society* (London, 1782), 337.

33 Hume, *Essays*, 1: 194.

34 Georg Simmel, *The Philosophy of Money*, 2d ed., trans. Tom Bottomore and David Frisby (New York, 1978), 67. According to William Robertson, the "motives which rouze men to activity in civilized life, and prompt them to persevere in fatiguing exertions of their ingenuity or strength . . . arise chiefly from acquired wants and appetites," wants which are a direct consequence of the natural affections of domestic union and men's desire to win women's favor and affection (*History*, 2: 314). Here, the desire for luxury is the displacement of men's desire for women: well before Freud, these writers offer a narrative of "civilization" as the product of sublimated eroticism.

35 *Georg Simmel: On Women, Sexuality, and Love*, ed. and trans. Guy Oakes (New Haven: Yale University Press, 1984), 134–35.

36 Rousseau's general outline of social transformation—if not his evaluation of it—was closely followed by the Scots. See, especially, his account of the acculturating effects of men's desire for women's esteem—a desire fanned by female modesty and heightened by biological need—in the First and Second Discourses. In the First Discourse, for instance, luxury is seen to corrupt morals and vitiate taste by prostituting male genius to the caprice of a feminine audience. As Rousseau writes in a footnote, "men will always be what women choose to make them"; therefore, women should be educated, their taste cultivated, to desire the finest of men's productions and self-productions; *The Social Contract and Discourses*, trans. G. D. H. Cole (New York: Dutton, 1968), 133. John U. Nef sees a new outlook on violence and cruelty, a "new sense of human responsibility for decent conduct in this world," originating in early modern Europe, which he links to "the discovery of woman" and new standards of elegant and polite living during the period; *Cultural Foundations of Industrial Civilization* (Cambridge: Cambridge University Press, 1958), 65–80, 128–55. See also Norbert Elias on women's role in the civilizing process: *The Civilizing Process*, trans. Edmund Jephcott, 2 vols. (New York: Pantheon, 1982), 1: 184–87. For an incisive critique of how contemporary scholarship on the "alleged feminization of society" is implicated in the rhetoric it purports to analyze, see Lora Romero, *Home Fronts: Domesticity and Its Critics in the Antebellum United States* (Durham: Duke University Press, 1997), 35–51.

37 Amos Chase, *On Female Excellence* (Litchfield, Conn., 1792), 13. All further references are to this edition.

38 Siegfried Giedion, *Mechanization Takes Command: A Contribution to Anonymous History* (New York: Norton, 1948), 313. Identifying a "feminization of rococo furnishings" in eighteenth-century France, Debora Silverman argues that "the rococo interior was inseparable from its female identity" and embodied an "ethos of la grace, a petite, amorous, and explicitly female form," noting that "furniture with anthropomorphic female names multiplied" during the period; *Art Nouveau in Fin-de-Siecle France* (Berkeley: University of California Press, 1989), 27–28.

39 The term "sensibility" had both a narrow medical and a diffuse general meaning during the period. Medically, as defined by Albrecht von Haller in 1762, "sensibility" referred to the reactiveness of sensory nerves. In broader cultural terms, "sensibility" meant, to paraphrase the *OED*, aliveness and receptivity to sensation and emotion, to the sublime and the pathetic. This association of bodily sensibility and emotional sensitivity is central to Lockean sensationalism, informing Hume's conception of "vivacity."

40 Kaplan, "Romancing the Empire: The Embodiment of American Masculinity in the Popular Historical Novel of the 1890s," *American Literary History* 2 (1990): 659–90.

41 For Lovejoy, see *The Great Chain of Being: A Study in the History of an Idea* (Cambridge: Harvard University Press, 1936), 201. Home (Kames), *Sketches*, 1: 410–11, 2: 150. According to many eighteenth-century physiologists, the female body was more delicate and less firm than the male body, its muscular and nervous "fibres" more loosely organized and hence less resistant to disease; and, in a characteristic rhetorical move which imbued physiological with moral categories, this constitutional infirmity was frequently seen to be exacerbated by women's "softer" lifestyles. In the words of the English physician Thomas Sydenham, women are more susceptible to hysteria "because they lead a softer life, and because they are accustomed to the luxuries and commodities of life and not to suffering" (as quoted in Michel Foucault, *Madness and Civilization*, trans. Richard Howard [New York: Vintage, 1973], 149). On eighteenth-century medical views of the degenerative susceptibility of the female body, see Ludmilla Jordanova, *Sexual Visions* (Madison: University of Wisconsin Press, 1989).

42 Scarry, *Body in Pain*, 293; *The Selected Writings of Benjamin Rush*, ed. Dagobert D. Runes (New York, 1947), 197, 259.

43 Robertson, *History*, 1: 305–7; Home (Kames), *Sketches*, 2: 141.

44 Analyzing the "feminization of American culture" in the antebellum period, Ann Douglas narrates this process as the unhappy (and inevitable) outcome of the "rise" of industrial production (*Feminization*). Instead, I contend that the Enlightenment categories discussed above structured transformations of both gender and commerce that were as essential to the spread of capitalism as the rationalization of production.

45 Werner Sombart writes of the "domestication of luxury," its relocation "after the seventeenth century" from the public pageantry and display characteristic of the Middle Ages to its confinement within the domestic sphere, an event that Sombart attributes to the "triumph of women"; *Luxury and Capitalism*, introduction by Philip Siegelman (Ann Arbor: University of Michigan Press, 1967), 95. Elias discusses the bourgeois privatization of an "aristocratic ethos" of courtesy, noting that "forms of sociability, the ornamentation of one's house, visiting etiquette, or the ritual of eating, all are now relegated to the sphere of private life"; *Power and Civility*, trans. Edmund Jephcott (New York: Pantheon, 1982), 306. On the dissemination of aristocratic ideals in late-eighteenth-century Anglo-American conduct material, see Ryan, *Womanhood in America*, 54–61, and Ruth Bloch, "American Feminine Ideals in Transition: The Rise of the Moral Mother, 1785–1815," *Feminist Studies* 4, no. 2 (1978): 101–26. These writers

suggest that aristocratic categories shaped middle-class self-formation even in the absence of a hereditary aristocracy.

46 Douglas Sloan, *The Scottish Enlightenment and the American College Ideal* (New York, 1971).

47 Jean-Christophe Agnew, *Worlds Apart: The Market and the Theater in Anglo-American Thought, 1550–1750* (New York: Cambridge University Press, 1986).

48 Ibid., 152.

49 Bourdieu, *Distinction,* ch. 1.

50 The erotic complexities of Scottish discourse are multiple, and I cannot attend to them fully here. In Smith's *Theory,* the erotics of public sympathy, produced through sympathetic exchange, are largely articulated through class differences and animate economic competition and emulation: in the passages discussed in the previous section, it is precisely the social distances of class distinctions that produce and regulate (homoerotic) desire. It would appear that property here, too, serves a regulatory function: it enables the splitting of identification from desire, of being from having, central to discourses of identification. (On the instability of this dichotomy in psychoanalysis, see Diana Fuss, *Identification Papers* [New York: Routledge, 1995].) However, this distinction is unstable: although the spectator is meant to identify with the property owner and desire his property, the sympathetic inscription of property objects as metonyms of subjective desire blurs that distinction. As I suggest in the introduction, in America, the feminization of taste, a discursive project completed by the 1830s, stabilized the distinction between "public" and "private" sympathies and regulated the homoerotics of taste and sentimental identification.

51 de Lauretis, *Alice Doesn't: Feminism, Semiotics, Cinema* (Bloomington: Indiana University Press, 1984), 137.

52 In the *Theory,* biological and social reproduction are assimilated to one another: "The family character [the similarity of familial disposition] which we so frequently see transmitted through several successive generations . . . like the family countenance, seems to be owing not altogether to the moral but partly too to the physical connection" (367).

53 Home (Kames), *Sketches,* 1: 320.

54 *Georg Simmel,* 134, 136–37, 147–48.

55 John Stuart Mill, "The Subjection of Women," in *Essays on Sex Equality,* ed. A. S. Rossi (Chicago: University of Chicago Press, 1970), 141.

56 Pateman, *Sexual Contract,* 33.

57 Mary P. Ryan, "Femininity and Capitalism in Antebellum America," in *Capitalist Patriarchy and the Case for Socialist Feminism,* ed. Zillah R. Eisenstein (New York: Monthly Review, 1979), 151–68; Brodhead, "Sparing the Rod."

58 Grossberg, *Governing the Hearth: Law and Family in Nineteenth-Century America* (Chapel Hill: University of North Carolina Press, 1985), 31ff.

59 Pateman, *Sexual Contract,* 18; Grossberg, *Governing the Hearth,* 34.

60 Kant, *Philosophy,* 239.

61 Samuel Richardson, *Clarissa* (New York: Penguin, 1985), 720, 77.

62 Jay Fliegelman, *Prodigals and Pilgrims: The American Revolution against Patriarchal Authority, 1750–1800* (New York: Cambridge University Press, 1982).

63 "On the Happy Influence of the Female Sex in Society and the Absurd Practice of Separating the Sexes Immediately after Dinner," *Universal Asylum* (Philadelphia) (March 1791), 153; Mitchell, *Address to the Fredes* (New York, 1804), 7.

64 Lewis, "Republican Wife," 701.

65 Enos Hitchcock, *Memoirs of the Bloomsgrove Family* (Boston, 1790), 1: 47–48. All further references are to this edition, identified as *Memoirs*.

66 Hemlow, "Fanny Burney and the Courtesy Books," *PMLA* 65 (1950): 732; Armstrong, *Desire*, 61.

67 Armstrong, *Desire*, 61–62, 71, 68.

68 Klein, "The Third Earl of Shaftesbury and the Progress of Politeness," *Eighteenth-Century Studies* 18, no. 2 (1984–85): 197.

69 Lewis, "Republican Wife."

70 *Advice to the Fair Sex; in a Series of Letters, Chiefly Concerning the Graceful Virtues* (Philadelphia, 1803), 17. All further references are to this edition, identified as *Advice*.

71 Foster, *The Boarding School; or, Lessons of a Preceptress to Her Pupils* (Boston, 1829), 23. All further references are to this edition. Chase, *Female Excellence*, 19.

72 Goffman, *The Presentation of Self in Everyday Life* (Garden City, N.Y.: Doubleday, 1959).

73 [For William Robertson, dress and reserve constituted parallel "arts of female allurement" (*History*, 1: 295).] The author's censure of Maria's architectural confusions reflects contemporary developments in household taste. In the seventeenth-century hall-and-parlor plan, the parlor served as the sleeping quarters of the head of the household, and usually held the most expensive bed and occasionally the head-of-household's wearing apparel; during the course of the eighteenth century, beds were gradually moved into chambers used exclusively for sleeping. Clifford E. Clark Jr., *The American Family Home, 1800–1960* (Chapel Hill: University of North Carolina Press, 1986), 12–15.

74 This tension, between antiformalism and the codification of social norms—or pietism and behaviorism—was the defining tension of Puritan social discourse. On this subject, see Breitwieser, *American Puritanism*.

75 David Marshall, *The Surprising Effects of Sympathy* (Chicago: University of Chicago Press, 1988); Agnew, *Worlds Apart*.

76 "Reflections on Courtship and Marriage," in *A Series of Letters on Courtship and Marriage* (Hudson, N.Y., 1804), 42. All further references are to this edition.

77 John Ogden, *The Female Guide* (Concord, N.H., 1793), 40.

78 J. Hector St. John de Crèvecoeur, *Letters from an American Farmer*, ed. Albert E. Stone (New York: Penguin, 1981), 46–47. Further references (in the conclusion, below) are to this edition.

79 Rush, *Selected Writings*, 221–22.

80 Chase, *Female Excellence*, 7; George Strebeck, *A Sermon on the Character of the Virtuous Woman* (New York, 1800), 9. All further references are to this edition.

81 Joyce O. Appleby, *Economic Thought and Ideology in Seventeenth Century England* (Princeton: Princeton University Press, 1978), 186.

82 Hyde, *The Gift: Imagination and the Erotic Life of Property* (New York: Norton, 1979), 34, 103.

83 In Enlightenment social discourse, the mother-child bond is consistently depicted as a site of "natural sociability" and the naturalized transmission of culture.

84 Strebeck, *Sermon*, 22, 14.

85 Hannah More, *Strictures on the Modern System of Female Education* (London, 1799), 1: 102; Strebeck, *Sermon*, 22, 14, 16.

86 Ellen K. Rothman, *Hands and Hearts: A History of Courtship in America* (Cambridge: Harvard University Press, 1987), 41.

87 Lydia Maria Child, *Letters from New York* (New York, 1845), 96.

88 Hannah Foster, *The Coquette*, ed. Cathy Davidson (New York: Oxford University Press,

1986), 107. All further references are to this edition. Carolyn Lougee, *Le Paradis des Femmes: Women, Salons, and Social Stratification in Seventeenth-Century France* (Princeton: Princeton University Press, 1976).

89 As Ruth Bloch summarizes this process: "If virtue was regarded as outside politics, what better way to conceive of it than as feminine? In an increasingly competitive male political system, the distinction faded between virtuous men committed to public service and unvirtuous men pursuing narrow self-interest. The new distinction between feminine virtue and masculine self-interest eased the process by which all white men (whether rich or poor, individually 'virtuous' or not) could become political actors and all women could not" ("Gendered Meanings," 57–58).

90 Lougee, *Paradis*, 31.

91 Hume, *A Treatise of Human Nature*, ed. P. H. Nidditch and L. A. Selby-Bigge (Oxford: Clarendon, 1978), 587, 602–3, 605. In the *Treatise*, politics are only invented because of a natural scarcity of sympathy (488–90).

92 Arendt, *The Human Condition* (Chicago: University of Chicago Press, 1978).

93 Cherniavsky, "Charlotte Temple's Remains," in *Discovering Difference*, ed. Christopher K. Lohman (Bloomington: Indiana University Press, 1993), 35–47.

94 On writing as the constitutive sign of "modern" subjectivity, see Armstrong, *Desire*.

95 Davidson, Introduction, *The Coquette*, xiv; Davidson, *Revolution and the Word: The Rise of the Novel in America* (New York: Oxford University Press, 1986). I am indebted to Davidson's fine readings of *The Coquette* as well as her historical contextualization of it. There are, however, important differences in our readings: I argue that the text exposes the mystifications of feminine "choice" as constitutive of freedom rather than reinscribes an ideology of choice; and I see the text as less concerned with critiquing coverture (the legal negation of married women's identity) than with exploring contradictions in republican forms of feminine civil subjectivity.

96 Spillers, "Mama's Baby, Papa's Maybe," 73.

97 Davidson, *Revolution*, 148.

98 Ronald L. Meek, *Social Science and the Ignoble Savage* (New York: Cambridge University Press, 1976).

99 On feminine loss (specifically, the loss of the mother) as feminine developmental imperative under patriarchy, and melancholia as constitutive of feminine subjectivity, see Butler, *Gender Trouble*.

100 Davidson points out that Eliza delivers "one of the earliest fictional critiques of the 'cult of domesticity' " (*Revolution*, 144). Notably, Sanford plays on this theme of domestic confinement to advantage (e.g., 36).

101 Davidson, *Revolution*, 146–47.

102 Ibid., 141–49.

2 *Gender, Domesticity, and Consumption in the 1830s*

1 Cartwright, *Autobiography*, ed. W. P. Strickland (New York, 1856), 251–52. All further references are to this edition.

2 See, for instance, Kenneth L. Ames, "Material Culture as NonVerbal Communication: A Historical Case Study," *Journal of American Culture* 3, no. 4 (1980): 628; Weber, *The Protestant Ethic and the Spirit of Capitalism*, trans. Talcott Parsons (New York, 1900), 51.

3 Lears, "Salvation," 4. In a more recent essay, Lears revises his earlier argument to account for the antebellum period's burgeoning consumerism, acknowledging that

"preliminary evidence suggests that it may be a mistake to argue a shift from the plodding nineteenth century to the carnivalesque twentieth: the carnival may have been in town all the time"; "Beyond Veblen: Rethinking Consumer Culture in America," in *Consuming Visions: Accumulation and Display of Goods in America, 1880–1920*, ed. Simon J. Bronner (New York: Norton, 1989), 77.

4 For "pious consumption" see note 42 to my introduction, above.

5 Giedion, *Mechanization*, 395.

6 Elizabeth Stuart Phelps, *The Gates Ajar* (Boston, 1869), 183–84.

7 See Horowitz, *Morality*, xxv (as discussed in my introduction); also Martin, *Standard*, and Blumin, *Emergence*, 138–91.

8 Douglas, *Feminization*.

9 The significance of art in Anglo-American Protestant religious experience has not been carefully studied, perhaps the legacy of simplistic notions of Protestant asceticism and iconoclasm. For an insightful discussion of Puritanism's "iconoclastic materialism," and the importance of "material shapes" in English and American Puritanism, focusing on the writings of John Cotton, see Kibbey, *Interpretation*. Jonathan Edwards is a crucial figure in the history of Protestant conceptions of the aesthetic, and played a central role in Protestant theology's complex negotiations with neoclassical aesthetic theories such as those of Shaftesbury and Francis Hutcheson. Crucially, eighteenth- and early-nineteenth-century pietistic Protestantism, and its secular counterpart sentimentalism, oversaw an apparent expansion in the array of material shapes—including luxurious artifacts, art, theater, and "civilized" bodily manners; social forms, especially sympathetic, loving human relations (e.g., romantic love, motherhood); and "living images" such as Native Americans, African Americans, women, children, madmen, criminals, and pets—deemed sanctified vessels of spirit.

10 Neil Harris discusses this revaluation of luxury and art and the growing consensus among American Protestants that "art objects were powerful means of bringing men to God"; *The Artist in American Society: The Formative Years, 1790–1860* (Chicago: University of Chicago Press, 1966), 134.

11 Webster, "Lecture before the Society for the Diffusion of Useful Knowledge," in *Writings and Speeches of Daniel Webster* (Boston, 1903), 13: 74. On Webster's vision of the productive interrelationship between democracy and consumption, see Horowitz, *Morality*, 8. Jonathan A. Glickstein discusses the Whig consumer ethic and antebellum arguments for increased leisure and higher wages based on the view that increased consumption would stimulate economic progress, in *Concepts of Free Labor in Antebellum America* (New Haven: Yale University Press, 1991), 272, 449, 466, 474.

12 Douglas, *Feminization*, 80–117.

13 James Deetz, *In Small Things Forgotten* (Garden City, N.Y.: Anchor, 1977), 120–25.

14 Colleen McDannell, *The Christian Home in Victorian America, 1840–1900* (Bloomington: Indiana University Press, 1986), 20–51; Handy, *Christian America*.

15 Gervase Wheeler, *Rural Homes* (New York, 1852), 276.

16 Specifically, this construction detaches class from (or at least qualifies its connection to) the realm of production. In addition, by establishing feminine civil subjectivity as both originary and politically salient, these texts reinforce a liberal, proprietary definition of political agency and "freedom" (defining "freedom" as proprietary authority) that could be used to discredit other ideas of public life and agency. Last, this domestic construction of class suggests the cultural import of domestic fictions in mobilizing forms of class identification. This definition of class is replicated in the work of feminist

historians, who emphasize the role of domesticity and domestic "culture" in (middle-) class formation (e.g., Ryan); in an important sense this work describes, rather than analyzes or historicizes, a newly hegemonic formation of class.

17 Lott, *Love and Theft.*

18 Caroline M. Kirkland, *A New Home, Who'll Follow? or, Glimpses of Western Life*, ed. Sandra A. Zagarell (New Brunswick: Rutgers University Press, 1990), 183, 32. All further references are to this edition.

19 In her study of the idea of the frontier in feminine literature, Annette Kolodny argues that "women [typically] claimed the frontier as a potential sanctuary for an idealized domesticity." According to Kolodny, men's dreams of possessing and exploiting a "virgin" continent "do not seem to have been part of women's fantasies. They dreamed, more modestly, of locating a home and a familial human community within a cultivated garden." Kolodny describes Kirkland as a key figure in the feminine reconstruction of the frontier, and discusses at length *A New Home*'s self-reflexive questioning of the conventions of male frontier writings and Kirkland's efforts to clear the literary ground for a distinctly feminine frontier narrative. According to Kolodny, "The most immediate impact of Kirkland's success was . . . that it made the west available for literary treatment by women." But in embracing the feminine ethos of cultivation and refinement as "saving and even liberating," Kolodny largely overlooks its restrictive, class-bound content and dependence on stereotypes of feminine gentility; more seriously, she fails to recognize how fully that ethos is implicated in the spread of capitalist enterprise she assails; *The Land before Her: Fantasy and Experience of the American Frontiers, 1630–1860* (Chapel Hill: University of North Carolina Press, 1984), xiii, 131–58.

20 See Slotkin: *Regeneration* and *The Fatal Environment: The Myth of the Frontier in the Age of Industrialization, 1800–1890* (Middletown: Wesleyan University Press, 1985).

21 Sigourney, *Letters to Mothers* (Hartford, Conn., 1838), 163.

22 Warhol, "Toward a Theory," 811–18.

23 Leverenz, *Manhood and the American Renaissance* (Ithaca: Cornell University Press, 1988), 151–64.

24 Steven Mintz, *A Prison of Expectations* (New York, 1983), 21–39; Kirkland, "Mrs. Kirkland's 'Essay on Fiction,'" *Bulletin of the New York Public Library* 64, no. 7 (1960): 397. As suggested in chapter 1, literary identification is viewed as a socializing, "civilizing" force precisely because textual objects of identification instantiate the "feminine" property relation essential to liberal subjection's interdeterminations of agency and subordination: enabling a fantasy of autonomy ("power over") that is also an identification with the dependent object of sympathetic possession.

25 Hulme, *Colonial Encounters*, 3.

26 Kirkland, preface to Eastman's *Dahcotah; or, Life and Legends of the Sioux* (New York, 1849), vi, vii. Eastman collected the Dakotah legends while living at Fort Snelling in the 1840s, where her husband was stationed as a soldier for seven years. Lucy Maddox analyzes Kirkland's preface as an expression of antebellum literary nationalism: *Removals: Nineteenth-Century American Literature and the Politics of Indian Affairs* (New York: Oxford University Press, 1991), 40–41. What Kirkland represents as the inevitable passing of the Indians and their inassimilability into white civilization — in the words of Francis Parkman, their "immutability" and "fixed and rigid" quality — was a commonplace of late-eighteenth- and early-nineteenth-century Anglo-American historiography and literature. Antebellum representations of Indian objectification and "stasis" ex-

emplify what Pratt calls the ethnographic "present tense," a rhetorical device which works, in this instance, to situate Indians in a "timeless present," thus fixing them in a temporal order distinct from the "progressive" historicity of the Anglo-Americans (*Imperial Eyes*, 64).

27 On the complex correlations between the sentimental memorialization of Native Americans in American literature and white Americans' fascination with Indian life, and Jacksonian policies that were violently forcing Native Americans' disappearance, see Maddox, *Removals*, and Fisher, *Hard Facts*, 22–86.

28 Smith, *Lectures on Justice, Police, Revenue, and Arms*, ed. Edwin Cannan (Oxford, 1896), 159–60.

29 Richard D. Brown, "Modernization and the Modern Personality in Early America, 1600–1865: A Sketch of a Synthesis," *Journal of Interdisciplinary History* 2 (1972): 201–28.

30 Adrian Forty, *Objects of Desire* (London: Thames and Hudson, 1986), 67–72.

31 Laqueur, "Orgasm"; Ruth Bloch, "Untangling the Roots of Modern Sex Roles: A Survey of Four Centuries of Change," *Signs* 4, no. 2 (1978): 237–52.

32 Christine Stansell, *City of Women*, ch. 10.

33 Harris, *Artist*. On the period's ornate "ruling style," see Giedion, *Mechanization*. Notably, most material culture historians who discuss the period's ornamental style offer a narrowly economic explanation for this phenomenon; both Giedion and Forty, for instance, attribute the profusion of ornament to technological advances that facilitated its cheap production. As I have suggested, however, ornament—and display pieces like the bibelot—were afforded widespread cultural legitimacy precisely because they satisfied new desires for "pious consumption" and spiritual materialism: signifying the superfluous and the (physically) useless, and they constitute material forms that minister to subjective (e.g., moral, aesthetic) wants.

34 Kirkland, "Comfort," in *A Book for the Home Circle* (New York, 1853), 198.

35 Norton discusses the predominance of images of eating and cannibalism in antebellum representations of the frontier, and notes that frontier life, as depicted in numerous legends, was "one long meal" (*Alternative Americas*, ch. 7).

36 Horace Bushnell, *Christian Nurture*, introduction by Luther A. Weigle (New Haven: Yale University Press, 1916), 12, 17.

37 Kenneth Cmiel, *Democratic Eloquence: The Fight over Popular Speech in Nineteenth-Century America* (Berkeley: University of California Press, 1990), 61–62.

38 Bailey, *The Family Preacher* (New York, 1837), 43.

39 Downing, *Cottage Residences*, 77–78.

40 William Ellery Channing, *Conversations in Rome* (Boston, 1847), 93.

41 Foucault has argued that bourgeois hegemony has been characterized by an "intensification of the body," an increased concern with bodily enjoyment and bodily health: "The bourgeoisie underscored the high political price of its body, sensations, and pleasures, its well-being and survival" (*History of Sexuality*, 1: 123, 49). While contemporary scholars have made ample use of Foucault's claims about the "political ordering" of the *sexual* body in nineteenth-century discourses, surprisingly little work has developed his idea of "biopower" in terms of *other* aspects of bodily life, *other* forms of bodily "sensations and pleasures" during the period—a fact which, ironically, bears out Foucault's point about our very obsession with sex. The nineteenth century oversaw the proliferation of cheap consumer goods for home and personal enjoyment, and held forth to an increased number of individuals new species of bodily enjoyment and

pleasure. But the century also witnessed the proliferation of printed materials—such as home decorating, architectural and etiquette manuals, cookbooks, and advertisements—which specified proper uses for these objects, and saturated their use with social value. By the end of the century, market research came into its own—a sociology of consumption practices which, particularly in its elaboration of consumer "types" and "identities," constitutes a discourse that strikingly resembles sexual science. These texts illuminate not so much the *suppression* of consumption by a culture committed to productivist asceticism as the *rationalization* of consumption practices, the "proliferation of specific pleasures" in accord with specific cultural imperatives. Foucault's work offers a provocative theoretical frame for considering consumerism's socialization of bodily pleasures during the last two centuries.

42 John Kasson, *Rudeness and Civility: Manners in Nineteenth-Century Urban America* (New York: Hill and Wang, 1990), 59.

43 Cf. Kirkland's contemporary, Eliza Farrar, on the categorical distinctions in conventions of borrowing, according to which certain objects qualify as lendable and certain others—in particular, one's most intimate belongings—are exempt from exchange; *The Young Lady's Friend*, ed. Leon Stein and Annette K. Baxter (1836; reprint, New York: Arno, 1974), 136–37. Elsewhere in *A New Home*, Kirkland suggests that one's personal property, laden with emotional significance, must be protected from the public gaze, and that exposure entails a violation and depreciation of objects (e.g., 124).

44 David Leverenz identifies a "relative prominence of gender consciousness over class consciousness in American self-perceptions," and argues that gender ideologies "refract" class tensions (*Manhood*, 88–89).

45 Antebellum aestheticians often noted how business, by fixing one's attention on the cash value of objects, restricts aesthetic associations and pleasure; in Kirkland's text, men are insensible to the pleasures of "reverie" and the "rare and delicate beauty" of wildflowers (they are often distracted, intent on moving forward) (5), and are unmindful of the pleasures of "hostess-ship" which women cultivate, viewing each newcomer "merely as an additional business-automaton" (64).

46 Kasson, *Rudeness and Civility*, 124–25.

47 The literature on antebellum "separate spheres" ideology is extensive. See Romero, *Home Fronts*.

48 Kirkland's narrative suggests an interpretation of the nineteenth-century beautification movements as constituting a gendered struggle over the definition and control of social spaces.

49 Pocock, *Machiavellian Moment*, 462–505.

50 Recycling Kirkland's own categories, Kolodny notes that "male migration patterns" on the frontier involved rapid mobility and traveling light as well as a commitment to converting the wilderness into "portable wealth," and she argues that if "women's fantasies [had] been in control," settlers would have transformed the wilderness not into capital but into a "sanctuary of domestic happiness" (*Land before Her*, 11). Substantiating Kirkland's characterization of men's economic behavior, Slotkin notes that "after 1800 . . . there seemed to be a clear tendency for a man who had 'gone west' once to be the first to pick up and go again, when the opportunity offered, even if his original acquisition was a prosperous one." This tendency, Slotkin argues, fostered a "universal nomadism" of white men on the frontier, in which "no acquisition is anything more than a coign of vantage for surveying future fields" (*Fatal Environment*, 127).

51 Poe, "The Literati of New York," *Essays and Reviews* (New York, 1984), 1180.

52 Judith Fetterley, introduction to *Provisions: A Reader from Nineteenth-Century American Women*, ed. Fetterley (Bloomington: Indiana University Press, 1985). As Fetterley notes, a favorite "theory" of American literary history—that romance gave way to realism as the dominant genre after the Civil War—requires revision once the work of nineteenth-century women is "admitted to the category of American literature" (10).

53 Sandra A. Zagarell, introduction to *A New Home*, by Caroline Kirkland (New Brunswick: Rutgers University Press, 1990), xxviii.

54 [Caroline M. Kirkland], "Novels and Novelists," *North American Review* 76 (1853): 104–23.

55 Arendt, *Human Condition*, 52.

56 Shorter, *The Making of the Modern Family* (New York: Basic, 1975), 255; Alan Macfarlane, *The Culture of Capitalism* (Oxford: Basil Blackwell, 1987), 123–43.

57 According to Scottish writers, the psychological condition of "savagery" is principally characterized by an insensibility to aesthetic and ethical value, what William Robertson called "the charms of beauty and the power of love": for the "savage" possessed by bodily need, *any* woman, food, or covering will do. The psychic impoverishment of the "savage"—his lack of foresight as well as emotional blankness—is concisely illustrated by the following example from Robertson's popular *History of America*: the savage trades his hammock in the morning for "the slightest toy that catches his fancy," only to find himself bereft of bedding when "on the approach of the evening, [he] . . . feels himself disposed to go to rest" (1: 292). "Savages," Robertson insists, betray their attenuated subjectivities by their inability to make rational predictions; even more shockingly, they lack "taste"—they don't know how to treasure and appreciate things, to establish long-standing relations with things that are continually deepened and developed. In the United States, such concepts could serve to justify what contemporaries called "Indian removal"—Native Americans' dispossession of their lands and geographical displacement, enforced by U.S. policies—at the same moment that the sentimental cult of the home and its affectional attachments was being widely promoted as characteristic of middle-class whites. On the racist political uses of the concept of private property as a tool of expropriation in the formulation of U.S. Indian policy, see Ronald T. Takaki, *Iron Cages: Race and Culture in Nineteenth-Century America* (Seattle: University of Washington Press, 1979).

58 Sara Ruddick, *Maternal Thinking: Toward a Politics of Peace* (Boston: Beacon, 1989). As suggested in chapter 1, the sentimental model reconfigures Puritan ideals of emotional constancy in semisecular, social terms.

59 Scarry universalizes this model of sentimental animism in *Body in Pain* (278–326). Cf. Peter Conrad on the "strange animism" of Victorian novelists; *Victorian Treasure House* (London: Collins, 1973), 76–77.

60 Butler, *Gender Trouble*.

61 Mintz, *Prison*, 23–24; for Beecher, see Daniel Walker Howe, *The Unitarian Conscience* (Cambridge: Harvard University Press, 1970), 83, 56–64.

62 In an early novel, Sedgwick articulates what she calls the "truth of philosophy," that "the senses are the most direct avenues to the heart"; *Clarence; or, A Tale of Our Own Times*, 2 vols. (Philadelphia, 1830), 1: 35.

63 Helper, *The Impending Crisis of the South: How to Meet It* (New York, 1857), 8.

64 Armstrong, *Desire*, 16.

65 Mintz, *Prison*, 45; Mary Kelley, *Private Woman, Public Stage: Literary Domesticity in Nineteenth-Century America* (New York: Oxford University Press, 1984), 14.

66 Michie, *The Flesh Made Word: Female Figures and Women's Bodies* (New York: Oxford University Press, 1987), 64–65.

67 Sedgwick, *Home* (Boston, 1835), 10. All further references are to this edition. Nina Baym, *Novels, Readers, and Reviewers: Responses to Fiction in Antebellum America* (Ithaca: Cornell University Press, 1984), 49. For a compelling account of fictional characters as a species of common property and thus objects of universal identification, focusing on interrelations of gender, property, and literature in eighteenth-century England, see Catherine Gallagher, *Nobody's Story: The Vanishing Acts of Women Writers in the Marketplace, 1670–1820* (Berkeley: University of California Press, 1994).

68 Harris, *Artist*, 186; Wheeler, *Rural Homes*, 277.

69 Katherine C. Grier, *Culture and Comfort: People, Parlors, and Upholstery, 1850–1930* (Amherst: University of Massachusetts Press, 1988), 120.

70 Weber, *Protestant Ethic*, 171, 276–77, nn. 79, 80, 81, 82; Joseph Haroutunian, *Piety Versus Moralism: The Passing of New England Theology* (New York: H. Holt, 1932).

71 As quoted in Grier, *Culture and Comfort*, 128.

72 This sentimental identification between the material and the affectional is apparent in the lexicography of the term "comfort": according to the *OED*, the use of the word "comfort" (in both noun and verb forms) to designate a physical state of well-being is "apparently only of modern use" and dates back only to the eighteenth and early nineteenth centuries. Previously, the term had principally applied to spiritual strengthening, heartening, and succor.

73 Giedion, *Mechanization*, 133.

74 Harris, *Artist*, 195.

75 Ryan, "Femininity and Capitalism," 151–68.

76 Bailey, *The Family Preacher*, 43.

77 The back of the card reads, "This illustration by Mary Engelbreit, who thanks you from the bottom of her heart for buying this card."

78 Sedgwick, *Live and Let Live; or, Domestic Service Illustrated* (New York, 1837), 45, 201.

79 The sentimental revision of Cartesian rationalism that expressly shaped the emergence of pet-keeping is central to the cultural revaluation of affect analyzed throughout this book. Against Descartes, numerous eighteenth-century philosophers contended that animals are not "machines"—wholly body and therefore subject to the laws of physics and mechanics—but rather that they have feelings and therefore require tenderness. On the Enlightenment origin of modern ideas about kindness and cruelty to animals, see Keith Thomas, *Man and the Natural World* (New York, 1983), 143–50, and Marc Shell, "The Family Pet," *Representations* 15 (summer 1986): 121–53. On the sentimental rehabilitation of the female body, see the introduction above and chapter 3 below.

80 As defined in the *OED*, pets are "the animal or nonhuman beings that cannot, or should not, be eaten." On the Protestant sanctions against pet-eating, and the tendency among Romantic and Victorian Christians to treat as identical pet-eating and cannibalism, see Shell, "The Family Pet," 135.

81 On the erotics of "cuteness"—a new aesthetic category in the nineteenth century—and sentimental proprietary relation it instantiates, see Lori Merish, "Cuteness and the Aesthetics of Modern Ownership," in *Freakmaking: Constituting Cultural and Corporeal Others*, ed. Rosemarie Garland Thompson (New York: New York University Press, 1996). The liberal inscription of "civilizing" heterosociality illuminates what critics have identified as the "incestuous" nature of sentimental eroticism, as well as the emphasis on brother-sister relations in sentimental fiction.

82 Blumin, in his analysis of the construction and symbolic import of middle-class identity, insists on a distinction between intellectual and manual labor as crucial (*Emergence*); Faye E. Dudden, in *Serving Women: Household Service in Nineteenth-Century America* (Middletown: Wesleyan University Press, 1983), sees a similar class division of labor within the middle-class household, between the middle-class domestic manager and the servants who execute the tasks she devises. But the distinction is not only (or primarily) one between intellectual and manual labor: it is rather one between different kinds of manual work, differences which turn on distinctions in the state of the body and the "refinement" of physical production and consumption. The middle-class heroine of much women's fiction—who, as Nina Baym has suggested (*Woman's Fiction*), must become economically self-sufficient before acceding to adulthood—supports herself chiefly by performing particular kinds of labor: giving piano lessons, selling embroidery or needlework, making household decorations, cultivating and arranging flowers. (Notably, the products of such ornamental labors most commonly figure as gifts during the period.) Numerous domestic manuals envision a similar division of labor structuring domestic cookery: servants prepare the substantial dishes—cooking the roast, stewing or boiling the vegetables—while the domestic woman turns her hand to dainties, sweets, condiments and preserves, culinary embellishments rather than the body of the meal. The crucial symbolic distinction would seem to reside in the wants the labor ministers to: in the characteristic language of the period, aesthetic or social vs. bodily wants. Such texts foreground the importance of "taste" in identificatory processes of class formation and in securing the hegemony of the middle class.

83 Cf. Washington Irving's sketch "Rural Funerals," on the grave as "the ordeal of true affection" through which love is "purified from every sensual desire"; *The Sketch-Book of Geoffrey Crayon, Gent.* (New York, 1897), 116.

84 Kasson describes the various "rituals of refinement"—all the "little gestures of bodily adjustment" and social consideration—surrounding genteel dining during the nineteenth century, such as avoiding commenting on the food (such remarks, one writer warned, would be too naked an expression of "animal and sensual gratification" over the "intellect . . . and . . . moral nature"), minimizing one's own appetites and touching the food as little as possible (*Rudeness and Civility*, 207–14). Kasson recounts Sedgwick's delighted account of her introduction in 1839 while traveling in Frankfurt to the new fashion of service *à la Russe*—a fashion that replaced the older home-style service in which guests arrived at table already laden with dishes and to which they helped themselves—as entailing the harmonious sequence of food rather than a promiscuous abundance, and a first arrival to table decorated with "fruits and flowers, instead of being stupefied with the fumes of meat" (*Rudeness and Civility*, 206).

85 A memorable example appears in Sedgwick's first novel, *A New-England Tale* (New York, 1822). The novel opens with "flourishing trader" Mr. Elton's bankruptcy—in Sedgwick's words, "he adventured rashly in one speculation after another, and failing in them all, his losses were more rapid than his acquisitions had been" (18)—and subsequent death; his wife, left destitute with her twelve-year-old daughter, heroine Jane Elton, dies shortly after her husband. Jane, now orphaned, is powerless and bereft, and the full sense of her losses is driven home in Sedgwick's depiction of the inevitable estate sale: "When every thing was in readiness, and the moment of departure arrived, [Jane] shrunk back from [her servant] Mary's offered arm, and sinking into a chair, yielded involuntarily to the torrent of her feelings. She looked around upon the room

and its furniture as if they were her friends. It has been said . . . that objects which are silent every where else, have a voice in the home of our childhood. Jane looked for the last time at the bed, where she had often sported about her mother, and rejoiced in her tender caresses— . . . at the footstool on which she had sat beside her mother; and the old family clock. . . . 'Oh, Mary!' said she, 'even my honey-suckle seems to weep for me' " (36–37). Finally, Jane, in a moment of forced and painful detachment from these early objects of love, "without allowing herself time to look again at any thing, hastily passed through the little courtyard in front of their house" (38).

86 On the persistence of such couplings—those between passive, virtuous heroines and hard, sometimes sadistic phallic males—in contemporary romances, see Tania Modleski, *Loving with a Vengeance: Mass-Produced Fantasies for Women* (New York: Routledge, 1988).

87 Ralph Thompson, *American Literary Annuals and Gift Books, 1825–1865* (New York, 1936), 7. Most antebellum conduct books included a chapter on the etiquette of gift selection and exchange. For an extended discussion of gifts as embodiments of sentimental value, and for the claim that gifts are a form of " 'female' property," see Hyde, *Gift*.

88 Cott, *The Bonds of Womanhood: "Woman's Sphere" in New England, 1780–1835* (New Haven: Yale University Press, 1977), 135.

3 Sentimental Consumption

1 Stowe, *The Minister's Wooing* (1859; rpt. New York: AMS, 1967), 264, 14. All further references are to this edition.

2 Stowe, *Agnes of Sorrento* (1862; rpt. Boston: Houghton Mifflin, 1896), 112.

3 Nathalia Wright, *American Novelists in Italy* (Philadelphia: University of Pennsylvania Press, 1965), 119.

4 Harris, *Artist*, 134.

5 Lears, "Salvation."

6 Gillian Brown describes Stowe's sentimental domestic economy as "anticonsumerist" because of Stowe's antipathy toward the "new" as destructive of domestic sentiment and her emphasis on the "self-sufficiency of home" (*Domestic Individualism*, 45–47, 52). Indeed, sentimental texts such as Stowe's rarely include incidents of women shopping: the most popular antebellum women's text to depict such a scene, Susan Warner's *The Wide, Wide World*, anxiously attempts to rescript that event within a female gift economy. However, although these texts decommoditize domestic property by inscribing it within sentimental bonds (thus translating, into affectional and moral terms, the republican equation of stable ownership and virtuous personality), this structure, instead of indicating an antipathy toward consumption, works to naturalize feminine taste: in sentimental texts, sentimentally engaging domestic objects are "always already" around. While Stowe's texts don't exhibit the fetishization of novelty characteristic of contemporary mass culture, they do encode a logic of identification and feminine taste central to consumerism's affective economy.

7 Wheeler, *Rural Homes*, 133.

8 Cf. note 47 to my Introduction, above.

9 On proslavery writers' attack on liberal models of economic and domestic freedom, see Stanley, "Home life," 74–96.

10 Warner, *The Wide, Wide World*, ed. Jane Tompkins (New York: Feminist Press, 1987), 9. All further references are to this edition.

11 Cummins, *The Lamplighter*, ed. Nina Baym (New Brunswick: Rutgers University Press, 1988), 128, 45–46. All further references are to this edition.

12 Architectural pattern books from the period represent the "house beautiful" as the essential basis of an emotionally gratifying domesticity, and offer advice on how to increase the home's seductive charms. According to Wheeler's *Rural Homes*, a manual about building and decorating rural homes "with truest refinement of taste" (preface), the creation of such an environment would be managed chiefly by the social (and literary) inculcation of increased demand for "articles of improved taste," and Wheeler supplies his readers with names and addresses of establishments from which the necessary articles of furniture and architectural embellishments and fittings could be acquired. On antebellum architectural pattern books as consumer manuals, see Dell Upton, "The Traditional House and Its Enemies," *Traditional Dwellings and Settlements Review* 1, no. 2 (spring 1990): 71–84.

13 Baym, *Woman's Fiction*, esp. 22–50.

14 Stansell, *City of Women*, 41, 193–216.

15 Several critics and historians have noted what Peter Conrad calls the "strange animism" of depictions of familiar objects in Victorian novels and stories. None, however, adequately accounts for this phenomenon; Conrad, for example, surmising that such depictions serve as a means of charming "potentially aggressive, painful things into acquiescence and friendship" and therefore "enlisting them as protectors," rhetorically amplifies rather than analyzes this anthropomorphizing impulse (*Victorian Treasure House*, 134).

16 Grossberg, *Governing the Hearth*, esp. 244–46.

17 My summary of Isabella's spiritualist experiences, recounted in her diary, is based on the discussions in Kenneth R. Andrews, *Nook Farm: Mark Twain's Hartford Circle* (Cambridge: Harvard University Press, 1950), 53–62, 223–24, and Jeanne Boydston, Mary Kelley, and Anne Margolis, *The Limits of Sisterhood: The Beecher Sisters on Women's Rights and Woman's Sphere* (Chapel Hill: University of North Carolina Press, 1988), 189–90.

18 Downing, *Architecture of Country Houses* (1850; rpt. New York: Dover, 1969), xix–xx; Giedion, *Mechanization*, 342–44.

19 On the shifting significances of "mean," see the *OED*. In *Culture and Comfort*, Grier discusses the "democratization" of artifacts embodying domestic comfort—such as upholstered furniture—during the antebellum period.

20 Analytic philosophers writing on love, as well as legal theorists and psychologists, often seem to assume that intimacy and material privacy are causally linked—that, in other words, an individual needs something like a middle-class home in which to "really" love. On this ideal of intimacy as a materially bounded, "indoor" activity, defined as a sharing of information and experience not shared with the public, see, for instance, Jeffrey H. Reiman, "Privacy, Intimacy, and Personhood," in *Today's Moral Problems*, ed. Richard A. Wasserstrom (New York: Macmillan, 1979), 392–407. These associations between domesticity and intimacy suggest why the nineteenth-century experiments in communal and collectivized living failed to take hold in America and displace the single-family dwelling. For a history of these experiments, see Dolores Hayden, *The Grand Domestic Revolution: A History of Feminist Designs for American Homes, Neighborhoods, and Cities* (Cambridge: MIT Press, 1981).

21 Douglas, *Feminization*, 255.

22 On the hegemony of the work ethic in antebellum America, see Daniel T. Rodgers, *The Work Ethic in Industrial America, 1850–1920* (Chicago: University of Chicago Press, 1978). In most studies, the "work ethic," with its paired emphases on industriousness and frugality (or "simplicity"), is read as an instrument of class and well as national self-definition, a means of affirming the unique character of a distinctly *American* middle class by distinguishing its practices from aristocratic—i.e., "European"—leisure and luxury consumption. "Property," in this account, expresses the personality of *homo economicus*, the rationality and industry of the bourgeois subject. However, in characterizing the work ethic and utilitarianism as Victorian America's dominant ethos, these authors miss the importance of gender—and a gendered sentimentalism—in nineteenth-century culture, and ignore the significance of sentimentalism in structuring class and national identifications and practices. Stowe, for instance, countered aristocratic "conspicuous consumption" not with frugality but with a sentimental ideal of intimate involvement with one's possessions; see below.

23 Hayden, *Grand Domestic Revolution*, 54–63; Brown, *Domestic Individualism*, 13–38. Beecher and Stowe, *The American Woman's Home* (1869; rpt. Watkins Glen, N.Y.: American Life Foundation, 1979), 215.

24 Stowe, "What Is a Home?" *House and Home Papers*, in *Household Papers and Stories* (New York: AMS, 1967), 53. All further references to *House and Home Papers* are to this edition. Discussing Stowe's explicit endorsement in her novels and advice literature of the woman of "faculty"—the homemaker who embodies order, precision, and competence in all domestic tasks—Rodgers observes that "even as [Stowe] pleaded for the dignity of work, she peopled her novels with examples of work gone to extremes—cross, austere, overclamped women, blind to beauty, obtuse to the promptings of the heart. . . . In the best and most deeply felt of her novels, in fact, it is not work that saves but love." Surmising that Stowe's "overt counsel" to women was dutifully borrowed from her sister Catharine rather than an adequate inscription of her own sense of women's needs, Rodgers argues that "love and compulsive industry, Eva and Stowe's toiling, always precise Aunt Esther [Lyman Beecher's sister, who ran the Stowe household after Harriet Porter Beecher died], were not complements but polar opposites" (*Work Ethic*, 188–89). Rodgers's account of Stowe's ambivalence toward, and partial rejection of, her sister's model of domestic economy may explain why she employs the distancing device of a male persona in much of her advice literature of the 1850s and 1860s, including *House and Home Papers*. In distinction from Rodgers, I am suggesting that Stowe in fact *synthesizes* these competing ideals of labor and love, and embodies that synthesis in her model domestic woman.

25 On the gendering of muscles and nerves in medical literature and physiological models during the period, see Jordanova, *Sexual Visions*, 44–52. Stowe's ideal body is a delicate balance of nerves and muscles, feeling and action (cf. the discussion of exercise in *American Woman's Home*). In fact, Stowe offers a complex theory of female agency in *House and Home Papers*, one in which actions and feelings are intimately interconnected, and in which actions are continually tested for their (domestic) social consequences and adjusted accordingly. Stowe's text thus maps onto the body the identificatory dynamic constitutive of feminine "taste" and civil subjectivity.

26 On Stowe's homemaking style, see the letters from Calvin to Harriet, 29 and 30 September 1845, in which Calvin criticizes Harriet for being messy and slack, while he is methodical and orderly. He likes to have morning prayers and meals on time; she

doesn't care when they have them. He likes to have the things in the house assigned to their places and left there; but it "seems to be your special delight to keep everything . . . on the move." He likes to have his newspapers "properly folded"; but she and Ann have vexed him "beyond all endurance" by "dropping them sprawling on the floor, or wabbling them all up in one wabble, and squashing them on the table like an old hen with her guts and gizzard squashed out." Harriet's lack of "rigid habit[s]" was the flip side of her powers of emotional absorption: "When your mind is on any particular point, it is your nature to feel and act as if that were the only thing in the world; and you drive at it and make every thing bend to it, to the manifest injury of other interests. For instance, when you are intent on raising flowers, you are sure to visit them and inspect them very carefully every morning; but your kitchen would go for two or three days without any inspection at all, you would be quite ignorant of what there was in the house to be cooked, or the way in which the work was done." According to Calvin, Harriet's inspired spontaneity determined her selection as well as her treatment of domestic objects, easily translating into impulse buying: " 'Naturally thoughtless of expense and inclined to purchase whatever strikes your eye, without much reflection on the proportion of expenditure to be devoted to such objects, this propensity was indulged and greatly increased by your relations with Kate [the austere Catharine Beecher!]. It can be corrected only by a rigid habit of keeping strict written accounts of all available income, of all absolute wants, and of all actual expense.' " Quoted from excerpts in Edmund Wilson, *Patriotic Gore: Studies in the Literature of the American Civil War* (New York: Oxford University Press, 1962), 46–47. For a discussion of Stowe's "chatty" prose style, see Warhol, "Toward a Theory."

27 Hayden, *Grand Domestic Revolution*, 67–89.

28 Like many of Stowe's *House and Home Papers*, "Raking Up the Fire" delineates an attack on consuming objects for status or show rather than sentimental involvement; in other words, the sketch denounces investing in objects which aren't readily incorporatable into—or to borrow from Stowe's vocabulary, "harmonized" with (76)—existing structures of familial emotional experience and which instead threaten to disrupt these structures. Rather than condemning consumption per se, Stowe's critique of "conspicuous consumption" constitutes a discursive strategy through which she distinguishes middle-class from aristocratic consumption practices.

29 Relaxation (or "unselfconsciousness") as a sentimental ideal was inscribed in domestic possessions of the period. On the production of relaxing and reclining chairs in mid-century, see Grier, *Culture and Comfort*.

30 Baudrillard, *For a Critique*, 45–46; Arendt, *Human Condition*, 52.

31 Thomas, *Man and the Natural World*, 240; Shell, "Family Pet." Most historians, including Thomas and Shell, describe pet-keeping as a distinctly middle-class phenomenon. The preservative love exhibited in pet-keeping distinguished middle-class practices from "brutal" and "savage" rituals of both the aristocracy (blood sports) and the working class (cat drownings, etc.), and gave moral sanction to middle-class domestic practices.

32 See chapter 2, note 80. Sentimental novels often represent hurting pets—and especially treating them as farm animals, as food—as a vivid sign of savagery and brutality; both Sedgwick's *Home* and Cummins's *The Lamplighter* contain scenes in which a kitten is plunged into a pot of boiling water by a cruel and "insensible" individual.

33 Stowe, "Rights of Dumb Animals," *Hearth and Home* 2 (January 1869): 203. Stowe published a number of children's stories involving animals; see, especially, "A Dog's Mission," in which a dog takes refuge in the home of an old Calvinist spinster with a

passion for neatness. "Blue Eyes" inspires Miss Avery's sentimental conversion—he "softens" and "win[s] . . . her heart"—and ultimately reunites her with her niece and long-alienated brother; *A Dog's Mission and Other Stories* (New York: Fords, Howard, and Hulbert, 1880), 7–65. Trine, *Every Living Creature; or, Heart-Training through the Animal World* (New York, 1899).

34 In his popular marketing manual, Carl Naether expressly advises advertisers to exploit feminine sympathetic identification in order to stimulate women to "buying action"; *Advertising to Women* (New York: Taylor, 1928), 44–55.

35 Fisher, *Hard Facts*, 58–59. Stowe, *Uncle Tom's Cabin*, ed. Ann Douglas (New York: Penguin American Library, 1981), 336. All further references are to this edition.

36 E.g. Karen Sanchez-Eppler, "Bodily Bonds: The Intersecting Rhetorics of Feminism and Abolition," *Representations* 24 (1988): 28–59.

37 Hartman, *Scenes of Subjection*, 17–21. Because Hartman's study is not focused on the instabilities of sentimental subjectivity, her argument ultimately replicates the binaristic terms of the debate about the sources of the "pleasures" of representations of suffering first formulated by eighteenth-century critics.

38 Simms, "The Morals of Slavery," in *The Pro-Slavery Argument* (Charleston: Walker, Richards, 1852), 270.

39 Williams, *Alchemy*, 220–21.

40 On new legal limits on traditional patriarchal property rights—limits most clearly legible in the reformulation of custody rights during the nineteenth century, and the flurry of laws and judicial decisions designed to protect women, especially wives—see Grossberg, *Governing the Hearth*.

41 Sentimental texts such as Stowe's characteristically conflate the proprietary and the affectional, and constitute "civilized" sentiments in expressly proprietary terms. The dangerous capriciousness of unlegalized sentiment—especially for women—is foregrounded by Stowe in much of her later work: see, for instance, her depiction in *Oldtown Folks* of the seduction of Emily Rossiter, who is undone by the radical—and French—doctrine of free love; her exposé of Byron's alleged incestuous relationship in *Lady Byron Vindicated* (1870); and her preface to the sensationalistic, autobiographical account of Mormon polygamy authored by Mrs. T. B. H. (Fanny) Stenhouse. These texts construct sentimental ownership as an expressly "American" formulation, defined in opposition to the proprietary practices of various (national/ethnic/religious) Others. Stowe herself strenuously opposed free love and liberal divorce laws on the grounds that they encouraged male promiscuity and sexual license, and she clearly viewed marriage—as did many nineteenth-century women—as a means to restrain and "civilize" male desire, so that it would adhere to the structure of (natural) constancy characteristic of feminine dependency.

42 Holmes, "Uncle Tom's Cabin," *Southern Literary Messenger* (December 1852): 728–29.

43 Elizabeth Ammons, "Heroines in *Uncle Tom's Cabin*," *American Literature* 49, no. 2 (1977): 161–79.

44 Stowe, who wavered throughout her life on the question of woman suffrage, unwaveringly defended women's property rights, endorsing them as a form of protection against male victimization. I am suggesting here that she presented a similarly delimited, protective configuration of African American subjectivity. Stowe's sentimentally inspired racial revisionism challenged antebellum stereotypes of black women's "insensibility" as well as material practices authorized by racist representations. America's most eminent gynecological surgeon during the period, Dr. J. Marion Sims, carried out

his lengthy and agonizing experimental operations on black women because they lacked, he contended, the ability to feel pain as white women did. G. J. Barker-Benfield, *The Horrors of the Half-Known Life: Male Attitudes toward Women and Sexuality in Nineteenth-Century America* (New York: Harper and Row, 1976), 91–119.

45 Downing, *Architecture*, 25.

46 Among Stowe's contemporaries, Hawthorne in particular explored the moral dangers (and eroticized pleasures) of voyeurism or psychologically intrusive, unsympathetic looking—a visual mode typically gendered "male" in his work; see below. This delineation of differently gendered gazes is familiarly reiterated in contemporary film theory. The responsive "female" look in Stowe's novel, however, must be paired with and followed by responsible and sympathetic action: the dangers of "just looking" are thematized in the novel in the history of Augustine St. Clare, a "dreamy neutral spectator" (450) who sees and feels much but does nothing.

47 Hawthorne, *The House of the Seven Gables* (New York: Penguin, 1981), 219. All further references are to this edition.

48 In the end, *Uncle Tom's Cabin* conspicuously situates blacks outside the bounds of the American polis, whether in heaven or in Liberia. In the novel's final chapter, "Concluding Remarks," where she directly appeals to her readers, Stowe explicitly outlines her final "solution" to race politics in America: African American emigration to Liberia, the African "refuge" which, she notes, God had so prudently provided (625–26). On welfare state "maternalism," see Paula Baker, "The Domestication of Politics: Women and American Political Society, 1780–1920," *American Historical Review* 89, no. 3 (June 1984): 620–47.

49 In *Stories, Sketches and Studies* (New York: AMS, 1967), 138.

50 Tompkins, *Sensational Designs: The Cultural Work of American Fiction, 1790–1860* (New York: Oxford University Press, 1985), 131.

51 James D. Hart, *The Popular Book: A History of America's Literary Taste* (Berkeley: University of California Press, 1950), 111–12. Spillers suggests that this proliferation of Uncle Tom poems, songs, dioramas, plates, and other memorabilia replicates the novel's "considerable display of massive *inarticulations* (the Topsies; the black young, piled in a corner of Uncle Tom's Cabin in a confused heap of noise and motion)," silent and silenced African Americans who supply the ground for Stowe's own discursive profusion; "Changing the Letter: The Yokes, the Jokes of Discourse, or, Mrs. Stowe, Mr. Reed," in *Slavery and the Literary Imagination*, ed. D. E. McDowell and Arnold Rampersad (Baltimore: Johns Hopkins University Press, 1989), 25–61.

52 James H. Collins, "The Topsy Element in Advertising," *Printer's Ink* 14 (Oct. 1908): 18.

53 Ward, *The Mormon Wife*, reprinted as *Female Life among the Mormons* (New York: Derby and Jackson, 1857), 221. All further references are to this edition.

54 Leonard J. Arrington and Jon Haupt, "Intolerable Zion: The Image of Mormonism in Nineteenth-Century American Literature," *Western Humanities Review* 22 (1968): 243–60.

55 Ibid., 249.

56 David Brion Davis, "Some Themes of Counter-Subversion: An Analysis of Anti-Masonic, Anti-Catholic, and Anti-Mormon Literature," *Mississippi Historical Review* 47 (1960–61): 205–24. Antebellum "white slave" narratives belong to the tradition of what Pratt calls Eurocolonial "survival literature," narratives of cultural contact that depict "Europeans enslaved by non-Europeans, Europeans assimilating to non-European societies, and Europeans cofounding new transracial social orders." Accord-

ing to Pratt, "The context of survival literature was 'safe' for transgressive plots, since the very existence of a text presupposed the imperially correct outcome: the survivor survived, and sought reintegration into the home society" (*Imperial Eyes*, 87).

57 Roediger, *Wages of Whiteness*, 68.

58 Ibid., 70, 72, 85.

59 This analysis is indebted to Benedict Anderson's understanding of national identity as "shaped by what it opposes" and requiring "some element of alterity" for its definition (*Imagined Communities*, 12).

60 J. H. Beadle, *Life in Utah* (Philadelphia: National, 1870), 359, 365.

61 Sedgwick, *Clarence*, 1: 152.

62 E.g., Tompkins, *Sensational Designs*, 3–39.

63 Kesserling, *Hawthorne's Reading, 1828–1850* (New York: New York Public Library Press, 1949).

64 The figure of Paul Pry appears in Hawthorne's "Sights from a Steeple," *Twice-Told Tales* (Columbus: Ohio State University Press, 1974), 192. On Hawthorne's recorded fears that he would become the cold observer portrayed in Paul Pry, see Arlin Turner, *Nathaniel Hawthorne: A Biography* (New York: Oxford University Press, 1980), 54–55.

65 Hawthorne, *The Scarlet Letter* (New York: Norton, 1982), 80. All further references are to this edition.

66 *The House of the Seven Gables* similarly registers, indeed literalizes the Scottish metaphorics of the animating power of commercial and domestic exchange (expressly opposed to the stifling captivity of feudal ownership). The text begins with the opening of the Pyncheon mansion—a house "conceived in the grotesqueness of a Gothic fancy" (11)—in which an elderly and reclusive aristocratic "maiden," Hepzibah Pyncheon, has lived for twenty-five years, waiting for her brother Clifford's return from prison, where he has unjustly served a lengthy sentence. Having spent a quarter century "taking no part in the business of life, and just as little in its intercourse and pleasures" (31), Miss Hepzibah resolves to reopen an old shop in the mansion and to enter the "galvanizing" realm of social exchange, severing her alliance with the idle "aristocracy" (54). Receiving her first "copper-coin," Miss Hepzibah experiences "a thrill of almost youthful enjoyment. It was the invigorating breath of a fresh outward atmosphere, after the long torpor and monotonous seclusion of her life. . . . That little circlet . . . had proved a talisman. . . . It was as potent, and perhaps endowed with the same kind of efficacy, as a galvanic ring! Hepzibah, at all events, was indebted to its subtile operation, both in body and spirit; so much the more, as it inspired her with energy to get some breakfast, at which—still the better to keep up her courage—she allowed herself an extra spoonful in her infusion of black tea" (51–52).

67 Hawthorne, *The Blithedale Romance*, ed. Annette Kolodny (New York: Penguin, 1983), 19. All further references are to this edition.

68 Newfield, *Emerson Effect*.

69 Lauren Berlant, "Fantasies of Utopia in *The Blithedale Romance*," *American Literary History* 1, no. 1 (spring 1989): 31–62.

70 Luther S. Luedtke, *Nathaniel Hawthorne and the Romance of the Orient* (Bloomington: Indiana University Press, 1989).

71 Lefcowitz, "Some Rents in the Veil: New Light on Priscilla and Zenobia in *The Blithedale Romance*," *Nineteenth-Century Fiction* 21 (1966): 263–75. The Lefcowitzes base their reading on the text's sexual symbology—particularly the symbolism of the silk purses

that Priscilla weaves and with which she is consistently associated — and the "ontological ambivalence" of Priscilla's characterization.

72 Hawthorne, "Sights from a Steeple," *Twice-Told Tales*, 192.

73 The author of one mid-nineteenth-century conduct manual contrasted the visual parameters of respect for another's privacy — what the sociologist Erving Goffman has identified as the genteel imperative to maintain the delicate stance of "civil inattention" — with the requirements of the "business" of detection: "The rule is imperative, that no one should see, or, if that is impossible, should seem to see, or to have seen, anything that another person would choose to have concealed; unless indeed it is your business to watch for some misdemeanor" (qtd. in Kasson, *Rudeness and Civility*, 223).

74 Significantly, Hawthorne's contemporaries responded with moral suspicion to what they characterized as the violence of his psychological realism. Mrs. Margaret Oliphant, for instance, complained that Hawthorne's Puritans "are exhibited to us as a surgeon might exhibit his pet 'cases,' [rather] than as a poet shows his men and women, brothers and sister the universal heart"; cited in Joel Pfister, *The Production of Personal Life: Class, Gender, and the Psychological in Hawthorne's Fiction* (Stanford: Stanford University Press, 1991), 56.

4 *Domesticating "Blackness"*

1 Tate, "Allegories of Black Female Desire, or, Rereading Nineteenth-Century Sentimental Narratives of Black Female Authority," in *Changing Our Own Words*, ed. Cheryl A. Wall (New Brunswick: Rutgers University Press, 1989), 107.

2 The concept of the "tactic" is borrowed from de Certeau. For de Certeau, "tactics" are improvisational maneuvers — calculated moves in a kind of guerrilla warfare — that enable the "weak" to contest the determinations of institutions and structures: a "tactic" is a "maneuver 'within the enemy's field of vision' . . . [that] takes advantage of 'oportunities' and depends on them. . . . It must vigilantly make use of the cracks that particular conjunctions open in the surveillance of the proprietary powers. It poaches in them" (*Practice*, 37).

3 Linda Brent [Harriet Jacobs], *Incidents in the Life of a Slave Girl, Written by Herself*, in *The Classic Slave Narratives*, ed. Henry Louis Gates Jr. (New York: Signet, 1987). Further references are to this edition. To avoid confusion, I will refer to the author of *Incidents* as Jacobs, but will use the pseudonym Linda Brent in analyzing the text and protagonist.

4 *Narrative of Sojourner Truth*, ed. Jeffrey C. Stewart (New York: Oxford University Press, 1991). All further references are to this edition. For the *Book of Life*, see note 44 below. There are, of course, scholarly problems involved with treating a dictated autobiography, and even transcriptions of speeches, as primary sources. The *Narrative*, for instance, contains numerous summary passages and moralistic statements that were almost certainly the independent contribution of Truth's amanuensis. But the text, as Jeffrey C. Stewart has pointed out, does contain vivid inscriptions of Truth's voice, especially in direct quotes; and he claims that, when approached with caution and examined in conjunction with collateral information such as transcriptions of her speeches, the *Narrative* offers crucial insight into Truth's personal and public self-constructions (introduction to the *Narrative*, xxxv). The problems involved in dealing with Truth's speeches are that transcripts of single speeches often vary widely; some texts of the 1851 Akron speech, for instance, are written in standard or "white" En-

glish, while others are written in rather crude Southern dialect (a dubious rendering, given that Truth was a bilingual ex-slave from the North). But it seems imperative that we struggle with all these texts, problematic though they are, since they constitute the only extant records of the voice of one of the most influential black women in American history.

5 On the categorical exclusion of black women from the construction of "true womanhood" during the period, see Hazel Carby, *Reconstructing Womanhood: The Emergence of the Afro-American Novelist* (New York: Oxford University Press, 1987). Carby argues that antebellum stereotypes of black femininity (especially the stereotype of the sexualized black woman) both legitimized the sexual exploitation of slave women and served to define antithetically the antebellum construction of white femininity. Other scholars have situated the problematic construction of black femininity within the specific material and social conditions of slavery. Angela Davis contends that plantation labor degendered the bodies of slaves; *Women, Race, and Class* (New York: Random House, 1981). Hortense Spillers examines this "ungendering" of the slave's body, and has contrasted the linguistically and culturally marked "captive body" with the undifferentiated and unnamed "flesh" in "Mama's Baby." Elizabeth Fox-Genovese observes that Southern courts persistently ruled that black slave women were outside the statutory rubric "woman"; *Within the Plantation Household: Black and White Women of the Old South* (Chapel Hill: University of North Carolina Press, 1988), 326.

6 The problematization of the categorical distinction between "autobiography" and "fiction" seems especially necessary when examining nineteenth-century African American narratives, since such texts have historically been evaluated against a critical standard of "authenticity," a standard which has been used to discredit more experimental, discursively complex autobiographical narratives (such as Jacobs's *Incidents*) while serving—especially during the antebellum period—radically to circumscribe the autonomy and literary authority of African American writers. On the preoccupation with "authenticity" in abolitionist culture and the narrative constraints that placed on ex-slave narrators and speakers, see William L. Andrews, "The Novelization of Voice in Early African American Narrative," *PMLA* 105, no. 1 (January 1990): 23–34.

7 Albert E. Stone, *Autobiographical Occasions and Original Acts* (Philadelphia: University of Pennsylvania Press, 1982), 10.

8 Ibid., 19. As Frances Smith Foster reminds us, writers of slave narratives, both men and women, were writing to a partly if not largely white audience, and their narratives were often edited by white editors (or, as in Truth's case, transcribed by white amanuenses) and framed by the authenticating documents and testimonials of other white persons; *Witnessing Slavery: The Development of Antebellum Slave Narratives* (Westport, Conn.: Greenwood, 1979), 65. Slave narratives were also formally shaped by their political purpose—to document and expose the evils of the institution of slavery; this intention and premise of slave narratives has been linked, for instance, to conventions of the genre, such as their episodic form. Robert B. Stepto examines the import of slave narratives' authenticating documents in *From behind the Veil: A Study of Afro-American Narrative* (Urbana: University of Illinois Press, 1991).

9 Spillers, "Mama's Baby," 79.

10 Valerie Smith, *Self-Discovery and Authority in Afro-American Narrative* (Cambridge: Harvard University Press, 1987); Claudia Tate, *Domestic Allegories of Political Desire: The Black Heroine's Text at the Turn of the Century* (New York: Oxford University Press, 1992).

11 Jacobs's complex negotiations with sentimental topoi and conventions have been much discussed. Hazel Carby, for instance, has argued that the specific content of Jacobs's experience as a black slave woman, and the particular forms of patriarchal abuse and exploitation to which she was subjected, forced her to reject the "conventional patterns" of popular domestic fiction (*Reconstructing Womanhood*, 42). Valerie Smith identifies generative gaps or lacunae inscribed and produced within Jacobs's narrative which mark her departure from sentimental topoi (*Self-Discovery*, 28–43). These critics focus, for the most part, on Jacobs's self-justifying "confession" of her loss of virtue, which is seen to signify her rejection of sentimental fiction's equation of chastity and virtue: Carby, for example, speaks of Jacobs's "subversion" of a "major narrative code of sentimental fiction": the punishment of loss of purity with death (59–60). As I argue in chapter 1, this code of sentimental narrative suggests the radical unthinkability of the female sexual subject—and of feminine consent—outside the normative patriarchal structures of gender.

12 Spivak, *In Other Worlds: Essays in Cultural Politics* (New York: Routledge, 1988), 145.

13 Claire C. Robertson and Martin A. Klein, eds., *Women and Slavery in Africa* (Madison: University of Wisconsin Press, 1984).

14 Fox-Genovese, *Within the Plantation Household*, 299.

15 Spillers, "Mama's Baby," 65–81.

16 David Brion Davis, *The Problem of Slavery in the Age of Revolution, 1770–1823* (Ithaca: Cornell University Press, 1975) and *Slavery and Human Progress* (New York: Oxford University Press, 1984).

17 Roediger, *Wages of Whiteness*, 27; Lott, *Love and Theft.*

18 On the paradoxical tension between free choice and ineluctably determined fate in representations of romantic involvement, see Niklas Luhmann, *Love as Passion: The Codification of Intimacy* (Cambridge: Harvard University Press, 1986), 181.

19 Mill, "The Subjection of Women," 141.

20 Douglass's and Jacobs's inscriptions of the cultural paradigms of gender and civic personhood constitute, at once, colonial "mimicry" and gender "masquerade" (or performance) and thus represent, in Homi Bhabha's formulation, both "resemblance and menace" of normalizing discursive formulations and identity categories; *The Location of Culture* (New York: Routledge, 1994), 85–92; emphasis in original. See the further discussion of Bhabha just below.

21 Williams, *Alchemy*, 220–21; emphasis added.

22 Bhabha, *Location*, 85–86.

23 *Narrative of the Life of Frederick Douglass, an African Slave*, in *The Classic Slave Narratives*, ed. Henry Louis Gates Jr. (New York: Signet, 1987), 325. All further references are to this edition.

24 Douglass's recuperation of this faculty, and his progression from chattel to free laborer, constituted a narrative rebuttal of proslavery arguments that slaves "needed" slavery because they would not respond to the free-market incentives which drove whites and because they were "naturally" indolent—an argument explicitly attacked in his speeches. For an example of this proslavery argument, see Simms, "Miss Martineau on Slavery," 654. For an example of Douglass's attack on this argument, see "The Future of the Negro People of the Slave States," in *Afro-American History: Primary Sources*, ed. Thomas R. Frazier (Chicago: Dorsey, 1988). Douglass's investment in liberal ideals of self-ownership is of course undercut by his (attenuated) account of the racism he encounters while a "free" laborer in New Bedford—racism that prevents him from

gaining employment as a caulker and forces him to work instead at diverse menial jobs. Describing his move to New Bedford, Douglass notes briefly that "such was the strength of prejudice against color, among the white calkers, that they refused to work with me, and of course I could get no employment"; he qualifies this statement in a footnote, where he claims that "I am told that colored persons can now get employment at calking in New Bedford—a result of anti-slavery effort" (325). But Douglass's documentation of racist employment practices in the North testifies to the market and social forces that make "free labor" little more than a mystifying slogan. Douglass's narrative simultaneously invests in the political fiction of "free labor" as a categorical alternative to slave chattel and a lever to extricate him from slavery, and evokes specific historical conditions that prevent free and equal access to capitalist economic opportunities, radically restricting a black "free" laborer's available markets so that he is forced to "do any kind of work I could get to do" (325). In Douglass's *Narrative*, free labor is thus an ideal or potentiality rather than the realized historical condition that it often appeared in more conservative representations, one which served as a critical index of contemporary social relations.

25 On Douglass's rhetorical uses of the revolutionary legacy, see Sundquist, *To Wake the Nations*. For critiques of the representation of gender in Douglass's *Narrative* and *The Heroic Slave*, respectively, see Jenny Franchot, "The Punishment of Esther: Frederick Douglass and the Constitution of the Feminine," and Richard Yarborough, "Race, Violence and Manhood: The Masculine Ideal in Frederick Douglass's 'The Heroic Slave,' " both in *Frederick Douglass: New Literary and Historical Essays*, ed. Eric J. Sundquist (New York: Cambridge University Press, 1990).

26 Franchot, "Punishment"; Fox-Genovese, *Within the Plantation Household*, 319.

27 Jacobs's awareness of the specific forms of her oppression as a slave *woman* is amply present in the text, and has been discussed in detail by Jean Fagan Yellin, "Text and Contexts of Harriet Jacobs' *Incidents in the Life of a Slave Girl*: Written by Herself," in *The Slave's Narrative*, ed. Charles T. Davis and Henry Louis Gates Jr. (New York: Oxford University Press, 1985), 262–82. According to Yellin, *Incidents* is, "to my knowledge, the only slave narrative that takes as its subject the sexual exploitation of female slaves—thus centering on sexual oppression as well as on oppression of race and condition" (263).

28 Berlant, "The Queen of America Goes to Washington City: Harriet Jacobs, Frances Harper, Anita Hill," in *Subjects and Citizens: Nation, Race, and Gender from Oroonoko to Anita Hill*, ed. Cathy N. Davidson and Michael Moon (Durham: Duke University Press, 1995), 455–80.

29 This rescripting can be read in numerous ways. Certainly, *Incidents* testifies that slaveowners frequently invoke the sentimental nature of relations between owner and owned as a defense of the "peculiar institution": the Flints' sentimental funeral ritual to commemorate the death of Aunt Nancy is a case in point, as is Emily Flint's young brother's claim, in a letter to Linda, that "the same heartfelt tie existed between a master and his servant, as between a mother and her child" (488). Slavemasters, as *Incidents* reveals—and as contemporary historians have demonstrated—were fond of characterizing slavery as a "beautiful 'patriarchal institution' " (*Incidents*, 403) modeled on an interracial family, as a way of blurring the distinction between these two institutions and binding slaves to masters. I am suggesting that this rescripting is enabling for Linda as well, and allows her to construct an identity as a feminine (sentimental) subject.

30 Pratt, *Imperial Eyes*, 101.

31 On the "legend of black sexual promiscuity" in antebellum America, see Eugene Genovese, *Roll, Jordan Roll: The World the Slaves Made* (New York: Random House, 1974), 458–75.

32 de Certeau, *Practice*, 37.

33 Thompson, *Appeal of One Half of the Human Race, Women, Against the Pretensions of the Other Half, Men, to Retain Them in Political, and Thence in Civil and Domestic, Slavery* (London: Longman, 1825), 56–57.

34 Spillers, "Mama's Baby," 73; Pateman, *Sexual Contract.*

35 Spillers, "Mama's Baby," 76.

36 Yellin, "Texts and Contexts," 263, 276. According to Yellin, Jacobs forged cross-racial female alliances in her personal life, especially with her Quaker friend and supporter Amy Post (who encouraged Jacobs to write her narrative and whose testimonial of its authenticity was appended to it), her editor, Lydia Maria Child, and her employer, Mrs. Willis (who appears in *Incidents* as "Mrs. Bruce").

37 Jacobs insists that any female "identification" between black and white women is only possible through an acknowledgment of the profound differences beween slave and free women. For an important analysis of the complexities of cross-racial sympathy in *Incidents*, see Dana Nelson, *The Word in Black and White: Reading "Race" in American Literature, 1638–1867* (New York: Oxford University Press, 1993).

38 Foster, *Written By Herself*. Jacobs's struggle for this "respect" was enacted, in part, on the level of writing and discursive authority: Jacobs insisted on writing her story as a book-length narrative and rejected Stowe's efforts to reduce her autobiography to a representative example or textual object-lesson in her *Key to Uncle Tom's Cabin*; and on more than one occasion she had to confront Child in order to retain control over the form, emphasis, and proofreading of her text. On the history of her manuscript, see Frances Smith Foster, *Written by Herself: Literary Production by African-American Women, 1746–1892* (Bloomington: Indiana University Press, 1993), esp. 106; Yellin, "Texts and Contexts."

39 My characterization of liberal feminine "freedom" as sentimental preference suggests that the Goldilocks story is a kind of ur-myth of modern (consumerist) femininity, one which pivots on the notion that even if one is too tall and one is too small, there will be one that is "just right." A more contemporary example of this idea is a board game I played as a young girl, "Mystery Date" (a game marketed to girls), where players took turns opening a "door" in the center of the board (the fantasy was that a man was coming to your house) behind which were pictures of a number of men—e.g., California surfer, prom king—one of whom would be exactly "your type."

40 While intelligible within the gendered constructs of her intended readers, this self-representation also encodes specifically African American traditions. On the voice of maternal outrage as a strategy of political protest in black women's autobiographies, see Joanne Braxton, *Black Women Writing Autobiography: A Tradition within a Tradition* (Philadelphia: Temple University Press, 1989). According to Deborah Gray White, for antebellum African American women, as for their African foremothers, motherhood was of greater significance than marriage in a young woman's coming of age and identity; *A'rnt I a Woman? Female Slaves in the Plantation South* (New York: Norton, 1985).

41 Lefebvre as quoted in Mary P. Ryan, *Women in Public: Between Banners and Ballots, 1825–1880* (Baltimore: Johns Hopkins University Press, 1990), 92. For historical analyses of the "living space" produced by slaves within the Southern slave system, see Michael J.

Cassity, "Slaves, Families, and 'Living Space': A Note on Evidence and Historical Context," *Southern Studies* 17 (summer 1978): 209–15.

42 hooks, *Yearning: Race, Gender, and Cultural Politics* (Boston: South End, 1990), 41–49.

43 Linda's ambivalent relationship to domesticity is suggested by the fact that the peephole she bores in the garret wall does not look inside but outside the house: unlike the female figures in Anglo-American window scenes discussed in chapter 3, Linda's gaze is more ambiguously directed and inflected.

44 The story of Isabella's renaming is told in the *Narrative*. In 1843, God called her to leave her home in New York City and travel and preach, and she announced herself "Sojourner"; later, He gave her "Truth." For purposes of clarity, I will refer to her with her public identity, Sojourner Truth, except when explicitly discussing the *Narrative*'s account of her personal history before her self-transformation. On the trope of naming in African American literature, see Kimberly W. Benston, "I yam what I am: The Topos of Un(naming) in Afro-American Literature," in *Black Literature and Literary Theory*, ed. Henry Louis Gates Jr. (New York: Methuen, 1984), 151–72.

As I suggest early in this chapter, Truth is a complex figure for any literary scholar to work with, chiefly because her words come down to us through the pens of others: like many other ex-slave narrators, her autobiography was dictated to and transcribed by a white amanuensis; in addition, her speeches and sermons are available today only as speech texts penned by diverse listeners. The issue is further complicated by the fact that Truth evidently considered print a technology of white domination; indeed, it appears that Truth featured the fluidity of the oral form, and oral *performance*, as a locus of personal and collective regeneration, positioned against the fixity of the written text controlled by a white editorial and publishing establishment. Truth certainly did exercise substantial control over how and when her words were "written": although she agreed, when approached by Olive Gilbert, to publish her autobiography in 1850 to aid the abolitionist cause, she rejected a later proposal by Theodore Tilton to write her life, reportedly stating that she expected to live a long time yet, was going to accomplish lots before she died, and didn't want to be "written up" at present; *Book of Life*, ed. Frances Gage, in *Narrative of Sojourner Truth*, ed. Jeffrey C. Stewart (New York: Oxford University Press, 1991). All further references are to this edition. Indeed, it is arguable that Truth exercised her agency most powerfully in her *performance* of this act of being "written" by whites; carrying with her on her travels the *Book of Life*, she would share with acquaintances and audiences its collection of signatures and testimonials by public figures, newspaper clippings, essays (such as Stowe's "Libyan Sibyl"), personal letters, and other documents about her life. I argue below that the *Book of Life* foregrounds this issue of being "written" by (predominantly white) others in complex and illuminating ways.

45 Higginbotham, "African-American Women's History and the Metalanguage of Race," *Signs* 17, no. 2 (winter 1992): 258.

46 Carby, *Reconstructing Womanhood*, 39.

47 Stowe's essay "Sojourner Truth, the Libyan Sibyl," was first published in the *Atlantic Monthly* in 1863 and then reprinted in the *Book of Life*. As Esther Terry notes, "It is very possible that Harriet Beecher Stowe gave Sojourner her widest audience" through this piece; "Sojourner Truth: The Person behind the Libyan Sibyl," *Massachusetts Review* 26, nos. 2–3 (summer–autumn 1985): 430. The influence of Stowe's characterization is perhaps indicated by a journalist's statement, first published in the *Rochester Democrat and Chronicle* and reprinted in the *Book of Life*, that Truth's "appearance reminds one vividly of Dinah in 'Uncle Tom's Cabin' " (*Book of Life*, 225). Stowe's inscription of the

bed incident, supposedly delivered in Sojourner Truth's own words, illuminates some of the issues scholars must struggle with in working with extant discursive records of the black preacher's self-representations. Stowe's account of the scene reads as follows: "[The Quakers] jes' took me in, an' did for me as kind as ef I'd been one of 'em; an' after they'd giv me supper, they took me into a room where there was a great, tall, white bed; an' they told me to sleep there. Well, honey, I was kind o' skeered when they left me alone with that great white bed; 'cause I never had been in a bed in my life. It never came into my mind they could mean me to sleep in it. An' so I jes' camped down under it, on the floor, an' then I slep' pretty well. In the mornin', when they came in, they asked me ef I hadn't been asleep; an' I said, 'Yes, I never slep' better.' An' they said, 'Why, you haven't been in the bed!" An' says I, 'Laws, you didn't think o' sech a thing as my sleepin' in dat 'ar' *bed*, did you? I never heerd o' sech a thing in my life' " (475). Stowe's account, notably written in dialect, exaggerates Sojourner's mystification when faced with the refinements of life (Stowe images Sojourner as being unaware of what the white bed is for, while the *Narrative*'s account stresses her reluctance to use it), appeals to stereotypes of black superstitiousness (the version in the *Narrative* says nothing of Sojourner's fear of the bed), and is overall a more comic depiction of the confrontation of poverty with wealth, a vignette with the overtones of a minstrel show. These representations were of a piece with Stowe's portrayal of Truth as an entertaining curiosity, an individual with "a droll flavoring of humor" who was "always ready to talk or to sing" (478–79); or they may have been the consequence of Truth's skill as a rhetorician, her ability to perform "blackness" as defined and desired by whites in order to appeal to her auditor. Certainly, Stowe's constructions reflect the importance of stereotypes in mediating whites' perception and understanding of African Americans and African American culture. It is important to point out, however, that Truth was capable of resisting Stowe's efforts to define her when she chose to. Stowe's characterization of her as a "living breathing impersonation" of "the Libyan Sibyl," a statue by William Wetmore Story which Truth's personal history supposedly inspired, was one that Truth apparently repudiated. Although she eagerly listened to newspapers read aloud to her, "she would never listen," Gage reports, "to Mrs. Stowe's 'Libyan Sibyl.' 'Oh,' she would say, 'I don't want to hear about that old symbol; read me something that is going on now, something about this great war' " (*Book of Life*, 174).

48 Douglass also noted that Truth "was much respected at Florence, for she was honest, industrious, and amiable. Her quaint speeches easily gave her an audience, and she was one of the most useful members of the Community in its day of small things"; Frederick Douglass, "What I Found at the Northampton Association," as quoted in Terry, "Sojourner Truth," 444. Both Douglass and DuBois characterize Truth as "primitive" racial type and an example of unrefined, uncultivated black womanhood; for both, Truth's public image is seen to be politically dangerous, because of its potential to be recuperated by racist stereotypes that black leaders (including these two men) were attempting to counter with positive representations. On nineteenth-century efforts by black writers to "reconstruct" the public image of the black racial self, see Henry Louis Gates Jr., "The Trope of the New Negro and the Reconstruction of the Image of the Black," *Representations* 24 (fall 1988): 136. The authenticity of Truth's famous rebuke, "Frederick, *is God dead*," discussed below is addressed in Nell Irvin Painter, *Sojourner Truth: A Life, A Symbol* (New York: Norton, 1996), 151–63.

49 W. E. B. DuBois, *The Seventh Son: The Thought and Writings of W. E. B. DuBois*, vol. 1, ed. Julius Lester (New York, 1971), 388, 519–20.

50 Sanchez-Eppler, "Bodily Bonds."

51 Stewart, Introduction to *Narrative of Sojourner Truth*, xxxiii.

52 On enactment, see Karlyn Kohrs Campbell, "Style and Content in the Rhetoric of Early Afro-American Feminists," *Quarterly Journal of Speech* 72 (1986): 435. Douglass, in *My Bondage and My Freedom* (1855), describes the division between mind and body, rational analysis and narrative representation, in his relationship with the Garrisonians during the 1840s, and discusses William Lloyd Garrison's reliance on Douglass to provide testimony of slavery—"tell your story, Frederick"—and living proof of its injustices. According to Douglass, his white co-workers tried to "pin [his speeches] down" to simple, factual narrations of his personal experience while he was "growing, and needed room" to express a widening array of subjects. Douglass notes that John A. Collins, general agent of the Massachusetts antislavery society, advised the ex-slave to "Give us the facts, we will take care of the philosophy"; and his status as embodied evidence or prize exhibit (or, in Douglass's words, "*brand new fact*") was underscored in the abolitionists' standard introduction of the black speaker as a "graduate from the peculiar institution with [his] diploma written on [his] back" and as "a '*chattel*'—a '*thing*'—a piece of southern '*property*'—the chairman assuring the audience that *it* could speak"; *My Bondage and My Freedom*, in *Frederick Douglass: The Narrative and Selected Writings*, ed. Michael Meyer (New York: Modern Library, 1984), 157–62.

53 On mid-nineteenth-century artisan republicanism's "cult of manliness," see Sean Wilentz, *Chants Democratic: New York City and the Rise of the American Working Class* (New York: Oxford University Press, 1984). Paula Baker examines the construction of partisan politics during the Jacksonian period as a masculine territory (a partial consequence of universal white male suffrage), and discusses the era's identification of partisan politics with the ritual performance of manliness ("Domestication"). On tropes of "manliness" in antebellum African American men's prose, see Franchot, "Punishment of Esther," and Yarborough, "Race, Violence, and Manhood." Truth's work enacts a feminine appropriation of the liberatory, indeed revolutionary potential of the tropes of "manly" heroism prevalent in African American men's work, even while she deemphasizes the potentially violent nature of that heroism and the connotations of violence presented by the "manly" black body. In an interesting way, Truth's use of these tropes constitutes a symbolic reconfiguration of her famous debate with Douglass about the legitimacy of black slave violence.

54 Dyer, *Heavenly Bodies: Film Stars and Society* (New York: St. Martin's, 1986), 138–39.

55 On the radical potential of religious conversion in African American women's autobiographical narratives, its power to grant self-authorization to an individual and negate the secular authority of earthly "masters," see William L. Andrews, *Sisters of the Spirit: Three Black Women's Autobiographies of the Nineteenth Century* (Bloomington: Indiana University Press, 1986), 2–4.

56 Stewart, Introduction to *Narrative of Sojourner Truth*, xxxviii–xxxix.

57 Scarry, "Consent and the Body: Injury, Departure, and Desire," *New Literary History* 21 (1990), esp. 874–84.

58 Susan B. Anthony, Elizabeth Cady Stanton, and Matilda Joslyn Gage, eds., *History of Woman Suffrage* (New York: Fowler and Wells, 1881), 2: 225.

59 This plan—for relocating African Americans to unoccupied western lands—was devised by Sojourner Truth after seeing the destitution and poverty of free Southern blacks during Reconstruction, and it became the centerpiece of her vision of equality and autonomy for blacks. She promoted this plan in speeches at religious and political

meetings around the country; several of her speeches from this period are transcribed or summarized in the *Book of Life* (for an especially moving and brilliant example, see 225–27). Truth's contention that all freemen had the right to independent freeholding or landownership invoked a familiar principle of agrarian republicanism, a principle which structured early-nineteenth-century land reform, culminating in the enactment of the 1859 Homestead Act.

5 *Fashioning a Free Self*

1 Tate, *Domestic Allegories of Political Desire: The Black Heroine's Text at the Century's End* (New York: Oxford University Press, 1992), 107. I have argued throughout this book that sentimental consumption narrativized (and socialized) a particular formation of feminine consumer desire; that narrative, of course, doesn't exhaust consumerism's political possibilities or the emotions it generates. For the argument that mass consumption, in fact, brought into view a different concept of the public sphere, that of a "social horizon of experience," see Oskar Negt and Alexander Kluge, *The Public Sphere and Experience*, trans. Peter Labanyi (Minneapolis: University of Minnesota Press, 1990), 143. Elizabeth Wilson sees in "fashion," as aesthetic and symbolic system, a rich structure of collective fantasy and vocabulary of visual expression in which "tabooed, fantastic, possible and impossible dreams" could be explored in blueprint; Wilson, "All the Rage," in *Fabrications: Costume and the Female Body*, ed. Jane Gaines and Charlotte Herzog (New York: Routledge, 1990), 31. The cultural/narrative space of desire offered by commodity culture may have been especially important for African American women, for whom, because of persistent stereotypes of black women as sexually lascivious, the representation of black female sexual desire was profoundly complicated and, indeed, fraught with cultural danger. Images of "tasteful," genteel consumption in nineteenth-century African American women's literature should also be seen as a response to stereotypes of African Americans as illicit, excessive, and irrational consumers. Anne Norton discusses two contemporary incarnations of this stereotype, the "welfare queen" and the "crack addict," observing that such images seem to evoke the prototype for illicit black consumption — the cannibal (*Republic of Signs*, 47–86); these images suggest that black women's consumption and consumer desire remain sites of political and cultural contest. Depictions of consumer "refinement" in postbellum and late-nineteenth-century black women's fiction should be read against this backdrop; in particular, they would have served to neutralize racist cultural representations, displacing stereotypes of rapacious orality and sexuality with images of taste and sentimental investment.

2 On interconnections between the emergence of the "cotton kingdom" in the South, the rise of manufacturing (beginning with textiles) in the East, and the appropriation of Indian lands in the West, see Takaki, *Iron Cages*, 76–79. As Takaki argues, "The removal of Indians and the expansion of black slavery made possible the Market Revolution" (78). On slave and free black women's role in textile production, see Jacqueline Jones, *Labor of Love, Labor of Sorrow: Black Women, Work, and the Family, from Slavery to the Present* (New York: Vintage, 1985).

3 Spillers, "Mama's Baby," 72.

4 Ibid., 79.

5 Robyn Wiegman, *American Anatomies: Theorizing Race and Gender* (Durham: Duke University Press, 1995), 4, 22; Nicholas Thomas, "Licensed Curiosity: Cook's Pacific Voy-

ages," in *The Cultures of Collecting*, ed. John Elsner and Roger Cardinal (Cambridge: Harvard University Press, 1993), 116–36.

6 Richards, *Commodity Culture.*

7 James D. Norris, *Advertising and the Transformation of American Society, 1865–1920* (Westport, Conn.: Greenwood, 1990).

8 Jan Nederveen Pieterse, *White on Black: Images of Africa and Blacks in Western Popular Culture* (New Haven: Yale University Press, 1992), 195–98.

9 McClintock, *Imperial Leather: Race, Gender, and Sexuality in the Colonial Contest* (New York: Routledge, 1995), 207–31.

10 Wilson, "All the Rage," 33.

11 Kaja Silverman, "Fragments of a Fashionable Discourse," in *Studies in Entertainment: Critical Approaches to Mass Culture*, ed. Tania Modleski (Bloomington: Indiana University Press, 1986), 139–52.

12 On sentimental codes of dress, see Karen Halttunen, *Confidence Men and Painted Women: a Study of Middle-Class Culture in America* (New Haven: Yale University Press, 1982), 72–80. Teresa de Lauretis, *Technologies of Gender* (Bloomington: Indiana University Press, 1987).

13 Steedman, *Landscape*, 67; Kathy Peiss, *Cheap Amusements: Working Women and Leisure in Turn-of-the-Century New York* (Philadelphia: Temple University Press, 1986).

14 Jones, *Labor of Love, Labor of Sorrow*, 68–69.

15 Spillers, "Mama's Baby," 66–67.

16 Bhabha, *Location*, 86.

17 Simms, "Miss Martineau on Slavery," 641–57.

18 Genovese, *Roll, Jordan, Roll*, 556; Fox-Genovese, *Within the Plantation Household*, 222.

19 Genovese, *Roll, Jordan, Roll*, 559; Fox-Genovese, *Within the Plantation Household*, 293.

20 William and Ellen Craft, *Running a Thousand Miles for Freedom; or, The Escape of William and Ellen Craft from Slavery* (Salem, N.H.: Ayer, 1981).

21 duCille, *The Coupling Convention: Sex, Text, and Tradition in Black Women's Fiction* (New York: Oxford University Press, 1993), 88.

22 Fox-Genovese, *Within the Plantation Household*, 177–85.

23 Sterling, ed., *We Are Your Sisters: Black Women in the Nineteenth Century* (New York: Norton, 1984), 96, 216–17.

24 Fox-Genovese, *Within the Plantation Household*, 184.

25 Keckley, *Behind the Scenes: or, Thirty Years a Slave, and Four Years in the White House*, introduction by James Olney (New York: Oxford University Press, 1988), 21. All further references are to this edition.

26 Jones, *Labor of Love, Labor of Sorrow*, 68–70.

27 John E. Washington, *They Knew Lincoln* (New York: Dutton, 1942), 218.

28 Referring to the conflation of violence and sex in the whipping scene in Douglass's 1845 narrative, Mae G. Henderson argues that "not only an object of exchange in a slave economy, the aunt is also an object of desire within a system unbound by legal or cultural restraints"; "The Stories of (O)Dessa: Stories of Complicity and Resistance," in *Female Subjects in Black and White*, ed. Elizabeth Abel, Barbara Christian, and Helene Moglen (Berkeley: University of California Press, 1997), 293.

29 Young, "Women Recovering Our Clothes," in *On Fashion*, ed. Shari Benstock and Suzanne Ferriss (New Brunswick: Rutgers University Press, 1994), 205–6.

30 Fox-Genovese, *Within the Plantation Household*, 315; Spillers, "Mama's Baby."

31 Such practices constitute forms of mimicry which, in Homi Bhabha's formulation,

both reinforce and destabilize the "normalizing" authority of colonial discourse (*Location*, 85–92).

32 This is, in part, the desire for black women's labor; see the analysis of the erotics of black male labor and its appropriations in Lott, *Love and Theft*.

33 Gates, *The Signifying Monkey: A Theory of African American Literary Criticism* (New York: Oxford University Press, 1985). On the Enlightenment association between "letters" and "civilization," see Gates, "Writing, 'Race,' and the Difference It Makes," in *"Race," Writing, and Difference*, ed. Gates (Chicago: University of Chicago Press, 1986), 1–20.

34 A similar moment in the narrative occurs during a trip to Richmond with the Lincolns during the Civil War, directly after that city surrendered to the North. During a conversation with a young African American boy, the party hears the word "tote" for the first time, and discovers that the African word, in its original sense, is "defined in our standard dictionaries" and accepted in its established usage by whites and blacks (168). In this seemingly incidental inclusion to her narrative, Keckley makes visible African American contributions to Southern (and by extension, national) culture.

35 Pratt, *Imperial Eyes*, 87–88. The erotic charge and exoticism associated with transgressive social experience is perhaps most clearly legible in the "social voyeurism" of nineteenth-century popular sensationalistic fiction. Urban-exposé novels about the "mysteries" of American cities such as George Lippard's *The Quaker City* and George Thompson's *Venus in Boston* popularized what David S. Reynolds has called the antebellum "voyeur style," and are replete with passages in which the author dwells lasciviously on the private parts of his heroines and describes women in full or partial dishabille. See Reynolds, *Beneath the American Renaissance: The Subversive Imagination in the Age of Emerson and Melville* (Cambridge: Harvard University Press, 1989), 214–15.

36 Keckley attempts to distance herself from the logic of the sensational exposé, in part by relating an anecdote. As modiste for Mrs. Lincoln, she notes, "parties crowded around and affected friendship for me, hoping to induce me to betray the secrets of the domestic circle" (92). One woman, posing as a client, offers Keckley a bribe of "several thousand dollars" to secure for her a position as Mrs. Lincoln's chambermaid (94–95). After relating her shock and indignant refusal of the offer, Keckley describes how she "afterwards learned that this woman was an actress, and that her object was to enter the White House as a servant, learn its secrets, and then publish a scandal to the world" (95). Keckley both acknowledges the privileged position she occupies as domestic worker and confidante—with evident access to the Lincolns' public life—and demonstrates her discretion and loyalty: unlike the unscrupulous and insincere "actress" who is willing to commercialize even the most intimate relations, Keckley would not willingly participate in such a scandal. While Keckley insists that "I simply record the incident to show how often I was approached by unprincipled parties" (95) and that it has mere documentary value, it is obviously included as evidence of Keckley's moral character, and is meant to serve as an index to her motives in discussing the "Lincoln Dress Scandal."

37 My summary of the publishing history of Keckley's narrative is indebted to Foster, *Written by Herself*, 117–30.

38 Ibid., 129–30; Washington, *They Knew Lincoln*, 232–35.

39 Gates, "Trope of the New Negro," 136.

40 Gutman, *The Black Family in Slavery and Freedom* (New York: Pantheon, 1976).

41 Barbara Christian, *Black Women Novelists: The Development of a Tradition, 1892–1976* (Westport, Conn.: Greenwood, 1980); Deborah E. McDowell, " 'The Changing Same':

Generational Connections and Black Women Novelists," *New Literary History* 18, no. 2 (winter 1987): 281–302.

42 Williams, "Club Movement among Colored Women," in *A New Negro for a New Century*, ed. Booker T. Washington and Fannie Barrier Williams (Chicago: American Publishing House, 1900), 374.

43 Ibid.

44 Paula Giddings, *When and Where I Enter: The Impact of Black Women on Race and Sex in America* (New York: Vintage, 1984).

45 Kaplan, "Romancing the Empire," 659–90.

46 Bhabha, *Location*, 85–92.

47 Frances Smith Foster, Introduction to *A Brighter Coming Day: A Frances Ellen Watkins Harper Reader*, ed. Foster (New York: Feminist Press, 1990), 4.

48 Harper, in Frances Smith Foster, ed., *A Brighter Coming Day: A Frances Ellen Watkins Harper Reader* (New York: Feminist Press, 1990), 285, 286, 288, 290, 292, 104.

49 Harper, *Iola Leroy*, introduction by Hazel Carby (Boston: Beacon, 1987), 98. All further references are to this edition.

50 Foster, ed., *Brighter Coming Day*, 103–4, 138–56.

51 Anna Julia Cooper, *A Voice from the South* (1892; rpt. New York: Negro Universities Press, 1969), 29.

52 Hopkins, *Contending Forces: A Romance Illustrative of Negro Life North and South*, introduction by Richard Yarborough (New York: Oxford University Press, 1988), 147. All further references are to this edition.

53 Hopkins, "The Test of Manhood: A Christmas Story," in *Short Fiction by Black Women*, ed. Elizabeth Ammons (New York: Oxford University Presss, 1991), and *Hagar's Daughter*, in *The Magazine Novels of Pauline Hopkins*, introduction by Hazel Carby (New York: Oxford University Press, 1988), 184. Cf. Charles W. Chesnutt's short story "The Wife of His Youth" (1899), in which the protagonist, Mr. Ryder, on the verge of marrying an educated, refined, and light-skinned African American woman from the nation's capital, is visited by his seemingly "ancient" and "very black" first wife, whom he had left behind on the plantation and who has been searching for him for twenty-five years. Mr. Ryder decides to reveal his identity to Liza Jane—who is clearly represented by Chesnutt as a mother or even grandmother figure—and acknowledges his obligation to her as the "wife of his youth"; *The Wife of His Youth and Other Stories of the Color Line* (Ann Arbor: University of Michigan Press, 1969).

6 Not "Just a Cigar"

1 Pratt, *Imperial Eyes*, 4.

2 Tracing a shift from scientific racism to "commodity racism" in the second half of the nineteenth century, McClintock argues that commodity racism "converted the narrative of imperial Progress into mass produced consumer spectacles" (*Imperial Leather*, 33, 207–31).

3 See, for example, the essays in Amy Kaplan and Donald E. Pease, eds., *Cultures of United States Imperialism* (Durham: Duke University Press, 1993).

4 Kaplan, "Romancing the Empire," 659–90.

5 Sedgwick, *Between Men: English Literature and Male Homosocial Desire* (New York: Columbia University Press, 1985).

6 Lott, "White Like Me: Racial Cross-Dressing and the Construction of American White-

ness," in *Cultures of United States Imperialism*, ed. Amy Kaplan and Donald E. Pease (Durham: Duke University Press, 1993), 481.

7 Ibid., 482; Bhabha, *Location*, 66–84.

8 Fanon, *Black Skin, White Masks* (New York: Grove, 1967), 177, 157, 170.

9 Lott, "White Like Me," 476.

10 Delany, *Blake; or, The Huts of America*, ed. Floyd J. Miller (Boston: Beacon, 1970), 62–63.

11 Robert E. May, *The Southern Dream of a Caribbean Empire, 1854–1861* (Baton Rouge: Louisiana State University Press, 1973). The "Africanization of Cuba" was a purported plot by Spain and Britain to free slaves and put blacks in power. People of African heritage did, in fact, constitute a majority of the island's population by midcentury: census figures for 1846 indicate that, out of a total population of nine-hundred thousand, over half (53 percent) were slaves or free people of color.

12 Edward W. Said, *Culture and Imperialism* (New York: Vintage, 1993), 136–37. Signaling Delany's literary and ideological investment in forms of masculinity, Paul Gilroy states that Martin Delany should be "recognised as the progenitor of black Atlantic patriarchy"; *The Black Atlantic: Modernity and Double Consciousness* (Cambridge: Harvard University Press, 1993), 26.

13 The passage underscores the (relative) racial fluidity of Cuban society, qualities the novel's revolutionary protagonist, Henry Blake, will attempt to harness for their transformative political potential. In *Blake*, Cuba occupies a central site in the novel's inscription of Pan-African identity and a multiracial, utopian politics. (Perhaps similarly acceding to this symbolic register of "creolization," both Cassy and George Harris in *Uncle Tom's Cabin* [the text Delany was revising in *Blake*] escape from slavery in Spanish disguises.) In the nineteenth-century United States, "Cuba" constituted a sign of national difference as well as ethnic creolization and thus, for Anglo-Americans, racial difference. The racialization of "Cuba" owed something to the racialization of Spain in the Anglo-American racial imaginary; see Roberto Fernández Retamar, *Caliban and Other Essays* (Minneapolis: University of Minnesota Press, 1989).

Like Delany's *Blake*, James Weldon Johnson's *Autobiography of an Ex-Colored Man* foregrounds "Cuba" (as well as cigars) in his narrative exploration of race politics. The unnamed narrator becomes a "stripper" and then a reader in a cigar factory in Jacksonville, after he drops out of a black college in Atlanta. Emphasizing the political radicalism cigarmakers were known for as well as the *mestizaje* culture of the Cuban-American borderland of Florida (where the narrator states with pride that he became more "Cuban" than the Cubans [see note 16 below]), the episode problematizes the narrator's racial identity, perhaps informing the text's final configuration.

14 On this usage, see Nancy A. Hewitt, " 'The Voice of Virile Labor': Labor Militancy, Community Solidarity, and Gender Identity among Tampa's Latin Workers, 1880–1921," in *Work Engendered: Toward a New History of American Labor*, ed. Ava Baron (Ithaca: Cornell University Press, 1991), 142–67.

15 By the late eighteenth century, in the United States, tobacco was a prominent sign of Anglo-American economic independence and was critical to America's revolutionary symbology; the judge translates that symbology to a different colonial context. On the politicization of tobacco in the late eighteenth century, see Timothy Breen, *Tobacco Culture* (Princeton: Princeton University Press, 1985). Breen suggests that by the late eighteenth century tobacco was inscribed in Virginia political discourse as a sign of Anglo-American liberty and was prominent within the revolutionary symbology of the new nation. Delany reconfigures this symbology in the new colonial "frontier" of Cuba.

In this passage, Delany also invokes the perceived revolutionary significance of smoking in the street—a practice closely linked to the popular ascendancy of the cigar in Europe and America. According to one writer, with the spread of cigar smoking in the nineteenth century "tobacco became ambulatory, and was regarded by the authorities as a sign of revolutionary tendencies and liberalism as compared with the conservative pipe, which preferred limited confines, quiet and sedentary habits"; [Count] Corti, *A History of Smoking* (New York: Harcourt, 1932), 246. Corti notes that smoking in the street was forbidden in the absolute monarchies of Europe—a restriction lifted after the revolutions of 1848.

16 On the Cuban national discourse of *mestizaje*, utilized by José Marti, among others, see Vera M. Kutzinski, *Sugar's Secrets: Race and the Erotics of Cuban Nationalism* (Charlottesville: University of Virginia Press, 1993). Antonio Benítez-Rojo analyzes the Africanization of Cuban culture in *The Repeating Island: The Caribbean and the Postmodern Perspective*, trans. James E. Maraniss (Durham: Duke University Press, 1992), esp. 61–71. Arguing that Cuba epitomizes Caribbean creole culture, Benítez-Rojo attributes the extensive African influence in Cuban culture to the relatively late date of the onset of the plantation system on that island (68).

17 That desire is articulated through class as well as through race. Unlike the United States, where (in Eric Lott's phrasing) "the formation of a northern working class depended on a common sense of whiteness" (*Love and Theft*, 67), the Cuban working class was chiefly comprised of workers of color. Free people of color (15–20 percent of the total population at midcentury) constituted a majority of workers in Cuba's skilled trades—an arrangement attributed by some scholars to the traditional Spanish stigma attached to manual labor. The differences in the racial constitution of the Cuban and U.S. working classes was not lost on U.S. travelers, who regularly commented on the extraordinary visibility of Afro-Cubans in manufacturing and other skilled trades. Hiram Hastings, U.S. consul to Trinidad, in 1842 described a Cuban "mechanic industry carried on by free labor, mostly by blacks and mulattoes"; quoted in Robert Paquette, *Sugar Is Made with Blood* (Middletown: Wesleyan University Press, 1982), 32.

18 Fiedler, *Love and Death in the American Novel* (New York: Stein and Day, 1966). Similarly foregrounding the problematic of black male *labor*, Lott examines this structure of white male cross-racial, homoerotic identification and disavowal at work in antebellum blackface (*Love and Theft*, passim).

19 For theoretical analyses of the erotics of national identity and for the view that "nationalism favors a distinctly homosocial form of male bonding," see the essays in Andrew Parker et al., eds., *Nationalisms and Sexualities* (New York: Routledge, 1992).

20 While most lynchings took place in the South, several scholars have attempted to recontextualize lynching as a national, rather than a regional, racial phenomenon, and an index of Northern as well as Southern white men's racial/sexual fears. Both Nina Silber and Gail Bederman, for example, argue that Northern white men saw a model of white manhood in the lynching scenario; see Silber, *The Romance of Reunion* (Chapel Hill: University of North Carolina Press, 1993), and Bederman, "Civilization, the Decline of Middle-Class Manliness, and Ida B. Wells' Anti-Lynching Campaign (1892–94)," in *Gender and American History since 1890*, ed. Barbara Melosh (New York: Routledge, 1993), 27–39. According to Silber, "many northerners responded to the South's racial hysteria not because of a deep and abiding fear of black rape, but because the southern message about sexual and gender disorder, and the need for

white men to play a greater role in reasserting the old boundaries, resonated with their view of the sexual changes they saw occurring in their own society" (156).

21 As quoted in Kevin Gaines, "Black Americans' Racial Uplift Ideology as 'Civilizing Mission': Pauline E. Hopkins on Race and Imperialism,'" in *Cultures of United States Imperialism*, ed. Amy Kaplan and Donald E. Pease (Durham: Duke University Press, 1993), 441–42.

22 Hazel V. Carby, "'On the Threshold of Woman's Era': Lynching, Empire, and Sexuality in Black Feminist Theory," in *"Race," Writing and Difference*, ed. Henry Louis Gates Jr. (Chicago: University of Chicago Press, 1986), 301–16.

23 Trudier Harris, *Exorcising Blackness: Historical and Literary Lynching and Burning Rituals* (Bloomington: Indiana University Press, 1984).

24 According to Hazel Carby, writers such as Ida B. Wells "knew that emancipation meant that white men lost their vested interests in the body of the Negro and that lynching and the rape of black women were attempts to regain control" ("'On the Threshold of Woman's Era,'" 308).

25 Harris, *Exorcising Blackness*, 13.

26 Jacquelyn Dowd Hall, "'The Mind That Burns in Each Body': Women, Rape, and Racial Violence," in *Powers of Desire: The Politics of Sexuality*, ed. Ann Snitow, Christine Stansell, and Sharon Thompson (New York: Monthly Review, 1983), 328–49.

27 Harris, *Exorcising Blackness*, 6.

28 Wright, *The Long Dream* (New York: Harper, 1987), 78–79.

29 Smith, as quoted in Harris, *Exorcising Blackness*, 23.

30 Ibid., 22.

31 Dance, as quoted in Harris, *Exorcising Blackness*, 22.

32 Videorecording, *Bill T. Jones: Dancing to the Promised Land* (New York: View Video, 1994).

33 An overtly phallic signifier, the cigar could be termed a racial fetish: like the sexual fetish in Freud's account, the racial fetish works to alleviate the fact of difference and lack—here the specifically racial lack under white hegemony of a relation between the races. Like the (female) object of the sexual fetishist's gaze, the black male body is the object of an erotic overinvestment which negates the identity of racial difference—thus making that body available as the projected site of repressed (white) eroticism and the repository of white male revivification.

34 Fernando Ortiz, *Cuban Counterpoint: Tobacco and Sugar* (New York: Knopf, 1947), 5.

35 Kutzinski, *Sugar's Secrets*, 11.

36 Robert Heimann, *Tobacco and Americans* (New York: McGraw-Hill, 1960), 89.

37 On the growing U.S. influence over the Cuban economy in the last quarter of the nineteenth century, see Jules R. Benjamin, *The United States and the Origin of the Cuban Revolution* (Princeton: Princeton University Press, 1990).

38 James, *The Bostonians*, Introd. Irving Howe (New York: Random House, 1956), 343. Many historians have examined this "crisis of masculinity." See Lears, *No Place of Grace*; and John Higham, "The Reorientation of American Culture in the 1890s," in *Writing American History: Essays on Modern Scholarship* (Bloomington: Indiana University Press, 1970), 73–100.

39 Lester D. Langley, *The Cuban Policy of the United States: A Brief History* (New York: John Wiley, 1968), 6, 10. Most U.S. policymakers rejected colonialism in favor of generalized economic imperialism. For instance, the Spanish American War journalist Trumbull

White, writing enthusiastically about the United States' acquisition of "our new possessions"—Cuba, Puerto Rico, Hawaii, and the Philippines—observed that "to dominate in commercial influence and in all things for the uplifting of a swarming population of alien races, is a function as worthy, and of more interest and consequence to most of our people, than the mere detail of official sway"; quoted in David Spurr, *The Rhetoric of Empire* (Durham: Duke University Press, 1992), 16, 118. By the late nineteenth century, commodity culture was officially identified as the primary terrain on which U.S. imperial desires and designs would be played out. Within the United States, the commodity served as a means through which national policy was inscribed on the bodies of U.S. citizens, a means through which individuals were enlisted to participate in "empire as a way of life."

40 Takaki, *Iron Cages*, 253–79.

41 Like sugar and coffee, tobacco found ready and expanding markets as a working-class ingestible in industrializing nations such as the United States. For a related discussion of the connections between the rise of working-class consumption, imperialism, and slavery, see Sidney W. Mintz, *Sweetness and Power: The Place of Sugar in Modern History* (New York: Vintage, 1985). Increased working-class demand for imperial commodities (such as the cigar) both restructured the nexus of international capitalism, and was directly linked to the development of empire and its racial divisions of labor.

42 During the war, Cuban soldiers were widely represented in American journalism as cowardly and undisciplined—in short, as unmanly—a representation which served to highlight the masculinity of American soldiers, and to justify the U.S. political decision to exclude the Cuban command from military operations and consequently from deciding on their future in the peace settlement with Spain. See Kaplan, "Romancing the Empire."

43 Higham, "Reorientation of American Culture."

44 Seton, as quoted in Mark Seltzer, *Bodies and Machines* (New York: Routledge, 1992), 149.

45 For examples of such revisionism in the sphere of literature, see the essays in Gustavo Pérez Firmat, ed., *Do the Americas Have a Common Literature?* (Durham: Duke University Press, 1990).

46 Ortiz, *Cuban Counterpoint*, 61, 46. For a critique of Ortiz's analysis, see Kutzinski, *Sugar's Secrets*.

47 L. Glenn Westfall, *Don Vicente Martinez Yor, The Man and His Empire: The Development of the Clear Havana Industry in Cuba and Florida in the Nineteenth Century* (New York: Garland, 1987), and Patricia A. Cooper, *Once a Cigar Maker: Men, Women, and Work Culture in American Cigar Factories, 1900–1919* (Urbana: University of Illinois Press, 1987).

48 Jean Stubbs, *Tobacco on the Periphery: A Case Study in Cuban Labor History, 1860–1958* (New York: Cambridge University Press, 1985).

49 Smith, "Visiting the Banana Republic," in *Universal Abandon?: The Politics of Postmodernism*, ed. Andrew Ross (Minneapolis: University of Minnesota Press, 1988), 139.

50 On the consolidation of the national market and the growth of a mass consumer society during this period, see the essays in Bronner, ed., *Consuming Visions*.

51 Robert Goldman, *Reading Ads Socially* (New York: Routledge, 1993).

52 Presbrey, *The History and Development of Advertising* (1929; rpt. New York: Greenwood, 1968), 382.

53 Neil Harris, "Iconography and Intellectual History: The Half-Tone Effect," in *New Directions in American Intellectual History*, ed. John Higham and Paul K. Conkin (Baltimore: Johns Hopkins University Press, 1979), 196–211.

54 Some of the best-known figures in commercial advertising got their start as war illustrators. For example, Howard Chandler Christy developed the "Christy girl" when illustrating a Spanish American War story by Richard Harding Davis for Scribners.

55 On such "fads" as the cigar-band dish (especially popular between 1900 and 1912), see Edmund B. Sullivan, *Collecting Political Americana* (New York: Crown, 1980), 154–55.

56 Blumin, *Emergence,* 183.

57 Cooper, *Once a Cigar Maker,* 13.

58 Slotkin, *Regeneration.* Neither Slotkin nor Norton deals with the homoerotics of this paradigm.

59 As I have argued throughout this project, the gendered constructions of "pious" and frontier consumption are constituted in relation to one another. Just as the "civilized" feminine consumer was often used, iconographically, to emblematize the moral superiority of the West and to legitimize imperial aggressions, the sentimental domestic ethos worked to neutralize, even while it discursively sustained, the violence of "masculine" imperial expansion.

60 E.g., *Cartoons of the Spanish-American War* (Minneapolis, 1899).

61 Pratt, *Imperial Eyes,* 56.

62 Lears, *No Place of Grace,* 141–81. On the origins of romantic "Anglo-Saxonism" and its links to imperialism, see Reginald Horsman, *Race and Manifest Destiny: The Origins of Racial Anglo-Saxonism* (Cambridge: Harvard University Press, 1981).

63 Hobsbawm, as seen in Kaplan, "Romancing the Empire."

64 Heimann, *Tobacco,* 106. Examples of the "American Presidents" series appear in Z. Davidoff, *The Connoisseur's Book of the Cigar* (New York: McGraw Hill, 1969).

65 Norris, *Advertising,* 130–31.

66 Smith-Rosenberg, *Disorderly Conduct: Visions of Gender in Victorian America* (New York: Oxford University Press, 1985).

67 For example, President Monroe described Cuba as the "mouth" of Mississippi, thus organically annexing Cuba to the national "body" of the United States. On Monroe's imperial metaphorics, see Wai-Chee Dimock, *Empire for Liberty: Melville and the Poetics of Individualism* (Princeton: Princeton University Press, 1989).

68 Ibid., 27.

69 José David Saldivar, *The Dialectics of Our America: Genealogy, Cultural Critique, and Literary History* (Durham: Duke University Press, 1991), 9.

70 See Norton, *Alternative Americas.*

71 William Atlee Burpee was a famous seedsman who collected seeds from all over the world; occasionally he commissioned explorers and missionaries to collect for him. Burpee sold the seeds through his mail order company, with advertisements for the seeds appearing in agricultural journals and religious periodicals. See Clare Shaver Haughton, *Green Immigrants: The Plants That Transformed America* (New York: Harcourt Brace Jovanovich, 1978), 218–19.

72 *Cartoons of the Spanish-American War,* 108.

73 Heimann, *Tobacco,* 96. For additional examples, see A. D. Faber, *Cigar Label Art* (Watkins Glen, N.Y.: Century House, 1949), esp. 32, 58, 64, 67, 71, 80.

74 E. R. Billings, *Tobacco: Its History, Varieties, Culture, Manufacture, and Commerce* (New York, 1875), 261.

75 Kaplan, "Romancing the Empire," 676–77.

76 Rosenberg, *Spreading the American Dream: American Economic and Cultural Expansion, 1890–1945* (New York: Hill and Wang, 1982), 47.

77 Saldivar, *Dialectics*, 24.

78 See Westfall, *Don Vicente*. Jean Stubbs notes that many Cuban cigar manufacturers emigrated to the United States to avoid the costly tariffs that were imposed on U.S. imports starting in the 1860s, and states that Key West and Tampa formed "part of a single 'Cuban' cigar making universe" at the turn of the century (*Tobacco on the Periphery*, xiii).

79 "The Repeating Island," in *Do the Americas Have a Common Literature?* ed. Gustavo Pérez Firmat (Durham: Duke University Press, 1990), 103. Benítez-Rojo describes the modern Caribbean as an "island bridge," an ontologically hybrid territory engendered "by the copulation of Europe—that insatiable solar bull—with the Caribbean archipelago," a cultural coupling which enabled capital accumulation and distribution (generated by the development of the Atlantic fleet system and the plantation) and through them the history of Western capitalism as we know it.

80 Said, *Orientalism* (London: Routledge, 1978).

81 Enloe, *Bananas, Beaches, and Bases: Making Feminist Sense of International Politics* (Berkeley: University of California Press, 1990), 133.

82 On anti-Spanish narratives such as *Rosamond*, see Jenny Franchot, *Roads to Rome: The Antebellum Protestant Encounter with Catholicism* (Berkeley: University of California Press, 1994).

83 Louisville *Daily Courier*, 19 February 1859, as quoted in May, *Southern Dream*, 7.

84 Pratt, *Imperial Eyes*.

85 Havelock Ellis, "Sexual Inversion in Women," in *Studies in the Psychology of Sex*, vol. 2, *Sexual Inversion* (Philadelphia: F. A. Davis, 1928), 250. For a relevant discussion of Krafft-Ebing, see Smith-Rosenberg, *Disorderly Conduct*.

Conclusion

1 Poovey, "Aesthetics and Political Economy in the Eighteenth Century," in *Aesthetics and Ideology*, ed. George Levine (New Brunswick: Rutgers University Press, 1994), 83–84.

2 Crèvecoeur, *Letters*, 70, Brown, "Wounded Attachments," 199–227. As in the eighteenth-century texts discussed in chapter 1, Crèvecoeur's text sutures together "Americanness," property ownership, "free" civil subjectivity, and whiteness. The constitutive, and racialized, ambivalence of this construction, discussed throughout this book, suggests a way of interpreting the place of the "wounded" black body in Crèvecoeur's *Letters*, spectacularly (re)presented in letter 9, and the forms of gothic terror and self-recognition in the white spectator which that body generates.

3 In Crèvecoeur's *Letters*, as I have suggested, the myth of class equality among whites depended implicitly on forms of racial difference (specifically, the political subordination and discursive objectification of blacks); but Crèvecoeur, in part because he imagines familial unity in an agrarian "household economy," doesn't problematize patriarchal authority (nor does he feminize sentiment). By the 1820s, with universal white male suffrage and new economic relations, at least in urban areas, gender was being produced as the only salient social difference among whites.

4 Lydia Maria Child. Hobomok and Other Writings on Indians, ed. Carolyn L. Karcher (New Brunswick: Rutgers University Press, 1992), 76. All further references are to this edition.

5 The novel's severe problematization of Mary's desire for Hobomok, and her consent to marry him, are symptomatic of the racial parameters of feminine consent and patri-

archal authority in the text, the suturing together of feminine conscience and (white) patriarchal law. When she agrees to marry Hobomok, Mary is depicted as desperate to the point of distraction, possibly mad, will-less, and "apparently unconscious" (125); Child even suggests that Mary's "decision" should be viewed as an atavistic relapse of the Puritans' "blind belief in fatality" (121). In evoking the "broken and confused mass" of thought, the "whirlwind of thoughts and passions" that precipitate Mary's action, narrative authority breaks down, generating a crisis in the sympathetic powers of the narrator: "It is difficult to tell what the feelings could have been, half bewildered as they were, which led her to persevere in so strange a purpose" (124). That the novel depicts Mary's decision as unrepresentable, indeed unimaginable, is symptomatic of the sentimental alignment of feminine conscience (and subjectivity) with patriarchal law.

6 It is in these terms that we are meant to view Mr. Johnson as the novel's true hero: unlike Mr. Conant, he cannot survive his wife's death, confessing on his deathbed, "God forgive me, if in sinful weakness, I have loved that dear woman even better than his righteous cause" (112–13).

7 Lawrence Grossberg, "History, Politics and Postmodernism: Stuart Hall and Cultural Studies," in *Stuart Hall: Critical Dialogues in Cultural Studies*, ed. David Morley and Kuan-Hsing Chen (New York: Routledge, 1996), 168.

WORKS CITED

Adorno, Theodor. *Prisms.* Trans. Samuel Weber and Shierry Weber. Cambridge: MIT Press, 1982.

Advice to the Fair Sex. Philadelphia, 1803.

Agnew, Jean Christophe. *Worlds Apart: The Market and the Theater in Anglo-American Thought, 1550–1750.* New York: Cambridge University Press, 1986.

Alarcon, Norma. "The Theoretical Subject(s) of This Bridge Called My Back and Anglo-American Feminism." In *Making Face, Making Soul/Hacienda Caras,* ed. Gloria Anzaldúa, 356–69. San Francisco: Aunt Lute, 1990.

Ames, Kenneth L. "Material Culture as Non Verbal Communication: A Historical Case Study." *Journal of American Culture* 3, no. 4 (1980): 619–41.

Ammons, Elizabeth. "Heroines in *Uncle Tom's Cabin.*" *American Literature* 49, no. 2 (1977): 161–79.

Anderson, Benedict. *Imagined Communities: Reflections on the Origin and Spread of Nationalism.* London: Verso, 1983.

Andrews, Kenneth R. *Nook Farm: Mark Twain's Hartford Circle.* Cambridge: Harvard University Press, 1950.

Andrews, William L. "The Novelization of Voice in Early African American Narrative." *PMLA* 105, no. 1 (January 1990): 23–34.

——. *Sisters of the Spirit: Three Black Women's Autobiographies of the Nineteenth Century.* Bloomington: Indiana University Press, 1986.

Anthony, Susan B., Elizabeth Cady Stanton, and Matilda Joslyn Gage, eds. *History of Woman Suffrage.* 6 vols. New York: Fowler and Wells, 1881.

Appleby, Joyce O. *Economic Thought and Ideology in Seventeenth Century England.* Princeton: Princeton University Press, 1978.

Arendt, Hannah. *The Human Condition.* Chicago: University of Chicago Press, 1958.

Armstrong, Nancy. *Desire and Domestic Fiction: A Political History of the Novel.* New York: Oxford University Press, 1987.

Arrington, Leonard, J., and Jon Haupt. "Intolerable Zion: The Image of Mormonism in Nineteenth-Century American Literature." *Western Humanities Review* 22 (1968): 243–60.

Bailey, Rufus William. *The Family Preacher.* New York, 1837.

Bailyn, Bernard. *The Ideological Origins of the American Revolution.* Cambridge: Harvard University Press, 1967.

Baker, Paula. "The Domestication of Politics: Women and American Political Society, 1780–1920." *American Historical Review* 89, no. 3 (June 1984): 620–47.

Barker-Benfield, G. J. *The Horrors of the Half-Known Life: Male Attitudes toward Women and Sexuality in Nineteenth-Century America.* New York: Harper and Row, 1976.

Basch, Norma. *In the Eyes of the Law: Women, Marriage, and Property in Nineteenth-Century New York.* Ithaca: Cornell University Press, 1982.

Baudrillard, Jean. *For a Critique of the Political Economy of the Sign.* Trans. Charles Levin. St. Louis: Telos Press, 1981.

——. *Selected Writings.* Ed. Mark Poster. Stanford: Stanford University Press, 1988.

Baym, Nina. *Novels, Readers, and Reviewers: Responses to Fiction in Antebellum America.* Ithaca: Cornell University Press, 1984.

——. *Woman's Fiction: A Guide to Novels by and about Women in America.* Ithaca: Cornell University Press, 1978.

Beadle, J. H. *Life in Utah.* Philadelphia: National, 1870.

Bederman, Gail. "Civilization, the Decline of Middle-Class Manliness, and Ida B. Wells' Anti-Lynching Campaign (1892–94)." In *Gender and American History since 1890,* ed. Barbara Melosh, 27–39. New York: Routledge, 1993.

Beecher, Catherine, and Harriet Beecher Stowe. *The American Woman's Home.* 1869. Reprint, Watkins Glen, N.Y.: American Life Foundation, 1979.

Beeman, William O. "Freedom to Choose: Symbols and Values in American Advertising." In *Symbolizing America,* ed. Hervé Varenne, 52–65. Lincoln: University of Nebraska Press, 1986.

Belsey, Catherine. *Critical Practice.* New York: Methuen, 1980.

Benítez-Rojo, Antonio. "The Repeating Island." In *Do the Americas Have a Common Literature?* ed. Gustavo Pérez Firmat, 85–106. Durham: Duke University Press, 1990.

——. *The Repeating Island: The Caribbean and the Postmodern Perspective.* Trans. James E. Maraniss. Durham: Duke University Press, 1992.

Benjamin, Jules R. *The United States and the Origin of the Cuban Revolution.* Princeton: Princeton University Press, 1990.

Benston, Kimberly W. "I yam what I am: The Topos of Un(naming) in Afro-American Literature." In *Black Literature and Literary Theory,* ed. Henry Louis Gates Jr., 151–72. New York: Methuen, 1984.

Berlant, Lauren. *The Anatomy of National Fantasy: Hawthorne, Utopia, and Everyday Life.* Chicago: University of Chicago Press, 1991.

——. "Fantasies of Utopia in *The Blithedale Romance.*" *American Literary History* 1, no. 1 (spring 1989): 31–62.

——. "The Queen of America Goes to Washington City: Harriet Jacobs, Frances Harper, Anita Hill." In *Subjects and Citizens: Nation, Race, and Gender from* Oroonoko *to Anita Hill,* ed. Cathy N. Davidson and Michael Moon, 455–80. Durham: Duke University Press, 1995.

Bhabha, Homi K. *The Location of Culture.* New York: Routledge, 1994.

Bill T. Jones: Dancing to the Promised Land. Videorecording. New York: View Video, 1994.

Billings, E. R. *Tobacco: Its History, Varieties, Culture, Manufacture, and Commerce.* New York, 1875.

Bloch, Ruth. "American Feminine Ideals in Transition: The Rise of the Moral Mother, 1785–1815." *Feminist Studies* 4, no. 2 (1978): 101–26.

———. "The Gendered Meanings of Virtue in Revolutionary America." *Signs* 13, no. 1 (1987): 37–58.
———. "Untangling the Roots of Modern Sex Roles: A Survey of Four Centuries of Change." *Signs* 4, no. 2 (1978): 237–52.
Blumin, Stuart M. *The Emergence of the Middle Class: Social Experience in the American City, 1760–1900.* New York: Cambridge University Press, 1989.
Bourdieu, Pierre. *Distinction: A Social Critique of the Judgment of Taste.* Trans. Richard Nice. Cambridge: Harvard University Press, 1984.
Boydston, Jeanne, Mary Kelley, and Anne Margolis. *The Limits of Sisterhood: The Beecher Sisters on Women's Rights and Woman's Sphere.* Chapel Hill: University of North Carolina Press, 1988.
Braxton, Joanne. *Black Women Writing Autobiography: A Tradition within a Tradition.* Philadelphia: Temple University Press, 1989.
Breen, Timothy. *Tobacco Culture.* Princeton: Princeton University Press, 1985.
Breitwieser, Mitchell Robert. *American Puritanism and the Defense of Mourning: Religion, Grief, and Ethnology in Mary White Rowlandson's Captivity Narrative.* Madison: University of Wisconsin Press, 1990.
Brodhead, Richard. "Sparing the Rod: Discipline and Fiction in Antebellum America." *Representations* 21 (1988): 67–96.
Bronner, Simon, ed. *Consuming Visions: Accumulation and Display of Goods in America, 1880–1920.* New York: Norton, 1989.
Brown, Charles Brockden. *Alcuin: A Dialogue.* Ed. Sydney J. Krause et al. Kent, Oh.: Kent State University Press, 1987.
Brown, Charles H. *The Correspondents' War: Journalists in the Spanish-American War.* New York: Scribner's, 1967.
Brown, Gillian. *Domestic Individualism: Imagining Self in Nineteenth-Century America.* Berkeley: University of California Press, 1990.
Brown, Richard D. "Modernization and the Modern Personality in Early America, 1600–1865: A Sketch of a Synthesis." *Journal of Interdisciplinary History* 2 (1972): 201–28.
Brown, Wendy. "Wounded Attachments: Late Modern Oppositional Political Formations." In *The Identity in Question,* ed. John Rajchman, 199–227. New York: Routledge, 1995.
Bruckner, Pascal. *Tears of the White Man: Compassion as Contempt.* Trans. William R. Beer. New York: Free Press, 1986.
Bushnell, Horace. *Christian Nurture.* Introduction by Luther A. Weigle. New Haven: Yale University Press, 1916.
Butler, Judith. *Gender Trouble: Feminism and the Subversion of Identity.* New York: Routledge, 1990.
———. *The Psychic Life of Power: Theories in Subjection.* Stanford: Stanford University Press, 1997.
Campbell, Colin. *The Romantic Ethic and the Spirit of Modern Consumerism.* London: Basil Blackwell, 1987.
Campbell, Karlyn Kohrs. "Style and Content in the Rhetoric of Early Afro-American Feminists." *Quarterly Journal of Speech* 72, no. 4 (1986): 434–45.
Carby, Hazel V. " 'On the Threshold of Woman's Era': Lynching, Empire, and Sexuality in Black Feminist Theory." In *"Race," Writing, and Difference,* ed. Henry Louis Gates Jr., 301–16. Chicago: University of Chicago Press, 1986.
———. *Reconstructing Womanhood: The Emergence of the Afro-American Novelist.* New York: Oxford University Press, 1987.

Cartoons of the Spanish-American War. Minneapolis, 1899.

Cartwright, Peter. *Autobiography.* Ed. W. P. Strickland. New York, 1856.

Cassity, Michael J. "Slaves, Families, and 'Living Space': A Note on Evidence and Historical Context." *Southern Studies* 17 (summer 1978): 209–15.

Channing, William Ellery. *Conversations in Rome.* Boston, 1847.

Chase, Amos. *On Female Excellence.* Litchfield, Conn., 1792.

Cherniavsky, Eva. "Charlotte Temple's Remains." In *Discovering Difference,* ed. Christopher K. Lohman, 35–47. Bloomington: Indiana University Press, 1993.

Chesnutt, Charles W. *The Wife of His Youth and Other Stories of the Color Line.* Ann Arbor: University of Michigan Press, 1969.

Child, Lydia Maria. Hobomok *and Other Writings on Indians.* Ed. Carolyn L. Karcher. New Brunswick: Rutgers University Press, 1992.

——. *Letters from New York.* New York, 1845.

Christian, Barbara. *Black Women Novelists: The Development of a Tradition, 1892–1976.* Westport, Conn.: Greenwood, 1980.

Clark, Clifford E., Jr. *The American Family Home, 1800–1960.* Chapel Hill: University of North Carolina Press, 1986.

Cmiel, Kenneth. *Democratic Eloquence: The Fight over Popular Speech in Nineteenth-Century America.* Berkeley: University of California Press, 1990.

Collins, James H. "The Topsy Element in Advertising." *Printer's Ink* 14 (Oct. 1908): 18–19.

Conrad, Peter. *The Victorian Treasure House.* London: Collins, 1973.

Cooper, Anna Julia. *A Voice from the South.* 1892. Reprint, New York: Negro Universities Press, 1969.

Cooper, Patricia A. *Once A Cigar Maker: Men, Women, and Work Culture in American Cigar Factories, 1900–1919.* Urbana: University of Illinois Press, 1987.

Cornell, Drucilla. *Beyond Accommodation: Ethical Feminism, Deconstruction, and the Law.* New York: Routledge, 1990.

Corti, Egon Caesar [Count]. *A History of Smoking.* Trans. Paul England. New York, Harcourt, 1932.

Cott, Nancy. *The Bonds of Womanhood: "Woman's Sphere" in New England, 1780–1835.* New Haven: Yale University Press, 1977.

Craft, William and Ellen. *Running a Thousand Miles for Freedom; or, The Escape of William and Ellen Craft from Slavery.* Salem, N.H.: Ayer, 1981.

Crèvecoeur, Hector St. John de. *Letters from an American Farmer.* Ed. Albert E. Stone. New York: Penguin, 1981.

Cummins, Maria. *The Lamplighter.* Ed. Nina Baym. New Brunswick: Rutgers University Press, 1988.

Cvetkovich, Ann. *Mixed Feelings: Feminism, Mass Culture, and Victorian Sensationalism.* New Brunswick: Rutgers University Press, 1992.

Davidoff, Z. *The Connoisseur's Book of the Cigar.* New York: McGraw Hill, 1969.

Davidson, Cathy N. Introduction. *The Coquette,* by Hannah W. Foster. New York: Oxford University Press, 1986.

——. *Revolution and the Word: The Rise of the Novel in America.* New York: Oxford University Press, 1986.

Davis, Angela. *Women, Race, and Class.* New York: Random House, 1981.

Davis, David Brion. *The Problem of Slavery in the Age of Revolution, 1770–1823.* Ithaca: Cornell University Press, 1975.

——. *Slavery and Human Progress.* New York: Oxford University Press, 1984.

———. "Some Themes of Counter-Subversion: An Analysis of Anti-Masonic, Anti-Catholic, and Anti-Mormon Literature." *Mississippi Historical Review* 47 (1960–61): 205–24.

de Certeau, Michel. *The Practice of Everyday Life*. Berkeley: University of California Press, 1984.

Deetz, James. *In Small Things Forgotten*. Garden City, N.Y.: Anchor, 1977.

Delany, Martin. *Blake; or, The Huts of America*. Ed. Floyd J. Miller. Boston: Beacon, 1970.

de Lauretis, Teresa. *Alice Doesn't: Feminism, Semiotics, Cinema*. Bloomington: Indiana University Press, 1984.

———. *Technologies of Gender*. Bloomington: Indiana University Press, 1987.

D'Emilio, John. "Capitalism and Gay Identity." In *The Gay and Lesbian Studies Reader*, ed. Henry Abelove, Michèle Aina Barale, and David M. Halperin, 467–76. New York: Routledge, 1993.

Dimock, Wai-Chee. *Empire for Liberty: Melville and the Poetics of Individualism*. Princeton: Princeton University Press, 1989.

Douglas, Ann. *The Feminization of American Culture*. New York: Anchor, 1988.

Douglass, Frederick. "The Future of the Negro People of the Slave States." In *Afro-American History: Primary Sources*, ed. Thomas R. Frazier. Chicago: Dorsey, 1988.

———. *My Bondage and My Freedom*. In *Frederick Douglass: The Narrative and Selected Writings*, ed. Michael Meyer. New York: Modern Library, 1984.

———. *Narrative of the Life of Frederick Douglass, an African Slave*. In *The Classic Slave Narratives*, ed. Henry Louis Gates Jr. New York: Signet, 1987.

Downing, A. J. *The Architecture of Country Houses*. 1850. Reprint, New York: Dover, 1969.

———. *Cottage Residences; Rural Architecture and Landscape Gardening*. New York, 1847.

DuBois, W. E. B. *The Seventh Son: The Thought and Writings of W. E. B. DuBois*. Vol. 1, ed. Julius Lester. Vintage: New York, 1971.

duCille, Ann. *The Coupling Convention: Sex, Text, and Tradition in Black Women's Fiction*. New York: Oxford University Press, 1993.

Dudden, Faye E. *Serving Women: Household Service in Nineteenth-Century America*. Middletown: Wesleyan University Press, 1983.

Dyer, Richard. *Heavenly Bodies: Film Stars and Society*. New York: St. Martin's, 1986.

Eisenstein, Zillah R. *The Color of Gender: Reimaging Democracy*. Berkeley: University of California Press, 1994.

Elias, Norbert. *The Civilizing Process. Volume One: The Development of Manners*. Trans. Edmund Jephcott. New York: Pantheon, 1982.

———. *The Civilizing Process. Volume Two: Power and Civility*. Trans. Edmund Jephcott. New York: Pantheon, 1982.

Ellis, Havelock. "Sexual Inversion in Women." In *Studies in the Psychology of Sex*. Vol. 2, *Sexual Inversion*. Philadelphia: F. A. Davis, 1928.

Enloe, Cynthia. *Bananas, Beaches, and Bases: Making Feminist Sense of International Politics*. Berkeley: University of California Press, 1990.

Faber, A. D. *Cigar Label Art*. Watkins Glen, N.Y.: Century House, 1949.

Fanon, Frantz. *Black Skin, White Masks*. New York: Grove, 1967.

Farnham, Eliza W. *Life in Prairie Land*. New York: Harper, 1846.

Farrar, Eliza. *The Young Lady's Friend*. 1836. Reprint, ed. Leon Stein and Annette K. Baxter, New York: Arno, 1974.

Ferguson, Adam. *An Essay on the History of Civil Society*. London, 1782.

Fetterley, Judith. Introduction. *Provisions: A Reader from Nineteenth-Century American Women*, ed. Fetterley. Bloomington: Indiana University Press, 1985.

Fiedler, Leslie A. *Love and Death in the American Novel.* New York: Stein and Day, 1966.

Firmat, Gustavo Pérez, ed. *Do the Americas Have a Common Literature?* Durham: Duke University Press, 1990.

Fisher, Philip. "Democratic Social Space: Whitman, Melville, and the Promise of American Transparency." *Representations* 24 (fall 1988): 60–101.

——. *Hard Facts: Setting and Form in the American Novel.* New York: Oxford University Press, 1985.

Fliegelman, Jay. *Prodigals and Pilgrims: The American Revolution against Patriarchal Authority, 1750–1800.* New York: Cambridge University Press, 1982.

Forty, Adrian. *Objects of Desire.* London: Thames and Hudson, 1986.

Foster, Frances Smith. Introduction. *A Brighter Coming Day: A Frances Ellen Watkins Harper Reader.* Ed. Foster. New York: Feminist Press, 1990.

——. *Witnessing Slavery: The Development of Antebellum Slave Narratives.* Westport, Conn.: Greenwood, 1979.

——. *Written By Herself: Literary Production by African American Women, 1746–1892.* Bloomington: Indiana University Press, 1993.

——, ed. *A Brighter Coming Day: A Frances Ellen Watkins Harper Reader.* New York: Feminist Press, 1990.

Foster, Hannah W. *The Boarding School; or, Lessons of a Preceptress to Her Pupils.* Boston, 1829.

——. *The Coquette.* Ed. Cathy Davidson. Reprint, New York: Oxford University Press, 1986.

Foucault, Michel. *Discipline and Punish: The Birth of the Prison.* Trans. Alan Sheridan. New York: Random House, 1979.

——. *The History of Sexuality.* Vol. 1, trans. Robert Hurley. New York: Random House, 1980.

——. *Madness and Civilization.* Trans. Richard Howard. New York: Vintage, 1973.

Fox-Genovese, Elizabeth. *Within the Plantation Household: Black and White Women of the Old South.* Chapel Hill: University of North Carolina Press, 1988.

Franchot, Jenny. "The Punishment of Esther: Frederick Douglass and the Constitution of the Feminine." In *Frederick Douglass: New Literary and Historical Essays,* ed. Eric J. Sundquist, 142–65. New York: Cambridge University Press, 1990.

——. *Roads to Rome: The Antebellum Protestant Encounter with Catholicism.* Berkeley: University of California Press, 1994.

Fraser, Nancy. *Justice Interruptus: Critical Reflections on the "Postsocialist" Condition.* New York: Routledge, 1997.

——. *Unruly Practices: Power, Discourse, and Gender in Contemporary Social Theory.* Minneapolis: University of Minnesota Press, 1989.

Fried, Marc. "Grieving for a Lost Home." In *The Urban Condition: People and Policy in the Metropolis,* ed. Leonard J. Duhl, 151–71. New York: Basic, 1963.

Fuss, Diana. *Identification Papers.* New York: Routledge, 1995.

Gaines, Jane. "Introduction: Fabricating the Female Body." In *Fabrications: Costume and the Female Body,* ed. Jane Gaines and Charlotte Herzog, 11–15. New York: Routledge, 1990.

Gaines, Kevin. "Black Americans' Racial Uplift Ideology as 'Civilizing Mission': Pauline E. Hopkins on Race and Imperialism." In *Cultures of United States Imperialism,* ed. Amy Kaplan and Donald Pease, 433–55. Durham: Duke University Press, 1993.

Gallagher, Catherine. *Nobody's Story: The Vanishing Acts of Women Writers in the Marketplace, 1670–1820.* Berkeley: University of California Press, 1994.

Gates, Henry Louis, Jr. *The Signifying Monkey: A Theory of African American Literary Criticism.* New York: Oxford University Press, 1985.
——. "The Trope of the New Negro and the Reconstruction of the Image of the Black." *Representations* 24 (fall 1988): 129–55.
——. "Writing 'Race' and the Difference It Makes." In *"Race," Writing, and Difference,* ed. Henry Louis Gates, 1–20. Chicago: University of Chicago Press, 1986.
Genovese, Eugene. *Roll, Jordan, Roll: The World the Slaves Made.* New York: Random House, 1974.
Giddings, Paula. *When and Where I Enter: The Impact of Black Women on Race and Sex in America.* New York: Vintage, 1984.
Giedion, Siegfried. *Mechanization Takes Command: A Contribution to Anonymous History.* New York: Norton, 1948.
Gilroy, Paul. *The Black Atlantic: Modernity and Double Consciousness.* Cambridge: Harvard University Press, 1993.
Glickstein, Jonathan A. *Concepts of Free Labor in Antebellum America.* New Haven: Yale University Press, 1991.
Goffman, Erving. *The Presentation of Self in Everyday Life.* Garden City, New York: Doubleday, 1959.
Goldman, Robert. *Reading Ads Socially.* New York: Routledge, 1993.
Gramsci, Antonio. The Modern Prince *and Other Writings.* New York: International Publishers, 1959.
Grier, Katherine C. *Culture and Comfort: People, Parlors, and Upholstery, 1850–1930.* Amherst: University of Massachusetts Press, 1988.
Grossberg, Lawrence. "History, Politics and Postmodernism: Stuart Hall and Cultural Studies." In *Stuart Hall; Critical Dialogues in Cultural Studies,* ed. David Morley and Kuan-Hsing Chen, 151–73. New York: Routledge, 1996.
Grossberg, Michael. *Governing the Hearth: Law and Family in Nineteenth-Century America.* Chapel Hill: University of North Carolina Press, 1985.
Gutman, Herbert G. *The Black Family in Slavery and Freedom.* New York: Pantheon, 1976.
Habermas, Jürgen. *The Structural Transformation of the Public Sphere.* Trans. Thomas Burger. Cambridge: MIT Press, 1991.
Hall, Jacquelyn Dowd. " 'The Mind That Burns in Each Body': Women, Rape, and Racial Violence." In *Powers of Desire: The Politics of Sexuality,* ed. Ann Snitow, Christine Stansell, and Sharon Thompson, 328–49. New York: Monthly Review, 1983.
Hall, Stuart. "The Toad in the Garden: Thatcherism among the Theorists." In *Marxism and the Interpretation of Culture,* ed. Cary Nelson and Lawrence Grossberg. Urbana: University of Illinois Press, 1988.
Halttunen, Karen. *Confidence Men and Painted Women: A Study of Middle-Class Culture in America.* New Haven: Yale University Press, 1982.
Handy, Robert T. *A Christian America: Protestant Hopes and Historical Realities.* New York: Oxford University Press, 1971.
Haraway, Donna J. *Simians, Cyborgs, and Women: The Reinvention of Nature.* New York: Routledge, 1991.
Haroutunian, Joseph. *Piety Versus Moralism: The Passing of New England Theology.* New York: H. Holt, 1932.
Harper, Frances E. W. *Iola Leroy.* Introduction by Hazel Carby. Boston: Beacon, 1987.
Harris, Neil. *The Artist in American Society: The Formative Years, 1790–1860.* Chicago: University of Chicago Press, 1982.

———. "Iconography and Intellectual History: The Half-Tone Effect." In *New Directions in American Intellectual History,* ed. John Higham and Paul K. Conkin, 196–211. Baltimore: Johns Hopkins University Press, 1979.

Harris, Trudier. *Exorcising Blackness: Historical and Literary Lynching and Burning Rituals.* Bloomington: Indiana University Press, 1984.

Hart, James D. *The Popular Book: A History of America's Literary Taste.* Berkeley: University of California Press, 1950.

Hartman, Saidiya V. *Scenes of Subjection: Terror, Slavery, and Self-Making in Nineteenth-Century America.* New York: Oxford University Press, 1997.

Haughton, Clare Shaver. *Green Immigrants: The Plants That Transformed America.* New York: Harcourt Brace Jovanovich, 1978.

Hawthorne, Nathaniel. *The Blithedale Romance.* Ed. Annette Kolodny. New York: Penguin, 1983.

———. *The House of the Seven Gables.* New York: Penguin, 1981.

———. *The Scarlet Letter.* New York: Norton, 1982.

———. "Sights from a Steeple." In *Twice-Told Tales,* 191–98. Columbus: Ohio State University Press, 1974.

Hayden, Dolores. *The Grand Domestic Revolution: A History of Feminist Designs for American Homes, Neighborhoods, and Cities.* Cambridge: MIT Press, 1981.

Hebdige, Dick. *Subculture: The Meaning of Style.* London: Methuen, 1979.

Heimann, Robert. *Tobacco and Americans.* New York: McGraw-Hill, 1960.

Helper, Hinton Rowan. *The Impending Crisis of the South: How to Meet It.* New York, 1857.

Hemlow, Joyce. "Fanny Burney and the Courtesy Books." *PMLA* 65, no. 5 (Sept. 1950): 732–61.

Henderson, Mae G. "The Stories of (O)Dessa." In *Female Subjects in Black and White,* ed. Elizabeth Abel, Barbara Christian, and Helene Moglen, 285–304. Berkeley: University of California Press, 1997.

Herrera-Sobek, María. "The Politics of Rape: Sexual Transgression in Chicana Fiction." In *Chicana Creativity and Criticism: Charting New Frontiers in American Literature,* ed. María Herrera-Sobek and Helena María Viramontes. Houston: Arté Público, 1988.

Hewitt, Nancy A. " 'The Voice of Virile Labor': Labor Militancy, Community Solidarity, and Gender Identity among Tampa's Latin Workers, 1880–1921." In *Work Engendered: Toward a New History of American Labor,* ed. Ava Baron, 142–67. Ithaca: Cornell University Press, 1991.

Higginbotham, Evelyn Brooks. "African-American Women's History and the Metalanguage of Race." *Signs* 17, no. 2 (winter 1992): 251–71.

Higham, John. "The Reorientation of American Culture in the 1890s." *Writing American History: Essays on Modern Scholarship.* Bloomington: Indiana University Press, 1970.

Hirschman, Albert O. *The Passions and the Interests: Political Arguments for Capitalism before Its Triumph.* Princeton: Princeton University Press, 1977.

Hitchcock, Enos. *Memoirs of the Bloomsgrove Family.* 2 vols. Boston, 1790.

Hoffman, Ronald, and Peter J. Albert, eds. *Women in the Age of the Revolution.* Charlottesville: University of Virginia Press, 1989.

Holmes, George Frederick. "Uncle Tom's Cabin." *Southern Literary Messenger* (December 1852): 721–31.

Home, Henry (Lord Kames). *Sketches of the History of Man.* 4 vols. Edinburgh, 1778.

hooks, bell. *Yearning: Race, Gender, and Cultural Politics.* Boston: South End, 1990.

Hopkins, Pauline E. *Contending Forces: A Romance Illustrative of Negro Life North and South.* Introduction by Richard Yarborough. New York: Oxford University Press, 1988.

———. *Hagar's Daughter.* In *The Magazine Novels of Pauline Hopkins,* introduction by Hazel Carby. New York: Oxford University Press, 1988.

———. "The Test of Manhood: A Christmas Story." In *Short Fiction by Black Women, 1900–1920,* ed. Elizabeth Ammons, 205–18. New York: Oxford University Press, 1991.

Horkheimer, Max, and Theodor W. Adorno. *Dialectic of Enlightenment.* Trans. John Cumming. New York: Continuum, 1988.

Horowitz, Daniel. *The Morality of Speaking: Attitudes toward the Consumer Society in America, 1875–1940.* Baltimore: Johns Hopkins University Press, 1985.

Horsman, Reginald. *Race and Manifest Destiny: The Origins of Racial Anglo-Saxonism.* Cambridge: Harvard University Press, 1981.

Howe, Daniel Walker. *The Unitarian Conscience.* Cambridge: Harvard University Press, 1970.

Hulme, Peter. *Colonial Encounters.* New York: Methuen, 1986.

Hume, David. *Essays, Moral, Political, and Literary.* Ed. T. H. Green and T. H. Grose. 2 vols. New York, 1898.

———. *A Treatise of Human Nature.* Ed. P. H. Nidditch and L. A. Selby-Bigge. Oxford: Clarendon, 1978.

Hyde, Lewis. *The Gift: Imagination and the Erotic Life of Property.* New York: Vintage, 1979.

Irving, Washington. *The Sketch-Book of Geoffrey Crayon, Gent.* New York, 1897.

Jacobs, Harriet A. *Incidents in the Life of a Slave Girl, Written by Herself.* In *The Classic Slave Narratives,* ed. Henry Louis Gates Jr. New York: Signet, 1987.

James, Henry. *The Bostonians.* Introduction by Irving Howe. New York: Random House, 1956.

Jameson, Fredric. *The Political Unconscious: Narrative as a Socially Symbolic Act.* Ithaca: Cornell University Press, 1981.

———. "Reification and Utopia in Mass Culture." *Social Text* 1 (1979): 132–48.

Jefferson, Thomas. *Notes on the State of Virginia.* Ed. William Peden. New York: Norton, 1972.

Jones, Alice H. *American Colonial Wealth: Documents and Methods.* 3 vols. New York: Arno, 1977.

———. *Wealth of a Nation to Be: The American Colonies on the Eve of the Revolution.* New York: Columbia University Press, 1980.

Jones, Jacqueline. *Labor of Love, Labor of Sorrow: Black Women, Work, and the Family, from Slavery to the Present.* New York: Vintage, 1985.

Jordanova, Ludmilla. *Sexual Visions.* Madison: University of Wisconsin Press, 1989.

Kant, Immanuel. *The Philosophy of Law.* Trans. W. Hastie. Edinburgh, 1887.

Kaplan, Amy. "Romancing the Empire: The Embodiment of American Masculinity in the Popular Historical Novel of the 1890s." *American Literary History* 2 (1990): 659–90.

Kaplan, Amy, and Donald E. Pease, eds. *Cultures of United States Imperialism.* Durham: Duke University Press, 1993.

Kasson, John. *Rudeness and Civility: Manners in Nineteenth-Century Urban America.* New York: Hill and Wang, 1990.

Keckley, Elizabeth. *Behind the Scenes: or, Thirty Years a Slave, and Four Years in the White House.* Introduction by James Olney. New York: Oxford University Press, 1988.

Kelley, Mary. *Private Woman, Public Stage: Literary Domesticity in Nineteenth-Century America.* New York: Oxford University Press, 1984.

Kesserling, Marion L. *Hawthorne's Reading, 1828–1850.* New York: New York Public Library Press, 1949.

Kibbey, Ann. *The Interpretation of Material Shapes in Puritanism: A Study of Rhetoric, Prejudice, and Violence.* New York: Cambridge University Press, 1986.

Kipnis, Laura. *Bound and Gagged: Pornography and the Politics of Fantasy in America.* New York: Grove, 1996.

Kirkland, Caroline M. "Comfort." In *A Book for the Home Circle.* New York, 1853.

———. "Mrs. Kirkland's 'Essay on Fiction.' " *Bulletin of the New York Public Library* 64, no. 7 (1960): 397.

———. *A New Home, Who'll Follow? or, Glimpses of Western Life.* Ed. Sandra A. Zagarell. New Brunswick: Rutgers University Press, 1990.

———. "Novels and Novelists." *North American Review* 76 (1853): 104–23.

———. Preface. *Dahcotah; or, Life and Legends of the Sioux,* by Mary Eastman. New York, 1849.

Klein, Lawrence. "The Third Earl of Shaftesbury and the Progress of Politeness." *Eighteenth-Century Studies* 18, no. 2 (1985): 186–214.

Kly, Y. N. *The Anti-Social Contract.* Atlanta: Clarity Press, 1989.

Kolodny, Annette. *The Land before Her: Fantasy and Experience of the American Frontiers, 1630–1860.* Chapel Hill: University of North Carolina Press, 1984.

Kovel, Joel. *White Racism: A Psychohistory.* New York: Columbia University Press, 1970.

Kramnick, Isaac. *Republicanism and Bourgeois Radicalism: Political Ideology in Late Eighteenth-Century England and America.* Ithaca: Cornell University Press, 1990.

Kutzinski, Vera M. *Sugar's Secrets: Race and the Erotics of Cuban Nationalism.* Charlottesville: University of Virginia Press, 1993.

Laclau, Ernesto, and Chantal Mouffe. *Hegemony and Socialist Strategy: Towards a Radical Democratic Politics.* Trans. Winston Moore and Paul Commack. London: Verso, 1985.

Langley, Lester D. *The Cuban Policy of the United States: A Brief History.* New York: John Wiley, 1968.

Laqueur, Thomas. "Orgasm, Generation, and the Politics of Reproductive Biology." *Representations* 14 (1986): 1–41.

Lazarus, Neil. "Doubting the New World Order: Marxism, Realism, and the Claims of Postmodern Social Theory." *differences* 3, no. 3 (1991): 94–138.

Lears, T. J. Jackson. "Beyond Veblen: Rethinking Consumer Culture in America." In *Consuming Visions: Accumulation and Display of Goods in America, 1880–1920,* ed. Simon J. Bronner. New York: Norton, 1989.

———. "From Salvation to Self-Realization: Advertising and the Therapeutic Roots of the Consumer Culture, 1880–1930." In *The Culture of Consumption: Critical Essays in American History, 1880–1980,* ed. Richard W. Fox and T. J. Jackson Lears, 3–38. New York: Pantheon, 1983.

———. *No Place of Grace: Antimodernism and the Transformation of American Culture, 1880–1920.* New York: Pantheon, 1981.

Lefcowitz, Barbara, and Allan Lefcowitz. "Some Rents in the Veil: New Light on Priscilla and Zenobia in *The Blithedale Romance.*" *Nineteenth-Century Fiction* 21 (1966): 263–75.

Leverenz, David. *Manhood and the American Renaissance.* Ithaca: Cornell University Press, 1988.

Levinson, Boris. *Pets and Human Development.* Springfield, Ill.: Charles C. Thomas, 1972.

Lewis, Jan. "The Republican Wife: Virtue and Seduction in the Early Republic." *William and Mary Quarterly* 44, no. 4 (1987): 688–721.

Lott, Eric. *Love and Theft: Blackface Minstrelsy and the American Working Class.* New York: Oxford University Press, 1993.

——. "White Like Me: Racial Cross-Dressing and the Construction of American Whiteness." In *Cultures of United States Imperialism,* ed. Amy Kaplan and Donald E. Pease, 474–95. Durham: Duke University Press, 1993.

Lougee, Carolyn. *Le Paradis des Femmes: Women, Salons, and Social Stratification in Seventeenth-Century France.* Princeton: Princeton University Press, 1976.

Lovejoy, Arthur O. *The Great Chain of Being: A Study in the History of an Idea.* Cambridge: Harvard University Press, 1936.

Luedtke, Luther S. *Nathaniel Hawthorne and the Romance of the Orient.* Bloomington: Indiana University Press, 1989.

Luhmann, Niklas. *Love as Passion: The Codification of Intimacy.* Cambridge: Harvard University Press, 1986.

Macfarlane, Alan. *The Culture of Capitalism.* Oxford: Basil Blackwell, 1987.

MacKinnon, Catherine A. *Toward a Feminist Theory of the State.* Cambridge: Harvard University Press, 1989.

Macpherson, C. B. *The Political Theory of Possessive Individualism: Hobbes to Locke.* New York: Oxford University Press, 1964.

Maddox, Lucy. *Removals: Nineteenth-Century American Literature and the Politics of Indian Affairs.* New York: Oxford University Press, 1991.

Marshall, David. *The Surprising Effects of Sympathy.* Chicago: University of Chicago Press, 1988.

Martin, Edgar S. *The Standard of Living in 1860: American Consumption Levels on the Eve of the Civil War.* Chicago: University of Chicago Press, 1942.

Marx, Karl. In *The Marx-Engels Reader,* ed. Robert C. Tucker. New York: Norton, 1978.

May, Robert E. *The Southern Dream of a Caribbean Empire, 1854–1861.* Baton Rouge: Louisiana State University Press, 1973.

McClintock, Anne. *Imperial Leather: Race, Gender, and Sexuality in the Colonial Contest.* New York: Routledge, 1995.

McCoy, Drew R. *The Elusive Republic: Political Economy in Jeffersonian America.* New York: Norton, 1980.

McDannell, Colleen. *The Christian Home in Victorian America, 1840–1900.* Bloomington: Indiana University Press, 1986.

McDowell, Deborah E. "'The Changing Same': Generational Connections and Black Women Novelists." *New Literary History* 18, no. 2 (winter 1987): 281–302.

McKendrick, Neil. Introduction. In *The Birth of a Consumer Society: The Commercialization of Eighteenth-Century England,* ed. Neil McKendrick, John Brewer, and J. H. Plumb. Bloomington: Indiana University Press, 1982.

Meek, Ronald L. *Social Science and the Ignoble Savage.* New York: Cambridge University Press, 1976.

Merish, Lori. "Cuteness and the Aesthetics of Modern Ownership." In *Freakmaking: Constituting Cultural and Corporeal Others,* ed. Rosemarie Garland Thompson. New York: New York University Press, 1996.

Meyer, D. H. *The Instructed Conscience: The Shaping of the American National Ethic.* Philadelphia: University of Pennsylvania Press, 1972.

Michie, Helena. *The Flesh Made Word: Female Figures and Women's Bodies.* New York: Oxford University Press, 1987.

Mies, Maria. *Patriarchy and Accumulation on a World Scale: Women in the International Division of Labour.* London: Zed, 1986.

Mill, John Stuart. "The Subjection of Women." In *Essays on Sex Equality*, ed. A. S. Rossi. Chicago: University of Chicago Press, 1970.

Millar, John. *The Origin of the Distinction of Ranks*. London, 1806.

Mintz, Sidney W. *Sweetness and Power: The Place of Sugar in Modern History*. New York: Viking, 1985.

Mintz, Steven. *A Prison of Expectations: The Family in Victorian Culture*. New York: New York University Press, 1983.

Mitchell, Samuel L. *Address to the Fredes*. New York, 1804.

Modleski, Tania. *Loving with a Vengeance: Mass-Produced Fantasies for Women*. New York: Routledge, 1988.

Morgan, Edmund. *The Puritan Family: Religion and Domestic Relations in Seventeenth-Century New England*. New York: Harper, 1944.

Naether, Carl. *Advertising to Women*. New York: Taylor, 1928.

Nef, John U. *Cultural Foundations of Industrial Civilization*. Cambridge: Cambridge University Press, 1958.

Negt, Oskar, and Alexander Kluge. *The Public Sphere and Experience*. Trans. Peter Labanyi. Minneapolis: University of Minnesota Press, 1990.

Nelson, Dana D. *The Word in Black and White: Reading "Race" in American Literature, 1638–1867*. New York: Oxford University Press, 1993.

Newfield, Christopher. *The Emerson Effect: Individualism and Submission in America*. Chicago: University of Chicago Press, 1996.

Norris, James D. *Advertising and the Transformation of American Society, 1865–1920*. Westport, Conn.: Greenwood, 1990.

Norton, Anne. *Alternative Americas: A Reading of Antebellum Political Cultures*. Chicago: University of Chicago Press, 1986.

———. *Republic of Signs: Liberal Theory and American Popular Culture*. Chicago: University of Chicago Press, 1993.

Ogden, John. *The Female Guide*. Concord, N.H., 1793.

"On the Happy Influence of the Female Sex in Society and the Absurd Practice of Separating the Sexes Immediately after Dinner." *Universal Asylum* (March 1791): 153.

Ortiz, Fernando. *Cuban Counterpoint: Tobacco and Sugar*. New York: Knopf, 1947.

Painter, Nell Irvin. *Sojourner Truth: A Life, A Symbol*. New York: Norton, 1996.

Paquette, Robert. *Sugar Is Made with Blood*. Middletown: Wesleyan University Press, 1982.

Parker, Andrew, Mary Russo, Doris Sommer, and Patricia Yeager, eds. *Nationalisms and Sexualities*. New York: Routledge, 1992.

Pateman, Carole. *The Sexual Contract*. Stanford: Stanford University Press, 1988.

Peiss, Kathy. *Cheap Amusements: Working Women and Leisure in Turn-of-the-Century New York*. Philadelphia: Temple University Press, 1986.

Pfister, Joel. "The Americanization of Cultural Studies." *Yale Journal of Criticism* 4, no. 2 (1991): 199–229.

———. *The Production of Personal Life: Class, Gender, and the Psychological in Hawthorne's Fiction*. Stanford: Stanford University Press, 1991.

Phelps, Elizabeth Stuart. *The Gates Ajar*. Boston, 1869.

Phillipson, Nicholas. "Adam Smith as Civic Moralist." In *Wealth and Virtue: The Shaping of Political Economy in the Scottish Enlightenment*, ed. Istvan Hont and Michael Ignatieff, 179–202. Cambridge: Cambridge University Press, 1983.

———. "Towards a Definition of the Scottish Enlightenment." In *City and Society in the*

Eighteenth Century, ed. Paul Fritz and David Williams, 125–47. Toronto: University of Toronto Press, 1973.

Pieterse, Jan Nederveen. *White on Black: Images of Africa and Blacks in Western Popular Culture.* New Haven: Yale University Press, 1992.

Pocock, J. G. A. "Cambridge Paradigms and Scotch Philosophers." In *Wealth and Virtue: The Shaping of Political Economy in the Scottish Enlightenment,* ed. Istvan Hont and Michael Ignatieff, 235–52. Cambridge: Cambridge University Press, 1983.

———. *The Machiavellian Moment: Florentine Political Thought and the Atlantic Republican Tradition.* Princeton: Princeton University Press, 1975.

———. *Virtue, Commerce, and History.* New York: Cambridge University Press, 1985.

Poe, Edgar Allan. "The Literati of New York." In *Essays and Review,* 1118–1222. New York: Library of America, 1984.

Poovey, Mary. "Aesthetics and Political Economy in the Eighteenth Century." In *Aesthetics and Ideology,* ed. George Levine. New Brunswick: Rutgers University Press, 1994.

———. *Uneven Developments: The Ideological Work of Gender in Mid-Victorian England.* Chicago: University of Chicago Press, 1988.

Porterfield, Amanda. *Female Piety in Puritan New England: The Emergence of Religious Humanism.* New York: Oxford University Press, 1992.

Potter, David M. *People of Plenty: Economic Abundance and the American Character.* Chicago: University of Chicago Press, 1954.

Pratt, Mary Louise. *Imperial Eyes: Travel Writing and Transculturation.* New York: Routledge, 1992.

Presbrey, Frank. *The History and Development of Advertising.* 1929. Reprint, New York: Greenwood, 1968.

"Reflections on Courtship and Marriage." In *A Series of Letters on Courtship and Marriage.* Hudson, N.Y., 1804.

Reiman, Jeffrey H. "Privacy, Intimacy, and Personhood." In *Today's Moral Problems,* ed. Richard A. Wasserstrom, 392–407. New York: Macmillan, 1979.

Retamar, Roberto Fernández. *Caliban and Other Essays.* Minneapolis: University of Minnesota Press, 1989.

Reynolds, David S. *Beneath the American Renaissance: The Subversive Imagination in the Age of Emerson and Melville.* Cambridge: Harvard University Press, 1989.

Richards, Thomas. *The Commodity Culture of Victorian England: Advertising and Spectacle, 1851–1914.* Stanford: Stanford University Press, 1990.

Richardson, Samuel. *Clarissa.* New York: Penguin, 1985.

Riley, Denise. *"Am I That Name?" Feminism and the Category of "Women" in History.* Minneapolis: University of Minnesota Press, 1988.

Robertson, Claire C., and Martin A. Klein, eds. *Women and Slavery in Africa.* Madison: University of Wisconsin Press, 1984.

Robertson, William. *The History of America.* 2 vols. London, 1777.

Rodgers, Daniel T. *The Work Ethic in Industrial America, 1850–1920.* Chicago: University of Chicago Press, 1978.

Roediger, David. *The Wages of Whiteness: Race and the Making of the American Working Class.* New York: Verso, 1991.

Romero, Lora. *Home Fronts: Domesticity and Its Critics in the Antebellum United States.* Durham: Duke University Press, 1997.

Rosenberg, Emily. *Spreading the American Dream: American Economic and Cultural Expansion, 1890–1945.* New York: Hill and Wang, 1982.

Rothman, Ellen K. *Hands and Hearts: A History of Courtship in America.* Cambridge: Harvard University Press, 1987.

Rousseau, Jean-Jacques. *The Social Contract and Discourses.* Trans. G. D. H. Cole. New York: Dutton, 1950.

Ruddick, Sara. *Maternal Thinking: Toward a Politics of Peace.* Boston: Beacon, 1989.

Rush, Benjamin. *The Selected Writings of Benjamin Rush.* Ed. Dagobert D. Runes. New York: Philosophical Library, 1947.

Ryan, Mary P. *Cradle of the Middle Class: The Family in Oneida County, New York, 1790–1830.* New York: Cambridge University Press, 1981.

———. *The Empire of the Mother.* New York: Haworth Press, 1982.

———. "Femininity and Capitalism in Antebellum America." In *Capitalist Patriarchy and the Case for Socialist Feminism,* ed. Zillah R. Eisenstein, 151–68. New York: Monthly Review, 1979.

———. *Womanhood in America from Colonial Times to the Present.* 2d ed. New York: New Viewpoints, 1979.

———. *Women in Public: Between Banners and Ballots, 1825–1880.* Baltimore: Johns Hopkins University Press, 1990.

Said, Edward W. *Culture and Imperialism.* New York: Vintage, 1993.

———. *Orientalism.* London: Routledge, 1978.

Saldivar, José David. *The Dialectics of Our America: Genealogy, Cultural Critique, and Literary History.* Durham: Duke University Press, 1991.

Sanchez-Eppler, Karen. "Bodily Bonds: The Intersecting Rhetorics of Feminism and Abolition." *Representations* 24 (1988): 28–59.

Scarry, Elaine. *The Body in Pain: The Making and Unmaking of the World.* New York: Oxford University Press, 1985.

———. "Consent and the Body: Injury, Departure, and Desire." *New Literary History* 21 (1990): 867–96.

Scott, William B. *In Pursuit of Happiness: Conceptions of Property from the Seventeenth to the Twentieth Century.* Bloomington: Indiana University Press, 1977.

Sedgwick, Catharine. *Clarence; or, A Tale of Our Own Times.* 2 vols. Philadelphia, 1830.

———. *Home.* Boston, 1835.

———. *Live and Let Live; or, Domestic Service Illustrated.* New York, 1837.

———. *A New-England Tale.* New York, 1822.

Sedgwick, Eve Kosofsky. *Between Men: English Literature and Male Homosocial Desire.* New York: Columbia University Press, 1985.

Sekora, John. *Luxury: The Concept in Western Thought, Eden to Smollett.* Baltimore: Johns Hopkins University Press, 1977.

Seltzer, Mark. *Bodies and Machines.* New York: Routledge, 1992.

Shammas, Carole. "The Domestic Environment in Early Modern England and America." *Journal of Social History* 14, no. 1 (1980): 3–24.

———. "How Self-Sufficient Was Early America?" *Journal of Interdisciplinary History* 13 (autumn 1982): 247–72.

Shell, Marc. "The Family Pet." *Representations* 15 (summer 1986): 121–53.

Shorter, Edward. *The Making of the Modern Family.* New York: Basic, 1975.

Sigourney, Lydia. *Letters to Mothers.* Hartford, Conn., 1838.

Silber, Nina. *The Romance of Reunion.* Chapel Hill: University of North Carolina Press, 1993.

Silverman, Debora. *Art Nouveau in Fin-de-Siecle France.* Berkeley: University of California Press, 1989.

Silverman, Kaja. "Fragments of a Fashionable Discourse." In *Studies in Entertainment: Critical Approaches to Mass Culture,* ed. Tania Modleski, 139–52. Bloomington: Indiana University Press, 1986.

——. *Male Subjectivity at the Margins.* New York: Routledge, 1992.

Simmel, Georg. *Georg Simmel: On Women, Sexuality, and Love.* Ed. and trans. Guy Oakes. New Haven: Yale University Press, 1984.

——. *The Philosophy of Money.* 2d ed., trans. Tom Bottomore and David Frisby. Boston: Routledge and Kegan Paul, 1978.

Simms, W. Gilmore. "Miss Martineau on Slavery." *Southern Literary Messenger* 3 (November 1837): 641–57.

——. "The Morals of Slavery." In *The Pro-Slavery Argument,* 175–285. Charleston: Walker, Richards, 1852.

Sloan, Douglas. *The Scottish Enlightenment and the American College Ideal.* New York: Columbia University Press, 1971.

Slotkin, Richard. *The Fatal Environment: The Myth of the Frontier in the Age of Industrialization, 1800–1890.* Middletown: Wesleyan University Press, 1985.

——. *Regeneration through Violence: The Mythology of the American Frontier, 1600–1860.* Middletown: Wesleyan University Press, 1973.

Smith, Adam. *Lectures on Justice, Police, Revenue, and Arms.* Ed. Edwin Cannan. Oxford, 1896.

——. *The Theory of Moral Sentiments.* Introduction by E. G. West. Indianapolis: Liberty Press, 1976.

Smith, Paul. "Visiting the Banana Republic." In *Universal Abandon? The Politics of Postmodernism,* ed. Andrew Ross. Minneapolis: University of Minnesota Press, 1988.

Smith, Valerie. " 'Loopholes of Retreat': Architecture and Ideology in Harriet Jacobs' *Incidents in the Life of a Slave Girl.*" In *Reading Black, Reading Feminist: A Critical Anthology,* ed. Henry Louis Gates Jr., 212–26. New York: Meridian, 1990.

——. *Self-Discovery and Authority in Afro-American Narrative.* Cambridge: Harvard University Press, 1987.

Smith-Rosenberg, Carroll. *Disorderly Conduct: Visions of Gender in Victorian America.* New York: Oxford University Press, 1985.

Sombart, Werner. *Luxury and Capitalism.* Introduction by Philip Siegelman. Ann Arbor: University of Michigan Press, 1967.

Spillers, Hortense. "Changing the Letter: The Yokes, the Jokes of Discourse, or, Mrs. Stowe, Mr. Reed." In *Slavery and the Literary Imagination,* ed. D. E. McDowell and Arnold Rampersad, 25–61. Baltimore: Johns Hopkins University Press, 1989.

——. "Mama's Baby, Papa's Maybe: An American Grammar Book." *diacritics* 17, no. 2 (summer 1987): 65–81.

Spivak, Gayatri Chakravorty. *In Other Worlds: Essays in Cultural Politics.* New York: Routledge, 1988.

Spurr, David. *The Rhetoric of Empire.* Durham: Duke University Press, 1992.

Stanley, Amy Dru. "Home Life and the Morality of the Market." In *The Market Revolution in America,* ed. Melvyn Stokes and Stephen Conway, 74–96. Charlottesville: University of Virginia Press, 1996.

Stansell, Christine. *City of Women: Sex and Class in New York, 1789–1860.* Urbana: University of Illinois Press, 1986.

Steedman, Carolyn Kay. *Landscape for a Good Woman: A Story of Two Lives.* New Brunswick: Rutgers University Press, 1988.

Stepto, Robert B. *From behind the Veil: A Study of Afro-American Narrative.* Urbana: University of Illinois Press, 1991.

Sterling, Dorothy, ed. *We Are Your Sisters: Black Women in the Nineteenth Century.* New York: Norton, 1984.

Stevenson, Olive. "The First Treasured Possession: A Study of the Part Played by Specially Loved Objects and Toys in the Lives of Certain Children." *The Psychoanalytic Study of the Child* 9, no. 1 (January 1954): 199–217.

Stone, Albert E. *Autobiographical Occasions and Original Acts.* Philadelphia: University of Pennsylvania Press, 1982.

Stowe, Harriet Beecher. *Agnes of Sorrento.* 1862. Reprint, Boston: Houghton Mifflin, 1896.

——. *A Dog's Mission and Other Stories.* New York: Fords, Howard, and Hulbert, 1880.

——. "Feeling." In *Stories, Sketches, and Studies.* New York: AMS, 1967.

——. *House and Home Papers.* In *Household Papers and Stories.* New York: AMS, 1967.

——. *The Minister's Wooing.* 1859. Reprint, New York: AMS, 1967.

——. "Rights of Dumb Animals." *Hearth and Home* 2 (January 1869): 203.

——. *Uncle Tom's Cabin.* Ed. Ann Douglas. New York: Penguin American Library, 1981.

Strebeck, George. *A Sermon on the Character of the Virtuous Woman.* New York, 1800.

Stubbs, Jean. *Tobacco on the Periphery: A Case Study in Cuban Labor History, 1860–1958.* New York: Cambridge University Press, 1985.

Sullivan, Edmund B. *Collecting Political Americana.* New York: Crown, 1980.

Sundquist, Eric. *To Wake the Nations: Race in the Making of American Literature.* Cambridge: Harvard University Press, 1993.

Takaki, Ronald T. *Iron Cages: Race and Culture in Nineteenth-Century America.* Seattle: University of Washington Press, 1979.

Tate, Claudia. "Allegories of Black Female Desire; or, Rereading Nineteenth-Century Sentimental Narratives of Black Female Authority." In *Changing Our Own Words: Essays on Criticism, Theory, and Writing by Black Women,* ed. Cheryl A. Wall. New Brunswick: Rutgers University Press, 1989.

——. *Domestic Allegories of Political Desire: The Black Heroine's Text at the Turn of the Century.* New York: Oxford University Press, 1992.

Terry, Esther. "Sojourner Truth: The Person behind the Libyan Sibyl." *Massachusetts Review* 26, nos. 2–3 (summer–autumn 1985): 425–44.

Thomas, Keith. *Man and the Natural World.* New York: Pantheon, 1983.

Thomas, Nicholas. "Licensed Curiosity: Cook's Pacific Voyages." In *The Cultures of Collecting,* ed. John Elsner and Roger Cardinal, 116–36. Cambridge: Harvard University Press, 1993.

Thompson, Ralph. *American Literary Annuals and Gift Books, 1825–1865.* New York: H. W. Wilson, 1936.

Thompson, William. *Appeal of One Half of the Human Race, Women, Against the Pretensions of the Other Half, Men, to Retain Them in Political, and Thence in Civil and Domestic, Slavery.* London: Longman, 1825.

Tompkins, Jane. *Sensational Designs: The Cultural Work of American Fiction, 1790–1860.* New York: Oxford University Press, 1985.

Trine, Ralph Waldo. *Every Living Creature: or, Heart-Training through the Animal World.* New York, 1899.

Truth, Sojourner. *Book of Life,* ed. Frances Gage. In *Narrative of Sojourner Truth,* ed. Jeffrey C. Stewart. New York: Oxford University Press, 1991.

——. *Narrative of Sojourner Truth.* Ed. Jeffrey C. Stewart. New York: Oxford University Press, 1991.

Turner, Arlin. *Nathaniel Hawthorne: A Biography.* New York: Oxford University Press, 1980.

Twain, Mark. *Adventures of Huckleberry Finn.* Berkeley: University of California Press, 1985.

Upton, Dell. "The Traditional House and Its Enemies." *Traditional Dwellings and Settlements Review* 1, no. 2 (spring 1990): 71–84.

Ward, Maria. *The Mormon Wife.* Reprinted as *Female Life among the Mormons.* New York: Derby and Jackson, 1857.

Warhol, Robyn R. "Toward a Theory of the Engaging Narrator: Earnest Intervention in Gaskell, Stowe, and Eliot." *PMLA* 101, no. 5 (1986): 811–18.

Warner, Susan. *The Wide, Wide World.* Ed. Jane Tompkins. New York: Feminist Press, 1987.

Washington, John E. *They Knew Lincoln.* New York: Dutton, 1942.

Weber, Max. *The Protestant Ethic and the Spirit of Capitalism.* Trans. Talcott Parsons. New York: Scribner, 1958.

Webster, Daniel. "Lecture before the Society for the Diffusion of Useful Knowledge." In *Writings and Speeches of Daniel Webster,* 13: 63–78. Boston, 1903.

Wendt, Lloyd, and Herman Kogan. *Give the Lady What She Wants! The Story of Marshall Field and Company.* South Bend, In.: And Books, 1952.

Westfall, L. Glenn. *Don Vicente Martinez Yor, The Man and His Empire: The Development of the Clear Havana Industry in Cuba and Florida in the Nineteenth Century.* New York: Garland, 1987.

Wexler, Laura. "Tender Violence: Literary Eavesdropping, Domestic Fiction, and Educational Reform." In *The Culture of Sentiment: Race, Gender, and Sentimentality in Nineteenth-Century America,* ed. Shirley Samuels, 12–32. New York: Oxford University Press, 1993.

Wheeler, Gervase. *Rural Homes.* New York, 1852.

White, Deborah Gray. *A'rnt I a Woman? Female Slaves in the Plantation South.* New York: Norton, 1985.

Wiegman, Robyn. *American Anatomies: Theorizing Race and Gender.* Durham: Duke University Press, 1995.

Wilentz, Sean. *Chants Democratic: New York City and the Rise of the American Working Class.* New York: Oxford University Press, 1984.

Williams, Fannie Barrier. "Club Movement among Colored Women." In *A New Negro for a New Century,* ed. Booker T. Washington and Fannie Barrier Williams. Chicago: American Publishing House, 1900.

Williams, Patricia. "On Being the Object of Property." In *The Alchemy of Race and Rights.* Cambridge: Harvard University Press, 1991.

Williamson, Judith. *Consuming Passions: The Dynamics of Popular Culture.* London: Marion Boyers, 1979.

Willis, Ellen. "Consumerism and Women." *Socialist Review* 3 (1970): 76–82. Reprinted in *Popular Writing in America,* ed. Don McQuade, 358–61. New York: Oxford University Press, 1974.

Willis, Susan. *A Primer for Daily Life.* New York: Routledge, 1991.

Wilson, Edmund. *Patriotic Gore: Studies in the Literature of the American Civil War.* New York: Oxford University Press, 1962.

Wilson, Elizabeth. "All the Rage." In *Fabrications: Costume and the Female Body,* ed. Jane Gaines and Charlotte Herzog. New York: Routledge, 1990.

Wood, Gordon S. *The Creation of the American Republic, 1776–1787.* Chapel Hill: University of North Carolina Press, 1969.

Wright, Nathalia. *American Novelists in Italy.* Philadelphia: University of Pennsylvania Press, 1965.

Wright, Richard. *The Long Dream.* New York: Harper, 1987.

Yarborough, Richard. "Race, Violence, and Manhood: The Masculine Ideal in Frederick Douglass's 'The Heroic Slave.' " In *Frederick Douglass: New Literary and Historical Essays,* ed. Eric J. Sundquist, 166–88. New York: Cambridge University Press, 1990.

Yellin, Jean Fagan. "Text and Contexts of Harriet Jacobs' *Incidents in the Life of a Slave Girl:* Written by Herself." In *The Slave's Narrative,* ed. Charles T. Davis and Henry Louis Gates Jr., 262–82. New York: Oxford University Press, 1985.

——. *Women and Sisters: The Antislavery Feminists in American Culture.* New Haven: Yale University Press, 1989.

Young, Iris Marion. "Women Recovering Our Clothes." In *On Fashion,* ed. Shari Benstock and Suzanne Ferriss. New Brunswick: Rutgers University Press, 1994.

Zagarell, Sandra A. Introduction. *A New Home, Who'll Follow? or, Glimpses of Western Life,* by Caroline Kirkland. New Brunswick: Rutgers University Press, 1990.

Zaretsky, Eli. *Capitalism, the Family, and Personal Life.* New York: Harper and Row, 1976.

INDEX

Lori Merish is Assistant Professor of English at Miami University.

Library of Congress Cataloging-in-Publication Data
Merish, Lori.
Sentimental materialism : gender, commodity culture, and nineteenth-century American literature / Lori Merish.
p. cm. — (New Americanists)
Includes bibliographical references and index.
ISBN 0-8223-2480-6 (cloth : alk. paper) — ISBN 0-8223-2516-0 (paper : alk. paper)
1. Women — United States — Social life and customs — 19th century. 2. Women consumers — United States — History — 19th century. 3. Sex role — United States — History — 19th century. 4. Material culture — United States — History — 19th century. 5. Women in literature. 6. Material culture in literature. I. Title. II. Series.
HQ1418.M47 2000 305.42'0973'09034 — dc21 99-050027